Hafeez Malik is Professor of Political Sciences, member of the Institute for Contemporary Arab and Islamic Studies, President of the Pakistan–American Foundation and Director of the American Institute of Pakistan Studies at Villanova University, Pennsylvania. Since 1962 he has been Visiting Professor at the Foreign Service Institute of the US State Department. He is also Executive Director of the American Council for the Study of Islamic Societies. Among his previous publications are *International Security in Southwest Asia* (editor); *Political Profile of Sir Sayyid Ahmed Khan*; *Sir Sayyid Ahmed Khan's History of the Bijnore Rebellion*; *Iqbal: Poet Philosopher of Pakistan* (editor); and *Muslim Nationalism in India and Pakistan*.

SOVIET–AMERICAN RELATIONS WITH PAKISTAN, IRAN
AND AFGHANISTAN

Also by Hafeez Malik

INTERNATIONAL SECURITY IN SOUTHWEST ASIA (*editor*)
POLITICAL PROFILE OF SIR SAYYID AHMED KHAN: A Documentary Record
SIR SAYYID AHMAD KHAN AND MUSLIM MODERNIZATION IN INDIA AND PAKISTAN
SIR SAYYID AHMAD KHAN'S HISTORY OF THE BIJNORE REBELLION
IQBAL: POET PHILOSOPHER OF PAKISTAN (*editor*)
MUSLIM NATIONALISM IN INDIA AND PAKISTAN

Soviet-American Relations with Pakistan, Iran and Afghanistan

Edited by

Hafeez Malik
Professor of Political Science
Villanova University, Pennsylvania

St. Martin's Press   New York

© Hafeez Malik, 1987

All rights reserved. For information, write:
Scholarly & Reference Division,
St. Martin's Press, Inc., 175 Fifth Avenue, New York, NY 10010

First published in the United States of America in 1987

Printed in Hong Kong

ISBN 0-312-00240-8

Library of Congress Cataloging-in-Publication Data
Soviet–American relations with Pakistan, Iran, and
Afghanistan.
Papers presented at a seminar held Dec. 7-8, 1984,
at Villanova University.
Bibliography: p.
Includes index.
1. Asia—Foreign relations—United States—
Congresses.   2. United States—Foreign relations—
Asia—Congresses.   3. Asia—Foreign relations—
Soviet Union—Congresses.   4. Soviet Union—Foreign
relations—Asia—Congresses.   I. Malik, Hafeez.
JX1 569.Z7U67   1987   327'.095   86-21898
ISBN 0-312-00240-8

Contents

Preface vii

Notes on the Contributors xi

1 Introduction 1
  Hafeez Malik

2 The Strategic Importance of Iran, Afghanistan and
  Pakistan to the United States 27
  George C. McGhee

3 Thinking South: Soviet Strategic Interests in Iran,
  Afghanistan and Pakistan 39
  Morris McCain

4 India's Relations with Pakistan, Iran and
  Afghanistan 54
  Craig Baxter

5 Ethnic Dilemmas in Pakistan, Iran and Afghanistan
  as Security Problems 70
  Jon W. Anderson

6 Buffer States on the Rim of Asia: Pakistan,
  Afghanistan, Iran and the Superpowers 90
  Lawrence Ziring

7 Soviet Intervention in Afghanistan and its Impact on
  Pakistan's Foreign Policy 127
  Hafeez Malik

8 Pakistan's Relations with the United States 163
  Agha Shahi

9 Soviet Relations with Pakistan 182
  Yuri V. Gankovsky, Railya Muqeemjanova,
  Vyacheslav Belokrenitsky, and Vladimir Moskalenko

10	Pakistan's Nuclear Options *Rodney Jones*	199
11	The United States and Revolutionary Iran *Richard W. Cottam*	217
12	The Soviet Union and the Islamic Republic of Iran *Shireen T. Hunter*	244
13	Relations between Iran and the Arab States *Andrew Killgore*	267
14	The International Political Economy of the Iran–Iraq War *Khosrow Fatemi*	281
15	The Afghan State and its Adaptation to the Environment of Central and Southwest Asia *Ashraf Ghani*	310
16	Communism in Afghanistan *Henry S. Bradsher*	333
17	Cultural Determinants of the Afghan Resistance to the Saur Revolution of 1978 *Louis Dupree*	355
18	The Demography of Afghan Refugees in Pakistan *Nancy Hatch Dupree*	366
19	Superpower Relations with Pakistan, Iran and Afghanistan *Kail Ellis*	395

Appendix: List of Seminar Participants — 421

Index — 423

Preface

Since the end of the Second World War two sets of conflicting strategic interests have steadily rocked the stability of the Middle East: the United States' determination to have unhindered access to the supply of oil, which is produced in the Persian/Arabian Gulf area, while simultaneously supporting the territorial integrity of the State of Israel by making it militarily the most dominant state in the region. The imperatives of the US strategic interests have now started to collide sharply with the security concerns of the USSR, especially on its southern flanks. As British imperial power started to evaporate into thin air in the late 1940s, the United States determined to replace Britain in the area and to keep the Soviet Union out of the Middle East, first through the instruments of the Baghdad Pact and then the CENTO. Upon the disintegration of both, and in the aftermath of the Soviet intervention in Afghanistan in December 1979, the United States established the Central Command (Rapid Deployment Force) to get there first before the presumptive Soviet occupation. In order to make the rapid deployment force effective and credible the United States acquired operational facilities in Egypt, Kenya, Somalia and Oman. Altogether nineteen countries became the ward of the Central Command.

For many years, however, the conventional wisdom dictated that the USSR (despite its capacity to produce and export indigenous oil) would be interested in grabbing the oil wells in the Arabian peninsula, and in establishing a firm access to the warm water port(s) in the region – a strategy implying the Soviets' ability to leapfrog the two contiguous states of Iran and Afghanistan. No one really seriously assessed the possibility of the Soviet march in the direction of the south to protect its southern flanks. Clearly in terms of Soviet security, Iran, Afghanistan and now Pakistan are the areas of prime concern, while the Middle East with its oil riches would not disappear from the Soviets' power calculations.

The Soviet Union (like the United States) nervously watches Iran, and remains alive to the future possibility of influence which might develop in the post-Khomeini period. The Soviet commitment of 110 000 troops in Afghanistan to fight the Afghan insurgents, the campaign to Sovietize Afghanistan, and the policy of carrot and stick being applied to Pakistan highlight the Soviet security concerns and the desire to turn these three states at some point in the future into the Soviet sphere of influence. One might ask a rhetorical question as to why a superpower should be so apprehensive of its security, especially when its southern neighbors happen to be small and militarily so ineffectual! The great power dilemma, however, is that the small powers' ability to involve the superpowers in their security arrangements ends up heightening insecurity for the superpowers themselves, which makes the small powers targets of their fears, frustrations, and antagonism. This peculiar psychological, as well as power, syndrome is ignored by the decision-makers of small powers to their own peril.

This book has been in gestation since May 1980, when I attended a politico–military simulation at the Pentagon under the sponsorship of the US Chairman of the Joint Chiefs of Staff. Civilian policy-makers and military officers at the ranks of assistant secretary, ambassador, lieutenant general, and general officer participated in these exercises. Through the courtesy of a friend at the Pentagon I also watched scenarios of a nuclear war between the United States and the Soviet Union which had actually originated in Iran. It then dawned on me that the long range US interests in Southwest Asia center on maintaining a viable and stable non-Soviet aligned Iran, and that the US was determined not to allow Iran to become the next Soviet Afghanistan. In line with this reasoning the outlines of American policy became vivid in bright colors: the US would attempt to recreate the old tripartite arrangement of cooperation among Turkey, Iran and Pakistan. Ayatollah Khomeini's Islamic Republic so far has thwarted the establishment of this three-state system. Despite the Ayatollah, Chief of Staff of the US Central Command at MacDill Air Force Base in Florida communicated to me in his letter of 20 September 1984 that the US was very much concerned with events in these three countries (Pakistan, Iran and Afghanistan), as they number among the 19 countries assigned to the United States Central Command. However, some crucial questions keep raising a gnawing fear: Would the United States demonstrate a commitment of support to Iran and Pakistan in order for them to withstand the Soviet pressure in the future? Can Afghanistan's present socialist status be reversed?

After delivering a stern warning to Pakistan's President Zia-ul-Haq in March 1985 on the occasion of Konstantin Chernenko's funeral for his support to Afghan insurgents, the Kremlin was supposed to be considering unspecified military action against Pakistan, if President Ronald Reagan continued his military pressure on Nicaragua. In a trade-off possibility between Nicaragua and Afghanistan, which country would the US choose? Clearly, the Soviet–American relations over the future of these three states would go through severe trials, which would threaten international equilibrium.

In order to examine these questions and other contours of Soviet–American relations with Pakistan, Iran and Afghanistan, I organized an international seminar on 7–8 December 1984 at Villanova University. Emulating the politico–military simulations of the Pentagon, I invited recognized specialists from the three constituencies of the US military, international diplomacy, and the academia. In addition to the invited guests, seventy specialists participated in the discussions; their names, positions and institutional affiliations are indicated in an appendix. Seventeen well-prepared papers were circulated among the participants, and they now constitute the core of this volume. An introduction was added to highlight the nature of superpower relations with small states, and to pull together specialists' divergent analyses in a coherent whole. The last chapter has synthesized the specialists' critique of each other's theses, and the superpowers' role in Southwest Asia. A book containing exceptional insights on international problems has developed, for which the authors of various chapters and other participants deserve our applause.

An international seminar of this caliber would not have been possible to organize without the help of the specialists, who graciously accepted my invitation to attend the seminar. Pakistan's Ambassador to the United States, Ejaz Azim, exchanged ideas on Pakistan's relations with the US and USSR at the banquet on 7 December with George C. McGhee, former US Under-Secretary of State, and Agha Shahi, former Minister of Foreign Affairs of Pakistan. The Soviet Union was represented by Igor V. Khalevinski, Senior Political Counsellor of the USSR Mission to the United Nations and India by Consul General, Arun B. Patwardhan. Professor Yuri V. Gankovsky, Head of the Department of Middle East Studies at the Institute of Oriental Studies in Moscow, was scheduled to participate in the seminar, but for some reasons unknown to us, he was unable to come. Co-authored by three of his colleagues at the Institute of Oriental Studies, Professor Gankovsky sent us a chapter on Soviet–Pakistan relations which was received after the seminar. The chapter is, therefore, included in the volume without any comments.

It is my pleasure to acknowledge with thanks the generosity of

Father John M. Driscoll, President of Villanova University, who has supported the American Institute of Pakistan Studies, *Journal of South Asian and Middle Eastern Studies* and the Pakistan American Foundation since 1972. Very kindly, Father Driscoll not only attended the banquet to welcome the guests, but also provided the Pakistan American Foundation Villanova University's institutional support without which none of our activities, including this international seminar, would have been possible. Father Lawrence Gallen, Vice President for Academic Affairs, and Father Kail Ellis, Director of Villanova University's Institute for Contemporary Arab and Islamic Studies, have always provided generously institutional and personal support.

For their unfailing help, support and affection, I owe a debt of gratitude to Nadia Barsoum, Magdy Barsoum, Dolores J. Kephart and Horace L. Kephart. I owe a special thanks to Lynda P. Malik, my wife, whose scholarly interest has now extended from Pakistan to Iran and Afghanistan. Other friends and colleagues, particularly Dr Justice Javid Iqbal, Fred Khouri, Jack Schrems, Ralph Braibanti, Riaz Ahmad, Afaq Haydar and Sharif ul-Mujahid, gave me valuable assistance and encouragement. As usual, my Administrative Assistant, Susan K. Hausman, managed the logistics and details of the seminar with remarkable skill. Many of my own ideas contained in this study were sharpened as a result of challenging views expressed by American diplomats and government officials who attended my lectures at the Foreign Service Institute of the US State Department during the last two and a half decades. Many thanks to all of them.

Villanova University HAFEEZ MALIK
Villanova, Pennsylvania

Notes on the Contributors

Jon W. Anderson is Associate Professor of Anthropology at the Catholic University of America, Washington, DC. He is an author of several books and his articles have appeared in learned journals in the United States and elsewhere.

Craig Baxter retired from the State Department as the Consul-General and is currently Professor of Political Science at Juniata College, Huntingdon.

Vyacheslav Belokrenitsky is a Senior Research Associate in the Department of Middle East Studies in the Institute of Oriental Studies of the Academy of Arts and Sciences, Moscow, USSR.

Henry S. Bradsher worked in Afghanistan as an Associated Press Correspondent in the early 1960s, visited the country again in the 1970s for the *Washington Star*, and has written about Afghanistan for *The Economist* and other well-known publications. Long a specialist on Soviet Affairs, Bradsher was AP Bureau Chief in Moscow from 1964 to 1968. In 1980–81 Bradsher was a Guest Scholar at the Kennan Institute for Advanced Russian Studies of the Smithsonian Institution's Wilson Center.

Richard W. Cottam, formerly a Foreign Service Officer at the American Embassy in Tehran, Iran, is now a Professor of Political Science at the University of Pittsburgh. He is an author and editor of six volumes and has published extensively in learned journals in the United States.

Louis Dupree is Professor of Social Sciences at US Military Academy, West Point. Since his first visit to Afghanistan in 1949, Dupree has lived and worked in that country for extensive periods – as Visiting Professor, American University's Field Staff, Journalist, Archaeologist, Industrial Consultant, and US Government Advisor. He has published several books on Afghanistan and his articles have appeared in learned journals in the United States, Europe and Asia.

Notes on the Contributors

Nancy Hatch Dupree is an anthropologist who has specialized on the demography of Afghanistan. She has lived in Afghanistan for at least two decades and has published extensively on the ethnic variety of the Afghan people.

Khosrow Fatemi is Associate Professor of International Business at Laredo State University, St Laredo, Texas. Before joining Laredo State University, he served for many years as a Senior Official of Iran's Ministry of Commerce in Tehran.

Yuri V. Gankovsky is Head of the Near and Middle East Department of the Institute of Oriental Studies, USSR Academy of Sciences, Moscow.

Ashraf Ghani is Associate Professor of Anthropology at the Johns Hopkins University in Baltimore and has published extensively on the history and cultural anthropology of his native land, Afghanistan.

Shireen T. Hunter is Deputy Director of the Middle East Project at the Georgetown University Center for Strategic and International Studies in Washington, DC. She was in the Iranian Foreign Service until 1979 and was also associated with the Brookings Institution and the Harvard University Center for International Affairs.

Rodney Jones is a Senior Research Associate at the Center for Strategic and International Studies of Georgetown University of Washington, DC. He is a specialist of Security Studies and has published extensively on the implications of nuclear weapons for foreign policy of the superpowers.

Andrew Killgore retired from the Foreign Service of the United States after twenty-five years. He was US Ambassador to Qatar and has written extensively on the problems of the states of the Persian Gulf.

Morris McCain is Professor of Political Science at the College of William and Mary, Williamsburg, and Research Associate at the Russian Center of Harvard University.

George C. McGhee is former US Ambassador to Germany and Turkey. He served in the Department of State for twenty years and retired as Under-Secretary of State.

Hafeez Malik is Professor of Political Science at Villanova University and editor of the *Journal of South Asian and Middle Eastern Studies*. Since 1962 he has been Visiting Professor at the Foreign Service Institute of the US State Department. He has authored or edited eight books published in the United States, Pakistan and India. He is President of the Pakistan–American Foundation and Director of the American Institute of Pakistan Studies.

Railya Muqeemjanova is a Senior Research Associate in the Department of Middle East Studies in the Institute of Oriental Studies of the Academy of Arts and Sciences, Moscow, USSR.

Vladimir Moskalenko is Head of the Pakistan Section in the Institute of Oriental Studies of the Academy of Arts and Sciences, Moscow, USSR, and author of *The Foreign Policy of Pakistan: Its Emergence and the Main Stages of Its Evolution*.

Agha Shahi resigned his position as the Minister of Foreign Affairs of Pakistan in 1982. Previously, he served for ten years as Pakistan's Ambassador to the United Nations and to the People's Republic of China. He is an internationally known statesman and diplomat of Pakistan.

Lawrence Ziring is Professor of Political Science at Western Michigan University, Kalamazoo. He is author or editor of six volumes published in the United States. Currently, he is Visiting Professor of International Relations at the University of Oxford, England.

1 Introduction
Hafeez Malik

This is essentially a three-dimensional analysis of interaction between the United States and the Soviet Union regarding their relations with Pakistan, Iran and Afghanistan; and the manner and style of relations of these three states with the superpowers; and finally, as neighbors of the USSR, the conduct of their relations with the Soviet Union, with each other, and the exogenous power, the United States. Despite the obvious dissimilarities in their political systems, (where the United States stands committed to free enterprise, multiple party system, and human rights and the Soviet Union espouses with an equal passion socialism, one-party rule, and classless social order), both superpowers have developed remarkable similarities in the conduct of their foreign policies.[1] Among the similarities or instrumentalities of foreign policy may be included economic and military aid, the right to articulate the strategic interests in other continents, and above all, the right to exercise intervention in the affairs of neighboring, as well as distant, states.

In two recently published studies, two groups of respected scholars projected twelve sets of conflict in the 1980s between the United States, and the Soviet Union, and articulated American strategic interests in Europe, the Persian Gulf and Southwest Asia, the Pacific, Latin America, Africa, Oceans and Space.[2] No part of the globe was excluded from the scope of the American national interest. Soviet scholars, however, have believed that 'the alignment of forces on the international scene [have been] steadily changing in favor of socialism' in the post World War II period, and attribute decline to 'the American position of dominance' in the 1960s.[3] In referring to the problems of economic development in the Third World, including energy development, raw materials, the exploration and use of the world ocean, and outer space, the Soviets categorically pose their challenge: 'These problems cannot be solved by any country alone, [they] require a collective effort'.[4]

Intervention is an old technique used in the conduct of international relations. In the state system of Europe, which lasted from 1815 to approximately 1945, correctness of intervention was admitted by the theorists of the system, including Lord Brougham, who stated:

Whenever a sudden and great change takes place in the internal structure of a state, dangerous in a high degree to all neighbors, they have a right to attempt, by hostile interference, the restoration of an order of things safe to themselves; or, at least, to counterbalance by active aggression, the new force suddenly acquired.[5] This definition of intervention was rooted in the theory of the balance of power,[6] which has not acquired the same degree of acceptance in the post World War II equilibrium. Nevertheless, President Ronald Reagan echoed Lord Brougham's thesis in October, 1983, when he defended his strategy of covert military activity in Central America. 'I do believe,' he said, 'in the right of a country, when it believes that its interests are best served, to practice covert activity'.[7]

Two weeks later the military action of the United States, and the organization of Eastern Caribbean states brought to a close the four-year rule of the New Jewel Movement on the Island of Grenada. The United States justified her actions by the need to protect American medical students residing in Grenada. The USA and the Caribbean states asserted that the intervention was valid because they had been invited in Grenada by the Governor-General, Grenada's head of state.

With a total land area of 344 sq. km. this micro-state can barely support slightly over 100 000 citizens. Was Grenada a threat to the security of the United States, and the states in the Caribbean basin? The Departments of State and Defense documented the affirmative answer in a white paper issued in September, 1984. 'The revolution [led by Maurice Bishop] that overthrew the Guiry regime in Grenada in April, 1979 was designed to create a communist society and to bring Grenada into the Soviet orbit . . . The close working relations the regime established with the Government of Cuba – both in Grenada and in Cuba itself – showed that Bishop intended to mold his revolution on that of the Soviet Union and, more immediately, of Cuba'.[8] In rejecting the similarity of this intervention to that of the Soviet intervention in Afghanistan, President Reagan described it as 'a rescue operation'.

In opposing the Sandanista regime in Nicaragua the United States has accused the Sandanistas of: (1) engaging in subversive activities against El Salvador; (2) receiving 3000 Cuban military advisers; (3) increasing its military force from 48 800 to 100 000; (4) receiving economic and military aid from the Soviet Union, East Germany, Bulgaria, Poland, Czechoslovakia, Hungary, Libya and PLO.[9] Embellishing Lord Brougham's views, the US Government has maintained that both in Grenada and Nicaragua 'a sudden and great change' took place which was potentially dangerous 'in a high degree to all neighbors', which justified American intervention in Grenada and great concern for the developments in Nicaragua.

In ignoring international law, the Soviet Union has come forth with a doctrine of intervention which legitimizes Soviet intervention on a global scale. This doctrine is rooted, at least in theory, in a long historical struggle against the West which was initiated by the October Revolution (1917) pitting socialism against capitalism in order to establish 'a socialist global system of international relations'.[10] In recent times, this doctrine assumed the forms of proletarian internationalism, peaceful coexistence, the Brezhnev doctrine (relevant to the socialist states of Eastern Europe), and the Asian collective security, designed to contain a fellow socialist state – the People's Republic of China. In the Soviet perception, these doctrines have established a higher order of legitimacy for intervention than that of international law. This is demonstrated by the Soviet intervention in Afghanistan, which took place in December, 1979.

The Charter of the United Nations (Chapter VII) has provided for collective intervention only, and under Article 2 (7) has forbidden intervention in matters which are essentially within the domestic jurisdiction of a member state. The General Assembly in its declaration on the inadmissibility of intervention in the domestic affairs of states, which was adopted in 1965 (with no negative votes and only one abstention) declared that no state shall 'interfere in civil strife in another state'.[11] The same view was expressed in the General Assembly Resolution 2625 (XXV) which was adopted by consensus on 24 October 1970. In violating this international consensus the Soviet Union intervened in Afghanistan, and justified her action by invoking the doctrine of intervention by invitation. The Soviet Union had offered similar justifications for its interventions in Hungary (1956), and Czechoslovakia (1968) to which the Brezhnev doctrine lent ideological legitimacy.

The intervention by invitation raises several problems of a factual nature. It is often difficult to determine whether the intervening state(s) marched in with the consent of the lawful government. Even when treaty arrangements of mutual help exist between states, it is at times hard to know if the consent was freely given and was not obtained through hidden pressures or individual influences of various kinds. In a civil strife, where the ethnic communities are likely to be fragmented, as was the case of the Israeli invasion of Lebanon in the summer of 1982, or in a state where no political system has achieved political stability, a weak government, despite its claims to legitimacy, is likely to invite foreign forces in order to boost its own shaky position.

In disregard of international law, the superpowers have imposed upon the present state system varieties of intervention, including: (1) collective intervention; (2) intervention by invitation; (3) intervention for access to natural resources of other states; (4) humanitarian intervention; (5) intervention to support or suppress movements of national liberation; (6) and intervention to remove ideologically noxious neighboring, as well as distant, states.[12]

In order to engage in the three-dimensional analysis of relations between the two superpowers and three states covering the southern flanks of the Soviet Union, forty scholars from three different constituencies of diplomacy, military and academia met together in a seminar at Villanova University on December 7–8, 1984. Seventeen specialists presented carefully prepared papers in four panels on clearly defined themes to preserve the integrity of the three-dimensional analysis with a sharp focus on the concepts of superpower roles, strategic interest, and intervention. Ample time was devoted to general discussions and the review of the themes that had been elaborated. (An overview of these synthesized themes appears in the last chapter).

STRATEGIC INTERESTS OF THE UNITED STATES AND THE SOVIET UNION AND INTERACTION WITH THE REGIONAL FORCES

George C. McGhee, Morris McCain, Craig Baxter and Jon W. Anderson analyzed these issues from the perspective of diplomats and professional scholars.

In addition to his systemetized exposition of the US strategic interests in Iran, Afghanistan and Pakistan, McGhee brought to the discussions his insights into Soviet–American relations that were based upon his lifelong experience as a former US Ambassador to Germany and Turkey. As a former Undersecretary of State, he contributed a great deal to the understanding of the foreign policy making process in the State Department, especially during the 1950s and the 1960s.

'Strategic importance, like beauty', states McGhee, 'is in the eye of the beholder'. Obviously, perception is the key to the understanding of the strategic interest. McGhee believes that since these three states are Islamic, the United States faces a barrier of understanding with the three states. Iran is relatively more important because of its reserves of 38.3 billion barrels of oil. With the overthrow of the Shah, Iran as a small non-industrialized state, could not have much local or regional power.

Highlighting the role of Afghanistan as a buffer state between the Indian sub-continent and the Russian/Soviet state, McGhee states that with the demise of the British empire there is no longer a need for a buffer state. India or Pakistan, with large populations in comparison with their natural resources, would not be an inviting object for conquest. However, according to McGhee, the USSR would like to see Pakistan demilitarized in order to remove any threat to the Soviet occupation of Afghanistan. There was also danger that Soviets would attempt to control Pakistani Baluchistan in order to achieve the closest striking distance to Iranian oil in the Persian Gulf. Consequently, 'any Soviet threat against Iran, through Baluchistan, would constitute a major strategic problem for the United States'.

Focusing his attention on the Soviet intervention in Afghanistan, McGhee believes that it put an end to the era of detente and the start of the second cold war. As long as the Soviet presence continues in Afghanistan, the fear will persist in the West that they will use Afghanistan as 'a stepping stone to the seizure of Iran and other Middle Eastern states'. In light of this, he recommends that the United States should 'provide military and economic aid to the Afghan freedom fighters and to Pakistan'.

In the final analysis, McGhee believes that the question of the strategic importance of Iran, Afghanistan and Pakistan is that of Soviet intentions. If the Soviets expand, the United States strategic interests would stay in these three states. If the Soviet policy changed, the US policy would shift to helping these three states in the development of their economies.

A Soviet specialist, McCain defines the strategic interests of the superpowers in terms of their capabilities to have global reach. 'For the Soviets, an ideology of universal socialist revolution provides the rationale; for the West, the deathly menace of Communism'. In other words, the struggle for power essentially underlines the definition of the strategic interests of the United States and the Soviet Union. However, McCain assigns ideology a subordinate position to Soviet political goals. Very much like the United States, the Soviet Union often has supported right-wing dictatorships if they served Soviet strategic interests. Essentially, according to McCain, 'security from attack and the extension of Soviet influence over other governments' is the name of the Soviet game.

The Soviet Union shares common borders with twelve states. In the West most of the Soviet boundaries are secured except southern frontiers with Iran, Afghanistan and Pakistan and extensive borders with China. 'In terms of proximity', McCain believes, 'Pakistan is to the Soviets as Cuba is to the Americans . . . as long as Pakistan remains allied with the West and China, Moscow will make sustained efforts to destabilize the Government in Islamabad'. In regard to Afghanistan, McCain believes that Soviet interests are more 'limited than is often recognized'. The Soviet goal is to prevent another hostile government from coming to power along the southern flanks of the Soviet Union. Afghanistan is unlikely to become the sixteenth Soviet Republic since there are already about 50 million Muslims within the Soviet Union.

While Iran remains a big prize for the Soviet Union, McCain believes the 'USSR will probably be frustrated in its efforts to improve relations with Tehran', while Ayatollah Khomeini remains at the helm of affairs. Iran is not about to become another Afghanistan, McCain asserts very confidently, whether the US builds its forces in the region or not. 'Soviet troops will neither march East nor West from Afghanistan. Their most likely direction is north'.

In addition to the US and USSR, India, a middle power, plays a significant role in the political developments of Southwest Asia. A close strategic partner of the USSR, India has had historically hostile relations with Afghanistan.

A former US Consul-General, Baxter, who has spent many years of his life in India and Pakistan, believes that in recent times the improvement of relations between India and Afghanistan was due to the emergence of Pakistan in 1947, a state which inherited disputed boundaries and divided ethnic groups with Afghanistan. This development turned India into a strategic partner of the Soviet Union and created close relations between Pakistan, the US and China. In light of the Soviet presence in Afghanistan, Baxter indicates that 'one permanent interest of India should be defense against incursions from the Northwest'. Rationally speaking, the disappearance of the buffer role of Afghanistan would be against the Indian interest. However, this has not happened and, Baxter indicates that India has 'justified Soviet intervention' in Afghanistan. While relations between Pakistan and Iran have been fairly cordial, India's relations with Iran have fluctuated from cordiality to indifference and even hostility. While Pakistan's relations with the Khomeini Government have not been exactly cordial, the 'converse, a close relationship between revolutionary Iran and India, has not been the result'.

Dealing with Pakistan's relations with India, Baxter points out that despite the lingering dispute over Kashmir, the two countries have resolved certain problems, including the delineation of the boundaries, the division of the Indus waters, and the territorial settlement in the Rann of Kutch. However, according to Baxter, India has shown a strong determination to claim a position of pre-eminence in South Asia and wishes to be acknowledged by other states in that position. Consequently, India has taken strong exception to the US military aid to Pakistan and Pakistan's program to achieve nuclear capability.

The newly established South Asia Regional Cooperation (SARC) is another arena where India has made it abundantly clear that while it will deal with its neighbors on a bilateral basis, India would do so on its own terms. In discussing 'a number of preconditions' for India's role in SARC, Baxter has described them as the 'Indira doctrine' which includes (1) strict bilateralism between India and its neighbors; (2) no security relationships between nations of South Asia and outside powers; (3) the Indian Treaty of 1971 with the Soviet Union is to be an exception – the US–Pakistan agreement on military assistance, however, is in violation of this aspect of the doctrine; (4) 'members of SARC should not disagree with India on major issues; although, it is not phrased so baldly'.

Although Baxter does not project this aspect of India's foreign policy, in the long run, the Indian conception of its dominance in South Asia, one is inclined to think, is likely to collide with the Soviet extension of influence in Southwest Asia.

An anthropologist who has done extensive field work in the three states, Anderson indicates that Pakistan, Iran and Afghanistan 'share characteristic internal ethnic diversities and national borders which cut across local ethnic groups in all directions'. These ethnic groups, called nationalities by the Soviet ethnographers, pose serious challenges to the three states, including (a) political, cultural and linguistic integration within the national culture; and (b) the possibility of exploitation of their grievances by the regional, as well as the major, powers. The latter situation is clearly demonstrated by the Soviet encouragement to Afghanistan for its support to the Pashtuns

Table 1.1 Ethnic dispersion among Pakistan, Iran and Afghanistan and the Soviet Union

Ethnic Community	USSR	Iran	Afghanistan	Pakistan	Divided Among States
Pashtun			x	x	2
Baluch		x	x	x	3
Nuristani (i.e. Kalash)			x	x	2
Kurd	x	x			4 (*Including Turkey & Iraq*)
Kazak	x		x		2
Tajik	x		x		2
Karakalpak	x	x	x		2
Kirghis	x		x		2
Turkoman	x	x	x		3
Uzbek	x		x		2
Aimak		x	x		2
Hazara		x	x	x	3
Qashqais		x			1
Arabs		x	x		2
Bakhtiaris		x			1
Lurs		x			1
Azerbaijanis	x	x			2
Punjabi (Muslim)				x	1
Sindhi (Muslim)				x	1
Kashmiri (Muslim)				x	2 (*Including India*)
Total 20	8	11	12	6	38

Sources: Hafeez Malik, *Sir Sayyid Ahmad Khan and Muslim Modernization in India and Pakistan* (New York: Columbia University Press, 1980), p. 18; Richard W. Weeks, Ed., *Muslim Peoples: A World Ethnographic Survey* (Westport, Conn.: Greenwood Press, 1984), Revised Edition, II Vols. Information condensed from the latter source.

(Pashtunistan) and the Kurdish people and the Azri Turks in Iran and Iraq, which reflected at different times in the form of the People's Republics of Azerbaijan (1920, 1945–46) and Mahabad (1943). This situation is further complicated by the fact that some ethnic groups are commonly shared between the three states and the Soviet Union, as is indicated in Table 1.1

None of these states has evolved any pragmatic policy to ensure parity of participation and parity of esteem for their ethnic or regional communities. This situation, therefore, shows a relative deprivation both cultural and material, which the ethnic groups endure across the boundary lines.

Anderson has highlighted this dilemma by stating that the Iranian state is identified with a kind of 'Persian mission' with regard to non-Persian and non-urban cultures within its domain. 'Drawing on that tradition as a hinterland version of the Persian state, the Afghan state has pursued various policies of Afghanization for the past one hundred years from military extension of state power and resettlement of Afghans in previous non-Afghan territories to establishment of Pashtu as a national language taught to all non-native Persian speakers'. By contrast, Anderson believes Pakistan is a 'modern, centralized, bureaucratic state' where diverse civil, military, bureaucratic elites define nationalism and expect other groups to conform.

SUPERPOWER RELATIONS WITH PAKISTAN

Lawrence Ziring, Hafeez Malik, Agha Shahi and Rodney Jones have dealt with various aspects of Soviet–American relations with Pakistan reflecting their backgrounds as academic specialists and diplomat.

A well known specialist of Pakistan, Ziring spotlights the role of buffer states. 'States do not choose to become buffers', maintains Ziring, 'it is a role thrust upon them by a hostile international environment over which they have no control'. Ziring believes that Afghanistan's role as a buffer state had not only preserved its territorial integrity, it had also been a measure of the region's security. 'Neither could be sustained', Ziring believes, 'after the epoch-making events of 1978–1979' when the Daoud regime was overthrown by the Afghan marxists and eventually the Soviet Union intervened. Since then, Afghanistan's sovereignty has become a fiction, while Iran and Pakistan are threatened by forces beyond their control.

'Iran, not Pakistan, was the first country to experience the loss of the Afghan buffer', according to Ziring, and he hypothesizes that Iraq struck Iran in September, 1980 because the Soviets had moved into Afghanistan and were maneuvering to exploit ethnic and sectarian conflicts within Iran. Pakistan attempted to reconcile the conflict between Iran and Iraq, but had difficulty relating to revolutionary Iran.

In discussing the consequences of Soviet military actions against the insurgents in Afghanistan, Ziring again hypothesizes that the

Soviets are engaged in ethnic, as well as geographic, engineering of Afghanistan. 'The Soviets seriously contemplate the reorganization of the geography of northern Afghanistan', believes Ziring, 'so that a section from a line south of Herat to Chaghcharan and just north of Kabul to the Pakistan frontier would become one with the Soviet republics'. This cartographic rearrangement of Afghanistan, according to Ziring, 'would imply the linking of the Pashtun and Baluch areas of Pakistan in a scheme for a greater Afghanistan'. This grand design obviously cannot be accomplished without dismembering Pakistan and Iran. Nevertheless, Ziring believes that 'it is well within the range of probability'.

In assessing the impact of Soviet intervention in Afghanistan on Pakistan's foreign policy, Malik indicates that Pakistan appeared determined to achieve the following objectives: (1) improvement of strategic relations with the United States, (2) indirect negotiations with Afghanistan through the United Nations; (3) support to the Afghan refugees for humanitarian and 'other purposes' and (4) improvement of relations with India. The pursuit of these objectives, Malik believes, has steadily soured relations between Pakistan and the Soviet Union.

When the Soviet Union intervened in December, 1979, US relations with Pakistan were at their lowest ebb because of American suspicion that Pakistan was making covert attempts to develop nuclear military capability. Relations between the US and Pakistan did not improve until President Reagan was elected in 1980. The Reagan Administration offered an economic and military aid package of 3.2 billion dollars beginning with October, 1982 and terminating in October, 1987. This aid injected a sense of security into Pakistan, while Pakistan reinvigorated its relations with the People's Republic of China. President Zia stated that 'we now have a trilateral strength from our association with China, our new relationship with the US, and our traditional relationship with other Islamic countries, headed by Saudi Arabia'. Has it really brought security to Pakistan? Malik has speculated extensively on this nebulous sense of security that Pakistan claims to have achieved.

Pakistan's support to the Afghan refugees has created a dreadful dilemma for Pakistan. Would 3 million Afghan refugees return to Afghanistan 'in conditions of dignity and honor' as Pakistan has demanded or would they eventually settle down in Pakistan? Most observers, including Malik, have now come to believe that given the most favorable conditions for the Afghan refugees, no more than 50 per cent would return to Afghanistan. Meanwhile, Pakistan's borderlands have become sanctuaries for the Afghan insurgents who have tied down 110 000 Soviet troops in Afghanistan. The negotiations between Pakistan–Afghanistan–Soviet Union through the United Nations have sputtered along for several years and they are unlikely to yield any results.

Despite Pakistan's best attempts to improve relations with India, not much has been achieved. Malik indicates that several formidable obstacles have retarded the improvement, including (1) Indian objection to US military aid to Pakistan; (2) the rise of militant Sikh nationalism in India for which India has partially blamed Pakistan; (3) the failure of negotiations over the no-war pact between the two states, heightening suspicions and finally (4) the Soviet friendship treaty of August, 1971 with India which obligated India not to establish relations with any third country which might be harmful to the security interests of the Soviet Union.

Sandwiched between the Soviet Union and India, Pakistan faces a precarious future much as Poland did in the 1930s when it was hemmed in by the two powerful neighbors – Germany and the Soviet Union.

A former Minister of Foreign Affairs of Pakistan and former Ambassador to the People Republic of China and the United Nations, Agha Shahi explains Pakistan's relations with the United States in the context of US–Soviet competition, Pakistan's traditional relationships with the Middle East and the triangular relationships of Pakistan with India and the United States.

The rivalry between the United States and the Soviet Union began to have repercussions in Southwest Asia soon after the withdrawal of the British imperial power in 1947. Pakistan signed a mutual defense agreement with the United States in 1954 and abandoned the non-alignment posture. From 1955 to 1960, according to Shahi, Pakistan 'enjoyed a kind of honeymoon relationship with the United States'. Pakistan, during this period, allowed the United States to conduct U-2 reconnaissance flights from Peshawer over the Soviet territory. However, this 'honeymoon' began to cool off when (1) President Kennedy 'hailed the non-alignment nations as bridge builders' between the NATO and Warsaw Pact nations; (2) President Johnson imposed an arms embargo against Pakistan in the aftermath of the 1965 India–Pakistan war and (3) Pakistan's developing relations with China were viewed with suspicions.

The relationship between Pakistan and the US improved in

1970–71 when Pakistan arranged a secret visit of Henry Kissinger to Beijing in mid 1971 which enabled President Nixon to visit China in 1972. That this would have very disturbing impact on the Soviet policy makers was unfortunately not taken into consideration, especially when it became known that Pakistan's Foreign Secretary personally chauffered Kissinger to the airport where he flew off in the President of Pakistan's plane to Beijing. This aspect of the arrangement is not mentioned by Shahi, but he pointed out that the Soviet Union was so irritated that 'it threw its support behind India and the secessionist movement in East Pakistan'. The Indo-Soviet Treaty of August, 1971, Shahi believes, was concluded 'to prevent China from assisting Pakistan in the ensuing war of secession'. In other words, Pakistan paid a rather heavy price for its indiscriminate support to American objectives in regard to China.

Pakistan had barely begun to 'bind its wound' after the amputation of 1971 when the Carter Administration began to exercise pressure on Pakistan to stop progress on its nuclear program. Consequently, US relations with Pakistan were downgraded and Pakistan turned toward consolidating its ties with China, withdrew its membership from SEATO, and cemented its fraternal bonds with the Islamic states in the Middle East. Soviet intervention in Afghanistan in 1979 prompted the Carter Administration to offer a military aid package of 800 million dollars to Pakistan which was however rejected.

At this critical stage, according to Shahi, Pakistan had three options: (1) to directly confront the Soviet Union by participating in the Afghan resistance; (2) to accept Soviet occupation of Afghanistan; (3) to protest the Soviet intervention in the forums of the United Nations, the Islamic Conference and the non aligned movement. Pakistan, according to Shahi, opted for the third course.

Despite the US economic and military aid to Pakistan since 1980, relations between the two states have occasionally suffered a jolt over the nuclear issue. 'In 1976', Shahi states, 'Henry Kissinger served notice to Pakistan that the Democrats would make a horrible example of Pakistan', if Pakistan did not stop its nuclear program. Shahi asked a rhetorical question: Why is Pakistan being singled out for this treatment when a more or less permissive attitude is maintained toward Israel, South Africa and India? Shahi believes that to make Pakistan's nuclear program a centerpiece of the new US–Pakistan relationship would be contrary to the interests of both states.

In regard to India, Shahi maintains that objecting to US military aid to Pakistan, India has chosen to predicate its own security, not on its military superiority over its neighbor, but 'on an offensive capability so overwhelming as to deprive Pakistan of any capability for defense'. Shahi remains committed to peaceful relations between India and Pakistan and has strongly recommended a no-war pact between the two states.

Finally, Shahi believes, the three states of Pakistan, Iran and Afghanistan would be able to best preserve their territorial integrity and independence if they continue to follow the policies of neutrality and non-alignment. 'Being the neighbors of the Soviet Union', Shahi advises, 'it would be hazardous for them to choose the camp of its adversary'.

Currently Director of Nuclear Policy Studies at the Center for Strategic and International Studies of Georgetown University, Rodney Jones unequivocally states that 'Pakistan's nuclear progress toward some sort of atom bomb capability is now almost universally recognized'. However, he cautions that if Pakistan can achieve 'credible status as a nuclear armed regional power, it becomes an important but disturbing precedence'.

Jones has pointed out that Pakistan has followed two routes for the development of nuclear weapons: (a) gaseous centrifuge facilities for uranium enrichment and (b) the plutonium route for the development of weapon-grade materials. He believes that Pakistan has the ability to produce 'enough material for 5-7 early generation atomic bombs per year'.

In Jones' calculations, Pakistan's threat perceptions are focused on India and not on the Soviet Union. Pakistan defense planners conclude that they don't have the capacity to defend against full scale invasion of Pakistan by the Soviet Union. On the other hand, the military force balance between Pakistan and India has steadily shifted in the favor of India. India has been able to perpetuate military superiority *vis-à-vis* Pakistan both qualitatively and quantitatively. With its nuclear capability, Jones indicates, India at some point may be able to impose on Pakistan an unconditional surrender. It is this particular situation that makes nuclear military option for Pakistan so attractive. Jones indicates that 'Pakistan's perceptions of safety would rise if Pakistan demonstrated nuclear explosive capability'. However, he doubts 'whether those perceptions are accurate', and then concludes that 'nuclear competition [between India and Pakistan] in the sub-continent will itself be a magnet for and more deeply engage Soviet influence in the sub-continent than its absence'.

SOVIET–AMERICAN RELATIONS WITH REVOLUTIONARY IRAN

Richard W. Cottam, Shireen T. Hunter, Andrew Killgore and Khosrow Fatemi have analyzed the relations of the superpowers with revolutionary Iran and examined Iran's relations with the Arabs with a sharp focus on the economic aspects of the Iran–Iraq war. These scholars have reflected in their analyses an invaluable experience of diplomacy and academic expertise on these issues.

A former US diplomat and a well-known scholar of Iranian nationalism, Cottam has attempted to offer an explanation of 'deep and persistent enmity' between Iran and the United States. After World War II, the US became a global power, and 'gradually replaced the British as the leading competitor of the Soviet Union for influence in Iran'. Cottam believes that with the passage of time 'American policy towards Iran began to manifest the same patterns that could be seen in earlier British policies'. In other words, the US became the imperial protector of Iran. This pattern of relations laid the foundation for deep enmity which surfaced during the Iranian revolution of 1979. Cottam has presented an extensive analysis of various phases of American–Iranian relations which illustrate his main thesis.

Cottam has indicated that since World War II American foreign policy had doggedly pursued three objectives in the Middle East: (a) contain and deter Soviet expansion; (b) maintain the flow of oil and petro dollars to the United States and its allies and (c) and maintain Israeli security. In order to achieve these objectives, the US sought to have *de facto* alliance with Middle East leaders who are conservative, anti-communist and willing to cooperate with multi-national corporations, American banks and to limit their opposition to Israel to a rhetorical level. Cottam indicates that American code words for these leaders are 'moderate' and 'responsible'. 'Any indication that they might be abandoned', Cottam maintains, 'could destroy the basis of American policy in the Middle East'.

Ayatollah Khomeini, on the other hand, was conservative and anti-communist, but was, in American terminology, unwilling to be 'moderate' and 'responsible'. The radical Islamic movement 'personified by the Khomeini regime was a threat to every American ally with a large Muslim population in the area'. In dealing with the Reagan Administration, Cottam has noted a tilt toward Iraq in the Iran–Iraq conflict. He believes that this conflict ranks 'with the Arab–Israeli conflict and the Afghan situation as those most likely to give definition to American policy in the area'. This crisis, in his judgement, affects 'all three basic American objectives and in contradictory ways'.

Summing up his main thesis, Cottam makes a couple of telling points: (1) Soviet and American policies have lost control of regional dynamics; (2) 'functionally, Soviet and Iranian policy are allied in the Eastern Mediterranean, and American and Iranian policy are allied in Afghanistan'. This strand of analysis suggests that Iran could make a case for a working relationship with either superpower. But, would it? Not as long as Ayatollah Khomeini is in the saddle.

A former Iranian diplomat and currently Deputy Director of the Middle East Program at the Center for Strategic and International Studies at Georgetown University, Hunter has traced Russian/Soviet relations with Iran since 1722; i.e. from the fall of the Safavid Empire to the end of the Qajar and Pahlavi dynasties. Moreover, she has devoted extensive efforts to analyzing the Soviet relations with the Islamic Republic of Iran.

In contemplating the landscape of Russo–Iran relations before the Soviet revolution of 1917, Hunter has discerned certain patterns of relationship between the two neighboring states, including (1) 'Whenever Iran was threatened by total domination by a rival power, Russia tried to prevent the occurrence while also securing advantages for itself'; (2) the Treaty of Turkmanchai (1829) decisively shifted the balance of power in the favor of Russia conceding to her extra territorial rights and a veto power over the succession issue; (3) in the 19th century, Britain emerged as the countervailing force to the Russian power and the rivalry between the two ensured Iran's independence; (4) Russian expansion in Central Asia eliminated small khanates (princedoms) as buffers and Iran had to face the Russian Empire across a 1200 mile border. This geopolitical reality, indicates Hunter, has determined Iran's political options regarding the Soviet Union, as well as other powers.

Like a tide, Soviet power ebbed and flowed in the direction of Iran from 1941 to 1946 when the Reza Shah came to power. Following the allied decision, the USSR forces occupied northern Iran and the British established their control in southern Iran in order to supply the Soviet Union with war material. However, Hunter maintains that the Soviets' ultimate objective was 'the Sovietization [of northern Iran] and incorporation within the Soviet empire'. This was vividly demonstrated when the Soviet Union encouraged the establishment of 'democratic republics in Iranian Azerbaijan and Kurdistan'. Simultaneously, 'Moscow tried to change the Iranian regime'. However, the US pressure forced the Soviets to withdraw from Iran.

During 1953–1962 the Soviet Union had very tense relations with Iran, but by 1972 a degree of stable *détente* had been established between the two states. As the Soviet relations with Iraq improved, serious tensions developed between Iran and the USSR.

Under the Islamic Republic, however, the Soviet relations have fluctuated from 'a mixture of ambivalence and expectancy' to a degree of antagonism. Despite the Soviet support for Iran in the hostage crisis when 52 American diplomats were seized in November, 1979, the Khomeini Government condemned the Soviet intervention in Afghanistan when Khomeini called the USSR 'the other great Satan'. By mid-1981, Soviet–Iranian relations improved because of the developments caused by the Iran–Iraq war. This *rapprochement* did not last very long and the relations between Iran and the Soviet Union slid back to occasional cooperation and occasional antagonism.

Hunter has projected the future relations between the two neighbors in a seesaw fashion: 'They are likely to remain volatile and pass through stages of relative *rapprochement* and estrangement, depending on Iran's internal developments, the shifts in regional and international politics'.

A former US Ambassador to Qatar, a Gulf state, and a diplomat with lifelong experience in other Gulf states, Killgore has noted a pattern of historical antagonism between the Iranians and the Arabs. To Killgore, even Islam, which replaced Zoroastrianism in Iran in the seventh century, 'assumed such a peculiarly Persian mold' that it is 'hardly a unifying force' with the rest of the Islamic world.

From this premise, Killgore analyzed territorial disputes between Iran and Iraq focusing on the Shatt-al-Arab, Khorramshahar, called Muhammarah by the Arabs, and the Province of Khuzistan, called Arabistan in the Arab world; and the Arab-owned Gulf islands of Abu Musa and the greater and lesser tunbs, which were occupied by the Shah in 1971.

Killgore has severely criticized the American policy of 1972 when the Nixon Administration sold the Shah 'all the arms he could buy, excepting nuclear weapons'. Essentially this policy, according to Killgore, set the stage for revolution in Iran. The US policy treated the Shah as the American surrogate in the Gulf and steadfastly refused to have contacts with the opposition in Iran. Persuaded by Israel and the Israeli lobby in the US, Killgore maintains Kissinger came to believe that 'a heavily armed Iran on one side and a heavily armed Israel on the other side would keep the Arab states in line and guarantee the security of Israel'. Commenting on the Iran–Iraq war, Killgore believes 'that it will probably end in a stalemate'. However, he has ruled out any negotiated solution of the war as long as Khomeini is alive.

A former Senior Economist at the National Iranian Oil Company and Director General of the Bureau of International Cooperation at Iran's Ministry of Commerce, Fatemi has analyzed various aspects of the international economy of the Iran–Iraq war. A part of his chapter is devoted to the analysis of the political factors that led to the current Iran–Iraq war. Most of the chapter, however, is devoted to energy problems at a global level and the way international finance has been affected by the ups and downs of the war.

Unlike Killgore, Fatemi maintains that the thesis of 'centuries of enmity' culminating in the Iran–Iraq war is hyperbolic. He admits racial, cultural and political differences between the Iranians and the Arabs, but for him the most frequent source of tension and conflict has been the geopolitical factors between the two neighboring states. The Shatt-al-Arab, according to him, has been the most frequent source of tension and war; but, whenever a degree of understanding was reached about its status, the Shatt-al-Arab became the stream of accord between Iran and Iraq.

Focusing on the current Iran–Iraq war, Fatemi has catalogued at least six main reasons: (1) in the aftermath of the revolution, Iran was perceived to be militarily a weak state by Iraq; (2) Iraq's leader, Saddam Hussein's uncontrolled ambitions to be the leader of the Arab world; (3) Iraq's demands that Iran should return to Arab sovereignty disputed islands of Abu Musa and the two tunbs, located in the Persian Gulf/Arab Gulf; (4) Khomeini's declared vows to export Islamic revolution to other states; (5) Iraqi calculations, especially in 1980, leading Saddam Hussein to think that the Iranian Army was about to mutiny and eventually disintegrate under the hammer blows of Khomeini's purges; and last, but not least, (6) Iraqi failure to pay any attention to Irani national sentiment and the Shiite resolve for martyrdom which have turned the initial Iraqi success to a stalemated war with Iran. No serious scholar of the Middle East scene would take exception to any of these explanations.

Dealing with the issues of international economy, Fatemi has focused on oil supply, trade, international finance, north-south relations, and finally, the long-term prospects for the international oil cartel, OPEC. Despite this drawn-out war between the two states causing the loss of production of oil (7 per cent of the world supply) in Iran and Iraq, there has been no shortage of oil in the international market. Why? He gives the following reasons: (1) overproduction of oil in Saudi Arabia; (2) conservation of energy in the industrialized states; (3) economic slowdown in the western countries; and (4) the glut of oil being used by the industrialized states for stockpiling purposes.

While the industrialized world has suffered no particular damage from the Iran–Iraq war, the two states have suffered enormous losses, including the stoppage of oil exports, nation-building activities and the destruction of oil refineries and other industries. Ironically, Fatemi believes that the Iran–Iraq war has infused new life into OPEC. The war reduced by 7–8 million barrels per day OPEC's total capacity and thus relieved the pressure of competition among the OPEC members, sparing them competition for the production of oil which would have not only bred suspicions among them, but would have reduced the price of oil.

SOVIET INTERVENTION IN AFGHANISTAN, DECEMBER 1979

Ashraf Ghani, Henry S. Bradsher, Louis Dupree and Nancy Hatch Dupree have discussed various aspects of the Soviet intervention in Afghanistan, its consequences for Pakistan and the response of the world to this intrusion. All four scholars have spent a large number of years in Afghanistan and are probably the most recognized experts on Afghanistan's development. With the exception of Bradsher, who is a Journalist-Scholar, the other three are anthropologists who have looked at the problems of Afghanistan from the grassroots level.

An Afghan national who is now on the faculty of Johns Hopkins University, Ghani has focused on the development of the Afghan state from 1880 to 1978, when the Afghan Communist Party overthrew the regime of Prince Muhammad Daoud, the first cousin and brother-in-law of the former King, Zahir Shah. Ironically, Daoud had toppled the monarchy in 1973 while his cousin, the King, was vacationing in Italy.

Very appropriately, Ghani has indicated that the struggle for power between Britain and Russia in Central Asia was primarily responsible for the emergence of Afghanistan as a buffer state, a thesis, which Lawrence Ziring has also expounded at great length in chapter six of this volume.

Ghani is forthright in stating that Afghanistan's frontiers with Russia/Soviet Union, Iran and Pakistan, were determined by the two imperial powers. While he recognizes the validity of Afghanistan's frontiers with Iran and the Soviet Union, he describes Afghanistan's frontiers with British India, and the successor state, Pakistan, as the product of unequal treaty between the overwhelming British India and Amir Abdur Rahman, King of Afghanistan. In this formulation, he has disregarded Pakistan's claim that the Durand Line established in 1893 (the boundary between Pakistan and Afghanistan) was ratified in 1905 by Amir Habibullah Khan, Amir Abdur Rahman's son, and then by King Amanullah in 1919 and then finally by King Nadir Shah in 1930.[13]

If all unequal treaties are to be considered null and void in the contemporary state system, then a very large number of states would have to be unscrambled – a highly destabilizing process for the world's equilibrium. Moreover, Pakistan, Iran and Afghanistan are multi-ethnic states as Jon Anderson has demonstrated in chapter five of this volume, and Ghani himself has highlighted in his chapter, stating that 'thirty two languages belonging to four linguistic families' are spoken in Afghanistan. How many ethnic-linguistic regions will have to be carved into states in order to satisfy varieties of irredentism?

In describing the process of state formation of Afghanistan, Ghani has underlined 'the potency of Islamic symbols assuming overwhelming importance, while descent and ethnicity remained equally salient'. In discussing the Afghan relations with American-armed Pakistan, which were clouded by Afghan territorial claims against Pakistan, Ghani points out that the Afghan rulers established closer links with the Soviet Union. This link eventually paved the way for the leftist revolution that occurred in 1978 and culminated in the Soviet intervention in December, 1979, essentially to protect the Afghan Communists who were about to be toppled by the insurgents.

An Associated Press correspondent in the early 1960s in Afghanistan, and the Bureau Chief in Moscow from 1964 to 1968, Bradsher has given a remarkably detailed description of the formation of the Communist movement in Afghanistan, its bifurcation into two factions (parties?), 'invitation' to the Soviet Union, and finally, an assessment of its future acceptance in Afghanistan. The People's Democratic Party of Afghanistan (PDPA) came to power thirteen years after its formation in 1966 and has never described itself as the Communist Party, nor has the Soviet Union ever enlisted it as a socialist/communist fraternal state, while it is true that the USSR has fostered its development since its infancy.

Bradsher has highlighted three views of Afghanistan's possible future development espoused by three groups which had emerged in 1958: (1) businessmen and technocrats who were dominant until 1978 and were supported by Daoud Khan and King Zahir Shah; (2) 'westernized' and educated elite with traditional Islamic orientations which eventually established the Jamiat-i-Islami in 1958; (3) the Communists who operated clandestinely, but surfaced on the political scene during the decade of democracy (1963–73). Of these three groups, so far the Communists have triumphed at an enormous cost of destruction of their fellow countrymen with the onset of the Soviet intervention.

The PDPA initiated its formation in Nur Muhammad Taraki's home in January, 1965 where Babrak Karmal assumed the second position of leadership. No two more disparate personalities could have been yoked together in one movement. Karmal hailed, maintains Bradsher, from 'Afghanistan's aristocrasy as the son of a royal general', and wanted to work within the royal system to expand the Marxist influence. Karmal was twice elected to the Afghan Parliament during the decade of democracy (1963–73). Taraki, on the other hand, Bradsher points out, 'wanted to gain supporters from a position of opposition'. Taraki was a Pashtun; however, Bradsher has given a very interesting, yet a peculiar description of Karmal's ethnic identity, saying that 'Karmal was Kashmiri, but appearing essentially Tajik and claiming Pashtun ancestry'. Karmal speaks Farsi/Dari and German, while Taraki spoke Pashto and some English.

Almost a year before the overthrow of the Daoud regime on 7 April 1978, the two factions of the PDPA (Parcham with Karmal as their leader and Khalq with Taraki and Hafeezullah Amin as their leaders) had restored 'unity'. Within two months after the takeover of Afghanistan by the PDPA, the facade of 'unity' disappeared and Karmal and his associates were posted as ambassadors abroad. Karmal, however, returned to Kabul in December, 1979 when the Soviet Union intervened.

Bradsher believes that the statistical information about the PDPA members is dubious and, in any case, 'communism in Afghanistan is limited to a fairly small number of persons'. Moreover, the PDPA has not been able 'to replace the throne as a symbol of national unity for the country's disparate ethnic, tribal and linguistic groups' and has not been able to eliminate dissensions within its own ranks. Bradsher has painted a rather bleak picture of the PDPA's future in Afghan society: 'The PDPA has no chance of breaking away from the Soviet Union, will remain weak and isolated in Afghanistan' and that 'Soviet Marxist-Leninism will [not] win widespread acceptance in a land of ruggedly unvanquished people'.

The description of the increasing dependence of the Afghan Government on Soviet support was beyond the scope of Bradsher's paper. However, recently, a substantial amount of information has become available to demonstrate that the Soviet Union has had some success in Sovietizing Afghanistan. The campaign to Sovietize Afghanistan includes emphasis on education and the counterpart advisory system. The school system from kindergartens to universities has been revamped. Several childrens' organizations have been created: One prominent one is Parwareshgah-i-Watan (Fatherland orphanage). This orphanage is established for children whose parents have been killed in the war. In November, 1984, 870 children from the orphanages were sent to the Soviet Central Asian Republics for ten years of education. Some 12 000 Afghans are now (1985) studying at various universities and training institutions in the Soviet Union.[14] Approximately 1500 university scholarships are offered to Afghan students each year by the Soviet Union. Socialist countries allocate some 500 scholarships a year to Afghani students. It is estimated that 350 Afghan teachers are sent annually to the Soviet Union and East Germany to learn how to teach communist ideas effectively. While some information has appeared that students are forced to go to the Soviet Union, actually, 'the Afghan Government is, in fact, swamped with applicants. It is estimated that 3000–4000 Afghans apply annually for the 1500 scholarships'.[15] Social contacts between the northern Afghan nationalities and their ethnic cousins in Soviet Central Asia are assiduously fostered. Uzbak and Tajik radio programs, newspapers and literature published in the Soviet Union are aimed at convincing northern Afghans that their historical links are across the Soviet border. Afghan Tajiks are now free to cross into Soviet Tajikistan for free medical care.

Many Soviet Central Asians and Russians participate in the counterpart advisory system in the Afghan Government ministries. According to some reports, the Soviet Union has sent Iranian Communist Party members into Afghanistan posing as Soviet Tajiks. These Iranians are supposed to help to reorganize the PDPA and build up its membership. The advisory system has been elaborated in all Afghan ministries, but more so in the Ministry of Foreign Affairs, where a diplomatic institute was formed to train diplomats. (The top Soviet advisor in the Ministry of Foreign Affairs, according to one latest report, is Vasily Safronchuk).[16]

Many professional associations, the unions of writers, musicians and artists, have been established. For an individual to make a living at those activities, membership is required. Also, there are unions of farmers and religious leaders and party-controlled trade unions. The fatherland front stands at the apex of the state's sponsored organizations.[17]

The secret police, Khad (known after its Afghan initials), modeled on the KGB, has been designed to watch over these organizations as well as private citizens. Its tentacles extend even into the Afghan refugee tent villages on the Pakistan side of the border. While the Afghan armed forces remain weak, they are being strengthened with the help of Iranian communists and other Soviet Central ethnic military experts, in addition to the Russians. In 1984–85, the Afghan armed forces number 160 000, including 60 000 in the army, 75 000 in paramilitary forces and 25 000 in secret police. Selig Harrison notes elsewhere after his visit to Afghanistan in 1984 that 'the army is still plagued by desertion, but the desertion rate appears to have leveled off'.[18]

Would the Soviet campaign to Sovietize Afghanistan succeed in Afghanistan, especially in face of these 'nation-building' endeavors that do not lend encouragement to those who continue to expect Soviet retreat across the southern borders?

The Soviet withdrawal from Afghanistan forced upon her by the insurgents on its southern borders would not only destroy the entire left movement in Afghanistan, but would also give a shattering blow to the Soviet reputation for military power. (Those who have consistently advocated the policy of establishing a *cordon sanitaire* around the USSR *a la* Baghdad Pact and CENTO may argue that destroying the Soviet military prestige on its southern borders may very well be the US foreign policy). However, the Soviet failure to maintain a 'friendly' regime on its southern flanks would also have serious repercussions on the stability of Soviet Central Asia, where Muslim nationalities have unhappily learned to offer a grudging loyalty to the Soviet regime. The image of overwhelming Soviet power coupled with policies of cooption of ethnic elites, economic and educational improvements, have succeeded so far in maintaining the Soviet system in Central Asia. The Soviet defeat at the hands of the Afghan insurgents would have the potential to unravel the Soviet empire in Central Asia – a risk that no Soviet regime is likely to take. This aspect of the Soviet dilemma has not been grasped either in Pakistan or in the United States. (Time alone will prove or disprove this assessment).

The recognition of this Soviet dilemma is not 'rationalization for the invasion of Afghanistan by Soviet-line sympathizers', as Louis Dupree asserts, nor an admission of 'defeat'. It is an act of realism, which is based upon the geopolitical realities of Central and Southwest Asia, along with a recognition that international conflicts are not necessarily zero-sum games. To be aware of one's adversary's dilemma in a difficult situation is the hallmark of rational pragmatism and statesmanship. Probably this Soviet dilemma can be best explained in a rhetorical question: If Vietnam had shared contiguous territory with the United States on any side of its borders, would it be conceivable that the United States would have conceded a defeat to the Viet Cong? Would it, in that case, have been prudent to have proposed a compromise with North Vietnam? Precisely for these analogous considerations, a strong case can be made for the Reagan Administration's support to the contras in Nicaragua and El Salvadore; even though these states are not exactly contiguous with the United States.

An internationally recognized scholar of Afghanistan who has spent almost 25 years of his life in that rugged country, Louis Dupree analyzes 'Afghan cultural reaction to the Soviet invasion'. Actually, Dupree never believed that the Soviet Union would intervene in Afghanistan and had, in fact, seen two kinds of communists before December, 1979 in Afghanistan: (1) 'political communists (revolutionists who wish to overthrow the constitutional monarchy and substitute an undefined government of their own) and (2) the economic socialists (evolutionists who wish to evolve a state-controlled economy within the already functioning system, but with free enterprise recognized in commerce)'. Quite authoritatively, Dupree had cautioned: 'Outsiders should not assume that either group will come under the direct control of Moscow or Peking, a mistake frequently made in the past concerning indigenous left wing elements in Afro-Asia and Latin America.'[19]

In discussing the Afghan reaction to the Soviet intervention, Dupree has highlighted the egregious errors of the Taraki-Amin regime which lasted until December, 1979. These errors included the regime's violations of the Afghan cultural norms, including 'freedom of the mouth', land reforms, womens rights, etc. These reforms were, according to Dupree, 'remarkably similar to those announced by President Daoud's Republic', who had used typically the Afghan idiom in explaining these reforms.

Like Bradsher, Dupree also reiterates that Taraki and Amin 'insisted they were not communists', but followed an ideologically distinct Afghan socialist party. Dupree leads us to think that 'the ultimate demise of Taraki and Amin as the result of Soviet machinations lends some credence to this claim'. He is silent in his description of Barbak Karmal, the current President of Afghanistan, whom he has known personally and who fits in the Dupree created category of 'economic socialists'.

In the earlier phases of the revolution, the population remained generally quiescent. This mood was related to economic activities during the summer and spring months. Students of warfare, Dupree believes, should have known better, but they underestimated 'the relationships between leisure time and fighting in the annual cycle of preindustrial peoples'. After the period of economic activity, the revolt broke out and the DRA overreacted in bombing and napalming the villages. Subsequently, the DRA tried to intensify ethnic rivalries to overcome the rebellion.

As the spring of 1979 approached, Afghan peasants and nomads, instead of returning to their traditional economic activities, continued to fight the government since much blood had been shed in the fighting. By the fall of 1979 draftees from the Afghan military units started to desert and its strength dropped to 20–30 000. 'The socialist interregnum', as Dupree describes, ended with the Soviet invasion in December, 1979. Typically, following their own historical pattern, 'the Afghans reacted against the Soviets in the 1980s just as they reacted to the British in the 1880s.'

In highlighting the role of Islam in 'all Afghan reactions', Dupree suggests that unlike the Shia, the Afghan interpretation of Islam teaches the warriors to kill the enemy in order 'to live and fight another day'. This philosophy is the life-blood of resistance against the Soviet occupation. Dupree concludes that the outside assistance to the Afghan insurgents was 'not necessary to precipitate and perpetuate' the Afghan resistance to Soviet intervention, and he sees no light at the end of the war tunnel. The victim of the conflict, however, is the Afghan refugee, who is now forced to live in the tent villages across the border in Pakistan.

Like her husband, Louis, Nancy Hatch Dupree lived in Afghanistan for almost twenty-five years and has developed remarkable expertise of Afghanistan's culture in her own right. Her analysis of the Afghan refugees in Pakistan is probably the most thorough study of their demography. What is the number of the Afghan refugees? Nancy Dupree believes that no one really knows. The Government of Pakistan has 'held to a consistently rising population of over 2.8 million', and she believes that the Government of Pakistan plans assistance to the refugees on the 'basis of the 10–15 per cent inflated figures in order to avoid shortfalls'. These figures are questioned by the monitors of international aid to Afghan refugees.

Nancy Dupree's description of the refugee population distribution in terms of area, density, age, sex and ethnic composition, is exceptionally detailed. However, she believes that the Afghan refugees' 'repatriation with honor would seem to be a long way off'. This negative assessment has now come to be shared by a very large number of analysts of the Soviet–Afghan conflict. However, she has raised a very crucial question which is in the back of most Pakistanis' minds: 'What political havoc would be generated if it were determined [that] there was no longer any hope for them to return to their homeland in Afghanistan?' On this issue, she leaves us with a hope and a prayer.

Notes

1. One scholar has singled out for scrutiny American and Soviet behavior in (1) aid relations with the Third World, (2) crisis management in the Middle East, and (3) nuclear non-proliferation. See Christer Jonnson *Superpowers: Comparing American and Soviet Foreign Policy* (New York: St. Martin's Press, 1984) p. 5
2. William J. Taylor, Jr., Steven A. Maaranen, and Jerrit W. Gong, *Strategic Responses to Conflict in the 1980s* (Lexington, Mass.: DC Heath & Co., 1984), p. 517. See also, Prosser Gifford, Ed., *The National Interests of the United States* (Washington, DC: Woodrow Wilson International Center for Scholars, 1981) p. 188.
3. Nikolai I. Lebedev, *Great October and Today's World* (New York: Pergamon Press, 1981), pp. 134–142.

4. *Ibid.*, p. 317.
5. Lord Brougham, *Works*, VIII, pp. 37–38 (Glasgow: 1955–57).
6. Edward Vose Gulick, *Europe's Classical Balance of Power* (Ithaca: Cornell University Press, 1955), pp. 62–65.
7. James Reston, 'Reagan on Subversion', *The New York Times*, 23 October 1983, p. 19.
8. This white paper contains more than 2000 pages of documents and statements of responsible officials of the US Government. See, *Grenada Documents: An Overview and Selection* (Washington, DC: Departments of State and Defense, 1984), p. 3. One study has expressed serious reservations about the 'legality of the use of force' in Grenada. William C. Gilmore, *The Grenada Intervention: Analysis and Documentation* (New York: Facts on File, 1984) p. 74.
9. *Background Paper: Nicaragua's Military Build-Up and Support For Central American Subvention*, (Washington, DC: Departments of State & Defense, July 18, 1984) p. 36. Malik attended a White House briefing on November 30, 1984, when an aide from the National Security Council stated 'that the Sandanistas plan to increase their armed forces to 250 000 far exceeding Nicaragua's needs for self-defense'.
10. Lebedev, *Great October*, pp. 32–34.
11. UNGA. Res. 2131 (XX).
12. Hedley Bull, Ed., *Intervention in World Politics* (Oxford: Clarendon Press, 1984) p. 195.
13. For Pakistan's position regarding the validity of the Durand line, see Liaquat Ali Khan, Prime Minister of Pakistan, Reply to a Question in the Constituent Assembly on 9 January 1950 published as *Pushtunistan: A Myth* (Karachi: Publications Department, Government of Pakistan, 1950) p. 9, *Durand Line* (Karachi: Government of Pakistan, 1956) p. 16, including a map of the Durand Line.
14. Richard Bernstein, 'Remaking Afghanistan in the Soviet Image', *The New York Times*, 24 March 1985, p. 53.
15. Christina Dameyer, 'In Campaign to Sovietize Afghanistan USSR Uses School Media and Ethnic Ties', *The Christian Science Monitor*, 26 March 1985, p. 13.
16. Bernstein, *Rémaking Afghanistan*, p. 55.
17. For the creation of the Fatherland national front, see Hafeez Malik, 'Memorandum of Conversation with Mr Shah Mohammad Dost', *Journal of South Asian and Middle Eastern Studies*, Volume V, #2, p. 71.
18. Selig Harrison, 'Afghanistan Stalemate: Self-Determination and a Soviet Force Withdrawal', *Parameters* (Journal of the US Army War College), Vol. XIV, #4, 1984, p. 36.
19. Louis Dupree, *Afghanistan* (Princeton: Princeton University Press, 1980 edition), p. 662.

2 The Strategic Importance of Iran, Afghanistan and Pakistan to the United States
George C. McGhee

Strategic importance, like beauty, is in the eye of the beholder. What is of strategic importance to one nation can be of no importance, – a void or wasteland – to another. In a world polarized in a global struggle between Communist and anti-Communist nations, gaining the cooperation or the ability to control even the least strategically important nations might be considered of value. On the other hand, many nations would undoubtedly be considered a liability. Strategic importance, however, is to the beholding nation based on an appraisal of elements of strength or weakness which could have a substantial favorable or adverse influence on its own security and well-being. This is more important if there is involved a potential leverage or multiplier result from the initial gain or loss, which would include any so-called 'domino effect'.

Are the Southwest Asian nations, Iran, Afghanistan, and Pakistan of strategic importance to the US? They are all relatively small and weak nations occupying an arid, hostile, mountainous terrain. They are all Islamic, which creates special barriers of understanding between us. Only Iran has any significant natural resources of interest to us. And even the oil of Iran, whose daily production of 2.5 million barrels is presently surplus to the world's needs and whose reserves of 38.3 billion barrels are less than 5 per cent of world reserves, is not as important as that of other Middle East states and cannot be considered of critical significance to us. We no longer own any Iranian oil or even purchase very much.

Iran's gas reserves of 370 trillion cubic feet or 10 per cent of the world's reserves, are more important, but mainly for the future since the current surplus of world gas is much greater than that of oil. Moreover, although it can be piped to the USSR or Western Europe or the intervening countries, it cannot be piped to us. We have, in addition to our own large gas reserves of 208 trillion cubic feet, more gas available from Canada and Mexico than we want. Seaborne gas is a glut on the market.

Iran, with a population of 40 million, Afghanistan with 15 million, and Pakistan with 97 million, aggregate only about 150 million, or $3\frac{1}{3}$ per cent of the world's 4.6 billion people. We have almost no investment in these countries, little trade with them. With scant mineral resources apart from the oil and gas of Iran, little industrial production, poor soil, and low educational levels, these countries could never constitute a significant military threat to the US. The British employed mercenaries from the area during the colonial era, particularly from that part of India which is now Pakistan. The inhabitants of these nations are, however, of military value today only in connection with their own defense. Pakistan was recently defeated by India, Afghanistan is occupied by the USSR, and Iran is able to achieve no more than a standoff in its hopelessly deadlocked war with Iraq, half its size.

The recent overthrow of the Shah illustrates better than anything else the fallacy of the illusion that a small non-industrialized state can have much local, much less regional power. The Shah's ego and ambition led him to acquire fabulously expensive weapons beyond the capability of his armed forces to maintain or use, which we furnished him on the basis of faulty political and strategic analysis. The Shah was encouraged by the subservient attitude of Presidents Nixon and Ford, the latter of whom complained publicly how tough the Shah was. The Shah was also encouraged by Security Advisor and Secretary Kissinger's seemingly unlimited commitments to him in support of Kissinger's theory of geopolitics. The Shah considered himself not only the leading Middle East and Indian Ocean power but also an African power, as he announced during a visit to Australia. He proclaimed that he would make Iran the sixth industrial power in the world.

The debris left after the Shah's fall leaves scant hope that any hopes of geopolitical power will in the foreseeable future arise from the lands that once supported Darius' conquest of half the world. It will take years for Iran to emerge from the introverted Islamic morass erected under Khomeini's iron will, and free itself from its war with Iraq.

What is there, then, of strategic importance left in the three ancient countries under discussion? The lands which now constitute Iran, Pakistan, and Afghanistan were, starting during the second millenium before Christ, not only important routes of conquest, but centers of great empires. The first civilization in the area of what is now known as Iran, was that of the Elamite Kingdom in the southeast starting around 2000 BC. The area was later conquered by many races including the Medes and the Persians and by the Persian Achaemenid, Cyrus the Great, who in the sixth century BC extended his rule over all of Asia Minor and Egypt as well. This empire reached its peak under Darius, who in the fourth century BC ruled from Greece to India from his twin capitals of Persepolis and Susa.

Later, Persia was to be conquered by Alexander the Great in the fourth century BC and made the capital of his empire. In the seventh century AD it was taken by the Arabs, who gave it the Shiite branch of Islam as its religion. After further subjugation by Turks, Mongols, and Afghans, parts of Iran during the nineteenth and early twentieth centuries came under the influence and often the control, of both Czarist Russia and Britain. In the early 1900s the predecessor to the British Anglo-Iranian oil company was given the oil concession for southern Iran.

Reza Shah Pahlavi was a military officer who, in 1921, became dissatisfied with a weak Iranian government, marched his troops to Teheran, and took control. In 1925, he forced the abdication of Ahmed Shah. And, with the approval of the Majlis, the legislative body elected under Iran's constitution, Reza Shah developed a program to modernize Iran and free it from foreign influence. He attacked the Imams and confiscated property left as religious endowments. Considerable progress had already been made before the outbreak of World War II. Reza Shah announced his neutrality in the war, but when he refused to allow the use of the Iranian railways for supply to the Soviet Union in 1941, the Soviets and British occupied Iran and forced his abdication.

The post-war period witnessed Soviet withdrawal from Azerbaijan in 1946 under US pressure, and denial by the Iranian Majlis under the leadership of Dr Mohammed Mossadeq of a Soviet oil concession in the north. There emerged a strong nationalist movement supported by the Communist Tudeh party, directed against all foreign interference in Iran, particularly by the British. The son of Reza Shah Pahlavi, Mohammad Shah Pahlavi, with whom the US enjoyed good relations after his accession in 1941, freed Iran from foreign control and made great progress in modernizing the country.

Afghanistan has existed as a state only since 1747, when it was carved by Ahmad Shah out of the conquests of Nadir Shah. The term

Afghan applies only to one ethnic group, the dominant tribe known as the Durani. The remainder are a mixture of various subject tribes including Turks, Tajiks, Hazars, Uzbeks, Kafirs, and the Pathans or Pushtu-speaking tribes who inhabit what was once the border area with British India. These various tribes have traditionally lived independent lives under their own tribal codes. Typically, they are warlike, hardy, sober, stern, and often cruel people. Traditionally they have prized their freedom and resisted taxation and incorporation into a modern state. Fiercely religious, their determined resistance to Soviet conquest could have been anticipated.

The history of Afghanistan has been dominated by a long sequence of conquests by the various South Asian empires. Geographically the country is divided by the northeast-southeast-trending massif, the Hindu Kush Mountains. To the north lies the plain of the Amu Darya (Oxus) River, the only natural barrier between Afghanistan and the Soviet Union. British influence in the area began in 1809 with a mission by the East India Company. Russian influence came shortly after.

After a brief British occupation, there resulted a virtual standoff between Great Britain and Russia, which was formalized by the Anglo-Russian Convention of 1907, permitting Afghanistan to remain relatively free of foreign control. Afghanistan was opened to Western influence following World War I by Amanullah, who seized power in 1919. Nedir Shah came to power in 1929, after a brief interregnum following Amanullah's abdication. When Nadir Shah was assassinated in 1933, he was succeeded by his son, Mohammed Zahir Shah Khan, who was overthrown by his cousin and brother-in-law, Prince Muhammad Daud Khan in 1973.

Civilizing influences began in India with the invasions of the Indo-Aryans around 2400 BC. Alexander the Great invaded around 326 BC. Although India has over the centuries spawned a variety of local dynasties, the true Indian empires were created by Muslim invaders, including Arabs, Iranians, and Turks, starting about AD 1000. India was sacked by the Mongol Tamerlane in 1398, and the great Mogul Empire created in 1526 by Babur of Faragana (which is now located in the USSR) lasted into the early eighteenth century, when Europeans gained control over important coastal areas; first came the Portuguese, then the Dutch, and then the British through the East India Company.

After many local and border wars, India came under the rule of the British Crown in 1858 and was ruled until 1947 by a British Viceroy.

After World War II, the UK understood that India must be granted independence. The Indian nationalist leader, Mohandas Gandhi, apostle of nonviolence, had been leader of the Indian National Congress since 1919. Independence was granted in 1946, and in 1947 India was partitioned into predominantly Hindu and Muslim states.

Pakistan was undergoing a parallel evolution. Following creation of the Muslim League in 1906, its president, Mohammed Ali Jinnah, headed a movement to found an independent Muslim state. The Dominion of Pakistan was created on 14 August 1947, with Jinnah as the first Governor-General. With partition, between six and seven million Hindus and a smaller number of Muslims were exchanged between the two countries. Tension between the two was exacerbated in 1947 by difficulties arising over Indian retention of control over Kashmir, which was predominantly Muslim. After armed clashes in 1948, the UN was asked to settle the dispute, but no progress has been made. Pakistan was greatly weakened by its separation from its more populous eastern segment through the creation of Bangladesh, after defeat of Pakistan by India in 1971.

The territory that is now Afghanistan was, during the period of British rule in India, a buffer between India and the Czarist regimes that were carving out a colonial empire in Central Asia. Although the dividing line between the two varied, the contest was a standoff. Britain feared Czarist expansion because it could threaten their control of India, whose wealth and cheap labor made it the jewel of the British Empire. Iran, in the 19th and 20th centuries, provided a similar buffer, with Russia usually controlling Azerbaijan and the north, the British the south.

With the demise of the British Empire there is no longer a need for such a buffer. India, with its teeming 700 million people and low living standards is not so attractive as to invite conquest. In 1962 Communist China challenged the northern gates of India, but after winning a few skirmishes and making such border changes as it desired, retired without further efforts to seize Indian territory. Pakistan, also, with its relatively large population in comparison with its natural resources, would not be an inviting object for conquest except for its enmity with India and the Soviet Union. There is fear that the Soviet Union, India's ally and arms supplier, might tempt India to attack Pakistan, India's traditional and only important enemy.

The USSR would undoubtedly like to see Pakistan demilitarized as an end to its threat to the Soviet occupation of Afghanistan, directly and through its support and arms supply to the Afghan resistance movement. The whole complex of possible developments in the relationships between India, Pakistan, and the USSR are, however, believed to be beyond the US ability to control. Soviet conquest and demilitarization of Pakistan would be a major strategic setback; however, it is unlikely that the USSR would wish to occupy and control Pakistan any more than India.

Iran, with its oil reserves and access to the Persian Gulf, is, however, a more inviting target for the USSR. At the end of the Second World War, the Soviets made an effort to seize Azerbaijan and were repulsed by Iran only with the strong support of the US. As will be discussed later, any attempt by the Soviets to invade or establish a friendly Communist regime in Iran through threat or subversion, would constitute a major strategic threat to US interests.

There has also, in theory, been a threat that the Soviets would attempt to control Baluchistan, the southwestern province of Pakistan, as a stepping stone to gaining control of Iran by providing military aid and/or troops to a separatist regime that might be created for the purpose of severing Baluchistan from Pakistan. Although this region has few natural resources, little water, and a sparse population, its possession would put the USSR within closer striking distance of Iranian oil and the Persian Gulf. Any Soviet threat against Iran through Baluchistan would constitute a major strategic problem for the United States.

There have been other threats to peace in the three countries under review. The drawing of the Durand line between India and Afghanistan and the creation of Pakistan in 1947 have exacerbated the ancient problem of the Pushtu-speaking tribes who inhabit the mountainous territory lying on both sides of the Pakistan-Afghanistan border. Afghanistan, since the creation of Pakistan, has favored the forming of an independent Pushtoonistan state for the tribesmen, who are closely related to the ruling Afghan tribe. Pakistan has naturally opposed this. We attempted, during Afghan independence, to dissuade the Afghans from pressing this issue, since it could have led to a war with Pakistan and created opportunities for Soviet intervention in both countries. Apart from these considerations the disposition of the Pathans has little strategic interest to us.

The US, in the aftermath of the Communist North Korean invasion of South Korea in the 1950s, considered that South Asia was threatened by both the USSR and Communist China. Massive military aid was supplied to Pakistan for self-defense. Pakistan joined

Iran, Turkey, and the UK in 1954 to create a defensive barrier against the Soviets. The Pakistanis pledged that under certain conditions they would supply forces to help defend other Southwest Asian nations threatened by Communist aggression. With the apparent reduction of this threat and the demise of the Central Treaty Organization, US strategic interest in Pakistan waned.

Iraq invaded Iran in September, 1980, after a dispute between the two countries over Iranian assistance to Iraq's Kurdish tribes and the control of the Shatt-al-Arab waterway. The war has had a disastrous effect on both countries and affects US strategic interests to the extent that it might remove Iraqi and Iranian oil from world markets and result in attacks by either country on tankers carrying Persian Gulf oil. As a result of the glut in world oil, however, this has so far not created a great problem except in raising present insurance rates. A serious strategic problem would be created if Iran, in retaliation against Iraq, would attempt to interfere with vessels transitting the straits of Hormuz. As will be discussed later, this would create a situation to which the US, Western Europe, and Japan would be forced to react.

A survey of the strategic importance to the US of Iran, Afghanistan, and Pakistan before December, 1979, would have highlighted Iran. This would have been based on the possibility that the Soviets might possibly move to control or occupy Iran. Although at that time this seemed remote, it could have led to a threat to the access by the West to Persian Gulf oil. In December, 1979, however, this evaluation was changed drastically by the unexpected massive invasion of Afghanistan by the USSR under the pretext of responding to a request for assistance by the 3-month Communist regime of Hafizullah Amin. Amin was killed soon after in a Soviet-backed counter coup and replaced by the more amenable Babrak Karmal as head of the revolutionary council.

The Soviet occupation was accomplished by 115 000 troops, who with Afghan government forces have suffered casualties estimated at 25 000, including 8000 deaths. There has resulted a continuing strong resistance by an estimated 50 000 Afghan Freedom Fighters, with a total of 30 000 killed so far in action. There have been over a million Afghan civilian casualties.

This invasion came as a surprise and a profound shock to the entire world and resulted in the strongest possible condemnation in the United Nations by all of the non-Communist nations. It has also been condemned by the organization of Islamic states, and unilaterally by most free world nations. Under the leadership of the US, strong economic sanctions were taken against the USSR and many countries followed the US in withdrawing from the Soviet Olympics.

The Soviet invasion of Afghanistan constitutes a most unfavorable landmark in post-war history. The era of *détente*, which had at least provided some hope for world peace, was over. It was concluded by many that the Cold War had been resumed. The Soviets had before exported revolution and had held on tenaciously to the Eastern European nations occupied during the war as well as the earlier Czarist Asian conquests. They had also through inducement and threat established strong positions in Angola, Ethiopia, Syria, and the Lebanon. The invasion of Afghanistan represented, however, their first post-war example of a classical mass invasion of a peaceful neighboring state which constituted no threat to them. The Soviets had made no effort to negotiate with the Afghans nor to justify their invasion to the UN or world opinion.

As a result some four million Afghan refugees have fled their country, mostly to Pakistan, in addition to a million internal refugees. The Afghan resistance fighters remaining have organized a determined underground which is supplied through Pakistan, mainly with covert US aid. According to a recent report by the Helsinki Watch, the Soviets are continuing their war against the Afghan people using terror and reprisal, bombing entire villages, Soviet soldiers killing indiscriminately non-combatant men, women, and children. The Soviets have imposed a totalitarian regime on the entire country. They now have 130 000 troops there.

This Soviet action, in itself, has created a real strategic problem for the US and the free world in the three countries under review. The Soviets have revived the Czarist and Stalinist imperative to seize border lands that do not threaten them, for the sake of having them as a buffer and as a means of access to lands beyond. This constitutes a reversion of a century to the age of colonial expansion, and a half-century to the era of Hitler's expansion. As long as the Kremlin is ruled by the political party and leaders who perpetuated the invasion of Afghanistan, there remains the possibility that they will use Afghanistan as a stepping stone to the seizure of Iran and other Middle East states.

I do not say that this is inevitable, even probable, but the threat cannot be ignored by the West. Almost no one would have thought the Soviets would invade Afghanistan. I do not believe the Soviets can gain control over Iran without invasion through the Communist Tudeh party. The Tudeh has never been a powerful force in Iran and was recently abolished by the Khomeini government and its leaders executed. And Iran, with over three times the population of Afghanistan, is accessible from the USSR only over long lines of communications through difficult terrain. Moreover, the Soviets would not be able to make use of Iranian oil even if they seized it. Indeed, as the world's single greatest producer of oil by far, they do not need it. To attempt to deny Persian Gulf oil to the West would guarantee immediate Western retaliation. President Carter so committed our country, and Europeans who depend almost entirely on Persian Gulf oil would have no choice but to join us.

Improbable as it is, however, as long as the possibility exists, we and other free world nations must consider Iran, Afghanistan, and Pakistan as being of strategic importance in keeping the Soviets from consolidating their hold on Afghanistan and in inducing them to retire from Afghanistan and turn their government back to the Afghan people. The West must seek to deter the Soviets from further expansion by demonstrating the certainty of the resistance they would encounter. We should also make clear the retaliatory measures we and others would take. I will try to sketch out the policy the US should follow in attempting to forestall such a Soviet move.

OUTLINES OF AN AMERICAN POLICY

This should, as a minimum, include a continuation of present sanctions against the Soviets arms supplies to Pakistan and the Afghan Freedom Fighters, and reaffirmation of President Carter's pledge to oppose any aggression against the Persian Gulf area and continued buildup of US and other Western forces that will be required.

The total of American aid to Afghanistan since the Soviet invasion is reported to be $625 million. In addition, the Saudis have contributed $100 million. The US Congress has doubled the amount requested by the administration for the current fiscal year which now totals $280 million. American officials say the fighting is not going well for the Soviet and Afghan government troops, despite their complete control of the air. The Freedom Fighters are well supplied, although their arms are limited to non-US sources, and are often obsolete. The Soviets only attempt to control the urban areas and transport routes, in which they are not always successful. They do not hope to defeat the Afghan guerillas but to cut them off from their base of support among the people.

Whatever the Soviet motive in invading Afghanistan was – to prevent the fall of a Communist regime once established, to create a buffer state under Soviet control between the USSR and Western-oriented Pakistan, or to achieve a jumping-off place for further conquests – it is believed that hindsight shows it to have been a mistake. Perhaps, with continued help from the UN, which has undertaken a peacemaking role on the Afghan question, the Soviets can be provided a face-saving plan of withdrawal, leaving a self-governing neutral Afghanistan. Until that occurs, however, it is believed that the US should continue to provide military and economic aid to the Afghan Freedom Fighters, and to Pakistan.

The use of Afghanistan and Iran as an invasion route to the Persian Gulf is, however, subsumed by the whole question of the possibility of such an invasion and how and where it would occur. President Carter announced on 23 January 1980:

> Let our position be absolutely clear: An attempt by any outside force to gain control of the Persian Gulf region will be regarded as an assault on the vital interests of the United States of America, and such an assault will be repelled by any means necessary, including military force.

Possible sites for stationing US military forces in the area still being considered no longer include Saudi Arabia, but center instead on the Sinai Peninsula and Egypt. Base rights for US use in the event of hostilities in the Persian Gulf area are being sought with Oman, Somalia, and Kenya. The US has also proceeded to develop a naval base on the island of Diego Garcia in the Indian Ocean, under rights obtained from the British.

Beginning in the Carter administration and continuing under President Reagan, the US has developed mobile forces to deploy to these bases in the event of hostilities. In addition to naval support forces, this Rapid Deployment Force, part of which is being trained at Fort Bragg, will in the event of emergency be transported by air to forward areas in Egypt and, one hopes, Saudi Arabia, where they can be deployed, if necessary, by parachute. Other forces can be landed by air in forward air bases in Egypt, Oman, or perhaps Saudi Arabia, with back-up forces arriving by sea.

As already stated, it seems highly unlikely that the Soviets would attempt a military invasion of the Persian Gulf area. They have never undertaken such an operation in an area distant from their borders. They do not have the logistical base to accomplish this by sea or air. It is unlikely that land invasion would be undertaken through Afghanistan and Iran for the reasons previously stated. A better route would be provided by Iraq. This would create, however, the disadvantage of exposing their flank of a long line of communications to their traditional enemy the Turks, whose 600 000 man army is one of the best. They would also face harassment by air by the US and our Western allies, who could be particularly effective if given use of Turkish as well as Saudi bases.

Even if a Soviet invasion of Iraq were preceded by a Communist coup in Baghdad, which would be used as a justification, we would treat it as being straight aggression. It would not seem likely that a Communist coup could succeed in either Iran or Iraq without direct Soviet military intervention. To forestall the Soviets 'leaning against any perceived weakness' in Middle East defense, the US should continue to provide substantial military aid to Turkey. When the Iraqi–Iranian war can be ended every effort should be made to repair relations with Iraq, with whom we have only recently established diplomatic relations, and eventually with Iran. As opportunity permits we should help both nations to stiffen their defensive forces, as appropriate, as a deterrent to Soviet subversion or aggression.

An interesting recent development is the announcement on 29 November 1984 by six Persian Gulf states – Saudi Arabia, Kuwait, Bahrain, the United Arab Emirates, Qatar, and Oman – that they would establish a rapid deployment force to help defend themselves against external military threats. This would be a standing force with a mandate for a limited period with a unified command, for dealing with an undefined emergency, not subversion. Although obviously created because of the threat of Iran and of limited strength, this force could play a supporting role in defense of the Persian Gulf and against a Soviet attack, the brunt of which would, of course, have to be borne by the US and other Western nations.

So, in the final analysis, the question of the strategic importance of Iran, Afghanistan, and Pakistan is that of Soviet intentions. As long as the Soviets continue their expanding aggressive policies they constitute a threat in this region. If this policy should ever be changed, if the Soviets could ever be persuaded to participate in a genuine *détente* with the West, US attention to these three countries can be shifted to helping with the development of their economies and societies. Although local rivalries and tensions among the three states will remain, and even local wars may break out, they will have only local significance and would not be a threat to us or world peace.

3 Thinking South: Soviet Strategic Interests in Iran, Afghanistan, and Pakistan
Morris McCain

Emerging from its Stalinist introversion in 1953, the USSR found itself for the first time a global power. With an efficiency no leadership in Moscow could achieve on its own, the Second World War had vanquished the traditional opponents of Russia. Stalin had crowned the compressed industrial revolution of the 1930s – a national mobilization of resources unequaled in history – with the world's second nuclear force. It remained to his successors to decide what to do with their newly acquired capabilities.

SECURITY, INFLUENCE, AND RISK

The result is eerie to recount. In the post-war world two superpowers, nearly self-sufficient in resources, separated by about the greatest distance the planet's girth will allow, and with roughly equal power, snarl and strain at each other for decades on end, as if their existence as nations were at stake. By the time Stalin died, the Soviets had ample buffering along the traditional invasion route from the west. To the east they faced a demilitarized Japan and a sympathetic, communist China. Their southern border confronted a series of impotent neighbors with natural sea and mountain defenses. The only foreseeable nuclear threat came from the US and could be deterred by putting a few nuclear weapons aboard submarines. For its part, the United States was born into the nuclear era just as secure.

If necessity is the mother of invention, sufficiency must be the father of greed. From the security of its own region, each power has ventured into the world at large to do battle with the other over 'interests' each describes as essentially global. For the Soviets an ideology of universal socialist revolution provides the rationale, for the West the deathly menace of Communism. In reality two nations inexperienced in the exercise of power, and with too few self-evident limits to their influence, turn an easily regulable competition into a fatal contest for every scrap of ground.

To some extent the fault is Lenin's. Discarding Marx's vision of socialist triumph in the most advanced nations for revolution 'at the weakest link in the chain,' he made insurgency in the colonial world a matter of obligation for the socialist. His 'national liberation movements' figured in Soviet foreign policy from the earliest days and were endorsed again by Khrushchev soon after Stalin's death. 'Peaceful coexistence', by ruling out war between socialist and capitalist camps themselves, directed their rivalry all the more forcefully toward the developing nations.

As recently as 1976, Leonid Brezhnev restated the Soviet commitment to wars of national liberation and to revolution on a world scale. He advised a Communist Party Congress in that year that, even as the nuclear arms race was being curtailed, Moscow would pursue socialist victory over capitalism by supporting 'the struggle of other peoples for freedom and progress.' Defending his aid to the MPLA in Angola, Brezhnev added, '*Détente* does not in the least repeal, it cannot repeal or alter, the laws of class struggle. No one should expect that in conditions of *détente* Communists will become reconciled to capitalist exploitation or that monopolists will become supporters of revolution.'[1]

From the start, however, ideology has been a poor guide to Soviet foreign policy, which pursues standard, if immodest, power-political goals. Where Marxist insurgency is expected to enhance Soviet influence it is supported. Where bitter right-wing dictatorship can be bent to the same purpose it is befriended. Among Soviet international priorities, two predominate: security from attack and the extension of Soviet influence over other governments.

Security comes first, and to it must be sacrificed all other ambitions. Taking as a premise that the USSR would be attacked from a number of quarters in the absence of an adequate deterrent, the Soviet military erects warfighting capabilities for a variety of scenarios. At the same time the country's leadership is at pains to avoid even the most limited, conventional engagement with the forces of the other great powers. If the priority of defense means stagnation in the Soviet civilian economy, the price must be paid. If war avoidance means reversal or humiliation in the third world, that too can be accepted.

Ruling a country with the world's longest land borders, the leaders in Moscow give unique attention to events along their perimeter. They use invasion periodically to ward off hostile governments in neighboring countries. Indeed they employ their massive ground forces outside the Soviet Union only in this context, where geographical contiguity gives them logistical supremacy and a clear spheres-of-influence rationale.

Far more often friendly neighbors can be assured through less desperate devices. To the northwest non-Communist governments are tolerated as long as they provide no platform for an assault eastward. In Communist Eastern Europe economic dependency and occasional leadership changes usually suffice to maintain Soviet domination. To the south, Turkey, Iran and Afghanistan have traditionally been handled with economic assistance and trade, whatever the nature of their governments. Only in the last of these could Moscow use force without fear of involvement in war with the West.

The USSR has failed to secure its borders only in the case of China. There, dozens of well-armed Soviet divisions stand guard, accompanied in recent years by a dense thicket of intermediate-range nuclear weapons. For reasons that are inscrutable, the Soviets refrained from a preventive strike against China's nascent nuclear capability in the 1960s. They now have to dread the modernization of their Communist rival's forces with American assistance. No wonder the Andropov leadership turned first to China in the face of growing international difficulties.

To emphasize Soviet fascination with security is not to discount their interest in expanded influence generally. Communists in Moscow behave much like other great-power leaderships in the modern era, when technology allows empires to circle the globe. They are cautious imperialists, whose risk aversion is too infrequently noted or taken advantage of by their opponents. As opportunities arise, the Soviet leaders pursue them, unless the costs seem too high or the risks too great.

The opportunity for expanded Soviet influence in developing nations often comes in the form of regional or civil conflicts compelling shaky governments to seek arms abroad. Israel's opponents in the Middle East are a prime example, as are Somalia and Ethiopia in Africa. The crown jewel of Soviet military-assistance policy, though, is India, which by the early 1970s did scarcely fifteen per cent of its trade with the Soviet Union and Eastern Europe but depended on Moscow as its principal external source of arms.[2] India's left-leaning neutralism exacts its price in Soviet inability to affect events in Pakistan. The most assiduous attempts to woo the two mortal enemies at once have failed, leaving Pakistan, like Somalia, wide open to US domination.

By the same token, antagonism between Afghanistan and Pakistan secured Soviet friendship with the former throughout the postwar era. Governments in Washington, less supple than the Soviets ideologically and perhaps a little less talented at opportunism, refused aid in any substantial amount to Afghanistan even when it was ruled by conservative monarchs.[3] Although the country might have achieved more independence if the successor to the Afghan kings, Mohammad Daud Khan, had stayed in power and if Iran's short-lived policy of assistance had been maintained, the events of 1979 again isolated Kabul from all but Soviet control.[4]

If proof is needed that influence outweighs ideology in Soviet global thought, none could be more conclusive than its treatment of Iran. The USSR has a history of choking down the destruction of Communist movements by 'bourgeois-nationalist' regimes in the Third World.[5] It can support, where necessary to keep its hand in, the most rabid reactionaries. Thus its largest trading partner in the Middle East was, until his fall in 1979, the Shah of Iran.[6] Thus also its painful efforts at evenhandedness in the war between Iraq, a longtime ally, and a violently anti-Marxist Islamic fundamentalist theocracy in Tehran. Events in Iran are simply too critical to Soviet interests for Moscow to keep its distance, no matter what the actions or ideologies of governments there.

SECURITY ALONG THE SOUTHERN BORDER

The Asian subcontinent has attracted Soviet attention throughout the post-Stalin period. Even as rival leaders were juggling for supremacy in Moscow, visits among Indian and Soviet heads of state in the mid-1950s accompanied growing development aid and trade southward. From the start, the threat from Pakistan has given Moscow influence in India. While Western sources predominate in supplying non-military aid to India, the USSR emphasizes 'cooperation in the area of defense.' In recent years an expanded US naval and airbased presence in the Indian Ocean, known to bother New Delhi, also comes in for Soviet condemnation. Speaking in that capital in March 1984, Soviet Defense Minister Ustinov referred to 'the militarization of a number of South Asian countries' by the United States and to a 'network of military bases' and 'interventionist Rapid Deployment Force troops' in the area. He concluded that 'Soviet-Indian cooperation in the military sphere serves to enhance India's defensive capability.'[7]

The USSR is not interested, however, in having India as its only friend in South Asia. For one thing, the Congress Party leadership is too good at mixing its foreign sources of support and balancing great-power friendships in the interest of neutrality. For another, India's long coastline is of little help to Soviet naval ambitions. While Soviet ships have access to Indian ports, Moscow has been offered no basing rights there.

The present western orientation of Pakistan obscures a long history of Soviet attempts to cultivate influence there as well. While they benefit from the expectation of recurring war between the two countries, Soviet leaders maintain an embarrassing neutrality when conflict between India and Pakistan actually erupts. As was the case on the Horn of Africa in the 1970s, the USSR hopes, usually unrealistically, to gain influence with both sides in third-world quarrels. Thus they have tried on a number of occasions to mediate disputes on the subcontinent. The 1965 war over Kashmir found the USSR unwilling to take either side, as had the Sino-Indian conflict of 1962.[8]

Only in 1971, as Indian victory in the war over the secession of Bangladesh seemed imminent, did Moscow abandon its evenhanded strategy. In December the United States, which described its policy as 'tilting against India', started a carrier task force on its way from the Pacific toward the Indian Ocean, according to some accounts in an effort to dissuade India from following its successes in Bangladesh with an attack on West Pakistan.[9] The Soviet Navy engaged in what Michael McGwire describes as a 'reactive deployment' of an anticarrier group, with which it traced the movements of US forces until they left the area.[10] For its support of India, the USSR was rewarded with a 20-year Treaty of Peace, Friendship, and Cooperation with the now clearly dominant power in South Asia. The price was enduring hostility in Pakistan, soon to become the base of resistance to Soviet actions in Afghanistan.

Events in Kabut went well from the Soviet standpoint through most of the postwar era. With the possible exception of Finland,

Afghanistan represented the best-disposed and least threatening of Moscow's neighbors until the 1970s. Its friendship was maintained at little cost, the Americans seeming to accept tacitly that the country was both insignificant and firmly in the Soviet sphere of influence. While life in Afghanistan remained medieval, a monarchy dependent on Soviet support allowed Moscow to build the roads over which it was later to invade.

This idyll of national security for the USSR came to an end during the 1970s. Hereditary rule in Kabul was supplanted by a series of modernizing regimes more interested in alternative sources of support and more evocative of internal resistance by Islamic forces. Fundamentalist Islam became a revolutionary force along Soviet borders. And an American wimp-complex, stimulated by defeat in Vietnam, led Washington to react to Soviet military occupation of Afghanistan as if it brought enemy troops right to the St. Lawrence.

The considerations behind Moscow's decision to intervene are still not fully clear. The Politburo seems to have hesitated before sending in its troops, as one faction in the Soviet-backed DPPA battled another and the Marxist regime's control weakened. Given the outcome of the Shah's fall a year earlier and the reactionary nature of the DPPA's opposition, it had to be expected that the collapse of Marxism in Kabul would mean another Islamic fundamentalist republic on the Soviet southern border. The supposition is common that leaders in the Kremlin felt the internal stability of their own Muslim areas threatened by the attraction of radical Islam adjacent to them.

The USSR does share Muslim ethnicities with both Iran and Afghanistan, but we have little evidence of unrest among them. Compared with Lithuanians or Georgians, they seem relatively well assimilated. Gail Lapidus points out that elites among Soviet Muslims are coopted by symbolic recognition and opportunities for status advancement, while modernization of Soviet Central Asia has meant far better material living conditions there than for fellow ethnics across the border.[11] Nevertheless, press campaigns in Soviet Muslim areas reflect the leadership's concern to discredit Islam. *Kommunist Tadzhikistana* gave the following account of life to the south in April 1984:

> Every day one sees 'morality patrols' on the streets of Iranian cities. If they spot a woman whose clothing, in their opinion, is not

in keeping with Islamic standards, they detain her and conduct a 'tribunal' on the spot with a mullah's participation. . . .

There have been frequent instances in which a 'court' presided over by a semiliterate rural mullah has sentenced women – even pregnant women – to death by stoning.[12]

Even if Kremlin leaders have little basis for their fears of Islam, they must have seen the Iranian revolution as raising the stakes for Moscow in Afghanistan. The advent of the mullahs also reduced the risk attendant on military action there. From an American client state, Iran turned swiftly into a threat to US interests in the Gulf. Cut off from Afghanistan in the west, the US could scarcely hope to participate directly in resistance to the Soviet incursion. The USSR could move in with no chance of a miscalculation resulting in war with the West.

In their panic at the Kremlin's boldness in Afghanistan, western observers began to wonder whether a Soviet invasion of Iran would be next. The country has long been a target of Russian expansionism and, like Afghanistan, formed a source of contention with Britain well before the Bolshevik revolution. Hitler and Stalin apparently discussed its fate, although some accounts suggest it was Hitler who proposed Iran as a future Soviet sphere of influence. The end of World War II found the armed forces of the USSR in northern Iran. That it did not become another partitioned country of the postwar era says something about Stalin's priorities. While he would do almost anything to keep Germany divided, Soviet control in northern Iran was not sufficient cause for war with his former Allies.

An independent Iran became a major prize in the post-war competition between Moscow and Washington for influence. No ideological differences could deter the Soviet leadership from courting the Shah, nor could the fact that, in Soviet terms, 'the Shah's government brutally suppressed the Kurdish national movement in Iran.'[13] Following a 1963 Agreement on Economic and Technical Cooperation, Moscow and Tehran developed a lively trading partnership. Even as Iran under its last Shah was becoming a well-armed US ally, it was selling gas to the USSR, which found it geographically more convenient to export its own gas surplus to European markets.[14]

The overthrow of the Shah put an end to US influence in Iran, since Washington had kept no channels open to either left or right among the Shah's opponents. The Soviets, who would have preferred victory for left-wing elements in the Iranian revolution, are nonetheless willing to deal with the government of Khomeini. Iraq's attack on Iran in 1980 faced Moscow with an agonizing choice. Baghdad had provided one of the first cracks in John Foster Dulles' encirclement arrangements to the Soviet south. It had depended on the USSR through most of the postwar period and provided port access for its ships in the Persian Gulf.

Nonetheless, the prospect of influence in Tehran was too alluring for the Soviets to support Iraq's war aims against the center of radical Islam. Through the first two or three years of the conflict, Moscow wrung its hands over the 'senselessness' of war between two nonaligned nations. The Soviet press covered the hostilities in a precisely neutral fashion, to the extreme of giving equal column-lengths to reports from each side. Accounts from Tehran and Baghdad were placed first on alternate days.[15]

What can we expect next from the Soviet Union along its southern border? The occupation of Afghanistan, as long as it succeeds, places Moscow's aircraft in closer proximity to the Persian Gulf. Will it try to cut off the supply of oil from there to the West? Will its next move be an invasion of Iran to eliminate a hostile regime there? Or will Pakistan find itself the next victim of attack from the USSR? What are the priorities of the leadership in Moscow, as it looks to its south?

CURRENT SOVIET INTERESTS IN IRAN, AFGHANISTAN, AND PAKISTAN

Two developments of the 1960s heightened Soviet interest in the Indian Ocean as a region. American deployment of strategic nuclear weapons on submarines made the oceans to the south a likely platform for strategic attack on the USSR. And the closing of the Suez Canal in 1967 lengthened the distance Soviet shipping had to travel between the European and Asian ports of the USSR, making it harder to protect a growing merchant marine fleet. More recently, the Soviet military press has been warning of US strategic aircraft on Diego Garcia and the American intent to maintain 'three gigantic aircraft carriers with support vessels' in the Persian Gulf.[16]

Beginning in about 1968, the flotilla maintained by rotation of Soviet naval vessels through the Indian Ocean underwent considerable expansion. Its port calls, made from Singapore to East Africa, increased in number, as did the average number of vessels in the area at a given time.[17] Albert Graham reports Soviet 'overtures' for access to port facilities in Sri Lanka, Malaysia, Singapore, Bangladesh, India, the Andaman and Maldive Islands, Iraq, South Yemen, and Mozambique.

At no time, however, has the USSR approached naval supremacy in the area. It lacks the technology to threaten western submarines to its south. Even before the current buildup by the US around the Persian Gulf, Soviet forces in the area would have been at a considerable wartime disadvantage.[18] Moscow's frequently reiterated proposal to turn the Indian Ocean into a 'zone of peace' probably indicates an interest in containing more successful American efforts there. A US rapid deployment force threatens Soviet ambitions even in peacetime, since it raises the estimated cost of Soviet support for its clients there and makes US intervention in favor of threatened allies more credible.

In Pakistan, where Moscow has had the least influence in recent years, its immediate interests are several. As the conduit for American aid to the Afghan resistance and the principal base for refugees from Afghanistan, Pakistan has to expect continued interdiction forays into its territory. To the extent that these come on the ground, however, they are unlikely to involve Soviet troops: US involvement in Pakistan imposes too high a risk for direct incursion.

In many ways, the situation is similar to that in Nicaragua. While Managua serves as a base for insurgency against US-dominated governments to its north, it will have to live with Washington-backed counterinsurgency within its own borders. It can expect various forms of limited assault from American military forces – reconnaissance overflights, offshore patrols, even limited bombing and mining – whether or not these violate international law. One could wish, though, for a little more certainty that Washington understands the limits of the game as well as Moscow – for example, that no US attacks on Soviet shipping to Nicaragua will be undertaken.

A second development of interest to the USSR in Pakistan is the possibility of an 'Islamic bomb' there, built with the practical assistance of the United States. In terms of proximity, Pakistan is to the Soviets as Cuba is to the Americans. It is foolish for either power to define as its gain any and all new causes for anxiety in the other. The USSR has no record or theory of preventive war of the sort, for example, that Israel uses to remove emerging threats in its region. It has stood fearfully by as China developed and deployed a nuclear capability and will probably do the same with Pakistan. But it is hard to feel sure of this.

As long as Pakistan remains allied with the West and China, Moscow will make sustained efforts to destabilize the government in Islamabad. The inherent shakiness of military government plays into their hands there, as does ethnic tension. The opportunity to encourage separatism in Baluchistan, for example, has been noted.[19] Should the regime in Pakistan show signs of discontent with its dependence on Washington, or should a leadership more open to Soviet assistance replace the current one, Moscow can be counted on to jump at the chance for improved relations.

In Afghanistan, Soviet interests are probably more limited than is often recognized. The country is an unlikely candidate to become the sixteenth Soviet republic; there are Muslims enough within the USSR at the moment. Nor is it a crucial launching pad for military expansion into the Persian Gulf. The limited commitment of troops by Moscow (Compare their involvement with that of the US in Vietnam after five years.) indicates more modest aims and an unwillingness to pay high costs in Afghanistan.

The overriding Soviet goal in Kabul is to prevent another hostile government from coming to power along the country's borders. As elsewhere in the Muslim world, the choice in Afghanistan seems now to be between revolutionary modernity and Islamic feudalism. Moscow's present attachment to the DPPA, riven as that party is by ethnic cleavage, would not keep it from supporting a moderate alternative, if one could be found. A second Daud, oriented toward incremental modernization, might be able to hold the country together well enough to allow a gradual withdrawal of Soviet troops. The same outcome might find favor in the United States, unless Washington is determined to foster whatever most threatens the interests of Moscow.

The neutral Soviet position in the war between Iran and Iraq has been getting less and less tenable over the past year or so. In 1983 the Islamic Republic began a roundup of Communists for trial on espionage charges. By the end of the year, *Pravda* was charging that 'reactionary groupings' in Iran were preventing 'the accomplishment of the social and economic reforms the masses expected after the anti-Shah revolution of 1979.'[20] Subsequently, Soviet news accounts have shifted blame to Iran for a war still described as a 'senseless' dispute between 'two states that belong to the nonaligned movement and that hold anti-imperialist positions in foreign policy.'[21] Iraq is said to be responding positively to UN peace initiatives, while Tehran demands Baghdad's capitulation. Iran is condemned for its worldwide revolutionary pretensions.

The tilt to Iraq reflects Soviet fears that the prolonged war will cost Moscow one of its best-established clients in the Middle East. French support for the Iraqi war effort and the resumption of diplomatic relations between Baghdad and Washington show just how far Iraq has slipped from the desired orbit. Nonetheless, Iran remains the real prize for the Soviets in the Gulf.

While the Ayatolleh Khomeini holds sway, the USSR will probably be frustrated in its efforts to improve relations with Tehran. Moscow's best chance is to cultivate Khomeini's successors, whatever their ideological bent. As long as radical regimes of either left or right control Iran, US policy is likely to leave the field open there for renewed Soviet influence, should an Iranian leadership want to end its isolation in the world. We can count on the Kremlin not to blush at whatever ideology it needs to embrace in the process.

One alternative is clearly ruled out in Iran, however. American interests there are far too apparent for the Soviets to consider direct military intervention in that country. They will do their best to curry favor in Tehran, but they will tolerate hostility there as long as they have to. Iran is not about to become another Afghanistan, whether the US builds up its forces in the region or not. Soviet troops will march neither east nor west from Afghanistan; their most likely direction is north.

CONCLUSION: STRATEGIC INTEREST AND EXPANSIONISM

The great powers of our world have by now enjoyed forty years of unstable peace. The instability – the expectation on the part of each power that it might soon find itself at war and the resulting piling up of weapons all round – stems from competing Soviet and American expansionism.[22] The more remarkable fact of peace among the powers must be attributed to several causes.

First among them, of course, is the changed nature of war. Since August 1945, no country has been able to go to war with a nuclear power without contemplating its own annihilation. Though it took years for governments in Moscow to acknowledge this publicly, and though some in Washington would still like to deny it, nuclear war cannot be won in any meaningful sense. Thus the 'interests' which once led so readily to war among nations may no longer do so. Even 'strategic' interests, those in some way more crucial to a country's prosperity, are whittled down to only a very few. They are basically those for which a nuclear power will risk its own destruction by another.

The geographical separation of the two superpowers makes easier the identification of interests which are not incompatible. Even global communications have not eliminated distance in this important sense. The United States and the Soviet Union share no common borders across which a conventional assault could occur, and there is no invasion corridor connecting them. Each can regulate events across its borders without penetrating a buffer zone of the other.

Far more than the dominant nations of the nineteenth and early twentieth centuries, the current nuclear superpowers are self-reliant in resources. Each possesses vast, if extravagantly wasted, natural resources. Though the mineral resources of, say, southern Africa, are attractive to both sides, each could do without them. The principal exception is oil, to which the United States and its allies are addicted. As long as they fail to develop renewable resources with any enthusiasm, the West will be constantly exposed to the threat of war in the Middle East.

A final, rarely-noted factor in our four decades of nuclear peace is the risk aversion which characterizes governments in Washington and Moscow, compared with earlier leaderships in Berlin, Rome, and Tokyo. Despite thunderous pronouncements on both sides, and countless engagements with lesser enemies, postwar governments of the US and USSR have learned how to avoid direct military collision between the superpowers. American forces stay out of countries bordering the Soviet Union, despite occasional optimistic statements about 'liberating' Eastern Europe or Afghanistan. Soviet troops go no place where they might encounter US forces, even if it means ignominious defeat for allies like Syria or Egypt. The mutual withdrawal of missiles from Cuba and Turkey twenty years ago marked a watershed in this great-power learning process.[23]

Thus I expect no deliberate assault on Western interests in regions such as the Persian Gulf by Soviet military forces. Improved naval capabilities in the Indian Ocean and forward bases for fighter aircraft in Afghanistan could be useful to interdict Western supplies in the event of war, but they will not be used to start one. Moscow may try to limit Western access to the resources of the Gulf by undermining governments there from within, but it is not likely to choose suicide as a strategy.

Conversely, the West must make better use of its non-military assets in the Middle East to secure both the survival of Israel and its own bloodlines for black gold. Support for conservative monarchies may be satisfactory for the moment, but oppositions which could provide future governments also need cultivating. Experience affords little hope that rapid deployment forces can keep an unpopular government in power forever.

When it does use force in the Middle East, the United States must keep geography in mind. Iran and Afghanistan are on Soviet borders; what Moscow tolerates in Lebanon it may not accept nearer home. While Washington can get away with support for armed insurgents in Afghanistan, it can do little more to prevent Soviet control there. Even a shutoff of oil from Iran will have to be endured if the alternative is putting US troops ashore. By the same token, the Kremlin would do well to avoid such a shutoff, should gratifyingly friendly governments overthrow Western clients along the Gulf.

If the Middle East is one place where confrontation between Soviet and Western interests will take some careful avoiding, the superpower competition elsewhere should be fairly easy to regulate. Moscow must make sure that when American forces are used in Latin America they find no armed Soviet resistance. Washington must take similar precautions in Eastern Europe, China, and Afghanistan.

The principal Soviet opportunity to the south lies in Iran, as the Kremlin's attitude to the war with Iraq indicates. A left-wing succession to Khomeini's rule would be ideal but seems improbable. Failing that, the USSR will try to use energy purchases and possibly arms sales as an opening to the next government in Iran. If Washington is smart, it will make sure neither the Iraqi war effort nor a collapse of demand for oil in capitalist markets plays into Moscow's hands.

Nor should the West consider Pakistan safely in its pocket. If the present military government there collapses, as military regimes have a way of doing, the Soviet leadership will try for influence there once again. That the war in Afghanistan stands in the way of progress with Islamabad is a substantial incentive to find a way out.

In the face of East-West competition in countless arenas, mutual interests of the superpowers are likely to be overlooked. The containment of Islamic fundamentalism is one such interest, giving Americans and Soviets alike reason to support moderate governments in

Iran, Afghanistan, and Pakistan. Though such regimes, like that in New Delhi, might not automatically become the clients of either side, both Washington and Moscow should find them preferable to the conflicts which radical Islam, radical Marxism, and military authoritariarism bring to the region.

Even the Soviet and Indian proposals for a zone of peace in the Indian Ocean may be useful in adjusting the interests of the superpowers. Excepting freedom of movement for ships of East and West, the interests of each in the region are peripheral. Since neither can maintain a growing naval presence there without great expense, both could benefit from a negotiated build-down of military capabilities. As with other aspects of the US-Soviet relationship, the competition for influence could be pursued more safely and with less resource drain if the threat of force were reduced.

Notes

1. *Pravda*, 25 Feb 1976, p. 4.
2. William J. Barnds, 'Soviet Influence in India: a Search for the Spoils that Go with Victory,' in *Soviet and Chinese Influence in the Third World*, ed. Alvin A. Rubinstein (Praeger, 1975).
3. As noted by Gerard Chaliand in his *Report from Afghanistan* (Penguin, 1982) pp. 26–7.
4. *Ibid.*, p. 33.
5. Egypt is a case in point. See Karen Dawisha, 'The USSR and the Middle East,' *Foreign Affairs* (Winter 1982/83).
6. Fred Halliday, *Soviet Policy in the Arc of Crisis* (Institute for Policy Studies, 1981) p. 29.
7. *Pravda*, 6 Mar 1984, tr. & excerpted in the *Current Digest of the Soviet Press*, 4 Apr 1984.
8. Barnds, pp. 28–32 & 41.
9. For a detailed account of deployment and counterdeployment, see James M. McConnell and Anne Kelly Calhoun, 'The December 1971 Indo-Pakistani Crisis,' in *Soviet Naval Diplomacy*, ed. Bradford Dismukes and James M. McConnell (Pergamon, 1979).
10. Michael MccGwire, 'The Navy and Soviet Oceans Policy,' in *Soviet Naval Influence*, ed. Michael MccGwire and John McDonnell (Praeger, 1977).
11. Gail Warshofsky Lapidus, 'Ethnonationalism and Political Stability: The Soviet Case,' *World Politics* (July 1984) pp. 555–80.
12. *Kommunist Tadzhikistana*, 27 Apr 1984, tr. in *Current Digest*, 6 June 1984. Lapidus refers to two articles dealing with efforts by the KGB to combat ideological subversion in Central Asia by S. Tsvigun in *Kommunist*, Sep. 1981, and Major Gen. Z. Yusif-Zade in *Bakinskii rabochii*, 19 Dec 1980.

13. Doctor of History M. Lazarev, 'The Kurds and the Kurdish Question,' in *Argumenty i fakty*, 24 Jan 1984, tr. *Current Digest*, 25 Apr 1984.
14. Halliday, pp. 46–8.
15. For example, see *Pravda*, 8 & 9 Nov 1982 p. 5.
16. 'Invasion Forces Augmented, *Krasnaia zvezda*, 11 Nov 1982, p. 3.
17. Albert E. Graham, 'Soviet Strategy and Policy in the Indian Ocean,' in *Naval Power in Soviet Policy*, ed. Paul J. Murphy (US Air Force, 1978) p. 278.
18. Robert Legvold, 'The Super Rivals: Conflict in the Third World,' *Foreign Affairs* 57, 4 (Spring 1979) p. 769.
19. See William E. Griffith, 'Super-Power Relations after Afghanistan,' *Survival* 22, 4 (Jul–Aug, 1980), and Zalmay Khalilzad, 'Afghanistan and the Crisis in American Foreign Policy,' *idem*.
20. K. Vitalyev, 'Who Needs This?' *Pravda*, 31 Dec 1983, p. 5, tr. *Current Digest*, 25 Jan 1984.
21. 'Who Benefits From the Bloodshed?' *Krasnaia zvezda*, 21 Apr 1984, p. 6, tr. *Current Digest*, 23 May 1984.
22. For the term 'unstable peace', and for the hope of something better, I am indebted to Kenneth Boulding. See his *Stable Peace* (University of Texas Press, 1978).
23. Charles A. McClelland studies the same kind of learning in the period before the Cuban missile crisis in 'Access to Berlin: The Quantity and Variety of Events, 1948–1963' in J. David Singer, ed. *Quantitative International Politics* (Free Press, 1968).

4 India's Relations with Pakistan, Iran, and Afghanistan
Craig Baxter

Relations between India and Iran and between India and the area which is now Afghanistan have been hostile throughout much of history, even in the period prior to historical times during an era which is clouded with myth. That relations with modern Afghanistan by an independent India have been close is an accident, one which resulted from the birth of Pakistan in 1947. It is evident from the past 37 years that relations between India and Pakistan have been less than cordial. It is necessary to look briefly at the past upon which the present is built and, perhaps, look at the future.

HISTORICAL CONFLICTS

If the usual interpretations of the migration of the Aryans from somewhere in central Asia are correct – and there is no reason to believe that they are not – the eastern branch of that tribal conglomeration moved together to a point somewhere in the area of Herat[1] and then divided, presumably with a quarrel. Evidence which is used to support this interpretation is generally linguistic, including the diametrically opposed use of the words *asura* (devil in Sanskrit; as *ahura*, god in Avestan) and *deva* (god in Sanskrit; devil in Avestan). Although similarities remained between the divided groups, such as the importance of fire or the fire god (Agni in Vedic India), the two streams divided with one moving west to Iran and the other east to what is now northern Pakistan.

The group moving eastward had constantly to be wary of further incursions from the northwest, through the Khyber and other passes. Invaders came often and the earliest of these, Huns, Kushans and others, were assimilated into Hindu society and made the northern reaches of India a melting pot of new entrants to the society. Nonetheless the incursions were often violent initially and were something to be guarded against. Movements did not always take place from the all but unknown interior of central Asia but also from the west, the most important of these being that of Alexander in the 4th century BC, but even these used the passes between Afghanistan and the Indus valley to gain entrance to India. Indeed the most important contacts of India with the outside world were those with the areas to the west and northwest. The Himalaya served as an effective barrier to the north; the mountains and jungle to the east. Even the transmission of Buddhism to Mongolia, Tibet, China, Japan and Korea was by the long route through Afghanistan. There were contacts to the east by sea; these should not be underemphasized, but they were limited both in time and degree even though the results of the expansion can still be seen.

Following the retreat of Alexander, there developed in north India the first major empire, that of the Mauryas. The tutor to Chandragupta Maurya, Kautilya, propounded a theory of international relations which can be seen to serve the present Indian government as well. The theory of concentric circles in which the center (India) is surrounded in the next circle by potential enemies (China, Pakistan) who are in turn enemies of those nations in the next circle (Soviet Union, Afghanistan) and who are therefore potential allies of the central nation (India) can be seen in present day Indian foreign relations as noted by the names of the countries in parentheses. In short, the plan of Kautilya can be summed up in the phrase 'my enemy's enemy is my friend'. He was not the only exponent in history of this theory and has earned the title 'the Indian Machiavelli'. While this theory is surely not the only explanation of Indian foreign policy in the region it can help an understanding of that policy – and it seems far too often to be overlooked by foreign-policy-makers in the West. One can suggest that post-independence India would look toward Afghanistan as a potential associate almost without regard to the type of regime in Afghanistan. The reverse would also be true, that is Afghanistan would look toward India, as 'enemy' Pakistan is sandwiched between the two.

Invasions from the northwest did not end with the groups which could be assimilated into Hindu society but continued when Iran and central Asia became Muslim. This new set of incursions brought a people with a clearly defined faith which was antagonistic to the very core of Hinduism. Assimilation was impossible; distinct differences would remain until the present. Beginning with the end of the 10th century AD and the raids of Mahmud of Ghazni, a series of Afghan,

Turkic and Mongol (Mughal) invaders arrived culminating in the Mughal victory at Panipat in 1526. Muslim rulers preceding and including the Mughals extended Muslim domination over all of the sub-continent except the extreme south. Later, raids from Afghan groups continued and some like the Rohillas settled in India. Persia was not absent from raiding in India as the attack of Nadir Shah in 1739 demonstrates. However, although Muslim dynasties controlled much of India much of the time and often had Hindu allies or subsidiaries, there was no union of social customs between the two religious groups.

The domination of the British, dated, not entirely accurately, from Clive's victory at Plassey in 1757, brought to India a new set of rivalries and with it a new set of international relationships. The extension of Anglo-French conflicts to India was short-lived as the British soon won out. However, as the British enlarged their rule up the Ganges and across to the Indus, their concerns, too, centered on the northwest. Buffers were set up. First, the Cis-Sutlej states, mostly Sikh, were brought into the system as a buffer against the Kingdom of the Punjab, also a Sikh power. Then, that kingdom was annexed in the mid-19th century, and Britain inherited its conflict with the Afghans.

The extension of Russian power into central Asia seemed to lead inevitably to direct conflict between the British and Tsarist empires. Afghanistan was to be the buffer between the two and the period described as the 'great game' and immortalized by Kipling in *Kim* dominated the latter nineteenth century. The British fought three wars with Afghanistan, the last in 1919, and never were able fully to bring it under control. The Anglo-Russian *entente* of 1907 had brought Russian agreement that Afghanistan was outside its sphere of influence and Russia would deal with Kabul only through Britain. (The same agreement also affected Persia in that the two powers recognized three zones, one for each and one neutral in Persia, all, of course, without actual Persian agreement.) In the 1919 Treaty of Rawalpindi Britain recognized the complete independence of Afghanistan. Russian, now Soviet, direct relations would be sanctioned regardless of what disposition the Soviets made of Tsarist treaties.

Thus as World War II was beginning the British Indian government had completed, not always successfully, an arrangement which would differ but little from that of independent India were it not for the partition of India and the creation of Pakistan. To the north, despite little likelihood of a threat, Tibet was a buffer between India and China although under the 'suzerainty' of China. To the east and south, the territory was under British or French control. To the west, Persia (now Iran) was weak and its principal source of income firmly under British control. The northwest was a problem still. Other nations, the Soviets, Germany and Italy, were meddling in what was once, at least on paper, a British preserve.[2] Beyond was the hostile Soviet Union, accused also of meddling in Indian internal affairs. While that problem would diminish after the German invasion of the Soviet Union, it would recur after World War II.

Internally in India, however willing the British may have been to carry out the promise of gradual movement toward dominion status proclaimed in the Montagu declaration of 1917, the seemingly insoluble problem of sharing of power by Hindus and Muslims was steadily exacerbated. This is not the place to detail the growing move toward a firm Muslim demand for a separate state but it is evident that following the Congress refusal to work within the Cripps offer of 1942 and surely after the failure of the Cabinet Mission plan of 1946 there was no course available to the British or to the Hindus and Muslims other than an India divided in hostility.

The creation of Pakistan in 1947 changed the equation for residual India. Pakistan and India became neighbors in enmity. Afghanistan placed claims against Pakistan which would have put Pakistan beyond the Indus in Afghanistan. India and Afghanistan became natural allies in the Kautilyan sense. It should have come as no surprise to policymakers that the same principle brought Pakistan and China together. The only surprise should have been that it took so long for a close relationship to develop, coming only in the 1960s. Equally, it should have been no surprise that, after the break between the Soviet Union and China (which the United States was slow to recognize) and the brief conflict between India and China, the already friendly relations between India and the Soviet Union should have become very close, culminating in the treaty of 1971 and contributing to India's reluctance to condemn unequivocally the Soviet invasion of Afghanistan of 1979.

Pakistan's earlier close relationship with the United States was based, from Pakistan's side, on its desire to compete on more even terms with India as was its *entente*[3] with China. That it now fits in with a Kautilyan arrangement following the opening and improvement in United States-China relations perhaps brings this *entente* into conformity with other relationships in the region. Taking Kautilya at his word one can see a series of relationships among the underlined countries in the following series opposed to those not underlined. Afghanistan, Pakistan, India, China, the Soviet Union, the United States. (One can even stretch this further. Vietnam and China are opposing each other. India has close relations with Vietnam and is almost alone among non-Soviet bloc nations in supporting the Vietnamese in Kampuchea. Bangladesh has found its international position but little altered since it won its independence from Pakistan and has close relations with Pakistan, China and the United States, and at best correct relations with India and is cool toward the Soviet Union.) A further point which needs to be made, perhaps here, is that Pakistan does not forget that Afghanistan alone voted against its admission to the United Nations.

It seems important to this writer that the historic relationships of the nations and their predecessors in the area be kept in mind when present-day relations are analyzed. It has been said that nations have neither permanent friends nor permanent enemies, but only permanent interests. It would appear that one permanent interest of India should be defense against incursions from the northwest, an interest which was clearly held paramount by the British when they ruled India. Thus one might expect that the destruction of the buffer role of Afghanistan would be something against which the Indians would react strongly if only verbally and diplomatically. Such has not been the case as India has often suggested that there were others interfering in Afghanistan and this justified Soviet intervention.

India's allegations of interference

The frequent allegations of interference in Indian affairs by outside powers is a paranoia which severely afflicted the regime of Indira Gandhi, and, if his early statements are a measure, may well be carried on by her son now that he is prime minister. The outside powers usually mentioned are the United States, Pakistan or both.

These allegations, however, have not extended to Iran even when there have been cases of Harijan ('untouchable') conversion to Islam or manifestations of Islamic fundamentalism. In the first months of 1981, perhaps a thousand Harijans converted to Islam in Tamilnadu and Hindu communal bodies and, to an extent, the generality of Hindus expressed fear that the conversions were only the beginning of a Muslim revival and expansion.[5] The conversions were clearly Sunni and not Shi'a and those concerned believed that 'gulf money . . . is today's Khyber Pass through which Muslims seek to gain domination over India'.[6] Government reports noted that the conversions were the result of discrimination by Hindus and the taking of steps by the Harijans to withdraw from the Hindu system, but the reports were also inconclusive about the possibility of foreign money. At any rate, Saudi Arabia seemed to be the most frequently named 'culprit'.

Communal problems have been a disconcerting feature of 1984 India. The Sikh problem culminating in the storming of the Golden Temple in Amritsar and the assassination of Indira Gandhi has far overshadowed Hindu–Muslim difficulties which have also flared up during the year. It should be noted, however, that many Indians, including officials, have accused Pakistan of assisting Sikh extremists and of aiding at least one group of hijackers of flights of Indian Airlines.[7] Pakistan has, of course, denied these charges, but has during the year levied some of its own by asserting that India has colluded with demonstrators in Sind province who are unhappy both with the military and unrepresentative government in Pakistan and with what is seen by them as discrimination against Sindhis by the dominant Punjabi group, linguistic factions in Pakistan are roughly equivalent to religious divisions in India in the sense of political competition which can turn to violence. It would, however, be unlikely, given the historic animosity between the two countries that at least some meddling is not present, either of India in Pakistan or of Pakistan in India, or, more likely, both.

There are other communal and political problems in India in which a Pakistani hand can easily be seen by those in India with a paranoid mind. The dismissal of a popularly elected government in Jammu and Kashmir by the Indira Gandhi regime has caused some unrest in that state where the hand of Pakistan is regularly imagined. The Muslims of India have, in the last decade or so, asserted their demands much more openly than before and these have been resisted more strongly by Hindus. It is not difficult for those who have already made up their minds to assert that Pakistan has a role in these demands which have included a reinstatement of the separate electorate system which existed before independence.[8]

The communal problems during 1984, in addition to that of the Sikhs in the Punjab, have included a major Hindu–Muslim riot near Bombay, the continuing problem of alleged Muslim infiltration into Assam from Bangladesh and even a dispute between Hindus and Christians in Kerala. The Bangladesh issue has hindered good relations between India and Bangladesh which were strained already on a variety of issues including the division of the waters of the Ganges and the Brahmaputra.

India and Iran

If the past relationships described earlier have application it might seem that India and Iran should be close in that both border Pakistan and each should have some degree of common enmity toward Pakistan. This has not been the case. First, common borders alone do not appear to cause enmity if the border is of less significance than other borders. For example, for Pakistan its common border with Iran has been of less importance than that with Afghanistan and its border with China of less significance than that with India. Other factors clearly override the mere existence of a common boundary. Second, there were no significant disputes between the Iran of the late Shah and Pakistan. In the region, each has been more concerned with Afghanistan and this, among other factors, has drawn them together.

Pakistan's problems with Afghanistan have been mentioned, but Iran, too, has concerns ranging from memories of the Afghan destruction of the Safavid empire in the 18th century to the relatively trivial dispute over the waters of the Helmand River. Iran was among the first Muslim nations to welcome Pakistan into the state system; for example, early on Iran agreed to allow Pakistan to take delivery of British aircraft purchased by Iran as a help to Pakistan in developing its armed forces against what it saw as an Indian threat. Third, both Iran and Pakistan have been more at home with the more conservative Arab governments and have, in the past, feared the more radical regimes of Nasser and the Baath. Fourth, Iran and Turkey have been alarmed at the prospect of Soviet moves against them and, following such steps as the Truman doctrine, have looked to the West and particularly the United States, for guarantees against Soviet action.

Pakistan joined with the other two in the Central Treaty Organization (ex-Baghdad Pact) ostensibly to secure the northern tier against the possibility of Soviet moves to the south, although it is clear Pakistan's motives, as noted earlier, were principally to gain strength against India. Fifth, there have been other specific moves such as the Shah's provision of aircraft to Pakistan during the 1965 war with India. The relationship has clearly been strained since the Iranian revolution and especially as the Khomeini government challenges Pakistan's close friends who are labor and goods markets in the Gulf through the Iran–Iraq war and other forms of pressure on the states in the area. But the converse, a close relationship between revolutionary Iran and India, has not been the result.

This is not to say that the contacts between India and Iran have not been correct. India at times has tried to moderate the close relationship between Iran and Pakistan. The Shah visited India for the first time in 1973 and Mrs Gandhi returned the visit the following year. The visits resulted in several agreements including one of great importance to India: Iranian credits to develop iron ore pelletizing in Rajasthan and the export of the pellets exclusively to Iran for a projected steel mill. The revolution in Iran and the decrease in exportable capital there have left the agreement incomplete. India also had Iran as its principal source of imported petroleum and has a major trade deficit with Iran. Iranian delegations to India in 1980 and 1981 have addressed these problems without any significant result, although an Indo-Iranian Joint Commission has been set up. The commission met most recently in New Delhi on 29 November 1984. India has stated that Iran would like Indian technology to replace European and American technology which has been withheld. These, however, are commercial arrangements which could not match the close relationships between Iran and Pakistan in political terms.

India on a number of occasions has called for a political settlement of the Iran–Iraq war. But it has also conceded that there is but a small role India can play in a settlement even in its present position as leader of the Non-Aligned Movement. Its concern is both for its citizens in the region of conflict and for continued access to Gulf oil including that from Iran.

Relations between India and Pakistan

The generally poor relations between India and Pakistan, which can from time to time improve, can not only be expected from the Kautilyan concept of hostility between neighbors but are also the outcome of the separation of the Muslim-majority areas of the sub-continent from the Hindu-majority and the creation of Pakistan. Pakistan was unhappy with the line which was drawn by a commission and which, for example, awarded all of the Punjab district of Gurdaspur to India, thereby, say the Pakistanis, giving India a direct access to Jammu and Kashmir. The Indians strongly opposed the concept of partition although in the end the Congress Party accepted it reluctantly. Pakistanis have feared that India might wish to undo partition by force, a fear which seems entirely unfounded to an outside observer if for no other reason than the inclusion of Muslim-majority areas in India would greatly upset the communal problem which is already difficult within India.

The disputes between the two successor nations began with the day of independence but many of those are of little importance today. One, the division of the Indus waters, was settled through outside mediation and financial assistance in 1960 in what is clearly the most successful agreement between the two (although it might be added that the Indians feel they were hurt by the agreement and this contributes to India's refusal to allow talks with Bangladesh on the Ganges waters to expand beyond the bilateral level). Kashmir remains as a sticking point on each side. India asserts that the entire state acceded to India and that Pakistan is in illegal occupation of parts of the territory (it also insists that China is as well in the Aksai Chin but that is a matter outside the scope of this paper). Pakistan states that the accession was conditioned on a plebiscite being held after a cease-fire and that India has not carried out that part of the resolutions of the United Nations Security Council. In a practical sense, the dispute has been settled, for India is not going to go to war to reclaim Pakistani occupied territories and Pakistan has shown that its resort to military action has failed in the past and, no doubt, would in the future if it were again attempted. Nonetheless, each country, especially Pakistan, insists on bringing up the subject from time to time in apparent violation of the Simla agreement of 1972. An example of this is Ziaul Haq's remarks at the meeting of the Non-Aligned Movement in New Delhi in 1983. It seems an unnecessary irritant to an already irritated situation.

The press in each country contributes greatly to the acrimonious climate between the two. In February 1984 a series of events preceded a noisy exchange. Pakistan expelled two servants of an Indian embassy employee and two officers of Indian Airlines, suggesting that some or all of those deported were involved in an alleged plot against Ziaul Haq. At the same time a Kashmiri was executed after trial and conviction on murder charges; the murderer was described by Zia as a 'martyr'. The 25 February 1984 issue of the *Overseas Hindustan Times* which reported these happenings also said that United States policy had changed following the revolution in Iran and the Soviet intervention in Afghanistan: 'The new policy attaches to Pakistan's military regime a degree of importance which was not previously there . . . and elevated Pakistan to the level of a major US security interest.'

But it is not only the Indian press which reports with regularity actions which are disapproved by the other country. The *Pakistan Times Overseas Weekly* of 12 February 1984, carried on its front page a detailed report of an address by former foreign minister Agha Shahi in which his topic was the dangers to the welfare of the smaller countries of the sub-continent posed by the disparity between India and the others – this at a multi-national seminar in Islamabad on the prospects for South Asian cooperation. Shahi went back through the Mauryas, Guptas, Mughals and British to suggest that India may wish to exercise its 'manifest destiny' to dominate and to exercise the right of intervention in the other states. (We will come back to this concept shortly in a section on South Asian cooperation.)

With the steady diet of venom against the other country in both India and Pakistan it is perhaps surprising that the two have not been at war more often than they have. Khushwant Singh, one of the delegates to the seminar at which Shahi spoke, commented on this in his column in the *Overseas Hindustan Times* on 3 March: 'despite the three bloody wars we have fought with them and despite the fact that our leaders spit abuse at each other and the air is thick with rumors of a fourth war . . . I return to the country where I was born.' Khushwant Singh portrays the nostalgia shown especially among Punjabis for the area but he, not alone, has stood for closer and more rational relations between the two countries. One in the Pakistani press who plays a similar role is Mazhar Ali Khan, editor of the leftist *Viewpoint*. It is unfortunate that such men are too few and far between and that they are of an age that indicates that they will not play such roles into the distant future. The venom may well be all that is known by the younger generations and for this political and military leaders will be properly blamed.

In addition to differing views on the Afghan issue to which we will refer shortly, India is concerned about one of the results of the Soviet intervention – the provision of American military assistance to Pakistan. India, cherishing the dominant place in the sub-continent for itself, maintains that the balance of weapons in the region has been and will be changed through the $1.6 billion American military program with Pakistan. India is also concerned, as are many others, about the possible (probable?) development of nuclear capability by Pakistan, although it should be recalled that many were also concerned about the Indian nuclear detonation in 1974.[9]

Despite the problems, the two countries have taken a number of steps to work out a better relationship on matters outside the political and military areas. Many of these stem from a short stopover in New Delhi by Ziaul Haq on 1 November 1982. He and Mrs Gandhi agreed to set up an India–Pakistan Joint Commission which would take up 'non-political' subjects such as trade, tourism, travel, telecommunications and sports and cultural exchanges. This served as a substitute for the time being to further discussions on the Pakistani offer of a 'no-war' pact and the Indian counter-offer of a treaty of peace, friendship and cooperation. A number of small but significant steps have been taken since, but these have usually been interspersed by periods of acrimony.

President Ziaul Haq attended the funeral of Mrs Gandhi and met briefly with the new prime minister, Rajiv Gandhi. The press reported that the conversation was friendly and that each leader pledged to work further for better relations between the two nations. Nonetheless, the statements of Pakistani complicity in the Sikh disturbances mentioned earlier followed this meeting.

One cannot help but think that if muzzles were placed on the leading political figures and some of the journalists in each country the climate for a measure of cooperation between the two would be greatly enhanced.

The Afghan intervention

India's position on the Soviet intervention in Afghanistan has not been completely consistent. If the proposition that Afghanistan is a potential friend of India as a result of India's antagonism toward Pakistan is correct, it should, as has been suggested, follow that the nature of the regime in Kabul is not an issue unless some unlikely event should occur which would place in office a government which was openly and actively friendly to Pakistan. A degree of agreement between the Daud regime and the Pakistanis was seen to be possible before the latter's overthrow in 1978, but the level contemplated, even if it included a recognition of the Durand line, was not likely to be inimical to India. However, the presence in Afghanistan of Soviet troops supporting the third in a series of post-Daud governments and moving Soviet presence much closer geographically to India might have been expected to receive a negative reaction in India.

The Soviet action took place at the end of December, 1979, just as India was going through an election campaign which would bring Mrs

Gandhi back to power after a nearly three-year absence. Shortly after taking office the government issued a statement:

> India has always opposed outside interference in the internal affairs of one country by another. It is also the Government of India's earnest hope that no country or external power would take steps which might aggravate the situation and that normalcy would be restored early.[10]

A month later, P. V. Narasimha Rao, then foreign minister stated before the Lok Sabha:

> We are against the presence of foreign troops and bases in any country. We have expressed our hope that the Soviet forces will withdraw from Afghanistan.[11]

However, it must be noted that these sentences were preceded by a declaration of opposition to American arms assistance to Pakistan which 'could convert the South Asian region into a theatre of great power confrontation and conflict.' By this time Pakistan had been proclaimed 'a front-line state' by the United States acting unilaterally and an offer of assistance had been made by the Carter administration, an offer which would be declined as 'peanuts' by Ziaul Haq.

The statement by the foreign minister illustrates clearly the two sides of the Afghan question as seen by the Indians. There was concern that one superpower, the Soviet Union, had intervened in another state which was close to India and part of the South Asia region as usually defined. But the greater concern for India was additional military power for Pakistan, an addition which would include the introduction of a new generation of aircraft, the F–16. The February, 1980, visit to India of Soviet Foreign Minister Gromyko built upon this fear of Pakistani arms increases when he said that Pakistan, if it went along with 'imperialist maneuvers', would 'undermine its position as an independent state'.[12] He added that the United States was the cause of the problem and the Soviets had acted against American activities in the region. India's request for a withdrawal timetable was ignored.[13] Campaigning in Uttar Pradesh by-elections in March, Mrs Gandhi said that India wanted the Soviets out but that the Soviets only acted after Pakistan had started training and arming rebels (presumably against the Taraki and/or Hafizullah regimes).[14]

India's public stance on Afghanistan remained very much the same for a time and it was unable to convince its Soviet ally to agree to a political settlement leading to a withdrawal. Mrs Gandhi told a visiting American Congressional delegation in June that pressure, apparently meaning guerilla operations, would not work. India, she said, wanted Soviet troops out but it must occur as the result of a political settlement acceptable to both the Afghans and the Soviets.[15] When Brezhnev visited Delhi in December, she apparently used much the same formulation to him and said an Afghanistan which is independent, sovereign and non-aligned must emerge from the negotiations. Brezhnev blamed the United States, Pakistan and Iran for the problem. The Indians simply noted that the positions of the two countries 'diverged'.[16]

There are perceptible changes in this series of public statements on the problem as they move from withdrawal to negotiated withdrawal and from Soviet action alone to the suggestion that others may have provided a reason for the Soviets to act. The Indian draft for the final statement at the Non-Aligned Movement meeting in New Delhi in February, 1981, displayed a clear association of 'other powers' as a causal factor in the Afghan question. The draft regretted the Soviet intervention but also regretted the role played by other powers as well and suggested that these began before the Soviet action.[17] The plenary session of the Non-Aligned Movement in March, 1983, said that the Afghan people should be allowed to determine for themselves their form of government without outside interference and that the refugees should be allowed to go home.[18] At the United Nations General Assembly, India has continued to support the Soviet Union against the large majority of members who have annually condemned the Soviet action.

The Indian stand, however it may be phrased to give an idea of neutrality or equal condemnation, is seen by outside observers, other than those who support the Soviet Union, as being highly favorable to the Soviet position. It must be recalled, however, that it is also part of a strong statement against additional arms for Pakistan from the United States.

South Asia Regional Cooperation

Both India and Pakistan, along with Bangladesh, Bhutan, the Maldives, Nepal and Sri Lanka, formally became members of the South Asia Regional Cooperation (SARC) through an agreement signed in New Delhi in August, 1983. The genesis of the new organization was in a series of visits made by Bangladeshi President Ziaur Rahman, who, so far as the writer can determine, was the only South Asian head of government to visit each of the other four major countries (India, Pakistan, Sri Lanka and Nepal) during his term of office. Ziaur Rahman, before his assassination in May, 1981, motivated a series of preliminary meetings before the final agreement was signed.

The members of the group agreed to consult on a wide variety of issues other than those which are strictly bilateral (as defined by either party) or which can be described as political, military or trade. This still leaves a number of areas in which cooperation can be undertaken, many of which are development-related, such as agricultural research, various technological and scientific subjects and meteorology, and travel. Initially India saw the group as ganging up on it and Pakistan feared Indian domination, but the persuasion of the smaller powers, Bangladesh, Sri Lanka and Nepal, was successful. Bangladesh, in particular, would like to see an expansion of the range of subjects and powers of the consultative bodies.

India has set a number of preconditions which will serve to limit the utility of SARC. These have been described by some as the 'Indira Doctrine'. First among these is that India insists on bilateralism in political or sensitive relations with its neighbors. For example, India will not permit discussions with Bangladesh on the Ganges waters question to be expanded to include Nepal and surely not to include nations outside the region as did happen during the negotiations on the Indus waters in the fifties. Second, there should be no security relationships between nations of South Asia and outside powers. The pre-existing Indo–Soviet Treaty of 1971 is conveniently excepted, but the United States–Pakistan agreement on military assistance is said to be in violation of this aspect of the doctrine. Third, there must be acceptance by the other nations of India's hegemonic position in South Asia. Other members of SARC should not disagree with India on major issues, although it is not phrased quite so baldy. They clearly do disagree, especially on Afghanistan and Kampuchea. None of the other nations is likely to accept this attempt at Indian domination of foreign policy, even at the cost of a decrease in the effectiveness of SARC.

Conclusion

In the past, notably during the first Indira Gandhi administration, India had been described as a nation which enjoyed poor relations with each of its neighbors. Those in the sub-continent saw, with some justification, the possibility of the recreation of an imperial Delhi. Much of this feeling was dissipated by the Janata administration led by Morarji Desai, even with foreign affairs in the hands of the Jana Sangh leader, Atal Behari Vajpayee. The second Indira Gandhi administration did not return fully to the relationship patterns of the first government but it is clear that India still has problems with each of its bordering countries, perhaps greater with Pakistan and Sri Lanka at the moment but clearly present with Nepal and Bangladesh. India, whether it wishes to or not, dominates the sub-continent to the discomfiture of its neighbors, particularly those which were once part of the Mughal empire and the British raj. No matter what Rajiv Gandhi's or some other government in India wishes, it cannot change the basic equation of Indian predominance.

Notes

1. See, for example, Arnold Toynbee, *Between Oxus and Jumna* (London: Oxford University Press, 1961), especially pp. 73–76.
2. For additional detail see Ludwig W. Adamec, *Afghanistan's Foreign Relations to the Mid-Twentieth Century* (Tucson: University of Arizona Press, 1974) and Leon B. Poullada, *Reform and Rebellion in Afghanistan, 1919–1929* (Ithaca: Cornell University Press, 1973), especially Chapters 10 and 11.
3. The term 'entente' is taken from the title of Anwar H. Syed's *China and Pakistan: Diplomacy of an Entente Cordiale* (Amherst: University of Massachusetts Press, 1974). It is also used by Yaacov Vertzberger, *The Enduring Entente* (New York: Praeger, 1983).
4. See Syed Nur Ahmad, *From Martial Law to Martial Law*, edited by Craig Baxter (Boulder, Colorado: Westview Press, 1985), pp. 294–295, for the aircraft arrangement and Jinnah's instructions to Pakistan's first ambassador, Raja Ghazanfar Ali Khan.
5. See Robert L. Hardgrave, Jr, *India Under Pressure* (Boulder, Colorado: Westview Press, 1984), pp. 38–42. It should also be recalled that in the fifties substantial numbers of Harijans in Maharashtra converted to Buddhism.
6. Hardgrave, p. 38.
7. For a recent expression, see *Overseas Hindustan Times* (hereafter *OHT*), 1 December 1984.
8. For a summary of the demands see Walter K. Andersen, 'India, a Case Study', in Philip H. Stoddard, David C. Cuthell and Margaret W. Sullivan, eds, *Change and the Muslim World* (Syracuse: Syracuse University Press, 1981), pp. 127–134.
9. See *Philadelphia Inquirer*, 1 December 1984, for a report on a study by Rodney W. Jones commissioned by the Department of Defense.
10. *OHT*, 10 January 1980.
11. *OHT*, 7 February 1980.

12. *OHT*, 21 February 1980.
13. *OHT*, 28 February 1980.
14. *OHT*, 6 March 1980.
15. *OHT*, 12 June 1980.
16. *OHT*, 18 December 1980.
17. *OHT*, 19 February 1981.
18. *OHT*, 24 March 1983.

5 Ethnic Dilemmas in Pakistan, Iran and Afghanistan as Security Problems
Jon W. Anderson

> 'The concept of the "ethnic" group, which dissolves if we define our terms exactly, corresponds in this regard to one of the most vexing, since emotionally charged concepts: the *nation*.'—Max Weber

Notwithstanding their profound historical and demographic differences, Pakistan, Iran and Afghanistan share characteristic internal ethnic diversities and national borders which cut across local ethnic groups in all directions. As elsewhere, these legacies of the past in current practice make ethnicity a security problem. The problem is usually conceived of as one of artificial frontiers. But ethnic identities pose issues which transcend frontiers here not only because ethnic groups transcend those boundaries; specific continuities between internal and external relations make ethnicity an issue, at its most vexed, of loyalties. To unravel what is at issue, it is necessary to relate what ethnicity means in Southwest Asia and how the states there have dealt with it as a problem for their security to a specific structure of relations whose most familiar but by no means only manifestation is the Great Game.[1]

WHAT IS ETHNICITY IN SOUTHWEST ASIA?

'Ethnicity' is an odd-job word in the social sciences. Its original application was as a substitute for overburdened ideas of 'race' in which cultural differences were interpreted as matters of degree of culture and seen to be rooted in biology, often as an extension of it. This association is retained in conceptions of ethnicity as a kind of cultural heritage that is stored and transmitted in traditions which differentiate populations that are articulated more by communication than by organization into a social institution like a state. Viewed as residues of extra-social, even pre-social, processes, ethnic identities are commonly seen to rest on primordial solidarities, or, alternatively, to be situational formations and in either case somehow closer to natural than to social orders.[2] In either specification, conceptions of ethnic groups as subnational communities are brought into analysis as variously dependent or independent variables and analytically fitted with diverse meanings of primordial attachments, interest groups, and 'culture'.

Such conceptions of ethnic groups as standing between nature and culture do not travel well. Blu has pointed out that 'none of the generalizations yet offered about "ethnicity" stands up under cross-cultural scrutiny',[3] and concluded that 'what sets "ethnic" groups apart from other symbolically differentiated groups with a strong sense of unity is not clear.'[4] The problem is not only 'the diverse factors that are hidden behind this seemingly uniform phenomenon', which Weber noted,[5] but, Blu observes, that the notion is based on American – and, one should add, on European – folk conceptions and in that setting reflects real experiences. The problem is that analytically this conception encodes a particular notion of society as based on primordial sentiments which leads to complementary situational views of ethnicity as indicative of some social structure in which it is a factor or to which it is an adaptation.

Superficial similarities to Western notions of ethnicity can obscure a variety of usage. In the Middle East, a plethora of identifications provide formats for the relations of individuals and groups. Drawing on material from the Southwest Asian borderlands in particular, Barth observed that ethnicity is a flexible marker which enters into social relations in diverse ways. Though he went on to argue for a view of ethnicity in terms of superordinate and limiting statuses,[6] data he adduces about the porosity of identities and group boundaries[7] bear a stronger resemblance to Rosen's finding in Morocco that 'ethnic identity serves to indicate some of the bases of possible relationship to those who choose to actualize such latent bonds while it defines in rather vague and minimal detail the essential features of those members of the opposite ethnic group with whom a direct tie of consociation has yet to be established.'[8] While such relations often include a political component, they also often do not.

In what they organize, ethnic identifications are themselves variable and complex in Southwest Asia; the more closely they are examined, the more diversely articulated they appear to be. In discussing a Kurdish-speaking group in Iraq, Vinogradov outlined how 'Different kinds of ties prevailed between them and the many groups in their environment; those with the Arab nomads were clear-cut and limited to the economic sphere. The ties with the landowners were ambiguous and transient; those with the urban landlords were more persistent and multiplex because, in addition to being landlords, the urban *sada* were in a position to guarantee the physical survival of the weak and scattered Shabak community against its powerful neighbors.'[9]

Throughout Southwest Asia, also, there are cases of 'ethnic' groups arising out of more diverse and shifting causes than ancestry.[10] Many of these are relationships of protection and sponsorship in which group identities evolve around economic, variously political, and often importantly religious relationships. Barth has noted how the Basseri in Iran were put together through the activities of Shiraz merchant patrons,[11] and Garthwaite how the Bakhtiari were formed through the political activities of their khans;[12] Canfield has described how Hazara identity in Afghanistan is fundamentally sectarian, and gone on to argue that those identities are often more important than ones which are ethnic only, which they often override.[13] 'Ethnicity' in such settings varies in both content and relevance alongside and in combination with many other identifications, most especially religious identities.

The contingent relations of religious, political and ethnic identities seem less apparent in officially Muslim Pakistan than Shia Iran, with its Sunni minorities, and in Sunni Afghanistan, with its Shia minorities; but it is no less the case in each that ethnic identities take on social relevance in combination with religious sectarian and, hence, political identifications. There are at best only family resemblances between identities compared as 'ethnic' rather than, say, sectarian or political ones with which they are often overlaid and easily confounded.

Examples could be multiplied, but the plain fact is that these are complex societies in which multiple identities are available and in which relations are diversely joined with others. Identities are not fixed, but rather become variously relevant in diverse contexts. Ethnic identities lack fixed content or relation with other identities. Any suggestion that ethnic identities represent something more primitive than the societies in which they figure is quite a false, even opposite, reading of their significance. Multilingualism and other abilities to move between different cultural settings are common features of the complexity of societies in this region.[14] As individuals move through a variety of settings, language and culture are rarely the agency of community and vary at least as much in their social significance. While there are continuities between ethnicity and kinship,[15] notions of ethnicity as a kind of sub-nationality encode a specifically Western sensibility about the nation as a sort of suprapersonality actualized in the state which apply poorly in Southwest Asia. Functional resemblances between identities compared as 'ethnic' in this sense arise when, from the perspective of local states, such identities appear as an impediment in the form of a generalized and alternative but not necessarily political loyalty with which states compete and, thereby, politicize. This dilemma emerges less from any primordial or superordinate nature of ethnic identities in this region than from the political characteristics of states there, and it has to be sought in those characteristics.

DILEMMAS OF STATES IN SOUTHWEST ASIA

To generalize about states is marginally easier though hardly less subject to qualification than generalizing about ethnicity. It would not do to obscure real historical and organizational differences between Pakistan, Iran, and Afghanistan. But there are similarities in more limited comparisons of specific institutions. In so far as those states as historically specific formations face dilemmas with respect to diversities in their populations, it is primarily in terms of hegemonies they represent. Each, although quite different, represents forms and legacies of conquest states whose primary imperatives include monopolizing political life, minimally police powers and primarily in forms of dividing and ruling various component communities within a plural society. Second, by virtue of their various imperial legacies, each of these states faces stratified frontiers where limited administrative reach falls short of claims to unlimited sovereignty, or abilities to act fall short of interests. Third, cultural chauvinisms in the forms of a civilizing mission claimed by these states intertwine with the dilemmas not only of borders which cut across otherwise culturally continuous local groups but also with the diversities of component communities. While the specific contents of these states' hegemonies vary, and their differences are as important as their similarities, the structures of their hegemonies are in various degrees each imperial rather than popular; broadly speaking, the terms of ethnic dilemmas they have faced are set by those degrees, which in turn provide a basis for comparison.

State and statecraft in Iran encode a long tradition of treating component populations as local and ethnic only, while denying that identity to the state itself, which is variously religious and/or political depending on period and circumstance. Classically, also, the Iranian state is identified with a kind of 'persianizing mission' with respect to non-Persian and non-urban cultures within its dominion. Drawing on that tradition as a hinterland version of the Persian state, the Afghan state has pursued various policies of Afghanization for the past hundred years, from military extensions of state power and resettlement of Afghans in previously non-Afghan territories to establishment of Pashtu as a national language taught to all non-native-Persian speakers. By contrast, the Pakistan state is a direct legatee of a different 'nineteenth-century imperial experience, which entailed the formation of a new kind of power in the subcontinent, a modern, centralized bureaucratic state.'[16] To a considerable extent, 'nation' represents the project of an ethnically and otherwise diverse civil-military bureaucratic elite who are the prime repositors of nationalism in each case.

These states lay claim to some profoundly different cultural traditions for their legitimacies. There is little comparison between the metropolitan Persian cultural chauvinism toward others in Iran, Afghanization as the state project of Afghanistan, and Pakistani nationalism;[17] in drawing on traditions of Persian culture in the case of Iran, Afghanization in Afghanistan, and national institutions in Pakistan, the form and operations of these states differ accordingly. But there are similar ambiguities in the relations of these traditions to the ruling institutions of these states which have historically been less the creators than inheritors of traditions they promote. The classic pattern in Iran of a succession of originally tribal military autocracies that seize on Persian cultural legitimacy in their course finds an ironic echo in the rulers of Afghanistan who, though profoundly persianized themselves, promoted parochial afghanization within their realms. And Pakistan's officials operate a British-derived bureaucracy.

Beneath the various Islamic legitimacies to which each of these states appeals, they bear other, more structural similarities in subordinating ethnic identities of component communities to their own. These similarities emerge forcefully in frontiers which are borders to limited power but not to claims to monopolize political life. Embree's description of Pakistan's inherited British imperial scheme of a three-fold frontier of administration, sovereignty and, beyond that, of influence,[18] could apply to Afghanistan and Iran as well. Administrative control rarely extended as far as the sovereignties they claimed or the influence they sought. Direct gave way to increasingly indirect rule, and then to what often amounted to protectorate relations in name only as the secondary frontiers of each state form the tertiary frontiers of the next. For this common structural pattern, it could also be said of each state in Southwest Asia that contemporary national governments differ from former imperial ones by 'their commitment, however haltingly it may be practiced, to social change. The political arrangements for an unadministered frontier, while suited to the limited social aims of the imperial power . . . were dysfunctional for a national state basing its legitimacy on an identity of territorial sovereignty and nationality'.[19]

Put differently, the problem is that in attempting to monopolize political life, a characteristic pattern of politics emerges especially along the structural borders of authority. It is best known in the wider regional version, which came to be called the Great Game between the British and Russian empires for Asian spheres of influence during the 19th century. That strategy of interventions, rule by proxies, and stratified frontiers in the long-distance contest between the British and Russian empires merges with less well-known forms of the same politics on local levels, where their other side includes common patterns of recruiting third parties into local contests. On that side, and at every level, third parties figure as resources for swinging a local balance of power, or so it is anticipated, without really entering those arenas in their own right. Superficially presenting the form of a three-party game, this is less a politics of alliance and collaboration than one of coopting and circumscribing arenas, which fragments them on the one hand and limits initiatives on the other in what amounts to monopoly politics. The process extends down to local levels in the form of attempting locally to secure unlimited spheres of authority by enlisting outsiders in limited, or limiting, capacities.

Even without the larger imperial contest, center-periphery relations typically took the form of a spidery state that is weak but facile at the periphery, where its participation in indigenous political forms mirrors collaboration with foreign powers. In Kurdistan and Baluchistan and in the tribal zone of eastern Afghanistan and the North-West Frontier, a certain symmetry emerges in relations by which states recreate their own forms, or those are mimicked, in local organizations. Thus, after the Kurdish emirates were abolished in the 19th century, *sheykhs* entered the roles vacated by deposed emirs, especially as mediators, while local Kurdish organization itself became 'more tribal'.[20] There is a similar political convergence of local with state structures in Baluchistan, where Harrison notes that 'Persian rulers were able to break the power of Baluch chieftains by first defeating them on the battlefield and then inducing them with carrot-and-stick techniques to act as middlemen for Teheran in dealing with their tribesmen. By contrast, British colonial administrators did not attempt to extend the administrative machinery of the Raj into the Baluch areas. . . . the *sardars* enjoyed virtually complete control of their tribal affairs and were paid subsidies as well.'[21] Comparing these two experiences, Harrison aptly concludes that 'by reinforcing the power and autonomy of the tribal chieftains, this permissive policy set the stage for subsequent conflict between the Pakistani Baluch and Islamabad.'[22] So the *sardars* became prominent exponents of nationalist sentiments among Pakistan Baluch. On the NWFP by comparison, the outcome between the British Raj and the Pakhtun of Swat was a reorganization of the latter's tribal forms as a princely state.[23] Similar symmetries emerge on interior frontiers as well, such as between the Iranian state and the tribal confederacies of Fars,[24] in Azerbaijan,[25] in the central Hazarajat of Afghanistan,[26] and in Afghan Turkestan.[27] Structurally, these are similar as forms of center-periphery relations. Although each is different, they are different in similar ways: these states intersect those parts of local organizations which mirror their own, and then exaggerate them. The relations become symmetrical by becoming unidimensional.

Symmetry is not stability, however. In each of these cases, other local structures of relationships obtain. Not all aspects of local organizations are joined in relation to the state; instead, all relations are brought under those around which the state's interest emerges. As Embree pointed out, nation-states develop interests in control that only begin with but extend far beyond the exercise of police powers. But in expanding their interests from ameliorating to changing social conditions, they tend to revert to imperial forms by which their authority was previously extended, and contests previously settled in one arena are joined in another. To take an extreme example, the radicalism of the revolutionary regime in Afghanistan in pursuing its claims to prosecute a new order presented a kind of autocracy not seen since the reign of Amir Abdur Rahman Khan

(1880–1901).[28] Much the same followed the Iranian revolution with the vastly expanded claims of government in the hands of clerical authorities, the *Velayat-e-Faghih*. Similarly, there is a sense in which remilitarization of government in Pakistan is a response to the expansion of its interests beyond those of the former imperial government. The organizational locus of this dilemma met in the best known but also the most extreme cases of Kurdistan and Baluchistan can be elicited by comparison with similar, though less well known, situations and in a unified historical perspective which permits a more comprehensive comparison than is available in more limiting cases.

TRIBE AND STATE IN EASTERN AFGHANISTAN

Afghanistan presents most of the kinds of dilemmas that involve the relations of ethnic identities and the security interests of states. The present borders of the country were drawn by and for the convenience of the Russian and British empires during the last century, and on every side cut through ethno-linguistic groups. The most troublesome has been the south-eastern frontier,[29] drawn through the homelands of the Pakhtun/Pashtun population in whose name the state of Afghanistan was proclaimed over two hundred years ago. This is as much a stratified frontier on the Afghan side as formerly on the British and now on the Pakistani side; central authority runs tenuously and erratically, limited largely to claims to sovereignty toward the international border and to residual interests beyond that are based more on historic conquests than on ethnic grounds alone.

It is essentially but not unambiguously as a conquest state that local tribes on the Afghan side of the border regard that state. The majority of these tribes belong to a confederacy which overthrew the Safavid empire of Persia in the 18th century, only to be superseded by another group of Pashtun tribes from the south and west which established the Afghan state and achieved its widest extent. The former also credit themselves with bearing the brunt of resistance to subsequent British encroachments during the 19th century. Although that state has represented a hegemony identified with the Pashtun/Pakhtun population over others, among eastern tribes it has also represented hegemony over them of Durrani Pashtun from the south and west which they have resisted in their area with varying degrees of success.

The most violent form of resistance has been a series of revolts following each of the three Anglo-Afghan wars and directed against reassertion of Durrani suzerainty in the southeastern area. A serious revolt against Amir Abdur Rahman after he took the Afghan throne following the second Anglo-Afghan war (1879–1881), which secured Afghan internal independence from British India, was crushed in concert with his Durrani allies. Once subjugated, Ghilzai were turned north against the then non-muslim population of what is now Nuristan and west against the Shi^{c}a population of the Hazarajat in state-sponsored *jihads*.[30] Another series of revolts broke out against a subsequent ruler during the 1920s among these same tribes, many of whom had taken up his cause in the third Anglo-Afghan war (1919–1921) which secured Afghan independence from British India in foreign affairs, and culminated in his overthrow in 1929.[31] In between these revolts against exertions of the state, both of which were prosecuted in the name of Islam and its own authority, a running resistance to the exercise of state authority within the region took the form of more minor 'troubles,' as they were called in British reports on the trans-border region. These, in fact, are the more typical manifestation of dilemma of the state's relations to the populations of this region, which were otherwise ethnic cogeners of the dominant Duranni, and are exemplified in the process by which state authority was reasserted during the 1930s, following the restoration of a Durrani monarchy.[32]

Ghilzai participation in both the overthrow of Amir Amanullah in 1929 and the restoration under Nadir Shah was mixed and less uniformly in tribal or 'ethnic' capacities than under religious leadership. Ghilzai revolts in 1883 and 1886–7 had been led by a Sayyid mullah with marital ties to the Andar tribe. Other Ghilzai had joined a rebellion originating in Khost in 1925, also led by a mullah, while others desisted and some supported then-Amir Amanullah at the behest of religious leaders in Kabul but then stood aside when that support was withdrawn in 1929 and Amanullah was deposed in revolution by a non-Pashtun. In neither the revolts against Amanullah nor in the subsequent restoration of the Pashtun monarchy under Nadir Shah do Ghilzai appear to have acted corporately as whole tribes; instead they participated more as something like factions forming and reforming temporary alliances. There are two major reasons.

First, tribes are not monolithic organizations. They are arenas of competition defined by common ancestry and joined over what common ancestry organizes, which is mostly land-tenure and a sense of community.³³ Such identities articulate parallel rather than common interests, and they emerge through divisions of which they are, in effect, the record. Consequently, Pakhtun tribes *never* act as units. Instead, factions within each unit, which is defined by division, make alliances with factions in others; 'tribe,' in its most specifically organizational sense as the framework of local organization through land-tenure, and in its most abstract 'ethnic' sense, is accordingly one of the prizes and goals, rather than the means, of indigenous, local-level politics. As an identity, it represents the residue of a former unity, but operationally arises itself in factionalism recast as political nostalgia, not for a prior state of affairs but for its abstracted form. Would-be local leaders compete in promoting this nostalgia, while their competitions are what make it problematic.

Second, up to this period, there appears to have been a relative increase in the influence of religious figures, who appeal to unities over the head of local tribal-ethnic identities. Kakar, for instance, notes that 'especially during the Second Anglo-Afghan war . . . some mullahs for the first time in many centuries emerged as leaders of the campaigns and in many cases offered more sound military opposition to the British than either the [Durrani] sardars or tribal elders did.'³⁴ A similar mobilization under religious leadership occurred contemporarily on the NWFP.³⁵ It is similarly ambiguous as well, with frequent declarations of *jihad*, countered in the Afghan case by others anathematizing revolt against a Muslim sovereign, while the most respected religious personages, often Sufi *pir* and *mian*, served mediatory roles as peacemakers at the behest of one or the other side, and in pursuit of their own interests. Ghani has recounted earlier efforts by Amir Abdur Rahman to assume the role of chief ᶜ*alim*,³⁶ and thus to coopt this cycle. This was neglected by subsequent rulers, who instead relied when necessary on religious mediation to smooth their own relations, especially in the eastern Pashtun tribal areas, which compounded the effect of continuing to forfeit appeals to ethnic Pakhtun solidarity by making that part of the issue between center and periphery.

The equivocal and changing significance of ethnic identities in center-periphery relations continued throughout the first decade under the next Afghan monarch.³⁷ Much as in the revolt against Amanullah, the subsequent restoration under Nadir Shah was supported by some but not all Ghilzai – again not in whole tribes. In fact his progress through the region toward Kabul was halting and marked by frequent and prolonged negotiations for support, in some cases for passage,[38] which was reportedly secured in the end through the intervention of Sher Agha, Hazrat of Shor Bazaar in Kabul. This same *pir* of a sufi order, the Naqshbandiyya, which was reputed to have wide adherence among Ghilzai, subsequently refused to repeat his earlier mediation during various 'troubles' that marked the early years of restoration in Ghilzai country; or that mediation was refused on account of his earlier identification with that restoration. The result was a gradual reorientation of center-periphery relationships around the fragmentary and limited character of the center itself and away from tribalism.

This restoration *cum* reorientation was marked by the same sort of 'troubles' that marked British assertions of authority in comparable parts of the NWFP, and were sufficiently similar to be all of a piece. They normally would originate in some local incident of internecine violence. Land-disputes, animal losses or thefts, violations of grazing rights, and various other, often interpersonal, aggrandizements would escalate into wider or prolonged violence as the principals recruited or were joined by other parties for their own reasons, often also aggrandizement. Upon reaching or being forced on the government, or by government choosing to take note of them when officials became involved, the issue would escalate further by the addition of that interest until it involved the police powers of the state. Government demands for surrender of weapons and reference of the case to state courts would be met by counter-demands for non-interference and respect for privileges of not having officials stationed in the territory that were granted, or claimed to have been granted, previously in return for support elsewhere. Eventually, the issue, which had become defined as an offense against public order – and, more subtly, over who had charge of it – would be reduced to something like its original proportions as the more expansive claims on all sides were quietly abandoned or allowed to drop. Government sovereignty would be acknowledged in principle, tribesmen would keep their guns, an unlucky few might go to prison or quietly slip away, officials would be withdrawn or restationed, some property might be confiscated and later returned or not, all under the cover of multiple reaffirmations of solidarity and mutual respect.

Trivial as it might seem when reduced to schematics, the pattern was common and persisting. Something as minor as a sheep theft or the report of a wanted person and something as local as disputed grazing rights or field boundaries, might be interpreted as 'rebellion' and escalate into years of inquiries, desultory police action, and even troop movements. In pursuit of conflicting claims over jurisdiction, bandits would become rebels and officials tyrants because, so abstracted, the issues were the government's authority. Not only was every act meaningful in these terms, any action had more than one meaning. The British had stood aside during the campaign of restoration in 1929, although tribesmen from their side of the international border – from their second frontier in Embree's terms – had played a large role in it. But they took a close interest in subsequent incidents and produced detailed reports both through their political agents on the NWFP and through their embassy to the government in Kabul. For its part, the Afghan government did likewise, and not only in response to British concerns for peace on their borders.

As the issues were the government's authority, the government came not to rely on the mediation of religious figures, precisely to reduce if not entirely to displace that role in its dealings with tribesmen. For their part, the British were concerned not only with the Afghan government's control, and with their influence over it as their farthest frontier, but also with agitation on the NWFP. This was a period of persistent, if sporadic, resistance among Frontier tribes, and occasionally also in concert with Congress agitation in which the Afghan government similarly took an interest because of its residual claims on Frontier territory. Both governments had interests in keeping Afghan government interest from becoming hostage to religious intermediation, and hence determination, though for different reasons. For Kabul, it was to break with trends since the 19th century toward that dependence; for the British, it was to break that determination one way on the other side of the international frontier and another way on its own.

Each of these separate contests in each of a multitude of similar local issues conformed to the double pattern which marked larger, regional contests. On the one hand, parties to local disputes would seek to swing a local balance by recruiting outsiders in limited capacities, more as resources than as allies, which implied some reciprocity; often just to demonstrate such abilities was as important as doing it. For their parts, outsiders to a particular issue would intervene to coopt the contest or to absorb local into a larger one that mattered to them; or they would intervene to preserve some other arena, and again to demonstrate the ability to do so. The game-like quality of such three-party politics is belied by the seriousness with which it is pursued. No issue was merely local when the stakes are attempts to monopolize political life and to deny such monopolization to others; so the spiral, or the potential of spiraling, is insured and in turn locally assures the value of collaboration with outside powers, on one side, and the counterpart imperative to prevent that on the other.

The stakes are also indicated by the long-term tapering-off of such incidents in Ghilzai country throughout the 1930s. Locally, the threshold appears to have risen with the extension of additional arms of the government besides its police into at least the fringes of tribal country and an eventual broadening of its interests from ameliorating conditions to changing them. Extension and improvement of the road network, which drained investment from agriculture into commerce,[39] was eventually followed by local development projects. What came immediately on the heels of reasserted police power was a renewed encouragement of ethnic Pashtun/Pakhtun to emigrate into previously non-Pakhtun areas of central and northern Afghanistan. The policy had been initiated by Amir Abdur Rahman's granting rights to graze and encouraging Pashtun/Pakhtun colonization in the Hazarajat, Nuristan and Turkestan. Large tracts adjacent to Ghilzai areas fell under Ghilzai sway,[40] and accelerated in the Hazarajat interior through expansions from pastoralism to landlordism through trade.[41] These and other moves sponsored by the government, proceeding to large-scale immigration into northern provinces,[42] had the impact locally of draining away population and turning potential rebels at home into active supporters of the government as colonizers.

The character of the terms in which such stakes emerge is suggested by Barfield's report that the favoritism shown Pashtun immigrants in the north by a government locally identified with that policy engendered 'a separatist movement in Qataghan demanding that Turkestan be for "Turkestanis" – basically anyone who was not Pashtun. . . . in part a backlash to the national government's incessant propaganda about Pashtunistan.'[43] Opposition to government in the Ghilzai homelands took the less ironic turn of plotting against the ossifying Durrani hegemony. The traditional avenue of reducing government to local terms by appealing to or permitting the intermediation of religious figures waned with the 1930s. From its beginning, the restoration government contrived to separate the institutional interests of religious figures from those of the tribes, starting with the establishment of a *Jamiyat-i-ᶜulema* in 1931 and proceeding through foundations of mosques and religious schools supported by government stipends to granting oversight of legal administration in re-established shari᥋a courts. The wide adherence to sufi orders and influence of *pir* among Ghilzai reported by the British in the 1920s and into the 1930s was no more evident in Ghilzai country by the early 1970s than was any separatist sentiment. Such affiliations did provide an individual alternative in some marginal areas and among displaced tribesmen in the cities,[44] and they occasionally complemented local identities much as submerged political affiliations did in another, also covert, mode.[45] If those religious identifications were formerly as wide and strong as reported, then with decline in their strength came a shift in significance from tension with the local tribal order to tension with the more evanescent order of society wrought by the state, where they were in competition with other voluntary affiliations of party for articulating opposition in a fashion that would engage the state on something like symmetrical terms.

SOME COMPARATIVE CONCLUSIONS

The short conclusion that emerges from examining such evidence in its own contexts is that while center-periphery relations emerge in the terms in which they are joined, the dilemmas in those relations arise less from those terms than from the structural patterns of those relations. The dilemma of the state's authority, and hence its security, in eastern Afghanistan was posed by its abstracting its relation to local populations to one that was political only. That is utterly familiar for making the state accessible as a player in a local game. The residue of each incident was the curve of escalation and de-escalation which provided part of the background for the next. The gain accrued to the state in the intermediate term but eventually focused the dilemma on that gain itself as opposition sought to re-establish some symmetry by transferring the game back to the government's own bailiwick, first through the new parliament and then, failing that, through submerged political parties. By comparison, the counterpoint of intervention in lesser and recruitment from greater arenas in the northern regions where the government sponsored colonization – itself a play against both sides – engendered a separatism on a scale parallel to what the state made its own policy elsewhere. Structurally viewed, the outcome of this pattern of attempted political monopolization, as in the case of Swat's trajectory from religious alternatives to consolidation as a princely state within the British Indian empire,[46] is to borrow just that leaf from an opponent's book which restores, or might conceivably restore, an essential measure of symmetry.

The more complex conclusion is that the irony is intended. Ethnic identities are not the dilemma. These are complex, multidimensional societies, and so are 'ethnic' identities, which are themselves variably infused with cultural meaning and social significance. The conflicts of identity usually attributed to ethnicity arise instead from such complexities and rest in each case on exaggerations of those limited features in which the state is present on the peripheries of its authority. Comparisons between northern and eastern Afghanistan, and between the two sides of the Afghanistan-Pakistan border, could be extended to more familiar, or infamous, cases to flesh out the monochromatic qualities those assume in isolation. Kurdistan and Baluchistan display similar double-sided processes along stratified frontiers. It is not just that imperial forms are dysfunctional for modern states, but that 'modernization' most immediately means expansion of the interests of the state, and thus a reprise of imperial method. Parallels between recruiting third parties into local contests as resources, on the one hand, and of intervening in such settings, on the other hand, do not go unnoticed locally as two sides of a unified pattern of attempting to monopolize political life. Max Weber seems to have had such convergence in mind in remarking that 'The concept of the "ethnic" group, which dissolves if we define our terms exactly, corresponds in this regard to one of the most vexing, since emotionally charged concepts: the *nation*, as soon as we attempt a sociological definition.'[47] It is precisely in the European setting that ethnicity has the meaning of sub-nationality which it lacks in Southwest Asia, with its different kinds of states. There, that meaning, which is attached to communities in Europe, attaches to political identities and emerges in the interplay of contests to monopolize political life joined by the state and countered in its terms; their repetition across many substantively different arenas makes those into dilemmas that are, at one level, all different. They are not always ethnic, and not all 'ethnic' groups pose dilemmas for states, while at another, structural level, these dilemmas do not derive a pattern of politics from something more basic but derive from a pattern of politics which itself makes security a problem of authority.

Notes

1. This paper is based in part on fieldwork in Afghanistan, 1971–1974, supported by US National Foundation grant No. GS-30275, and on archival research at the India Office Library, London, 1980, supported by the Etnografisk Museum of the University of Oslo (Norway).
2. The primordialist view of ethnicity, and its application to the third world, is developed by Clifford Geertz in 'The integrative revolution: primordial sentiments and civil polities in new states' in Clifford Geertz, ed. *Old Societies and New States* (New York: Free Press, 1963) from Edward Shils's formulation in 'Primordial, personal, civil and sacred ties' *British Journal of Sociology* 8: 130–145, 1957. The complementary situationalist view of ethnic identities as responses arises out of more socially-oriented anthropological perspectives. For example, Elizabeth Colson's 'Contemporary tribes and the development of nationalism' in J. Helm, ed. *Essays on the Problem of Tribe* Proceedings of the 1967 Annual Meeting of the American Ethnological Society (Seattle: University of Washington Press, 1968) and Abner Cohen's *Custom and Politics in Urban Africa. A Study of Hausa Migrants to Yourba Towns* (Berkeley: University of California Press, 1969); for a recent summary, see Anya Peterson Royce, *Ethnic Identity: Strategies of Diversity* (Bloomington: Indiana University Press, 1982).
3. Karen I. Blu, *The Lumbee Problem: The Making of an American Indian People* (Cambridge: Cambridge University Press, 1980) p. 219.
4. *Ibid.*, p. 224.
5. Max Weber, (Guenther Roth & Klaus Wittich, eds) *Economy and Society: An Outline of Interpretive Sociology* (2 vols. Berkeley: University of California Press, 1978) p. 394.
6. Fredrik Barth, 'Introduction' in *Ethnic Groups and Boundaries*. (Oslo: Universitetsforlaget, 1969).
7. 'Pathan identity & its maintenance,' *ibid.*
8. Lawrence Rosen, 'The social and conceptual framework of Arab–Berber relations in central Morocco' in Ernest Gellner and Charles Michaud, (eds) *Arabs and Berbers* (London: Duckworth, 1973) p. 177.
9. Amal Rassam Vinogradov, 'Ethnicity, cultural discontinuity and power brokers in northern Iraq: the case of the Shabak' *American Ethnologist* 1: 207–218, 1974, p. 216.
10. See Fredrik Barth, *Nomads of South Persia* (London: Allen & Unwin, 1961); Daniel Bradburd, 'Never give a shepherd an even break: class and labor among the Komachi' *American Ethnologist* 7: 603–620, 1980 and 'National conditions and local-level political relations: patron–client relations in Iran' *American Ethnologist* 10: 23–40, 1983; Lois G. Beck, 'The Qashqai confederacy' in R. Tapper, (ed.) *The Conflict of Tribe and State in Iran and Afghanistan* (London: Croom Helm, 1983).
11. *Ibid.*
12. Gene Garthwaite, 'Tribes, confederation and the state: an historical overview of the Bakhtiari and Iran' in *The Conflict of Tribe & State in Iran & Afghanistan* (London: Croom Helm, 1983.)

13. Robert L. Canfield, *Faction & Conversion in a Plural Society: Religious Alignments in the Hindu Kush* (Anthropological Papers No. 50. Ann Arbor: University of Michigan Press 1973); cf. 'Religious myth as ethnic boundary' in J. W. Anderson & R. F. Strand, (eds) *Ethnic Processes & Intergroup Relations in Contemporary Afghanistan*, (Occasional Paper No. 15 of the Afghanistan Council. New York: The Asia Society, 1977); another side is developed in Richard F. Strand's 'Ethnic competition and tribal schism in eastern Nuristan,' *ibid*.
14. Two case studies which deal with what 'ethnic' identities and cultural traditions mean in complex Middle Eastern social settings are Fredrik Barth's, *Sohar: Culture and Society in an Omani Town* (Baltimore: Johns Hopkins University Press, 1983) and Thomas J. Barfield's *The Central Asian Arabs of Afghanistan: Pastoral Nomadism in Transition* (Austin: University of Texas Press, 1981). Dale Eickelman develops the implications of such data in broader perspective for more general understanding of Middle Eastern societies in *The Middle East: An Anthropological Approach* (Englewood Cliffs: Prentice-Hall, 1981) esp. pp. 175–199.
15. For instance in the generalized notion of *gawm*, see Jon W. Anderson, 'Introduction and overview' in Jon W. Anderson and Richard F. Strand (eds) *Ethnic Processes and Intergroup Relations in Contemporary Afghanistan* (New York: The Asia Society, 1978).
16. Ainslie Embree, 'Pakistan's Imperial Legacy' in A. T. Embree, ed. *Pakistan's Western Borderlands* (Durham: Carolina Academic Press, 1977) p. 25.
17. Anecdotal references suggest parallels by conveying monochromatic impressions of hostility, but more nuanced accounts emerging from actual case studies show how different these cases are, and how diversely each locates and valorizes cultural differences. E.g., for Iran see Lois Beck, 'Nomads and urbanites: involuntary hosts and uninvited guests' *Middle Eastern Studies* 18: 426–444, 1982; for Afghanistan, G. Whitney Azoy, *Buzkashi: Game & Power in Afghanistan* (Philadelphia: University of Pennsylvania Press, 1982) and Thomas J. Barfield *Central Asian Arabs*; for the NWFP, Akbar S. Ahmed, *Religion and Politics in Muslim Society: Order and Conflict in Pakistan* (Cambridge: Cambridge University Press, 1983). For comparative of the cultural and structural components of intergroup relations, see R. Tapper 'Introduction' in *The Conflict of Tribe and State in Iran and Afghanistan*, 'Ethnicity and class: dimensions of intergroup conflict in North-Central Afghanistan' in M. N. Shahrani & R. L. Canfield, (eds) *Revolutions & Rebellions in Afghanistan: Anthropological Perspectives* (Berkeley: Institute of International Studies, 1984), and Jon W. Anderson, 'Introduction and overview' in *Ethnic Processes and Intergroup Relations in Afghanistan*.
18. 'Pakistan's imperial legacy.'
19. *Ibid*. p. 37.
20. Martin M. van Bruinessen, *Agha, Shaikh and State: On the Social and Political Organization of Kurdistan* (Utrecht: Doctoral Dissertation, 1978) pp. 371–3. This is the most comprehensive study of Kurdish

organization as it relates to national revolts within the Iranian, Iraqi, and Turkish contexts. See also van Bruinessen, 'Kurdish tribes and the state of Iran: the case of Simko's revolt' in *The Conflict of Tribe & State in Iran & Afghanistan*.

21. Selig S. Harrison, *In Afghanistan's Shadow: Baluch Nationalism and Soviet Temptations* (New York: Carnegie Endowment for International Peace, 1981) p. 21.
22. *Ibid*. The structure of the Baluch chieftains in Persia is analysed in Philip C. Salzman's 'Why tribes have chiefs: a case from Baluchistan' in *The Conflict of Tribe and State in Iran and Afghanistan*; for Pakistan Baluch, see Robert N. Pherson's *The Social Organization of the Marri Baluch* (Viking Fund Publications in Anthropology Number 43. New York: Wenner-Gren Foundation, 1966) and Nina Swidler's 'Brahui political organization and the national state' in *Pakistan's Western Borderlands*. The only study of Baluch in Afghanistan is Erwin Orywal's *Die Baluch in Afghanisch-Sistan: Wirtschaft und socio-politische Organisation in Nimruz, SW-Afghanistan*, (Berlin: Dietrich Reimer Verlag, 1982).
23. See Fredrik Barth, *Political Leadership among Swat Pathan* (London: Athlone Press, 1959) and Akbar S. Ahmed, *Millennium and Charisma among Pathans: A Critical Essay in Social Anthropology* (London: Routledge and Kegan Paul, 1976).
24. See Lois G. Beck, 'The Qashqai confederacy' in *The Conflict of Tribe and State in Iran and Afghanistan* and Gene R. Garthwaite, 'Tribes, confederation and the state: an historical overview of the Bakhtiari and Iran' *ibid*.
25. Richard Tapper *Pasture and Politics: Economics, Conflict and Ritual among the Shasevan Nomads of Northwestern Iran* (New York: Academic Press, 1979).
26. Robert L. Canfield, *Faction & Conversion in a Plural Society: Religious Alignments in the Hindu Kush* (Anthropological Papers No. 50. Ann Arbor: University of Michigan Press, 1973).
27. Thomas J. Barfield, *The Central Asian Arabs of Afghanistan* (Austin, Texas: University of Texas Press, 1981) cf. M. Nazif Shahrani, 'Ethnic relations and access to resources in Northeast Badakhshan' in *Ethnic Processes and Intergroup Relations in Contemporary Afghanistan*. (New York: The Asia Society, 1978) Jon W. Anderson and Richard F. Strand, Eds., pp. 15–25.
28. The best documented analysis is Asta Olesen's *Soldiers, Peasants & Revolution: Political Strategies and an Analysis of the 7 Saur Revolution* (Project Re-Construction Saighanchi, Aarhus: Australian Scientific Mission to Afghanistan, 1980).
29. See Leon B. Poullada, 'Pushtunistan: Afghan domestic politics and relations with Pakistan' in *Pakistan's Western Borderlands*, 1977. The counterpart to the Pushtunistan controversy on the other side of the border was the 'scientific (*i.e.*, ethnic) frontier' advocated by some British officials: e.g., Sir W. K. Fraser-Tytler, *Afghanistan: A Study of Political Developments in Central and Southern Asia* (3rd edition, London: Macmillan, 1967), esp. pp. 48–54.

30. See M. Hassan Kakar, *Afghanistan: A Study in International Political Developments, 1880–1896* (Lahore: Panjab Educational Press, 1971).
31. See Leon B. Poullada, *Reform & Rebellion in Afghanistan, 1919–1929* (Ithaca: Cornell University Press, 1973).
32. For this period, I draw both on informants' statements and on reports by political agents on the then-Indian side of the border to Delhi and to the India Office, deposited in the IOL (L/P&S/12 nos. 1738, 1739, 1740, 1568 and R/12/126). Some of this material is summarized in *Military Reports on Afghanistan*, Part 1-History (Simla: General Staff of India, 1941). Historical studies covering this restoration period lack detail on the eastern tribal region, but see Vartan Gregorian's *The Emergence of Modern Afghanistan: Politics of Reform & Modernization, 1880–1946* (Stanford: Stanford University Press, 1969), esp. Ch. 11. Comparable material for the earlier restoration period under Amir Abdur-Rahman is provided in M. Hassan Kakar's *Government & Society in Afghanistan: The Reign of Amir 'Abd al-Rahman Khan* (Austin: University of Texas Press, 1979); for the end of the first Anglo-Afghan (1838–1842), see Malcolm Yapp, 'The revolutions of 1841–2 in Afghanistan' *Bulletin of the School of Oriental and African Studies* XXVII: 333–381, 1964.
33. See Jon W. Anderson, 'Tribe and community among Ghilzai Pashtun' *Anthropos* 70: 575–601, 1975; 'Khan and khel: dialectics of Pakhtun tribalism' in *The Conflict of Tribe and State in Iran and Afghanistan*. Comparable material from the lower Kunar is reported by Asger Christensen, 'The Pashtun of Kunar: tribe, class and community organization' *Afghanistan Journal* 7(3): 1980. For the neighboring Mohmand in the NWFP see Akbar S. Ahmed, *Pukhtun Economy and Society*(Cambridge: Cambridge University Press, 1980); cf. Asger Christensen, 'Organization, variation and transformation in Pukhtun Society' *Ethnos* 1–2: 96–108, 1981.
34. *Afghanistan*, p. 153.
35. See C. Collin Davies, *The Problem of the North-West Frontier, 1890–1908, with a Survey of Policy since 1849* (London: Cambridge University Press, 1932); cf. Ahmed *Millennium & Charisma*, 1976.
36. Ashraf Ghani, 'Islam and state-building in a tribal society: Afghanistan, 1880–1901' *Modern Asian Studies* 12: 269–284, 1978.
37. I ignore here the brief Saqaoist interregnum in 1929 between the fall of Amanullah and the installation of Nadir Shah as monarch. Popular Ghilzai representations simply reject the usurpation by a non-Pashtun as of no real impact, whether because of its brevity or because it simply did not impinge significantly on the Ghilzai regions. Poullada's analysis, which emphasizes the roles of non-Ghilzai Shinwari and Khogiani Pashtun of the Kabul valley in the revolt against Amanullah and of the non-Ghilzai Mangal, Zadran and Wazir to their east in the campaign of restoration, also paints an equivocal picture of Ghilzai 'remaining aloof' and 'wintering in India' (*Reform & Rebellion*, pp. 197–8); this might reflect instead the relatively greater prominence in the British reports on which he relies of the border tribes in comparison to more shadowy images of Ghilzai, whom the British knew mostly – and reported separately – as nomads who descended annually to India. Some Ghilzai

families maintain traditions of having supported the anti-Saqaoist campaign, while at least some of those who opposed or did not support the Durrani restoration subsequently emigrated to the north; see, Hugh Beattie, 'Kinship and ethnicity in the Nahrin area of Northern Afghanistan' *Afghan Studies* 3/4: 39–51, 1982, and Asen Balikci's 'Pastoralism and class differentiation among the Lakenkhel' *Journal of Asian and African Studies* XVI: 150–157, 1981.
38. The blow-by-blow account by Shah Wali Khan of the march on Kabul is summarized by Poullada, (*Reform & Rebellion*, 1973) pp. 183–198.
39. More precisely, it drained the investment of rural landowners away from the countryside and into cities and towns; see Jon W. Anderson, 'There are no khans any more: economic development and social change in tribal Afghanistan,' *The Middle East Journal* 32: 167–183, 1978.
40. For evidence that such displacement had been going on since the 18th century, see D. M. Balland 'Vieux sedentaires Tadjik et immigrants Pachtoun dans le sillon de Ghazni (Afghanistan Oriental),' *Bulletin de l'Association des Geographes* 417/418: 171–180, 1974.
41. See Klaus Ferdinand "Nomad expansion and commerce in central Afghanistan," *Folk* 4: 123–159, 1962.
42. See Thomas J. Barfield, 'The impact of Pashtun immigration on nomadic pastoralism in Northeastern Afghanistan' in *Ethnic Processes and Intergroup Relations in Contemporary Afghanistan*; Nancy Tapper, 'Abd al-Rahman's North-West Frontier: the Pashtun colonisation of Afghan Turkestan' in *The Conflict of Tribe and State in Iran and Afghanistan*; Hugh M. Beattie, *Afghan Studies* 3/4: 39–51, 1982.
43. *The Central Asian Arabs of Afghanistan*, pp. 161–2.
44. See Jon W. Anderson, 'How Afghans define themselves in relation to Islam' in M. Nazif Shahrani and Robert L. Canfield, (eds) *Revolutions and Rebellions in Afghanistan: Anthropological Perspectives* (Berkeley: Institute of International Studies, 1984).
45. The social characteristics of PDPA members adduced in Anthony Arnold's *Afghanistan's Two-Party Communism* (Stanford: Hoover Institution Press, 1983), esp. pp. 26–31 and Ch. 9, appear similar in some respects to those second sons and younger brothers, and other sorts of marginal tribesmen, who were also attracted by religious alternatives.
46. *Political Leadership among Swat Pathan*; cf. Ahmed, *Millennium & Charisma*.
47. *Economy & Society*, p. 394.

6 Buffer States on the Rim of Asia: Pakistan, Afghanistan, Iran and the Superpowers
Lawrence Ziring

States do not choose to become buffers. It is a role thrust upon them by a hostile international environment over which they have no control. Buffer states are lesser actors sandwiched between more powerfully endowed, ambitious, and often aggressive entities. The purpose of the buffer state is established by these external competitors. They become sacrificial elements in a larger contest. Their particular interests are ignored, often treated with indifference or disdain by the greater actors who set the dimensions and lay down the guidelines of confrontation. To be designated a buffer state therefore is to witness the diminishing of a state's sovereignty, to acknowledge that its national destiny is influenced from without, and that its territorial integrity is neither fully respected nor legally protected from alien intruders. Buffer states are extensions of balances of power, not international law. As such, they are protected by military–political conditions, not moral–legal procedures. Where their status as buffer states is respected their precarious existence is sustainable. However, in circumstances where the pattern of regional relationships undergoes significant change, buffer states are usually the first victims. Buffer states pay the price for temporary larger power equilibrium, a cost which oscillates between a loss of national pride on the one side and extinction on the other.

Eighteenth-century Poland is the classic European buffer state. Powerless to defend its sovereignty against the combined machinations of Russia, Prussia and Austria–Hungary, it suffered three traumatic episodes before disappearing as an independent entity. Today, despite the permanent presence of the Red Army in Eastern Germany, Poland remains a buffer state, frustratingly hostage to the protracted conflict between East and West.

AFGHANISTAN: CENTRAL ASIAN BUFFER

Afghanistan was perceived a buffer state between British and Tsarist imperial interests in the nineteenth century. Russia's transcontinental ambitions brought its legions into Central Asia and in due course long-ruling Muslim khanates were defeated and their territories absorbed within the spreading Slavic empire.[1] Britain's power in India was consolidated during this same period and the two imperiums eyed one another suspiciously, neither being prepared to accept the other's statements about 'peaceful coexistence.' The British colonial office was convinced the tsar would not be content until his forces broke through to the warm water of the Indian Ocean and their strategy centred on containing Russian forces in Central Asia, but on the northern side of the Oxus River (Amu Darya).[2] Afghanistan could not avoid becoming a buffer state given the posturing of its powerful neighbors. Moreover, Britain developed its 'Forward Policy' which envisaged the stationing of British-Indian contingents in Afghanistan as well as the subordination of its government to alien diktat.

Afghan resistance to this British intrusion resulted in the Anglo-Afghan War of 1838-1842. Kabul concluded its primary enemy was Britain and when tsarist emissaries were invited to Kabul following the British withdrawal, London initiated the Second Afghan War of 1878. In the latter conflict, the Afghan leader, Sher Ali, sought refuge in Russia as the British occupied Kabul. The British were forced to decide on either annexing Afghanistan directly or fashioning a 'friendly' government guaranteed to ensure the security of India and the Persian Gulf. After the 1838-42 war London had assured the Afghans they would not again interfere in their internal affairs. But the 1878 War only added to the fury of the tribal nation. The British realized the permanent garrisoning of Afghanistan against the will of the Afghan nation would bleed their treasury as well as their limited forces, and in time weaken rather than strengthen their hold over India. The British, therefore, opted for Afghanistan as a buffer state, and to ensure its 'neutrality,' a personality loyal to the British Crown was placed upon the throne.

The British chose Sardar Abdur Rahman to reign in Kabul while they continued to maintain a strong garrison in Kandahar. Kabul was restricted in its relations with other governments, especially imperial Russia. In 1880 Britain pledged to defend Afghan territory from either northern or western threats and British suzerainty was recognised in the Treaty of Gandamak.

Given its buffer status, Afghanistan achieved relative stability despite continuing tribal disorders. By 1893 Abdur Rahman was prepared to enter into border discussions with the British Indian government and a legal frontier between British India and Afghanistan was drawn by a boundary mission led by Sir Mortimer Durand. Prior to this agreement, Britain entered into another treaty with Tsarist Russia (1887) delineating the Oxus River and the southern Pamirs as the northern frontier of the mountain state. The finger of territory in the north eastern corner, the Wakhan Corridor, was designed by the British to prevent Russian territory from bordering on British India.[3] The buffer state was thus given the sanctity of international law and although the Russians continued to probe for weaknesses in the agreements they remained intact well into the twentieth century.[4] Afghan national consciousness was provoked by the maneuvers of the British and Russians. The former faced staunch resistance from the tribal Pushtuns on India's northwest frontier and the Kabul government strained to assert its independence. The assassination of Amir Habibullah, Abdur Rahman's successor, in 1919, brought his brother Nasrullah to the throne. Nasrullah proved totally inept and yielded to his brother Amanullah whose burning ambition was the elimination of British tutelage. The Third Anglo –Afghan War was the immediate outcome of Amanullah's call for a *Jihad* against the English in India as well as Afghanistan. Although unsuccessful in his military campaign against the British, Amanullah obtained a new agreement from London and dreamed of transforming Afghanistan into a contemporary state.

In 1921 Britain entered into a new treaty with Afghanistan which recognized its sovereign status, and Amanullah launched a high-minded but disastrous reform program. By 1924 the Amir had provoked sufficient dissatisfaction among his people to cause rebellions to break out in numerous parts of the kingdom. He hastily called a Loy Jirga or Great Assembly of tribal leaders in order to repair the damage and agreed to back away from his modernization schemes. In 1927, however, he reneged on this promise, urged the acceptance of his reform package, and caused a renewal of the fighting. Amanullah lost the support of his courtiers as well as the tribal leaders and when a non descript brigand by the name of Habibullah Khan led a small army into Kabul the remnants of his Royal Army collapsed. Habibullah Khan, Bachha-i-Saqao, replaced Amanullah on the Afghan throne.

Amanullah had dreamed of a Central Asian Confederacy which would have linked Afghanistan with the Muslim territories of Soviet Central Asia. Indeed there was reason to believe the Muslims of Central Asia would regain their independence following the Bolshevik Revolution.[5] But by 1924 Moscow dashed all hopes that the region would be offered the right to self determination. Moreover, the Red Army had crushed the Basmachi Movement and Amanullah's support for those Muslim, mostly Pan-Turanian revivalists brought a stern rebuff from the Kremlin. Amanullah was threatened with a Soviet invasion of Kabul if he did not cease and desist from his support to the rebels.

By 1926 Soviet power in Central Asia was assured and Amanullah agreed to enter into a non-agression pact with Moscow. In 1927, before Amanullah's demise, Afghanistan and the Soviet Union signed trade and transportation agreements which were perpetuated by the successor government. Britain, however, had reason to believe the Bachha-i-Saqao was a contrivance of and therefore in league with the Russians. Both London and New Delhi feared the loss of their Afghanistan buffer and the possible spread of the 'Red tide'. They therefore plotted the removal of Habibullah Khan. Britain's hopes rested with Nadir Khan, a Durrani Afghan, whose ties to the Pashtun tribal community were judged important assets in the restoration of the monarchy. With British assistance, Nadir Khan organized Wazir and Mahsud tribesmen on the Indian side of the frontier and began his trek to Kabul. Joined by Afghan tribal units they entered Kabul in October 1929, chased the pretender from the throne, and proclaimed Nadir Khan, King of Afghanistan.

Nadir Shah gave Afghanistan its first constitution in 1931 and also assembled a bicameral legislature. Other reforms aimed at raising the level of political consciousness of the less tribal elements in the Afghan population, but his association with the British opened him to sustained criticism. After a plot on his life was foiled, Nadir Khan ordered the death of the conspirators, including one Ghulam Nabi. In 1933 Nadir Shah was felled by an assassin's bullets, said to have been fired by a son of Ghulam Nabi.

Nadir's son Zahir assumed the throne on the death of his father but did not begin to exert power over the government until 1946. Britain began its retreat from empire during this period and in 1947 India and Pakistan became independent, thus removing British presence from the subcontinent. It also eliminated the British role in Afghanistan. Significantly, the Soviet Union reiterated its commitment to boundary agreements entered into earlier and in 1946 an agreement to that effect was signed with Kabul. Zahir sensed the need to deal with the Soviet Union on a new basis. Afghanistan wished to remove its buffer status and Zahir Shah turned to his cousin Sardar Mohammad Daud whose ties to the Pashtun population as well as his apparent knowledge of the Soviet Union seemed beneficial in the country's new circumstances.

Afghanistan believed it would be granted an outlet to the sea prior to the British departure from South Asia.[6] The Kabul leaders had supported Indian Congress Party efforts in that belief. Moreover, Kabul envisaged linkages with the Pashtun population on the Indian side of the frontier.[7] They had championed both the Khudai Khidmatgar and its call for Pushtunistan as well as the Congress government in the Northwest Frontier Province. Afghanistan opposed the Muslim League's conception of Pakistan because it threatened to deny them their national objectives. Furthermore, the establishment of Pakistan prevented the country from shedding its buffer condition. Kabul therefore opposed the formation of Pakistan, and later cast the only negative vote when the new Muslim state sought admission to the United Nations.

Daud became Prime Minister of Afghanistan in 1953 and virtually monopolized power. Security treaties were arranged with the Soviet Union in 1954 and 1956, a period when Pakistan entered into military alliance with the West and gained guarantees of assistance from the United States. Pakistan's orientation toward the United States was influenced by its fear of India.[8] Afghanistan, however, argued the Pakistanis had betrayed the people of the region by replacing the British with the Americans. Although Afghanistan avoided formal alliance with the Soviet Union, its dependence on Moscow *vis à vis* potentially hostile neighbors was apparent. Daud had been invited to join the Baghdad Pact with Pakistan, Iran and Turkey, his northern tier Muslim 'kinsmen', but he rejected the offer, believing the pact would only increase tension in the region and place Kabul in direct confrontation with Moscow.[9] Instead he was drawn closer to the Soviet Union. Afghanistan became the First Third World nation to receive Soviet arms following World War II, but it also continued to obtain United States aid. American technical assistance had begun in 1946 but Daud skirted commitments that could disturb the Kremlin.

Soviet leaders visited Kabul in 1955 and pledged long-term economic assistance. The Afghan–Soviet treaty of non-aggression was renewed during this period and in 1956 Daud signed a major arms agreement with Moscow which called for the development of the

Afghan airforce as well as the modernization of its army. Thereafter, Kabul was the recipient of significant transfers of Soviet tanks, artillery and jet aircraft. The small American military mission in the country was terminated and a Turkish military assistance program was also phased out. In military affairs, therefore, Afghanistan became solely dependent on the Soviet Union.[10]

In addition to building an army of 100 000, both Kabul and Moscow labored to circumvent tribal independence by nurturing the expansion of the urban elite. The Soviets also engaged in a major road-building program linking Soviet Uzbekistan with Afghanistan's principal cities. The United States contributed to this road network by constructing the highway from the Khyber Pass at the Pakistan frontier to Kabul. With the completion of these projects, including the opening of the Salang Tunnel, the Soviets and Afghans enjoyed all-weather roads between their two countries.[11] Afghanistan thus became a more intimate extension of Soviet-dominated Central Asia. The U-shaped road network with its American contributed spur also placed Moscow's forces in Uzbekistan within eighteen motorized hours from the Pakistani border. The Soviet Union also assumed major responsibility for the development of Afghan airfields, as well as telephone, telegraph and radio services. The United States contribution was on a smaller scale. Washington was permitted to construct an airstrip at Kandahar, and a US-sponsored Helmand River Valley Project was concerned with land reclamation and the expansion of Afghanistan's agricultural sector. West German, Communist Chinese, British and Japanese aid-givers also assisted in a variety of development schemes, but their combined efforts were considerably less than the Soviet program.

The Muslim world paid little attention to Afghanistan. No Muslim nation was equipped in the 1950s and early 1960s to provide economic or technical assistance. Financial aid was limited to pledges made by the Shah of Iran. But even the latter was of minor importance during that period. Moreover, Daud was suspicious of a Tehran–Islamabad axis, especially as both countries were linked to the West's Central Treaty Organization. The Afghan Prime Minister, therefore, was more inclined to perceive his immediate Muslim neighbors as foes rather than friends. And he continued to pressure Pakistan on the Pushtunistan issue, both to emphasize Afghan irredenta, and to signal Moscow that he was a trustworthy neighbor.

IRAN AND PAKISTAN

With hostile neighbors on its sensitive eastern and north-western frontiers, Islamabad looked to the Shah of Iran for an ally and support base. Unlike Afghanistan, Iran acknowledged Pakistan's attempts to develop intimacy with the Muslim world. Tehran was an immediate neighbor and a potential source of financial assistance. Moreover, Pakistan's dependence on Middle East oil supplies made Iran a useful associate. Pakistan received preferential treatment in oil pricing and in return provided moral support for the Shah's administration. Islamabad displayed no difficulty in identifying with the more conservative Muslim states and its interaction with the Shah also paved the way for its support to traditional Arab governments, particularly Jordan and the Gulf states.

Iran assumed regional importance after August 1953, when following a brief exile, the Shah was returned to his throne in what has been described as an American-organized countercoup.[12] The Shah emphasized his liberal credentials and declared his intention to distribute crown land to peasant-cultivators. He also sustained the 1950 nationalization of the oil industry but permitted a consortium of foreign companies to exploit the country's petroleum reserves. In return the United States granted Tehran substantial grants and loans to help tide it through an economic crisis. The American CIA also assisted the government in assembling the Sazman-i-Amniyat va Kishvar (SAVAK) which was concerned with internal as well as foreign security. Savak's chief responsibility, however, was the protection of the Shah and the monarchial institution.[13]

The Iranian armed forces also underwent dramatic expansion and modernization. The Army was doubled in size and the airforce and navy received similar attention. Pakistan's development paralleled that of Iran in the military field, and both countries became committed to United States policies opposing the spread of international communism. Iran, however, did not envisage itself in a buffer role. Rather, it saw itself as the last line of defense against a Soviet thrust toward the oil lands of the Persian Gulf. Thus the Central Treaty Organization (CENTO) was conceived as a link in a chain of alliances anchored by NATO in Europe. Pakistan provided the tie to the Southeast Asia Treaty Organization (SEATO) and bilateral arrangements between the United States and Taiwan as well as Japan completed the American-sponsored containment network.[14] Iran and Pakistan therefore were significant actors on the rim of Asia. Paki-

stan's problems, however, were more complex than those of Iran's.
  Pakistan was less concerned with the Soviet threat and communist subversion, and more interested in its differences with India. Iran wanted to champion Pakistani interests but it drew a line where Indo-Pakistani antagonism was a dominant feature. The Shah perceived a Pakistan engaged in self-fulfilling prophecy and swept along by its own rhetoric, especially its allusions to Islam and the need to safeguard the Muslims of Kashmir. The Iranian monarch wished to avoid such emotional remonstrances, lest he unleash religious forces within his own society. Moreover, the Shah refused to consign New Delhi to the communist camp, and his instincts informed him that the Indians required cultivation. In time, the Shah anticipated mediating the Indo-Pakistani dispute and Islamabad never disabused him of such purpose. By the same token, the Shah endeavoured to play the role of honest broker between Kabul and Islamabad, given the fervent belief that local quarrels only played into the hands of their powerful northern neighbor.
  Iran and Pakistan along with Turkey organized the Regional Cooperation for Development (RCD) in 1964.[15] RCD headquarters was placed in Tehran and the organization emphasized its indigenous character and socio-economic and cultural purposes. The member states also sought to disassociate RCD from CENTO which was an internationally recognized military alliance. Nevertheless the two organizations reinforced one another. CENTO'S secretariat was housed in Ankara. CENTO emphasized military preparedness and cooperation, the construction of communication and transportation links, and dependence on the United States. RCD stressed economic development and social interaction, as well as the building of a broader community in West Asia. Efforts were made to highlight the regional character of RCD and its pacific objectives, but in practice the projects of the two organizations tended to intertwine. Moreover, as CENTO began to lose its appeal, RCD strained to sustain its purpose. Neither organization lived up to its billing, but it was CENTO's failure to assist Pakistan in its 1965 war with India that signalled the eventual demise of both organizations.[16] Informal relations between Pakistan and Iran, as with Turkey, however, were largely unaffected.
  Prior to the Iranian revolution of 1978–79, Pakistan was the more unstable of the two countries. Contrasted with the turmoil that overwhelmed Pakistan, Iran was relatively tranquil. Although the Shah's policies were challenged by aggressive factions, the threat to

his pre-eminence appeared minimal. Pakistan, however, suffered from a combination of internal and external disorders. And in 1971 civil war ripped through the country, provided India with an opportunity to settle old scores, and Pakistan was unceremoniously defeated, dismembered, and left in a demoralized condition.[17] Forced to confront the reality of India as the preponderant power in South Asia, Pakistan seemed temporarily content to lick its wounds and repair the damage caused by the war. Moreover, Pakistanis welcomed their first civilian ruler since General Mohammed Ayub Khan wrote an end to the country's initial parliamentary experiment in 1958.

During this same period, Iran loomed large as a regional military power and the Shah began casting glances at the Indian Ocean as well as the Arabian peninsula. Tehran's forces yielded the Bahrain's independence but it hastened to seize the islands of Abu Musa and the Greater and Lesser Tunbs in the Strait of Hormuz.[18] Moreover, the United States accelerated and expanded its arms transfer program to Tehran following the mercurial rise in world oil prices. The Shah also convinced the Iraqis it was in their interest to sign a treaty acknowledging Tehran's sovereignty over the waters of the Shatt-al-Arab that washed its shores. In a display of military prowess the Iranian monarch despatched troops to Oman where they played a crucial role in containing insurgents threatening the rule of the sultan. The Shah used his petrodollars to purchase commercial and financial properties in Western Europe and the United States. He also offered funds to well-wishers, and Pakistan was among the more prominent beneficiaries of this largesse.

Zulfikar Ali Bhutto had reason to be impressed with his powerful neighbor and he 'borrowed' some of the Shah's techniques. Most significant was Bhutto's development of the Federal Security Force (FSF). Although he came to power on a wave of popular approval, Bhutto believed it necessary to bolster his authority. Conditioned to anticipate assaults on his leadership, and determined to secure the time necessary to recreate Pakistan in his own image, Bhutto ordered the FSF to neutralize all potential opposition. Although it is alleged the Shah encouraged him to follow such a course, it is doubtful that Bhutto required convincing.[19]

Bhutto, however, also took positions which disturbed the Shah. The Pakistani leader's emphasis on socialist reconstruction, his subtle references to Maoism, and his often overt anti-Americanism were painful reminders that their philosophies were at variance. Bhutto's bilateralism in foreign policy, his desire to become the leading spokesman for Third World causes, his determination to win 'friends' in the Soviet Union and North Korea as well as China, troubled the Shah. No less worrisome was Bhutto's Middle East orientation which not only drew Pakistan closer to Saudi Arabia, it also opened the region to Libyan revolutionary doctrine. The Islamic Summit over which Bhutto presided in 1974 angered the Shah. He refused to attend the conference, ostensibly because Muammur Qaddafi was present. But the Shah was even more concerned that the Summit legitimated the resurgence of politico-religious forces, although he apparently did not grasp how they could specifically impact on Iran or the extended area. Nevertheless, in an effort to exploit socio-political conditions, Bhutto was perceived fueling a potentially explosive condition. Despite these problems, however, relations between Tehran and Islamabad remained in place, and the Shah hoped to temper Bhutto's emotional excesses by offering Pakistan large sums of money.

THE SHAH AND DAUD

Iran's association with the West, and especially the United States, placed the country in the international spotlight. The Shah's regime could not conceal from the world press the widespread opposition to the monarchy. Nor could it prevent the dissemination of news concerning the often brutal methods employed in counteracting dissidents. Savak was particularly vulnerable to criticism, and journalistic commentary characterized the secret police organization as an uncivilized, savage organization bent solely on causing pain and grief. With hundreds and often thousands of persons detained without charges and secreted in dismal prisons, international agencies like Amnesty International and the International Commission of Jurists were compelled to cite the brutalities committed by the Iranian police. Death sentences had become more numerous in the 1970s and executions more prevalent. Links between Iranian students studying in European and American universities with their foreign hosts, and especially with their student counterparts, dramatized the unpopularity of the Shah, his administration, and policies. The United States government's decision to increase military assistance to the Shah during this period only affirmed the perception of the opposition that the Americans were the defenders as well as the creators of the Iranian dictatorship.

In 1975 the Shah issued a decree establishing Iran as a one-party state. But this act neither won him friends nor increased support for his administration at home. In many respects it brought the violence-prone dissidents into coalition with more moderate political opposition. The Shah nevertheless pressed ahead with his *Rastakhiz* (National Resurrection) party. The monarch apparently believed his police and military establishments were capable of dealing with those refusing to accept his fiat. Criticism of the one-party state was generally treated with contempt and those rejecting it were summarily judged enemies of Iran and in league with foreign powers. The new party quickly drafted and approved a constitution, and a major movement was inaugurated to centralize power. Moreover, the increased revenue from petroleum began to alter the Shah's otherwise more cautious approach to both domestic and foreign affairs. The Shah now publicized a vision of Iran as a great power.[20]

The country's new five-year plan (1973–1978) was hastily altered to reflect this objective and the heaviest emphasis was placed on upgrading the armed forces. In March 1975 Iran entered into a $15 billion military and economic package with the United States which Henry Kissinger said symbolized 'the deep political bonds which exist between our two countries.' Involved in the package was an American promise to build several nuclear reactors and power stations in Iran. Electronic equipment, telephone systems, and a vast representation of modern weapons were at the heart of the arrangement. Supersonic fighter aircraft, advanced naval ships, contemporary battlefield weapons – all were destined for the Middle East nation.[21]

The Shah also displayed a willingness to share his riches with friendly governments. Pakistan was assisted with loans, and joint ventures promised to facilitate trade to and through Iran. Tehran also provided loans to Morocco and Egypt. Turkey was pledged assistance in the construction of a pipeline carrying Iranian natural gas to the Mediterranean, and Afghanistan was added to the list of recipients as funds were allocated for the development of its irrigation and agricultural projects. By 1975 the Shah had offered approximately $8 billion in loans, making it one of the world's leading creditor nations.[22]

It was just at this juncture, when Iran began to loom large as a power with worldwide interests, that the Shah's inflated ambition, his belief in his infallibility and indispensable role, caused him to take actions that threw into question his stability as a leader. A major anti-government demonstration which the security forces were determined to crush was organized in June 1975 in the holy city of Qum. The affair was significant because it represented the first serious effort by both leftists and rightists, radical revolutionaries and alienated religious elements, to combine forces. The government refused to publicize figures of casualties and prisoners, but the Qum episode revealed government resolve to deal harshly with every form of political opposition. Moreover, it cast the Shah and his government in the character of heretical forces, opposed to Islamic tradition. It also provided a degree of legitimacy for the role of the Marxists who sought to capitalize on the confrontation between secular and religious authority, always a pronounced conflict in Shiite Iran. The government crackdown therefore merely energized more extensive terrorist activities against the state, and the tally of such assaults multiplied in 1976–77. Inside and outside the country the picture began to emerge of a beleaguered but powerfully ruthless regime headed by the Shah and nurtured by the American CIA.

President Jimmy Carter did not dispel this widely-held perception. He visited Iran on 31 December 1977 and at a New Year's Eve banquet the American president spoke glowingly of the Shah and declared Iran was an 'island of stability' in a turbulent sea. He also stressed he had closer personal relations with the Shah than with any other world leader.[23] He departed Tehran noting that Iran's friendship was 'irreplaceable'. Despite these public statements, law and order in Iran was rapidly disintegrating. The Shah directed his forces to root out the Marxists, but he was equally determined to eliminate his Islamic fundamentalist foes. The main thrust of the government attack against the latter group was mounted in Qum. Casualties were said to be heavy and allegedly thousands were arrested. The conflict in the spiritual city epitomized the classic nature of the struggle and solidified the perception that truth and faith were pitted against greed and evil. The religious leaders sent an open letter to Prime Minister Jamshid Amouzegar vowing that the sacrilege committed by the government would not go unpunished. The mullahs declared the closing of all Tehran mosques for one week in tribute to the fallen martyrs of Qum. From then on funeral processions were transformed into popular expressions of hatred for the Shah and his followers both inside and outside the country.

The coalition of opposition forces looked to the Shiite religious leaders for guidance and direction, and the mullahs ordered their followers and supporters to increase the level of violence against the monarchy. The general disorder in the country gave all the appearance of being out of control. Extremists saw no reason to compromise, and the days of constitutional monarchy, unbeknownst to the Shah and his American supporters, had dwindled to a very few.[24] The mullahs let it be known they wished to rid Iran of both the Shah and his American associates. A total break with the West, with its influence, culture, and physical presence was on the immediate horizon. On 16 January 1979, the Shah departed Iran never to return. And on 1 February 1979 Ayatollah Khomeini triumphantly returned from exile and assumed direct leadership of a revolutionary government. Forces loyal to the throne resisted the mullah-led takeover but by 11 February they had been defeated. Despite its vaunted military establishment, the Shah's government collapsed before the popular forces led by the Ayatollah.

The Afghan monarchy met its denouement several years earlier. King Zahir Shah had eased his cousin, Daud, from the Prime Minister's office in 1963 and had enlisted the support of tribal leaders by getting them to approve a new constitution. The king proceeded to make all key appointments to the army, bureaucracy, and judiciary, however, and in time of emergency could suspend the constitution. Royal family members were prevented from participating in political parties, nor could they hold ministerial office, or obtain a seat in the parliament or Supreme Court. The King's actions in effect laid the groundwork for the abolition of the monarchy itself. Zahir could not manage the political forces which he himself had spawned. Moreover, given Soviet presence in the country, political organization was destined to follow a radical Marxist course. The formation of the People's Democratic Party of Afghanistan (PDPA), the Khalq, developed from this incubus. Its splinter group, the Parcham, also had its origin in this period. Faced with increasing political opposition and lacking the support base normally provided by the family, Zahir refused to sign the political parties bill in 1969 and provoked social unrest, especially from the student population of Kabul. Moreover, sophisticated Afghan youth made willing candidates for the more revolutionary parties, and all of them were dedicated to the liquidation of the monarchy.

Both the Khalq and the Parcham had little difficulty in enlisting the support of the country's educated and professional classes. The monarchy insisted on its own pre-eminence, and despite promises about sharing political power with the larger public, the administration remained frozen in its archaic, autocratic form. Economic progress was painfully slow, and corruption and inept management prevented genuine development despite efforts by international agencies and foreign governments. The failure of the Afghan government was written large in the famine that swept the central and northern regions of the country in 1972. 'Operation Help' was prompted by United States Ambassador Robert G. Neumann, however, government action was only generated after riots erupted in Kabul.

It was during this period of domestic difficulty that King Zahir Shah attempted to extricate his government from the Soviet web woven by his cousin, Daud. In December 1971 the King visited London and the two governments agreed to terminate their long period of enmity. The King also promised the British government that his military establishment would not take advantage of Pakistan, given Islamabad's then preoccupation with a civil war in its eastern province, and India's entry into the conflict in December 1971. Indeed, rumors had circulated that Sardar Daud had aroused the Afghan army and the tribal people on the frontier, and that he had called for the 'liberation' of Pushtunistan. (The Soviets later asserted that it was they that had restrained the Afghan forces).[25] This new relationship with Britain, combined with increased American efforts at feeding the famine-stricken Afghans disturbed Moscow as well as its supporters in the mountain state. However, it was not until the Shah pledged joint cooperation between Afghanistan and Iran, and urged Zahir to resolve his differences with Pakistan, that the King's fate was sealed.

The Soviets had invested heavily in Afghanistan. In 1967, Zahir Shah and Aleksei Kosygin entered into an agreement to send Afghan natural gas to the Soviet Union in return for the construction of Afghanistan's airfields and highways. The Soviets now sought to guarantee their role in the country and when Zahir Shah visited Moscow in March 1972 the Soviet premier insisted on their countries signing a collective security arrangement. The King's hesitation in responding affirmatively to the Soviet demand proved to be his final undoing. Zahir left Afghanistan for medical treatment on 17 July 1973. During his absence from the country, Sardar Mohammad Daud reasserted himself. With assistance from the Afghan armed forces he disarmed the royal garrison, proclaimed an end to the monarchy, and described Afghanistan as a republic dedicated to 'real democracy' and Islam.

Both the Khalq and Parcham proclaimed their support for the

coup. Daud immediately addressed the question of Afghanistan's foreign policy. Among his first public statements was a declaration concerned with liberating the Pushtuns on the Pakistan side of their mutual frontier. He reiterated his old call for an independent Pushtunistan and heightened tensions with Pakistan. While the United States and other Western nations followed the Soviet and Indian lead in recognizing the new regime, Communist China delayed recognition, citing Afghanistan's bellicose intentions toward Pakistan and the influence exerted by Moscow. Daud denied complicity with the Soviet Union and appointed himself President of Afghanistan.[26] Daud, however, could not avoid intimate entanglement with the Kremlin. In June 1974 he visited Moscow and obtained a higher price for Afghan natural gas. The Kremlin also pledged more than half a million dollars to support Afghanistan's development program. Moreover, the Russians offered to build an oil refinery, a chemical and fertilizer factory, and irrigation and other agricultural systems. There was also a general agreement on joint efforts at locating the nation's natural resources. The various agreements meant that even more Soviet citizens, officials, and military personnel would be domiciled in the country.

While these developments were moving forward, across the border in Pakistan an insurgency in Baluchistan necessitated the deployment of several of Pakistan's crack army divisions.[27] The Pakistan government took note of the Afghan government's repeated calls to the Pushtuns and Baluch to demand self-determination. It was also apparent that Baluch dissidents had taken refuge in Afghanistan and a number of leaders had established propaganda offices in Kabul. Bhutto and his government were convinced that Daud and the Soviet Union were behind the turbulence in the frontier region and they publicly accused the former of fomenting revolution and sanctioning terrorist activities that had reached all the way to Islamabad.

In an interview with *Le Monde* in February 1974, Daud argued that Baluchistan and Pakistan's Northwest Frontier Province had 'always been an integral part of Afghanistan.'[28] The British, he insisted, had severed these regions from Afghan control and sovereignty through unequal and unjust treaties that could never be sanctioned by his government. Thus with the outbreak of hostilities in Baluchistan, the Pakistani government was convinced of Afghan complicity. Bhutto also publicized Afghan attempts to assassinate him while he was touring the troubled area. He appealed to the United Nations and sent a personal message to UN Secretary-General Kurt Waldheim detailing Afghan intrigue, sabotage, and terrorist activities. Kabul had also become a haven for numerous Pakistani opposition leaders especially those identified with the National Awami Party (NAP). The NAP had been founded in 1957 on the principle of greater provincial autonomy for the units comprising the Pakistani state. It assumed new importance among the Pushtuns under the leadership of Wali Khan, the son of Abdul Ghaffar Khan, the venerated leader of the Khudai Khidmatgar and a co-founder of the NAP. Ghaffar Khan's long-term residence in Kabul seemed to confirm Pakistani fears. NAP complicity with Daud's government, therefore, could not be refuted or denied.

Bhutto visited Moscow in October 1974 with the express purpose of reducing tensions between Islamabad and Kabul. The Soviet authorities informed Bhutto that the initiative for a peaceful settlement lay with his government, and they urged the Pakistani Prime Minister to settle his outstanding differences not only with Afghanistan, but with India too. Premier Kosygin implied that the condition of conflict on Pakistan's frontier was a product of Islamabad's bellicose intentions and that only broad settlement aimed at terminating territorial claims could relieve the situation. Bhutto accepted the Kremlin's intimacy with Afghanistan and India and he understood the Soviets would not satisfy Pakistan's needs at the expense of those countries. He was therefore compelled to put a bright face on conditions by noting that all disputes in the region should be settled through negotiations and on the principles of peaceful coexistence. At the same time he declared his forces would step up their counter-insurgency campaign in the mountains of Baluchistan. Reinforced Pakistani army units finally achieved the upper hand in 1975 and despite evidence of increased Afghan support to the dissidents, the insurgents were forced to surrender or flee into Afghanistan where they were provided sanctuary.

The Shah of Iran had cause to worry about the fighting in Pakistani Baluchistan. Iranian Baluch could not be insulated from the conflict and its spread to Iran was a predictable outcome of the protracted conflict. The Shah insisted the entire problem was a Kremlin plot aimed at destabilizing the region as a prelude to a Marxist putsch. On the one side, the Shah sought to mediate the dispute between Afghanistan and Pakistan. On the other, he insisted on the rapid modernization and expansion of his own armed forces.

The Shah's peace efforts suffered a setback when, in February 1975, Prime Minister Bhutto's chief political supporter and Home

Minister in the Northwest Frontier Province, Hyat Mohammad Khan Sherpao, was assassinated while delivering a lecture at Peshawar University. Bhutto was in the United States at the time of the incident. He cut short his visit and flew directly back to Pakistan. Within hours of his arrival Bhutto accused the NAP of Sherpao's murder.[29] The NAP was banned, its assets were seized, and hundreds of its leaders and workers were imprisoned. Provincial government in the Northwest Frontier Province was suspended, and the Pakistan army assumed its administrative responsibilities. Bhutto's supporters echoed their leader's view that the Afghan government was behind the turbulence and that it wanted to subvert and divide Pakistani society. Daud's response to these accusations was hardly defensive. He took note of the decision by the American President, Gerald Ford, to lift the arms embargo against Pakistan that the Lyndon Johnson administration had imposed ten years before. Daud voiced the opinion that the reason for the restoration of military sales and transfers to Pakistan was United States intentions to influence the Pakistani army. Daud condemned the decision and declared the American action would further retard the process of normalization in Southwest Asia. Moscow repeated the same view.

By the summer of 1975 Daud was wedded to policies with a socialist orientation. Domestic programs were aimed at eliminating Afghanistan's economic elite. Banks were nationalized, and land reforms broke the back of the privileged landlords. Agricultural cooperatives were established and government bureaucrats placed in charge. The Soviet Union expanded its assistance program to Afghanistan and by 1975 was providing the Afghan government with $400 million in aid annually. These figures did not include even higher military expenditures. The Afghan army and airforce came under almost direct Soviet supervision, and their ranks were swelled by broader recruitment.[30] But segments of the Afghan population were unreconciled to the transformation of society, or the Soviet involvement, and violence was a prominent way of signalling dissatisfaction. Ali Ahmed Khoram, for example, Daud's Minister of Planning since 1974 was shot and killed outside his office in Kabul.

Daud, however, refused to yield to his detractors. He gave the country still another constitution. He also created the National Revolutionary Party (NRP) and dominated its Central Council. Daud also tried to ward off influences of the Khalq and Parcham. The NRP was declared the only legally recognized party in the country. Parcham, which up to this time had fully supported Daud's dismantling of the traditional institutions now sensed a threat to its fortunes. Daud was capable of acting ruthlessly, and only the Khalq and Parcham were perceived potential threats to his rule. Also, unlike the Khalq which chose to remain in the background, the Parcham had worked in close harmony with Daud. Parcham was more intimately associated with the Soviet Union, but the weaker of the two leftist factions. It was also totally dependent on its leader, Babrak Karmal.[31]

By contrast the Khalq had penetrated the civil service, the military and the professional and student populations. Through Hafizullah Amin it had also established standing among the tribal Pushtuns, especially among the numerous Ghilzai. Daud could not be oblivious to these activities of the extreme left. Although somewhat constrained by his ties to Moscow, he began to re-examine his policies. And when the Shah of Iran offered his good offices in the Afghanistan–Pakistan dispute, Daud displayed greater interest. Moreover, the Pakistani army had suppressed the rebellion in Baluchistan, and Bhutto's military intelligence and FSF had neutralized the more active terrorists. Daud agreed to meet with Bhutto in an effort to normalize Afghanistan's external policies. Conditions within Afghanistan necessitated a consolidation of his authority and a tranquil border with Pakistan was judged essential. The Shah also pledged financial support to Afghanistan in order to provide Kabul with the needed leverage in its dealings with Moscow.

Daud's negotiations with Bhutto, however, were cut short when Pakistan's high-ranking generals overthrew and arrested their leader and placed the country under martial law in July 1977. The leader of the Pakistani junta, General Mohammad Zia-ul-Haq, declared the coup an internal affair and said the deliberations begun by the Bhutto government with the Afghan leaders would continue uninterrupted.[32] Daud could not ignore the sudden shift in forces in Pakistan. Nor could he avoid the realization that his own army had been infiltrated by elements that were determined to oust him.

On 20 February 1978, Daud revealed that a number of persons involved in a plot to kill him and overthrow the government had been arrested. Both the Khalq and Parcham were implicated in the conspiracy. The leftists had merged their operations in 1977 in opposition to Daud's intensifying conservatism, and under orders from the Kremlin. Daud had been criticized for his new intimacy with the Americans and for his cooperative posture toward the Shah. The Marxists propagandized the view that Daud wanted their assistance in order to impose an absolute dictatorship on the country. The Afghan public was also told the Americans and the Shah had instigated the coup against Bhutto in the hope of thwarting progressive forces in Pakistan. These attacks were similar to those emanating from the Soviet Union. Thus Daud after a protracted flirtation with radical forces, now sought to disassociate himself from these same elements. But the leftists were too deeply entrenched, and given Soviet involvement in the country, Daud's awakening came too late to save him or his regime.[33]

Daud visited Pakistan in March 1978, and both governments publicized the need to sustain communications and to reconcile their differences. Zia spoke optimistically about Pakistan's relations with Kabul and suggested that a peaceful settlement of their long-standing dispute might be near. Daud returned to Kabul cognizant of the criticism that was mounting against his rule, but he still believed he could control the situation.

On 17 April 1978, Mir Akbar Khaibar, a leader of the Parcham was assassinated in the capital. His funeral precipitated a wild demonstration by several thousand leftists. Daud used the occasion of the riots to order the arrest of Khalq and Parcham leaders. Noor Mohammad Taraki, Hafizullah Amin and Babrak Karmal were all imprisoned and threatened with trials for acting in a manner 'prejudicial to national security'. Daud then called his cabinet to assemble on 28 April to examine the instability in the country and to decide on action against the Afghan leftists. Before that meeting could be convened, however, disaffected elements of the Afghan armed forces favorably disposed toward the Khalq and Parcham, as well as influenced by Soviet advisors, moved against the government. On 27 April 1978, President Mohammad Daud was killed along with his brother Naim and approximately thirty members of their family and other high placed officials in the government.[34] This was no palace revolution. The military units that perpetrated the coup had no intention of imposing their own rule. The leaders of the Khalq and Parcham were given their immediate release, and Taraki, leader of the Khalq formed the new government. Hafizullah Amin and Babrak Karmal were made deputy prime ministers and Khalq and Parcham members filled other positions in the cabinet and government.[35] The political nature of the takeover, and the role played by the Afghan military dramatized the involvement of the Soviet Union in the destruction of Daud. Afghanistan ceased to be a buffer state and seemed destined to assume all the trappings of a Soviet satellite.

Taraki endeavored to minimize the Marxist character of the coup and publicized his government's intention to redistribute wealth, root out corruption and promote genuine Islamic tradition. The regime's Islamic posture was important in holding the confidence of the armed forces, few of whom had participated in the coup and who continued to follow fundamental Muslim practices. The Soviet propaganda machine also added its voice to the debate. Tass, the official Soviet news agency, denied any involvement in the coup. The world was informed that the revolution in Afghanistan was 'a direct expression of the people's will, without the slightest interference'.[36]

With Daud removed from the scene the Marxists attempted to consolidate their revolution but clashes over doctrine and policy were highly personalized and the Soviet-engineered unity of Khalq and Parcham in 1977 was quickly undone. Taraki proved unable to mediate between the doctrinaire Amin and the pragmatist Karmal. Amin also stood in the way of Soviet efforts to gain mastery over the Afghan armed forces.

Pakistan remained relatively silent on the sudden shift of forces in Afghanistan. But the Islamic League in Jeddah, Saudi Arabia, denounced what it envisaged as an act of violence against the Muslim people. Iran, still under the rule of the Shah, began supplying arms to tribal elements in Afghanistan. Tehran also called for more intensive Muslim solidarity. But there was little reaction in the Muslim world. Divided between traditional and radical regimes, Muslim governments showed little inclination to take sides. The Afghan situation, therefore, was treated as a purely internal affair.

Khalq policies, especially those pressed by Hafizullah Amin, however, began to have a telling effect on the tribal people of Afghanistan. Moreover, the more conservative tribes quickly concluded that Islam was in mortal danger in Afghanistan and that the Kabul Marxists had to be resisted. When Babrak Karmal sensed the magnitude of this problem he cautioned Amin to slow his reform program; but this only infuriated the Khalqi leader and Karmal was forced from the cabinet. Taraki assigned him to an ambassadorial post in Czechoslovakia in a vain effort to hold the coalition together. But there was no repairing the Khalq–Parcham marriage; and despite Taraki's efforts, Amin moved ahead with his 'modernizing' program. Moscow too was disturbed with these developments and with the Islamic revolution threatening to destroy the Shah's regime, it was judged necessary to impose other restraints on Amin.

By this time a fundamentalist Islamic resistance had intensified against the Kabul Marxists. Direct assaults on Afghan army units caused high losses. Tribal guerrillas also killed unprotected foreigners who were taken for Russians, their prime targets.[37] The defection of Afghan army elements also troubled the regime and its Soviet advisors. But the Khalq played down resistance to its authority and admitted only to running battles with smugglers and conventional malcontents. In the meantime, Kabul remained under curfew, and members of the bureaucracy, the professions, and intelligentsia disappeared from the streets of the capital. The government arrested hundreds of suspects and rumors spread about summary executions in and around Kabul. And somewhat in an effort to deflect public attention, Amin renewed the Pushtunistan controversy, arguing that the Pushtun and Baluch people should be given the right to decide their own future.

The Kremlin called Taraki to Moscow in December 1978 and a twenty-year treaty of friendship and cooperation was signed between the two governments. The agreement reaffirmed their treaties of 1921 and 1931, and the two governments agreed that each would respect the sovereignty of the other and would not interfere in the other's internal affairs. The 1978 treaty recognized Afghanistan's nonaligned character. Moreover, the respective leaders promised to consult one another on all issues affecting their security, independence and territorial integrity. Continued military cooperation was high on the list of priorities and article 8 revived the proposal that Aleksei Kosygin had made to Zahir Shah in 1972 concerning a Soviet-sponsored security system for Asia. In a final communique the Soviet government pledged to assist Afghanistan in its new five-year plan and offered 'every assistance to the friendly Afghan people in building a new society'.[38]

Taraki returned from Moscow with orders to reduce Amin's authority and to reinstate Karmal in the government. These efforts proved a total failure as Amin assumed the posts of Prime Minister and Foreign Minister in March 1979. The Soviets countered by making Taraki president of the Supreme Council for the Defense of the Country, but he was unable to gain the necessary support in the army high command. This contest of wills between Amin and Taraki was played out against a background of tumultuous events in Iran. The Shah had been forced to flee his country and a broad combination of revolutionaries, headed by the Shiite clergy had taken control of Iran. Moreover, the Afghan tribal resistance had multiplied and, fired by religious yearnings, it began to assault government positions with more reckless abandon. Given the severity of the fighting, the reluctance to take prisoners, the destruction of the innocents through indiscriminate bombing and shelling, the families of the Afghan rebels, the mujahiddin, were put to flight. Many sought refuge in Iran, but the great majority sought sanctuary across the border in Pakistan. By August 1979 approximately 142 000 refugees had arrived in Pakistan, only a trickle in the tide that was to inundate the country in subsequent years.

Pakistan did not and could not prevent the influx of Afghan refugees, the Islamabad government noting that its concern was purely 'humanitarian'. Pakistan's President Zia-ul-Haq publicized his government's intention to remain neutral and he pledged non-interference in the domestic affairs of Afghanistan. At the same time be believed his government could not turn its back on terrified, impoverished people who were seeking shelter from a storm that was ravaging their country.[39]

The Soviets, however, had another view of the Pakistani role. The ratification of the 1978 treaty between Moscow and Kabul was also the occasion for Soviet authorities to condemn the actions of the guerrillas. They hinted at Pakistani complicity, and cited a meeting in Peshawar between Afghan dissidents and representatives of foreign governments. The Soviets also cited the Karakorum Highway between China and Pakistan, opened in 1978, and called it a principal artery for the flow of Chinese weapons to the insurgents. Some Arab regimes were also accused of aiding the Afghan revolutionaries. Moscow declared Egyptian representatives in Pakistan regularly met with leaders of the Muslim Brotherhood and supplied them with money to purchase weapons. The Afghan government was reassured by its Soviet ally that it could count on its strong support in crushing the rebellion.

On 21 March 1979, *Pravda* directed its criticism at the United States and West Germany, as well as Egypt, China and Pakistan. All these countries, it stated, were using Islam as a pretext for the reinstitution of the monarchy, and this the Soviet Union would never countenance. The kidnapping and death of American ambassador, Adolph Dubs, in Kabul during this period had all the signs of a Soviet plot. Rumors were rife that Hafizullah Amin and Dubs had developed a close rapport and that the Afghan leader was planning new overtures to the United States. Dubs' death, however, brought the curtain down on American-Afghan cooperation. It also sealed the fate of both Taraki and Amin.

Taraki was summoned to Moscow in August 1979 and ordered to get rid of Amin. But when he returned to Kabul, Amin had him arrested, held in a residence near the presidential palace, tortured, and finally killed. Amin then sought to consolidate power in anticipation of a renewed Soviet threat. Amin appealed to his armed forces for support. He also called upon the Afghan mujahiddin to join with him in the restoration of Afghanistan's equilibrium. But the excesses of the Khalq regime prevented reconciliation.

When Afghan officers sought to regain control of their units, Soviet 'advisors' found themselves easy targets. Many died at the hands of their Afghan 'colleagues.' Moscow rushed more military contingents to Afghanistan when it appeared its grip on the army was being loosened. In December 1979 Viktor Paputin, a Soviet First Deputy Minister of Internal Affairs, and a high ranking member of the KGB, was despatched to Kabul to plot the overthrow of Hafizullah Amin and to guarantee the establishment of a government in Kabul favorable to Moscow. The Soviet Committee for State Security (KGB) in Afghanistan, under Paputin's direction, prepared the groundwork for still another coup. His reported death remains hidden behind a wall of secrecy and deception. Some reports suggest he was murdered in Afghanistan by forces loyal to Amin. The Soviets insist he committed suicide on his return to Moscow, but offer to further explanation.[40] Whatever the correct version, the Soviet maneuver forced Amin to retreat behind the walls of his palace, surrounded by his loyal bodyguard.

The Soviet invasion of Afghanistan was apparently ordered when the Kremlin realized it could no longer trust the Afghan armed forces. On 27 December 1979 approximately 80 000 Soviet troops moved into Afghanistan by road and air. Amin was assaulted in his quarters and killed, the Kremlin justifying the action by asserting that the Afghan government had invited the Soviet forces to assist them in beating back a foreign conspiracy. Moscow wished the world to believe that Amin was a usurper and that the only legitimate leader of the Afghan nation was Babrak Karmal, leader of the Parcham. Karmal and his Soviet associates were determined to ensure the survival of Marxism in the Muslim country. The mujahiddin were just as determined to continue the struggle, irrespective of the odds against them.

REVOLUTION, ISLAM AND WAR

The revolutions that convulsed both Iran and Afghanistan set the scene for the 1980s and beyond. But the issues were far broader than the circumstances being played out within those respective countries. Moreover, Pakistan was directly affected by the magnitude of the instability that threatened the broader region. Afghanistan's buffer state role had not only promoted the integrity of the Central Asian state, it had also been a measure of the region's security. Neither could be sustained after the epoch-making events of 1978–1979. Afghanistan's sovereignty had become fiction, while Iran and Pakistan were threatened by forces that they could only minimally control. For all intents and purposes, Afghanistan was at war with its superpower neighbor. Only the artificial government in Kabul lent credence to the notion that the country was engaged in an externally encouraged civil war and that the Red Army had merely offered its services to a beleaguered government. The Kabul-Moscow claim that Pakistan and the United States wished to perpetuate the war in Afghanistan in the hope of 'bleeding' Soviet forces, is belied by the determination of the vast majority of Afghans to struggle against an alien oppressor. The defection of two-thirds of the Afghan armed forces, the flight of more than twenty-five per cent of the Afghan population to Pakistan and Iran, the constant erosion of Afghan leadership, underlines the popular character of the encounter. The fact that the mujahiddin have received weapons and supplies from abroad cannot alter this conclusion. Indeed, judging by the degree of Afghan sacrifice, the assistance provided to the resistance from outside has been limited in the extreme.

Iran, not Pakistan, was the first country to experience the loss of the Afghan buffer. The Iraqi invasion of Iran may well have been prompted by Baghdad's fear that the Shiite Muslim nation, under Ayatollah Khomeini's leadership, was bent on spreading its brand of revolution.[41] Khomeini's link with the Iraqi Al-Dawa and the latter's call to the faithful to assist in the overthrow of the Baathist government of Saddam Hussain has been well publicized. Nevertheless, it can be hypothesized that Iraq struck across the Shatt-al-Arab in September 1980 because the Soviets had moved into Afghanistan, and appeared to be maneuvering to exploit ethnic as well as sectarian conflict within Iran.

The cutting edge of the Iranian revolution had been provided by the Marxist Fedayeen-i-Khalq and the Mujahiddin-i-Khalq. Both groups had received aid and encouragement from the Tudeh Party, the long-time political instrument of the Soviets in Iran. Baghdad conjectured that there would be a link-up between these organizations with Soviet assistance and that the mullah-dominated government would soon wither and yield political power to a people's government. Iraq, therefore, believed the time was right for it to make its presence felt in the region. Moreover, given the physical destruction of the Iranian officer corps by the revolution, the desertion of significant army units, Baghdad anticipated only token resistance to its invasion. It also had reason to believe its thrust into oil-rich Khuzistan, what the Iraqis called Arabistan, would be welcomed by the region's inhabitants who would eagerly join in common Arab cause against the despised Persians.[42]

Baghdad, therefore, set itself limited objectives. It also decided to conserve its weapons and frontline forces. As a consequence of this conservatism as well as Iranian Shiite resolve, the Baathists seriously miscalculated their venture. Iran took considerable punishment in the opening drive of the war, but given time to regroup and mass its force of Shiite devotees and regular army personnel, it proved capable of launching a successful counter-attack. In 1982 the Iraqis were driven back across the Shatt-al-Arab and virtually all of Iranian territory was recaptured. When Baghdad indicated its desire to call off the fighting, the Iranian response was both emphatic and determined. The war had become a religious crusade, and the Tehran government declared it would end only after Saddam Hussain had been destroyed and Iraq agreed to rebuild the Iranian cities it had devastated as well as compensate the victims of its aggression. Saddam Hussain had no intention of yielding to such demands, hence the war became a protracted affair.

By the close of 1984 the Iran–Iraq War was considered among the most costly Middle East struggles in this century. Estimates of dead and wounded on both sides ran from 250 000 to just under one million. Nevertheless, there was no sign of it abating, despite feverish efforts by the Muslim Conference, the Ummah Committee, and the United Nations. Moreover, given both Iranian and Iraqi attacks on shipping in the Persian Gulf during 1984, the world community was moved to assert its concern about the spreading nature of the conflict. The UN Security Council approved a resolution in the late Spring of 1984 calling for restraint and moderation from the warring parties.[43] But there was virtually no indication that Iran would treat this call any differently than those made earlier.

Rumors circulated about Iranian plans for an all-out assault on Iraqi defenses around Basra, but the Iranians refused to oblige the forecasters and continued to build up their reserves. Their probe of the Meimak area near the border in Elam province in late October 1984 was the first significant encounter in several months.[44] The war was described by observers as static, 'with bursts of gunfire and the chances of sudden martyrdom punctuating long days of routine digging in for the coming winter.' The Basij and Pasdaran (revolutionary guards, or militias of the Iran Republican Party) had earlier engaged in numerous human wave attacks with the consequent loss of thousands of their members. Their tactics now, however, seemed to be gaining in sophistication. More caution was demonstrated.

The war is believed to have had a positive effect in stabilizing the Islamic revolution in Iran. The clergy-dominated government has had the time as well as the justification to strike at its internal enemies. Iranian opposition sources report the slaughter of more than 15 000 of their followers and the imprisonment of almost 50 000.[45] The Mujahiddin, the largest of the Marxist–Islamic organizations apparently has been neutralized and its leadership forced to take refuge in France. Similarly, the Tudeh Party which initially sought to cooperate with the mullahs, became implicated in conspiracies against the regime and was ruthlessly purged in 1983. The Iranian action against the Tudeh convinced Moscow that it ought to favor Iraq, with whom it entered into a treaty of cooperation and friendship in 1972. Indeed, Soviet assistance to Iraq has been added to that of France and Italy. Moreover, Saudi Arabia and Kuwait have bankrolled the Iraqi war effort. They have compensated Iraq for the loss of its oil production by allowing Iraq to sell their supplies as part of its own. It is estimated Iraq has received between $30 and $40 billion in assistance from these Arab sources.[46]

Iraqi superiority in combat aircraft (4:1), and tanks and armored personnel carriers (3:1), in addition to many of the other implements of modern warfare have not discourage the Iranians, nor cramped their war effort. Khomeini remains the respected and revered patriarch and his perception of the war is totally moral–religious. In a recent comment he declared: 'They do not know the views of God and the prophets, how they dealt with oppressors . . . To compromise with oppressors is to oppress the oppressed.' The Ayatollah continued: 'Our revolutionary guards who lead a less than normal life do not fear war. Our military men who lead a normal life do not fear war. War would not do them any harm. It is those who live in palaces and the like who should fear war.'[47]

Khomeini's control over the very young is judged the source of his strength. It is also the key to the Islamic revolution that he and his followers have launched. It is estimated that every year some 442 000 Iranian males attain the age of 18. It is therefore argued that Iran will have little difficulty in drawing manpower or motivating it to action. If Iran displays weakness, it is in the realm of weaponry, their use and maintenance. Nevertheless, most observers believed the prediction of Supreme Defense Council spokeman, Hajatoleslam Hashemi Rafsanjani that an all-out drive will be launched against Iraq no later than 1985.

Iraq is perceived not only defending its own position, but also that of the conservative Arab states of the Arabian peninsula. Khomeini's references to the 'palaces' refers to the reigning families in Saudi Arabia, Jordan, Kuwait, the United Arab Emirates, Bahrein, Qatar and Oman. Moreover, this purpose of the Iranian revolution is judged preliminary to the final assault on Israel. And interestingly, it dovetails with Soviet objectives in weakening, if not destroying the pro-Western states of the Middle East. Howsoever, the war is concluded, Moscow believes forces are in train which will significantly alter the correlation of power in the region.

The Pakistani reaction to the unending war between Iran and Iraq is one of dismay and frustration. As a long-time friend of Iran, Pakistan endeavored to mediate the conflict and President Zia has consistently pressed the goal of Muslim unity. As recently as September 1984, addressing an International Seminar on Islamic Solidarity and World Peace, he cited the Iran–Iraq War as a most debilitating activity.[48] But Islamabad has had difficulty relating to revolutionary states. It has always been more comfortable with conservative, traditional governments, and its difficulty in adjusting to the Shiite Islamic revolution in Iran is as apparent to the Iranians as it is to others in the Muslim world.

Zia's program to transform Pakistan into an Islamic state, to manifest the Nizam-i-Mustafa, the Rule of the Prophet, has been met with derision in Tehran and among other radical states. Moreover, it appears that Zia's vision of Islam is at total variance with the Iranian mullahs. Zia's military status, his association with the United States, does not endear him to the Iranian leaders. Therefore his Islamic state is judged a subterfuge, if not a direct assault on Muslim principles and lifestyle. Pakistani Shiite resistance to Zia's reforms is often linked with Iranian revolutionaries, and Pakistani authorities have cited numerous occasions where either Tehran officials in Pakistan, or Iranian students supposedly studying in the country, have engaged in conspiratorial and/or violent activities. Zia has been unceremoniously attacked by Muslim radicals who caustically refer to him as the would-be Amir or Khalifah of Islam. The Pakistani president therefore has been singularly unsuccessful in his attempt to relate to the Iranians. Furthermore, his 1983 domestic security agreement with Saudi Arabia and the stationing of approximately 20 000 Pakistani troops in that country, and others in a variety of Gulf states, does not appear to the Iranians as even-handedness.[49]

Iran continues to see more support for its cause in the secular–revolutionary states of Libya and Syria. It also believes the Shiite communities of the Muslim world will eventually join with it in common action. Even token success against the Iraqis would enhance its role as the most important revolutionary power. It remains to be discerned if the split within the ranks of the ruling clergy will bring a change in this belligerent posture. It is argued by none other than Abolhasan Bani-Sadr that a 'moderate' element among the mullahs has gained the upper hand in Tehran, and that they have not only been responsible for reducing the effectiveness of the Marxists, they have also shown signs of willingness to reopen channels to some western nations.[50] If such forces have emerged within the feuding hierarchy, and if they are desirous of a respite from conflict, Pakistan may yet have a diplomatic role to play.

But if the situation in Iran was bleak, conditions in Afghanistan were becoming more ominous. Despite the second year of indirect talks in Geneva between Pakistan's foreign minister and his Afghan counterpart, the last series having been completed in August 1984, progress has been wanting. The UN Secretary General launched this initiative with some expectation of success. After the 1983 'proximity talks,' Diego Cordovez, the UN mediator, was openly optimistic. Rumors circulated that the Soviet Union would begin a scaling-down of its forces in Afghanistan to signal its satisfaction with the negotiations. But tangible results were not forthcoming. In fact, in 1984 the Soviets added to their forces, and engaged in an expanded offensive against guerrilla units, especially in the Panjsher Valley. The Soviets are estimated to have had no less than 120 000 men in the country and some observers believed the figure could be as high as 180 000. Kremlin efforts to seal the Afghan border with Pakistan, in part, was given as explanation for the higher troop levels.[51]

The Afghan mujahiddin suffered serious losses as a consequence of the concerted Soviet campaign, but their response was to increase the pressure on the Red Army, not fade away. The Soviets also tried to get the guerrillas to agree to a cessation of hostilities near the Salang Tunnel in return for a Soviet pull-back in a region northeast of Kabul, but the offer was rejected by the resistance leaders. The guerrillas brought some of the bitterest fighting of the war to the very gates of Kabul in 1984. In October, the Soviet press for the first time acknowledged the ferocity of the war, and cited the house-to-house battles in the villages. One *Pravda* account described a battle in and around the capital. The correspondents in the field displayed surprise that the 'dushmens' (enemy) had penetrated the Kabul suburbs. Another account spoke of troops in the countryside, surrounded by guerrillas, and 'sighing for beautiful nights on the Dneper River.'[52] Such Soviet frankness can be interpreted in two ways. It could simply be the account of correspondents describing the character of the war in Afghanistan. Or it could be part of a government effort to prepare not only the Soviet people, but the attentive world, for more determined Red Army action. The term 'war' describing the situation in Afghanistan had not been used before in the Soviet Press. Moreover, the Soviets were accustomed to gaining something from 'war,' given the sacrifices that it demands. This latter point will be elaborated below.

With 12 000 to 14 000 Soviet troops in Paktia province along the Pakistan frontier, and Soviet helicopter gunships hunting Afghan mujahiddin on both sides of the frontier, Islamabad had ample cause for concern. The Pakistani border town of Teri Mangal, near Parachinar and deep in tribal territory, suffered a series of attacks from both the ground and air. Islamabad cited at least 40 separate incidents in 1984 and tallied 130 deaths by October. Despite such cross-border raids, Pakistan practised restraint. Moreover, because of the remoteness of the area, there was speculation that some of the explosions and resultant casualties were due to actions either of rival bands, or agents of the Kabul secret service, the Khad. Mujahiddin in the area, however, insisted it was an enemy attack brought on by a successful raid against a Soviet–Afghan convoy that took 300 lives.[53] One report said there had been between 4000 and 5000 guerrillas in the area of the Kurram Agency. President Zia publicized his inability to close the border area with Afghanistan. He declared his government could not be held responsible for mujahiddin raids from such historically autonomous regions. Moreover, there were some 300 000 Afghan refugees in that Pakistani tribal agency, and Islamabad was in no position to limit their movement.

The plight and role of the Afghan refugees in Pakistan is multidimensional and difficult to chart. It is a monumental dilemma for the Islamabad government. Three million people, the vast majority located in the frontier area, have been provided with basic needs at considerable expense to the nation. The Pakistani administration has received high marks for this act of compassion. And although the Islamabad government strives to find a formula that would permit the refugees to return to their country and homes, there is little indication that it will be successful. Although permanent residence in Pakistan is not entertained at official levels, privately many knowledgeable Pakistanis believe the refugees may be in Pakistan to stay. If such is the case Pakistan and Afghanistan will have undergone momentous social change. It could be argued that the Soviet Union would like to shift the Pushtun population of Afghanistan eastward across the Durand Line. The Pushtunistan issue would be truly a Pakistan problem. Moreover, the congregating of the Pushtuns in a particular geographic region makes it possible to rationalize tribal policy in Afghanistan proper. Nationalities split between Afghanistan and Soviet Central Asia could be rearranged. The Soviets seriously contemplate the reorganization of the geography of northern Afghanistan so that a section from a line south of Herat to Chaghcharan, and just north of Kabul to the Pakistan frontier, would become one with the Soviet republics. Such geographic engineering would entail the re-drawing of Afghanistan. It would also imply the linking of the Pushtun and Baluch areas of Pakistan in a scheme for a 'Greater' Afghanistan. Although such a program will be at the expense of both Pakistan and Iran, it is well within the range of probability.[54]

Islamabad has tried to reduce the ire of the Soviets by moving mujahiddin headquarters outside Peshawar. In August 1984, the government announced that it did not recognize the Afghan Tanzimat (organizations) in Peshawar as offices of the resistance movement.[55] Judged to be refugee headquarters, they were therefore governed by rules of international law. Pakistan was only required to provide shelter for refugees fleeing from their occupied land. The Afghan resistance, it was reiterated, was entirely indigenous. A government spokesman noted: 'We will not allow, as we have stated repeatedly, Pakistan territory to be used for this [warlike] purpose.' The refugees must conform to laws and regulations of the host country, noted the government directive. Moreover, the headquarters were ordered to be shifted outside the Peshawar city limits because they were said to be in crowded areas. Many Afghans visited them each day, making normal life in that part of the city difficult for the local inhabitants. But as of the end of 1984 there were said to be 350 refugee camps in Pakistan, with only 10 camps in the Punjab containing 100 000 persons. Six to seven thousand refugees continued to arrive each month and government costs in sustaining the population was placed at $414 million annually, $200 million supplied from outside the country.

Moscow knows the history of the Afghan tribal people. It understands they have never been defeated in protracted conflict in spite of their having lost numerous military campaigns. The Kremlin's strategy, therefore, has been to avoid an all-out drive, but to sustain sufficient pressure in order to maintain the flow of refugees to Pakistan and Iran. Given an estimated 200 000 to 400 000 dead, and the flight from the country of more than four million, Afghanistan is being rapidly de-populated. Soviet comments attributed to statements of Hafizullah Amin that he could rebuild Afghanistan 'with one million Afghans,' may also describe Moscow's perception of its own policy. The Soviets look scornfully on tribalism and claim 'holy mission' as their cause. It is they who are 'charged' with bringing civilization to a primitive region, to instill it with new purpose, and to guide its future development. 'Mongoliaization' is a term heard in Moscow to describe the current Soviet role in Afghanistan. It can be concluded therefore, that the Soviets anticipate their 'eventual' success through a multi-faceted policy that also involves the depopulation of the Central Asian State.[56]

Evidence that the Soviets may have designs on Afghanistan (and Pakistan as well) beyond the destruction of the mujahiddin is found in the formation of the Ministry of Tribes and Nationalities which has been made an extension of the Khad, the Afghan equivalent of the KGB.[57] The purpose of the ministry is several-fold: (1) to destroy the religious and ethnic character of the different tribes; (2) to alienate the tribes from one another so as to make them more dependent on central government authority; (3) to educate the younger generation to accept a new order of life; and (4) to inculcate Marxist–Leninist values. The ministry has three central divisions: (1) The *Akhwam* which incorporates all the frontier areas bordering Pakistan. The central purpose of this body would be to re-draw administrative regions and to impose a centralized bureaucracy managed by local commisars; (2) The *Tribal Department*, which includes the Pushtun tribes in Pakistan. Its objective would be to win over tribal leaders through bribes and other inducements; and (3) the *Nationalities Department*, an office charged with supervising all the non-Pushtun tribes of Afghanistan, i.e., Tajik, Uzbek, Hazara, Turkeman, Kirghiz, Aimaq, etc. Interaction between these more settled Afghans and their compatriots in the Soviet Union has been under way for years and is being accelerated. Moreover, indoctrination of young Afghans is enhanced by the war. Many have been orphaned by the conflict and the Soviet Union is now busily engaged in providing places for thousands of young Afghans in its own schools. A November communique from Kabul noted that 870 war orphans ages 7 to 9 were flown to the Soviet Union for ten years of schooling, only a small part of a larger process.[58] Moscow sees deep social changes obtaining in Afghanistan, and the rebuilding of the primitive society along less tribal, more sophisticated lines is not only envisioned, it is also official policy.

And if evidence is needed that the Soviets covet Afghan territory it need only be noted that following the Stationing of Forces Agreement between Moscow and Kabul in April 1980, the Soviets and Afghan authorities entered into and signed a treaty (16 June 1981) in which the Wakhan Corridor was ceded to Moscow.[59] The Soviets claimed the region was never under Kabul's control. Moscow officials say the local 'warlord' fled in advance of Soviet troops and was now residing in Turkey. There was therefore no reason to maintain the fiction that Wakhan had ever been an integral part of Afghanistan. Furthermore, Afghanistan was no longer a buffer state and the incorporation of the Wakhan Corridor into the Soviet Union confirmed this fact. In geopolitical terms it is clear that, by annexing the Wakhan, the Soviets have effectively closed China's border with Afghanistan. No less significant, the Soviet Union now borders directly on Pakistan, is within range of the Karakorum Highway and in general proximity to the Indus Valley and Kashmir.

The near-presence of the Soviet Union on its western frontier has made it imperative that Pakistan seek a *rapprochement* with India.[60] The assassination of Indira Gandhi in October 1984 brought her son Rajiv to the helm of the Indian state. President Zia's gesture of friendship to Rajiv was aimed at reducing tensions between their two countries. It is in India's interest to realize that although the Afghan buffer is gone, Pakistan has assumed that unenviable position. And although Pakistan does not cherish the role, it is the only means which currently guarantees the long-term survival of the Muslim nation. It is necessary for India to recognize, however, that Pakistan can only play its full role with New Delhi's cooperation. The realities of geopolitics on the rim of Asia in these waning years of the twentieth century require new attention to the 'Great Game' that has spread to South and Southwest Asia.

Notes

1. Arthur Stein, *India and the Soviet Union: The Nehru Era* (Chicago: Chicago University Press, 1969) p. 2.
2. W. K. Fraser-Tytler, *Afghanistan: A Study of Political Developments* (London: Oxford University Press, 1953) and Owen Lattimore, *Pivot of Asia* (Boston: Little, Brown, 1950).
3. From 1880 to 1884 the Russian Empire for the first time had extended its area of effective control as far as the Merv oasis on the northern frontier of Afghanistan. Since neither the British nor the Russians wanted a conflict to develop, they agreed to set up a border commission to demarcate the Russo–Afghan border. A settlement was finally reached in 1887 and the boundary was formally agreed upon. The British agreed in 1895 to delimit the southern borders of Afghanistan, and the Durand Line was drawn to demarcate the Indo–Afghan border. A strip of land was ceded to Afghanistan [Wakhan Corridor] in the Pamir Mountains region in order that the British and Russian controlled territories would not come into contact with each other. Stein, *India and the Soviet Union* p. 3.
4. The foreign policy of the British rulers of India was directed towards securing the alliance, integrity, or neutralization of the borderlands and minor states covering the land approaches to the Indian Empire. The system which resulted in these efforts came to be known as the 'ring fence' and comprised two more or less concentric circles. The 'inner ring' consisted of the Himalayan kingdoms of Nepal, Bhutan, and Sikkim, and the tribal areas in north and northeast Assam and on the northwest frontier. The 'outer ring' consisted of the Persian Gulf sheikhdoms and of Persia [Iran], Afghanistan, Tibet and Siam. The 'inner ring' was gradually brought under varying forms of control, while intensive diplomatic activity, backed by the threat or use of force, denied a foothold in any of the 'buffer' states in the 'outer ring' to a major power without compensating advantage. Lorne J. Kavic, *India's Quest for Security: Defence Policies, 1947–1965* (Berkeley: University of California Press, 1967) p. 9.
5. There was little geostrategic reason to believe the Russians, whether tsarist or Bolshevik, would ever relinquish control over Central Asia. So long as the Russians sustained their power in Central Asia, no genuine security threat could be mounted from South or Southwest Asia northward. The deserts of Central Asia and the Caucasus Mountains were formidable barriers. On the other hand, Central Asia was a natural location from which to marshal forces and press drives south, either

toward the Persian Gulf or India. Lord George E. Curzon, *Russia in Central Asia in 1889 and the Anglo–Russo Question* (London: Longmans, Green, 1889) and Michael Edwardes, *High Noon of Empire: India Under Curzon* (London: Eyre & Spotiswoode, 1965).
6. The Afghans have consistently argued against Pakistani claims that it is the rightful successor state to British India, citing Kabul's 18th-century hold over the northwest frontier, Baluchistan and Kashmir. Prior to and immediately following partition, therefore, they joined with Abdul Ghaffer Khan in calling for Pushtunistan for the Pushtuns. And in June 1947 Hashim Khan, the Afghan Prime Minister, demanded that Britain provide Afghanistan with an outlet to the sea before its withdrawal from the Indian subcontinent. Zalmay Khalilzad, 'Security in Southern Asia 1,' *The Security of Southwest Asia* (London: Institute for Strategic Studies, 1984) pp. 139–140.
7. The Kremlin joined the Afghans in demanding the creation of an independent Pushtunistan to be formed from the Pushtu areas of Pakistan. No mention was ever made of the Pushtu areas of Afghanistan, however. *Pravda*, 5 April 1954. Cited in Richard B. Remnek, *Soviet Policy Toward India: The Role of Soviet Scholars in the Formulation of Soviet Foreign Policy* (Durham: Carolina Academic Press; published in Lucknow, India by Oxford and IBH Publishing, 1975) p. 22.
8. Shirin Tahir-Kheli, *The United States and Pakistan: The Evolution of an Influence Relationship* (New York: Praeger Special Studies, 1982) pp. 1–3.
9. India's reaction to the Baghdad Pact was similar to that of Afghanistan. Both feared the Cold War was being brought into the region needlessly. Robert C. Horn, *Soviet-Indian Relations: Issues and Influence* (New York: Praeger Special Studies, 1982) p. 10.
10. Lawrence Ziring, *Iran, Turkey and Afghanistan: A Political Chronology* (New York: Praeger Special Studies, 1982) A considerable portion of the historical narrative in this chapter has been drawn from the above work.
11. S. P. Seth, 'Russia's Role in Indo-Pak Politics,' *Asian Survey* Vol. IX, No. 8, August 1969, pp. 620–621. See also: Zubeida Mustafa, 'Afghanistan and the Asian Power Balance,' *Pacific Community* January, 1975.
12. Kermit Roosevelt, *Countercoup: The Struggle for Control of Iran* (New York: McGraw-Hill Book Company, 1980).
13. Barry Rubin, *Paved With Good Intentions: Iran and the American Experience* (New York: Oxford University Press, 1980).
14. W. C. Eveland, *Ropes of Sand: America's Failure in the Middle East* (New York: W. W. Norton and Company, 1980).
15. A critical view of RCD is expressed in Sangat Singh, *Pakistan's Foreign Policy: An Appraisal* (Delhi: Asia Publishing House, 1970) p. 100.
16. Although Pakistan was dismayed by CENTO's failure to lend assistance in time of need, the organization survived until the Shah was forced to yield to revolutionary forces. By contrast, Pakistan abandoned SEATO after the loss of Bangladesh (East Pakistan), almost eight years earlier. While SEATO was disbanded in 1977, a security pact remains operational through the Manila Pact of 1954. Pakistan's mutual assistance agreements with the United States begun in 1953–54 and reiterated in

1959 also remain intact. *The Military Balance 1984–1985* (London: International Institute for Strategic Studies, October 1984) pp. 94–95.
17. Lawrence Ziring, 'Pakistan; The Yayha Khan Interregnum,' *Asian Affairs*, Vol. 1, No. 6, July–August, 1974, pp. 402–420.
18. K. G. Fenelon, *The United Arab Emirates* (London: Longman Group, 1976) p. 3; and J. C. Hurewitz, *The Persian Gulf After Iran's Revolution* Foreign Policy Series 244 (New York: Foreign Policy Association, 1979) and John R. Countryman, 'Iran in the View of the Persian Gulf Emirates,' *Study Project Paper*, US Army War College, Carlisle Barracks, Pennsylvania, May 1976.
19. Interviews in Pakistan, 1981 and 1983.
20. Lawrence Ziring, ed., *The Subcontinent in World Politics: India, Its Neighbors and the Great Powers* (New York: Praeger Special Studies, 1978) p. 144.
21. Edward Kennedy, 'The Persian Gulf: Arms Race or Arms Control,' *Foreign Affairs*, Vol. 54, No. 1, October 1975, pp. 14–35; and the *New York Times*, 19 July 1977.
22. The *New York Times*, 12 July 1977. The superheated economy, however, caused Iran to borrow money to meet its obligations.
23. James Bill commented on President Carter's visit to Iran and noted his avoidance of the human rights issue and the alienation of groups heretofore hopeful that the United States government would force the Shah to relax his repressive measures. James Bill, 'Iran and the Crisis of '78', *Foreign Affairs*, Vol. 52, No. 2, Winter 1978/1979, pp. 338–339.
24. The American Assistant Secretary of State for Near East and South Asian Affairs, Alfred L. Atherton, Jr, declared before a congressional subcommittee on international organizations that: 'Relatively little is known about the number of terrorists involved – they are not particularly large we are told . . . Neither do we know a great deal about the various political programs of these groups, for their principal motivation appears to be the destruction of the current society and its leaders; these groups have not promoted constructive alternatives.' Department of State, *Statement by Alfred Atherton*, 'Iran: Reform and Human Rights', 8 September 1976, p. 5.
25. Lawrence Ziring, *Pakistan: The Enigma of Political Development* (Kent, England: Dawson Publishing Company, 1980) p. 237.
26. Zubeida Mustafa, *op. cit.*, p. 283.
27. Government of Pakistan, *White Paper on Baluchistan* (Islamabad: Printing Corporation of Pakistan Press, 1974).
28. *Le Monde*, (Paris), 3–4 February 1974.
29. Lawrence Ziring, 'Pakistan: A Political Perspective', *Asian Survey*, Vol. 15, No. 7, July 1975, p. 642.
30. US Department of State, 'Soviet Dilemmas in Afghanistan', *Special Report* No. 72, June 1980, p. 3.
31. *Ibid.*, p. 2.
32. Bhutto did not believe his successors could successfully negotiate with the Afghans. Zulfikar Ali Bhutto, '*If I Am Assassinated*' (New Delhi: Vikas, 1979) pp. 126–129; See also: Victoria Schofield, *Bhutto: Trial and Execution* (London: Cassell, 1979) p. 208.

33. The *New York Times*, 28 April 1978.
34. *Ibid*.
35. Louis Dupree, 'Afghanistan Under the Khalq', *Problems of Communism*, Vol. 28, July-August 1979, pp. 57–62.
36. *Tass*, 6 May 1978.
37. The *New York Times*, 11 September 1979.
38. *Keesings Contemporary Archives*, 16 February 1979, p. 29459.
39. *Dawn* (Karachi), 5 June 1980.
40. Marshal D. Shulman, 'Tales of Afghanistan: Moscow Style', US Department of State, Current Policy, No. 143, March 1980. The author also obtained certain impressions in conversations in Moscow in September 1981.
41. Godfrey Jansen, 'The Gulf War: The Contest Continues', *Third World Quarterly* Vol. 6, No. 4, October 1984, pp. 950–952.
42. *Ibid.*, p. 952.
43. *Pakistan Affairs* (Washington), 16 June 1984.
44. The *Guardian* (London), 31 October 1984.
45. *Iran Liberation*, a Mujahiddin Khalq publication, 19 July 1982; *The Times* (London) 1 July 1982. These sources are also cited in Khalilzad *op.cit.*, p. 59.
46. The *Washington Post*, 4 August 1984.
47. *The Sunday Times* (London), 30 September 1984.
48. *Dawn* (Karachi), 18 September 1984.
49. *The Military Balance 1984–1985* (London: International Institute for Strategic Studies, October 1984) p. 107.
50. The *Washington Post*, 4 August 1984.
51. The International Institute for Strategic Studies places the Soviet troop figure in Afghanistan (including 10 000 KGB and MVD personnel) at 115 000. *Military Balance, op. cit.*, p. 22. By contrast Soviet force levels in Mongolia are placed at 75 000.
52. The *Guardian* (London), 12 October 1984.
53. *International Herald Tribune*, 8 October 1984. See also: The *Washington Post*, 29 August 1984.
54. I first presented this argument in Lawrence Ziring, 'The Contemporary Pivot of History', in R .G .C. Thomas, ed., *The Great Power Triangle and Asian Security* (Lexington, Mass.: Lexington Books, D. C. Heath Company, 1983) pp. 21–46. Nothing has occurred since that writing to alter my analysis or conclusions.
55. *Dawn* (Karachi), 17 August 1984.
56. 'Mongoliaization' was a term used by the Soviets during a 1983 visit to Moscow. It was made in the context of Afghanistan's future, and it was declared to be more useful than the term 'Finlandization,' which was earlier heard in the West, and said to be a solution to the Afghan dilemma. See also: Richard Reeves, 'Journey to Pakistan', The *New Yorker*, 1 October 1984, p. 75.
57. Material for this section has been drawn from the research of Azmat Hyat Khan, Research Associate, Area Study Centre, Central Asia, University of Peshawar, Pakistan, 1983–84.
58. The *Guardian* (London), 7 November 1984. A more lengthy article on

this subject acknowledged the presence of the wife of Babrak Karmal and 'weeping parents' at the Kabul airport. Indeed not all the Afghan children destined for long domicile in the Soviet Union were orphans. The Karmal government is reported describing the airlift of the children to school in the USSR as a 'magnificent friendly gesture by the Soviet Union toward the Afghan people'. The Soviet and Afghan authorities also announced that many similar groups of young children were to leave for the Soviet Union in subsequent weeks and months. The *Guardian* (London), 14 November 1984.

59. Azmat Hyat Khan, 'Afghanistan: A Springboard for Soviet Expansion?' (manuscript prepared for The *Muslim*, 27 September 1984.
60. In one of his last articles prior to his death in September 1984, A. T. Chaudhri, Pakistan's leading political analyst struck a note of considerable despair. He conjectured whether India was acting in concert with the Soviet Union and questioned whether 'another Indo-Soviet "collusion" with shades of the 1971 trauma – may be in the offing'. He gloomily noted the increasing rigidity of the Soviet position in Afghanistan and the 'most ruthless onslaught of the trigger-happy Soviet–Afghan troops.' Citing the 'abnormal deployment' of Soviet troops on the Pakistan–Afghan border near Chaman and the failure of the UN-inspired Geneva conversations, he closed with the thought that Pakistan's survival may have brought closer the moment to say 'goodbye to non-alignment' and to grant 'bases to the United States'. Pakistan, he opined, may have to make a pact with the 'lesser evil.' He did not, however, examine if Washington would respond affirmatively to a Pakistani offer of bases. Perhaps he held the view that the Americans could not ignore the gesture. A. T. Chaudhri, 'Shadows on National Landscape', *Dawn* (Karachi), 25 August 1984.

7 Soviet Intervention in Afghanistan and its Impact on Pakistan's Foreign Policy
Hafeez Malik

The Soviet intervention of December, 1979 in Afghanistan initiated an intense debate within both Pakistan and the United States regarding the Soviet intentions in Southwest Asia. One view asserted that Soviet intervention was essentially a defensive operation and that President Carter had overreacted[1] to the Soviet concerns regarding their southern borders. In other words, this view maintained that 'no serious account appears to have been taken of such specific factors as geographical proximity, ethnic affinity of the people on both sides of the border, and political instability, in what is, after all, a border country of the Soviet Union'.[2] This view has essentially remained a minority view in the United States. In Pakistan, this view is fairly broadly shared by some of the political parties.

A second view maintained that 'the invasion of Afghanistan seems to have contained defensive and offensive elements'. Russian czars and Soviet commissars alike have traditionally considered the northern tier of Afghanistan to be within their sphere of influence. 'The Russians intervened in Afghanistan on a limited scale in 1885, 1928, and 1930 . . . yet, the Russians never attempted a full scale invasion until 1979. Soviet concerns must be viewed in the wake of the US deployment off the coast of Iran in 1979. In addition to any defensive motives was the Soviet desire to be in a better position to exploit future opportunities in unstable Iran.'[3] To Pakistan's foreign policy makers, this subtle distinction between offensive and defensive nature of the intervention remained irrelevant.

The third view was espoused by the Carter and Reagan Administrations. Presidents Carter and Reagan believed that the Soviet intervention is a measured step to acquire a favorable strategic position in the Indian Ocean and the Persian Gulf. Carter stated quite emphatically on 24 January 1980: 'An attempt by any outside force to gain control of the Persian Gulf will be regarded as an assault on the vital interests of the United States. It will be repelled by use of any means necessary, including military force.' (In pursuit of this policy, the Rapid Deployment Force was established to provide security to 19 countries in the Gulf and the areas around the Gulf.) Looking upon herself as the backyard of the Persian Gulf, Pakistan readily accepted the view of the American administration.

The Soviet view was explained on 12 January 1980 by the architect of the Soviet intervention in Afghanistan, Leonid I. Brezhnev. He analyzed the Soviet decision in global terms and in the light of developments within Afghanistan, Iran and the bordering states. Brezhnev saw the Afghan revolution of April, 1978 as the genuine socialist revolution threatened by what he called 'the forces of the past' and supported by the 'reactionaries' in Pakistan, Iran, the United States, Egypt and China. He blamed Hafizullah Amin, who was executed on the eve of the Soviet intervention on 27 December 1979, for the domestic problems of Afghanistan. The Soviet Union responded, according to Brezhnev, to honor the Treaty of Friendship and Cooperation which the two countries had signed in December, 1978. Lack of action on the part of the Soviet Union, Brezhnev believed, would have turned Afghanistan 'into an imperialist military bridgehead on our country's southern border'.

In discussing the Soviet relations with the West, Brezhnev catalogued several grievances: (1) the United States encouraged its NATO partners in May, 1978 to increase their military budgets until the end of the twentieth century; (2) American reluctance to ratify the SALT II agreement; and (3) the United States pressure in December, 1979 on NATO allies to deploy on their soil new medium range missiles.[4] To this catalogue may be added two additional considerations for the Soviet policy-makers: (1) the triumph of the Islamic fundamentalist revolution in Iran with potential for negative influence in the Soviet Central Asian Republics and (2) US attempts to strengthen relations with the People's Republic of China, involving the delivery of 'benign', as well as lethal, weapons to China. All these factors are interrelated and the Soviet intervention in Afghanistan can be understood only against the background of these interlocking relations between regional and global variables.

Brezhnev stated categorically that the Soviet Union did not have any expansionist design on Pakistan, Iran or other countries in Southwest Asia. Despite these reassuring words, no one in Pakistan, Iran or elsewhere was convinced that the Soviet power would not expand beyond the Durand Line. When empires expand, the reasoning continued in Pakistan, they create new peripheries. Yesterday, Afghanistan was a periphery on the Soviet borders; today, Pakistan has acquired this dubious status. Internal upheavals in Iran and Pakistan could create new justifications for further Soviet interventions if instability in these peripheral areas threaten the core areas of the socialist states in central Asia. This political logic led Pakistan to seek a counteralliance with the United States and the People's Republic of China. With the additional support of the Afghan insurgents, Pakistan's government sought to roll back the Soviet power from Afghanistan. In order to pursue this grand strategy, Pakistan's foreign policy was activated to achieve the following objectives: (1) improvement of strategic relations with the United States; (2) indirect negotiations with Afghanistan through the United Nations; (3) support to the Afghan refugees for humanitarian and other purposes and (4) the improvement of relations with India. The pursuit of these objectives has steadily soured relations between Pakistan and the Soviet Union.

STRATEGIC RELATIONS WITH THE UNITED STATES

From 1977 to 1979, relations between the United States and Pakistan were less than friendly. There were two main issues that divided them. First, Bhutto Government's charge of 28 April 1977 that the Carter Administration had attempted to destabilize his government[5] for his endeavors to establish a nuclear reprocessing plant in Pakistan with French assistance. The second issue related to American insistence that Pakistan should not attempt to develop nuclear weapons.

In order to persuade Pakistan to accept American policy on the nuclear issue, the United States Government suspended all new development aid and project assistance in April, 1977. American action was presented, not as a cutoff of aid, but merely as a suspension of new development assistance. The United States continued to provide some economic aid to Pakistan.[6] Almost two months later on 5 April 1977, a military *coup d'etat* removed Prime Minister Bhutto's Government. Consequently, personal friction between the Carter Administration and Pakistan disappeared. But the nuclear issue remained. Under American pressure, the French Government canceled the contract for the reprocessing plant in August, 1979 and the United States Government was partially satisfied. Subsequently,

President Zia-ul-Haq offered to open all Pakistan nuclear facilities for international and Indian inspection if India reciprocated. Since India did not oblige, Pakistan refused to open her nuclear facilities to full scope safeguards. However, President Zia has publicly and privately assured the United States Government that Pakistan does not plan to develop nuclear weapons. Despite these assurances, American suspicion on this issue about Pakistan's intentions has remained.

Responding to intelligence information that Pakistan was making covert attempts to develop nuclear facilities for the production of weapons, the United States suspended for a second time on 7 April 1979 economic (non-food) and military assistance, including the military training program. (For this action, the Symington and Glenn Amendments of 4 August 1977 were invoked). Four months later relations between the two countries became bitter. Pakistan had summoned the US Ambassador in August, 1979 and expressed to him Pakistan's 'serious concern over the escalation of the campaign of threats and intimidation in regard to Pakistan's peaceful nuclear program'.[7] Pakistan also suspected that in light of Ambassador Gerard Smith's recommendations, the United States might encourage India or use paramilitary forces to damage the uranium enrichment facility at Kahuta.[8] The State Department stated categorically that the United States had 'no intention to use force or extra legal means to disable Pakistan's uranium enrichment facility'. At this point in time, Pakistan found 'American friendship' more threatening to her interests than reassuring to her security. In this climate of fear and antagonism of the United States, an infuriated mob in Islamabad burned the American Embassy, when rumors circulated that the United States and Israel had participated in the seizure of the Holy Mosque at Mecca. Pakistan apologized for the incident and offered to pay 13.94 million dollars for the cost of rebuilding the destroyed US Embassy and the American Center in Lahore. Pakistan–American relations had indeed reached their lowest point.

The socialist revolution in Afghanistan in April, 1978 and the fall of the Shah of Iran in 1979 changed American, as well as Pakistani, attitudes toward each other and toward the Soviet Union. From April, 1978 to December, 1979, Pakistan and the United States shared a common perception that the Afghan revolution was essentially a Communist takeover, but they differed in regard to the handling of future developments in Afghanistan. While Pakistan was anxious to evolve a contingency plan in cooperation with the United

States to deal with the Afghan developments, the United States Government maintained a wait-and-see position. In fact, American diplomats in Islamabad saw in Afghanistan the Soviet Vietnam. The United States position then radically changed when the Soviet Union intervened in Afghanistan in December, 1979.

Problems of Pakistan's security: The 1959 Executive Agreement

The fall of the Shah and the Soviet intervention in 1979 prompted the United States to recognize the security interdependence of three zones of strategic importance to them: Western Europe, the Far East and the Middle East. Since Pakistan was viewed as the backyard of the Persian Gulf, the Carter Administration now switched its position toward Pakistan. Zbigniew Brzezinski, National Security Advisor, and Warren Christopher, Undersecretary of State, were sent to Pakistan in 1980 to refurbish the eroded strategic relations with that country. Pakistan asked for assurances of her security and would have preferred to have a guarantee of security freshly restated through a congressional resolution, but it was not forthcoming.

While Brzezinski recognized Pakistan to be located in the Persian Gulf region, he refused to commit American power to the security of Pakistan, if it was threatened. President Zia publically described his dialogue with the American envoy:

> So I asked 'Where does Pakistan lie, in the Gulf or outside the Gulf, in your concept?', President Zia recalled. And Dr. Brzezinski told me 'It lies in the Gulf'. So I said, 'Just let me ask you one question. If there is a threat to the Gulf, will the United States go to war?' He said, 'Yes.' I then said 'If there is a threat to Pakistan, will the United States go to war?' He looked at me. So I said, 'You don't have to say anything.' (*Dawn Overseas Weekly*, 4 Oct 1980.)

Consequently, Pakistan accepted the administrative reaffirmation of the Executive Agreement of 1959 which was designed to offer security assistance against a communist power, or a communist-supported power. Article I of the 1959 agreement provided: 'The Government of Pakistan is determined to resist aggression. In case of aggression against Pakistan, the United States Government in accordance with the constitution of the United States of America will take such appropriate action, including the use of armed forces as may be mutually agreed upon and is envisaged in the joint resolution to promote peace and stability in the Middle East in order to assist the Government of Pakistan at its request.'

In the 1950s and again in the 1980s, Pakistan wanted this agreement to be applicable in case of war with India, as well as act of war by a communist country. The United States then and now maintains a rather ambiguous position in regard to India, while Pakistanis in their wishful thinking, look upon this agreement as a guarantee of security against India, as well as a communist country. Henry Kissinger has highlighted the nature of this security relationship between these two countries in the light of the 1959 agreement: 'The fact was that over the decades of our relationship with Pakistan, there had grown a complex body of communications by the Kennedy and Johnson Administrations[9] going beyond the 1959 pact, some verbal, some in writing, whose plain import was that the United States would come to Pakistan's assistance if she was attacked by India'.[10] These assurances included (a) a letter from President John F. Kennedy to Pakistan President Mohammed Ayub Khan on 26 January 1962; (b) an *aide memoir* presented by the US Ambassador on 5 November 1962; (c) a public statement by the State Department on 17 November 1962 and (d) an oral promise by President Lyndon Johnson to Ayub Khan on 16 December 1965.

President General Yahya Khan had invoked Article I of the 1959 agreement as the basis for United States aid to Pakistan against India in 1971. The United States argued that no such binding obligation existed. In 1980 President Zia-ul-Haq accepted the reaffirmation of the 1959 agreement, without it's being applied to India, with an additional understanding that Pakistan would collaborate 'more closely with other Muslim countries in opposing the Soviet occupation of Afghanistan'. Also, he asked for American good offices in enhancing Saudi-Pakistani cooperation. Obviously, the strategy was to persuade the Saudis to 'facilitate Pakistani arms purchases in return for a Pakistani military input to Saudi security.'[11]

Recently, American envoys have given vague assurances of security for Pakistan against India, which Pakistanis had been eager to accept and even to exaggerate their meaning. Responding to a question in a seminar on 10 October 1984, the US Ambassador to Pakistan stated the US position in regard to Pakistan's possible conflict with India:

> Pakistan is on the front line. That is why we listen to what the Indians say about our military assistance program, even though in

the end we must proceed to do what we think is in the interest of Pakistan and the United States. I don't think we are neutral in the sense of not having a vision of the kind of world that we would like. I don't think we would be neutral in a policy sense if either Pakistan or India were to commit an outright act of aggression. We attach importance to the sovereignty, independence and territorial integrity of both Pakistan and India, so one would have to examine the circumstances, but we are not neutral on the issue of aggression and the first use of force.[12]

The Pakistani press, however, eliminated the ambiguity in the American ambassador's statement and covered his speech in unambiguous terms: 'The US would also come to Pakistan's help if India committed aggression . . . in case of aggression from East or West against Pakistan, the United States would not remain neutral.'[13] In the event of a crisis with India, the foundations of Pakistan's national disappointment and grievance against the United States had been once again laid.

However, the Carter Administration's offer of 400 million dollars divided equally between economic and military assistance to Pakistan was rejected by President Zia as 'peanuts', who offered two reasons for this contemptuous rejection: (a) he believed the offer was 'devoid of credibility of a US–Pakistan relationship, nor was the package commensurate with the magnitude of the threat'. President Zia added that the US offer did not insure 'security and buys you greater animosity, particularly of another country, and a superpower, which now happens to be our neighbor'.[14] Actually, what Pakistan had hoped was a NATO-like security commitment which the United States did not think was possible or realistic. Consequently, negotiations over American aid to Pakistan between the Carter Administration and Pakistan were terminated.

The Reagan Administration moved rather swiftly to establish closer relations with Pakistan. For that purpose, the Administration moved an amendment to the Symington Amendment making it possible for Pakistan to receive economic and military aid from the United States. After four rounds of discussions, spanning over six months, the United States offered an aid package of 3.2 billion dollars beginning with October, 1982 and terminating in 1987. (for details, see Table 7.1).

Also, the United States made it clear that Pakistan's non-aligned status would not be affected and she would have no interest in

Table 7.1 Proposed US assistance to Pakistan, FY 1983–FY 1987
(in millions of US dollars)

Fiscal year	FMS	IMET	ESF	DA	Public Law 480	Total military	Total economic	Budgetary outlay	Total disbursements
1983	275	0.8	125	75	50	275.8	250	250.8	525.8
1984	300	0.8	125	100	50	300.8	275	275.8	575.8
1985	325	1.0	125	125	50	326.0	300	301.0	626.0
1986	325	1.0	125	150	50	326.0	325	326.0	651.0
1987	325	1.0	125	150	50	326.0	325	326.0	651.0
TOTAL	1550	4.6	625	600	250	1554.6	1475	1479.6	3029.6

FMS: Foreign Military Sales.
IMET: International Military Education and Training Programme.
ESF: Economic Support Fund.
DA: Development Assistance.

Source: US House, 97th Cong., 1st sess., Committee on Foreign Affairs and its Subcommittees, Hearings and Markup, *Security and Economic Assistance to Pakistan* (Washington, 1982), 21.

establishing any military bases in Pakistan. The military aid program was designed to replace Pakistan's 'aged and obsolete equipment'.[15] Consequently, Pakistan formally accepted the United States aid package on 15 September 1981 and five days later the US Congress passed the Reagan Administration's aid package to Pakistan. Since then, relations between the two states have improved steadily and Pakistan has more or less moved into the position of the Shah of Iran by extending its military aid programs to the small Persian Gulf states, and has established a close military relationship with Saudi Arabia. Pakistan now feels a sense of security in this combination of China and the United States. President Zia stated that 'we now have a trilateral strength from our association with China, our new relationship with the United States, and our traditional relationship with other Islamic countries, headed by Saudi Arabia'.[16]

Has it really brought security to Pakistan? That remains to be seen. (However, the problems of security relationship between the United States and Pakistan are reviewed later).

SUPPORT TO THE AFGHAN REFUGEES

By 31 March 1981, 1 827 036 Afghan refugees had achieved asylum in Pakistan averaging during 1980 between 80 000 and 90 000 refugees monthly. These figures represent approximately 7–10 per cent of the total Afghan population. Actually, the refugee influx to Pakistan started in 1973 when Daud Khan overthrew the monarchy. Consequently, about 2000 loyalists and political dissidents sought asylum in Pakistan. When, on 30 April 1978, Nur Mohammad Tarakai toppled Daud, a larger exodus of political dissidents into Pakistan occurred. By June, 1979, Pakistan had 109 000 Afghan refugees in Pakistan. The third coup of 14 September 1979, led by Prime Minister Hafeez Ullah Amin against Tarakai, increased the refugee figure in Pakistan to 193 000. During Amin's brief tenure of three months, the number of Afghan refugees in Pakistan doubled to 386 916. Since the Soviet intervention in Afghanistan in December, 1979, refugees in much larger number have continued to cross the border into Afghanistan. Now, (1984) these 2.9 million refugees are sheltered in 348 tent villages located in the 16 border districts/agencies along the 1500 miles of the Pakistan–Afghanistan border. Practically every ethnic variation within the Afghanistan population is represented among the Afghan refugees, and the Government of Pakistan has attempted to settle refugees in homogeneous tent villages.

From April, 1978 to January, 1980, the Government of Pakistan supported the refugees exclusively from its own resources. Subsequently, the United Nations agencies (the UNHCR, WFP, UNICEF, WHO and FAO) joined to establish relief programs. From August 1980 to 1984 the US Government has contributed more than $350 million for the refugees. During the initial stages of the relief programs, the Government of Pakistan provided cash subsidies (Rs 120 or $US 12 per head per month) and tents for shelter. When the UN and other private relief organizations joined in, the cash subsidies were reduced to Rs 50 per head per month with a maximum of Rs 500 in reverse proportion to the provision of commodity aid. In Gilgit, a cash allowance of Rs 120 per month per head is still being paid because of difficulties in transporting commodities to northern areas.[17]

In addition to cash allowances and commodity aid, the Government of Pakistan has established primary schools in each tent village where a religious teacher is also attached to give instruction in Islam. Vocational centers for carpet weaving, embroidery work for women and training in other occupations are also provided in each tent village. An elaborate international, as well as Pakistani, bureaucratic structure has been created which administers relief programs in the refugee tent villages. This bears similarities to the United Nations administration of the Palestinian refugee camps in Palestine, Israel, Jordan and Lebanon. Although the refugees have experienced a traumatic wrench from their homeland, each one is provided for, and is perhaps comparatively better off than some underprivileged Pakistanis. Afghan refugee life has now begun to have an autonomous existence in northern areas, the North West Frontier Province and Baluchistan.

The insurgency against the Tarakai government, i.e. the Khalq regime, started in 1978, and has continued more vigorously since the Soviet intervention. The Afghan insurgents can be divided into three categories: (1) ethnic minorities, including the Hazaras, Uzbeks, Tajiks, Kirghiz, Karakalpak and others who are either Basmachi, who fought the Bolsheviks in the 1920s in Central Asia or the sons and grandsons of Basmachi who had settled in Afghanistan. They were inflamed by the Khalq regime's emphasis on Pashto (one of the languages of Afghanistan) and the promotion of Pashtuns (Pashto speakers) in the bureaucracy and the armed forces; (2) Islamic fundamentalists who were enraged by measures that they believed were detrimental to their devoutly-held religious convictions; (3) property holders in rural areas who violently opposed land reforms instituted by the socialist government. Agrarian reforms sliced up large land holdings and parcelled them out to landless tenants in 2.5-acre lots. The usury system under which moneylenders had kept peasants in perpetual debt by forcing them to borrow against future crops was abolished, yet no method of crop financing was substituted. No compensation was promised for agricultural land which was confiscated.

Highly conservative families rebelled against new rules mandating school attendance for young girls. Traditional marriage payments and large cash dowries were also banned. In their revolutionary enthusiasm the Khalqi cadres spread out in the rural areas to preach the virtues of 'scientific socialism' and denounced religious 'superstitions'. This was conceived to be an open attack on Islam, which alienated even those classes which benefited from the well-intentioned reforms of the regime. Moreover, the Khalqi government changed the green color of the national flag to red, implying the triumph of red revolution over Islam. Parenthetically, one might add that a half century ago, King Amanullah had launched a crash program of modernizing Afghanistan that had some similarities to the Khalqi regime's reforms, but in 1929, after he had been on the throne only ten years, a civil war broke out driving Amanullah into exile.[18]

In Pakistan, the Afghan refugees have already created ecological, economic and cultural problems which will be further aggravated if they are not repatriated to their homeland. Refugees brought with them approximately three million cattle and sheep creating a serious threat to the scarce pasture lands and water resources in the North West Frontier Province and particularly in Baluchistan. Consequently, the Government of Pakistan has initiated plans for the regeneration of pasture lands and reforestation of plains through small-scale irrigation schemes. A great deal more needs to be done in view of the damage to the environmental and ecological resources of the two provinces. To remedy the water supply problems, particularly in Baluchistan, special projects have been undertaken to establish potable water supplies to the refugees and their livestock. These include tube wells, open surface wells, mono-pumps, hand pumps and gravitational supply systems. A number of refugees managed to bring 4000 trucks and buses with them from Afghanistan. They immediately started to participate in the transportation system of northern areas and the North West Frontier Province, without paying any tax to the Government of Pakistan. This situation immediately created friction between the refugees and the Afrides, the Pakistani Pashtuns, who very nearly monopolize the transportation industry.

Moreover, some feelings developed among the local population in the two provinces regarding the 'privileged' position of the refugees for whom the Government of Pakistan and other relief agencies have systematically provided elementary education, facilities for provisional settlement and economic resources. Hospitality is an essential element in Pakistan's culture and especially in the Pashtun culture in the North West Frontier Province. Whether this tradition will endure in the face of economic competition and a sense of relative deprivation remains to be seen. The Peshawar-based Afghan political organizations are also acquiring stable identities of their own. A prolonged stalemate between Pakistan and Afghanistan would strengthen these groups, and they would become partners in future negotiations and would be able to exercise a great deal of influence on the Government of Pakistan's policies. The possibility of these political groups evolving into a quasi-government in Pakistan *à la* the PLO cannot be ruled out.

In the Frontier Province, public opinion regarding the Red Revolution in Afghanistan is hostile, especially among the (1) land owning classes; (2) business community; (3) entrepreneurial classes; (4) intelligentsia and (5) *ulama* (the traditional religious scholars and leaders). Naturally, the Pashtun classes provide much moral and material support to the Afghan refugees and more so to the Pashtun elements among them. Despite this present solidarity between the Afghan refugees and Pakistani Pashtuns, according to the Government of Pakistan, the Kabul Government has managed to penetrate, through its agents, the refugee tent villages creating the potential for riots and generating antagonism between the refugees and the locals. In Baluchistan the Baluchis at some point in the future may perceive the non-Baluchi arrivals as a threat to their numerical strength in the province, and as competitors for the scarce economic resources of Baluchistan.

In Baluchistan, however, a substantial separatist sentiment has always existed which at some point in the future could be encouraged by the Soviet Union in order to cause a breakdown of relations between the Afghan and Baluchi populations. Baluchistan would then present a serious political problem for Pakistan. During the period of decline and fall of the Shah, and since the advent of the Islamic Republic of Iran, Iranian Baluchistan has demonstrated its will for autonomy and separatism. This nationalistic aspiration among the Pakistani and Iranian Baluchis could be substantially aided by the Soviet Union. Conversely, the Pashtunistan issue, which at one time had a great deal of appeal among some Pashtuns in the North West Frontier Province, has lost its attraction, thanks to the rise of the socialist regime in Afghanistan. This, however, does not mean that Afghanistan has lost its interest in Pashtunistan. Both the Tarakai and the Karmal regimes have celebrated Pashtunistan days in Kabul.[19] Under a different set of circumstances the issue could be revived again with Soviet support.

The Afghan resistance movement had started to organize itself politically before the Soviet intervention. In fact, the insurgency had achieved a remarkable success by the time Hafeez Ullah Amin and his cohorts assassinated Tarakai in September, 1979. From September to December, 1979, the resistance movement had developed so much self-confidence that they expected the Amin regime to collapse under their hammer blows. Indeed, this was one of the very strong reasons why the Soviet Union decided to intervene militarily and to install Babrak Karmal, the leader of the rival parcham faction of the People's Democratic Party.

Pakistan's borderlands have become a sanctuary for the Afghan guerrillas fighting against the Soviets. To a degree, this situation is beyond Pakistan's control. Repeatedly, the Government of Pakistan has suggested to the Soviet Union that it should seal the Pakistan-Afghanistan borders, if that is their preference. However, airspace violations by Soviet and Afghan aircraft are frequent. It is reported that the Government of Pakistan often keeps violations secret when deaths are few or when the incursions are minor ones, such as reconnaissance flights.[20]

However, the insurgents' strength has also increased, and they have been able to secure more sophisticated weapons, including rockets and explosives of all kinds. According to one estimate, 400 million dollars were appropriated by the US Government to the Afghan covert-aid program during the last five years.[21] The US Senate also established a precedent on 3 October 1984 by adopting the Afghan Effective Support Resolution with a roll-call vote of 97 to 0. The following day, the House of Representatives passed the same resolution unanimously and thus committed Congress to support the insurgents against the Soviet intervention in Afghanistan. The Department of State maintains that the insurgents control 75 per cent of the countryside and have become particularly 'effective against Soviet/DRA [Democratic Republic of Afghanistan] supply convoys, and Soviet helicopter and aircraft losses have risen significantly'.[22] In November, 1984, the insurgents succeeded in demolishing high-powered electric towers which supplied electricity to Kabul, and thus brought the economic warfare to the capital of Afghanistan.

The Soviet Union and DRA have also acknowledged the magnitude of damage inflicted upon Afghanistan by the insurgents. The Prime Minister of DRA stated on 11 April 1983: 'In the post-revolutionary years the bandits [Soviet/DRA euphemism for the insurgents] had destroyed or put out of operation 50 per cent of schools, half of all hospitals, 14 per cent of state transport, three quarters of all communication lines and several power stations. The damage is estimated at 24 000 million Afghanis, which equals half of all capital investments in economy during the 20 years preceeding the revolution.'[23] Commenting on the activities of the insurgents, President Zia, probably for the first time, obliquely acknowledged in

November, 1984, the role of the Afghan refugees as insurgents. He said: 'The bombing of Afghan refugee camps by the intruding Afghan planes was in fact an indication of the successes of the Afghan Mujahideen in their struggle against the occupation forces'.[24]

The Soviet Union is convinced not only that Pakistan's borderlands are guerrilla sanctuaries, but that the Government of Pakistan has become a conduit to the insurgents for the supply of heavy weapons, which are supplied by the United States, China and some Arab states. The US Government estimates that unless the Soviets substantially increase the present size of their troops (110 000–115 000), the military stalemate will continue.[25] Meanwhile, Soviet casualties continue to mount, and Soviet soldiers are taken as prisoners of war. Some evidence suggests that while the Soviet/DRA troops have not attacked the Pakistani military posts across the border, the Soviet 'hot pursuit of guerrillas into Pakistan' has begun.[26] In addition to Soviet diplomatic warnings to Pakistan, Soviet publications are now specifically castigating Pakistan's policy. V. Stepanov stated in *International Affairs* (Moscow: May, 1984, p. 30): 'By waging an undeclared war against the DRA, Pakistan in effect puts itself in a position of confrontation with the Soviet Union.'

Since Pakistan, for better or worse, is committed to the support of Afghan refugee/insurgents, several scenarios can be constructed to highlight the probable Soviet–Pakistan confrontation:

1. With vast material and ideological resources, the Soviet Union has the ability to destabilize Pakistan by exacerbating contradictions in the Pakistani society. Some of these contradictions are: the martial law regime's antagonistic relations with the political parties, especially the late Prime Minister Bhutto's Pakistan People's Party (PPP). General Zia-ul-Haq twice postponed general elections, in October, 1977 and in November, 1979. For the third time on 12 August 1983, President Zia said that the four-stage election process will begin in 1983 with polls to local bodies and end by 23 March 1985 with elections to the provincial and national assemblies, and the Senate, when Martial Law will be lifted.

At the end of 1984, Zia held a referendum for his own election which he won with overwhelming majority of the votes cast. The referendum was a yes or no answer to the continuation of the policies of Islamization in Pakistan. No Pakistani Muslim would have said no to Islam. Finally, the elections to the provincial and federal legislatures were held in February, 1985 without the participation of the political parties. Zia also amended the 1973 constitution in order for him to become a constitutional President with increased powers at the expense of the office of the Prime Minister.

Despite widespread public acquiescence to General Zia's rule, Pakistanis in General question the legitimacy of the Martial Law rule. In defiance of General Zia, the PPP has criticized Pakistan's foreign policy toward the Soviet Union in Afghanistan, declaring that 'Pakistan must not interfere in the internal affairs of Afghanistan'. Even the more pliable National Democratic Party [NDP] has stated that 'the Afghan problem is the most serious threat to Pakistan's stability and security', and called for 'diplomatic recognition of Babrak Karmal's government, concessions at peace talks, informal relations with the Soviets and a return of 3 million Afghan refugees to Afghanistan.[27]

Most observers agree that in a free general election the PPP would achieve electoral victory. If power were transferred to the PPP, it would establish a *modus vivendi* with Afghanistan and the Soviet Union. If other political parties were to come to power, even then the possibility of a settlement with the USSR over Afghanistan would greatly improve.

2. Since the execution of Bhutto, provincial tensions have been greatly accentuated in Pakistan. The Sindhis not only hold the Punjabi generals responsible for the *coup d'état* against Bhutto's elected government, but also fault the judges of the Punjab High Court for sentencing him to death, and the Punjabi judges of the Supreme Court of Pakistan for rejecting his appeal. In their perception, a Sindhi statesman became a victim of judicial execution in order for the Punjabi generals to establish their dictatorship over Pakistan. In this tense political atmosphere, the Bhutto family's personal vendetta against the martial law regime was blamed for the highjacking of a PIA aircraft flying to Afghanistan in March, 1981. Subsequently, even the Reagan Administration joined the chorus of criticism against the Soviet Union which emanated from Islamabad. In 1983 the Movement for the Restoration of Democracy [MRD] in Pakistan launched a civil disobedience movement in the four provinces. The agitation became violent in Sindh, but fizzled out in the other three provinces. However, at an appropriate time, the Soviet Union could profit by sharpening the provincial contradictions.

3. The provincial tensions in Baluchistan had ignited an insurgency from 1973 to 1977 when Bhutto was the Prime Minister. Very unwisely, Bhutto had dismissed the freely-elected National Awami

Party's [NAP] government and then incarcerated the Baluch leaders, including the Chief Minister Atta Allah Mangal and the Governor, Gaus Bakhsh Bizanjo. Another Baluchi armed struggle for independence in western Pakistan and eastern Iran with the support of the Soviet Union remains a high probability. One observer has asserted that '7500 guerrillas are ready for combat in Baluchistan and that 15 000–20 000 more could be fielded within a matter of weeks'.[28] With Baluchistan as an independent state, the Soviet Union could possibly in the future acquire naval facilities at the Gawader Port, which lies directly across the Strait of Hormoz, the world economic choke point, at the entrance to the Persian Gulf.

4. The Soviet and Afghan forces can attack refugee tent villages in order to push these villages away from the border. These actions could also dramatize the Government of Pakistan's inability to protect the guerrillas and the refugees.

5. The Soviet-Afghan forces could capture salients of Pakistani territory, forcing the Pakistanis to counterattack. The Durand Line follows an irregular course, and there are several salients of Pakistani territory jutting into Afghanistan. At present, these salients are not defended. Similarly, several mountain passes which are not fortified could be captured by Soviet–Afghan forces. These developments could demoralize the Pakistanis.

6. India, in collusion with the Soviet Union, could attack Pakistan in disputed Kashmir and threaten the security of the main population centers in the Punjab from Islamabad to Sialkot to Lahore. India would achieve total domination over the South Asian subcontinent, and the Soviet Union would thus crush the Afghan insurgency.[29]

India's military predominance over Pakistan is unquestioned. It might be added that the Pakistani inventory until 1982 was primarily based on 1950s American and Chinese technology. In May, 1980 India signed an agreement with the USSR to receive, according to the Government of Pakistan's estimate, ten billion dollars worth of additional weapons, further upsetting the quantitative ratios with Pakistan.

7. The last scenario is fraught with substantial international complications, and one does not project it without fearing the outbreak of World War III. However, the possibility exists, at least in Pakistan's perception, that India and the Soviet Union might launch a coordinated attack from the east and the west to totally dismember Pakistan. The Soviet objective would be to achieve access to the Persian Gulf and surround unstable Iran by controlling Afghanistan's borders

with Pakistan and Iran. India's objective would be to undo the partition of 1947 and extend its frontiers to the River Indus. Consequently, Afghanistan would have achieved the extension of its territory to include the so-called Pashtunistan.

Would the US Executive Agreement of 1959 cover all of these scenarios, and others that might emerge in the future? Much really would depend on the nature of the US–USSR relations at the global level, and the triangular India–US and China relations at the regional level. In the US perception, the scope of the agreement does not apply to India, who has fought at least three wars with Pakistan since 1947, and maintains durable strategic consensus with the Soviet Union. It is, however, doubtful that even in a worst case scenario the United States would go to war against the Soviet Union in order to keep Afghanistan out of the Soviet orbit, or to ensure the security of Pakistan in an India–Soviet collusion against Pakistan. The US would indeed give political, moral and even military hardware to Pakistan to fight for its own survival, and then hope for the best outcome.

In order to prevent these developments from occurring, and to forestall the Soviet–India collusion against her, Pakistan's diplomacy resorted to strengthening its armed forces with US help, (which we have already discussed), and to negotiating with the DRA/USSR the withdrawal of the Soviet armed forces from Afghanistan, with the support of world public opinion expressed through the United Nations and the Islamic countries.

A brief review of the strategies is in order.

NEGOTIATIONS WITH AFGHANISTAN AND THE SOVIET UNION

In relation to Afghanistan, Pakistan has formulated a maximum negotiating position, including: (1) unconditional withdrawal of Soviet forces from Afghanistan and repatriation of the Afghan refugees; (2) restoration of the Islamic character of Afghanistan and (3) maintenance of the non-aligned status of Afghanistan's foreign policy. Ever since 27 December 1979, when the Soviet intervention occurred, three-track negotiations on Afghanistan were undertaken. Pakistan took the initiative for mobilizing the United Nations and the Islamic world against Soviet intervention. The General Assembly of the United Nations on 14 January 1980, 'strongly deplored', by a vote of 104–18, the intervention and called for 'the immediate, unconditional and total withdrawal of the foreign troops in Afghanistan'. For the fifth time, the General Assembly adopted on 15 November 1984 the same resolution by a vote of 119 in favor to 20 against, with 14 abstentions. The text of the resolution had been endorsed by the foreign ministers of the Islamic Conference organization.

To follow up on the General Assembly's disapproval of the Soviet intervention, on 28 January 1980 foreign ministers from thirty-four Muslim countries condemned the Soviet intervention as 'a flagrant violation of international law'. The Islamic foreign ministers also suspended Afghanistan's membership in the international Islamic organization. On 20 November 1980 the General Assembly of the United Nations adopted another resolution calling for the immediate withdrawal of the foreign troops from Afghanistan and the return of Afghan refugees to their homes. The resolution also stipulated that the Secretary-General should appoint a special representative to promote a political solution of the Afghan conflict. Unfortunately, however, both Afghanistan and the Soviet Union rejected the resolution as constituting interference in Afghanistan's internal affairs. The Soviet Union insisted that no third party should either mediate or arbitrate the points of dispute between Afghanistan and Pakistan, but that they must be settled through bilateral negotiations.

The second track of the negotiations was the European initiative. In May and July 1980, Chancellor Helmut Schmidt of West Germany and President Valery Giscard D'Estang of France visited Moscow to find a solution for the Afghan conflict. While the United States cancelled grain sales and industrial contracts worth three billion dollars, the NATO allies of the United States rushed to do more business with the Soviet Union. In March the Soviet Union announced a $118 million deal with the French for offshore drilling rigs to be used in the Caspian Sea. Afghanistan created a view in Europe that the concept of *détente* is divisible. American foreign policy, under Carter, declared the Persian Gulf to be an American lake where any future Soviet expansion would be resisted with a force of arms if necessary. Under Reagan, the US Administration resorted to large-scale armament programs, hoping to deal with the Soviet Union once again from a position of strength. None of these negotiations has yielded any results, either for the repatriation of the refugees, or for the political status of Afghanistan. Had the three-track negotiations been coordinated, some solution might have been found; although by no means along the lines of maximum demands enunciated by Pakistan. Pakistan has refused to recognize the Babrak Karmal regime, while enigmatically the two countries continue to maintain diplomatic missions in their capitals.

The United Nations' mediation effort between Pakistan and Afghanistan started in April, 1981, when Kurt Waldheim sent Javier Perez de Cuellar to the region as his special representative. Following his election as Secretary-General, de Cuellar appointed Diego Cordovez as his Special Representative for the task of mediation. So far, six proximity meetings at Geneva have been held between the foreign ministers of Afghanistan and Pakistan, with the UN representative shuttling between the suites of the two foreign ministers. The other parties to the dispute – USSR, USA, China and Iran – have not participated in the negotiations, while they have materially affected the conduct, as well as the substance, of these negotiations. The foreign ministers of Afghanistan and Pakistan have in fact conducted these negotiations for the approval of their principal supporters, while subordinating their regional interests to the global rivalries of the two superpowers. A medium-size regional state, so goes the diplomatic reasoning in Islamabad, cannot negotiate in a meaningful way with a superpower unless her interests are protected by the countervailing force of the other superpower. Unavoidably, the interests of both regional states have thus become subordinate to the global strategies of the superpowers. No settlement can take place without the consent of the United States, the Soviet Union, and possibly China. (A review of these negotiations would highlight these diplomatic dilemmas).

Initially, the DRA demonstrated flexibility to facilitate the negotiations. Through its proposals of 14 May 1980 and 24 August 1981 the DRA: (1) accepted Pakistan's demand for indirect negotiations with the UN representative; (2) agreed to include Iran in the negotiating process (although Iran chose not to participate in these negotiations, but to be briefed on their progress); (3) agreed to discuss the refugee issue comprehensively, and (4) accepted Pakistan's demand to discuss 'other matters' of dispute between the two countries, especially the status of the Durand Line, the British established border between Afghanistan and Pakistan.

Diego Cordovez succeeded in securing the approval of Afghanistan and Pakistan for a framework of substantive negotiations in April, 1983. The three principal points of the framework included: (1) mutual guarantees of non-intervention and non-interference, backed by international guarantees (to be affirmed by the United

States and China); (2) repatriation of the Afghan refugees from Pakistan and assurances of their rights; (3) withdrawal of Soviet troops from Afghanistan. After the second round of negotiations at Geneva in April, 1983, Cordovez indicated that 95 per cent of a draft agreement had been drawn up. A month later an 'official leak' from Washington, DC stated that the United States had 'stepped up the quantity and quality of covert military support for Afghan insurgents'.[30] The third round of talks ended on 24 June 1983 with no sign of major progress on any of the issues. However, by this time the differences had been clearly defined, not only by Pakistan and Afghanistan, but by the principal supporters of both states. This divergence of policies and objectives can be explained around the core issues:

Withdrawal of Soviet troops

While the Soviet Union remained committed in principle to the withdrawal of its troops from Afghanistan, the timetable for the withdrawal became part of a comprehensive settlement, which included international guarantees of non-interference in the internal affairs of Afghanistan. Pakistan and the United States wanted a rapid withdrawal over a period of 3 to 6 months. The Soviet Union favored a longer period of 18 months. Anything less than a rapid pullout, according to Ronald Spiers, former US Ambassador to Pakistan, was 'unacceptable to the Afghan insurgents'.[31] Obviously, without Soviet agreement Afghanistan could have produced no mutually acceptable timetable for the withdrawal of Soviet troops.

Yuri V. Andropov asserted on 19 April 1983 in an interview with the West German news magazine, *Der Spiegel*, that the Soviet military presence in Afghanistan is analogous to the US efforts to protect its national interests in Central America. He said: 'Washington even considers itself authorized to judge what government should be in Nicaragua, since this allegedly affects the vital interests of the United States. Nicaragua, however, is more than 1000 kilometers away from the United States, while the Soviet Union and Afghanistan have a long common border. Thus, rendering assistance to our friends, we think at the same time of safeguarding the interests of our own security'.[32] In referring to Pakistan's attitude towards its negotiations with Afghanistan, Andropov maintained that Pakistanis 'are held by the sleeve by their overseas friends.'[33]

The Soviet Union has always believed that the Saur Revolution of Afghanistan in 1978 was a genuine socialist revolution, and it was its fraternal obligation to protect it from its sworn enemies, both internal and external. The cost for this intervention might be high, but the Soviet Union seems to be determined to lead the Afghan revolution to safety. In exploring this theme, Demitri Ustinov, Marshall of the Soviet Union, stated: 'The Soviet Union has always been opposed to the export of revolution. But we cannot agree and never will agree to the export of counter-revolution. Our attitude to the events in Afghanistan is based on it. Imperialism has been attempting to bring about the export of counter-revolution to that country.'[34]

Consequently, the Soviet Union has adopted the position that its armed forces would be withdrawn from Afghanistan only after the support to the Afghan insurgents has been completely withdrawn; reliable guarantees against future support have been furnished, and the Socialist Government in Kabul is firmly secured.[35]

In rejecting the thesis of 'counter-revolution', Pakistan and the United States have asserted that it is primarily an indigenous, self-perpetuating rebellion, and that Pakistan has no choice but to support the 'Afghan refugees'. (Pakistan's official position is that it does not support the guerrillas of the Afghan resistance.)

Repatriation of the Afghan refugees

All sides to the dispute agree in principle for an early return of refugees to their homes. One proposal envisaged a two-stage repatriation: (a) the refugees return to a demarcated and demilitarized zone inside Afghanistan; (b) the refugees in the second stage are visualized to be fully reintegrated into the Afghan society following the withdrawal of the Soviet troops. Most observers, however, believe that given the opportunity for repatriation to Afghanistan no more than 50 per cent of the refugees would return. In recognition of this psychological change in the refugees the Government of Pakistan has quietly undertaken measures to permanently settle the refugees in the North West Frontier Province, Baluchistan, and the contiguous districts of the Punjab. In addition to alloting small plots of land for the construction of houses in the Punjab, the Government of Pakistan has encouraged the Afghans to 'join occupational areas such as trades (shopkeeping), transport services, and skilled and unskilled wage labor'. In August, 1982 about 4500 Turkish speaking Kirghiz and Turkaman were airlifted to Turkey for permanent settlement.[36] Obviously, neither the resistance leadership nor the refugees are particularly anxious to return to their homes, especially when guerrilla warfare makes civilian life most hazardous in Afghanistan.

International guarantees of non-interference

There are indications that the DRA/USSR want the United States and China and some Arab states to be co-signatories of the pledge of non-interference and non-intervention in the internal affairs of Afghanistan. If these guarantees are provided and support for the insurgents is withheld the Soviet troops would be withdrawn from the embattled country. Pakistan, on the contrary, has stated that the three issues – the withdrawal of Soviet troops, repatriation of the Afghan refugees, and the international guarantees – constitute a package. All three issues must be simultaneously resolved.

Further complicating the problem is the American Congress' independent support to the Afghan refugees/insurgents. For the fiscal year 1984–85 the Congress earmarked 280 million dollars in covert military aid for the Afghan guerrillas. American dollars are used to purchase at exorbitant price Soviet-made arms from countries such as China, Egypt, and Israel. Very reliable sources in the United States indicate that 'the supplies pass to Pakistani control for delivery to the political leaders of the Afghan insurgency in Peshawar, Pakistan, and elsewhere. They in turn are supposed to pass them to the guerrillas'.[37] This support is motivated by the desire to make the Soviet Union 'pay a price' for its intervention in Afghanistan, let it bleed through a protracted conflict, while the international pressure, through the United Nations, and the Organization of Islamic States, is directed at the Soviet Union. Pakistan, like the US, believes that this strategy may force the Soviet Union to negotiate an acceptable package of agreement with Pakistan.

RELATIONS WITH INDIA

Soon after the Soviet intervention in Afghanistan, Pakistan began to realize that its strained relations with India could lead Pakistan to the brink of a 'two-front' situation.[38] Consequently, Pakistan made three major proposals to India to normalize their relations, including (a) exchange of mutual guarantees of non-aggression; i.e. non-aggression pact; (b) joint statement pledging nuclear nonproliferation and (c) an agreed ratio between the two countries' armed forces.

After nearly four years of negotiations, relations between the two countries, instead of improving, have visibly deteriorated, especially in the aftermath of the Indian Army's occupation of the Golden Temple in Amritsar in the summer of 1984 and the assassination of Mrs Gandhi by three Sikh dissident bodyguards on 31 October 1984. This setback to Pakistan–India dialogue was attributed, by India, to five 'provocative developments' involving Pakistan: (1) In September, 1984, a report from Washington stated that India was considering a preemptive strike to destroy Pakistan's nuclear plant at Kahuta, near Islamabad.[39] While in Washington, Pakistan's Minister of Foreign Affairs, Sahabzada Yaqub Khan, stated forthrightly that any pre-emptive strike by India against Pakistan's nuclear facilities would be an act of 'naked aggression' and that it would prompt Pakistan to undertake 'immediate retaliation'[40]; (2) Another report from Washington published in Pakistan on 5 October and in India on 10 October 1984 indicated that the United States was thinking of bringing the Pakistanis under its nuclear umbrella if they gave up their nuclear program; (3) A statement attributed on 10 October 1984 to Deane Hinton, the American Ambassador to Pakistan, 'that the United States would aid Pakistan if India attacked'[41]; (4) A disclosure was made in Washington on 11 October 1984 that Pakistan wants to buy an airborne early warning system built around the E2–C Hawkeye plane. India stated that Pakistan buys advanced military equipment, not to counter a potential Soviet threat from Afghanistan, but for possible use against India; (5) As India's troubles with its Sikhs worsened, India accused Pakistan of fomenting the trouble.

These accusations and counter-accusations reflect the pervasive mistrust that deeply permeates India and Pakistan; leading them to have differing perceptions regarding the Soviet intervention in Afghanistan, and Pakistan's efforts to forge closer economic and military relations with the United States. India's troubles with the Sikhs are rooted in the historical development of modern India when Muslims broke away from united India to create Pakistan and the Sikhs, in India's perception, are following a similar separatist route.

Negotiations for the no-war pact

When Pakistan made a formal proposal to India in November, 1981 for a no-war pact, Mrs Indira Gandhi viewed this offer as a 'trap'.

Pakistan perceived the Soviet military intervention in Afghanistan as a threat to regional security and decided to acquire sophisticated arms from the United States. India viewed Pakistan's policy as an encouragement to superpower rivalry in the Indian sub-continent. Moreover, India believed these weapons would be used against her.[42]

The *aides mémoire* that the two governments exchanged during 1981–82 on the non-aggression proposal reflected their diametrically opposed views. India proposed (a) that a no-war pact should not be a mere exchange of declarations; (b) it should create a definite framework of proposals to reduce tension and promote stability in the region; (c) a mechanism should be created to make on-going assessment of the implications of introducing foreign arms into the region; (d) that neither country should provide military bases to foreign powers; (e) that Pakistan should offer assurances in regard to its nuclear policy. India's *aides mémoire* of 24 December 1981, among other things, sought a reaffirmation of the Simla agreement emphasizing bilateral approach to the settlement of India-Pakistan disputes.[43]

The perennial Kashmir problem was raised by Pakistan in the UN Human Rights Commission demanding self determination for the people of Kashmir. Describing Pakistan's action as a violation of the Simla agreement, India postponed indefinitely high level negotiations relating to the no-war proposal.

This deadlock was broken when President Zia visited Mrs Gandhi on 1 November 1982 on his way to Southeast Asia. During this meeting, the two countries agreed to establish a joint commission for which a formal agreement was signed in March, 1983.[44] The Commission recommended to expand trade ties between the two countries, and an elaborate program for trade and information was designed. This trend to normalize relations between the two countries received a jolt when Mrs Indira Gandhi and her Minister of Foreign Affairs made statements of support for the political agitation which had been initiated by the Movement for the Restoration of Democracy [MRD] in Pakistan. Organized principally by the Pakistan People's Party in 1983, these agitations were in full swing in the province of Sindh. This support was not only a kiss of death for the MRD, but was construed to be a blatant intervention in the internal affairs of Pakistan, and on 27 August 1983 the Government of Pakistan lodged a strong protest with the Indian Government.

Probably Indira Gandhi had been advised that General Zia would fall during the agitation – which proved to be wrong – and in that eventuality India would have earned the goodwill of the PPP and other political parties. Not appreciating the extent to which Pakistanis are allergic to the appearance of Indian paternalism, some members of Indian Parliament also exercised pressure on Indira Gandhi to make some expression of support for the restoration of democracy in Pakistan.

Sikh nationalism

However, throughout 1983-84 Sikh nationalism asserted itself to destabilize the Punjab with its demands (which were articulated by the Akali Party), including (1) an amendment of Article 25 of the Indian Constitution which classified Sikhs as a Hindu sect; (2) a large share for the Punjab from the interstate rivers; (3) compulsory teaching of the Punjabi language in schools; (4) and a special status for Amritsar, the Sikh Holy City. In order to contain Sikh violence, Indira Gandhi imposed tough new laws in the Punjab allowing up to six months detention without reason being given, and imprisonment without trial for two years.[45]

The Sikh movement, which originally used tactics of non-violence, was gradually taken over by the more militant Sikh nationalists identified with Jarnail Singh Bhindranwale. Obviously, at this stage, Indian strategy was to crush the militants first and then return to the Akalis' moderate political demands and settle them in short order. In pursuit of this strategy, Indira Gandhi exercised conspicuously bad judgement in ordering a frontal assault on the Golden Temple in Amritsar on 6 June 1984. This blunder terminated the Hindu-Sikh alliance which had lasted from the death of illiberal Muslim Emperor, Aurangzeb, in 1707 to the contemporary period.

Hypothetically speaking, if the Sikhs had remained in Pakistan after 1947, they would have pressed for the creation of Khalistan (a proposed name for a sovereign Sikh state) even earlier.

Just as Pakistan had failed to recognize Bengali nationalism in East Pakistan in 1971, Indira Gandhi, in a similar fashion, refused to come to terms with Sikh nationalism. After occupying the Golden Temple, Indira Gandhi also blamed the moderate Sikhs for failure to do anything about terrorism, implying that the moderates' 'credibility and intentions were suspect' and that she might adopt a tougher line in future talks with them.[46] The tragedy of the Golden Temple was then blamed on the CIA and Pakistan. The latter was accused of having trained Sikh guerrillas in the Pakistani control sector of Kashmir, as well as on the Indian side of the disputed territory. China also came to share some of the blame.

Addressing a special session of the Punjab Provincial Council on 25 October 1984 in Lahore, President General Zia-ul-Haq reviewed Indian–Pakistan relations from 1980–1984. His speech for the first time reflected the view that Pakistan's road of friendship with India does not run directly to New Delhi, but detours through Moscow. He stated that both India and the Soviet Union had canceled the scheduled meetings of ministers of Foreign Affairs and foreign secretaries of their countries with Pakistan.[46] Rebutting India's charges of interference in the internal affairs of India, President Zia said that India had established a precedent of interfering in her neighbor's affairs in 1970–71 when the Bangladesh crisis surfaced.

Pakistan's litany of grievances in President Zia's language included five Indian actions: (1) 'an alliance with the Soviet Union'; (2) a propaganda campaign that India had to care for a large number of Bengali refugees; (3) sent saboteurs into East Pakistan; (4) gave military training to the refugees and sent them into East Pakistan for military action and finally, (5) attacked East Pakistan with nine divisions of the Indian Army.[47] A week later Indira Gandhi was assassinated and relations between the two states entered a new phase.

The Soviet factor

To this game of mutual recrimination and interference intermittently played between India and Pakistan should be added the additional weight of the Soviet Union's 'Treaty of Peace, Friendship and Cooperation' with India which was signed at the height of the crisis over Bangladesh on 9 August 1971. This treaty has been one of the serious factors in developing a strategic consensus and a commonality of outlook between India and the Soviet Union. The United States Government's decision to offer a military and economic package of 3.2 billion dollars to Pakistan for a period of five years provided an additional incentive to India to share Soviet perceptions in regard to Pakistan and Afghanistan.

When Agha Shahi, Pakistan's former Minister of Foreign Affairs, visited India in 1982, Indira Gandhi offered him a Soviet style treaty of friendship and cooperation for Pakistan's consideration. India proposed that in addition to Pakistan's no-war draft pact, India's preferred draft treaty of friendship should be negotiated simultaneously. India insisted that the two countries should develop a concrete framework of relationship which would enable the two countries to make on-going assessments of the implications of introducing foreign arms in South Asia. India also proposed that neither country should provide military bases to foreign powers.

However, India's perception regarding the solution of the Afghan problem was diametrically opposed to that of Pakistan's. Unlike Pakistan, India recognized the Babrak Karmal Government in Afghanistan and advised Pakistan to recognize it and to negotiate with it directly.

India believed that the Afghan resistance was unable to defeat the Soviet armed forces in Afghanistan. Consequently, they have no other alternative but to create favorable conditions for the withdrawal of Soviet armed forces. Implied in the Indian view is the assumption that American involvement in Afghanistan is against Pakistan's long-range interests and the interests of other South Asian states.

India also accepted the Soviet perception of the Afghan crisis, which has been generated by the superpower rivalry at global level. For instance, American endeavors to establish bases in Somalia and Oman were perceived to be an attempt at the encirclement of the Soviet Union. In a similar fashion, the Soviet Union and India believed that the quantum of military buildup had increased considerably in Diego Garcia and that the United States naval presence in the Indian Ocean included nuclear warheads.[48]

Reaffirming Soviet interpretation regarding the internal developments of Afghanistan in December, 1979, Indira Gandhi believed that 'what happened in Afghanistan is an internal matter of the country'. She believed that President Hafizullah Amin, who was overthrown in a Soviet-supported coup on 27 December 1979 had invited Soviet military help against the insurgents.

After the assassination of Mrs Indira Gandhi, power has passed to her son, Rajiv Gandhi. He has pledged closer relations with Pakistan and improvement of relations with China. However, it is doubtful if he would be able to disregard the 'Treaty of Peace, Friendship and Cooperation' with the Soviet Union and seek better relations with Pakistan and China at Soviet expense.

Articles 9 and 10 of the Friendship Treaty of 1971 are most relevant. Article 9 enjoins the two countries 'to refrain from giving any assistance to any third party taking part in an armed conflict with another party'. The Soviet Union has stated time and again that Pakistan is in virtual confrontation with the Soviet forces in Afghanistan. In light of this, Article 10 has special meaning which provides that the two countries 'shall not undertake any commitment secret or open with regard to one or more states incompatible with the present treaty'. By signing a no-war pact with Pakistan, India would virtually disregard her treaty commitments. A pragmatic question may be asked: What advantages would India derive in signing a no-war pact with Pakistan? After humbling Pakistan in 1971, India has become eight times bigger than Pakistan and has more than double the size of the armed forces of Pakistan. The inflow of modern weapons into Pakistan since 1981 does not tip the balance of power in Pakistan's favor. Pakistan has a lot to gain by signing a no-war pact with India, but Indian advantages are quite dubious. Consequently, why should India antagonize the Soviet Union by neutralizing herself in the Afghan conflict which would enable Pakistan to concentrate her efforts through the Afghan guerrillas on the Durand Line?

The Soviet Union views China as the greatest threat to her security. The United States is another major adversary of the Soviet Union playing an active role in South Asia through Pakistan. As long as the Pakistan–China–America connection persists, the Soviet Union would maintain the counterbalance in its association with India. There is a mutual recognition of the importance and reliability of relations between India and the Soviet Union.[49] In his very brief comment on India's relations with the Soviet Union, Rajiv Gandhi stated: 'We highly value the wide-ranging and time-tested relationship with the Soviet Union, based upon mutual cooperation, friendship and vital support when most needed.'[50] Despite Rajiv Gandhi's assurance to Pakistan for the improvement of relations, it is highly unlikely that a no-war pact between the two countries would be signed.

Finally, the one big question remains. What are the prospects for the resolution of the Afghan conflict? Can Pakistan make an autonomous contribution towards its solution? Here opinions would differ, but a few alternative approaches deserve some consideration:

(1) Pakistan needs to talk directly to the Karmal regime in Kabul. The diplomatic recognition need not be construed as an act of approval. The United States did not recognize the Soviet Union from 1917–1933, and withheld recognition from the People's Republic of

China from 1949–1979. Ironically, when President Carter's National Security Adviser, Brzezinski, visited Beijing in May, 1977, Chinese lectured him about the dangers of 'Soviet hegemonism', a phrase 'the Chinese spat out with the same venom an earlier generation of Americans had reserved for Godless atheistic communism'.[51]

When the two governments were recognized neither state had abandoned socialism. The United States, and the NATO allies established diplomatic relations with the East European states, who had become one-party socialist states after the Soviet troops ejected the Nazi forces from their soil in 1945. Even truncated German states established diplomatic relations with each other, and finally the Federal Republic of Germany had to quietly abandon the famous Holstein doctrine, which was designed to discourage other states from recognizing the Democratic Republic of East Germany. Last, but not least, didn't Pakistan recognize a part of its own territory as an independent and sovereign state when it became Bangladesh in 1971?

(2) The Soviets claim to have 'legitimate security interests' in Afghanistan, and Southwest Asia, and they seem determined to have this claim recognized by the US and Pakistan. The disappearance of Afghanistan as a buffer state between the Soviet Union and Pakistan might be a very uncomfortable prospect for the leading classes of Pakistan, but Pakistan need not be afraid of ideological subversion if it can develop an Islamic–capitalist society without sharpening its societal contradictions.

Finland may be considered as an appropriate paradigm for Pakistan to emulate, both diplomatically and for internal non-socialist-capitalist development. Pakistan should continue to maintain friendly relations with the United States, but should abandon policies which might lead the country toward a confrontation with the Soviet Union. The United States is unlikely to war against the Soviet Union in order to eject its troops from Afghanistan.

During the long-drawn-out war of Vietnam, the United States could not get Soviet help to extricate itself from that quagmire with honor. Understandably so, the United States would like to see Afghanistan become a Soviet Vietnam. The outraged sentiments of the Afghan insurgents strengthen this Vietnam syndrome. If the United States had shared 1500 miles of common border with Vietnam (which the Soviet Union does with Afghanistan), the outcome of the war would have been decidedly a different one. A Soviet defeat on its southern borders would have the potential of unraveling the Soviet–

Muslim society in Central Asia, and would irreparably undermine its military prestige in the world. Hypothetically speaking, even with very generous American support, does Pakistan realistically believe that the Afghan insurgents' victory is possible?

Nearly 3 million Palestinian refugees, scattered widely over the Arab states, are today a living monument to the exercise of power by a superpower's surrogate in the Middle East. No moral claim repeated *ad infinitum* by the Palestinians has shaken the resolve of the United States to deny them the right of self-determination. Admittedly, the Arab–Israeli conflict is a complex one, and does not lend itself to an equitable solution. With the passage of time, the position of the Afghan refugees has become just as complex. The continuation of the stalemate would add more to their miseries and homelessness.

(3) With incremental increase in the power of the Afghan insurgents, they will become a state within the volatile borderlands of Pakistan. (Elsewhere I have described this development as very similar to the role of the PLO in Lebanon). Already in 1984, the US Senate studies have predicted that 'any successor to Zia would face the practical fact that the refugee population is quite well armed, and would certainly act to defend its interests if it felt threatened.'[52] Also, a formal proposal to the US Senate has been made for the future recognition of an Afghan Government-in-exile.[53] If such a development were to come to pass, it would transfer any residual diplomatic initiative that Pakistan may possess to an insurgent state within Pakistan.

(4) Despite desultory attempts to create good neighborly relations between India and Pakistan, old suspicions and doubts about mutual intentions continue to persist. The situation would not change unless both countries adopt policies which would create an environment of friendship and trust in South Asia, eventually eliminating their threat perceptions. In order to create this environment, the Soviet Union can play a crucial role. The United States had recognized, with some felicitous understanding, the Soviet interests and her mediating role in the India-Pakistan war of 1965.

The Tashkent Conference, which was convened by the Soviet Union, and was attended by India and Pakistan in January, 1966, was the first diplomatic landmark of the Soviet role in the international security of South Asia. In welcoming Pakistan's President Ayub Khan, and India's Prime Minister Lal Bahadur Shastri, Premier Kosygin called them 'our southern neighbors', and reminded them that the Soviet Union has 'long maintained the closest trade and cultural contacts with the peoples of Pakistan and India.' Kosygin established the precedent of 'shuttle diplomacy' by personally moving between the hotels of Ayub and Shastri. Finally, both leaders signed the Tashkent Agreement that included their 'firm resolve to restore normal and peaceful relations'.[54] This Soviet interest in the security relationship between India and Pakistan is not likely to disappear in the 1980s.

Eventually, the Soviet and Indian strategic interests in South Asia would diverge, especially if India did not disintegrate due to her internal dissentions, and continued to develop industrially and economically. At that point in time, Pakistan would have room to maneuver between the Soviet Union and India, as well as China. If India disintegrated, this process would generate fierce revolutionary forces, which may not be conducive to strengthening Pakistan's independence and territorial integrity.

(5) The concept of 'war as a continuation of diplomacy' between the two countries can be best eliminated if Pakistan succeeded in developing nuclear weapons. This suggestion is not as radical as it might sound. President Ronald Reagan has offered in February, 1983, the most convincing arguments in support of deterrence as a nuclear policy. He said: 'The United States would not have dropped the atomic bomb on Japan in 1945 if Japan had its own nuclear weapon ready then as a deterrent'. In a brutal candor, President Reagan pointed out that the United States was 'the only country that ever dropped one of those', and then added: 'But, we were the only country that had it, and you have to ask yourself: Would we have dropped it if we had known they had one they could have dropped on us? I think we all know the answer to that'.[55]

In order to negotiate the nuclear issue with India, Pakistan has made five specific proposals:

(1) Pakistan and India to sign the Nuclear Non-proliferation Treaty
(2) Accept full safeguards of IAEA
(3) Establish nuclear weapons free zone in South Asia
(4) Jointly renounce the acquisition or production of nuclear weapons
(5) Accept mutual inspection of each other's nuclear facilities.

While these proposals give Pakistan a modest edge over India in diplomacy and world public opinion, they hope to achieve the impossible – strategic or nuclear parity with India without demonstrable nuclear capability on the part of Pakistan. Indian Prime Minister, Rajiv Gandhi, has 'demanded' that Pakistan abjure nuclear weapons capability in order to achieve 'friendship' with India. In other words, Pakistan must guarantee India a position of inferiority, both in conventional forces (an existing reality) and in strategic and nuclear weapons. In exercising pressure on Pakistan to abandon its nuclear weapons program, there has emerged a convergence of interest between United States, Soviet Union and Indian policies.

Clearly, the international pressure on Pakistan will not abate until the Government of Pakistan signs the Nuclear Non-proliferation Treaty and brings all of its nuclear installations under full scope safeguards designed by the superpowers, or, the Government of Pakistan convincingly demonstrates that Pakistan has achieved nuclear weapons capability. Like Eve's sin in the Garden of Eden, the latter position of Pakistan would not be reversible. The international power structure and India will have to recognize this 'sin' and then accept its logical consequences:

(1) Pakistan's nuclear parity with India would finally establish a political stalemate, where territorial, and irredentist claims will freeze to death;
(2) Pakistan would have established, even against the superpower(s) a proportional deterrence which would make the price of conquest of Pakistan irrational;
(3) A stable peace would eventually emerge between India and Pakistan which would not depend on the no-war pact with India.

In pursuit of the nuclear stalemate Pakistan would be well advised to convince the international community and the regional power(s) that Pakistan will not launch the first strike. In other words, Pakistan's nuclear weapons capability will be achieved to guarantee peace and not war. The balance of terror between India and Pakistan would lend credence to Pakistan's assurances on this score. Pakistan's benefactor, the United States, would also realize at some point in the future that Pakistan's proportional deterrence would contribute a little to stabilizing the borders and relations with Afghanistan where the Soviet Union has acquired political and military preeminence. The Soviet Union would also learn not to tread upon spunky little Pakistan's territorial integrity. Superpowers also respect small states, especially those who appear to be 'reckless' in the defense of their territorial integrity and sovereignty. Pakistan can earn this perceptual deference through demonstrable nuclear weapons capability.

Notes

1. The *New York Times*, 6 February 1980 (The James Reston column).
2. George F. Kennan, 'Washington's Reaction to the Afghan Crisis: Was This Really Mature Statesmanship?', The *New York Times*, 1 February 1980.
3. Jiri Valenta, 'From Prague to Kabul: The Soviet Style of Invasion', *International Security*, Fall, 1980 (Volume 5, #2), p. 120.
4. Saying that his public statements expressed to 'a varying degree the Soviet concepts, ideals, and objectives', Chernenko reiterated the same view in 'Trust and Cooperation Among Nations – The Guarantee of Peace and Security', *International Affairs* (Moscow, No. 8, 1980); see also Konstantin Chernenko, *Selected Speeches and Writing* (New York: Pergamon Press, 1982) p. 241.
5. Bhutto's suspicion stemmed from an incident when the Deputy Chief of the Mission of the American Embassy in Islamabad contacted an elected member of the National Assembly belonging to the Pakistan Peoples' Party (PPP) and then stated that the US Diplomatic Mission in Islamabad had substantial evidence that the elections were rigged in March, 1977. The American diplomat then asserted: 'Now the game is over'. A transcript of this conversation was given to Prime Minister Bhutto, but a few days after this conversation, three members of the National Assembly belonging to the PPP resigned. (Personal interview with the former MNA from Lahore).
6. This aid included about 57 million dollars-worth of PL480 commodities in 1977, 86 million dollars-worth of commodity credit corporation credits for the import of wheat; a 40 million dollar loan for a fertilizer plant and a 25 million dollar agreement for import of fertilizers. Arthur W. Hummel, Jr (US Ambassador to Pakistan), at a meeting of the English speaking Union of Pakistan, Karachi, 6 December 1978, *Morning News* (Karachi), 7 December 1978.
7. Statement of the Government of Pakistan of 14 August 1979 appearing in *Dawn*, 16–17 August 1979.
8. Richard Burt, 'U.S. Will Press Pakistan To Halt Nuclear Arms Projects' The *New York Times*, 11 August 1979.
9. Henry Kissinger, *White House Years* (Boston: Little, Brown and Co., 1979) p. 1488. For explanatory statements of the Eisenhower Administrative officials see Rajendra K. Jain, Ed., *US-South Asian Relations 1947–1982*, (Atlantic Highlands, NJ: Humanities Press, 1983).
10. *Ibid*, p. 895.
11. Zbigniew Brzezinski, *Power and Principle* (New York: Farrar, Straus, Jiroux, 1983) p. 449.
12. Deane R. Hinton, US Ambassador to Pakistan, 'Question and Answer Session after Ambassador Hinton's October 10, 1984 address to the Council on Security Studies in Lahore', (Islamabad-text sent to Malik by Ambassador Hinton on 7 November 1984) p. 8.
13. *The Pakistan Times Overseas Weekly*, 10 October 1984, and *Haft Roza Mashriq International*, 14 October 1984.

14. 'Face the Nation', a CBS program, 18 May 1980, President Zia-ul-Haq's interview with Walter Cronkite.
15. *Department of State Bulletin* (Washington, DC, August, 1981) p. 83. Contains US-Pakistan joint statement of 15 June 1981.
16. *Far Eastern Economic Review* (16–22 October 1981), p. 46, Rodney Tasker's Interview with President Zia-ul-Haq.
17. Chief Commissioner for Afghan Refugees, *Refugee Situation at a Glance*, (Islamabad: Government of Pakistan, 1981), typed draft, 26 pp; *Some Facts Regarding Afghan Refugees* (Islamabad: Chief Commissioner for Afghan Refugees, n.d.), 2 pp.
18. For King Amanullah's failure to modernize Afghanistan's tribal society see Leon B. Poullada, *Reform and Rebellion in Afghanistan, 1919–1929* (Ithaca: Cornell University Press, 1973); for details of the decrees and the *ulama's* declaration of opposition to King Amanullah see Rhea Talley Stewart, *Fire in Afghanistan, 1914–1929* (New York: Doubleday & Co., 1973), pp. 425–443.
19. Afghanistan's Minister of Foreign Affairs stated to Malik: 'We have come to recognize that the Pashtunistan issue was a mistake. We have stopped talking about it. This is strictly an internal issue for Pakistan. What the Baluchis and the Pashtuns want, that is their business, not ours.' Hafeez Malik, 'Memorandum of Conversations with Mr Shah Mohammad Dost, 30 September, 1981'., *Journal of South Asian and Middle Eastern Studies*, (Volume V, No. 2, 1981) p. 73.
20. Frederick Kempe, 'Soviet "Hot Pursuit" of Guerrillas Into Pakistan Could Draw Islamabad Into Afghan Fighting', The *Wall Street Journal*, (12 November 1984), p. 28.
21. The friends of the Afghan insurgents have maintained that 'only a fraction has reached the guerrillas in effective military hardware'. Mathew D. Erulkar (Executive Director, American Afghan Education Fund, Washington, DC) 'CIA is less than topnotch in Afghanistan', The *New York Times*, 26 November 1984. In order to support the insurgents some private American citizens have contributed material to Ahmad Shah Masaud in the insurgent-controlled Panjsher Valley in Afghanistan. For the activities of American Aid for Afghans, a non-profit Portland-based organization, see 'Gear Donated to Guerrillas', The *Philadelphia Inquirer* (14 April 1984) p. 16–A.
22. Bureau of Public Affairs, Department of State, *Gist*, Washington, DC, August, 1984.
23. *Anis*, (Kabul, 12 April 1983).
24. The *Pakistan Times Overseas Weekly*, 4 November 1984.
25. *Gist*, p. 1.
26. Kempe, *Op.Cit*, p. 28.
27. See 'Gear Donated to Guerrillas', *Philadelphia Inquirer*.
28. Selig Harrison, *In Afghanistan's Shadow: Baluch Nationalism and Soviet Temptations* (New York: Carnegie Endowment for International Peace, 1981) p. 75.
29. For the details of scenarios 5 and 6, see Francis Fukuyuma, *The Security of Pakistan: A Trip Report* (Santa Monica: Rand Corporation, September, 1980) pp. 1–45.

30. Leslie H. Gelb, 'US Said to Increase Arms Aid for Afghan Rebels', The *New York Times*, 4 May 1983.
31. The *New York Times*, 16 June 1984.
32. Yuri V. Andropov, 'Der Spiegel Interview', *Pravda*, 25 April 1983 in *Speeches & Writings* (New York: Pergamon Press, 1983) p. 323.
33. *Ibid*, p. 324.
34. D. F. Ustinov, *Serving the Country and the Communist Cause*, (New York: Pergamon Press, 1983) p. 14.
35. *Ibid*, p. 15.
36. Azhar Masood, 'Afghan Refugees for Turkey Today: In Search of New Home', *The Muslim*, 3 August 1982.
37. Gelb estimates that the earmarked amount of $280 million 'will bring total American aid to $625' since 1979. Citing intelligence sources, he asserts that '15 to 40 per cent of the arms aid is being skimmed off by the Pakistanis, and by Afghan exiles'. Leslie H. Gelb, 'US Aides Put '85 Arms Supplies To Afghan Rebels at $280 Million', The *New York Times*, 28 November 1984.
38. *Dawn*, 4 May 1981, (Agha Shahi's statement).
39. Philip Taubman, 'Worsening India-Pakistan Ties Worry US', The *New York Times*, 15 September 1984.
40. *Dawn*, 14 October 1984.
41. The *New York Times*, 21 October 1984: For extensive coverage of Ambassador Hinton's statements before a special meeting of the Council of National Security Studies in Lahore on 10 October 1984, see The *Pakistan Times Overseas Weekly*, 14 October 1984.
42. *Times of India*, 18 December 1981.
43. *Indian Express*, 14 February 1982; *Dawn*, 2 February 1982.
44. The first meeting of the Joint Commission was held in June, 1983 and four sub commissions were formed dealing with the following subjects: Sub-Commission I (economic matters, including industry, agriculture, communications, health, science and technology); Sub-Commission II (trade); Sub-Commission III (information, education, culture, sports and social sciences); Sub-Commission IV (travel, tourism and consular matters) *Strategic Studies*, (Islamabad, Vol. 7, #3, Spring, 1984) p. 7.
45. The *New York Times*, 6 April 1984.
46. The *New York Times*, 8 June 1984.
46a. In an interview, President Zia stated: 'We have an arrangement with the Soviet Union for an annual exchange of views between our foreign secretaries before the United Nations meets. The Soviet Union cancelled this year's meeting [i.e. 1984] without any explanation. The moment the news of cancellation was out, Madame Gandhi cancelled a joint India-Pakistan Foreign Ministers' meeting and a joint ministerial committee that was being prepared. Somehow I feel that the Soviet cancellation and Madame Gandhi's decision were closely related.' The *Pakistan Times Overseas Weekly*, 25 November 1984.
47. The *Pakistan Times Overseas Weekly*, 28 October 1984.
48. 'External Affairs Spokesmen Briefing on Gromyko Visit', *India News*, (Washington, DC) 18 February 1980, p. 3; The *New York Times*, 31 January 1980.

49. Robert H. Donaldson, 'The Soviet Union in South Asia: A Friend to Rely On?', *Journal of International Affairs*, 34:1, Spring/Summer, 1980, p. 235.
50. 'Excerpts from an address from Rajiv Gandhi', The *New York Times*, 13 November 1984.
51. Robert D. Schulzinger, *American Diplomacy in the Twentieth Century*, (New York: Oxford University Press, 1984) p. 327.
52. John B. Ritch, III, *Hidden War: The Struggle for Afghanistan* (A Staff Report prepared for the Committee on Foreign Relations, United States Senate, Washington, DC, 1984) p. 24.
53. *Ibid*, pp. 41–42.
54. 'Tashkent Declaration', appendix IX in Sangat, Singh, *Pakistan's Foreign Policy* (Lahore: Farhan Publishers, 1977) pp. 224–234.
55. Francis X. Clines, 'Reagan Calls Rebuff to Adelman Very Irresponsible and Injurious', The *New York Times*, 26 February 1983. Under this misleading caption coverage was provided of President Reagan's comments on the US nuclear policy.

8 Pakistan's Relations with the United States
Agha Shahi

While the subject of this chapter is Pakistan's relations with the United States, it must necessarily range over a wider field to include India–Pakistan relations and Soviet–Pakistan differences as well as the conditioning influence exercised on the US–Pakistan connection by the United States–India relationship. Moreover, neither Soviet policies towards Southwest and South Asia nor those of the United States can be analyzed without reference to their contention as superpowers for influence in the two regions.

US–SOVIET COMPETITION AND US–PAKISTAN RELATIONS

The competition between the United States and the Soviet Union for influence in South Asia broke out soon after the withdrawal of the British imperial power from the region with the emergence of Pakistan and India as independent states. In 1949, President Truman invited Prime Minister Jawaharlal Nehru to pay an official visit to the United States. Shortly afterwards, Soviet Premier Joseph Stalin extended an invitation to Prime Minister Liaguat Ali Khan of Pakistan to visit the Soviet Union. These invitations at once signalled the interest of two great powers in the strategic India Pakistan subcontinent.

It was not long before India gravitated towards the Soviet Union and Pakistan opted for security alliances with the United States. The Jammu and Kashmir dispute confirmed this alignment with the respective superpowers because India needed a Soviet veto to block the implementation of the UN pledge of a plebiscite to settle the dispute.

In 1954, Pakistan signed the Mutual Defense Assistance Agreement with the United States to qualify for non-reimbursable military aid, undertaking to cooperate with the United States in the defence of the area in which Pakistan was situated. Later that year, Pakistan became a member of the South East Asia Treaty Organization, a loose military alliance led by the United States to check communist expansion in that region and more specifically to prevent South Vietnam, Laos and Cambodia from being overrun by North Vietnam after its decisive victory over France at Dien Bienphu. In 1955, Pakistan acceded to the Baghdad Pact initiated by Britain and Iraq for an unspecified kind of defense cooperation against communist aggression. The United States, while fully supporting the Pact, did not formally join the arrangement but became a full member of its Military Committee.

From 1955 to 1960, Pakistan enjoyed a kind of honeymoon relationship with the US even though the quantum and quality of military equipment supplied to it was carefully limited so as not to enable Pakistan to achieve military parity with India. Also, the US permitted India to purchase military items under a separate legislation for mutual defense assistance. President Eisenhower was at pains to assure Prime Minister Jawaharlal Nehru that US military aid was not only for US allies but also for its friends. Nevertheless, the US–Pakistan alliance was so solid that when Soviet Premier Khrushchev threatened to drop an atom bomb on Peshawar, from where Gary Powers had taken off in his U–2 for Norway, and was shot down over the Soviet Union, President Ayub Khan's reaction was 'so what?'

Pakistan began to have second thoughts about its alliance relationship with the United States when President Kennedy reversed the Dulles policy and hailed the non-aligned nations as bridge builders between the two antagonistic military blocs – the NATO and the Warsaw Pact – confronting each other in the Cold War. Kennedy also rushed military assistance to India including US air force cover after the brief India–China clash near the end of 1962 without requiring India to commit itself against China in a defense alliance.

In the 1965 seventeen days war between India and Pakistan, President Johnson imposed an arms embargo against Pakistan which effectively deprived it of military aid, though to maintain an appearance of evenhandedness he also stopped the small-scale US military supplies that India had been receiving until then. The United States even lost interest in promoting an India–Pakistan settlement on Kashmir and encouraged Soviet mediation at Tashkent in early 1966. The two superpowers found themselves at one in denying to the People's Republic of China any role in the affairs of the region.

Pakistan's developing ties with China were another source of friction with the United States. With the growing involvement of the Johnson administration in Vietnam and the exacerbation of hostility towards China for its support to North Vietnam, and Pakistan's reluctance to align itself as a SEATO ally with the United States, the relationship came under strain. The United States' arms embargo against Pakistan remained unlifted.

It was President Nixon who saw in the Pakistan–China *entente* the possibility of using Pakistan as a bridge in his policy of *rapprochement* with China so as to gain leverage with the Soviet Union and to use both the Communist powers in ending the Vietnam war. Pakistan was instrumental in arranging the secret visit of Dr. Henry Kissinger to Beijing in mid-1971 which paved the way for Nixon's historic visit to China in the following year.

The Soviet Union, which for over a decade was locked with China in a bitter ideological and political controversy leading to their armed clash along the Ussuri river border in 1969, became so concerned over what was perceived to be a shift in the balance of power in favor of the United States, and so irritated by Pakistan's role, that it threw its support behind India and the secessionist movement in East Pakistan and Indian interference in Pakistan's internal crisis in 1971. The Indo–Soviet Treaty of August, 1971, was soon concluded to prevent China from assisting Pakistan in the ensuing war of secession by raising the threat of Sino-Soviet conflict if China were to intervene. The famous US 'tilt' towards Pakistan in the India–Pakistan war of 1971 was motivated more by a US desire to impress China that US friendship was dependable, than with a serious intention to prevent the dismemberment of Pakistan. President Nixon's willingness to lift the embargo on arms supplies on payment was frustrated by the force of opposition in the US Congress and American public opinion which had turned massively in favor of the independence of Bangladesh.

Premier Chou En-lai's admonishment to the United States not to forget Pakistan – the bridge which made possible the US opening to China, had little effect on the subsequent American stance towards Pakistan. Nixon in his reports to the Congress downgraded South Asia as an area of security interest to the United States and Henry Kissinger moved to rebuild its relationship with India by implicitly conceding India's claim to have emerged from the war with Pakistan as the predominant power in the region.

Pakistan began to bind its wound after the amputation. The Ford administration lifted the arms embargo in 1975 and agreed to sell some military equipment to Pakistan on a case by case basis. Pakistan began to look for its military equipment from China, France and other sources.

The relationship was improving when a new issue precipitated a serious rift. In the 1976 presidential election campaign, the Democratic candidate, Jimmy Carter, made nuclear non-proliferation a principal plank in his election platform. Although it was India which had in 1974 exploded a nuclear device built with some US technical assistance in plutonium separation technology and supplies of burnt uranium rods from an unsafeguarded Canadian-supplied reactor, it was Pakistan which was singled out for massive US pressure to force it to cancel its agreement with France for the acquisition of a fully safeguarded reprocessing plant. The United States saw no advantage in pressing India on non-proliferation and took the explosion as a *fait accompli* which could not be reversed, rather than bring its relationship with India under strain. Instead, even economic aid to Pakistan was cut off until the reprocessing agreement was reneged upon by France under unrelenting American pressure. This aid was again halted before long. Acting under US legislation, President Carter demanded that Pakistan forego uranium enrichment though he exempted India from the application of US law by continuing the supply of enriched uranium to its US-supplied power reactor at Trombay.

The Carter Administration downgraded its relationship with Pakistan. President Carter carried forward the earlier administrations' policies of concentrating on the build up of the political importance of selected nations as 'regional influentials' – Saudi Arabia, Israel, the Shah's Iran and India.

During the 1970s, Pakistan turned towards consolidating its time-tested ties with China, the normalization of its relations with India and improving its relations with Afghanistan which had become a Republic under President Daoud after the fall of King Zahir Shah in 1973. Considerable progress was made towards finding an amicable solution to the question of recognition by Afghanistan of the Durand Line as the frontier between the two countries, only to be abruptly reversed after the communist coup in 1978 led by Nur Mohammad Taraki and Hafizullah Amin. And Pakistan's foreign policy became increasingly oriented towards the Persian Gulf region and the Middle East with the loss of its eastern wing which had emerged as the independent state of Bangladesh.

The Pakistan–US connection during this period was not disrupted but survived as an adversarial relationship. Earlier, in 1972, Pakistan had withdrawn from SEATO after the loss of East Pakistan. In March, 1979, coordinating her action with the Islamic Revolutionary Republic of Iran, Pakistan ended its membership of the Baghdad Pact, which since, 1958 had been redesignated as CENTO. As this military alliance lost its regional character, it was quietly dissolved by its remaining members, including Turkey and Britain, with the concurrence of the United States.

In 1959, the United States and Pakistan had concluded a bilateral security arrangement in parallel with similar US bilateral agreements with Turkey and Iran. The United States chose to affirm to Pakistan that this bilateral pact would remain in force despite the end of CENTO. This security relationship did not create any obstacle to Pakistan's admission to the Non-Aligned Movement in September 1979; consequently, Pakistan pledged itself not to be a member of any multilateral military alliance concluded in the context of great power conflicts.

The degree to which the Pakistan–US connection had declined during the Carter administration became apparent when Deputy Secretary of State, Warren Christopher served notice to Pakistan that President Carter was not concerned with the past ties between the two countries and that in the future US–Pakistan relations would hinge upon Pakistan's willingness to cease and desist from its venture into the nuclear fuel cycle, and the degree to which Pakistan would comply with US legislation, forbidding plutonium reprocessing and uranium enrichment to recipients of economic aid from the United States.

The Soviet invasion of Afghanistan at the end of 1979, and Pakistan's instant reaction to it calling for the immediate and unconditional withdrawal of the Soviet forces from that country, at once transformed the Carter administration's cold attitude. Pakistan at once emerged in the US view as a front-line state in the path of a Soviet southward drive and the 'third central strategic zone' of potential superpower confrontation. President Carter quickly promulgated his security doctrine for the Persian Gulf. Pakistan was offered a military and economic aid package of 800 million dollars to bolster its security.

While Pakistan welcomed the easing of US pressure, it found this offer and its indicative list of the military equipment that might be supplied to be incommensurate with the gravity of the security threat to which it had become exposed. Pakistan, therefore, decided to reject it and turned towards mobilizing the international community against the Soviet action as an issue between the Soviet Union and the regional and Third World states in order to insulate it from superpower confrontation.

Much as Pakistan deplored the Soviet invasion and stood resolute in calling for the withdrawal of Soviet forces from Afghanistan it was in no position to confront a superpower. That its big neighbor India, an ally of the Soviet Union, viewed the Soviet action in a permissive light, added a new dimension to Pakistan's security predicament.

Several grave consequences ensued for Pakistan from the Soviet military intervention: first, the dangerous precedent of invasion by a larger neighbor to reorder the government and social and political system of a smaller country in violation of the norms of international law; second, the deterioration of the security environment of Southwest Asia as a result of the disappearance of a century-old buffer state and the advance of a superpower to the Pakistan border; third, the ambivalent Indian response to the Soviet action underlining its refusal to acknowledge Pakistan's concerns over the changed security environment of Southwest Asia; and fourth: the influx of Afghan refugees into Pakistan and Iran.

In recognition of these developments, Pakistan had three options: (1) to directly confront the Soviet Union by participating in the Afghan resistance; (2) to acquiesce in the *fait accompli* imposed by the Soviet Union with all its attendant security and political implications; (3) to protest the Soviet action for its violation of accepted international norms in the forums of the United Nations, the Islamic Conference and the Non-Aligned Movement without direct confrontation with this superpower, while seeking simultaneously to strengthen Pakistan's security politically and its defensive capability but without aligning itself with one side or the other in the superpower confrontation.

Pakistan opted for the third course. It was the one dictated by the geo-political circumstances of the region. Admittedly, this course was difficult to sustain, especially in the deteriorating political climate of East-West relations. The emotional urge to demonstrate Islamic solidarity more substantively had to be restrained, since a military solution to the problem was not possible. The only hope of withdrawal of Soviet forces lay in the force of international public opinion and the exercise of political and diplomatic pressure.

The preferred option of negotiation was also encouraged by the declarations of Soviet leaders that the Soviet forces would be withdrawn from Afghanistan provided that transborder incursions from Pakistan by the Afghan Mujahideen (insurgents) ceased and guarantees provided against (what was called) 'interference' from Pakistan and Iran. The Soviet leadership also believed that the military intervention was a link in a chain of events starting from non-ratification by the United States of SALT II Treaty, the decline of *détente*, the concentration of US naval and military forces in the vicinity of the Persian Gulf for possible intervention in Iran following the fall of the Shah and the taking of American diplomats as hostages, as well as invocation of the Soviet-Afghan Friendship Treaty for military assistance against the Afghan mujahideen by the Marxist Kabul regime. While the Soviet leaders were reticent about the repercussions in Soviet Central Asia of the Islamic Revolution of Iran, sources close to them indicated that this Islamic reassertion was also a conscious factor in the Soviet decision to intervene militarily in Afghanistan to prevent the overthrow of its Marxist governmental system.

Whatever the motivations behind the Soviet occupation of Afghanistan, Pakistan was convinced that there was no justification for the invasion of a neighboring and non-aligned Muslim country belonging to the Third World. The mujahideen (insurgents) constituted no threat to the security of their big neighbor. Afghanistan had always pursued a policy of friendship and cooperation with the Soviet Union. The Soviet Government had frequently cited the example of Soviet relations with Afghanistan as a model of peaceful coexistence of states with different social, economic and political systems. Nor could Pakistan accept the doctrine that the mandate of history overrode the norms of international law to entitle a Marxist superpower to intervene by force in the internal affairs of another state to decide the outcome of a struggle for power in favor of a Marxist faction over its opponents, or to change its Marxist leadership.

World opinion could not but be outraged by the Soviet invasion of Afghanistan. But the only hope for redress against acts of international lawlessness for the small and non-aligned states of the Third World lay in recourse to international diplomacy, to seek through the peaceful settlement procedures of negotiations, good offices and mediation, the adjustment of situations arising from the use of force. Pakistan had perforce to opt for a political solution of the Afghanistan problem through recourse to the Islamic Conference, the United

Nations and the Non-Aligned Movement, for the withdrawal of the Soviet forces from Afghanistan, the return of the Afghan refugees in Pakistan and Iran to their homes in conditions of honor and safety, the restoration of Afghanistan's independence and non-alignment and to secure respect for the right of the people of Afghanistan to determine for themselves their own form of government. These principles of settlement have been repeatedly endorsed by the United Nations General Assembly with overwhelming majorities and by the Islamic Conference and the Non-Aligned Movement.

It was in recognition of this principled but non-confrontational opposition to the Soviet military presence in Afghanistan, and of Pakistan's intention to open indirect negotiations with the Kabul regime through an envoy of the UN Secretary General, that the Reagan Administration proposed to Pakistan, in March 1981, its $3.2 billion offer of military sales and economic aid, in equal proportions over a five-year period. The military component was to include sales of high-performance aircraft to mitigate Pakistan's vulnerability in air defense against increasingly dangerous air strikes. Contrary to the earlier Carter offer, acceptance by Pakistan of full-scope nuclear safeguards was not made the centre-piece of this Reagan package, while the United States maintained its reservations regarding Pakistan's nuclear activities. Pakistan's right to acquire the means of self-defense against aggression from any quarter was acknowledged. The US also stated that it could not remain an idle spectator if Pakistan became a victim of unprovoked aggression from any quarter. By way of reciprocity, Pakistan was asked to show consideration for the US interests in the Middle East.

In President Reagan's offer, Pakistan discerned a possible basis for a new relationship with the United States consistent with its posture of non-alignment. Nevertheless, in order to eliminate any ambiguities in the expectations of each side, which otherwise could lead to misunderstandings, Pakistan explained to the US Government that given the geo-political decline and the inability of Pakistan to align itself with US policy towards the Middle East, (where Pakistan's interests were intertwined with the aspirations of the peoples of the Middle East for security, self-determination and the withdrawal of Israel from the occupied Arab territories), there could be no symmetrical reciprocity in the relationship of the two sides, which were developing from the proposed military sales and economic aid agreement between the United States and Pakistan.

In the talks held in Washington to define the new relationship, the

United States undertook to respect Pakistan's policy of non-alignment. The United States did not ask to establish bases in Pakistan, nor did Pakistan offer any bases to the United States. That Pakistan should not be expected to align itself with a Middle East 'strategic consensus', which was then being promoted by the US, was clearly understood. It was also understood that Pakistan could not agree to becoming a conduit for the supply of arms to the Afghan mujahideen (insurgents). Consequently, the US-Pakistan relations entered a new phase.

It is within this new framework that negotiations for the terms and conditions of US military sales and economic aid were concluded in September, 1981. In the Joint Statement issued in September 1981, on the conclusion of the agreement between Pakistan and the United States, (for a $3.2 billion military sales and economic aid package to strengthen Pakistan's security), it was expressly stipulated that this agreement was concluded without prejudice to Pakistan's policy of non-alignment. Simultaneously, as a token of Pakistan's commitment to peace with India and to address India's concerns over US military sales to Pakistan, an offer of a no-war or non-aggression pact was made to this militarily far more powerful neighbor of Pakistan.

While it is a matter of satisfaction that US deliveries of military equipment and economic aid are proceeding according to schedule, US officials have voiced the fear that Pakistan's stance on the Arab–Israeli conflict and its nuclear program could undermine its relations with the United States. On Pakistan's side, forebodings exist of the US–Pakistan connection being viewed as secondary to the pursuit of US objectives in regard to India which the US regards as the predominant power in South Asia.

PAKISTAN'S TRADITIONAL POLICY TOWARDS THE MIDDLE EAST: DIVERGENCE OF VIEWS WITH THE UNITED STATES

Pakistan's stand on the Middle East issues never figured as an impediment to the close relationship with the United States for more than two decades of their partnership in military alliances. If it were now to become an issue between them, a new condition would have been interposed by the US which would militate against Pakistan's geo-political interests, and would entail a reversal of its traditional policy towards the Middle East. This development would result in the disruption of the fraternal ties which bind Pakistan to the Muslim states of the Middle East. No nation is sufficient unto itself. Pakistan's national interest precludes an attitude of indifference to developments in the Middle East.

Since the birth of Pakistan, when Quaid-i-Azam Jinnah wrote to President Truman protesting against the injustice inflicted on the people of Palestine by the establishment of the state of Israel, successive governments in Pakistan, have found themselves in disagreement over US and western policies towards the Arab–Israeli conflict. In a letter of 8 December 1947, Jinnah wrote to President Truman:

> 1. At this hour when the Muslim world has received a terrible shock owing to the most unfortunate decision of the United Nations Organization to enforce partition of Palestine, I would like to address to you, Mr. President, this personal appeal.
>
> 2. The decision is ultra vires of the United Nations charter and basically wrong and invalid in law.
>
> 3. Morally it is untenable. Politically, historically, geographically and practically it would be impossible to enforce partition against the united resistance of the Arabs who have the full sympathy and support of over three hundred million Mussalmans and many non-Muslim countries and not only those who voted against UNO decision.
>
> 4. In the long run it will and must fail. The very people for whose benefit this decision is taken – the Jews, who have already suffered terribly from Nazi persecution – will I greatly fear, suffer most if this unjust course is pursued. Moreover, the decision presents a great danger to world peace.
>
> 5. May I, therefore, at this eleventh hour, appeal to you and through you to the great and powerful American nation, which has always stood for justice, to uphold the rights of the Arab race. The Government and the people of America can yet save this dangerous situation by giving a correct lead and thus avoid the gravest consequences and repercussions.
>
> 6. May I, Mr. President, with your permission, release this telegram to the press.[1]

Equity and even-handedness which marked the stand of President Eisenhower and the realistic approach of President Kennedy dictated by the US national interest, ended with the Johnson Administration.

The consequences of the Six-Day War of 1967 still bedevil all attempts to promote a comprehensive peace in the Middle East.

In the Nixon Administration, Secretary of State Rogers put forward a peace plan that would not 'reflect the weight of conquest'. But it soon withered away for lack of President Nixon's endorsement.

In the Ramadan war of 1973, the United States swung its support decisively behind Israel to turn the tide of war against Egypt and Syria. Henry Kissinger ordered a nuclear alert of the US strategic forces around the globe in order to deter Soviet military intervention to impose a cease-fire on Israel. The search for a comprehensive peace settlement was abandoned in favor of separate disengagement agreements between Israel, Egypt and Syria. The Palestinian problem which was and still remains the crux of the Arab–Israeli conflict, was relegated to the background.

President Carter no doubt approached the Arab–Israeli deadlock with good intentions. Step by step, diplomacy having run out of steam, he reverted to the idea of a comprehensive Middle East settlement. In October, 1977, Secretary of State Vance and Foreign Minister Gromyko issued a joint statement in favor of a renewed Geneva Conference for the establishment of a comprehensive peace, focusing on Israel's withdrawal from the occupied Arab territories and self-determination for the Palestinians as its goal. But this quest was abandoned no sooner than it was conceived. President Sadat preempted further efforts by announcing his dramatic visit to Jerusalem.

The Camp David Accords of 1978 and the Egyptian–Israeli Peace Treaty of 1979, have turned out to be no more than a bilateral settlement which recovered the Sinai for Egypt with what the other Arabs regarded as a sell-out of the Palestinian cause. It eliminated Egypt from the Middle East power balance, leaving the rest of the Arab world too weak and disunited to dislodge Israel from the occupied territories. Sadat's failure to secure recognition of the legitimate rights of the Palestinian in any form and Menachem Begin's flouting of the Camp David Accords by proceeding with accelerated establishment of Jewish settlements in the West Bank despite Carter's remonstrances, led to Sadat's tragic end. The United States found itself ineffective in fulfilling the pledge of 'full autonomy' which did not amount to even a semi-sovereign 'bantustan' for the Palestinians.

With Egypt eliminated from the Middle East equation, Israel

launched its massive invasion of Lebanon, in June 1982, to destroy the PLO and its leadership in Lebanon. The United States did not thwart the aggression. Instead, it eagerly embraced what it saw as the opportunity to reorder the politics of the Middle East by the imposition of a New Order on Lebanon under Israeli control. The fact that the problem of Lebanon was a political and an internal one, of a more equitable sharing of power among its different confessional communities, was ignored in favor of a solution imposed on the country by force.

The US-Israeli strategic alliance for across the board cooperation, is strongly opposed by the Arab States of the region, conservative and radical alike. They fear that this cooperation would lead to the establishment of Greater Israel from the Nile to the Euphrates. Israeli Defense Minister Moshe Dayan, while visiting Israeli troops in 1967, exhorted them to achieve Greater Israel:

> Our predecessors made the state of Israel of the 1948 frontiers; our generation that of the 1967 frontiers; (i.e. Israel with the addition of Golan Heights, Sinai, the West Bank and the Gaza strip); it is up to you to make Greater Israel.

Recently, Israel Foreign Minister Shamir, when asked about the frontiers of Israel, is reported to have said: 'But they are all defined in the Bible'.

In view of this fundamentalist attitude prevalent in Israel and even in the United States where the influence of the Moral Majority is a factor to be reckoned with, (even President Carter is on record as saying that the establishment of Israel was ordained by God), the difficulties of finding a comprehensive and just Middle East settlement based on the principles of inadmissability of acquisition of territory by war, are being compounded and all the more since the United States has reversed its historical stand that Israeli settlements in the occupied Arab territories were illegal and an obstacle to peace.

Pakistan cannot condone the policies of expansion, repression and denial of self-determination to the Palestinians. Islamic law enjoins on believers to resist oppressors who drive away men, women and children from their homes. Hundreds of thousands of Palestinians have been driven away from their homeland. Both Pakistan's interests and Islamic law dictate that their just cause be supported. Furthermore, public sentiment in the Muslim countries and international opinion as reflected in numerous United Nations resolutions are factors which no government of Pakistan is in a position to ignore.

THE NUCLEAR ISSUE

An even more serious issue between the United States and Pakistan is the nature of Pakistan's nuclear activities. Pakistan has been greatly concerned over the propaganda about the 'Islamic Bomb' depicting Pakistan as the villain and inciting Israel and India to acts of aggression aimed at the destruction of the Kahuta facility. For nearly a decade, US pressure on Pakistan to forego plutonium reprocessing or uranium enrichment has been intense and unrelenting. In 1976, Henry Kissinger served notice to Pakistan that the Democrats would make a horrible example of Pakistan. One may ask the question: 'Why is Pakistan being singled out for this treatment when a more or less permissive attitude is indulged towards Israel, South Africa, and India?' The characterisation of the Bomb as Islamic suggests it is because Pakistan is a Muslim country. Is Pakistan's peaceful nuclear program to be made the centerpiece of the new US–Pakistan relationship despite assurances of the Government of Pakistan to the contrary?

Pakistan is more concerned over the threat of horizontal proliferation of nuclear weapons than any other state. This is a matter of record. Twenty years ago, Pakistan warned the United Nations of the danger of such proliferation implicit in the peaceful uses of nuclear energy. It called upon the international community to establish a United Nations non-proliferation regime with effective guarantees for non-nuclear weapons by those states which already were or about to become nuclear weapon powers. Concrete proposals were submitted in this regard to the United Nations but to no avail. Pakistan's proposal for a nuclear-weapon-free zone comprising South Asian countries remains circumvented. Full scope inspection of nuclear facilities on a non-discriminatory or bilateral basis – another Pakistani initiative – has not been taken up nor has its proposal for joint renunciation of nuclear weapons evoked any interest. Now that the superpowers are about to resume their interrupted dialogue over a broad range of issues separating them, including the control of nuclear arms and horizontal non-proliferation, would it be too much to expect that they reappraise their past negative attitude towards the establishment of a truly credible non-proliferation regime under the aegis of the United Nations, which would provide non-nuclear states with credible guarantees against nuclear aggression or blackmail?

The non-proliferation policies thus far pursued by the superpowers are fraught with potentially grave consequences for the peace, freedom and stability of the South and Southwest Asian regions. Their inability or unwillingness to forge a universal, equitable and effective international non-proliferation regime, is leading to the emergence of two regional nuclear monopolies – one in the Middle East and the other in South Asia. The emergence of these regional superpowers with their own thinly-veiled ambitions for hegemony, domination or tacitly divided spheres of influence, is a new development of the power politics of their sponsors. The weaker nations in between feel themselves being strategically maneuvered towards the brink of fragmentation and reduction to marginal international existence and a permanent hostage to the nuclear blackmail of the two regional hegemonial states.

PAKISTAN-INDIA-US RELATIONS

A third element which has for long been a cause of instability in the Pakistan–US relationship has been the persistent trend in US South Asian policy to defer to India's wholly subjective perceptions of Pakistan–US relations. This tendency has been especially striking where US supplies of military equipment to Pakistan are concerned. During the 1950s and early 1960s while Pakistan was a member of US military alliances, India was seen as the key to the outcome of the competition between the democratic and the communist alternatives to development, which would decide the future of Asia. Consequently, the US was eager to accord preponderant weight to India in its South Asian policies. The Carter Administration gave unequivocal expression to its preference by designating India as the 'regional influential' of South Asia.

Another critical factor in the equation is the strategic nature of India's alliance with the Soviet Union under the Indo–Soviet Treaty of Friendship and Cooperation of 1971 and the availability to India of open-ended supplies of the most sophisticated conventional weapons on highly concessionary terms and conditions from the Soviet Union. If the military imbalance is tilted still further to deprive Pakistan of effective defense capability, it will be forced back in to an existence of undiminished insecurity.

Since the Simla Agreement of 1972, Pakistan has been striving to pursue a *modus vivendi* with India based on the principles of respect for political independence, state sovereignty, non-interference in internal affairs and sovereign equality. Fortunately, since the loss of East Pakistan in 1971, there has been no breach of the peace between

India and Pakistan, but the peace that has prevailed has remained fragile and sometimes precarious. A few major differences between the two countries continue to persist, including (a) Pakistan's references to the Jammu and Kashmir dispute in international forums, calling for an equitable settlement; (b) the sovereign right of Pakistan to provide for itself with the means for self-defense; (c) mutual recriminations about interference in internal affairs; (d) the plight of the Muslim minority in India; (e) the respective perceptions about the Soviet military intervention in Afghanistan and (f) nuclear non-proliferation. Consequently, this period of uncertain peace has alternated with alarms and relative normality with periodic rise and decline of tensions in bilateral relations.

It is disconcerting to Pakistan that India chooses to predicate its own security not on its military superiority over its neighbor and a non-aggression treaty, but on an offensive capability so overwhelming as to deprive Pakistan of any capability for defense. If the United States' concept of a balanced relationship with the two countries approximates towards the Indian view of the equilibrium, the interests of peace and stability in the region will not be safe-guarded. Consequently, the US–Pakistan relations would suffer a precipitous decline.

Since the security of Pakistan is of geostrategic significance to the stability of the Persian Gulf region, US military sales to Pakistan should be determined according to the objective requirements of Pakistan's defense capability and not the susceptibilities of third States which are oblivious to the geo-political sea change that has taken place.

With the beginning of a new era in India under Prime Minister Rajiv Gandhi, it is understandable that the United States should seize the opportunity to develop closer relations with that country. But initial reports suggest that it is unlikely the new leader would be more disposed than was his late mother towards developing Indo–US relations at the cost of weakening India's traditional ties with the Soviet Union. India would rather predicate an improvement of relations with the US on how the US manages its relations with Pakistan. It would appear to be implicit in this stance that the United States should interrupt or restrict deliveries of military equipment to Pakistan, the F–16 aircraft in particular.

The United States is of course fully conscious of the enormous disparity of military power between the two countries and has given no indication of a disposition to renege on its commitments to

Pakistan in order to accommodate India. The high-performance aircraft of the Indian Air Force outnumber by more than five to one, and are not inferior in quality to what Pakistan may come to possess. To this decisive edge must be added the factor of great superiority enjoyed by India in land and naval forces, and a monopoly of nuclear weapons capability matched to delivery systems.

President Zia ul Haq went to India to pay his last respects after Prime Minister Indira Gandhi's tragic assassination and to pledge in person his cooperation to her son and successor in making our own subcontinent safe for peace. One devoutly hopes that under its new Prime Minister, India will accept the good faith of Pakistan and bring India's strength to the struggle to banish the threat of war from this region. It is the fervent hope of the peoples of the two countries that the dialogue over the proposals for a non-aggression pact and a Friendship Treaty will be resumed and carried to a successful conclusion. At the same time the people of Pakistan fear that the competitive wooing of India by the superpowers may nullify President Zia's efforts by tempting India to extract maximum benefits from both to achieve a position of hegemony through the projection of growing military power.

PROBLEMS OF SOVIET INTERVENTION IN AFGHANISTAN

Pakistan–US relations had touched the lowest point at the time of the Soviet invasion of Afghanistan in December, 1979. Pakistan had withdrawn from the CENTO and had extended political and moral support to the Islamic Revolution of Iran. The Carter Administration had cut off economic aid in order to enforce US legislation directed against Pakistan's uranium enrichment program. In November, 1979, the US Embassy in Islamabad had been attacked and set on fire in reaction to inflammatory foreign broadcasts of American complicity in the violation of the sanctity of the Great Mosque in Mecca. It was in these circumstances that the decision to deplore the Soviet violation of Afghanistan's sovereignty and territorial integrity and to call for the withdrawal of Soviet forces from that country was taken by Pakistan. The decision was uninfluenced by any prompting, blandishment or pressure from outside. (The compelling considerations in adopting this stand have been mentioned earlier.)

The Geneva indirect negotiations between Pakistan and the Babrak Karmal regime for a political solution of the Afghanistan crisis were initiated in 1981. For the first two years the talks registered some progress but since April 1983, they have hardly moved forward.

Border provocations by the Karmal regime have been inflicting death and destruction on Pakistani citizens and Afghan refugees. While the Soviets continue to profess interest in the Geneva talks and have offered to enhance their economic cooperation with Pakistan, Foreign Minister Gromyko has accused Pakistan of 'increasing regional tension', 'undertaking dangerous preparations for war' and 'hostile actions' against 'the friendly state of USSR'. The Soviet Union persists in making Pakistan's attitude towards the Karmal regime, the litmus test of Soviet-Pakistan relations.

President Zia ul Haq stated to the *Wall Street Journal* last July that the Soviet Union has come to stay, and that time is on the side of the Russians. According to Diego Cardovez, the Personal Representative of the United Nations Secretary General, the deterioration in the political climate of relations between the United States and the Soviet Union, was exercising a negative influence on the progress of the Geneva proximity talks. The UN representative has a long way to go before a package agreement on Soviet withdrawal, guarantees of non-interference and conditions for the return of the Afghan refugees appears on the negotiating horizon. And even then, will remain the question of the complexion of the regime in Afghanistan before the refugees can be persuaded to return from Pakistan to their homes. It is becoming increasingly apparent that Pakistan could not possibly be the sole architect of a settlement. A question may be asked: 'What role would the two superpowers be willing to play in producing a settlement?' The signs point to a reversal of the breakdown of arms control talks between the United States and the Soviet Union. Even more relevant to Pakistan's particular concerns, Secretary of State Schultz is reported to have offered to discuss regional issues, presumably Lebanon, Middle East and Afghanistan with the Soviets. There have also been indications that the United States is not unmindful of Soviet concerns in regard to Afghanistan. A trend towards a new *détente* may hence be said to have set in.

The prospects of a political solution of the Afghanistan problem would be greatly enhanced if the competition between the superpowers for influence in the Middle East and South West Asia were to be moderated. Since the Ramadan War, the political strategy of the United States has been directed at excluding a Soviet role in the peace-making process in the Middle East. This policy has led the prospects of a settlement to a cul de sac. Strategic cooperation with

Israel will not enable the United States to establish a 'New Order' in that region as was conclusively demonstrated in Lebanon. A Soviet contribution has become essential to the establishment of a comprehensive, just and lasting peace in the Middle East.

The climate of distrust in US-Soviet relations can be transformed by a recognition of an indispensable Soviet role for a Middle East settlement and a corresponding Soviet willingness to facilitate a political solution of Afghanistan which would reconcile its concerns with Afghan self-determination and the security interests of Pakistan and Iran. The Soviet Union must seek an early solution of the Afghanistan question because this problem has now started to hurt the Soviet Union in the international arena, especially the United Nations, in the same manner as over the years the issues of Palestine and South Africa led to the erosion of American influence in the United Nations and other international fora.

The involvement of the United States in the mujahideen struggle against Soviet occupation cannot but affect Pakistan's relations with the Soviet Union, compound its security concerns, and jeopardize its good faith in the Geneva negotiations. A change from a policy of raising the costs of Soviet occupation, or excluding that superpower from the peace-making process to one of enlisting its cooperation in arriving at peaceful settlements based not on power politics but the principles of law and justice, is urgently needed in the interests of peace, security and stability in Southwest Asia and the Middle East. Concomitantly, the Soviet Union must withdraw from Afghanistan, allowing that country to pursue a policy of non-alignment and neutrality.

It is necessary to emphasize that peaceful settlements need to be based not on power, but principles. The realpolitik of Metternich which is credited with assuring the peace of Europe and a colonized world for more than fifty years is hardly relevant to the nuclear era of the late twentieth century, which has to find an answer to the problems of peaceful coexistence of over a hundred decolonized nations with the two superpowers. What none of the states of the two regions and, for that matter, the peoples of the world wish to see, is a second Yalta, carving out new spheres of influence, interference and intervention by the two superpowers or their strategic regional allies and surrogates.

The struggle for the independence and security of Pakistan, Iran and Afghanistan would be best pursued, in the light of past experience, within the framework of the principles and policies of neutrality and non-alignment. Being the neighbors of the Soviet Union it would be hazardous for them to choose the camp of its adversary. No less dangerous would it be for them to risk the antagonism of the United States by adopting a pro-Soviet orientation when that rival superpower considers its vital interests to be at stake in the Persian Gulf region. Having opted for non-alignment, a neither East nor West affiliation, Pakistan and Iran have only one viable option of choosing genuine non-alignment. This is a course dictated by their supreme national interests. Nor would this posture be detrimental to the interests of either superpower. A policy of positive neutrality would enable these regional states to enter into constructive relations with both without affording them cause or pretext for hostility or intervention by the use of force. A principled solution of the Afghanistan problem could lead concomitantly to the proclamation of Pakistan, Iran and Afghanistan as constituting a zone of peace and neutrality, and freedom from the military presence of the superpowers.

The attainment of these objectives, which in my view are in the best interest of the three regional states, as well as the two superpowers, is possible only when:

(1) the two superpowers agree to respect the neutrality and non-alignment of the three states;
(2) the three states forge a commonality of interest in the preservation of each other's independence, neutrality and non-alignment;
(3) the three states build intrinsic political economic and military strength to resist outside pressures and make cost of interventions or attempts at destabilization too high to be contemplated.

This perspective is a different one from that of the one or the other superpower. It is a perspective of geo-politics in the interest of peace and progress of the Southwest Asian region.

Note

1. Transmitted to the Department by the Chargé in Pakistan in telegram 198, 9 December 1 p.m. with this introduction: 'In letter dated December 8, Secretary Foreign Affairs has requested me transmit following message from Governor General Jinnah to President Truman and asks Department deliver copy Ambassador Ispahani his information (verbatim text):'. *Foreign Relations of the United States*, Vol. V., The Near East and Africa (Washington, DC, Government Printing Office, 1971), p. 1305.

9 Soviet Relations with Pakistan

Yuri V. Gankovsky,
Railya Muqeemjanova,
Vyacheslav Belokrenitsky
and Vladimir Moskalenko

We will first juxtapose the general aspects of the Soviet policies in South and Southwest Asia; and then focus on relations between Pakistan[1] and the Soviet Union. During the past few decades the scope and functions of the Soviet foreign policy have become much broader. This phenomenon is explained by a fast-moving integration of world economic, scientific, technological, cultural and other ties, a natural process which has involved all nations of the world.

SOVIET POLICIES IN SOUTH AND SOUTHWEST ASIA

The essence and the principles of the Soviet foreign policy have been outlined in Article 28 of the Soviet Constitution which says that

> the foreign policy of the USSR is aimed at ensuring international conditions favorable for building communism in the USSR, safeguarding the state interests of the Soviet Union, consolidating the positions of world socialism, supporting the struggle of the peoples for national liberation and social progress, preventing wars of aggression, achieving universal and complete disarmament, and consistently implementing the principles of the peaceful co-existence of states with different social systems.

The consistent nature of the Soviet foreign policy, invariably based on the principle of trying to solve all disputable issues peacefully, was reaffirmed at the 26th Congress of the Soviet Communist Party held in February–March 1981. The decisions of the 26th Congress reflect the global problems underlying the contemporary world and their growing significance for future generations. The Congress arrived at a conclusion that international cooperation had to be promoted in all possible ways, particularly in the questions of war and peace, something that the Soviet Union regards as the most crucial problem of our times.

The Peace Program for the 1980s contained a variety of proposals to prevent war and promote peace. These included: (1) Proclaiming an attempt by any state to use nuclear weapons first a grave crime against mankind; in advancing this initiative the Soviet Union unilaterally pledged not to use nuclear weapons first; (2) A complete and universal ban on all nuclear weapons tests and creating nuclear-free zones in various parts of the world; (3) Banning the deployment of any weapons in outer space; (4) Ensuring a limitation of nuclear weapons in Europe and a limitation and reduction of strategic arms; there are no weapons which the Soviet Union would not be prepared to limit and ban on a reciprocal basis; (5) Turning the Mediterranean into a zone of a lasting peace and cooperation; (6) The nonproliferation of NATO and Warsaw Pact's zones of activity to Asia, Africa and Latin America; (7) Attaining a fair and lasting peace in the Middle East; (8) Promoting trust-building measures to the whole of Asia, and reducing military activities in the Pacific and Indian Oceans.

It is appropriate to recall here that while proclaiming its backing of the idea to turn the Indian Ocean into a zone of peace, the Soviet Union also declared that the Indian Ocean was and is still a sphere of vital interests of no other states but the littoral states. The 26th Congress of the Soviet Communist Party reaffirmed the Soviet backing of the nonaligned proposal to turn the Indian Ocean into a zone of peace. At the 37th session of the UN General Assembly Soviet Foreign Minister Andrei Gromyko reaffirmed a proposal by Indira Gandhi made during her visit to the USSR that states whose ships ply the waters of the Indian Ocean should not wait until a world conference on the Indian Ocean was called; they should instead refrain from any steps that might complicate the situation in that part of the world and avoid sending large naval formations there, holding war games or expanding and modernizing military bases of those non-littoral states which already had such bases in the Indian Ocean.

The Soviet Union also proposed that all the states, including the western powers, China and Japan, agree not to build foreign military bases in the Persian Gulf countries and on the Gulf islands; not to deploy nuclear and other mass destruction weapons there; not to use or threaten to use force against the Gulf countries and not to interfere in their internal affairs; respect the status of nonalignment chosen by the Gulf states and avoid involving them in military alliances having nuclear powers among their members; respect the sovereign right of the Gulf states to their natural resources; not to prevent or threaten a normal commercial exchange and the use of sea lanes connecting the Gulf area with the rest of the world.

The Soviet Union has repeatedly declared its preparedness to back any initiative to defuse tensions and promote peace in Asia and the whole world. The Soviet Union backed Mongolia's proposal to sign a convention banning aggression and the use of force in relations between Asian and Pacific states. The USSR also supported a proposal by the Foreign Ministers of Vietnam, Laos, and Kampuchea (July 1982) to call a world conference to debate a settlement in Southeast Asia and to be attended by the countries of Indochina, the ASEAN members, Burma, India, and also the USSR, China, the United States, France and Great Britain.

The proposals made by the Soviet Union to the world community of nations in the recent past indicate that the chief goals of the Soviet foreign policy are to avert a military threat and curb the arms race. However, the newly-freed nations of the East are playing a prominent role in contemporary international relations, and their role in world politics will grow in the future. This applies equally to the countries of South Asia, including Pakistan.

Undoubtedly, the Soviet Union recognizes the differences between the foreign policies of various South, and Southwest Asian states. These differences may be attributed to an array of factors to be traced in the recent and past developments of these countries. The foreign policies of all states lying in this vast area of the world have been noted for their participation in the movement of nonalignment. The states in South and Southwest Asia want to strengthen their national independence, won in a long and hard struggle; they want to overcome the difficulties they have inherited from their colonial past, and promote their economic, scientific, technological and cultural progress. All South and Southwest Asian nations want world security and peace to be promoted and strengthened, and they seek a new and fair world economic order, and a complete elimination of the remnants of colonialism and racism. South and Southwest Asia would surely benefit enormously from the curbing and termination of the arms race on global and regional scales, something that may allow the countries concerned to stop wasting their natural resources and channel more means into solving their acute socio-economic problems.

Recently, the foreign policies pursued by the South Asian countries have been increasingly dominated by a new factor; i.e. their desire to establish and promote a multilateral cooperation on a regional scale. Undoubtedly, there are still some outstanding issues and differences between some countries of the region. However, these differences are hardly antagonistic in their essence and can be solved constructively, provided there is enough goodwill on both sides.

The origins of multilateral, mutually beneficial and fruitful ties, whether cultural, economic or political between the Soviet Union and Pakistan (as well as other South Asian nations), can be traced to ancient times. One can hardly overestimate those ties and their contribution to the cultural advance of the peoples of South Asia and the Soviet Union.

In recent times, the relations between the Soviet Union and South Asian nations have undoubtedly been promoted by the Soviet foreign policy (whose founding principles were elaborated by Vladimir Lenin) seeking to establish friendly ties with all states. These relations have also benefited from a sympathetic attitude of the South Asian nations towards the peoples of the USSR who played a prominent role in routing Nazism and opposing colonialism; and from the Soviet diplomatic and political backing of South Asia's bid for independence. During the past few decades Soviet ties with South Asian nations have developed into a major factor promoting the cause of peace in Asia and the rest of the world. These ties have helped South Asian countries to strengthen their sovereignty and independence. Relations between the USSR and South Asian nations have also been promoted by reciprocal visits by parliamentary delegations and official visits by statesmen.

Cooperation between the Soviet Union and South Asian nations, including construction of major industrial, power and communications projects, with Soviet financial and technical assistance, joint ventures in prospecting minerals, assistance in training scientific and technical staffs, has been conducive to the development of their economies. Soviet loans and credits, as well as other forms of economic, scientific and technical assistance, largely help transform the key branches of the South Asian economies on a modern scientific and technological basis, develop new enterprises and expand the existing ones. Cooperation with the Soviet Union helps not only to consolidate their economic independence, but also to create thousands of new jobs. At the same time, Soviet assistance to the Third

World is a no-strings-attached affair and is based on equality of states.

The relations between the Soviet Union and Pakistan, as well as other countries of South Asia, is a history of relations between partners, based on the principles of equality, solidarity and respect for each other's interests. These relations have been developing within the framework of the international division of labor.

SOVIET–PAKISTANI RELATIONS

Soviet–Pakistani relations can be divided into several stages: (1) the establishment of relations between the two countries during the late 1940s and early 1950s; (2) the tension-filled relations between the two countries due to Pakistan's involvement in military and political alliances created by the West with a distinct anti-Soviet bearing during the 1950s; (3) the improvement of relations and contacts in various fields in the 1960s; (4) the emergence of some negative aspects in Soviet–Pakistani relations because of the separation of Bangladesh from Pakistan in 1971; (5) the delicate relations as they are at the present stage in the 1980s.

Although relations between the Soviet Union and Pakistan plunged to their lowest in the late 1950s and then improved within the 40-year period, they have invariably been based on the principle of peaceful coexistence which means avoiding wars as a means to settle disputable issues and their settlement through negotiations, equality, mutual understanding and trust; considering each other's interests; respect for each other's territorial integrity and national sovereignty; and noninterference in each other's internal affairs. Soviet–Pakistani relations have never been at variance with national interests of either the Soviet Union or Pakistan and they have always been conducive to peace and security in the region. It is, perhaps, for that reason that slumps in relations between the two countries have never been protracted.

Relations between the Soviet Union and Pakistan were established at a time when Pakistan had just been taking its first steps in the international arena as an independent nation. On 30 September 1947 the Soviet delegation to the 2nd Session of the UN General Assembly voted for Pakistan's admission to the United Nations. Two months later, in late November 1947, when the Foreign Ministers of the anti-Hitler coalition met in London, in spite of manoeuvring by some

Western states, the Soviet Union insisted that Pakistan be consulted on matters of concluding a peace treaty with Germany. By so doing the Soviet Union implicitly admitted South Asia's contribution to defeating Nazism. The Soviet move stemmed from a desire to promote Pakistan's status as an equal and sovereign nation, and to establish and develop goodneighborly relations with that newly-freed country.

During the first few years of its independence, Pakistan's interests in the Soviet Union were represented by Britain; the fact that undoubtedly impeded progress in Soviet–Pakistani relations and was at variance with Pakistan's status as an independent nation. So when in April 1948 the Foreign Minister of Pakistan, Muhammad Zafrulla Khan, who was visiting New York City, passed his government's message to Andrei Gromyko, then First Deputy Foreign Minister of the USSR, suggesting that diplomatic relations be established between the two countries, the Soviet government agreed without hesitation. On 1 May 1948, the Foreign Ministries of the USSR and Pakistan exchanged notes on establishing diplomatic relations and instituted their representations at the rank of embassies. The two countries exchanged their ambassadors in 1950; the Soviet Ambassador handed his credentials to the Governor-General of Pakistan in March 1950.

The establishment of diplomatic relations with the Soviet Union was welcomed by many prominent Pakistani public figures and businessmen as a move to promote friendly ties and economic cooperation between the two countries. The Pakistani public also hailed news circulated by the press of Pakistan in the summer of 1949 to the effect that the Soviet government had invited Prime Minister Liaquat Ali Khan of Pakistan to visit the USSR. Regrettably, the trip was cancelled due to circumstances beyond the control of the Soviet side. In late April and early May, 1950, Pakistan's Prime Minister chose to visit the United States and Canada, although an invitation from Washington followed that from Moscow.

Even so, in the late 1940s and early 1950s Pakistan and the Soviet Union established cooperation in many fields. Events were positively influenced by the Soviet government's consent to supply Pakistan with some 120 000 tons of grain. This helped the country cope with the food crisis, as Prime Minister Liaquat Ali Khan had recognized. Trade between the two countries increased which was very important for Pakistan for two reasons. First, the Soviet Union agreed to import some raw materials (cotton, jute and leather) which Pakistan could not sell elsewhere, and exported to Pakistan industrial plant. Second, in dealing with the Soviet Union Pakistan always had a trade surplus, a real asset for a newly-freed country which badly needed foreign currency. When in the summer of 1952 the Pakistani government, faced with an imminent famine, asked several developed countries for help, the Soviet Union was one of the first to respond to the appeal. The Soviet government agreed to buy from Pakistan cotton and jute in exchange for 150 000 tons of wheat. The Soviet–Pakistani cooperation did not have political or any other strings attached to it and was mutually beneficial.

During the early 1950s the Soviet Union and Pakistan also established some cultural contacts. These were largely promoted by the fact that the peoples living in Soviet Central Asia and those living in Pakistan have had traditional ties since ancient times, while the mutual influence of their cultures upon literature and especially poetry, music and architecture is clearly visible even at the present time.

However, the obstacles impeding Soviet–Pakistani relations during this period also grew. The US and its NATO allies used the difficulties faced by Pakistan at home and abroad to involve it into a network of anti-Soviet alliances. Although Pakistan's real motives in joining SEATO in September 1954 and the Baghdad Pact, later known as CENTO, in September 1955 had nothing to do with anti-Sovietism (the fact frankly admitted and extensively commented on by various Pakistani and Western authors), its membership in both alliances involved it in Cold War against the socialist nations and made it support various anti-Soviet military, political and other moves attempted by the West. According to Khalid B. Sayeed, an analyst of Pakistani political problems, Pakistan was involved in the Western strategy to lock Soviet Russia into a ring of air force and ground-based military bases. It may be recalled that the notorious U–2 flight over the Soviet Union in 1960 started in Peshawar. Under such conditions concern had been mounting in the Soviet government over Pakistan's growing involvement in the activities of military and political groupings in the immediate vicinity of the southern borders of the USSR. It repeatedly sent to the Pakistani government notes of protest and statements which exposed the real plans of the US-led imperialist powers dominating the Baghdad Pact and SEATO and proposed ways to normalize Soviet–Pakistani relations which were deteriorating due to Pakistan's involvement in military alliances.

In the early 1960s the Pakistani government decided to sever its military and political links with the US and cut its activities in SEATO and CENTO. Some policies were initiated to promote Pakistan's ties with other nations of the world, making its foreign policy more independent, which created favorable conditions for the improvement of Soviet–Pakistani relations. Also, during the 1960s the flourishing economic cooperation was accompanied by growing political contacts largely promoted by encounters between the leaders of both countries. President Ayub Khan of Pakistan visited the Soviet Union in 1965, 1966 and 1967, while the late Soviet Premier Alexei Kosygin also paid an official visit to Pakistan. The growing Soviet–Pakistani contacts promoted better understanding, and revealed global political issues upon which both countries held similar views. Similarity of views on such issues as the eliminating of imperialism, colonialism and racism, and condemning the Israeli aggression against the Arab countries, promoted political contacts between the two countries. Such contacts were also furthered by the Soviet Union's constructive attitude towards the settlement of the 1965 armed conflict between India and Pakistan. The President of Pakistan praised the role of Soviet diplomacy in arranging a meeting between the Pakistani and Indian leaders in Tashkent in 1965, which also proved to be an important landmark in Soviet-Pakistan relations.

Having played a prominent role in stabilizing the political situation in South Asia in the mid 1960s, the Soviet Union continued to lay great stress on goodneighborly relations with Pakistan. The Pakistani government reciprocated by regarding good relations with the USSR as a lever to bolster the independence of its foreign policy. The Ayub Khan government's bid to further improve relations with the Soviet Union was manifest in its decision in May 1968 to shut down the US military base at Badaber near Peshawar. The base was dismantled in January 1970.

Progress in Soviet–Pakistani relations was again impeded in 1971 by the tragic events in South Asia, with the Soviet government and the Yahya Khan Administration holding totally different views on the situation. After its advent to power in December 1971 the Bhutto government displayed political realism by preferring to mend breaches in relations with the USSR, although its bid was frustrated by some political forces at home and abroad. In trying to improve Soviet–Pakistani relations the Bhutto government took into account the growing prestige of the Soviet Union in the international arena, including South Asia. After the political upheavals of 1971 an improvement of

Soviet–Pakistani relations was of utmost importance to Islamabad as a lever to bolster its prestige around the world.

A rehabilitation of goodneighborly relations was exactly what the Soviet Union sought with Pakistan, a nation in the immediate proximity to the Soviet southern borders. Some positive trends in Pakistan's foreign policy and its government's efforts to behave independently in the international arena were appreciated and backed by the Soviet Union, since in Soviet perception this attitude was to help Pakistan eliminate the bonds imposed on it by the imperialists. Many Soviet statements made at the time pointed out that Pakistan and the Soviet Union were not divided by any conflicts or contradictory interests and, therefore, could improve their relations. Numerous official documents, including joint communiques released after talks between the leaders of the USSR and Pakistan, the USSR and India, the USSR and Bangladesh, maintained that the Soviet Union was eager to help improve relations between South Asian countries.

President Bhutto's visit to the USSR on 16–18 March 1972 was crucial to increasing understanding between the two countries. During the Soviet–Pakistani talks in Moscow views were exchanged frankly and beneficially concerning bilateral relations and their prospects for the future. The leaders of both countries declared that they were convinced that goodneighborly relations between the Soviet Union and Pakistan would promote the interests of the two nations and contribute to the cause of peace in Asia and the rest of the world. An agreement was reached to maintain regular contacts on questions of mutual interest, and expand economic and technical cooperation between the USSR and Pakistan. During the Moscow talks both sides debated at length the situation in South Asia and other international issues.

Bhutto again visited the Soviet Union now as Prime Minister on 24–26 October 1974, to hold talks which contributed immensely to improving relations between the two countries. In a joint communique both sides stated that the situation in South Asia had been gradually getting back to normal and the South Asian governments should continue to translate into life the agreements they had signed to improve relations between states in the region. The communique also said that the governments of South Asia must take more constructive steps to promote peace and security in that part of the world.

The Soviet–Pakistani communique of 1974 also stated that both sides held similar (or close to similar) views on some global issues, including the Mideast problems and future peace settlement. Describing the situation in Indochina, the communique said that the problems facing Vietnam, Laos and Cambodia must be dealt with by these three countries on their own without any foreign interference and with a strict observance of their people's legitimate rights.

For Pakistan, whose attitude on some global problems, including the Mideast and Indochina, substantially differed from that of the US, the Moscow talks were a tangible political backing for Pakistan's position.

SOVIET–PAKISTANI ECONOMIC COOPERATION

Since its independence, Pakistan has made some spectacular economic achievements, with its economy in many respects developing faster than those of other newly-freed nations in the East. Pakistan's economic successes can be, to a certain extent, attributed to Soviet assistance.

Soviet economic assistance to Pakistan focused on key industries; on the transfer of technical expertise, and the training of general manpower. Soviet assistance was extremely beneficial for Pakistan because the costs of the contracts were low, with no political or any other selfish and profit-seeking strings attached to them. The segments of Pakistan's economy which required Soviet assistance included metallurgy, exploration for oil and gas, the power industry and industrial infrastructure.

Metallurgy was a key branch for which Pakistan needed Soviet assistance. Since the 1950s the government of Pakistan had been trying to approach various Western companies and corporations for financial and technical assistance to develop its own steel industry. All such attempts had failed. When the Soviet Union was asked to help, it agreed in 1971 to build near Karachi an iron and steel mill with the initial capacity of 1.1 million tons of steel and pig iron a year, with a view to boosting the project's capacity to 2 million tons. The USSR granted a loan for the project and helped with design and construction. It also provided equipment and building machines.

Despite the great difficulties faced by the builders of Pakistan's first iron and steel mill in completing a production cycle – these included a lack of skilled labor and experience in building big industrial projects – the mill became fully-operational by 1985. In 1981 the first blast furnace was put into operation and started to yield pig iron. By August, 1984, 99.3 per cent of the planned amount of work had been completed.

For Pakistan, the effect of a chance to produce its own steel can hardly be over-emphasized. It helped to save foreign currency and provided a powerful impetus to the country's industrial development. Pakistan's economy had developed to such a degree that it could not advance further without heavy industry. An iron and steel mill forms a basis for the entire range of such industries, including construction, the building of transport machinery, ship building, the production of electrotechnical equipment and the exploration and production of minerals. That Pakistan has acquired such a basis is clearly seen from the projections of the 6th Five-Year Plan for 1983–1988 and the private industrial investment program for the same period endorsed by the government.

The first sphere of Soviet–Pakistani economic cooperation was oil and gas exploration. The cooperative effort was launched after signing a bilateral agreement in 1961. The Soviet Union granted credits to enable Pakistan to arrange geological surveys, and provided deep-well drilling rigs, slim-hole drills, road transport and other equipment, materials and implements. It also sent specialists to help, and arranged the training of Pakistani workers and foremen. The joint Soviet–Pakistani effort to explore oil and gas resulted in the discovery of more than 30 oil and gas bearing structures, five gas fields, one oil, and one oil and gas condensate field. Soon after the discovery in the late 1960s of the oil field at Tut and two gas fields at Hundi and Sari the commercial production of oil and gas was started there. By 1977 the capacity of the oil field had reached 60 000 tons of oil, and two gas fields over 100 million cu.m. of gas a year. As the development of the Tut field progressively increased in 1983–1984, it yielded over 130 000 tons of oil – about a fifth of the amount produced by Pakistan. The Soviet Union also helped Pakistan develop its power industry by mounting the third 210MW unit at the Guddu thermal-electric power plant. The first two units had been erected by Czechoslovakia.

Soviet assistance has to some extent contributed to the development of Pakistan's infrastructure. In 1976 a Soviet-assisted 1000kW medium-wave broadcasting station was put into operation near Islamabad to become the biggest radio station in the country. The

Soviet Union also supplied three medium-wave and two short-wave transmitters and several ultrashort-wave stations.

Should one compare Soviet economic aid to Pakistan with that rendered by other major developed countries of the world, one cannot fail to notice that Soviet assistance has always advanced Pakistan's economy towards new frontiers, encouraged structural shifts in its economy and made it comprehensive and capable of growing independently. Meanwhile, assistance rendered by the leading Western countries tended to focus on supporting the existing economic structure in Pakistan, which was tantamount to retarding economic development and preventing Pakistan's departure from industrial backwardness. It is true that the US and US-controlled international financial institutions provided much more money to Pakistan than did the Soviet Union. Yet Soviet financial aid materialized in big joint ventures, while American aid turned into debt whose burden weighs heavily on Pakistan's economy and prevents the country from conducting an independent foreign policy.

In order to help Pakistan to advance its economic and social progress, the Soviet Union has always laid great stress on the transfer of technological expertise, mechanical know-how, and the training of skilled labor. This became obvious in the first few joint ventures which were undertaken to explore oil and gas; the Soviet geologists and drillers trained quite a few local workers and technicians on the spot, with Pakistani geologists and engineers also learning much from the experience of joint work.

The Soviet contribution to training skilled manpower in Pakistan was particularly tangible in the steel industry. The program for building the Soviet-assisted iron and steel mill in Pakistan provided for the setting up of a training center and sending the Pakistanis for training at similar projects in the Soviet Union. By the early 1980s the training center at the Pakistani mill was producing up to 800 technicians and operators on an annual basis. Moreover, over a thousand Pakistani engineers attended advanced training courses in the Soviet Union.

In addition to helping Pakistan develop its key economic segments the Soviet Union loaned it funds on favorable terms. Most of Soviet loans to Pakistan were granted at 2.5 per cent interest rate with a period of repayment of more than 12 years. The Soviet Union always agreed that Pakistan pay back its debts in kind – not raw materials but rather manufactured goods. By rendering economic assistance, the Soviet Union has never sought to make the Pakistani economy depend on foreign capital and drain Pakistan's financial resources by withdrawing profits. Thus the Soviet-assisted iron and steel mill near Karachi became an undisputed property of Pakistan after being put into operation, as well as the Guddu thermal-electric power plant and other Soviet-assisted projects.

The Soviet Union and its foreign trading organizations do not control the resources invested in Pakistan's economy and do not seek to make their partnership binding on Pakistan, thus giving it a free hand to choose its own partners in all future joint ventures. It is in form, not in essence, that Soviet economic aid may seem identical to that of the capitalist powers. In actual fact these are but two totally different patterns of international economic relations.

The Western countries provide Pakistan with loan capital on hard terms, and the industrial capital is to be invested in the private sector of the Pakistani economy. Soviet economic assistance is not the export of surplus capital since the Soviet credits are granted on easy terms to enable the borrower to buy equipment and pay for the imported technology and know-how. Commercial and economic cooperation with the Soviet Union is in fact a transfer of resources, a conveyance of property to another country, sales on easy terms, rather than the investment of capital.

In cooperating with Pakistan the Soviet Union tends to deal with the country's public sector which has largely consolidated its position owing to this cooperation. Thus the 1961 Soviet–Pakistani agreement resulted in the emergence of Pakistan's State Corporation for Oil and Gas. All the matters pertaining to the construction of the Soviet-assisted iron and steel mill near Karachi were firmly controlled by Pakistan's State Steel Corporation.

While promoting cooperation with Pakistan, the Soviet Union considers in full measure the nature of the Pakistani economy which is dominated by the private sector. Soviet economic agencies have accumulated vast experience in dealing with various private companies in Pakistan which have imported Soviet textile equipment, mills and Belarus tractors. A recent agreement on the construction of a Soviet-assisted tractor plant was a new step in Soviet cooperation with the Pakistani private sector. While promoting businesslike cooperation with Pakistani private firms, Soviet economic agencies do not depart from the principles of assistance on which the aid policy is based. They do not in fact become shareholders in a private company, but rather render the latter financial and technical assistance. That this assistance is rendered on really easy terms has been noted by the Pakistani press reflecting the views of the local business community. According to the Karachi-based magazine *Economic Review*, Soviet organizations do not make Pakistani firms pay for the trademark and the right to use a patent.

It is appropriate to mention here that a tractor plant to produce Soviet Belarus tractors in Pakistan, as well as Soviet exports of such tractors to Islamabad, are of great significance to Pakistan's agriculture. As agriculture is still one of the crucial branches of the Pakistani economy, mechanization is one of the chief levers to boost the efficiency of agricultural production.

Thus Soviet–Pakistani cooperation helps solve the key economic and social problems faced by this newly-freed nation, reconstruct its economy inherited from imperialism and to diversify its one-sided dependence on the world market.

THE DECLINE OF SOVIET–PAKISTANI RELATIONS

The political crisis of 1977 in Pakistan led to one more military coup and the eventual advent to power of a military regime led by General Zia-ul-Haq. The new government opted for strengthening the country's ties with conservative Middle East regimes and Western powers. After a short spell of uneasiness, Pakistani–American relations improved rapidly. The April revolution in Afghanistan, the collapse of the Shah regime in Iran and the disintegration of CENTO bolstered the role of Pakistan in the US military-strategic plans. After lifting its restrictions on economic aid to Pakistan, which had been imposed upon Pakistan earlier, because of violations of human rights in that country and its nuclear ambitions, Washington offered economic and military aid to Islamabad. This enabled Pakistan to buy the latest weapons, including F–16 fighter bombers. Pakistan has been included in the area assigned by the US to the Central Command (CENTCOM), which was established in 1983. The territory of Pakistan has been turned into a major bridgehead for aggression against the Democratic Republic of Afghanistan.

Changes in Islamabad's foreign policy (closely related to the home policies pursued by the military administration) bore a heavy imprint on Soviet–Pakistani relations. After its advent to power in July, 1977 the new military government proclaimed its intention to maintain friendly and goodneighborly relations with the Soviet Union in all fields. The Soviet Union continued to pursue its principled policy with regard to Pakistan, reaffirmed at the 26th Congress of the Soviet Communist Party, and aimed at promoting cooperation with the newly-freed countries for mutually beneficial trade, economic, scientific, technical and other ties.

The USSR and Pakistan held traditional consultations between their Foreign Ministries to debate the issues of mutual interest. While attending the 36th Session of the UN General Assembly in New York in September, 1981, Soviet Foreign Minister Andrei Gromyko received Pakistani Foreign Minister Aga Shahi at his request. The Ministers debated the situation in Southwest Asia, other global issues and Soviet–Pakistani relations. The problems arising from the situation in and around Afghanistan were discussed in principle on 15 November 1982 during a brief encounter between General Secretary of the Soviet Communist Party's Central Committee Yuri Andropov and President Zia-ul-Haq of Pakistan, who both attended Leonid Brezhnev's funeral. In July 1983 First Vice-Chairman of the Council of Ministers of the USSR and Soviet Foreign Minister Andrei Gromyko held talks with Foreign Minister of Pakistan, Yakub Khan.

The Ministers exchanged views on some global issues of mutual interest and Soviet–Pakistani relations. Great stress was laid on a settlement of problems arising from the situation in Afghanistan. Andrei Gromyko insisted that a political settlement would be possible on condition that armed or any other foreign interference in the internal affairs of Afghanistan was stopped. Pakistan, from whose territory armed incursions into Afghanistan are made, can and must play a significant role in defusing tensions around that independent and nonaligned country. It was stated that a political settlement of the problems arising from the situation in Afghanistan would also remedy the situation in Southwest Asia as a whole and help normalize the relations between Pakistan and its neighbors. It would also create favorable conditions for the development of Soviet–Pakistani relations in various fields. During this time, too, the Soviet Union has behaved as a reliable commercial and economic partner firmly standing by its previous commitments and eager to help the Pakistani people eliminate the legacy of colonialism, develop their national economy and alleviate the plight of their people.

It would be worthwhile to say a few words about trade between the Soviet Union and Pakistan. Although the Soviet share in Pakistan's foreign trade was insignificant, the USSR continued to rank as one of Pakistan's key commercial partners. Bilateral trade never failed to promote Pakistan's economic interests. The Soviet imports were dominated by manufactured goods which met the interests of Pakistan's growing industry. Machinery and equipment made the bulk of the Soviet exports and seemed to help Islamabad cope with many economic problems. The most important agreement of the period was signed by the two countries in October 1979 and concerned the merchant marine, with the most favored nation treatment to be granted in all questions pertaining to commercial shipping.

During the initial period of the present military government, the cultural relations between the USSR and Pakistan had developed rather vigorously. In December 1977 the two countries signed a program for cultural and scientific exchange for 1977–1979. Delegations of cultural workers and members of friendship societies were exchanged on a regular basis. In 1979 the Soviet Union and Pakistan signed three important documents opening up broad vistas for cultural and scientific exchange. In March 1979 a program of cooperation for 1979–1981 was concluded between the USSR State Committee for Radio and TV Broadcasting and the Pakistani Radio Broadcasting Corporation and TV Corporation. In June 1979 both sides signed a protocol admitting that education and academic degree certificates issued in the USSR and Pakistan were equivalent, which indicated that cooperation in the field of education between the USSR and Pakistan had reached a high level. In December 1979 both sides signed a program for scientific and cultural exchange for 1979–1981.

However, Pakistan's involvement in US military and strategic plans and its policy with regard to Afghanistan adversely influenced Islamabad's foreign policy in general and Soviet–Pakistani relations in particular. At the request of the Pakistani authorities the diplomatic, administrative and technical staffs at the Soviet Embassy in Islamabad and Consulate General in Karachi were cut by a third. (At first the Pakistani side demanded that the staffs be cut by half.) Publication of the Soviet news magazine *Tulu* published since 1967 was suspended and the press department in Karachi was closed down. Then the immigration authorities refused to extend visas to a group of Soviet technical specialists working according to contracts with various local firms within the framework of economic and commercial cooperation between the two countries. The Soviet proposals to expand commercial, economic, scientific and technical cooperation were either ignored or turned down, including a proposal to build several Soviet-assisted industrial and energy-generating facilities, which would have promoted Pakistan's economic progress and improved the welfare of its people. Trade between the two countries was curtailed.

Agreements on cultural exchanges were left unfulfilled, through the fault of the Pakistani side. The sales of Soviet books and periodicals in Pakistan were prevented in every possible way. Those advocating better relations with the USSR were subjected to repressions by the military administration, while the Soviet–Pakistani Friendship Society was virtually outlawed. Pakistani mass media launched a hostile propaganda campaign against the Soviet Union. Biased reporting of the USSR and its home and foreign policies were based on dubious sources. Thus, Soviet–Pakistani relations deteriorated and bilateral contacts decreased, through no fault of the Soviet side. However, we hope that this period will not be a protracted one as Soviet–Pakistani relations based on equality, goodneighborliness, noninterference in each other's internal affairs, respect and mutually beneficial cooperation have the potential to promote the national interests of Pakistan and the cause of peace and international security.

Note

1. The problems of Soviet–Pakistani relations have been thoroughly analysed by scholars in Soviet centers for Oriental Studies in Moscow, Leningrad, Tashkent, Dushanbe and other cities of the Soviet Union. It would be impossible to review in so short an article all the works in print on the subject, so we will attempt to sum up the basic conclusions drawn by Soviet researchers who studied and still study the past and present of Soviet–Pakistani relations.

10 Pakistan's Nuclear Options
Rodney W. Jones

Pakistan's technical progress toward some sort of atom bomb capability is now almost universally recognized.[1] Questions remain about whether Pakistan has the intent or capacity to produce militarily serviceable nuclear devices, or even whether its reckoning is military at all. But few doubt that Pakistan is a nuclear threshhold state in some sense, or that its leaders wish to convey an impression that it is nuclear-weapon-capable in some fashion.[2] If that impression is also consciously enigmatic, it may have some virtue for Pakistan partly because it invites the sort of speculation this chapter involves. And if the world believes Pakistan is nuclear-weapon-capable, that belief acquires a life of its own. Beliefs become facts in politics, and political facts have political consequences. The question of what are Pakistan's nuclear options is, in part, a question about what Pakistan wishes to do with the political facts and what political consequences it hopes for.

The matter is unquestionably of great importance to regional security. It has wider ramifications, too, for US international security interests. If Pakistan can achieve credible status as a nuclear-armed regional power, it becomes an important but disturbing precedent. Pakistan is the only nuclear threshold state in the developing world about which there is an element of surprise.

For China in the 1960s, or India and Argentina more recently, to become nuclear-weapon-capable entails no great surprise. Each got into the nuclear technology enterprise shortly after World War II, and each had an industrial and scientific base of substance decades ago. Israel and South Africa are not quite developing countries in the same sense; despite their small size, their scientific and industrial capabilities were quite advanced in the post-war period for different historical reasons. Taiwan and South Korea could be regarded as threshold developing countries even if they are not pressing the matter currently. But again the prodigious post-war industrial and technical development in each – emulating Japan on a smaller scale – tells its own story. But in Pakistan's case the limited early technical endowments, the agrarian character of industrial development priorities, and even the evolution of military planning before about 1972 do little to foretell that Pakistan would be on the nuclear threshhold in the 1980s.

WHAT ARE NUCLEAR OPTIONS?

It is important at the outset to distinguish peaceful nuclear energy options from those of a military nature, partly because Pakistan appears to be interested in both and because they do interact technologically, economically and politically.[3] It should be recognized that nuclear energy is an economically valuable and potentially more important part of the global energy supply picture. Moreover, while it will not be the focus of this paper for obvious reasons, Pakistan does have a stake, admittedly at this stage a small one, in the development of nuclear energy, and the official position of the Government of Pakistan is that its nuclear activities are exclusively dedicated to peaceful purposes. The point for making the peaceful *vs.* military use distinction, however, is that embrace of military options tends to constrain if not foreclose options in the peaceful use of nuclear energy.

But what do we mean by military options?[4] Before relating them to Pakistan's circumstances, consider military options analytically. Nuclear weapons involve a change in the scale and suddenness of destruction of targets if they are used in the conduct of a war. By their nature, nuclear weapons also involve a certain indiscriminateness of destruction – what we call collateral effects. Their use against military targets or combatants may not, typically would not be, isolatable from civilian destruction and casualties. Conventional weapons can also have collateral effects, but they can be used in such a way as to minimize such effects and they are prone to be less indiscriminate by their nature to begin with. There are inherent limits on so using nuclear weapons.

These features of nuclear weapons make them inherently less serviceable for the conduct of limited war, whether for some political gain or even merely for the defense of a country. Thus nuclear weapons involve a paradox. They are best not used in the conduct of a war. Their plausible defense policy purpose is to prevent resort to war, or deter war. The problem is, however, that they can be used for war, and cannot credibly deter unless they are usable for war. Given those conditions, there is never any way for two nuclear-armed rivals to be sure their nuclear weapons will not be used for war. If they could be, they may be, and preparations against those contingencies will occur.

In asymmetrical situations, there will be little stability. In symmetrical situations, stability will be uncertain and temporary at best unless it is actively maintained, and maintaining it produces new uncertainty and effort, not to mention great cost. Moreover, the world does not always fall out neatly among pairs of enemies. There are intersections that give rise to three-cornered, and more-cornered, and many-cornered situations, the dynamics of which can be confusing and precarious indeed.

One nuclear military option then, abstractly speaking, is to acquire a nuclear arsenal and deploy it for national defense. While the usual motive would be for defense in the sense that deterrence of war contributes to defense, one cannot rule out that the rulers or policies of nuclear-armed countries would have aims that go beyond deterrence. In any case, deterrence is not a tangible commodity and maintaining it may not be so simple. Once inducted into that situation, other issues come into play. Do nuclear weapons deter war, or do they merely deter the use of nuclear weapons by the opponent, leaving him free to wage conventional war? Do they deter escalation from limited conventional war to all-out conventional war, or only escalation of a nuclear sort? Do they deter unconventional war? Do they deter, or do they provoke? How much do the answers change if the opponent is nuclear-armed or not, generally weaker or stronger, or with or without major allies?

What we have just said makes clear that going nuclear in the sense of acquiring and deploying nuclear weapons opens up a variety of new risks and new dangers. That also suggests something about why so few countries have ventured on that path.[5] It is a momentous decision to proceed, and seldom arrived at without soul-searching, at least so we must conclude from the fortunately small sample of cases we know much about. But it is also clear that it is not the only way to express nuclear military options. There is something short of deploying a nuclear arsenal, and it may have less to do with military options than political ones, albeit ones that bear on security and defense directly or indirectly.

The political use of nuclear weapons is possible with a symbolic nuclear weapon capability, or perhaps even with the reputation for having such a capability. The risks can be much lower, particularly if there is ambiguity about the symbol or reputation, though not so much (or little) ambiguity that no one pays any attention. Many observers are convinced that we are entering a world in which ambiguous situations more than the bomb are proliferating.[6] Israel's situation for the last decade and a half usually is singled out as a case in point – the reputation for a 'bomb in the basement,' no physical proof, and no declaratory policy that would lend confirmation.[7] South Africa more recently, some believe, has acquired a similar reputation.[8]

For the political option of an ambiguous nuclear capability to matter, of course, there has to be some perception of gain. One can speculate about what such gain might consist of in the Israeli and South African cases, but it is not a trouble-free issue. Can one show, for instance, that Israel's security has improved, or at least has not deteriorated as much as it otherwise might have, because of the 'bomb in the basement' reputation? It is doubtful that you would find many Israelis who believe this to be the case. South Africa's bomb reputation is not quite so visible or long-standing, but evidence of political gain is sparse at best.[9] It has done nothing to reduce its isolation in the world community. But proof of gain is not the end of the issue. It is perception of gain, and perhaps speculative expectation of gain. Thus each country in question must be looked at separately, and Pakistan might be quite different.

There is one other issue of nuclear spread that needs to be touched on because it falls into the category of political nuclear options, and that is the option of 'nuclear terrorism'. Nuclear weapons are terrifying and naturally have the potential for use as terrorist weapons. There are even those who view nuclear weapons as quintessentially terrorist. 'Terrorism' is best defined not by the weapon, however, but by purpose. The purpose is to force the powerful to yield what a weaker group wants passionately enough to attack helpless innocents without warning. 'Nuclear terrorism' is an implausible option for most states, though there may be exceptions from time to time of 'rogue states.' Pakistan certainly is not a 'rogue state', and is not likely to become one. So we can dismiss that from this chapter. But 'nuclear terrorism' can also be an option for sub-national or subversive groups if they succeed in pirating nuclear material or devices. No socially diverse, nuclear-capable state, including Pakistan, can be wholly immune to this danger. This fact does not so much create a 'nuclear option' for a state as it colors foreign perceptions of dangers that might emanate from a state. This in turn adds a measure of interest and perhaps political influence to a state that can be attributed to its possession of nuclear-weapon-capable assets.

PAKISTANI NUCLEAR CAPABILITIES

Nuclear options, whether political or military, are constrained by technical factors. A state cannot acquire a real or even symbolic nuclear military capability unless it has a credible means of access to nuclear weapons. Since states customarily do not sell, rent, or loan nuclear weapons to each other, nor pass along weapons material and bomb-building kits to one another, the access to nuclear weapons usually is through 'self-help', that is, the national procurement or development of independent nuclear capabilities. The key capabilities are those that make weapons-grade nuclear material accessible.

In today's world, sufficient means for domestic production of nuclear energy are available without treading on the boundary of nuclear weapons. Safeguarded nuclear fuel and reactor maintenance services can be purchased on the open market less expensively than they can be replicated by less developed countries. Thus when a less developed country with only a nominal investment in nuclear energy invests heavily, surreptitiously, and uneconomically in unsafeguarded sensitive nuclear facilities, the inference that it has decided to develop a nuclear weapon capability is compelling. This happens to be the situation in Pakistan.

Because Pakistan's sensitive technology acquisitions have been surreptitious, their theoretical capacity cannot be reliably described in the same fashion as, for example, can India's. But it is now well-established that Pakistan has been endeavoring to construct gaseous centrifuges facilities for uranium enrichment, the centrifuge technology being based on the designs of URENCO equipment to which the head of the Pakistani program, Abdul Qadir Khan, gained access in the early 1970s.[10] Pakistan's centrifuge facility reportedly is located in Kahuta, a small town near Islamabad. The capacity of the enrichment program estimated from the scale of Pakistani procurement before 1981 ultimately could be sufficient to produce enough material for 5 to 7 early generation atomic bombs per year.[11] In June 1984, US Senator Alan Cranston announced that Pakistan had begun operating 1000 centrifuge, theoretically enough to produce one 'critical mass' (bomb-load) of highly enriched uranium in a year.[12]

The alternative route to weapons-grade material is the plutonium route. Pakistan appears to be pursuing this capability as well. The sensitive technology associated with plutonium is chemical reprocessing, the means of separating it from irradiated or spent fuel taken out of nuclear reactors. Pakistan has sought to develop this technology in three forms. The first, established quite some time ago, was a laboratory or research-scale facility in PINSTECH which is far too small to be a basis for military production, but is a means of familiarizing personnel with the methodology. The second was the French contract for a commercial-scale reprocessing facility under safeguards at Chashma. Though the French contract apparently was cancelled in 1978, some technology transfer and partial construction of the facility had occurred. The third venture, since Chashma was shelved, was to build through unsafeguarded avenues of procurement a facility at what is called New Labs, a small-scale facility capable of separating from 10 to 20 kilograms of plutonium a year. There are reports that this facility was completed in 1981 but that it probably has not been put into regular operation. If its total capacity of throughput was realized, the quantity of plutonium might suffice for about 3 nuclear devices a year.[13]

The usability of the New Labs separation facility depends on the availability of an irradiated fuel source. Both KANUPP and the 5MW HEU research reactor at PINSTECH are under IAEA safeguards. If material from either were routed to New Labs, technically Pakistan would be obligated to have IAEA safeguards on New Labs. This fact may account for the decision thus far not to start up the New Labs facility on a regular basis.

There was a possible loophole with KANUPP. It had to do with the fact that safeguards could be enforced on KANUPP as a practical matter because the supply of fabricated fuel had to be imported. In 1981, however, Pakistan evidently began to fabricate a small quantity of fuel domestically. This theoretically could have been cycled in and out of KANUPP without notice and routed to New Labs without IAEA inspection or detection. There is some possibility that this may have occurred. But the IAEA sought upgraded KANUPP safeguards to which Pakistan finally agreed in 1983, so that this avenue could not be exploited on a significant scale without abrogating safeguards.

A hypothetical means of getting weapons-usable plutonium is to build a dedicated reactor for this purpose. Such a reactor probably could be built domestically with Pakistan's technical skills if it were a graphite-moderated type reactor and the materials and components were purchased in pre-assembled form. Recently there were reports, never however reliably confirmed, that Pakistan was in the market for such materials and components.[14]

In the absence of such a facility, therefore, Pakistan would have to find an external source for plutonium or spent fuel. There are several aspects of sensitivity to the question of possible Chinese nuclear assistance to Pakistan. One that has not been commented upon is China's receptivity to receiving, storing, and possibly disposing of spent fuel from European nuclear installations for a service fee. A natural concern about this prospect is that such spent fuel might end up in other countries. Pakistan being a neighboring country, and one on good terms with China, the possibility here cannot be ignored.

What does all of this add up to? Some clues seem to have been provided in early 1984 when Abdul Qadir Khan, the head of the enrichment program, gave press interviews which seemed to indicate that Pakistan had made an operational breakthrough with the use of centrifuges to successfully enrich uranium.[15] If true, the iterative use of this equipment should enable Pakistan to raise enrichment levels to weapons-grade. Experience with the technology should also enable Pakistan to expand the facility and its capacity. Between now and the end of the decade, this capacity may grow from a level of being able to produce enough material for one nuclear device (or weapon) in a year to a level of about 5–7 such devices (or weapons). In short, a small-scale but militarily significant stockpiling process may be beginning.

If the plutonium route (a production source and New Labs) also can be brought into play, the annual capacity theoretically could be brought to about 10 such devices a year. One could do various extrapolations from that, ranging from a handful to a dozen or so devices in 1990 to over a hundred by the turn of the century.[16] On the other hand, it should be kept in mind that technical difficulties may impede the process, as it evidently has since 1979, when US administration forecasts indicated that Pakistan might well be by 1980 at a stage that it appears it may only be reaching in 1984 or 1985.[17] A change in policy, of course, could also do away with this approach altogether.

DEFENSE OPTIONS VERSUS INDIA

Pakistan's primary military threat perceptions continue to focus on India, despite the Soviet invasion of Afghanistan. This one would have to conclude, at least, if one looks at the deployment of Pakistani armed forces. While this may not make good sense from a Western point of view, it can be readily understood from a Pakistani standpoint. On one hand, Pakistan has been at war with India three (some would say three and a half) times since 1947, and was, as a larger national entity, dismembered by India in 1971. These were, to be sure, limited wars in terms of intensity, duration, and impact on non-combatants. But they are the only wars Pakistan has had, and they were with India.

On the other hand and looking at the Soviet threat side of the equation, Pakistani defense planners appear to conclude that they do not have the capacity to defend against a large-scale Soviet invasion anyway; such defense would depend on large-scale external assistance, which could not be counted on. This does not mean Pakistan could not defend against limited incursions, or will not try. But the policy implication that has been drawn, it appears, is to use diplomatic means to minimize the Soviet interest in mounting military threats to Pakistan, seek a political settlement in Afghanistan, and hope the Soviet military presence will be withdrawn. Political threats to Pakistani security, of course, may not be so easy to neutralize. But the means in that case are not primarily military.

In essence, then, Pakistan feels compelled to defend itself militarily against India, and plausibly can do so under most conditions. It may rely on diplomacy to avert war with India, but it has the military fall-back option. In the case of the Soviet military threat, at least that threat in a major form, Pakistan does not have prospects for adequate military defense. It must rely more fundamentally on the diplomatic option. It is in this sense that the Pakistani defense planners continue to focus on the Indian threat as the primary one.

If one examines the military force balances between Pakistan and India, one will find that the major ground forces on both sides (we are dealing with those that India apparently dedicates to the Pakistan side of its own defense equation) have been roughly the same in size historically, even in armored divisions and brigades. But we also see that the force balance has begun to shift markedly in India's favor, quantitatively, but especially qualitatively. India recently has begun to effectuate a lead in ground force modernization (mobility, firepower, organic air defense, and air support). Moreover, India has been able to perpetuate a roughly 2:1 superiority in modern combat aircraft and is now beginning to widen the gap in the air with sophisticated ground-attack as well as fighter-interceptor aircraft. If present trends continue, India may achieve a ratio of 4:1 or 5:1 in high-performance combat aircraft, with greater mission flexibility than Pakistan can achieve also buried in those figures.[19] This could be so despite the sale of F–16s to Pakistan, at least in the small numbers currently promised.

The strategy for conventional forces this Indian modernization and buildup makes feasible is not merely one of punching some limited distance into Pakistan to bargain for a termination of the conflict on favorable terms but, if India so chooses, to carry the war deep into Pakistan and potentially threaten to impose an unconditional surrender, or something approaching it. This capability could mean a war of much greater scope, intensity, cost, and perhaps duration. It also forces Pakistan either to acquiesce to unmistakable Indian military superiority or compete in force buildups that greatly strain its far more limited resources.

So far Pakistan has sought to avoid a clear choice between these unpleasant alternatives. It seems to be here that part of the attractiveness of a nuclear military option arises. One of the puzzles about Pakistan in fact is why the Generals seem to have fallen in behind the nuclear military option. It is clear that their predecessors through the 1960s were not, and that the initial push was by a civilian head of government, Prime Minister Z. A. Bhutto, and not a matter of pressure from the professional military.[20] In the late 1970s and early 1980s, the growing Indian advantages in technically sophisticated military forces and numbers of such forces are apparent, but hard to compete with.[21] Theoretically at least, Pakistan eventually could deploy a minimal nuclear deterrent and then feel more relaxed about the growing conventional force imbalance, declining to compete where it could not afford to. This could well be a rationale that some of Pakistan's military leaders and defense planners have come to find attractive, and may to some degree account for the shift in attitude of the military on the nuclear issue.

One must also consider the issue of the nuclear threat India poses to Pakistan's defense. Whereas it is believed in the West that India has not 'weaponized' its nuclear capability or stockpiled nuclear weapons as such, Pakistani planners would have to assume that India could make the transition to weapons production and deployment with delivery systems in a matter of one or two years, or perhaps just a few months. India detonated a nuclear device in 1974 and must be presumed to have drawn militarily relevant information from that test. If India went nuclear in this fashion, it might, as Pakistanis perceive the situation, use force to take the rest of Kashmir and use the implicit threat of use of nuclear weapons to prevent Pakistan retaliating militarily or defending Kashmir effectively. Thus the case could be made for Pakistan getting itself ready to be able to move into a similar weapons production and deployment program on short notice. This too may have become part of the rationale for the shift in military attitudes.

It should be added, however, that it is doubtful that Pakistan's acquisition of nuclear weapons would have much relevance to defense against major Soviet military threats. The asymmetry there is such that Pakistan would have to fear that nuclear weapons used against Soviet forces would bring unbearable retaliation in kind.

NUCLEAR POLITICS, STABILITY, AND STATUS

The discussion of the nuclear defense and military options may have some relevance to the longer term choices of Pakistan for national defense. But they probably are not operational choices for the moment, and very well may not be for a matter of some years. They do not in any case exhaust the discussion of Pakistan's nuclear options, nor address those most salient today, which are essentially of a political nature. Though political, these are not necessarily trivial because, arguably, they still have something to do with the security of the country, and to that extent cannot totally be divorced from issues of defense.

In the current environment, there are two ways Pakistan is playing nuclear issues politically for some sort of gain versus India, and one way that it is playing them domestically. These are not mutually exclusive options but rather ones that can be adopted simultaneously up to a point. They do entail risks and possible tradeoffs, and in this sense are alternatives to approaches that avoid those risks. The first option versus India is to use the threat of proliferation as a means of bargaining for a mutual pact on nonproliferation. The second option versus India is to arrive at a mutual stalemate around the idea that both countries have a 'bomb in the basement' but that neither needs more if both accept the status quo. Actually, this option, because it freezes ambiguity, can be regarded as a variant of the first. The third option is to do something to convince the Pakistani public that Pakistan enjoys a nuclear deterrent and the security that goes along with it without jeopardizing Pakistan's important international connections, which also add to Pakistan's security and status.

Pakistan has a strong compulsion to be treated as an equal by India. This compulsion arises from nationalism and its expressions in domestic politics. It is a matter that opposition groups seek to test the fidelity to of the government in power by seizing on bilateral issues that come up. The first and second options would both be ways of satisfying this test and thus would be politically attractive in that respect to any government in Islamabad. Only the second option, however, is really compatible with the third.

The first option consists of bargaining for nonproliferation by threatening proliferation. It emulates, in a sense, what India has done on the world scene, but applies it to India. It has a broader purpose, however, of bargaining for *détente* and all the benefits that would entail for Pakistan in recognition of its formally equal status, reduction of tension, and relaxation of military competition. Pakistan has proposed to India not only the concept of a nuclear-free zone (NFZ) for the region but also that both countries sign the NPT and implement its provisions simultaneously. Recognizing India's resistance to these latter ideas, Pakistan has also proposed a bilateral arrangement for mutual nonproliferation assurances and reciprocal inspection of nuclear facilities.

Though it seems unlikely that India would accept bilateral arrangements any more than the NPT or a subcontinental (or even Indian Ocean) NFZ, and though Pakistan undoubtedly is aware of this, the posture of Pakistan therein probably serves Pakistani security interests by drawing international attention to the fact that its own proliferation threat is driven by India's, and that the two are coupled in such a way that dealing with one requires dealing with the other at the same time. It is not impermissible to test this posture of Pakistan. It is clear that only India can do so. Pakistani nationalism could be satiated by a mutual nuclear weapon capability stand-down since it would implicitly be an equal obligation.

Perhaps the more likely course of events would be a tacitly understood or even secretly agreed, mutual freeze of latent nuclear weapon capabilities, i.e., both with some sort of reputed but undeclared 'bomb-in-the-basement' capability. Commentaries by well-known publicists on both sides are indicators of thinking about the desirability of achieving such an understanding.[23] This would not necessarily result in perceptions of physical or political equality between the two nations nor entail any formal acknowledgement of equality, but it would be open to the leaders of either side to promote an interval view that the situation is satisfactory and better than the risks of alternatives, and to finesse the issue of equality in their own ways.

Unfortunately, a mutual freeze of ambiguous capabilities without an inspection system would be fragile and probably unstable. It would be subject to shocks or disturbance from irritants in bilateral relations. It probably could not work if clandestine nuclear procurement and aggressive development of nuclear weapon-relevant capabilities was known to continue or disclosed in one way or another. It might be more stable, however, if both sides accepted the so-called 'fullscope safeguards' (comprehensive IAEA safeguards on nuclear facilities and activities), or an equivalent. The advantage of such safeguards is that there would be a neutral international entity monitoring the situation; an entity, moreover, which has a reputation for judiciousness rather than hasty conclusions.

The advantage of such a freeze would be that it would head off as long as it survived a 'nuclear arms race'. This would also have major beneficial implications for international security and stability. Unfortunately, it probably would not check conventional nuclear arms competition. But it would moderate conventional arms competition to the extent that a 'nuclear arms race' would not be exclusively nuclear, but would, in fact, stimulate conventional weapons and military technology acquisitions[24] for two additional, nuclear-related (more costly) reasons: One reason would be that nuclear warfare conditions require special preparations, not to speak of delivery systems and survivability measures for the delivery systems. The second reason would be that tremendous incentives would come into play to avert nuclear weapon use except *in extremis*, but to achieve that either state would want conventional capabilities that raise the nuclear threshhold to that level, a requirement that would be formidable if it is even achievable for Pakistan.

In short, a mutual freeze of ambiguous capability would not be an inherently attractive option. But it might be attractive as the lesser of evils.

This raises, however, the issue of nuclear explosive testing. India did test in 1974. So far Pakistan has not. Are the mutual-nonproliferation and mutual-freeze of ambiguity options feasible if Pakistan tests, or unless Pakistan tests? There is no easy answer to this question, except on the technical level. It is becoming widely recognized that a nuclear weapon capability can be imputed without demonstrating it by an explosive test. It is recognized about Israel. It is recognized in India about Pakistan. It is recognized within Pakistan among experts and the better-informed publicists. It may even be what Abdul Qadir Khan was driving at when he gave his interviews earlier this year and what President Zia-ul-Haq implicitly endorsed by letting it be made clear that Abdul Qadir Khan was so much in favor that the program he directs henceforth would be named after him.

It is an open question whether India would or, in the face of domestic political reaction, could respond with equanimity to a Pakistani nuclear explosive test. It is more uncertain given the recent violence in India and the tragic events connected with leadership succession. There are those who believe, however, that a single Pakistani test could be accommodated by India.[25] But it must be doubted this would be the case because India has a certain openness and pluralism of view, and its response would not be predictable. There is, in fact, great risk that a Pakistani test would trigger an Indian reaction with resumed testing of its own, and lead inexorably to a 'nuclear arms race'.

We spoke earlier of a way that Pakistan is playing the nuclear issue domestically. It is an option to continue on the same course, which, implicitly, suggests that Pakistan would when it can demonstrate a nuclear explosive capability to clarify for public consumption that the capability exists. The appeal of this is well-stated by Akhtar Ali:

> If Pakistan explodes a nuclear device, so-called peaceful or otherwise, it would nullify the Indian superiority, at least temporarily, and would destroy the basis of the confidence generated in the Indian mind in the wake of events of 1971 and 1974; a psychological climate so necessary to bring about a stable political relationship and a detente of its own type.[26]

What Akhtar Ali is getting at is the psychological balance of perceived risk (and relative national self-confidence) between India and Pakistan. The Pakistani view would be that national self-confidence that Pakistan's immunity from the threat of Indian aggression is high depends on an Indian risk calculus that its own resort to coercive actions against Pakistan would be imprudent. Pakistani perceptions of safety would rise if Pakistan demonstrated nuclear explosive capability. The difficulty an outside observer has with this view is whether those perceptions are accurate. Admittedly Pakistani self-confidence would rise. It is not so clear that Indian self-confidence would diminish or its calculation of risk rise correspondingly.

There are two related observations and subsequent questions. First, there is an important sense in which Pakistani security hinges on resolving internal political divisiveness based on regional ethnolinguistic differences. To the extent that any improvement in defense capability improves the morale of national political leaders and organizations and changes the pitch on which they deal with elements that threaten secession, one can see that reputed nuclear defense capability would strengthen the unity of the country and, in that sense, its security. But the fact is, it is unclear how nuclear politics of this sort really works in Pakistan. If the Bhutto episodes are looked at for lessons, it is just as easy to draw the conclusion that nuclear politics engenders new tensions in national life.

The second issue is whether the political morale-building effects of nuclear politics work to strengthen or rather undermine the possibilities of stable, representative political institutions. There is a longstanding, though exaggerated, charge that foreign military assistance to Pakistan has not only strengthened the military as an interest group in Pakistani politics but predisposed it to political intervention and government takeover. Would not nuclear capability possession reinforce such a tendency to the extent it exists, or institutionalize military control of government in a way that was not true before? This is a serious question because of the intense psychological aura that surrounds nuclear weapons. Who would control them? Who would control the controllers? In a political system where clear civilian control of the military is not a given fact, and where episodes of domestic political instability have chronically reappeared, these questions would not find easy answers, and the results are unpredictable.

THE 'ISLAMIC BOMB' ISSUE

The journalistic treatment of the term 'Islamic Bomb' in Pakistan's case has sometimes been tendentious. Pakistan has not showed any proclivity to want to spread atom bombs through some Islamic network, nor is there evidence that it would want to. But we are faced with certain difficulties here when the issue is treated in strictly symbolic terms. There is no question that Pakistan's acquisition of nuclear capabilities would not be perceived with greater interest by

Islamic countries than by most of the non-Islamic world. It would excite curiosity. It would invite open-ended speculation. It would put Pakistan more in the limelight. Arguably, it would enhance Pakistan's status. It would be unnatural if Pakistani leaders were unconscious of this or studiously brushed aside whatever new elements of influence flew their direction spontaneously from other states.

Zulfiqar Ali Bhutto was a flamboyant leader. There is always some reason to discount political flamboyance. But there is no reason to doubt Bhutto's nationalism. It is of more than usual interest, then, when a former head of government advertizes the fact that he believed in the symbolic importance at least of a nuclear weapon capability in the hands of Pakistan as meaningful in some way to the Islamic world. Once asserted, such statements are very difficult to live down.[27]

Here then lives another political option of nuclear capability in Pakistan, to play on the symbolism of bomb capability for regional status and influence. It can be played in different ways. One may doubt it has military importance. But from a nonproliferation standpoint, it is anything but stabilizing. Fortunately, one might add, this option is one that the current government of Pakistan appears to reject. The problem that remains with it at this time is the expectations of other states in the region.

LEVERAGE ON SECURITY ASSISTANCE

As Shirin Tahir Kheli has pointed out,[28] Bhutto used the threat of nuclear proliferation to seek greater foreign security assistance for Pakistan. Arguably, there is leverage in the threat of proliferation up to the point that the threat is not exercised so that ambiguity remains. In that sense, it may be an unstated element in Pakistani negotiations today over the forms, content, and rate of delivery of Western security assistance.

This is a very troublesome area, however, because it seemingly poses a serious dilemma. It seemingly forces Westerners to weigh nuclear risks to Pakistani and regional security against the risks to security posed by Soviet pressure on the same region, from Afghanistan, and from its own borders on neighbors elsewhere. The complication for Pakistan is that the risk calculus also entails, indeed gives primacy to, perceived threats from India. This problem deserves further study, but in that light it should be questioned whether the problem should be stated in that form. A case can be made, and it is this author's view, that nuclear competition in the subcontinent will itself be a magnet for and more deeply engage Soviet influence in the subcontinent than its absence.

As for the leverage on security assistance providers, this is a matter of skating on very thin ice.

Notes

1. Rodney W. Jones, *The Proliferation of Small Nuclear Forces*, Report for the Defense Nuclear Agency (Washington, DC: Georgetown University Center for Strategic and International Studies, 30 April 1984) pp. 22–23; Leonard Spector, *Nuclear Proliferation Today* (New York: Random House, for the Carnegie Endowment for International Peace, 1984) Richard K. Betts, 'India, Pakistan, and Iran', in Joseph A. Yager (ed.) *Nonproliferation and U.S. Foreign Policy* (Washington, DC: The Brookings Institution, 1980) chs 5–7.
2. For Indian recognition of the capability, see D. K. Palit and P. K. S. Namboodiri, *Pakistan's Islamic Bomb* (New Delhi: Vikas Publishers, 1979); and P. B. Sinha and R. R. Subramanian, *Nuclear Pakistan: Atomic Threat to South Asia* (New Delhi: Vision Books, 1980).
3. Akhtar Ali, *Pakistan's Nuclear Dilemma* (Karachi: Economist Research Unit, 1984); Zalmay Khalilzad, 'Pakistan: The Making of a Nuclear Power', *Asian Survey*, Vol XVI, No. 6, June 1976, pp. 580–592.
4. For more extensive discussion, see Rodney W. Jones, *Small Nuclear Forces* (New York: Praeger Publishers, The Washington Papers, No. 103, 1984), chs 2–3; Rodney W. Jones, 'Atomic Diplomacy in Developing Countries', in John J. Stremlau (ed.) *The Foreign Policy Priorities of Third World States* (Boulder, Co: Westview Press, 1982) pp. 67–96.
5. For a rigorous discussion of motivations and incentives for proliferation and nonproliferation, see Stephen M. Meyer, *The Dynamics of Nuclear Proliferation* (Chicago: The University of Chicago Press, 1984).
6. Lewis A. Dunn, *Controlling the Bomb: Nuclear Proliferation in the 1980s* (New Haven: Yale University Press, 1982).
7. Shai Feldman, *Israeli Nuclear Deterrence: A Strategy for the 1980s* (New York: Columbia University Press, 1983); Henry S. Rowen and Richard Brody, 'The Middle East', in Yager (ed.) *Nonproliferation and U.S. Foreign Policy*, op. cit., chs 8–10.
8. See Richard K. Betts, 'A Diplomatic Bomb? South Africa's Nuclear Potential', in Yager (ed.) *Nonproliferation and U.S. Foreign Policy*, op. cit., ch. 12.
9. Richard K. Betts, 'A Diplomatic Bomb?'.
10. For a somewhat sensational but plausibly detailed account, see Steve Weissman and Herbert Krosney, *The Islamic Bomb* (New York: Times Books, 1981).

11. Rodney W. Jones, *Nuclear Proliferation: Islam, the Bomb, and South Asia* (Beverly Hills, Calif.: Sage Publications, The Washington Papers, No. 82, 1981), see pp. 29–32, especially note 19.
12. Spector, *Nuclear Proliferation Today*, *op. cit.*, p. 100. Cranston did not specify the level of enrichment that Pakistan's operation could reach.
13. Spector, *ibid.*, p. 89.
14. *Nucleonics Week*, Vol. 25, No. 31, 2 August 1984, p. 1.
15. 'Scientist Affirms Pakistan Capable of Uranium Enrichment, Weapons Production', *Nawa-i-Waqt*, 10 February 1984; translated in FBIS/NDP, 5 March 1984; excerpted in Spector, *op. cit.*, p. 99.
16. Jones, *The Proliferation of Small Nuclear Forces*, *op. cit.*, pp. 22–23; Arnold Kramish, 'The Bombs of Balnibarbi', in Rodney W. Jones (ed.) *Small Nuclear Forces and U.S. Security Policy: Threats and Potential Conflicts in the Middle East and South Asia* (Lexington, Mass.: Lexington Books, 1984) chp. 2, especially pp. 27–29.
17. Thomas Pickering, Assistant Secretary of State, 'Nuclear Proliferation: the Situation in India and Pakistan', Hearing before the Subcommittee on Energy, Nuclear Proliferation and Federal Services of the Committee on Governmental Affairs, US Senate, 96th Congress, 1st Session (Washington, DC: US Government Printing Office, 1979).
18. Rodney W. Jones, 'Defense Policy and Modern Weapons in Pakistan,' in Rodney W. Jones and Steven A. Hildreth (eds) *Third World Regional Powers: The Future of Conflict*, (New York: Praeger, forthcoming); Stephen P. Cohen, *The Pakistan Army* (Berkeley and Los Angeles: University of California Press, 1984).
19. Jones, 'Defense Policy and Modern Weapons in Pakistan', and the companion piece, Rodney W. Jones, 'Defense Policy and Modern Weapons in India', in Jones and Hildreth (eds) *Third World Regional Powers*, *op. cit.* (forthcoming).
20. See the traditional military view in Lt.-Gen. (retd.) M. Attiqur Rahman, *Our Defence Cause* (London: White Lion Publishers, 1976); and Bhutto's autobiographical account in Z. A. Bhutto, *If I am Assassinated . . .* (Delhi: Vikas Publishers, 1979); also Weissman and Kropsey, *The Islamic Bomb*, *op. cit.*
21. Jones, 'Defense Policy and Modern Weapons in India', *op. cit.*
22. For recent Indian speculation about this and related prospects, see the symposium 'Pakistan and the Bomb: The Benefits of Ambivalence' in *World Focus Monthly Discussion Journal* Vol. 5, No. 7, July 1984 (especially the contributions by K. Subrahmanyam and A. M. Vohra).
23. For Pakistan, see Akhtar Ali, *Pakistan's Nuclear Dilemma*, *op. cit.*; and for India, see *'Pakistan and the Bomb: The Benefits of Ambivalence,'* *op. cit.*; and Bhabani Sen Gupta, *Nuclear Weapons: Policy Options for India* (New Delhi: Sage Publications India, for Centre for Policy Research, 1983).
24. See George Quester, 'Regional and Worldwide Military Balances, Arms Control and Crisis Management', chp. 9, and Rodney W. Jones, 'Small Nuclear Force Delivery Systems', chp. 3, in Jones (ed.) *Small Nuclear Forces and U.S. Security Policy*, *op. cit.*
25. Bhabani Sen Gupta, *Nuclear Weapons*, *op. cit.*

26. Akhtar Ali, *Pakistan's Nuclear Dilemma, op. cit.*, p. 77.
27. See Bhutto, *If I am Assassinated . . ., op. cit.*
28. *The United States and Pakistan: The Evolution of an Influence Relationship* (New York: Praeger, 1982).

11 The United States and Revolutionary Iran
Richard W. Cottam

For more than a decade prior to the Iranian Revolution, the government of the Shah, Mohammad Reza Pahlavi, had been the primary American surrogate in southwest Asia. Then in January 1979 the Shah was compelled to leave his country. The government of the Islamic Republic of Iran since that time has charted its own course in foreign policy, fully independent not only of the United States but also of the two governments that had for more than a century interfered regularly in Iranian affairs, Britain and Russia. It might be expected that years after the revolution the memory of external control and the bitterness toward the United States would be fading. Yet Iranian soldiers fighting Iraq and large Iranian crowds attending Friday prayer continued to chant 'Death to America'. Iranian officials continued to describe the United States as their greatest enemy. How can this deep and persisting enmity be explained?

BACKGROUNDS OF ANTI-AMERICANISM

The image Iranians held of Americans and American government policy toward Iran through 1951 was close to the opposite of that held today. On several occasions in the early years of American–Iranian relations, the United States government was or seemed to be siding with Iran in its efforts to establish sovereign independence. Iran had been the victim of British and Russian imperialist competition for more than a century before that. In their struggle for influence pre-eminence in Iran, both governments interfered in Iranian domestic affairs. But at critical moments, either Americans or the American government acted to counter the British and/or the Russians. Morgan Shuster, the American financial adviser to the constitutional government of Iran in 1911, was viewed as a hero in the anti-imperialist struggle.[1] In 1919, Woodrow Wilson's Secretary of State, Robert Lansing, ordered the American legation in Tehran to make clear publicly American opposition to the Anglo-Persian Agreement of 1919 which would have institutionalized a semi-colonial relationship in Iran.[2] Then in World War II American diplomats on many occasions opposed both British and Russian policies.[3] Most dramatic of these episodes was the strong American stand in the United Nations insisting on a Soviet military withdrawal from Iran in accordance with a wartime promise to do so. Iranians, especially those most committed to the struggle for real independence, came to see the United States as one western power true to its ideology and a defender of Iranian aspirations for international freedom and dignity.

But this American policy occurred in a period during which American interests in Iran were of low intensity. After World War II, the United States gradually replaced the British as the leading competitor of the Soviet Union for influence in Iran. As this process occurred, American policy toward Iran began to manifest the same patterns that could be seen in earlier British policies. Now, far from viewing sympathetically a strong Iranian nationalist movement and one led by men who fully subscribed to enlightenment values, American policymakers saw that movement as destabilizing and weakening Iran and thereby increasing its vulnerability to Soviet subversion. Harry Truman's secretary of state, Dean Acheson, believed that, however obstreporous and irrational, the Iranian national movement led by Dr Mohammad Mossadeq was more capable of defending Iran's independence than was any possible alternative regime.[4] But Dwight Eisenhower's secretary of state, John Foster Dulles, saw the Mossadeq movement as the British government saw it – a menace to western interests and a functional invitation for the aggressive Soviet purpose.

The decision of the American government to accept the British proposal to plan and orchestrate a coup to remove Mossadeq and his national movement from power in Iran was of historic importance. It involved an alliance with the Iranian traditional elite seeking to establish a tight dictatorial control over a popular movement whose leaders espoused the very ideology the so-called 'free world' claimed to be defending. Furthermore, although the CIA had hoped for non-attributability, the coup was so large and so clumsily executed that it was essentially overt.[5] The American public preferred not to see it. But the rest of the world was a fascinated spectator.

The consequences of that decision affected greatly the form the revolution in Iran was to take and the persisting view of the United States in Iran. First of these consequences was the destruction of the belief that the United States, unlike other western powers, was generally true to its ideology. From this point on, those Iranians who opposed the successor regime to Mossadeq, and even many who favored it, now saw the United States as ideologically hypocritical and in fact motivated by capitalist interests seeking to exploit Iran's resources and people.[6] It follows that America's natural allies in Iran were seen as those individuals willing to trade Iranian national interests for self-interests.

A second consequence was that those individuals, most particularly General Fazlollah Zahedi and the Shah, who were the beneficiaries of a coup supported by foreigners and directed against the man, Mossadeq, who had come to symbolize Iran's quest for independence and dignity, lost forever their nationalist legitimacy. They could be forgiven no more than could Quisling in Norway or Pierre Laval in France. This meant they were denied the ability to appeal to the patriotism of the Iranian people should they be confronted with a serious crisis. It was a source of enduring vulnerability.

But a third consequence had an important offsetting effect to the denial of nationalist legitimacy. In the Iranian view, Americans and Britons had easily manipulated the Iranian political system and removed a leader with a popular appeal that was at the charismatic level. This granted the western imperialists an aura of omnipotence that became an essential ingredient in the longevity of the royal dictatorial regime. Opponents of the Shah simply lacked a sense of efficacy for achieving their desired end. Indeed for several years they concentrated their efforts almost exclusively on convincing the United States that it had made the wrong decision.

The fourth consequence, however, was far and again the most important. Iran was undergoing fundamental change, and the process was both accelerating and close to being irreversible. One of its most important aspects was the development of a predisposition for political participation by an ever-growing percentage of the population. What would be the political values and the preferred political elite this newly awakening mass would embrace? When Mossadeq and the Iranian National Front were in power, they served as the political socializing agents of those entering the system. The norms thus embraced were those of a liberal, democratic, nationalist system. After Mossadeq was abruptly removed and his philosophical allies suppressed, socializing access passed primarily to religious leaders. In 1963, great anti-government demonstrations in urban Iran revealed the fact that a large proportion of the awakening mass was looking to the clerical leadership and specifically to Ayatollah Ruhollah Khomeini for guidance. Since Mossadeq had bested Khomeini's friend and like-thinker, Ayatollah Abol Qassem Kashani, in the access struggle in 1953, it is a fair assumption that Khomeini's pre-eminence would not have developed had the Mossadeq regime survived and consolidated power.

From 1964 through 1976, the Shah's control of this country appeared to him, to most outside observers and to almost all of his countrymen to be almost unshakably stable. The presence of urban guerillas and the Shah's inability to relax expensive and dangerous totalitarian control testified to an underlying lack of positive support and some desperate opposition. But his control system obviously was working, and it rested on two coequal factors.

The first of these factors was the internal coercive system. The Shah's survival in 1963 was due entirely to the effectiveness of his security forces. This included both the military and a number of civilian organizations, most important of which was known best by the acronym SAVAK. The coercive system was in fact a relatively efficient one. But of greatest significance was the popular image it gained. It was perceived as being omnipotent, omniscient and omnipresent. The point was reached that were an individual to risk an open oppositionist stance, friends and colleagues would suspect that he was an agent of SAVAK. No one not its agent, they could reason, would have the temerity to oppose it.

The other aspect of the control system, however, was one that Americans, with little memory of American policy in the 1950s rarely comprehended. This was the persisting belief in Iran that should SAVAK ever falter in its control, the American superpower would come to the Shah's assistance. This belief further reduced any likelihood that opposition elements would directly engage SAVAK. Even if successful, the regime would be saved. The parallel is closer to Eastern Europe than Americans cared to acknowledge. There too, leaders denied nationalist legitimacy could survive because of the popular expectation that the regime would always be saved by its superpower mentor. The American lack of geographical proximity did not reduce credibility in Iran because the illusion of CIA's omnipotence was comparable to that of SAVAK's.

Of equal importance in explaining the regime's longevity was its ability to satisfy at least minimal material demands of its people. Thanks largely to the oil income, the economy of Iran grew at a rate comparable to that of Taiwan and South Korea.[8] Furthermore, until the explosion in the price of oil in late 1973 and 1974, the inflation rate in Iran was acceptably low. The large majority of Iranians could believe that they would be better off next year than this. Landless peasants, most of whom flocked to Tehran and other cities, lived in terrible squalor.[9] But employment opportunities were sufficient to attract foreign labor to Iran. The educated middle class that provided the professional and technocratic base for the society and economy and the element that had a generation earlier provided Mossadeq's support base were coopted by the regime. As events were to demonstrate, they bore it little affection, but they had accommodated. Non-industrial labor and the lower middle class was better described as acquiescent. Real income for them was improving, but the income gap separating them from elements that were profiting at close to the optimal level was widening. These were, more than incidentally, the groups to which most of the newly awakened belonged and to which clerical leaders had their most natural access.

Positive, even occasionally enthusiastic, support for the regime came from those who owed the regime their upward mobility and who profited from it in both economic and influence terms. This included especially officers of the security forces and the newly rich. Easily underestimated is the vital importance of unofficially sanctioned corruption as a control factor. The cognoscenti were well aware of the system of corruption and of those able to preside over it. The struggle for access to those powerful individuals became one of the most significant elements of the political process. And the participants were inextricably tied to the regime.[10]

But the lack of nationalist legitimacy denied the regime a mode of control that in times of crisis can be vital. That is the ability to manipulate symbols to attract the support of the people and to ask them to make great sacrifices to keep the regime alive. Certainly the Shah made every effort to develop an effective set of symbols. For example, his extravagantly financed celebration of 2500 years of kingship in Iran was a failed effort to tie the Pahlavi dynasty symbolically to the Achemenid and Safavid dynasties and the Shah to some of the glorified shahs of the past.

Then when in 1974 Iran began suffering a high inflation rate and some moderately serious economic difficulties, he was unable to make a credible request of his people that they tighten their belts. Economic distress began to develop within the most deprived sections of the population and, as it did, the willingness of these people to acquiesce was reduced. It follows that with a declining utilitarian appeal and an inability effectively to manipulate symbols, the Shah had only one alternative available, and that was to intensify coercive control. Specifically, that required preventing clerics, with their access to increasingly dissatisfied people, from engaging in oppositionist activities, particularly in the form of sermons. The Shah's mystifying failure to do this was in large degree responsible for the particular form the revolution was to take.

It is within this context that Carter's human rights program as it was perceived in Iran must be viewed. Knowledgeable Iranians, and none less than the Shah, were very much aware of the fact that the decision to overthrow Mossadeq was rejected by the Democratic Truman and accepted by the Republican Eisenhower. They also believed that John Kennedy, another Democratic president, had favored a diminution of the Shah's authority in the 1961–62 period. Now another Democrat, Jimmy Carter, had been elected and had announced that a concern for human rights would be a central concern for his foreign policy. For both the Shah and his opposition, the portent of this policy was momentous. The United States was the Shah's mentor. His dictatorship, a direct consequence of an American action, had drastically reduced the expression of human rights in Iran. Continued American support was essential to the Shah's image of invulnerability and especially so given the economic difficulties. It follows that the Shah would believe he must accommodate Carter and, therefore, had no alternative to engaging in a tentative liberalization policy. When he did so, his opposition was doubly encouraged. This was a clear sign that American policy had indeed finally changed to conform once again with American ideology. The Shah now had to accommodate American wishes, and this meant that the latitude granted the opposition was suddenly much expanded. And they acted on this assumption. An underground press appeared, and groups made open demands for greater freedom and a restoration of the rule of law.

In fact, however, there is nothing in American statements or policy that would suggest an understanding of this Iranian reaction. For the Carter administration, the overthrow of Mossadeq, if they were even aware of the American role, was ancient history and had no bearing on the current situation. The rationale – that liberalization such as the Shah was engaging in would lead to a broadening of his support – was universally applied to friendly authoritarian regimes and was entirely innocent of an understanding of historical context. Carter's appointment of William Sullivan, a man with a reputation for a no-nonsense support of anti-communist regimes, as ambassador and his pressure on Congress to approve an AWACS sale to Iran were clear signs of strong support for the Shah. There is indeed no evidence to suggest that the administration was in contact with or even seriously aware of the makeup of the Iranian opposition.[11]

The Shah in his book, *Answer to History*, claims he was receiving mixed signals from the Americans – from Zbigniew Brzezinski encouragement to be tough, from Ambassador Sullivan periodic admonitions to proceed with his liberalization policies.[12] The Shah's response reflected serious ambivalence. He was at times repressive and brutal in dealing with the opposition. But he released political prisoners and certainly improved the treatment of those incarcerated. Most important, though he must have known which of the clerics was involved in the early revolutionary activity, he failed to arrest those such as Ayatollah Mohammad Beheshti, the best organizer and functionally the director of communications for the religious opposition. On the other hand, the Shah did sentence to prison Ayatollah Taleqani, the second most popular of the clerics and a man with excellent relations with the liberal and left secular and religious opposition. In following these patterns, the Shah projected an image of indecisiveness and arbitrariness but also of brutality. He actually, though probably inadvertently, strengthened the radical activists of the Khomeini stripe *vis à vis* the more liberal clerics and the religious laity.

CARTER'S DIPLOMACY

Jimmy Carter as president was inclined to be highly programmatic. He was very much the technocrat, concerned with detail and attentive to execution. But the philosophical underlay was uncertain and often varied sharply from programmatic area to area. This was true of his foreign policy as well. He had prominent in his foreign policy decisional entourage individuals with sharply differing, often contradictory, definitions of the situation. Carter sometimes turned to one view and other times to another, giving full backing to each. Thus, the rationale that underlay policy varied from geographic area to area. There was, as a consequence, no general strategy but rather an uncomfortable mix of regional strategies and tactical schemes.

With regard to dealing with the rapidly developing revolutionary momentum in Iran in 1977 and 1978, three points of view can be identified. Weakest of the three in terms of decisional clout was that associated with advocates of human rights. The suspicions, especially of the Soviet Union, that Carter's concern with human rights was simply instrumental for achieving cold war objectives – a new version of Dulles' roll back strategy – was surely overly cynical. The fact that Carter institutionalized his concern by establishing human rights sections in the Department of State and the National Security Council and peopled them with human rights advocates indicates his sincerity of purpose. As suggested above, this concern had had the inadvertent effect of adding to revolutionary momentum in Iran. But there is little policy evidence to suggest that the human rights section was directly influential in decisions regarding Iran in this crisis period. They were advocates of further liberalization on the Shah's part, but this view appears never to have prevailed. The 'mixed signals' the Shah saw were apparently the result of routine requests for information regarding human rights that all embassies were required to make.

Far more significant in terms of the strength of its advocates was the view that the force of the revolution was sufficiently strong that some form of accommodating it and still maintaining basic governmental stability should be found. Advocates of this view saw the revolutionary forces as entirely indigenous and not directed by the Soviet Union or any other external source. They included Ambassador Sullivan and the Iran Desk of the Department of State. This view coincided with the wishes of what can be described as the reformist wing of the revolutionary movement, that composed of secular and religious liberals who dominated the central leadership of the revolution inside Iran. This group concentrated its efforts on working out a transitional plan that would result in a cabinet dominated by the reformist group with the Shah accepting the position of constitutional monarch. The cabinet would call for free elections and, at that point, a reformist majority was a realistic possibility since most of the leaders were well known individuals and the religious leaders had yet to develop an electoral strategy. After the election, Khomeini would be given a triumphal welcome and the future of the monarchy would be decided, probably by referendum. There were many variations of such a plan proposed, but they all had essentially this outline. The American role would be that of insuring the Shah's acceptance of the plan.[13]

But American policy in the revolutionary period followed rather a third view of which Brzezinski was the primary advocate. According to this view, the Soviet role was a substantial one in the developing revolution. It would be going too far to describe the process as Soviet-orchestrated, although Soviet direction of some participants was apparent. It followed that American policy should be single-mindedly in reinforcing the Shah's position and in encouraging him to take strong measures to defend his position. Jimmy Carter's famous New Year 1978 Tehran statement of extravagant praise of the Shah was fully in tune with this policy. Indeed, the only evidence of any uncertainty was a rhetorical lapse on Carter's part that was probably inadvertent. The seeming acceptance of the transitional plan approach in January 1979 with Shapur Bakhtiar as prime minister was illusory. It came after Iranian advocates of the plan understood that, whatever the prospects for the plan earlier, it had no chance of success in January 1979. The Carter administration acceptance of it was a last, desperate effort to save the army. Brzezinski reportedly subsequently advocated a military coup but by then the military was already in the process of collapse. Many Iranians are convinced that the visit of General Robert Huyser to Iran in these final days was for the purpose of forcing an acceptance of Khomeini on Iran. But supporting evidence for that interpretation is non-existent. The evidence rather supports the purported purpose of the trip, i.e., to assess the state of morale and the viability of the Iranian military.[14]

In the immediate aftermath of the revolution, evidence of hostility toward the United States was overwhelming. But so was evidence of a suspicion and distrust of the Soviet Union. Even the Marxist left, with the exception of the Tudeh Party, which was making its obeisances to the new regime, was hostile to Soviet policy. The view that the revolution was to some degree a product of Soviet planning largely disappeared within Carter's decisional entourage. The most that remained was the non-controversial assumption that the Soviet Union was seeking to ingratiate itself with and to penetrate the new regime.

In the months between the success of the revolution and the taking of American diplomats as hostage, the prevailing view in Washington was that associated with the Department of State's Iran desk. There was apparent to all a fierce power struggle in Iran between the self-proclaimed reformist, Prime Minister Mehdi Bazargan, and his cabinet on the one side, and those who controlled the revolutionary institutions established after the revolution on the other. Equally apparent to all was the fact that the decisive factor in the struggle was Ayatollah Ruhollah Khomeini. Khomeini was at the time a leader whose charismatic appeal seems to have reached a larger percentage of his people than had that of any other leader in human history. That the Iranian people would accept whatever judgment he might make regarding these contending forces was not in question. What was in question was an explanation of why Khomeini failed for so long to make a choice.

The prevailing view in Washington was that Bazargan conceivably could consolidate power, that this was the most desirable outcome and that the United States could play some small role in encouraging that outcome. There was for once an understanding of the historically derived Iranian perception of American intentions in Iran and a realization that any indication of support for Bazargan would damage his prospects. Official policy, therefore, was correct diplomatically – one entirely congruent with the relations of two sovereign, independent governments. But quietly American commercial interests were encouraged to continue or to re-establish operations in Iran, and the administration was responsive to Iranian government overtures in economic matters. The assumption was that economic recovery and a non-threatening American stance would be beneficial to Bazargan's prospects.

However, the American press was following events in Iran with much fascination and very little effort at comprehension. The activities of the revolutionary institutions, especially the courts, received most of the attention. Body counts of the number of executions of individuals tried without benefit of counsel or indeed much else relating to due process were a feature of evening television. The focus of reporting was the bizarre and the excessive. Only rarely did a journalist take note of Bazargan's desperate struggle to gain control over the totality of governmental operations.[15] The lack of any obvious Soviet inroads being made in this troubled Iran made such disinterest possible. Only once in this period was there a strong reaction and then one largely confined to the American Jewish community. Habib Elghanian, a wealthy merchant who had been arrested for corruption by the Shah's regime, was suddenly executed. He was charged, in addition to corruption, as being in touch with leading Israelis and hence an Israeli agent. There was reason to fear that the execution was the beginning of an anti-Jewish campaign. The United States responded to the execution with a resolution of condemnation[16] on the assumption that public opinion pressure could reduced this likelihood.

But the resolution in fact had the result of weakening the position of the Bazargan forces, and Bazargan's foreign ministry responded furiously. The Senate resolution was condemned as blatant interference in Iranian affairs by an American government that apparently could not break its old habits. In retaliation, the Iranian government announced it would not accept as ambassador Walter L. Cutler, who had been selected for that post by the Department of State. Efforts to re-establish American-Iranian relations on a routine formal basis had been set back badly. It can only be a matter of speculation, but it was conceivable that had an ambassador been able to establish good personal relations with Khomeini the hostage crisis could have been avoided.

In this period, too, there was a difference of opinion between Brzezinski and the Iran desk. Brzezinski reportedly saw in Khomeini a man fiercely opposed to Soviet inroads and able to rally his people to that end as well.[17] He was less concerned with the objective of reinforcing the Bazargan reformists, whose view of the Soviets reflected little sense of threat. He could argue effectively the case that the reformists were sure losers in the power struggle and that even a subtle linking of American fortunes to theirs was a mistake. Without question, the indications all pointed to a victory for the clerical revolutionaries. But was that victory inevitable? The answer to that question rested primarily on one's assessment of Khomeini. If he was, as increasing numbers of secular Iranians believed, devious, cunning and calculating, the case could be made that he was engaged in a strategy of weakening the liberal wing and would soon liquidate it without suffering any repercussions. But if the answer was that Khomeini respected and trusted Bazargan and hoped to see a consensus of sincere Muslims regarding a program, the prospects for Bazargan were far from hopeless. The question really was to what extent did Khomeini see fundamental differences in the factional conflict. The prolonged support of Bazargan, long after it was apparent that his one-time base of support had dwindled to a pathetic remnant, argues that he did not see basic philosophical differences. But the fact that again and again when forced to choose between the positions of the contending factions, Khomeini sided with the radical clerics argues that he did.

The case of the three Iranians who were with Khomeini in Paris and who apparently gained his respect and even affection is evidence for the view that Khomeini valued consensus within the Islamic community far above a particular interpretation. Abol Hassan Bani Sadr, Sadeq Qotbzadeh and Ibrahim Yazdi were all to some degree proteges of Bazargan. Yet all three seemed to conclude that their association with Khomeini could be parlayed into their gaining great influence in post-revolutionary Iran and that they could dispense with Bazargan's support. Lacking any real independent base of support in Iran, the three had very little to offer Khomeini in return for his favors other than a promise of effective and loyal leadership. Whereas it is possible to see that a calculating Khomeini could believe he needed to move slowly to erode Bazargan's position – although this involves an assumed overestimating of Bazargan's support base – it is difficult to see why he should have bothered much with the three, knowing, as a clever man would, that they were, like Bazargan, more reformist than revolutionary.

In any event, the point of dispute became moot when on 4 November 1979 the American Embassy was seized for the second time in a year, this time by young students proclaiming themselves 'followers of the line of the Imam'. The immediate cause of the takeover, of course, was anger at the admission of the Shah to a New York hospital for medical treatment. A refusal to admit the Shah was a political impossibility for Jimmy Carter, whose standings in the polls were at an all time low. But soundings had been taken with the Iranian government of probable negative consequences and, although the possibility of an embassy takeover was seen by American diplomats in Iran as a real one, the overall Iranian government attitude did not appear too threatening. However, Khomeini responded to the Shahs' arrival with a harsh, condemnatory speech and his student followers, who had long found the idea an appealing one, made their move. The immediate response of both governmental and revolutionary officials in Iran was that, just as in the earlier takeover, the Americans would quickly be released.[18] Khomeini's decision to sanction the takeover and inaugurate the hostage crisis was a surprise to most of his closest political associates.

The reason Khomeini gave for his action tells much about his mind set. Reportedly, he saw the takeover as clearly in tune with patterns he associated with a divine plan. The United States, one of the two great oppressor states, despite the shock it had received at being unable to keep the Shah on the throne, continued to overestimate its ability to impose its will on the oppressed people of Iran and of the world. This act of taking over the embassy would be another shock and a particularly humiliating one. Hopefully, both the great oppressor and the oppressed peoples would see the illusory basis of oppressor power hegemony in the inability of the United States to free its people. Khomeini opined that this shock too would be insufficient. More would be necessary. But the Americans would be held hostage until Khomeini could see that the United States government had learned the most it would learn from the experience. Then they would be released.[19]

To the Carter administration, the Iranian action was in tune with an Iranian policy of uncertain rationality and bewildering in terms of purpose. How does one respond to such an act? The response came in five phases, the first of which was to impress on the Iranians the minimal price they must pay. Obviously, the demanded turning over to Iran of the Shah was unthinkable and so were any other obvious concessions.[20] This was a phase of unilateral economic punishment. It was not accompanied by a major effort to persuade and cajole others into joining the United States in so punishing Iran. Nor was there a serious threat to carry the reprisals to a military level. This was a period of rapidly growing tensions with the Soviet Union and the likelihood of a Soviet move into Afghanistan was being assessed. A strong American response could not be viewed in isolation by either superpower from the overarching cold war conflict. Furthermore, third world sympathy for Iran, seen as a long-time victim of American interference, would have made a precipitous military move a costly one in terms of popular, though not necessarily in terms of third world governmental, response.

The Soviet occupation of Afghanistan inaugurated the second phase of American policy. Khomeini's response to the Soviet action was one of outrage, and the Iranian government took the lead among Islamic states in condemning the invasion. Since the American world view was essentially one colored by an image of an aggressive Soviet Union, an image sharply reinforced by the move into Afghanistan, the absurdity of the conflict with an Iran, at least as bitterly opposed to the Soviet aggression as the United States, was even more apparent. Therefore, the Carter administration in this phase was willing to explore the possibilities of a settlement with Iran even to the point of risking Carter's domestic political vulnerability.

What these explorings revealed was a strong desire on the part of both the post-Bazergan government and the revolutionary council to bring the crisis to an end but a sensitive awareness of the fact that it would continue as long as Khomeini saw its purpose unfulfilled. Sadeq Qotbzadeh, foreign minister and member of the revolutionary council, advanced a plan for resolution of the crisis.[22] Accepting the conclusion that the prime essential requirement for that purpose was convincing Khomeini that the Americans had learned a lesson in the desired direction, Qotzadeh argued that American policy must at least appear to have changed. Policies that could give such an appearance included acquiescing in a United Nation's preliminary look at evidence of the Shah's criminality, a letter that could be interpreted as something of an apology, and a tolerance of a formal but not real effort to extradite the Shah from Panama. The other worldly quality of these proposals notwithstanding, the Carter administration went along.[23] But it continued with such real world policies as getting a Security Council condemnation of Iran and mobilizing an economic boycott of Iran. On at least three occasions, Qotbzadeh came close to setting in motion the steps leading to the hostage release. Each time, the effort faltered because of the difficulty of orchestrating the Iranian political scene. By April 1980, it was increasingly evident that Qotbzadeh's position was deteriorating and, more ominously, that the hostage issue was becoming intricately enmeshed in Iranian political rivalries.

Washington had had enough of Qotbzadeh's formula.[24] Now the rhetoric sharpened and a brief third phase of American policy was inaugurated. It had all the markings of the strategy that had come to be known as graduated compellence.[25] This involved signalling a condition that must be met – in this case release of the hostages – and an initial punishment that would occur if the condition were not met. Additional signals, purposely vague, would suggest what acts of retribution might be resorted to should the initial punishment prove insufficient. The sharpest signal concerned a threat to blockade Iranian oil shipments passing through the Persian Gulf. More distant threats were possible military action against Iranian ports and airfields.

This period was too short really to go beyond the initial rhetorical or signalling stage. But Iranian responses were those that could be expected from a regime that glorified martyrdom. But there was to be no testing of either the American initiatives or Iranian responses because the main theme of this phase was in fact a rescue attempt of the hostages. The idea of a rescue attempt occurred as soon as it was clear that the crisis would be a prolonged one. But the operation involved monumental difficulties, and planning had to be very refined before top decision-makers could be convinced that the probabilities for success were sufficiently high.

The failure of the attempt strongly reinforced Khomeini's view that he was acting in accordance with divine patterns. How else could the failure at its early stage as a result of mechanical difficulties and a collision be explained?²⁶ The Iranian response, therefore, was almost serene. American impotence had been demonstrated again and dramatically. The resignation of Cyrus Vance as secretary of state and the appointment of Edmund Muskie who vowed that he, and by implication not Brzezinski, would be the primary foreign policy formulator meant an end to a bellicose third phase of policy toward Iran.

The fourth phase, lasting from May until 12 September 1980, was really a period of no new initiatives. Elections for parliament were held in Iran, and the victorious candidates overwhelmingly were those associated with the Islamic Republic Party. That 'party' was in fact an umbrella association that included individuals whose views ranged from radical revolutionary to conservative in terms of institutional change and policy. The liberal reformist element that was elected was a tiny minority and clearly the end was in sight for President Bani Sadr, but once this struggle was over, new ones would quickly occur. Khomeini's leadership style was consistently one of avoiding close association with any of a number of evolving factions. The result was sustained conflict with factional fluidity a characteristic feature. The one clear focus was that of the president versus the parliamentary majority.

In this milieu, strong leadership in foreign policy, such as Sadeq Qotbzadeh had for a time exercised, was no longer possible. Indeed, there was nothing in the way of an Iranian policy position that the Carter administration could respond to. Then on 12 September the administration was told by the West German government that Khomeini would make an important statement.²⁷ He did. What he had to say appeared to confirm the Qotbzadeh interpretation. He said in effect that Iran had demonstrated American inability to impose its will on the oppressed people. Having done so, a settlement could be negotiated by his government around four terms, which he had long understood would be acceptable to the American government and indeed were the terms ultimately agreed to. But he gave his government full freedom to get the best terms possible. He in effect was now washing his hands of the affair. Apparently, he had concluded that America had learned all it would learn from this shock.

Khomeini's statement inaugurated the fifth and final stage of American policy in the hostage crisis. It was essentially one of responding to any movement from the Iranian government to put into effect Khomeini's instructions. The Algerian representative in Tehran, Abdel Karim Gharaieb, was probably the most respected and influential member of the diplomatic community. He and his government understood quickly that Khomeini's statement provided the basis for successful mediation on their part. But the negotiations were going to be exceedingly difficult for two reasons – Iraq's attack on Iran nine days after the speech and Iran's internal political struggle.

President Bani Sadr and his opponents in parliament were in full agreement on one point: the Iraqi attack was part of an American orchestrated plan to punish and overturn the Khomeini regime.[28] Khomeini had made clear in countless speeches his conviction that the great oppressor states, although their rivalries were real, would unite to attempt to defeat so fundamental a challenge to their hegemony. Thus, it should come as no surprise that Iraq, long a client of the Soviet Union, should appear as primary executor of an American plan. The fact that Iraq was supported by Jordan, a premier example of an American puppet state, was simply unnecessary confirming evidence of the case. Israel's hand, too, was apparent to the Iranians in the conspiracy although the case here was almost entirely a logical one – the small oppressor, tool of the United States, had to oppose Iran, the leader of the oppressed peoples. Therefore, the Iranian government announced a freeze on hostage negotiations and for several weeks no progress was possible.

Once Iran's ability to withstand the attack was apparent, movement began again with the negotiations. But now the obstacle was more internal. The lead in negotiations was taken by opponents of Bani Sadr and, despite his earlier efforts to release the hostages, the president now sought to take some demagogic advantage at the expense of the negotiations. Compromise with the great oppressor was by now hardly the most popular path to follow, and Bani Sadr made the most of his advantage.[29] It began to appear, in fact, that the negotiations could not produce a settlement before the inauguration of President Reagan. However, suddenly the Iranians became more cooperative. Why they did so is not fully explained. But the best thesis is that someone, probably Ayatollah Mohammad Beheshti, persuaded Khomeini to issue strong instructions that negotiations be completed before Carter left office.[30] Because of the complications resulting from the internal conflict, the settlement could easily have fallen apart. But the hostages finally left Tehran on the American presidential inauguration day.

REAGAN'S DIPLOMACY

The Reagan campaign for the presidency in 1980 argued the case that Carter had allowed America's great friend, the Shah of Iran, to fall and promised there would be no such lapses in a Reagan administration. The case for their contention was not developed, however, and it was never clear what they felt Carter could have done to keep the Shah in power. Nor was any indication given of what kind of policy a Reagan administration would adopt for dealing with the Islamic Republic of Iran. After the election, the Reagan transition team was deluged with suggestions from Iranian exiles as to the kind of policy that should be followed.[31] Although innumerable groups were represented, each with its own preferred candidate to lead a future Iran, all agreed that the United States government should support a coup against Khomeini.

There is no reason to question the administration's sincerity in its insistence that no other friends of America would be allowed to collapse. Indeed, Arab leaders with a relationship to the United States comparable to that the Shah had had were given explicit guarantees of support. But the Iranian exiles were disappointed in the response to their appeals. Reagan administration officials were no more inclined to accept a contention that the Khomeini regime was weak, vulnerable, unpopular and easily overturned than Carter officials had been. The situation was not comparable to that of 1953. Then the percentage of the population that was politically participant was small, probably no more than 10 to 15 per cent. Traditional elites were able to control the countryside, provincial towns and the means for bringing into the streets of the cities large mercenary mobs. In 1979, the level of political participation was close to European standards. Traditional elites had lost most of their influence. Whereas it may well be true that Khomeini was down to a 15 to 30 per cent core support base, that support was at a level of intensity at which people were ready to risk their lives for the regime. Furthermore since the support base was urban lower and lower middle class, it was easily mobilized by political leaders. Huge crowds could be turned out in any of the large Persian or Turkish-speaking cities. The regime clearly was unpopular among Kurds and Baluchis, but control elsewhere was secure. The majority may well have disliked the regime, but it was thoroughly intimidated and lacking in any sense of efficacy. The regime's immediate vulnerability was a product of factionalized leadership, incomplete institutionalization and excessive reliance on a charismatic leader for mobilizing support. But as long as Khomeini lived and the various factions were unreceptive to making alliances with elements opposed to the regime, prospects for success for any coup plan were poor.

But if the option of supporting a coup to overturn Khomeini was not realistic, what should a policy toward the Islamic Republic of Iran be? American policy in the Middle East since World War II has been one of seeking to achieve three basic objectives: contain and deter perceived Soviet expansionism, maintain the flow of oil and of petrodollars to the United States and its friends and allies, and maintain Israeli security. Over time, a general policy evolved by which these three objectives with their implicit contradictions could be reconciled. The formula for doing so was one of forming a *de facto* alliance with a group of Middle East leaders who were conservative, anti-communist, open to full cooperation with multinational corporations and western banks and willing to limit their opposition to Israel to a rhetorical level. These leaders, always described by the American code words 'moderate' and 'responsible', it follows, had to be supported. Any indication that they might be abandoned could destroy the basis of American policy in the area.

Regional leaders, such as Hafez Assad of Syria, who were opposed to this conservative alliance, normally saw as their only option one of establishing a working relationship with the Soviet Union. They were, therefore, likely to be perceived by American policymakers as Soviet clients and the instruments of Soviet policy in regional affairs. But Khomeini and his regime could not be so easily classified. Their anti-Soviet attitude was given policy expression in Afghanistan, in dealing with domestic communists and in the difficulties placed in the Soviet path in such matters as the sale of natural gas. Yet the radical Islamic movement personified by the Khomeini regime was a threat to every American ally with a large Muslim population in the area. If the Reagan administration really meant to support its friends in the face of internal challenges, some plan for dealing with radical Islamic forces should be developed.

In sharp contrast to the Carter administration, which included in important positions individuals with significantly different world views, the Reagan administration was very much of one mind. Soviet policy in the Middle East could be described as 'cautious', but no one in the Reagan administration doubted the ineluctable quality of its aggressive intent. A basic strategy thus was easily designed: oppose firmly every manifestation of Soviet efforts to enlarge its influence in the area. But the tactical plans for accomplishing this strategy were not at all self-evident. Except for Afghanistan, none of the regional crises could be translated easily in terms of a Soviet challenge. Indeed, the radical Islamic element was more of a constant feature, and this was true even in Afghanistan. Thus, whereas the Carter policy in the area tended to be a set of tactical programs that often were strategically contradictory, the Reagan policy was a strategy with only an occasional supporting tactical plan. The result was a loss of control of the dynamics of the situation. The Reagan administration was in a position of responding to the initiatives of others.

The best the analyst can do given this lack of defined policy is to identify some tendencies in American reactions to events that could crystallize into a firm policy. The first of these tendencies is that of tilting toward Iraq in the Iran–Iraq conflict. That conflict ranks with the Arab–Israeli conflict and the Afghanistan situation as those most likely to give definition to American policy in the area. It is a crisis that affects all three basic American objectives and in contradictory ways.

When Saddam Hossein invaded Iran in September 1980, he did his best to describe the conflict in Arab vs. Iranian terms. But his efforts were unsuccessful. Saddam Hossein only two years earlier had taken initiatives in opposing Sadat's diplomacy that gave him a major claim to being the chief defender of the progressive and Arab nationalist position in the Arab world. Then in a sharp reversal, he shifted his alliances away from Syria, Libya, Algeria, the PLO and South Yemen toward Saudi Arabia, Jordan and Morocco. This move was accompanied by a weakening of his ties to the Soviet Union. He took severe action against local communists and condemned the Soviet Union for its invasion of Afghanistan. Everything indicated a shift toward the United States. Saddam's attack on Iran and the expected easy victory should have restored whatever standing with Arab nationalists he may have lost as a consequence of his close association with regimes viewed as American clients. Not only would Khomeini have been eliminated, and with him the challenge from Islamic radicalism, but the oil-rich province of Khuzistan, which he called Arabistan, would be incorporated in Iraq.[32] A secular and subordinate Iranian regime, probably under Shapur Bakhtiar, would make peace with Iraq. Saddam Hossein would be the number one leader of the Arab nation;[33] his Arab enemies would be isolated; his new found friends would have no recourse to accepting his leadership. His bargaining position with the two superpowers would be very strong.

But it was not to be. Saddam Hossein had badly underestimated the strength of the Islamic movement in Iran. After a few weeks, it was obvious that Iran would not be defeated and that the most Saddam Hossein could hope for, and that with the support of his friends, would be survival. The Syrian–Iranian alliance was strengthened, and, in 1982, it appeared briefly likely that Iraq would be defeated. At that point, there was open speculation about the consequences of such an eventuality, especially in the Arabian peninsula. But no clear policy response emerged from Washington even though America's closest Arab friends appeared to be in jeopardy. Then, as the Iranian inferiority in weaponry made any early Iranian victory unlikely, the sense of urgency evaporated.

The case was further complicated by improved Soviet–Iraqi relations and the shipment of increasing amounts of Soviet military equipment to Iraq. Then, when the Iranians arrested and began prosecuting Tudeh Party officials, Soviet–Iranian relations deteriorated. This coincided with increasing evidence of an American tilt toward Iraq. Iraq was removed from the list of governments aiding terrorists thus opening up trade possibilities; and diplomatic contacts intensified until the restoration in November 1984 of diplomatic relations. At the same time, the United States was not only withholding the sale of arms from Iran, but also urging all of its friends to do likewise. Defense assistance was granted to Gulf states threatened by Iranian retaliation for supporting Iraq. The United States and the Soviet Union almost seemed to be allies in an effort to contain the military advance of Islamic activism.

Relating American policy toward the Iran–Iraq conflict to the three basic objectives in the Middle East poses some real difficulties. *De facto* cooperation with the Soviet Union in support of an Arab regime, Iraq, that Israelis have seen as seriously threatening appears to contradict two of the three objectives. Furthermore, it is Iraq, not Iran, that is the initiator in attacking oil shipping in the Persian Gulf. The alliance with conservative Arab states, which was in the past seen as instrumental for the achievement of the three objectives, seemed now to be an end and one damaging to the three objectives.

American policy in Afghanistan was unequivocally anti-Soviet, but there the forces of Islamic activism were primary instruments for containing or at least tormenting the Soviet occupation forces. This brought the United States into *de facto* alliance with Iran since the Iranians were supporting some of the same Afghan rebel forces.

Moving to the Arab–Israeli conflict area, the overall picture is further muddied. In Lebanon, both the Americans and the Israelis have suffered setbacks at the hands of indigenous Lebanese forces. Of these, Shiite activists are now most important. Increasingly, they are following the lead of men with close relations with the Iranian leaders. Since the Syrian–Iranian alliance has been strengthened and Soviet–Syrian relations have remained close, the circle is completed. The Soviets stand as *de facto* allies with Islamic activism and with Iran in the Lebanese theatre.

What this picture of gross foreign policy contradictions reflects is the point made above: American policy has lost control of regional dynamics. The same point can be made of Soviet policy. Of regional factors, the PLO and Iraq have suffered serious losses of influence. Far more surprising, Israeli policy, for many years one of the major determinants of regional dynamics, has begun to lose that determining force. The reason for that is a growing awareness that the Israeli incursion into Lebanon resulted in a serious, resource-draining over-extension. This, in turn, has led to a diminution of the Israeli capability image. To be sure, Israel continues to be seen as overwhelmingly powerful in her own sphere. It is the size of that sphere that is now more in question.

The one obviously growing force behind regional dynamics is Islamic political activism. Here again, however, the contradictory trends and responses noted above are accurate reflections of the inchoate nature of the Islamic movement. Every government in the area is aware of the growth in Islamic political activism among its people, and each has developed a strategy of its own for dealing with it. But they are aware as well of the highly diverse manifestations of this activism. Sectarian and factional differences stand in the way of any close coordination of activities from one state to the next and even within states. The triumph of a clerical leadership in Iran has alerted opposition secular elements to the danger of a secular–sectarian alliance, thus weakening somewhat overall opposition strength. Yet there is no compensating assistance from an established religious government in Iran. Except in some Shia areas, Khomeini has not achieved anything approaching the charismatic appeal he has in Iran. Thus, an initial fear that Islamic activism would overturn additional regimes has declined, and there is in the region an underestimation of the force of Islamic activism in regional and international affairs.

Iran's great achievement in this equation is scarcely recognized. Iraq is receiving external assistance from conservative oil-producing

Arab regimes, from Egypt and Jordan, from France, from the Soviet Union and indirectly from the United States. Iran, on the other hand, confronted with a major effort by the United States to block military sales and indeed all sales with any technical military potential, must struggle to purchase arms and spare parts. She does so primarily from mercenary arms agents, some of whom ironically have been in the employ of the Israeli government. Nevertheless, despite the resulting advantage to Iraq in terms of weaponry, Iran not only has had no difficulty in containing the Iraqis but is in a position to take the initiative on the long front. Were Iran to break out of her diplomatic isolation, the military advantage could shift rapidly in her direction.

The ambivalence of both Soviet and American policy toward Iran and toward Islamic political activism is obvious. Functionally, Soviet and Iranian policy are allied in the eastern Mediterranean, and American and Iranian policy are allied in Afghanistan. This suggests the Iranians could easily make a case for a more explicit working relationship with either superpower. But, given Ayatollah Khomeini's rigidly held view of the superpowers as the nucleus of oppressor hegemony over the oppressed, such a move by Iran is unlikely.

Less easily explicable is Iran's neglect of the potential for allying with other Islamic movements, especially the Islamic Brotherhood in the eastern Arab states. Khomeini has been adamant in his insistence that the movement he leads is broadly Islamic, not simply Shiite. Yet in both Afghanistan and the Arab world, Iranian foreign policy has not, at least on the surface, made any serious effort to build an alliance among Islamic forces generally. With regard to the Islamic Brotherhood, for example, the Iranians chose to back Hafez Assad in his moment of confrontation with the Brotherhood at Hamma in 1982.

That decision can be explained as one of several that reflect the pragmatism of the Iranian foreign office and of Foreign Minister Velayati in particular. Other policies on the list are the purchase of military supplies from agents of the Israeli government, and efforts to establish good relations with Turkey and Pakistan, both close allies of the United States. But that explanation could be too facile. Dr Velayati, in explaining Iran's policy, argued the Brotherhood by weakening Syria at the very moment that Israel was obviously planning its invasion of Lebanon was in effect aiding the cause of the oppressors by weakening the one regime in the oppressed Arab world willing to stand up to the challenge. His argument went to the core of the dilemma faced not only by the Brotherhood but by Khomeini as well.

Believing as he does that he is serving divine purpose by demonstrating to the oppressed peoples that they can overturn the domination and exploitation of the oppressors, Khomeini has looked with great favor on regimes such as that of Syria whose policies have been true to this objective. But Khomeini sees his purpose as well one of demonstrating to the peoples of the world that the divine plan, as revealed in the Qoran, is the one path for achieving true self-realization. How then is one to deal with individuals and regimes which fight the oppressors but which are unalterably secular? In Iran, Khomeini dealt with his one-time secular allies brutally, effectively purging them from even a significant societal role. The Brotherhood, by identifying secular nationalists as more of an obstacle to the achievement of their objectives – not dissimilar from Khomeini's – allied with conservative forces that in turn were the allies of the great oppressor, the United States. But Iranians are not impressed.

The Iranian definition of the situation doubtless reflects Iranian preoccupation with the conflict with Iraq. But it is as well essentially true to the highly abstract world view of Ayatollah Khomeini. As he sees it, the oppressors must make the effort to destroy the primary challenge to their hegemonic control – the government of the Islamic Republic. They, therefore, must bury their own rivalries and amass their forces against Iran. Their primary instrument is Saddam Hossein and his 'Baathist clique'. But the entire array of regional puppets is being mobilized to support that instrument. Even so, this satanic policy has failed to subdue Iran, and this is clear evidence of divine assistance.[34]

With such an integrated picture, specific policies are easily explained. Iraqi attacks on Iranian oil shipments, for example, are treated in the western press as designed to provoke the United States and European states into confrontation with Iran, thus benefiting Iraq. But in the official Iranian explanation, Saddam Hossein is following American directives, as he always does and the design is to make a direct American attack on Iran more acceptable to the world public.[35] Yassir Arafat's effort to marry the PLO with conservative Arab policy simply reveals him as a minor actor in the oppressor stable. And, it follows, the Brotherhood's cooperation with Arafat and King Hossein reveals them as being under the control of particularly insidious leaders – leaders who attempt to clothe Satan's purpose in Islamic garb.

The option available to Iran of developing a strategy focused on the objective of coordinating Islamic forces throughout the region appears on the surface to be unexplored. Velayati's statement regarding the Brotherhood, however, did reveal a detailed picture of the Brotherhood leadership and pointed to the erring individual leaders. This suggests that the tactic of becoming involved in internal factional conflicts within such organizations may be being explored. If so, Iran's importance in regional affairs could increase suddenly and decisively. More likely, though, is Iran's following the lead of indigenous Islamic forces in various states and responding to their requests for assistance. The extraordinarily rapidly developing strength of the political expression of Shia Islam in south Lebanon is a case in point. As Syria loses control of events in south Lebanon, the attraction of the movement to anti-Assad Sunni Lebanese grows and a Sunni–Shia alliance becomes a possibility. Iran predictably will come under conflicting pressures – to restrain Shiite militance from Syria, to give full support to a uniting movement from the Shiite Lebanese.

The scenario suggests an even more basic probability: that events, the product of indigenous forces, will produce a crystallization of American and Soviet policies in the region. The crystallization for the United States is likely to be one that results in a new formula for reconciling the three major American objectives in the area. Most easily predictable of the type of event that could result in such crystallization is that of terrorist attacks. Predisposed as it is to see terrorism as the preferred tactic of groups with ties to the Soviet Union, the American government could easily perceive acts of terrorism carried out by militant Islamic groups as ultimately, if indirectly, Soviet orchestrated. Or the orchestration could be seen as Iranian. In either event, retaliatory attacks could follow against Syria and/or Iran. These in turn could lead to a closer, and for Iran a direct, working relationship with the Soviet Union. Pushing militant Islam toward the Soviet Union would, in turn, have serious consequences for every American ally in the Islamic world. All are confronted with strong Islamic political movements, and each has followed its own strategy for dealing with the movement in its borders. The American action would, hence, be destabilizing and could easily lead to new strong appeals for assistance from an America already concerned with being overextended.

There are many other types of events that could lead to somewhat different response patterns on the part of the United States. An

Israeli inability to extricate herself from Lebanon, for example, could lead to serious counter-pressures on the United States – on the one side from Israel and on the other from Islamic states friendly to the United States. The overturning of a secular government of important Arab states and its replacement by an Islamic government would force the United States to develop a major policy response. Escalation in the Persian Gulf to the point of an Iranian effort to close the Strait of Hormoz would do the same. But probably most compelling of a major American response would be an Iranian military breakthrough in Iraq. Any of these events would be likely to produce a policy toward Iran and politically activist Islam that could well determine the nature of American's relations with Iran and Islam for some time to come. There are no indications that a policy will evolve without some such precipitating event.

In spite of Khomeini's efforts to alter capability images in the Middle East, there remains an exaggerated view of American capability in the area and an underestimation of Iranian capability. Another set of events comparable in importance to the overthrow of the Shah, the invasion of Afghanistan and the Israeli incursion into and then retreat from Lebanon, however, would be likely to produce an altered perspective – one closer to power realities. The result would be fewer options available to the United States in the area and more available to the Islamic Republic of Iran.

Notes

1. Morgan Shuster, *The Strangling of Persia* (New York: 1912).
2. See for this episode Abraham Yeselson, *United States–Persian Diplomatic Relations, 1883–1921* (New Brunswick: Rutgers University Press, 1956) p. 164.
3. See American diplomatic correspondence concerning Iran 1941–45 for innumerable comments to this effect. Compiled in *Foreign Relations of the United States*. See for an extended, but typical, example 11 February 1943, *Foreign Relations of the United States*, 1943, Volume IV, pp. 331–36.
4. Dean Acheson, *Present at the Creation* (New York: Norton, 1969).
5. Kermit Roosevelt, *Countercoup: The Struggle for Control of Iran* (New York: McGraw Hill, 1979) The book illustrates the point rather than making it.
6. For an Iranian perspective, typical of left nationalists, see Bahman Nirumand, *Iran: The New Imperialism in Action* (New York: Monthly Review Press, 1969).

7. Richard Cottam, *Nationalism in Iran* (Pittsburgh, University of Pittsburgh Press, 1979) See the discussion of the Iran Party Manifesto, pp. 234–35.
8. For an advocate's picture of the economic and social accomplishments under the Shah, see Jehangir Amuzegar, *Iran: An Economic Profile* (Washington: Middle East Institute, 1977).
9. Farhad Kazemi, *Poverty and Revolution in Iran* (New York: New York University Press, 1980).
10. Robert Graham, *Iran: The Illusion of Power* (New York: St. Martin's Press, 1978) This is an excellent account of the influence system operating in the Shah's Iran.
11. See Richard Cottam, 'Arms Sales and Human Rights: The Case of Iran', in Peter G. Brown and Douglas MacLean (eds) *Human Rights and U.S. Foreign Policy* (Lexington, MA: D.C. Heath, 1979).
12. Mohammad Reza Pahlavi, *Answer to History* (New York: Stein and Day, 1980).
13. Ambassador Sullivan's account is a candid appraisal of the decisional locus, William Sullivan, *Mission to Iran* (New York: Norton, 1981) It should be read along with Zbigniew Brzezinski, *Power and Principle* (New York: Farrar, Straus, Giroux, 1983) pp. 354–400.
14. See the discussion of Huyser's mission in Iran in Sullivan, *op. cit.*, pp. 36–37 and Brzezinski, *op. cit.*, pp. 376–96.
15. Oriana Fallacci's interviews with Khomeini and Bazargan are examples of some excellent reporting, *New York Times* 7, 28 October 1979.
16. *New York Times*, 10, 13, 16, 21 May 1979.
17. This was Bazargan's recollection of a conversation with Brzezinski in Algiers. Interview, Tehran, November 1979.
18. Mohammad Beheshti told an Iranian political leader interviewed in November 1979, and better not named, that the hostages would be released in six hours. Sadeq Qotbzadeh in an interview the same day told me he alone of the Revolutionary Council members understood that Khomeini would sanction the taking of hostages.
19. This was explained to me by Qotbzadeh in a series of interviews in Tehran in November 1979. I remained in regular trans-Atlantic telephonic contact with him for the next fourteen months.
20. Qotbzadeh stated at my first interview in November 1979 that Khomeini fully understood that the American government could not under any circumstances return the Shah to Iran.
21. Meeting with Hamilton Jordan, Pittsburgh, January 1980.
22. Qotbzadeh's thinking is well summarized in Pierre Salinger, *America Held Hostage: The Secret Negotiations* (Garden City, NY: Doubleday, 1981).
23. Hamilton Jordan, *Crisis: The Last Year of the Carter Presidency* (New York: Putnam, 1982).
24. *Ibid.*, pp. 245–46.
25. The theory of graduated compellence is advanced in Thomas Schelling, *Arms and Influence* (New Haven: Yale University Press, 1966).
26. This theme runs through a large percentage of Khomeini's speeches. Apparently the episode was very reinforcing for him.

27. Jordan, *op. cit.*, p. 341.
28. This view was expressed repeatedly and examples can be found in almost any week. For example, on 21 January 1981 Bani Sadr, in a speech at Qazvin, reported in *Keyhan* 25 January 1981 developed the case at some length. The Tehran Radio, under control of his enemies, developed the case very similarly a few days later, 4 February 1981.
29. Bani Sadr's attitude was reflected in his newspaper, *Enqellab Islam*. See, for example, that of 25 January 1981 for his response to the hostage release.
30. This was a thesis advanced to me by Qotbzadeh in a telephonic conversation January 1981.
31. The consensus of Iranian exiles interviewed on this subject was that General Gholam Ali Oveissi was most effective in dealing with the transition team but that even he was deeply disappointed.
32. See for Iraqi statements on the war, Tareq Y. Ismail, *Iran and Iraq: Roots of Conflict* (Syracuse: Syracuse University Press, 1982).
33. For a description of Iraqi television depiction of Iraq as the leader of the Arab world in Fall 1980 see Daniel B. Tinnin, 'Iraq and the New Arab Alliance', *Fortune*, 3 November 1980, pp. 44–46.
34. See Khomeini's address to the nation, 15 February 1983, for a full development of this theme.
35. This point is developed at length in an article by H. Musavian, 'From Persian Gulf War to World War', *Tehran Times*, 6 June 1984, p. 3.

12 The Soviet Union and the Islamic Republic of Iran
Shireen T. Hunter

For two centuries, one of Iran's principal preoccupations has been relations with Russia/the Soviet Union. During this period, basic patterns of political and economic interaction have developed between the two countries – patterns whose essential features have survived changes in their respective ideologies and regimes while responding and adapting to new circumstances.

This long interaction has left a deep imprint on Iranian perceptions of Russian intentions and on the Russians' perceptions of their vital interests in Iran, significantly affecting their policy choices concerning each other and other countries. This interaction and its results are likely to continue. Thus an analysis of present Soviet–Iranian relations requires prior understanding of traditional patterns of Russo–Iranian relations and deep-rooted perceptions. Therefore, while the primary focus of this paper will be on Soviet relations with the Islamic Republic, it will place these relations in their historical and psychological context.

RUSSO–IRANIAN RELATIONS FROM THE FALL OF THE SAFAVID EMPIRE TO THE END OF THE QAJAR DYNASTY (1722–1925)

The basic pattern of Russo-Iranian relations was laid down when the once-powerful Safavid Empire crumbled, heralding a long period of Iranian decline, while the Russian Empire was entering a new phase of expansion under Peter the Great. Taking advantage of Iran's chaos in the wake of the Afghan invasion, Russia occupied Iran's northern provinces, thus establishing a long-term pattern of incursion and expansion.[1] Yet Russia also faced a formidable rival in the Ottoman Empire.[2] Russo–Turkish rivalry significantly influenced Russian strategy towards Iran. This indicated another long-term pattern, namely, the impact of rivalry with other powers on Russian strategy towards Iran. Whenever Iran was threatened with total domination by a rival power, Russia tried to prevent that occurrence while also securing advantages for itself.[3]

Yet the rivalry of other powers was seldom strong enough to preclude their accommodation at Iran's expense, as indicated by Russo–Turkish agreement in 1729 to partition Iran, thereby establishing another recurring pattern in Russo–Iranian relations.[4] European politics played a role in this, illustrating the vulnerability of Russo–Iranian relations to European power politics. This, too, was to become an important aspect of Russo–Iranian relations.

Following the fall of the Safavids, however, Iran's total disintegration was averted by the emergence of a new military leader, Nadir Shah Afshar, who later became Iran's king. Nadir reunited Iran and restored its old borders.[5] Nadir's successes, including those *vis à vis* Russia, illustrated the significance of Iran's internal conditions, especially the strength of its central government, on the state of its relations with Russia. But Nadir's successes were also due in part to the fact that, by this time, Peter the Great had died and Russia's expansionist thrust had slowed. This, too, was an early indication of the impact of internal changes in Russia on the state of Russo–Iranian relations.

QAJAR DYNASTY AND RUSSIA'S TERRITORIAL AND POLITICO-ECONOMIC EXPANSION IN IRAN

Soon after Nadir's death, conditions deteriorated in Iran. Only after a long period of internal turmoil and short-lived dynasties did Agha Mohammad Qajar restore some measure of internal stability to Iran and succeed to its throne. However, instability and rebellion in many of Iran's outer provinces, especially Georgia, did not end and finally involved Iranian and Russian military intervention.[6] But the Georgian question remained unresolved because of the deaths of Catherine the Great and Agha Mohammad Khan.[7]

RUSSO–IRANIAN WARS, 1804–1826

The unresolved Georgian problem was the immediate cause of the first round of Russo–Iranian wars.[8] But the underlying reason was that the Russian Empire, under the leadership of Alexander I was again on the march.

The first round of wars started in 1804, lasted nine years, and ended with the Treaty of Gulistan.[9] The second round began in 1826 over disagreements regarding certain provisions of the Gulistan Treaty and Russian mistreatment of the Muslims in conquered territories. It lasted three years and ended with the Treaty of Turkmanchai. The treaty proved to be disastrous for Iran's political future. In fact, in the Iranians' view the Treaty of Turkmanchai is second, in terms of national humiliation, only to the Arab victory over the Sassanid empire.[10] The most damaging aspects of the treaty were its non-territorial provisions, which granted Russia extraterritorial rights, significant trade concessions, heavy war reparations, and an actual veto power over the succession issue.

The Treaty of Turkmanchai thus ushered in a very long period of Russian domination of Iran's economic and political life, clearly illustrated by the following statement nearly a century after the conclusion of this treaty:

> Northern Persia was now to all intents and purposes a Russian province . . . Little by little the whole machinery of administration had been placed in the hands of the Russian consuls. The Governor General of Azerbaijan was a mere puppet who received and carried out the orders of the Russian Consul General and the same might be said of the Governors of Rasht, Kazvin, and Julfa. They were one and all agents of the Russian government and acted in entire independence of the central government in Tehran. Large numbers of Persians were being converted into Russian-protected subjects and the taxes were being collected by the Russian Consul to the exclusion of the agents of the Persian financial administration.[11]

In addition, Iran was heavily indebted to Russia, and Russia controlled the only viable military force in Iran, the Persian Cossacks.

Moreover, the treaty further undermined Iran's independence, because other powers claimed privileges similar to those granted to Russia. Russo–Iranian wars also marked the beginning of Iran's greater involvement with other Europeans. Britain ultimately emerged as the other dominant power in Iran. The preponderance of Russian and British influence in Iran, with no other countervailing power, thus put Iran's destiny at the mercy of the vagaries of

Russo–British relations. In the final analysis, Russo–British rivalry maintained Iran's nominal independence, but whenever this rivalry subsided Iran's independence was seriously threatened. Russian advances in Caucasia and later in Central Asia also created new geopolitical realities for Iran that still persist. Thus, instead of having small princedoms (Khanat) as buffers, Iran came to face the Russian Empire across a 1200-mile border. Over the years, this geopolitical reality has greatly affected Iran's policy choices *vis à vis* Russia/the Soviet Union and other powers.

To sum up, the basic pattern of Russo–Iranian relations in this period was one of domination and expansion by Russia, and submission and retrenchment by Iran. It was affected by (1) The growing power of Russia and the declining force of Iran; (2) Russian rivalries with other powers, particularly Britain; (3) The state of European politics; (4) Domestic conditions in Russia and Iran; and (5) Geopolitical realities, especially the growing proximity of Russia.

However, there were gradations in the underlying pattern of Russian domination and expansion. In other words, Russia pursued both minimalist and maximalist goals in Iran. The latter – such as the total domination of Iran and access to the Persian Gulf – were thwarted by British power and presence in southern Iran. But the lesser objective was thoroughly achieved, as illustrated by the following statement made by Russia's Foreign Minister in 1909:

> we have tried gradually to subject Persia to our dominant influence, without violating the external symbols of its independence or its internal regime. In other words, our task is to make Persia politically obedient and useful – i.e., a sufficiently-powerful instrument in our hands – and, economically, to keep for ourselves a wide Persian market, using Russian work and capital freely.[12]

THE RUSSIAN REVOLUTION OF 1917: IMPACT ON RUSSO–IRANIAN RELATIONS

The Bolshevik Revolution in Russia inaugurated a new phase in Russo–Iranian relations, and its impact was equal to that of the treaty of Turkmanchai. The Revolution introduced new complexities (ideology) into Russo–Iranian relations and posed new threats to Iran. But its immediate impact on Iran's political destiny was positive.

First, the revolution ended the Russo–British *entente*, prompting

Russia to force the withdrawal of British troops from Iran. Second, relying more on popular revolutions for the expansion of Bolshevik influence in Iran – and beyond – the new government made a number of friendly and highly significant gestures towards Iran.[13] These included opening negotiations for the withdrawal of Soviet troops from Iran and Trotsky's denunciation of the Anglo-Russian agreement of 1907.[14] These acts generated a strong sense of relief in Iran, plus considerable sympathy and enthusiasm for the Bolshevik government, as illustrated by the following statement of a famous Iranian political and literary figure of the time:

> Two enemies, each pulling one side of a rope, were trying to strangle a man. Suddenly, one of them let the rope go and said 'poor man, I am your brother', and the unfortunate man was released. The man who let the rope go from our throat was Lenin.[15]

In fact, the Russian revolution initially saved Iran's independence and territorial integrity. As the treaty of Turkmanchai had opened the way for Iran's penetration by other powers, Bolshevik repudiation of Tsarist privileges enabled Iran to extract similar concessions from other foreign powers. It also introduced a new pattern into Russo–Iranian relations, namely that of acquiring influence by offering advantages and not relying solely on pressure and intimidation.

SOVIET–IRANIAN RELATIONS IN THE PAHLAVI ERA

Russo–Iranian relations had already entered a new phase by the time of the establishment of the Pahlavi dynasty in 1925. The new Bolshevik government had renounced Tsarist privileges in Iran, and the two governments had signed a treaty in 1921 laying the foundations for the new relationship.[16]

THE REIGN OF REZA SHAH (1925–1941)

From the Iranian perspective, Soviet–Iranian relations in this period benefited from a number of factors. First, the more pragmatic Bolsheviks – who were most concerned with the consolidation of the new regime – gained more influence. Consequently, the promoting of world revolution became less important.[17] Second, the Soviets viewed Reza Shah as a nationalist and anti-imperialist (anti-British) leader, and the Pahlavi regime as progressive in changing Iranian society from feudalism to capitalism, thus in time creating a better chance for socialist change in the country. Third, Reza Shah's success in establishing order and a relatively efficient central government in Iran, plus his efforts to eliminate British privileges, was reassuring to the Soviets. In other words, Iran was becoming more credible as a buffer state. Fourth, trade and economic relations between the two countries remained extensive.

However, the Soviets' decision not to pursue the goal of Iran's sovietization did not mean abandonment of their quest for economic and political influence there. The Soviet Union's pressure on Iran to grant it a fisheries concession is a good example.[18] Yet despite a number of thorny problems, including Iran's concern over its communists, Soviet–Iranian relations in this period were marked by a mutual willingness to iron out differences.

However, as the traditional imperial pattern of Russian behavior reappeared in Soviet foreign policy, Iran became one of its early victims. For example, after the Soviet–Nazi *rapprochement*, Iran was put in the Soviet sphere of influence. In a conversation with Molotov on 13 November 1940, Hitler recognized 'The Asiatic area to the south of the Soviet Union as Russia's sphere of influence.'[19]

THE REIGN OF MOHAMMAD-REZA PAHLAVI

Mohammad Reza Shah came to power in 1941 when, once again, Iran was occupied by foreign forces, its neutrality was overlooked this time on the grounds of its links with Germany.[20] Russian troops occupied northern Iran, and the Soviet Union used this opportunity to consolidate its power inside Iran, with the ultimate goal of its sovietization and incorporation within the Soviet empire. To this end, the Soviets' encouraged separatist movements among Iran's minorities in Azerbaijan and Kurdistan and used communist propaganda.[21] In addition, the Soviets resurrected a demand for oil concessions in northern Iran.[22]

The most concrete evidence of the USSR's ultimate objectives in Iran surfaced in 1945–46 when two so-called Democratic Republics were established in Iranian Azerbaijan and Kurdistan, with active Soviet support,[23] and when Moscow tried to change the Iranian regime.²⁴ To prevent Soviet encroachments, Iran appealed to the newly-established world body (the United Nations). But ultimately it was US pressure that forced the Soviets to withdraw from Iran.²⁵ In turn, US pressure reflected the changed atmosphere in global politics caused by the gradual dissolution of the wartime Soviet–American alliance and the beginning of the Cold War. Thus, once again Iran's destiny was determined by changes in the state of big-power relations. The withdrawal of Soviet forces from Iran, however, did not end Soviet efforts to influence events there, primarily through use of the Tudeh Party. The Tudeh was outlawed in 1949 after an assassination attempt on the Shah. But it continued to operate freely in the volatile and turbulent atmosphere of the Iranian political scene during this period. It organized mass demonstrations, tried to mobilize the workers and intellectuals, and heavily infiltrated the army. During the period 1951–53, the Tudeh initially supported Dr Mossadegh. But later, thinking that the time had come for a communist takeover in Iran, it undermined his nationalist government.

The heavy-handed policies of the USSR towards Iran during the period 1941–53 ultimately proved harmful to Moscow's long-term interests. These policies eliminated any remaining illusions regarding the real intentions of the communist regime; dissipated the good will generated by the early actions of the Bolshevik government; caused divisions within the Iranian communists;²⁶ and made the neutrality option less attractive to Iran. But more important, they provoked the United States' intervention in Iran in order to save the monarchy, caused the collapse of Mossadegh's nationalist, neutralist government, and paved the way for Iran's alliance with the United States.

CONFRONTATION AND ACCOMMODATION: 1953–1962

The *coup d'état* that restored the Shah's power was a serious setback for Soviet ambitions in Iran. After regaining power, the Shah purged the Tudeh's sympathizers in the military and bureaucracy and embarked on a policy of alliance with the United States. A number of reasons, including considerations of domestic politics, were behind the Shah's American policy, but disenchantment with past policies of neutrality and fears of Soviet intentions dominated. As opposed to earlier times, the US policy of containing the Soviet Union and of building alliances around its periphery led Washington to respond to Iran's efforts.

Thus in this period, Soviet–Iranian relations became dominated by the issues of growing US influence in Iran and Iran's membership in the Western-sponsored Baghdad Pact. The USSR viewed these developments with apprehension, fearing that they would lead to the stationing of long-range bombers and intermediate-range missiles close to its borders.[27] The Iranian government responded by emphasizing the defensive character of the Pact and by reassuring the Soviets that Iran would not grant nuclear bases to the West. However, these reassurances only partially calmed Soviet anxieties,[28] and Soviet–Iranian relations remained tense.

Nevertheless, a number of practical steps were taken to resolve some of the outstanding problems, including trade and boundary issues. The initiative came from the Soviets and relected their new policy of peaceful coexistence. The Shah visited Moscow in 1956 and was offered economic aid. Fearing the domestic implications of a large Soviet economic presence in Iran, however, he did not accede to Soviet offers. Rather, he skilfully used Soviet overtures to press the United States into signing a security agreement with Iran in March 1959. This act chilled Soviet–Iranian relations, prompting Moscow to attack the Shah personally.[29] The chill lasted until 1962.

Iran's policy of alliance with the United States and its exploitation of Soviet offers of cooperation were largely responsible for the chill. However, the Soviet policy of differentiating between state-to-state relations and those between fraternal communist parties put limits on the possible degree of improvement in Soviet–Iranian relations.

SOVIET–IRANIAN DÉTENTE: 1962–1972

These relations improved dramatically in 1962, when in an official note of 15 September Iran promised the USSR that it would not permit the stationing of missiles on Iranian soil. The real factors behind this improvement in relations, however, were the easing of global tensions and improved US–Soviet relations; changes in nuclear weaponry; strains in US–Iranian relations; and Iran's growing concern over its southern borders, because of the Iraqi revolution and increased Egyptian activity in the Persian Gulf.[30] During this period, Soviet–Iranian relations in trade, plus economic, financial, and technical cooperation, reached unprecedented levels, and Iran signed its first arms agreement with the USSR.

GROWING TENSIONS: 1972–78

During this period, Soviet–Iranian economic cooperation continued to expand. In fact, it was the Shah's strategy to prevent Soviet attacks against Iran by giving Moscow such economic incentives that such an option would become too costly. But underlying Iranian misgivings remained and even grew stronger.

By 1972, significant regional changes began seriously to strain Soviet–Iranian relations. These changes included Iran's growing role in the Persian Gulf and the Indian sub-continent; the growing reach of Soviet military and naval power; and the increasing Soviet presence in regions of vital interest to Iran (such as the Persian Gulf and the Indian Ocean). Moreover, the following specific events convinced Iran that the Soviet threat to its security was no longer confined to the north; rather, the USSR was following a policy of encircling Iran with unfriendly countries: (1) the development of close Iraqi–Soviet relations and the signing of the Iraqi–Soviet Treaty of Friendship, coupled with Iraq's subversion in Khusistan and Baluchistan;[31] (2) the dismemberment of Pakistan in 1971, the growing separatist movement in Pakistan, and the signing of the Indo-Soviet Treaty of friendship in 1972; (3) the growing Soviet presence in Somalia and South Yemen, plus the Marxist rebellion in Oman's Dhofar Province; and (4) Soviet support for Libya, Syria, and the PLO, which actively subverted the Shah's regime.

Moreover, these changes were taking place against the backdrop of Western retrenchment from the region, symbolized by the British withdrawal from the Persian Gulf and the enunciation of the Nixon Doctrine. The Soviets tried to assuage Iran's fears, but the Shah was not willing to take any risks. He accelerated Iran's new arms buildup. And after the oil price increase of 1973, he took an active role in regional politics, principally trying to counter Soviet and radical threats.[32]

The Soviets grew increasingly unhappy with Iran's policies, seeing the Shah as a tool of Western imperialism. Another irritant was the establishment of diplomatic relations between Iran and the PRC in 1972. But both Iran and the Soviet Union were careful not to let these differences undo the positive results of a decade of cooperation. The USSR had come to appreciate the stability on its southern border, the Shah's predictable, business-like diplomacy, and the economic benefits accruing to it and to Eastern Europe.

For Iran, having stable relations with the USSR was a *sine qua non* for its ability to pursue an activist policy elsewhere. Thus it is not surprising that the Soviet Union was concerned about political disturbances in Iran and was one of the last countries to withdraw its support from the Shah.

THE LEGACY OF THE PAST

Two centuries of Soviet–Iranian relations have left a heavy legacy. Iran has become convinced of Soviet expansionist tendencies; Soviet unwillingness to see Iran strong and independent;[33] the Soviet Union's role as another exploitative great power; Soviet unreliability (a view shared even by many Iranian leftists); Soviet opportunism; and the need for Iran to keep in mind Soviet proximity and power.[34] For the Soviet Union, two centuries of expansion and influence has convinced it that Iran is its natural sphere of influence. But this experience has also given the USSR great flexibility to shift from minimalist to maximalist policies or to pursue both of them simultaneously at different levels.

THE SOVIET UNION AND THE ISLAMIC REPUBLIC

Until recently, the Soviet attitude toward Iran's revolutionary movement was a mixture of ambivalence and expectancy. Now, after six years of revolutionary rule, the expectancy has died down and ambivalence has turned into serious doubt; but Soviet interest is still keen.

Initially, the Soviet Union's ambivalence was caused by its suspicions of the US role in the anti-Shah movement. The Soviets suspected that the United States wanted to pressure the Shah into more submission or to replace him with another pro-American regime. But as these fears did not materialize, the USSR became optimistic about the impact of the Iranian revolution on its strategic and other interests in Iran and beyond, only to become badly disappointed.

The Soviet Union's policy towards the Islamic Republic has thus reflected its assessment of the impact of the revolution on its interests, as the revolution has passed through several stages in the last six years. In turn, the Iranian response has been affected by the ideology of the revolution, by the power equation within its leadership, and by external events, while both Iran and the Soviet Union have shown in their attitudes the influence of their history.

THE TRANSITIONAL PERIOD: THE BAZARGAN GOVERNMENT

Once the demise of the Shah's regime became inevitable, the USSR quickly changed its attitude, welcomed Khomeini's return to Iran, and recognized Bazargan's provisional government. Later, it tried to establish friendly state-to-state relations with the new regime, and got encouragement from some of the regime's members. But the Ayatollah Khomeini remained indifferent to Soviet overtures. The Soviet policy of trying to ingratiate itself with the new regime was determined by the following factors: (1) a number of policy changes were made in Iran, including its withdrawal from CENTO; the closure of American listening posts; the drastic reduction in the US presence; Iran's abandonment of the role of the Persian Gulf's gendarme; and its anti-Israeli stand. These amounted to significant strategic gains for the Soviet Union. Moreover, the Tudeh was now allowed to operate freely; (2) the USSR considered the revolution in Iran as a first stage toward a true socialist revolution – the USSR had bitter memories of its not having supported the nationalist regime of Mossadegh, and it did not want to repeat the same mistake; and (3) the Soviet Union considered Khomeini as playing a progressive role in Iran's development.

However, during Bazargan's tenure, Soviet expectations of expanded cooperation, leading to increased influence, did not materialize. This prompted cautious Soviet criticism of the regime, although it left out Khomeini. Several factors accounted for this development: (a) traditional Iranian suspicion of Russian intentions, as well as the determination of Iran's new leaders to follow a policy of equal-distance from East and West, as symbolized by their slogan, '*na sharghi, na gharbi*'. The Soviet Union considered this policy unfair, arguing that it had supported the revolution. In fact, it believes that any equation of the two superpowers is suspect and that 'even-handedness is a mask for subservience toward the West'.[34] Soviet suspicions became stronger when the Bazargan government tried to normalize relations with the United States, including the famous

Bazargan-Brzezinski meeting in Algiers. Another disquieting incident was Foreign Minister Ibrahim Yazdi's meeting with Secretary of State Vance at the United Nations. (b) Soviet heavy-handedness in regard to certain issues of special concern to Iran. Soviet insistence on the validity of Articles V and VI of the 1921 Treaty, which had been repudiated by both the Shah's government and the revolutionary regime, was particularly important in rekindling old Iranian suspicions of Russian ambitions. (c) Soviet attitudes towards Iran's ethnic minorities. The Soviet Union had traditionally used Iran's ethnic minorities and their autonomist tendencies to increase its influence in Iran. A fragmentation of Iran along ethnic lines, even within a loose confederal system, would increase Iran's vulnerability to Soviet pressures, if not become a prelude to its gradual sovietization. Past Soviet behavior in Azerbaijan and Kurdistan bore witness to this Soviet proclivity. The Soviet Union was also irritated by some pan-Iranist claims to parts of the USSR with Persian-speaking peoples. Thus the Soviet Union supported the rights of Iran's minorities. The following extract from a 1973 Tudeh Party document on minorities also reflects Soviet views. It expresses support for:

> full equality of rights for all the peoples, ethnic groups, and national minorities living in Iran and their voluntary unity within a single homeland based on preserving the territorial integrity of the Iranian homeland . . . This can be achieved by securing autonomy for the deprived peoples and nationalities.[35]

However, the degree of the Soviet Union's support for Iran's minorities or its manipulation of Iran's ethnic diversities had generally depended on the state of Soviet relations with the Iranian government. Thus, when first the disturbances occurred among Iran's Turkman and Kurdish minorities, the Soviets attributed this to imperialist plots and cautioned the Kurds. But as they became disappointed with the Bazargan government, the Soviets began to support the Kurds. (d) the invasion of Afghanistan and the Iraqi connection. The communist *coup d'état* in Afghanistan in April 1978 had caused great anxiety in Iran, but the Shah's government was not able to do much about it. The new regime criticized Soviet intervention in Afghanistan's internal affairs, and even Khomeini personally warned the Soviet ambassador in their meeting on 12 June 1979 against such interference. In addition to the impact of Islamic solidarity both on Khomeini and on general Iranian attitudes, the Iranians thought that

Afghanistan was a prelude to Soviet advances into Baluchistan. Khomeini also warned the Soviet ambassador against helping Baluch and Kurdish autonomists. The Soviet Union's friendship with Iraq also hurt relations with Iran, since leaders in Teheran suspected the USSR of being involved in Iraqi subversion among the Arab minorities of Khusistan.

THE HOSTAGE CRISIS AND THE FALL OF THE BAZARGAN GOVERNMENT

The Soviets were not alone in being unhappy about the policies of Bazargan's government, especially his efforts to normalize relations with the United States. Rather, a mixed group of ultra-religious clerics, a variety of leftists, and even certain moderate secular leaders were against him (the opposition of the first two groups was based on ideological grounds, whereas personal ambitions motivated the last-named).

The instrument used to eliminate Bazargan was the 4 November 1979 seizure of 52 American diplomats by a group of students who called themselves followers of the Imam's line. Bazargan resigned on 6 November, the provisional government was dissolved, and preparations were begun for elections for president and parliament, which elected Bani-Sadr president. Given their view of the Bazargan government – reflected in the following assessment by the Tudeh leader, Kianuri – the Soviets were pleased with these developments:

> A certain period following the revolution's victory was characterized by a dualism of power. There was, on the one hand, the revolutionary center headed by Ayatollah Khomeini, and on the other hand there was the government of the liberal opportunistic bourgeoisie . . . The revolutionary center around Ayatollah Khomeini resolutely declared itself against any compromise with US imperialism . . . Khomeini also declared himself in favor of a change in the political and economic life of the country to the advantage of the working masses . . . The liberal bourgeoisie by no means liked this situation and began to obstruct the revolutionary movement for the sake of its own economic interests.[36]

The Soviet Union used the hostage crisis to ingratiate itself with the Iranian regime. It also believed that, as long as the hostages were in

Iran, US–Iranian relations would not be normalized.[37] Yet the Soviets were concerned about possible US military action against Iran that could then be used to install a pro-American government there. In January 1980, Brezhnev even stated that the Soviet Union would not tolerate any outside interference in Iran's internal affairs. However, coming as it did after the December 1979 Soviet invasion of Afghanistan, this statement did not reassure the Iranians but instead worried them. They thought that the USSR might use the pretext of an American threat to invade Iran. To try preventing this from happening, the Iranian ambassador in Moscow informed Soviet foreign ministry officials that:

> in the likely event of an attack on Iran by America, we can defend ourselves alone, and we will not allow a single foreign soldier to enter the country on whatever pretext and by virtue of whatever friendship treaty.[38]

Moreover, despite Soviet support for Iran in the hostage crisis, the Iranian government continued to condemn the Soviet invasion of Afghanistan, it withdrew from the 1980 Moscow Olympics, and Khomeini called the USSR the 'other Great Satan'. Consequently, the Russians grew increasingly dissatisfied with Bani-Sadr, suspecting him of being another bourgeois nationalist; but they continued to praise Khomeini himself. Thus the USSR and its mouthpiece, the Tudeh, along with other leftists joined hands with clerical factions to undermine Bani-Sadr.

Despite lingering Iranian fears and verbal abuse of the USSR, during 1980 a number of events forced Iran to move closer to the Soviet Union. Gradually, economic and other relations between Iran and the USSR began to expand.

The first event was the Western economic embargo, which increased the importance of the Soviet Union and some East European countries for Iran. Thus efforts were made to regularize trade and economic relations. In April 1980 the Iranian Minister of Economy and Finance visited Moscow and, following further talks, a number of agreements on transit, trade, and other issues were signed, although some thorny problems remained unresolved.[39] The second event was the American hostage rescue mission, which gravely exacerbated Iranian fears of American military intervention. The third event was the Iraqi invasion of Iran in September 1980. Happening as it did while the hostage crisis was continuing, Iranians believed that the attack had been sanctioned – if not instigated – by the United States. However, they equally accused the USSR of complicity, albeit for different reasons. For example, then Foreign Minister Qotbzadeh thought that the major powers wanted to use Iraq to isolate Iran: the United States, so that it could regain its influence; and the USSR, so that it could force Iran to enter the Eastern camp. Some Iranian officials feared a Soviet–American agreement to divide the region into spheres of influence in the traditional pattern of Russo–British agreements.[40]

The Soviet Union tried hard to dispel these fears and suspicions, but found it a difficult task. In a meeting with the Soviet ambassador, the then prime minister, Mohammad Ali Rajai, recalled the USSR's stand *vis à vis* Mossadegh and the Shah's regime; he also reiterated Iran's anxieties over Soviet arms deliveries to Iraq and over Iraqi Deputy Prime Minister Tariq Aziz's visit to Moscow.[41] But the Soviets continued to befriend Iran. In addition to wanting to bring Iran into their sphere of influence, Soviet-Iraqi relations had grown tense because of Baghdad's policy shifts and its Westward trend.

By mid-1981, however, both Iran's domestic conditions and developments caused by the war resulted in a significant Soviet–Iranian *rapprochement*. First, there were the economic and military necessities of the war. Iran's most important port, Khoramshahr on the Persian Gulf, was destroyed, thus making Iran seriously dependent on overland routes through Soviet territory. A number of high-level meetings took place between Iran and the USSR and several economic and technical cooperation agreements were signed. By the end of 1981, the transit of commodities to and from Iran through Soviet territory had increased from 1 million tons in 1978 to 3.9 million tons in 1981, and the volume of trade had risen to 800 million roubles (over $1 billion) from 671 million roubles in 1978. Shortages of foreign currency in Iran were in part responsible for this increase, with Iran's bartering oil for other commodities. In fact, in 1981 Iran bartered 2.2 million tons of oil for Soviet goods.

Similarly, Iran's inability to procure arms from Western sources forced it to turn elsewhere. There is no hard evidence of any direct Soviet arms deliveries to Iran, despite claims by some Iranian exile groups. But, indirectly, Soviet-made arms found their way into Iran through the intermediary of Soviet allies, such as Syria, Libya, North Korea, and a number of East European countries. According to some reports, the Soviets also became involved in training the Revolutionary Guards, and a number of Soviet intelligence advisers arrived in Iran in 1981.[42]

In addition to Iran's very real economic and military needs, its *rapprochement* with the Soviet Union was also due to political changes taking place inside Iran. By late 1981, the clerical factions in Iran scored a final victory over the remnants of the secular-moderate forces when Bani-Sadr was forced to leave Iran. Moreover, within this group those clerics with a more radical and pro-Soviet outlook seemed to dominate, and they also had allies among the technocrats.[43] But the new group was faced with challenges both from the Islamic left (the Mujahedin-e-Khalgh, whose leader had fled with Bani-Sadr to Paris) and from the royalist and other secular groups, with coup plots reportedly being discovered fairly regularly. Thus these clerics felt they needed the support of the Tudeh and the USSR.

For its own reasons – including the desire to weaken other leftist groups and increase its own influence – the Tudeh party was prepared to accede. This policy did pay off and the Tudeh party made significant inroads into the Iranian bureaucracy and military. But its success proved to be short-lived and was not without associated costs.

GROWING RIFT: 1983–84

Soviet–Iranian *rapprochement* did not last very long. Soon the same factors that had led to the improvement in Soviet–Iranian relations led to their deterioration.

First, there was the evolution of the war with Iraq. By the end of 1982, Iran had expelled Iraqi forces from its territory, and the debate in Teheran was whether to agree to peace or to pursue the war into Iraqi territory. The Soviet Union was apprehensive about this turn of events and viewed an Iranian victory as detrimental to its interests. For example, such a victory would make Iran less amenable to Soviet pressures. It could also mean the establishment of an Islamic government in Iraq which – from the Soviet perspective – would be worse than the present Baathist regime. Consequently, by summer 1982 the Soviet Union resumed arms deliveries to Iraq. This step, in turn, strained Soviet–Iranian relations, particularly after Iraq began during 1983–84 to bomb Iran's civilian population. Iranian leaders, including the speaker of the Majlis, Hashemi Rafsanjani, frequently stated that Iran would remember that Russian missiles were killing Iranian children. In addition, thinking that the peace faction within the Iranian leadership was strong, the Tudeh openly called for peace with Iraq.

The second factor leading to the deterioration of Soviet–Iranian relations was the improvement in Iran's economic conditions and a significant expansion in its trade and economic relations with countries such as West Germany, Japan, and Britain. For example, in 1983 the volume of trade between Iran and West Germany reached the $4 billion level. This development, plus expansion of Iran's trade and economic ties with smaller countries in West and East Europe and the Third World, reduced its economic dependence on the USSR. In addition, Iran had succeeded in controlling regional and ethnic unrest.

The third factor was growing Soviet disappointment with many aspects of Iran's foreign policy. These included Iran's refusal to accommodate the Soviet invasion of Afghanistan, plus some Iranian involvement with the Afghani Shias;[44] Iran's close and friendly relations with Pakistan and Turkey; and Soviet doubts about Iran's Gulf policy. The Soviets initially welcomed Iran's revolution because they thought it would reduce American influence in the Persian Gulf and weaken the conservative Gulf regimes. But this did not happen. Rather, the Gulf countries' fear of Iran prompted them to become engaged in closer defense and security cooperation within the framework of the Gulf Cooperation Council. They also drew closer to the United States.

The fourth factor was the evolution of Iran's domestic politics. The elimination of the moderates did not lead to greater influence for the leftists or the so-called progressive Muslims. Quite the contrary, the Iranian regime became increasingly dominated by the conservative clerics, and the tempo of Islamization quickened. This increased the Soviets' ambivalence *vis à vis* the Iranian regime. Some Soviet experts, including Yevgeni Primakov, believed that – unlike Bani-Sadr and his supporters who 'were oriented towards the United States . . . towards the West, towards Europe' – the fundamentalist clerics adopted 'patriotic' positions on a wide range of issues and thus were preferable. But others, including Bovin, pointed out that, while this was so, the struggle 'against the Western devil' appeared together with 'a struggle against the Eastern devil'.[45]

Nevertheless, as time passed the Soviet Union's appraisal of Islam as a positive revolutionary force and of Iran's Islamic revolution became more negative.⁴⁶ There is some indication that the Soviets began to worry more about the impact of Iran's Islamic revolutionary ideology on their own Muslims.⁴⁷ In addition, the new revolutionary interpretation of Islam in its absolutist and totalitarian form was a challenge to socialism in all Muslim countries.

More important, the strong anti-communism and social and economic conservatism of many of Iran's influential clerics was behind the Soviet–Iranian rift. A number of specific incidents contributed to this rift. The first was the expelling of eighteen Soviet diplomats from Iran in April 1983 on charges of spying. According to some reports, the information about Soviet activities was passed on by the British, who had obtained it from a Soviet ex-vice consul in Teheran and a senior KGB official, Vladimir Andreyevich Kuzichkin, who defected to Britain.⁴⁸ The latter also disclosed that Tudeh members and other Soviet agents had infiltrated in great numbers the revolutionary organization, the bureaucracy, and the military. This information put the Iranian regime on alert and led to extensive purges. Among those discovered as Soviet sympathizers were Captain Bahram Afzali, the commander of the Iranian navy, and the special assistant to Majlis Speaker Rafsanjani.

Following these events, the Tudeh Party was banned and its leaders were arrested. The trials of some of the Tudeh members were televised, and their leaders confessed to their pro-Soviet and anti-revolutionary activities and repented. The themes they emphasized included Tudeh's subservience to the USSR even when Soviet-armed Iraqis attacked Iran; its spying for the USSR and infiltration of the bureaucracy and the military; its collaboration with the Kurdish rebels; and its plans to seize power.⁴⁹

The message the Iranian government wanted to get through was that Marxism and the Soviet model are irrelevant to Iran. This view is encapsulated in the following statement by the Tudeh leader Kianuri: 'no leftist trend should infiltrate into Iran as it means affiliation to foreigners, to aliens. It is the mother of all treason'.⁵⁰

The USSR reacted sharply to the Khomeini regime's treatment of the Tudeh, unlike many other previous occasions when the Soviet Union had overlooked the mistreatment of communists in other Middle Eastern countries. In fact, the Soviet Union's reaction reflected its general unhappiness with Iran. The Soviets also warned Iran through intermediaries, such as Libya and Syria, against executing the Tudeh leaders. The nature of these warnings is not quite clear, but they were obviously strong enough to prevent the executions. The latest trial, scheduled for 11 November 1984, was cancelled on the 7th, and no new date has yet been set.[51] It is not clear, however, whether the USSR played any role in this decision.

PERSISTING PRAGMATISM AND LOWERING OF TENSIONS

Throughout this period of rift, both Iran and the USSR have demonstrated a considerable degree of pragmatism and have not let political differences affect other aspects of their relations, especially in economics. For example, Moscow did not retaliate against Iran by curtailing transit and other trade, and approximately 2000 Soviet experts continue to work on a number of projects. In their broadcasts to Iran, the Soviets also continue to emphasize the benefits of Soviet–Iranian economic cooperation. For their part, the Iranians have tolerated certain Soviet activities on Iran's eastern border with Afghanistan.[52]

In addition to mutual efforts to keep lines of communications open and to avoid jeopardizing economic ties, Soviet–Iranian relations have begun to improve, albeit very slowly. The Iranians took the initiative when the official equivalent to Assistant Secretary for Europe, Sadr, visited Moscow in June 1984 and met with Andrei Gromyko. This visit was prompted by the growing Iraqi attacks on shipping in the Persian Gulf, by statements made by the United States and other Western countries that they would not allow the flow of Persian Gulf oil to be interrupted, by the delivery of US Stinger missiles to Saudi-Arabia, and, finally, by the shooting down of an Iranian F4 by Saudi F14s. Both Iran and the USSR feared American intervention in the Gulf; and their communique reflected this fear, by stating that both countries opposed foreign intervention in the Persian Gulf.

This meeting was followed by a number of visits to Iran by Soviet energy officials, and agreements have been reached to resume work on a number of projects. There has even been a rumor that Gromyko and the Iranian Foreign Minister may meet, but so far this has not happened. However, while all the developments discussed above have narrowed the Russo–Iranian rift, they have not led to any dramatic improvement – as was the case in 1982 – and Soviet–Iranian relations remain cool.

FUTURE OUTLOOK

How Soviet–Iranian relations will develop in the future is not easy to predict. But if the past is a reliable guide, they are likely to remain volatile and pass through stages of relative *rapprochement* and estrangement, depending on Iran's internal developments, the shifts in regional and international politics, and changes in the Soviet Union's strategic and political calculations.

Meanwhile, Soviet–Iranian relations will continue to be affected by certain more constant geopolitical and psycho-historical factors. This, in turn, would put limits on the degree of both *rapprochement* and estrangement, barring, of course, drastic changes in one or more of the other variables. The record of Soviet–Iranian relations in the post-revolutionary period clearly illustrates this point. In fact, although the Islamic revolution has added a new factor – militant Islam – to Soviet-Iranian relations, the essential features of these relations have had strong continuities with the past.

The Soviet Union has applied past policies of intimidation and ingratiation toward Iran; it has followed both maximalist and minimalist goals in that country; and – despite its policy of accommodation with the existing regime and maximization of existing benefits to the USSR – it has not abandoned the goal of gaining greater influence in Iran, although for now its hopes of early success have been disappointed.

For its part, Iran has been conscious of Soviet power and proximity, even when challenging Soviet influence. It has also used economic and political advantages offered by the USSR whenever needed and possible, including at times, the use of these advantages as counterweights to American pressures against Iran and American influence in the region. Yet at the same time, Iran has been conscious of incompatibilities between its economic, political, and ideological interests and those of the USSR, as well as possible dangers of too-close relations with the USSR as a trigger to more active Western hostility against the Islamic regime.

In all likelihood, this pattern of interaction will continue. In particular, the Soviet Union will keep a close watch on Iran's internal evolution, so as not to miss any significant opportunities, while trying to preserve past gains and to avoid setbacks.

At the beginning of Iran's revolution, a Soviet expert, Ul'yanovskii, expressed the opinion that 'full of contradictory potential, the revolution contains within itself the possibility of sharp turns in the future'.[53] So far, the turns have not served Soviet interests, but they may still prove advantageous in the future. The USSR would want to be ready, when and if such a turn occurs.

Notes

1. Rouhollah K. Ramazani, *The Foreign Policy of Iran: A Developing Nation in World Affairs, 1500–1941*, (Charlottesville: University of Virginia Press, 1966) pp 21–22.
2. *Ibid.*, p. 20.
3. In 1723, Russia agreed to help Iran in exchange for Gilan, Mazandaran, Astarabad, Baku, and Derbend. *Ibid.*, p. 21.
4. France mediated this agreement. *Ibid.*, p. 22.
5. According to some historians, Nadir received some military help from Russia against the Turks.
6. *Ibid.*, p. 43.
7. *Ibid.*, p. 44.
8. Some scholars, including R. K. Ramazani, attribute the war to Iran's irredentism and unrealism. Ibid., pp. 44–45.
9. The treaty was signed in 1813. In addition to Iran's territorial losses, it established Russian military exclusivity on the Caspian Sea.
10. The treaty in Iran is known as the 'Shameful Treaty' of Turkmanchai.
11. This is how the British Ambassador to St. Petersburg, Goerge Buchanan, explained the situation to the Tzar in 1914. Quoted in Aryeh Y. Yodfat, *The Soviet Union and Revolutionary Iran* (New York: St. Martins Press, 1984) p. 8.
12. Quoted in *ibid.* p. 6.
13. The Bolsheviks, including Lenin, considered the revolutionizing of Iran essential to revolution in the East, as the following illustrates:

    The Persian revolt can become the key to a general revolution in the East . . . This precious key must be in our hands; at all costs Persia must be ours. Persia must belong to the revolution. (Quoted in R. K. Ramazani, *Iran's Foreign Policy, 1500–1941* p. 141).

14. *Ibid.*, pp. 92–93.
15. Mohammad-Taghi Bahar, *Tarikh-e-Ahzab Siassi*, Teheran: 1323 (1945) Vol. 1, p. 27.
16. The key articles of the Treaty are Articles V and VI, justifying Russia's military intervention in Iran should the former find its security threatened.
17. Partly because of this, Russia withdrew its support for the Gilan Republic. In a letter to its leader, the Soviet Ambassador in Tehran said that:

    Soviet Russia at this time regards revolutionary movements as not only fruitless, but also harmful. (Quoted in R. K. Ramazani, *Iran's Foreign Policy, 1500–1941, op. cit.*, p. 91.)

18. *Ibid.*, pp. 225–227, for details.
19. Iran became very alarmed by the Nazi-Soviet Pact and approached the German Ambassador in Tehran. See R. K. Ramazani, *Iran's Foreign Policy 1941–1973* (Charlottesville: University of Virginia Press, 1975) p. 26.
20. *Ibid.*, pp. 27–28, for details.
21. The Soviets dropped leaflets on Iranian towns, glorifying the lot of Soviet peasants and workers. See *Ibid.*, pp. 91–92.
22. The renewed Russian interest seems to have been caused by Iran's efforts to attract American oil companies. The Russians felt that nobody else should be allowed to explore for oil in northern Iran and they have succeeded in preventing that so far. See Ibid., p. 107.
23. *Ibid.*, pp. 110–153, for details.
24. Averell Harriman reported that the Soviets wanted to change Iran's regime because they felt it did not have popular support. See *ibid.*, p. 111.
25. In an article in 1957, President Truman said that he had sent an ultimatum to the Russians over Iran. See *ibid.*, pp. 138–139.
26. The Tudeh party's advocacy of a security perimeter for the Soviet Union in Iran, and its support for separatist movements, caused deep splits within it, illustrated by Khalil Maleki's breakaway 'Third Force' party, the forerunner of the theory of different roads to socialism. See Sepehr Zabih *The Communist Movement in Iran* (Los Angeles: University of California Press, 1966) p. 135.
27. Alven Z. Rubinstein, *Soviet Policy Toward Turkey, Iran, and Afghanistan* (New York: Praeger, 1982) p. 67.
28. *Ibid.*, p. 66.
29. Khrushchev said that the Shah was not frightened of the USSR, but of his own people. *Ibid.*, p. 299.
30. For details see R. K. Ramazani, *The Persian Gulf: Iran's Role* (Charlottesville: University of Virginia Press, 1973) and Shireen T. Hunter, 'Arab-Iranian Relations and Stability in the Persian Gulf', *Washington Quarterly*, Summer 1984, pp. 67–76.
31. R. M. Burrell & A. J. Cottrell, *Iran, Afghanistan, Pakistan: Tensions and Dilemmas* (California: Sage Publications, 1974) p. 7.
32. For Iran's use of oil revenues as a tool of influence. See Shireen T. Hunter, *OPEC and the Third World: The Politics of Aid* (Bloomington: Indiana University Press, 1984) pp. 106–123. One aspect of this policy that was particularly disturbing to the Russians was Iran's efforts to distance Afghanistan from the Soviet Union. See Selig S. Harrison, 'Dateline Afghanistan: Exit through Finland', *Foreign Policy*, Winter 1981–82, pp. 163–187.
33. Shireen T. Hunter, 'Iranian Perceptions and a Wider World', *Political Communication and Persuasion*, Fall 1984.
34. Shahram Chubin, 'The Soviet Union and Iran', *Foreign Affairs*, Spring 1983, p. 930.
35. Aryeh Yodfat, *The Soviet Union and Revolutionary Iran*, *op. cit.*, p. 57.
36. *Ibid.*, pp. 65–66.
37. For example, Kianuri, The Tudeh leader, told Eric Rouleau that, 'as

long as the hostages are in Iran, normalization of relations with the United States, as some politicians are dreaming of, will not be possible.' *Le Monde*, 18 April 1980.
38. Quoted in the Tehran daily, *Ettela'at* of 12 May 1980.
39. One of these problems was the issue of Iran's gas exports to the Soviet Union.
40. For example, in an interview in October 1980 with *An Nahar al-Arabi wa ad Duwali*, an adviser to Bani-Sadr, talked of a Soviet-American agreement to divide the region.
41. Aryeh Y. Yodfat, *The Soviet Union and Revolutionary Iran*, op. cit. p. 94.
42. *Ibid.*, p. 98.
43. For an excellent analysis of intra-clerical divisions, see Shahrough Akhavi, in Nikki R. Keddi (ed.) *The Iranian Revolution and the Islamic Republic*, Middle East Institute/Wilson Center, 1982, pp. 17–28.
44. *Le Monde*, 17 October 1984.
45. Quoted in Aryeh Y. Yodfat, *The Soviet Union and Revolutionary Iran*, op. cit., p. 117.
46. Muriel Atkins, 'Moscow's Disenchantment with Iran', *Survey*, Autumn/Winter 1983, pp. 248–250.
47. Alexander Bennigsen, 'Mullahs, Mujahidin, & Soviet Muslims', *Problems of Communism*, November/December 1984, pp. 28–44.
48. Aryeh Y. Yodfat, *The Soviet Union and Revolutionary Iran*, op. cit., p. 132.
49. Muriel Atkins, 'Moscow's Disenchantment with Iran', op. cit., p. 251.
50. Foreign Broadcasting Information Service (FBIS) South Asia, 3 May 1983, p. 13.
51. *Iran Times*, 16 November 1984.
52. Some reports have claimed that Iran has allowed a Soviet listening station in Baluchistan, enabling the Soviets to assess activities on the Soviet–Afghan border. *Time*, 8 March 1982, p. 32.
53. Quoted in Muriel Atkins, 'Moscow's Disenchantment with Iran', op. cit., p. 260.

13 Relations between Iran and the Arab States
Andrew Killgore

Some scholars believe that the Iran–Iraq War arose from a differentiation between Shi'a and Sunni Islam about 450 years ago;[1] some trace the origins back a thousand years or more. The real origins go back at least 4000 years and, indeed, into pre-history. There is a geographic, cultural and linguistic divide somewhere along the current Iraqi–Iranian frontier, a division made all the more immutable by the Zagros Mountains barrier between the two countries. East of that divide is the great Iranian plateau, the heartland of Persian civilization. To the west of it is the vast Tigris–Euphrates river basin and great deserts beyond and in between, peopled by Semites. The basin has been dominated for 1400 years by Arab and Turkish rulers. It has been peopled by Semitic speakers long before that.

LEGACY OF THE PAST

The Persian heartland is ruled by the descendants of Indo–European tribes who speak Farsi, Persian. The people of Iraq speak mainly Arabic, a Semitic language. The Iranians view the world from the perspective of a settled people, and their traditions and institutions reflect this. The Tigris–Euphrates basin throughout history was infiltrated or invaded by Semitic tribes from the desert. The traditions and institutions of the nomad thus have a strong hold in that riverine system and in the encompassing deserts.

There is almost no perceptible racial difference between the peoples on either side of the ancient divide. But the old conflict between the desert (the Arabs) and the sown (Iran) seemingly abides forever, while the linguistic difference between Indo–European Persian and Semitic Arabic constitutes a strong barrier to greater mutual understanding. The fact that these conflicting forces were contending with each other even in pre-history and continue to do so today suggests that misunderstanding and war will last as long as the geographic divide in that area between the settled and the nomadic endures.

We know little about the ancient Sumerians, except that they did not speak a Semitic language. We do know that Sargon of Akkad, who spoke a Semitic tongue, established hegemony over the Sumerian city states. According to the *Encyclopedia Britannica*, Sargon named himself Sharru-Kin (Rightful King) in support of an accession not achieved in an old-established city through hereditary accession. Heredity was the Persian way of one ruler succeeding his blood-kin previous ruler. This was the tradition of a settled people. The Semitic way, or way of the desert nomad, was that successorship went to the strongest contender, often chosen by consensus, and not necessarily related by blood to the previous ruler.

One can see the unending contest between Iran and the Arab states as dating back to Sargon, and probably before. The contesting sides were not even known at that time as Iran and the Arabs. Sargon established an empire all the way to the Mediterranean and maybe into present-day Greece. He dominated Susa, the capital city of the non-Semitic Elamites in the Zagros Mountains of western Iran. An interesting sidelight is that Sargon, like Moses in the Bible story, was supposedly found as a baby floating in a basket in the river.

Looking back into history the Zagros Mountains barrier between the Iranian plateau and the Tigris–Euphrates basin, plus desert, has never been permanently breached politically, and has never been breached linguistically. Cyrus the Great and his successors did it in the sixth to fourth centuries BC, when they ruled the Semitic people between Persia and Greece. This thrust was ended in bloody conflict by the Macedonian, Alexander the Great, called Alexander the Terrible in Iran.

The thrust went the other way in the seventh century AD when the Arabs and their new religion of Islam took over Persia and lands to the east. Islam replaced Zoroastrianism as the religion of Persia, but Islam in that country gradually assumed such a peculiarly Persian mold that Islam there was and is hardly a unifying force with Islam as observed by the great majority of the Arabs.

For several centuries the Persians wrote in Arabic, and the Farsi language today is perhaps one-third Arabic, certainly when used for political discussion. But this infiltration of Arabic was resented by many Persians. Their greatest poet Ferdowsi whose Shahname, (Book of Kings), written about the middle of the eleventh century, was written in Persian and whose theme was old Persian history and legends. These predated the advent of Islam and Ferdowsi came to personify the revival and indeed the indestructibility of the Persian language and the Aryan Persians as opposed to the Arabic language and the Semitic Arabs.

The long-enduring rivalry between Semites and Aryans along the Zagros divide did not cease even in the great days of the Abassid Empire (749–1258) in Baghdad when Persia was part of an Arab empire. Persians, Greeks and Jews achieved great influence at the Imperial Court – too great in the view of many Arabs. It was during this period, it appears, that the Arabic word Ajami came to mean Persian. It also meant barbarian and non-Arab. It sometimes is used in this pejorative sense in Arab politics today.

Something called the Arab States did not exist until this century, and some of today's Arab countries only gained their independence in the 1970s. The name Iran, deriving from Aryan, is also relatively new. But social and cultural differences on either side of the great divide provided and still provide background for repeated clashes.

Ottoman Turks and Persian Safavids fought each other in the sixteenth century. The same rivalries continued in the eighteenth century, most notably when Nadir Shah besieged Basrah and Baghdad and when Karim Khan Zand captured Basrah in 1774. Tension and border clashes continued in the nineteenth century but under prodding from Great Britain, survey teams eventually brought stability along the divide. But it makes little difference who rules on either side of the divide; the tensions have become a part of the atmosphere. I hope I have firmly established the idea that war and bad blood between Persians and Arabs is a simple concomitant of their living next to each other.

THE FOCUS OF TENSION BETWEEN IRANIANS AND ARABS

The greatest problem between Iranians and Arabs lies along the Shatt-al-Arab River, which flows 130 miles from the conjunction of the Tigris and Euphrates Rivers to the Gulf. Iran's most important river system, the Karun, joins the Shatt 45 miles from its mouth. For its last 55 miles that Shatt is the Iranian–Iraqi border. Iraq's port of Faw is just across the river from Iran and its main port, Basra, is very close to Iranian territory.

Iran's most important port of Khorramshahr (called Muhammarah by the Arabs), lies just at the confluence of the Shatt and the Karun rivers. Khorramshahr is also the southern railhead of the Trans-Iranian railway system.

In the Iraqi view, Iraq has been short-changed in its access to the sea, which consists of only 50 miles of swampy frontage. Most of Iraq's oil exports have to pass under Iranian guns, while Iran's export terminal for petroleum is down south at Kharg Island, far away from Iraq. Since the Iraq–Iran War began in September 1980, Iraq has not exported oil via the Gulf, dramatizing Iraq's strategic vulnerability.

Efforts to demarcate the Iran-Iraq border along the Shatt have not removed tension. By the nineteenth century Iran was recognized as the east or north bank and Iraq the west bank. The 1913 Constantinople Accords fixed the line as the low water mark on the Iranian side. The Thalweg or center of the river was recognized in 1937 as constituting the border around Abadan. Under pressure, Iraq in 1975 accepted the Thalweg as its common border with Iran along the Shatt-al-Arab.

Other problems causing tension between Iran and Iraq are that the cities of Karbala and Najaf, considered by some Shiites to be as important as Mecca and Medina as places of pilgrimage, are located in Iraq. More than half of Iraq's population are Shiites, many of whom look to Iran as the center of Shiism. A large part of the population of Iran's major oil-producing province of Khuzistan, called Arabistan in the Arab World, are Arabs. Finally, millions of Kurds inhabit both sides of the Iranian–Iraqi border. These problems that spill across borders tempt both countries to interfere in the affairs of the other, and each has done so.

Other Arab states, especially those in the Gulf, have had their trouble with Iran. In 1971 the late Shah, Muhammad Reza Pahlavi, invaded and seized the Arab-owned Gulf islands of Abu Musa and the Greater and Lesser Tunbs. About that time he more or less relinquished Iran's claim to Bahrain, whose population is more Shia than Sunni. But this did not stop Iran's diplomatic but ostentatious continued interest in Bahrain, which many Bahrainis and Arabs elsewhere regarded as vaguely threatening.

All the Arab states of the Gulf have significant Shia populations, in the case of Iraq and Bahrain amounting to more than half. The Shiites in Kuwait are 15 per cent to 30 per cent; in Qatar 10 to 20 per cent; and in Saudi Arabia 5 per cent to 10 per cent. In the latter case, however, the Shiites are heavily concentrated in the Eastern Province, Saudi Arabia's oil-producing area. Ayatollah Khomeini's calls for Muslim solidarity against Iraq constitute an attempted extraterritorial interference in the affairs of these Arab states, in the view of the governments of those states. The prerevolutionary government of Iran, in the view of the Arab states of the Gulf, did the same thing, although less openly and less specifically via Islam.

GREAT POWER MACHINATIONS

In going back to 1898, one would like to speculate on what might have been if only certain things had not happened about that time and in later years. It might even be the case that the Iraq–Iran War would not have happened if the Great Powers had not interfered in one or the other of these two countries for their own interests.

Great Britain took the Shaikhdom of Kuwait under its protection in 1898. It was detached from the Ottoman Empire's Governerate of Basra because the Turks were too weak at the time to do anything about it. The British move was designed to prevent Imperial Germany from having a proper Gulf outlet for its ambitious Berlin to Baghdad Railway scheme. The fact that huge reserves of oil were later discovered in Kuwait was serendipitous to an extreme degree.

The British served their imperial aims at the time and the modern state of Kuwait has done a fine job of using its great wealth wisely. But one result is that Iraq, which fell heir to Basra and its environs, feels cheated of a natural outlet to the Gulf. In the early 1960s Iraq laid public claim to Kuwait. This created an uproar in the Arab World and in the West. The issue was smoothed over without war, but Iraq's felt need for a safe outlet to the Gulf is a problem the world will have to reckon with in the future.

More Great Power interference occurred in 1953, this time in Iran by the United States. Muhammad Mossadeq overthrew the Shah who fled to Rome. The CIA paid for mob disturbances in Tehran and the Shah was brought back to his country. If Mossadeq, nothing more than a Persian nationalist, had not been overthrown, events arguably would have followed a less turbulent course. The ill-starred American intervention in Iran's internal affairs to overthrow Mossadeq haunts the United States to this day. It is well to remember, especially in the light of the situation for the United States in Iran today, that for twenty-five years Iran was pointed to by the Central Intelligency Agency as *the* great success story of US intervention in the affairs of other countries. It is also worth remembering, in view of the continuing stability of neighboring Arab regimes and in light of President Carter's personal distaste for the Shah, that Carter publicly called Iran an island of tranquility in a sea of turmoil.

Mossadeq, a member of the conservative landlord class, wanted Iran to gain control of its petroleum resources from the British. This doesn't seem to be a very revolutionary idea today, but Mossadeq was portrayed in the West as a dangerous leftist, if not perhaps a secret Communist. He was also a passionate man, given to tears when much moved. This struck Westerners, especially Americans, to whom lack of visible emotion is regarded as strength, as comical and weak. The real reason for wanting to destroy Mossadeq's regime was of course that the desire to nationalize the oil industry might have been infectious, especially in Saudi Arabia.

The Shah later seized the estates of all the landlords under the guise of land reform. His real objective was to remove the landlord class as rivals for power. The disastrous result was the crippling of Iranian agriculture and flight from the land to the cities by the Iranian serfs. Unemployed farmers filled the cities, particularly Tehran. These masses of people formed the mobs which Khomeini used to bring about the 1978–79 political cataclysm in Iran.

I come now to the final 'if only' something had not happened. This was the fateful American decision of 30-31 May 1972 to sell the Shah all the arms he could buy, excepting nuclear weapons. President Nixon and Secretary of State Kissinger, seemingly almost on a lark, flew from Kiev to Tehran on 30 May, had dinner with the Shah that night, told him he could buy what he wanted and flew off to Warsaw on 31 May.

All the old restraints were removed and Muhammad Reza Pahlavi, Shahinshah Aryamehr, King of Kings and Light of the Aryans, bought American arms in prodigious quantities and at a frantic pace. About $25 billion was expended on US arms alone in the next five years. These gigantic military expenditures diverted funds from an increasingly crippled agricultural sector and sucked into the military skilled manpower that might have been used to bolster economic development. The American love affair with the Shah had only one restraint. (In view of the association of the Nazis with Aryanism, we did not ourselves use the Shah's title of Light of the Aryans, limiting ourselves to King of Kings only.) But otherwise it was 'whatever the Shah wants the Shah gets'. The stage had been set for revolution in Iran.

The American policy of making the Shah its chosen instrument in the Gulf had nothing to commend it, not even 'redeeming social value' as they used to say about an otherwise objectionable film that had at least one aspect the censors felt the public might usefully view. The British were pulling out from 'east of Suez' and some sort of terrifying 'vacuum' was deemed to be lurking around waiting to descend over the Gulf the moment the last Briton pulled out. Or so one would have thought from reading the American press or listening to State Department spokesmen.

The US Government was uninformed about the realities of Iran, for one reason because our Embassy had foolishly let itself be persuaded by the Shah in 1968 that talking to the Iranian opposition constituted a lack of US confidence in the Shah's competence to rule. The Shah himself was surrounded by sycophants and sadly out of touch with the true conditions in his country. So both the US and the Shah were ignorant. As if this were not enough, Henry Kissinger had been persuaded by Israel and the Israel Lobby in the United States that a heavily armed Iran on one side and a heavily armed Israel on the other side would keep the Arab states in line and guarantee the security of Israel.

The United States was truly ignorant of reality in Iran. This alone might not have been enough to bring on the disastrous decision to make the Shah our chosen instrument in the Gulf. The other factor was Israel which views bad US relations with the Arabs as necessary to its security. Our policy in Iran and the Gulf was fatally flawed as are so many of our decisions in the Middle East, which these days are always made with an eye to what Israel wants.

THE IRAN-IRAQ WAR

The situation was ripe for an Iraqi attack on Iran when President Saddam Hussein moved in September 1980. There was growing chaos in Iran. Tehran looked weak and vulnerable, but in spite of this the Shiite revolution might spread to Iraq's majority Shias. The Iranian military officer corps was dead or in exile. US arms supply had been cut off. The balance of power seemed to have moved in Iraq's favor. The Camp David Accords had removed President Anwar Sadat from Arab leadership and thrown it to Saddam. The United States was preoccupied with the diplomatic hostage crisis. The Soviet Union was bogged down in Afghanistan.

An attack now might win for Iraq a revision of the 1975 Thalweg deal which Saddam had had to accept to induce the Shah to stop supporting a revolt by Iraq's Kurds, who lived next to one of Iraq's important oil fields. (I know now but I did not know in 1972–74 when I was Political Counselor at the US Embassy in Tehran that the United States was also secretly supporting the Kurds in conjuction with the Shah). Certainly in retrospect the US had made another short-sighted and foolish decision. Supporting the Kurds may have forced Iraq in 1975 to make a decision on the Thalweg favoring our man, the Shah, but a desire to revise that decision appears to have been a contributing cause to Iraq's decision to make war in 1980.

The war has consumed 300 000 to 500 000 lives. Many things that had been expected to happen did not happen. If Saddam Hussein thought his attack would bring down the Ayatollah Khomeini, he was wrong. The evidence suggests the attack brought on a surge of Iranian patriotism which actually strengthened Khomeini. If Saddam expected the Arabs of Khuzistan to revolt and come over to the Iraqi side, his expectations did not eventuate. If Iraq's army had had the capability of seizing all of Khuzistan the result may have been different. As the situation actually developed on the ground, Iranian Arabs stayed loyal to Iran.

Ayatollah Khomeini's call for Iraq's Shiites to revolt apparently had little effect. The Shiites had their traditional grievances against the Sunni-dominated government in Baghdad. But they have displayed little tendency during the war to see their fate as linked to Tehran. One reason for this is that whatever its other faults may be, the Saddam Hussein regime has run an effective economic development program from which all elements of the population benefited.

Iran would appear to be stronger than Iraq. It has 40 million people, Iraq only 14 million. Its territory is also much larger and it has been able to maintain a larger volume of oil exports than Iraq. Why, then, has Iraq not collapsed? The answer is that the other Arab states have helped Iraq with money and manpower. Iraq is smaller than Iran, but its effective hinterland is much larger. It includes Egypt, Jordan, Saudi Arabia, North Yemen, the Sudan and the other Arab states of the Gulf.

The war encouraged Israel to attack the Iraqi nuclear reactor. Israel has supplied Iran with arms and spare parts. How effective this has been in propping up the Khomeini regime is questionable, and the Ayatollah publicly links Israel with the 'Great Satan' America. Whether effective in helping Iran or not, Israel's aid has had the great advantage from its point of view of contributing to further bad blood between the United States and the Arabs. I have never talked to an Arab in my many visits to the Gulf who did not believe that the US was encouraging Israel's actions and was in fact itself secretly supplying Khomeini. Arguments that this would be counter to America's interests are always brushed aside.

Syria has been odd-man-out in the Iraq–Iran War due to its age-old rivalry with Iraq and its minority Alawite regime which tends to sympathize with Shiism and Shiite Iran. But the Arab oil exporting states in the Gulf, plus Jordan and Egypt, have stood by Iraq. This is not because any of them particularly like the Saddam Hussein regime, but rather because an Iranian victory over Iraq is seen as a grave danger to the Arab World as a whole.

Nothing could more dramatically highlight general Arab antipathy toward Iran and Persians in general than the display of Arab solidarity in the Gulf War. The same Iraq which earlier supported the Popular Front for the Liberation of Oman and the Arabian Gulf (PFLOAG) has received billions of dollars from the United Arab Emirates, Qatar, Kuwait and Saudi Arabia. The traditional rulers of these states whose overthrow Iraq and PFLOAG had supported, now threw their support to Iraq. Similarly, an Egypt which had been practically read out of the Arab World by Iraq in the aftermath of Camp David, now rallied to Iraq's support with arms, pilots and other manpower. The explanation is that these earlier quarrels were viewed as inter-Arab quarrels – in the family as it were. The Arab quarrel with Iran, on the other hand, was ancient and implacable. Negative Arab feelings toward Iran are fully reciprocated by negative Iranian feelings toward Arabs.

A notable development among the Arab states of the Gulf, always affected by what happens in Iran and to a lesser extent by developments in Iraq, is the formation of the Gulf Cooperation Council (GCC). The Iran–Iraq War served as a catalyst for establishing the GCC, made up of Kuwait, Saudi Arabia, Qatar, Bahrain, the United Arab Emirates and Oman.

The Iranian revolution, the Mosque incident in Mecca and the Soviet invasion of Afghanistan alarmed the Gulf Arabs. While they had never really liked the Shah, and were uneasy over his grandiose dreams of a new Persian Empire, he had represented legitimacy and stability. His downfall was thus profoundly unsettling. Khomeini's plans were unknown but his apparent ambitions to lead a resurgent Islam across international boundaries left the traditional Arab rulers in the Gulf, Sunni to a man, cold as ice. With both Iran and Iraq at war, the six remaining Arab states could huddle together for mutual protection, and they did so in February 1981 when the GCC was officially announced.

THE FUTURE OF RELATIONS

The Iran–Iraq War will probably end in stalemate. The current military advantage seems to be with Iraq, but it does not have the strength to occupy and hold large areas of Iran, especially not Khuzistan. One of the reasons is that the other Arabs would not support this. Helping Iraq to avoid defeat at the hands of Iran is one thing. Assisting Iraq to strengthen its resources and population base by seizing and holding Iran's oil-rich Khuzistan might make Iraq too strong and create an unstable imbalance of forces in the Gulf.

A related factor is that the Gulf Arabs know they must get along with Iran in the future. They have gone to considerable lengths to conceal the magnitude of their support for Iraq, although everybody including Iran knows their assistance has been large. The small Arab states in the Gulf sense that their safety may be enhanced if Gulf forces are in some kind of a balance.

Contributing to stalemate is Iran's shortage of friends. The Soviet Union has strengthened Iraq with arms while supplying few to Iran. The United States is prepared, after dawdling indecisively, to do something in its own interests by looking favorably on Iraq. This has just led to the re-establishment of diplomatic relations between Baghdad and Washington.

Pakistan is generally well disposed towards Iran. However, it has heavy financial and security interests in the Arab states of the Gulf. It also has a substantial Shiite population. Moreover, Pakistan is very deeply involved in funneling assistance from the Muslim world and from the West to oppose the Soviets in Afghanistan. In these circumstances Pakistan cannot take sides, but has to pursue a carefully neutral course.

Ayatollah Khomeini has a powerful personality, and his hold on the Mullah class and their millions of poverty-stricken supporters in Iran apparently cannot be shaken. If he dies some kind of negotiated solution with Iraq may be worked out, but as long as he lives he will insist on the departure of Saddam Hussein as one of the prices of peace. Saddam clearly has no intention of stepping aside.

While Khomeini still plays the dominant role in Iran, he has limited ability to rally to his banner Islamic fundamentalism outside his borders. Syria's action in closing Iraq's oil pipeline to the Mediterranean, to help Iran, may seem to refute this statement. Syria's population is heavily Sunni Muslim, however, and President Hafez al-Assad's policy of helping Iran is unpopular with Syria's masses and with the other Arab states.

Assad is some kind of political genuis, but he heads a regime dominated by the Alawites, hardly more than ten per cent of the total population of Syria. Also his health is not strong. For these reasons it is not likely in the long run that Iran can count on much help from the Syrian connection.

Speaking very generally, the Arabs have a fundamentally different vision of Islam from that of the Iranians. Islam in Iran has a hierarchical structure and a very large priestly class very close to the poor Iranian masses. That this class has come to rule in Iran is not surprising, given the unconcern and ineptitude of the Shah's regime with respect to those suffering from poverty, a neglect that cost the destruction of the monarchy and the classes that supported it. But this system would be foreign to the Arab states, too 'Persian' ever to be looked on favorably. This severely limits Ayatollah Khomeini's effort to gain influence in the Arab states for his brand of Islamic fundamentalism.

Unless experienced at first hand, it is all but impossible to understand how incompatible are the Arabs and the Iranians. The fact that both peoples are Muslim may seem to be a unifying force. But from the very beginning of Islam, an abyss appeared. That was over the issue of successorship to the Prophet Muhammad.

According to the Persians, Ali, Muhammad's son-in-law, was the proper Caliph. This followed the bloodline as was the Persian wont. Ali indeed became successor, Khalif in Arabic, but only after three other long-term friends and supporters of Muhammad had been Caliph first. In the tradition of the desert Arabs, the fact that the first three were not related by blood to Muhammad was of little consequence. In the Persian view the first three were usurpers, a stand not designed to gain the friendship and understanding of most Arabs.

So the split between Persians and Arabs came at the very beginning, not over some esoteric point of religious doctrine, but over ingrained differences in ways of looking at the world, of what is fitting and proper, that long pre-dated Islam. Then bitterness was added by much spilling of blood. Ali's two sons, Hassan and Hussein, were lost, Hassan through some mysterious poisoning, Hussein in bloody battle. Martyrdom was the fate of other of Ali's relatives, and the theme of martyrdom became a powerful theme in Persia and Shiite Islam.

Nothing better illustrates the basic incompatibility between Persians and Arabs than the issue of the American diplomatic hostages in Tehran. Khomeini's supporters no doubt felt vengeful over US policies that had restored the Shah to power and helped to keep him there. Holding the diplomats prisoners was sweet revenge to Iranians, who did so in the name of Islam, as they perceived the religion.

In the general Arab view, taking and holding prisoners is all but unthinkable. The code of the desert is that even your worst enemy must be given succor and sent safely on his way. This is the established way of survival in a cruel environment where failure to give hospitality might well mean death to the one turned away.

In the Arab view taking prisoners was bad in itself. But as it gradually dawned on them that the Khomeini regime would hold the US diplomats all but indefinitely, they were deeply affronted. Khomeini's call for Muslim solidarity over this issue fell on deaf ears. In 1979 and 1980 I was often told by Qataris, including the most high ranking, that what the Iranians were doing to American diplomats was a violation of everything Islam stood for. They said, 'This is not Islam'.

During this period the US Government did not fully understand how opposed the Arabs were to what Iran was doing to our diplomats. From my Embassy in Doha I sensed that a US military rescue attempt was contemplated. I tried to assure the Department of State that a military rescue would not excite an unfriendly Arab reaction even if Iranian lives were lost in the process. But seemingly convinced that Arab Muslims would react violently against Americans if Iranian Muslim were hurt, our families were uselessly evacuated from the Gulf and kept away for months.

The two peoples are divided profoundly even in the area of personal style. A 1973 incident in Tehran illustrates this. A Saudi Arabian cabinet minister was due to visit Tehran and call on the Shah. My friend the Ambassador of Saudi Arabia related to me the instructions he had received from the Shah's protocol officers. The visiting minister was to advance to the edge of a certain carpet, stop and bow deeply to the Shah and then shake hands.

The problem was, the Ambassador told me, his minister looked on bowing as humiliating. Thus he was sure he would not bow to the Shah or anyone else. When asked my advice I suggested his minister simply walk up to the Shah and shake hands. This is what happened. Royal protocol may have been offended, but the Shah simply shook hands politely.

Pomp and circumstance simply go against the Arab grain. An informal democracy is their personal style. The late King Faisal of Saudi Arabia was addressed simply as Faisal even by the most humble of his subjects. He is buried today in a grave with no marker, nothing to differentiate his grave from hundreds of others just like it. The founder of the Saudi dynasty, King Abdul Aziz al-Saud, ibn Sa'ud in the West, was addressed simply as Abdul Aziz. Anyone who knows the Iranians and their sensitivity to status recognizes that the Arab way does not at all fit in with the Iranian outlook.

One could go on at great length with examples of this kind, but I think the point has been sufficiently made. The Iranian way of doing things does not commend itself to the Arabs. Its brand of Islamic fundamentalism does not, in my view, threaten Arab regimes. Iranian military power may have been a serious threat in the immediate past, but a rarely seen Arab solidarity turned back the threat.

This is not to say that the political cataclysm in Iran has not had a strong impact in the Arab World. Greater attention will be paid to Shiites than hitherto. The Shiites of Lebanon, formerly neglected by the Beirut government but now the most numerous religious group in the country, have gained additional respect because of events in Shiite Iran. But Arab Shiites generally will remain Arabs first and Shiites second.

It cannot be denied that an Islamic resurgence, as the journalists call it, is taking place in the Arab states. Modes of dress and pious behavior attest to it. To some extent it reflects events in Iran. But the larger reason is a bitter reaction against the United States for what the Arabs perceive as a blind American favoritism for Israel. What we see is a going back to the basics by many Arabs that does not augur well for the United States unless our policy changes soon. But a strong Arab reaction against US policy in the Middle East does not presage a real or long-term *rapprochement* with Iran.

Before closing, an irony should be mentioned, one that may affect Israel and, to a lesser extent, the Arabs. That is that Israel's occupation policies in south Lebanon have provoked the deep enmity of that region's Shiite Muslims. Iran has been assisting its fellow Shiites in Lebanon, according to reports. This support may well continue, no matter what complexion the regime in Iran ultimately assumes.

On this point Iran and the Arab states may be able to cooperate to their mutual advantage. Israel, which traditionally has maintained good relations with Tehran, may now have earned the ill will of Iran and of other Shiites in the Middle East who tend to look towards Iran.

To conclude, in my view not too much has been changed between the Iranians and the Arab states by the overthrow of the Shah and the advent of a religious-centered regime in Iran. That regime will fall because of incompetency, and a man on horseback, a man with a gun, as they say, will come to power, as has always been the case in the past. The Arabs will still be on their side of the Gulf, the Iranians on their side. The two disparate peoples will continue to coexist because neither is strong enough at this time to overcome the other. They are unlikely, however, to develop much real rapport.

Meanwhile, the United States seems to be reacting to events in the area from the wrong premises, as is usually the case. Several newspaper articles in the last few days assert that our restoration of diplomatic relations with Iraq stems in part from a desire to stop the spread of what is called Islamic fundamentalism from Iran to the Arab states. There does seem to be a movement among the Arabs to go back to the basics of Islam. This results, however, not from admiration of things Iranian but from Arab disgust with American policies in the area. If US policies in future are not more closely attuned to realities, American interests will be even more gravely endangered.

Note

1. For example see, Christine Moss Helms, *Iraq: Eastern Flank of the Arab World* (Washington, DC, The Brookings Institution, 1984) Stephen R. Grumman, *The Iran-Iraq War: Islam Embattled* (New York: Praeger, 1982).

14 The International Political Economy of the Iran–Iraq War
Khosrow Fatemi

> Iran's failure to implement its agreement to withdraw its forces from Iraqi frontier territories has obliged Iraq to recover them by force . . . I am, therefore, declaring the 1975 Algiers Agreement between the two countries null and void. . . . *Shatt al-Arab* is, henceforth, totally Iraqi and totally Arab.
>
> President,Saddam Hussein of Iraq in a televised speech before the Iraqi National Assembly on 17 September 1980.

And with that final prelude began a war which even before its conclusion has earned the infamy of being one of the costliest regional wars in history.[1] Soon thereafter, rhetorical pronouncements gave way to accelerated action and, finally, full-scale war erupted on 22 September 1980 when Iraqi planes bombed and strafed several military and civilian targets deep inside Iran. Iran's response was in kind, if not in severity. Its retaliatory raids the following day included aerial attacks on Iraqi oil and industrial centers as well as military complexes. In the first weeks of the war, Iraq scores some *bona fide* military victories by capturing Iran's major port city of Khorramshahr, encircling the oil city of Abadan and setting its refinery, the world's largest, on fire. The Iraqi army was also able to drive as much as 70 miles inside Iranian territory, and, at one point, reached within artillery range of the provincial capital of Ahvaz.

However, once Iranian forces recovered from the initial shock of the war, they were able to regroup and effectively reverse the direction of the war. In the ensuing months, the stalemate of the war, which began after the incipient Iraqi success, was only broken by Iranian offensive attacks forcing additional Iraqi withdrawals. In fact, twenty months after its incursion into Iran, Iraq was forced to withdraw all of its forces from Iranian territory it had captured in the early stages of the war.

Iran responded to the withdrawal of Iraqi troops from its territory by staging a counter-invasion of its own. Starting on 13 July 1982, with its first phase lasting for three weeks, Iran 'opened four offensives, two of them major, multidivision assaults'. However, the Iraqi forces, who had earlier been less then willing to put up any resistance against the Iranians while fighting in Iran, 'fought tenaciously to hold their positions, and . . . managed to blunt the Iranian attacks.'[2] Despite heavy fighting in July and additional bloody skirmishes in the following months, during which Ayatollah Khomeini used suicidal and human-wave attacks by his fanatical supporters, he was unable to achieve his main objective of capturing the Iraqi port and oil city of Basra. The price of this adventure – by all accounts one of the bloodiest battles since World War II – has been high: 'According to Western estimates, (during this three-week period) between 16 000 and 20 000 Iranians (and) . . . several thousand Iraqis were killed and an unknown number wounded.[3]

As the war began, the armed forces of the two sides were in sharp numerical, organizational, and operational contrast to each other. Numerically, Iraq had a superior army, including 50 000 more soldiers and three times as many tanks, but inferior air and naval forces. Its 230 MIG–21s and MIG–23s could not challenge Iran's 354 F–4s, F–5s, and F–14s neither could its navy match Iran's supremacy in the Persian Gulf (For a comparison of the armed forces of the two countries see Table 14.1).

Organizationally, the Iraqi command was completely integrated and the power of its field commanders fully consolidated. There were no major coordination problems, nor was communication a perplexing issue. In contrast, the Iranian high command was fragmented and demoralized, lacked logistical support and responsive coordination, and was in a general state of disarray.

Operationally, Iraq's armed forces were well-equipped, well-disciplined, and their morale was high. Iran's military establishment, on the other hand, was only a vague shadow of its past. Its ranks dwindled by 50 per cent through desertion of soldiers and officers; its crack units – The Imperial Guards and Commando Brigades – dismantled; its arsenal half-empty because of the Western, especially American, boycott precipitated by the hostage crisis; its generals executed, jailed, or retired; and its leadership taken over by military morons.[4]

Whatever the relative strengths and weaknesses of the two armies, the undeclared war between Iran and Iraq has had devastating effects

Table 14.1 Selected statistics: Iran and Iraq 1980

	Iran	Iraq
Population (mid-year, in millions)	37.45	13.08
Area (000 square kilometers)	1 648	438
Military Forces:		
Army:		
Personnel	150 000	200 000
Tanks[1]	1 125	2 600
Air Force:		
Personnel	70 000	38 000
Combat Aircraft[2]	445	332
Navy:		
Personnel	20 000	4 250
Ships[3]	14	12

Notes:
1. Including 875 Chieftains and 250 Scorpions for Iran and 100 T-34s and 2500 T-54s/T-55s/T-62s for Iraq.
2. Including 188 F-4s and 166 F-5s for Iran and 80 MIG-23s and 150 MIG-21s for Iraq.
3. Including 3 destroyers, 4 frigates and 7 large patrol crafts for Iran and 12 missile-armed fast attacks crafts for Iraq.

Sources: International Institute for Strategic Studies as quoted by *The Times* (London, 23 September 1980) for military figures; International Monetary Fund. *International Financial Statistics* (1981 Yearbook) Washington, DC: International Monetary Fund, 1981.

on both countries, in human as well as in economic terms. Casualty figures for the first two years of the war are estimated to have been 'nearly 80 000 troops killed, 200 000 wounded, and 45 000 captured'.[5] Added to this are tens of thousands of civilian casualties and hundreds of thousands who were made homeless by the war. (Iran estimates its war-related refugees to be over 2.0 million). In human terms, the savagery of the war intensified after its first year. Fatality estimates of the war's first four years (September 1980–September 1984) range as high as 500 000 and are conservatively placed at 300 000. Because of its wreckless management of the war and its 'martyrdom' philosophy, Iran bears the brunt of casualty numbers, at least two Iranians for every Iraqi dead or wounded.

The international political economy of the Iran–Iraq war has been even more staggering and as disheartening and tragic as its casualty figures. The physical destruction of the economies of the two countries in the first year of the war, including the opportunity cost of severely impaired economies, is estimated to be over $100 billion for Iran and half as much for Iraq. The gravity of these figures is further revealed when measured in *per capita* terms or compared with other economic indicators such as gross national product (GNP) of the warring parties. In *per capita* terms, the cost of the war in its first year was about 3000 dollars for every Iranian and $4000 for every Iraqi. Moreover, total cost of the first year of the war was equivalent to 18 months of total production (GNP) in the two countries. (A comparable damage to the economy of the United States would be $2 700 000 000 000). During its second year, the war was much more savage in human terms, but far less damaging in economic terms. This was mostly because during its first year it had so thoroughly destroyed everything in the border region or within easy reach of the combatants' bombers that there was little left to destroy. Nevertheless, the aggregate figures for the economic damages of the war suffered by the two countries, including lost income, for the first four years of the war exceed $300 billion.[6]

AN HISTORICAL PREVIEW

The claim that the 1980 war between Iran and Iraq was the culmination of 'centuries of enmity' between the two countries is hyperbolic, but it is indeed a varacious one. The two neighboring counties are separated by racial, cultural, religious, and political differences, as well as by conflicting geopolitical ambitions. Of all the manifestations of this rancor, the most frequent source of tension, but also the most enduring reason for accord, has been the control of the *Shatt al-Arab* Estuary.[7] (See Map 14.1.) In fact, one of the first known treaties initiated in the region was the demarcation of the Ottoman and Persian Empires signed in 1639, creating a zone rather than a line to separate the two states. Changing circumstances of the region, notably the introduction of shipping in the estuary and the discovery of oil, rendered this pact obsolete by the early twentieth century. As a result, in 1913, under pressure from the great powers of the time, Great Britain and Russia, a new accord was reached redefining the southern part of the border between the two countries 'from a point about four miles above the mouth of the Qarun (River) to a point about one mile below it.'[8] This agreement was later revised and

285

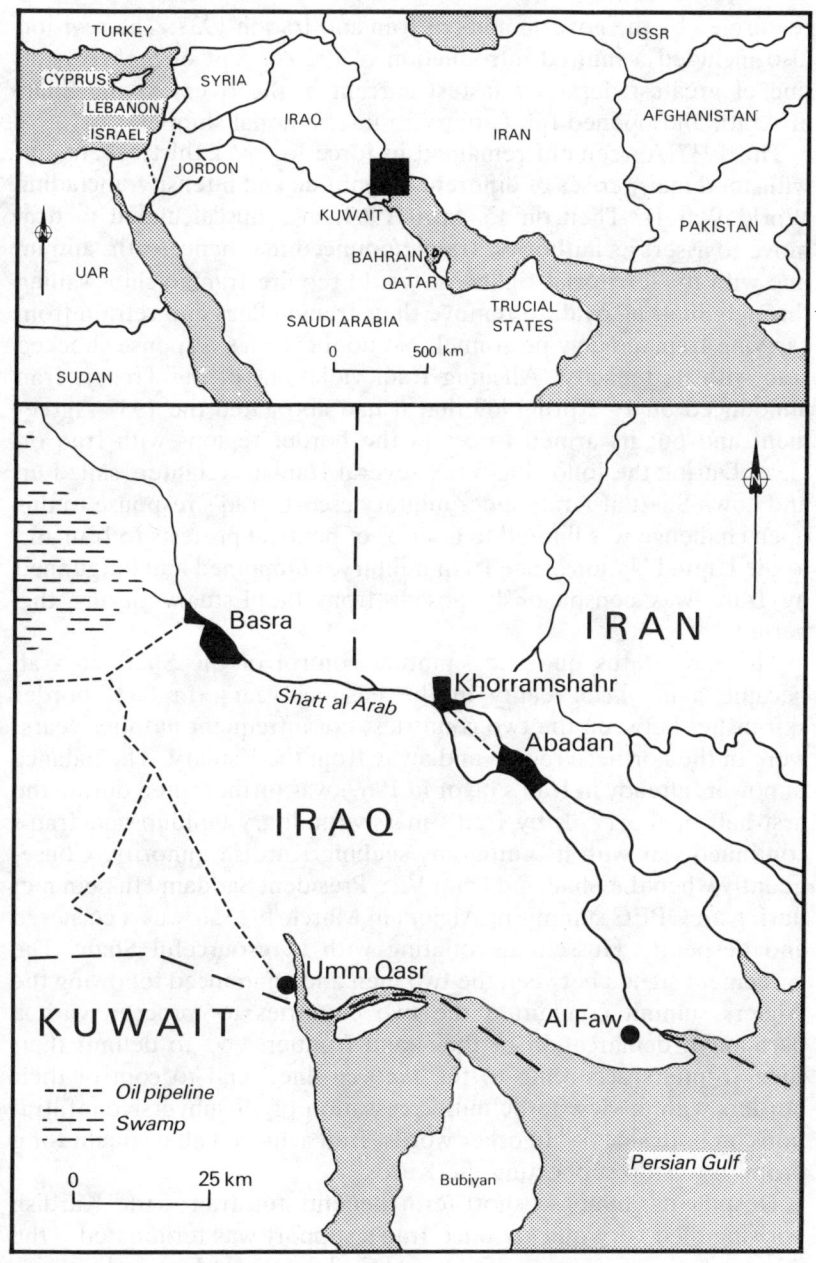

Map 14.1 Iran–Iraq Border and the Shatt al-Arab Estuary

reaffirmed by the governments of Iran and Iraq in 1937. The revision also included a limited introduction of the concept of *thalweg* (the line of greatest depth or fastest current in the river) to the Shatt al-Arab, and opened the Estuary to international shipping.

The 1937 Agreement remained in force for over thirty years and withstood many crises of different magnitude and intensity, including World War II. Then on 15 April 1969, in a miscalculated tactical move to assert its authority, Iraq announced that henceforth, and in line with its 'territorial rights', it would require Iranian ships sailing through Shatt al-Arab to remove their Iranian flags and refrain from carrying Iranian Navy personnel. No doubt, Iran's response shocked Iraq with its tenacity. Alleging Iraqi violations of the Treaty, Iran announced on 19 April 1969 that it had abrogated the 1937 Agreement and put its armed forces in the border regions with Iraq on alert. During the following week several Iranian freighters sailed up and down Shatt al-Arab under military escort. Iraq's response to this open challenge was limited to a series of political protests to Iran and to the United Nations. The Iraqi military, outmanned and outgunned by Iran, was conspicuously absent from the Estuary during this period.

The new status quo, i.e., mutual control of the Shatt al-Arab became a *de facto* reality in the ensuing years. In fact, border skirmishes between the two countries, not infrequent in those years, were in the northern region and away from the Estuary. The balance of power, already in Iran's favor in 1969, was further tilted during the first half of the 1970s by Iran's massive military buildup and Iraq's continued war with its autonomy seeking Kurdish minority. Consequently when the Shah and Iraqi Vice President Saddam Hussein met during an OPEC summit in Algiers in March 1975, it was a cornered and desperate Hussein negotiating with a resourceful Shah. The agreement signed between the two men and announced following the Algiers summit committed the two countries to 'proceed with a permanent demarcation of their land frontiers . . . to delimit their river frontiers according to the *thalweg* line,' and to control their borders with 'a view to definitive cessation of all subversive infiltrations on both sides'. [9] In other words, Iran achieved all it sought for a promise to stop supporting the Kurds.

Despite its immense short-term benefits for Iran – the Kurdish uprising died very quickly once Iran's support was terminated – the Algiers Agreement was a serious political defeat for Iraq and a major source of embarrassment and personal humiliation for Saddam Hussein. His opportunity for revenge came with the revolution in Iran and the effective disintegration of the Iranian military apparatus. Saddam Hussein's vendetta and his desire to regain both territory and prestige lost to the late Shah, however, provided only partial explanation for the Iraqis' all-out incursion into Iran. Other factors contributing to this decision included:

1. Saddam Hussein's fervid craving to become the *de facto* leader of the Arab world. This elusive objective became realistically attainable when President Sadat isolated himself and Egypt in the Arab world by signing the Camp David Accords with Israel. Saddam Hussein had already postured himself in a particularly advantageous position to capitalize on this issue. His *rapprochement* with moderate Arab states and his centrist policies in the latter half of the 1970s had placed Iraq in the mainstream of Arab politics more than at any other time since the overthrow of the monarchy in 1958. Defeating Iran and especially silencing Khomeini's 'racist' regime could have been the final step in Iraq's quest for leadership. The Ayatollah's open vows to 'export' his version of Islamic government around the world, especially 'to liberate our Muslim brethren in the neighboring countries,' had been particularly worrisome to the leaders of the Persian Gulf littoral states which have large Shiite minorities.[10] Many of these leaders would have been indebted to Saddam Hussein for this punishment and disposing of Khomeini.

To capitalize on this racial issue, Iraq claimed that its reason for the abrogation of the Algiers Agreement and its subsequent attack on Iran was 'to return Shatt al-Arab to total Iraqi and *total Arab* control'. Furthermore, it demanded the return of the islands of Abu Musa and the Greater and Lesser Tunbs to 'Arab motherland' as a precondition for any cease fire or peace with Iran.[11] The islands are strategically located in the Strait of Hormuz and were occupied by Iran in 1971. They are also claimed by the Sheikdoms of Sharja and Ras al-Khaima, both of the United Arab Emirates. These and other declarations of 'Arabism' were designed to appeal to the Arabs' sentiments and to convert the Iran–Iraq war into an Arab–Persian racial conflict.

2. The revolution in Iran created yet another power vacuum, this one in the Persian Gulf, in which Saddam Hussein had definite interests. He had competed with the late Shah for the dominance of the Persian Gulf during the latter's reign, but to no avail. The fall of the Shah, however, gave significant credence to Iraq's claim of primacy in the region. Here again, a defeat of Iran would have

accomplished the objective of establishing Iraq as the pre-eminent power of the Persian Gulf.

3. Tactically, the timing of the invasion seems to have been the result of a shrewd calculation by Iraqi military planners. By the summer of 1980, there were persistent reports of mutiny and disarray in the Iranian military.[12] There were also indications that an initial defeat could be a *coup de grace* for Khomeini's regime in Iran. With no central authority in Tehran, Iraq's goal of forcing a favorable settlement on Iran would not be far from realization. This was a simple miscalculation which plainly backfired on Iraq and also some of Mr Khomeini's internal opposition.[13] To the surprise of the former and the detriment of the latter, the Iraqi attack only helped to solidify the ayatollahs' regime and prolong their rule.

Iraq also misjudged the resolve and effectiveness of the Iranian military as well as the determination and fanaticism of Khomeini's paramilitary Revolutionary Guards.[14] The nationalistic sentiments of the Iranian military, galvanized in the face of an invasion by an old nemesis, were highly underestimated, as were Iran's war capabilities and its ability to improve them by 'improvisation' and 'cannibalization' of military spare parts and also by black-market purchases. Finally, the resolve and fanaticism of the Revolutionary Guards – who fought as much to win the war as to be 'martyred' for Islam – was another factor ignored or greatly underestimated by Iraq and its military planners.

Whatever the causes of the war, its effects are numerous, widespread, and staggering, in both political and economic terms. It is to the analysis of the impact of the war on the political economy of the world that the remainder of this Chapter addresses itself.

A CONCEPTUAL FRAMEWORK

Even though the greatest impact of the Iran–Iraq war was in the field of energy – both in pricing and supply availability – other areas of international political economy were not left fully intact. For instance, in international trade, the two countries had a combined total trade (exports and imports) of $18.7 billion in the third quarter of 1980; it was reduced to $7.4 billion in the fourth quarter of the year. More significantly, even when reactivated in 1981 and beyond, the trade patterns of both countries remained mostly redistributed and aimed at meeting short-term, indeed immediate, objectives of the war. In international finance, the two countries' foreign exchange reserves were estimated at approximately $50 billion ($35 billion for Iraq) when the war erupted; recent estimates are only a fraction of that figure. In North-South relations, when the first round of the Dialogue opened in Paris in 1975, both Iran and Iraq were among the most active delegations representing the developing nations. In round two of the talks in Cancùn, Mexico, (1981) neither country was present. The significance of these reversions to the political economy of the world notwithstanding, the greatest impact of the war was felt in the field in which the two countries were among the most important policy formulators; that is, oil. (In September 1980, when the war erupted, Iraq ranked second only to Saudi Arabia, and Iran was ninth among oil exporting countries.)

ENERGY

During the 1970s, Iran and Iraq increased their combined oil production from 5.4 million barrels per day (MM b/d) or 11.8 per cent of the world's total in 1970 to 8.3 MM b/d or 14.3 per cent of the world's total in 1976. Production in both countries tapered off slightly in 1977 to 8.0 MM b/d. (See Table 14.2) After that, while production in Iran continued to decline due to internal problems in that country – down 7 per cent in 1978, 40 per cent in 1979, and another 54 per cent in 1980 – Iraq reversed its trend and reached its highest production level, 3.5 MM b/d, in 1979. Together, the two countries averaged 6.6 MM b/d in 1979 and about 5.3 MM b/d during 1980 before the war interrupted their operations. This was substantially less than their production capacity or the peaks reached earlier. However, even at this depressed level, Iran and Iraq together produced 8.7 per cent of the world's total oil before the war's eruption in 1980. (See Table 14.3) in comparison, they averaged 1.8 MM b/d or 3.2 per cent of the world's total during the first six months of the war, i.e., October 1980–March 1981. This was mostly because of the two governments' violation of a long-standing 'gentlemen's agreement' between the two countries not to attack each other's oil installations. When in 1980 they broke this understanding, the impact of the war on oil production in both countries was immediate and severe.

In contrast to all previous skirmishes, the first reports of the 1980 war included destruction of oil centers in the two countries. During October 1980, the first full month after the inception of the war,

Table 14.2 Oil production in Iran and Iraq: 1970–1984

Year	Iran	Iraq	Total	World Total	Percentage[1]
	(000 barrels per day)				
1970	3829	1549	5378	45 720	11.8
1971	4539	1694	6233	48 219	12.9
1972	5023	1466	6489	50 850	12.8
1973	5861	2018	7879	55 802	14.1
1974	6022	1971	7993	56 088	14.3
1975	5350	2262	7612	53 384	14.3
1976	5883	2415	8298	57 883	14.3
1977	5663	2348	8011	59 863	13.4
1978	5242	2562	7804	60 142	13.0
1979	3168	3477	6645	62 679	10.6
1980	1467	2646	4113	59 741	6.9
1981	1316	897	2213	56 028	3.9
1982	2391	1012	3403	53 830	6.3
1983	2425	1005	3430	52 885	6.5
1984[2]	2230	1150	3380	53 948	6.3

Notes: 1. Production in Iran and Iraq as a percentage of the world's total.
2. January through May average.

Sources: Organization of Petroleum Exporting Countries, *Annual Statistical Bulletin*: 1982 (Vienna Organization of Petroleum Exporting Countries, 1983); US Department of Energy, *Monthly Energy Review*. (Washington, DC: August 1984) (1983–1984 Data).

Iran's production was 600 000 b/d and Iraq's was a meagre 150 000 b/d. In either case, production was not sufficient to meet the normal daily demand for domestic consumption. In other words, oil production in Iran and Iraq decreased by some four million b/d or 84 per cent from August to October 1980, and both countries ceased to be oil exporters. To alleviate the situation, other suppliers increased their production but not enough to provide immediate compensation for the entire loss. Global production which in August 1980 was 59.5 MM b/d, dropped to 56.0 MM b/d in October. In the ensuing weeks, despite the continuation of the fighting, both Iran and Iraq recovered from the initial shock of the conflict and found alternative means of exporting their oil. By early summer of 1981, total production in the two countries had reached 2.5 MM b/d – a level more or less

Table 14.3 Oil production in Iran and Iraq: 1980–1981

Month	(000 barrels per day)			World	Percentage[1]
	Iran	Iraq	Total	Total	
1980:					
January	2295	3400	5695	61 831	9.2
February	2500	3400	5900	62 130	9.5
March	2350	3400	5750	61 527	9.3
April	2200	3300	5500	60 481	9.1
May	1700	3300	5000	60 046	8.3
June	1500	3000	4800	59 703	8.0
July	1700	3100	4800	59 511	8.1
August	1600	3100	4700	59 482	7.9
September	1400	3000	4400	58 682	7.5
October	600	150	750	56 034	1.3
November	800	350	1150	56 778	2.0
December	1360	450	1810	58 018	3.1
1981:					
January	1600	600	2200	57 975	3.8
February	1700	700	2400	58 095	4.1
March	1700	1000	2700	58 410	4.6
April	1600	1000	2600	57 425	4.5
May	1500	1000	2500	56 635	4.4
June	1600	1000	2600	55 865	4.6
July	1400	1100	2500	54 360	4.6
August	1100	1100	2200	53 770	4.1
September	1100	1100	2200	53 620	4.1
October	920	1100	2020	54 385	3.7
November	930	1100	2030	53 400	3.8
December	1200	1100	2300	54 100	4.2

Note: 1. Production in Iran and Iraq as a percentage of the world's total.

Source: US Department of Energy *Monthly Energy Review*. Washington, DC: August 1982.

maintained until Iran's incursion into Iraq in July 1982. The rest of the lost production in Iran and Iraq was offset by increased exports by other producers, notably Saudi Arabia. All in all, global production of oil which had reached its lowest level since 1975 in October 1980 (the first full month of the war), recouped itself in a surprisingly orderly manner and approximated its pre-war levels in about six months.

What enabled the world to cope with the shock of losing more than 7 per cent (4.0 MM b/d) of its oil was an oversupply of crude which continued to prevail through the war and the ensuing years. According to industry sources, the world supply of oil in September 1980 exceeded global demand by some three million barrels per day. This was caused partly by overproduction in many countries, but mostly by conservation measures and also the economic slow down of Western countries. Before the war, this glut was being used by several importing countries for stockpiling purposes. The loss of production in the warring countries only slowed down or eliminated this process.

Considering that Iran and Iraq had a combined production of almost five MM b/d when the war erupted, the loss of their exports could have resulted in major disruption of oil markets and eventually large price increases not different from those of 1973 and 1979.[15] Yet, with the exception of the 'panic' buying and the $3.00 per barrel price increase of the last week of September, oil prices generally remained unaffected by the war between two major oil-producing countries. In fact, spot prices, which had been forced down by the large oversupply of summer months, had reached their lowest level of the year in August ($31.25 for lighter Iranian and Iraqi crudes) and had begun their moderate and seasonal surge early in September – three weeks before the beginning of the conflict. (See Table 14.4) However, the outbreak of hostilities, and particularly early reports of severe damage of oil installations of both countries, did result in a mild buying spree in the market; and spot prices registered increases of up to 10 per cent in the first week of the war, i.e., the last week of September. This increase could also be attributed to the reports that Iran might, in the face of a major defeat, attempt to block the strait of Hormuz, thus stopping oil exports from all Persian Gulf exporting countries. At any rate, this upward move was very brief and returned to normalcy and its seasonal pace after that. By mid-November, the price of average Persian Gulf oil was about $42 per barrel – a $7.00 or 20 per cent increase from early September. This increase is not, however, much higher than normal seasonal fluctuations of spot prices and cannot be necessarily attributed to the war.[16]

In fact, the most remarkable characteristic of the war in the energy area is what it did not produce, i.e., the absence of major price escalations. This moderation of response by the world oil markets can be best elucidated in terms of the oversupply of oil which was persistent at the war's inception and has remained in effect since.

Table 14.4 Weekly spot prices[1] – selected Iranian and Iraqi crudes: June–November 1980

	(US dollars per barrel)			
	Iranian light		Iraqi light	
Period	34	API	34	API
June (4-week average)		36.13		36.00
July (5-week average)		34.60		34.60
August:				
First week	33.00		33.00	
Second week	32.25		32.25	
Third week	31.25		31.25	
Fourth week	31.25		31.25	
4-week average		31.94		31.94
September:[2]				
Second week	31.75		31.75	
Third week	32.00		32.00	
Fourth week	35.00		35.00	
4-week average		32.92		32.92
October (4-week average)		38.00		38.00
November (4-week average)		41.25		41.25

Notes: 1. All prices on 30-day credit basis.
2. No quotations given for the first week of September.

Source: Syndic Oil as quoted in Organization of Petroleum Exporting Countries, *OPEC Bulletin* (monthly) (Vienna: Organization of Petroleum Exporting Countries) (Various 1980–1981 issues.)

This glut was caused, on the one hand, by expanded production capacity in many oil producing countries; and on the other, by a transitional stagnation of demand in the consuming nations. The supply side of the glut can be traced to the need, or greed, of OPEC states and some non-OPEC producers which continued to increase their production, and production capacity, not only in total disharmony with each other, but also in absolute dichotomy to global economic dictates. This excess – and excessive – production capacity contributed heavily to the phlegmatic response of oil markets during the early stages of the Iran–Iraq war. It created the general perception among the buyers of the willingness and *ability* of other producers to increase their production to counter the loss of oil from Iran and Iraq. In fact, an OPEC decision was announced on 26 September 1980 that the implementation of a planned 10 per cent production cut

Table 14.5 Global oil production: 1975–1984

	OPEC	(MM b/d) Mexico/ Britain	World total	OPEC as % of total
1975	27 155	717	52 880	51.4
1976	30 738	1076	57 312	53.6
1977	31 298	1749	59 685	52.4
1978	29 805	2291	60 057	49.6
1979	30 928	3029	62 535	49.5
1980	26 891	3558	59 538	45.2
1981	22 646	4124	55 900	40.5
1982	18 784	4866	53 162	35.3
1983	17 575	4975	52 885	33.2
1984[1]	17 975	5230	53 948	33.3

Note: 1. January–May Average.

Source: US Department of Energy, *Monthly Energy Review* (Washington, DC: August 1984).

by most member states, agreed to earlier in the month, had been indefinitely postponed.[17] The willingness of different oil exporting countries to capitalize on the misfortunes of other exporters had never been in doubt,[18] but their ability to do so on short notice had been. What distinguished 1980 from other supply interruptions was the large excess capacity which prevailed in most producing countries – thus enabling them to happily oblige and compensate for whatever shortages were created by the curtailment of supply from the warring countries.

A second supply factor contributing to the moderate behavior of world oil markets in 1980 was the role of non-OPEC producers, particularly Mexico. During the epoch of OPEC power in the early and mid-1970s, non-OPEC exporters were small in number and insignificant in capacity. By 1980, however, the largest two of these countries, Mexico and Britain, were producing more than 3.0 MM b/d and were competing with OPEC in some markets (See Table 14.5). Consequently, the aggregate crude exports of all OPEC states which had peaked at 27.6 MM b/d in 1977 dropped to 22.9 MM b/d in 1980. This falling trend has continued during the Iran–Iraq war and the agreement reached by OPEC member states in November 1984 to limit their total production to 16.0 MM b/d will assure the continuation of this trend, at least in the foreseeable future.

Table 14.6 US Oil imports by source: 1975–1984

	Volume			Percentage	
	OPEC	non-OPEC	Total	OPEC	non-OPEC
1975	3601	2454	6056	59.5	40.5
1976	5066	2247	7313	69.3	30.7
1977	6193	2614	8807	70.3	29.7
1978	5751	2613	8363	68.8	31.2
1979	5637	2819	8456	66.7	33.3
1980	4300	2609	6909	62.2	37.8
1981	3323	2672	5996	55.4	44.6
1982	2146	2968	5113	42.0	58.0
1983	1862	3189	5051	36.9	63.1
1984[1]	2055	3408	5463	37.6	62.4

Note: 1. January–June Average

Source: US Department of Energy, *Monthly Energy Review* (Washington, DC: August 1984).

On the other hand, the demand side of the glut was precipitated by a global decline in demand for 'foreign', particularly OPEC, oil. Whether caused by an economic slowdown or by effective conservation, this drop in demand has contributed heavily to the oil glut of the late 1970s and early 1980s. The United States has been particularly effective in diminishing its dependence on foreign, specifically OPEC oil. American imports of foreign oil which had peaked in 1979 at about 8.5 MM b/d dropped to 5.1 MM b/d in 1983. This was a reduction of 3.4 MM b/d or 40 per cent (See Table 14.6). More significantly, share of OPEC as a percentage of total oil imports into the United States has fallen from 70.3 per cent in 1977 to 37.6 per cent in the first half of 1984. In volume, this translates to a reduction of more than 4.1 MM b/d in OPEC potential exports. A similar trend, albeit not as pronounced, can be established for the other major consuming nations. Total consumption of oil by other member countries of the International Energy Agency (IEA) was 14.5 MM b/d in 1983. This is a decrease of 2.9 MM b/d or 17 per cent from its peak level of 1979.

In addition to this precarious situation of lower demand and higher supply and the resultant glut both before and so far during the Iran–Iraq war, what further kept the calm of oil markets was that in

Table 14.7 Petroleum stocks and consumption rates – major energy consuming countries: September 1980

	Petroleum stocks (Billion barrels)	Daily consumption (Million barrels)	Ratio[1] (Days)
USA	1447	16.60	87
Japan	508	4.12	123
Germany	306	2.54	120
France	264	1.74	152
Italy	192	1.65	116
Canada	183	1.71	107
Britain	173	1.27	136
TOTAL	3073	29.63	104

Note: 1. Petroleum stocks divided by daily consumption.

Source: US Department of Energy, *Monthly Energy Review* (Washington, DC: August 1982).

1980 all major oil importing countries were better prepared than ever to counter and manage any foreign oil shortages. Stung by their earlier inability to cope with oil supply interruptions, they began stockpiling larger inventories. Consequently, by 1980 these counties could rely on the security of 100, in some cases 150, days of oil reserves (See Table 14.7). This, plus the energy-sharing provisions of the International Energy Agency,[19] were the final impediments to any superfluous buying which could have accompanied the loss of Iranian and Iraqi oil in 1980 – hence the mature behavior of oil-consuming nations in the face of what could have been a major crisis.

TRADE

During the 1970s Iran and Iraq increased their aggregate international trade (imports and exports) by 746 per cent from $7885 million in 1971 to $66 698 million in 1980 (See Table 14.8). Contrary to general perception, only one-half of this was attributable to expanding oil sales (See the Second on Energy) and the rest was caused by

Table 14.8 International trade of Iran and Iraq: 1971–1983

(Million US Dollars)

Year	Iran Exports	Iran Imports	Iraq Exports	Iraq Imports
1971	3 825	2 219	1 139	702
1972	4 040	2 805	1 108	705
1973	6 182	3 383	1 944	905
1974	21 575	5 433	6 600	2 372
1975	20 211	10 343	8 297	4 215
1976	23 507	12 894	9 272	3 470
1977	24 260	14 645	9 649	3 899
1978	22 101	13 549	11 061	4 213
1979	19 976	9 738	21 431	7 230
1980	14 107	12 246	26 278	14 067
1981	12 612	12 499	10 530	20 922
1982	16 445	18 119	10 250	21 280
1983	19 498	18 227	9 785	11 712

Sources: Organization of Petroleum Exporting Countries, *Annual Statistical Bulletin*: 1980 (Vienna: Organization of Petroleum Exporting Countries, 1981) (1971–1973 data); International Monetary Fund, *Direction of Trade Statistics: 1982 Yearbook*. (Washington, DC: International Monetary Fund, 1984) (1977–1983 data) and 1981 (1974–1976 data).

other changes in the trade pattern of the two nations, *inter alia* the following:

1. The most obvious change in the trade picture of the two countries was the distortion of their import composition away from industrial and non-food products and towards heavy concentration on war material and food items. A natural consequence of a modern-day war is to expeditiously deplete the war chests of the belligerents and enhance their requisites for weapons and military spare parts. The warring parties of the Persian Gulf have been no exception to this rule and have expanded their military purchases and food imports to levels unparalleled in their recent history. In the light of their diminished export earnings and impoverished foreign currency reserves, this revamping of priorities has resulted in drastically reduced imports of non-food, non-military items by the two countries, particularly by Iran.

2. Another impact of the war on import patterns of the two countries has been their geographical dislocation. Iran's trade, heavily oriented towards the Western industrial countries during the Shah's reign and in the first five quarters of the Islamic Republic, reversed its trend in 1980. This was partly because of the revolutionary and anti-Western rhetoric of the ayatollahs, but mostly because of the Western embargo – even though only partially effective – placed on the country in the wake of the hostage crisis. Iran's imports from industrial countries, which had peaked in the second quarter of 1978 at $4510 million, fell by 63.7 per cent to $1639 million during the first three months of the war, i.e., the fourth quarter of 1980.

On the other hand, Iran's trade with the socialist and non-oil LDCs which had increased substantially because of the revolution were further enhanced by the war. Imports from the Soviet Union and other socialist countries, under 4.0 per cent of the total during the Shah, increased to 11.3 per cent in 1979 and remained at about 10 per cent until 1983 when it fell to 5.8 per cent.[20] Similarly imports from non-oil LDCs, only 10.4 per cent of the total in 1978, reached 18.8 per cent in 1980 and peaked at 28.2 per cent in 1982 before falling to 25.0 per cent in 1983. Lacking a complete breakdown of Iran's trade figures, and based on fragmented information from Iranian sources, this author's conjecture is that much, if not most, of the increase in imports from non-oil LDCs comes from re-exportation of industrial products from these countries to Iran. Many Iranian importers of western products simply re-route their imports through third countries, thus avoiding both the western embargo (1979–1981) and the ayatollahs' wrath of trading with the 'great and little satans'.

In the early stages of the Islamic Republic, most of this re-routed trade was with Iran's Persian Gulf neighbors. For example, in 1980 Iran's officially reported imports from the United Arab Emirates – which did not include black-market trade estimated at over $1.0 billion – amounted to $402 million. This was equal to one-third of that country's total non-oil exports. Following the expansion of the war into the Persian Gulf, Turkey became Iran's main source of Western, particularly American, goods. Iran's imports from Turkey increased from $41 million in 1977 to $257 million in 1981 and to $978 million in 1983.[21]

Iraq's initial decision, on the other hand, was to keep its imports of consumer goods at their pre-war levels, thus minimizing the war's impact on its citizenry. To accomplish this, Iraq relied heavily on its financial backers (see next section on international finance). In 1983,

Iraq's credit was 'exhausted' and imports were curtailed by 45 per cent, from $21 280 million in 1982 to $11 712 million in 1983. The information available on the breakdown of Iraq's post-war trade pattern and the impact of the war on its geographical distribution is fragmented and incomplete. What is available, however, indicates a continuation of the trend established in the second half of the 1970s. During that period, imports from industrial countries increased continuously from 59.2 per cent of total in 1974 to 78.1 per cent in 1980. Reduced during the same period were imports from the Soviet bloc and also from non-oil LDCs. In 1974, 12.9 per cent and 27.4 per cent of Iraq's imports came from these two blocs respectively. Comparable figures in 1981 were 2.5 per cent and 16.1 per cent.[22] This trend was reversed after 1980 and by 1983 only 57.5 per cent of Iraq's total trade was with industrial countries compared with 27.4 per cent from non-oil LDCs. Trade with the Soviet Union and the socialist bloc has stabilized at under 2.0 per cent.[23]

3. A final ramification of the war on the trade patterns of the two countries was to reduce their reliance, however temporarily, on oil exports. For Iran, the ratio of oil exports as a percentage of total exports during the first three months of the war (fourth quarter of 1980) was 89.9 per cent, compared with 95.3 per cent in the preceding quarter. It was also lower than that of any other time during the past decade. For Iraq, oil exports fell from 99.5 per cent of total exports in the third quarter of 1980 to 97.4 per cent in the fourth quarter. It is particularly ironic that the two nations' long-sought objective of less reliance on oil exports could be accomplished only by a war between them. This 'accomplishment' was very short-lived for both countries and by 1982 reliance on oil was even greater than before.

To summarize the impact of the war on the trade patterns of Iran and Iraq, a comparison of pre-war and war-affected trade statistics of the two countries indicates major structural and geographic shifts in both cases. It is however, too early to determine how much of this change is a consequence of the war and how much of it is due to unrelated international policies or isolated domestic events.

INTERNATIONAL FINANCE

For several years before the war, rapidly increasing oil prices enabled both Iran and Iraq to achieve surpluses in their balance of trade and also balance of payments, and to accumulate large reserve of gold,

SDRs, and foreign currencies. Estimates of total reserves of the two countries at the beginning of the war were $15–20 billion for Iran and twice as much for Iraq. Both countries are reluctant and slow to publish financial figures. (For example, the October 1984 issue of *International Financial Statistics* published by the International Monetary fund has no 'total reserves' figures for Iran after the first quarter of 1981 and after 1977 for Iraq.) Despite their secrecy, partial figures, unofficial estimates, and also deductions from related activities of the two governments, reveal the immense impact of the war on foreign exchange reserves of the two countries. Iraq's solution has been to 'borrow' from other Arab states, including interest-free loans and grants totaling more than $20 billion during 1981–1982.[24] Lacking international credit – and domestic credit, for that matter – the Iranian government has relied heavily on its printing presses and has curtailed non-military, non-food imports. Consequently, the claim by the Central Bank of Iran on the government, that is, the amount of money owed to the Bank by the government, almost tripled in the first year of the war. It stood at 1072 billion Rials ($15.3 billion) at the end of September 1980, then increased to 1636 billion Rials ($22.8 billion) by the end of the year, and 3003 billion Rials (38.5 billion) by December 1981, at which time the publication of the figure was suspended.[25] Even though the significance of this parameter is more in the microeconomic behavior of the economy, in cases such as Iran's it also reveals shortages of foreign exchange earnings.[26] While no official figures are given, it is estimated that during the first year of the war alone, the reserves of the two nations were depleted to less than one-third of their pre-war levels.

NORTH–SOUTH RELATIONS

When the first round of North–South Dialogue, officially known as the Conference on International Economic Cooperation (CIEC), opened in Paris in October 1975, Iran and Iraq were among the 19 representatives of the Third World countries.[27] They were both active in negotiations which followed in the ensuing 20 months and, in fact, Iran was elected, along with the European Economic Community, as the Co-Chairman of the Finance Commission of the Conference.[28] In contrast, when the next round of the Dialogue opened in Cancun, Mexico in October 1981 both countries were conspicuously absent. Although the two were not the only countries from the Paris Conference not to be present in Cancun.[29] they were among the most important ones. While Iran's absence was as much a consequence of its object leadership as it was to its war with Iraq,[30] the latter's non-attendance can only be attributed to its war with Iran. Considering the significance of the two countries to any ongoing dialogue between the poor and rich nations of the world, their elimination from Cancun has to be viewed as a political setback for both nations and as an indication of their new and pejorative status in the community of nations.

LONG-TERM PROSPECTS AND CONCLUSIONS

Even though the Iran–Iraq war is regional in scope and binational in nature, its consequences on the political economy of the world are far-reaching and not necessarily confined to the borders of the warrying states. This, despite the fact that, at least in the short-run, the impact of the conflict on the global energy situation was much less severe and more tame than it might have been. Considering the usual delicate balance between the supply and demand for oil, under most circumstances a war of this magnitude between two major oil-producing countries would have resulted in major panic buying, *à la* 1973, and substantial price increases. However, the incidence of the war with (1) a diminished demand for oil caused by the economic slowdown of the West; and (2) the existence of a major oversupply of oil in international markets, averted such a crisis. It was because of this coincidence that the experiences of 1973 and 1979 – when supply interruptions of smaller significance resulted in major price increases – were not repeated in 1980.

In the longer run, and from a different perspective, the war seems to have bred new life into OPEC. As an international oil cartel, OPEC has survived more than a decade of economic manipulation of the world because there has always been much mutuality of interest and little cause for discord among its members,[31] that is, always except in 1980–1984. In the three years preceding the Iran–Iraq war, global demand for OPEC oil had diminished by almost 20 per cent – from 29.4 MM b/d in 1977 to 24.9 MM b/d in 1980. This reduced demand was creating considerable tension among OPEC states, who found themselves competing in the unfamiliar surroundings of a buyers' market for the first time since OPEC rose to primacy in the early 1970s. Consequently, OPEC members began resorting to unusual

Table 14.9 OPEC oil production and exports: 1975–1984

	Production M b/d	Change	Total exports M b/d	Change
1975	27 155	—	25 624	—
1976	30 738	+13.2%	29 333	+14.5%
1977	31 298	+1.8%	29 392	+0.2%
1978	29 805	−4.8%	27 977	−4.8%
1979	30 928	+3.8%	28 910	+3.3%
1980	26 891	−13.1%	24 889	−13.9%
1981	22 646	−15.8%	20 282	−18.5%
1982	18 784	−17.1%	16 409	−12.6%
1983	17 575	−6.4%	15 175	−7.5%
1984	17 200	−2.1%	14 700[1]	−3.1%

Note: 1. Estimated by the author.

Sources: US Department of Energy, *Monthly Energy Review*. (Washington, DC: August 1984) (for production figures); Organization of Petroleum Exporting Countries, *Annual Statistical Bulletin: 1982*: (Vienna: OPEC, 1983).

tactics, including hidden discounts and long credit terms, to undermine each other and increase their own sales. Continuation of this situation could have, and in the judgment of the author would have, led to OPEC's demise – if not its total disintegration – at least to its termination as a strong cartel. The war reduced OPEC's total production capacity by some 7–8 million barrels per day and relieved most of the pressure of competition on its members.

This war-induced reprieve, however, was very short-lived. The continued decline in demand for OPEC oil further reduced the cartel's total exports to 20.3 MM b/d in 1981, 16.4 MM b/d in 1982 and to 15.2 MM b/d in 1983 (See Table 14.9). OPEC members' initial response was panic and undercutting of each other. Eventually most members agreed on a 'temporary' production scheduling whereby OPEC's total production would be limited to 17.5 MM b/d, with Iran and Iraq receiving identical quotas of 1.2 MM b/d. Iran vowed from the beginning that it would not abide by its allocated production level and was soon joined by some others. After several months of bickering, Iran's quota was raised to 2.4 MM b/d in March of 1983. At the same time, total OPEC quota was kept at 17.5 MM b/d. Even this reduced production total proved to be more than the world markets would absorb and downward pressure persisted on the spot market prices. This culminated in the fall of 1984 with a British/Norwegian decision to lower their North Sea prices and they were quickly followed by a Nigerian – an OPEC member. The emergency meeting of OPEC which followed the Nigerian action succeeded in temporarily averting the crisis by lowering its total production limit to 16.0 MM b/d.

What makes the above particularly alarming to OPEC is that all of this price cutting and in-fighting takes place when two of its members are at war with each other and are, consequently, unable to produce but only a fraction of their pre-war capacity.[32] In reality, the war has been a blessing for OPEC. By curtailing its production capacity by about 6.0 MM b/d (20 per cent) it has downgraded the cartel's chaos to disarray and has enhanced its effectiveness.

Undoubtedly, the termination of hostilities between Iran and Iraq will change the picture. Both countries have to increase their oil revenues rapidly merely to survive their post-war and war-related economic problems. They can possibly reach their combined pre-war production capacity of 8-9 MM b/d within a few months after the cessation of hostilities. In comparison with present production estimates, these figures would indicate an increase in the production capacity of oil exporting countries of some 5–6 MM b/d, in an already depressed market. At present prices, the world oil market will not be able to absorb any of this increase. That being the case, the response of the world oil markets would depend on the incidence and timing of (1) the economic recovery of the Western industrial countries, and (2) the resolution of the Iran–Iraq war. For an analysis of this interrelationship, the following scenarios have been developed:

1. *The increased exports in Iran and Iraq to generally coincide with an economic upswing in the West.* Under this scenario, once the Western economies recover from their present problems, then (a) demand for OPEC oil will expand rapidly; (b) this increase in demand will absorb not only the added exports of Iran and Iraq, but also the expected production increases in other hard-pressed OPEC countries such as Nigeria; and, (c) the absorption of these production increases by the market will necessitate no change or very minor changes in the price structure of oil.

2. *The parties to prolong the war to outlast current demand short falls.* Under this rather pessimistic scenario, the increased demand for oil will be met by higher utilization of production capacities of other exporting countries. There will be no oil shortages and oil prices will remain essentially constant.

3. *The war between Iran and Iraq to end before there is an end to the current economic problems and before there is any additional demand for oil.* Under such circumstances, any increase in production in Iran and/or Iraq could come only at the expense of other producers, notably Saudi Arabia. Others are either heavily populated and are too dependent on their already depressed oil income to afford any revenue losses, or are such small producers that any changes in their production levels would not appreciably alter the overall picture. Algeria, Indonesia, Nigeria, and Venezuela comprise the first group; while Ecuador, Gabon, Kuwait, Libya, Qatar, and the United Arab Emirates, with a combined production quota of about 3.4 MM b/d, fall in the second category.

Except in the case of Scenario 1, and even then only if materialized to its fullest extent, the impact of the resolution of the Iran–Iraq war on the world energy situation would depend on the response of Saudi Arabia to the renewed pressure on it to cut production. If the Kingdom is willing, and able, to reduce its exports by as much as 2.5–3.0 MM b/d, then increased exports by Iran and Iraq would not have any important effects on the world energy picture.[33] Otherwise, the resolution of the Iran–Iraq war would be accompanied, within a few months, by a serious, indeed – 'cut-throat' – competition among oil exporting countries. This would, in turn, lead to sharp price reductions and a serious weakening of OPEC. Whether this would be a permanent alteration of the international energy picture, or whether it would last until oil markets again become a sellers' market, would depend on the severity of competition in the interval and the extent of the damage suffered by the losers of this intra-OPEC competition, something which can be assessed only in *ex post facto* terms.

The consequences of the Iran–Iraq war on other aspects of international political economy are less complex and more predictable. In the area of international trade, the war has resulted in substantial and long-term increases in the two countries' reliance on trade, particularly with the Western industrial countries. Replacement of tens of billions of dollars-worth of destruction in the two countries cannot be accomplished without Western know-how, Western technology, and even Western capital; thus the two countries' long-term dependence on trade with – and, in fact, general dependence on – the West. In this context, the West can be assured of a multi-year, 100-billion dollar market for its industrial and infrastructure products in Iran and Iraq once the war is over. The Soviet bloc countries can also count on a captive, albeit substantially smaller, market for their food and light industrial products. The developing countries, on the other hand, might end up being the trade losers of the war. Except for food, there was little that either country imported from other developing countries and even those marginal figures will be further reduced while rebuilding plans are under way in both countries.

Finally, in the area of international finance, both Iran and Iraq will be net borrowers of funds in the international financial markets, particularly in the short-run. Both countries need more hard currency than their exports would provide them, even considering an expanded oil production, and both will have to rely on international lending institutions to meet their financial requirements. Their entry into the loan markets, however, will not produce any serious competition for other borrowers. Iraq has traditionally relied on Arab sources and will most likely continue to do so. Iran's credit rating is currently very low. (A recent survey places Iran 95th among the 101 countries appraised.) Regardless of the outcome of the war and the timing of its conclusion, Iran's creditworthiness will not improve much until its domestic political problems are solved and sanity returns to its leadership – or its leadership returns to sanity.

Notes

1. *The Washington Post*, 20 September 1981 quoting Western analysts estimated Iran's loss during the first year of the war to be 'over $100 billion', and Iraq's to be 'probably half that amount'. The *Baltimore Sun* quoted by The *Iran Times* 25 September 1981 gives a similar assessment of the war's total cost for its first year. The total figure of $150 billion translates into $411 million for every day, that is one million dollars for every 3.5 minutes of the war. Iran's estimates its war-related losses for the first three years to be $163 696 750 000.
2. For journalistic accounts of this phase of the war, see *Time*, 2 August 1982. pp. 26–27; The *New York Times*, 5 August 1982. P. A5; and *Newsweek*, 2 August 1982. p. 27.
3. The *Christian Science Monitor*, 3 August 1982. pp. 1, 8.
4. At the inception of the war, the Commander-in-Chief of the Iranian armed forces was Ayatollah Khomeini and his chief deputy and the president of the country's Supreme Defense Council – in charge of planning and implementing the country's military affairs – was Abol-Hassan Bani-Sadr. Both were military illiterates, as were several other members of the Council, including Prime Minister Rajai, Khomeini's personal representative on the Council, Ayatollah Khamenei, and Majlis Speaker, Ayatollah Hashemi Rafsanjani. The combined military expertise of the five was Rajai's brief tenure with the Iranian Air Force which

culminated in a dishonorable discharge. Only a minority of the Council members, i.e., its less powerful *ex officio* members were trained military men.
5. The *New York Times*, 5 August 1982. p. A5. Iranian opposition forces place the number of casualties for Iran alone at over '200 000 killed and similar number wounded or captured'.
6. Iran officially places its losses during the first three years at $163.7 billion, broken down into the following categories:

Oil and petrochemical	$53.7
Agriculture	40.7
Industries	8.2
Energy (non-oil)	3.7
Others	57.4

Source: *The Interim Report of the Special Commission on the Estimation of Economic Damages of the War* (Tehran, Summer 1984).
7. The *Shatt al-Arab* River is formed by the confluence of the Tigris and Euphrates rivers at the town of al-Qurhan in Iraq. It is later joined by the Karun (Qarun) River on the Iranian side and flows southeastward for 120 miles to the Persian Gulf. For about the last half of its course, flowing through Iraqi port cities of Basrah and al-Fao (al-Faw) and Iranian port cities of Khorramshahr and Abadan, the estuary forms the Iranian-Iraqi border. It is on this part of the river that all the conflict centers.
8. For a detailed discussion of all the agreements over the *Shatt al-Arab* see Alexander Melmid, 'The *Shatt al-Arab* Boundary Dispute,' *The Middle East Journal*, Vol. XXII, No. 3, 1968. pp. 350–7.
9. The *New York Times*, 8 March 1975.
10. There are large Shiite minorities in Kuwait, Bahrain, Abu Dhabi, Dubai, Qatar, and Oman. Shiites are, in fact, the majority in Iraq, but the government is under the control of the Sunni minority. There were numerous pro-Khomeini demonstrations in many of these countries during much of 1979 and early 1980.
11. See, for example, Edward Cody, 'Three Islands in the Persian Gulf Emerge as Issues in the War', The *Washington Post*, 26 September 1980.
12. An attempted coup by Air Force officers, for example, was discovered in July 1980 and resulted in the execution of scores of Iran's top pilots and technicians and the arrest of hundreds more. Many of those arrested were released during the early stages of the war to fly bombing missions over Iraq – usually accompanied by a Revolutionary Guardsman to foil any defections.
13. There were, in fact, many reports that some opposition leaders were in Iraq waiting for their opportunity or 'the right moment' to enter Iran and take over the reigns of government. *The Times* (London) reported on 26 September 1980 that 'a committee has been set up in London by a number of Iranian generals in exile with the aim of making contingency preparations for what they see as the imminent collapse of the Islamic Republic in Iran'. The paper identified the leader of the group as General Bahram Aryana, a former Chief of Staff of the Iranian military

under the Shah. According to this report, the generals maintain contact with General Oveisi, former commander of the Iranian Army, who 'has just returned from the United States to Iraq', and also with Shahpour Bakhtiar, who was also reported to have been in Baghdad when the war erupted.
14. An unusual illustration of this point is provided by a letter written to the editor of The *Iran Times* (9 October 1981, p. 14) purportedly by a member of the Revolutionary Guards. In this letter, the Guardsman discusses an 'incident' he claims to have witnessed while fighting at the war front. However absurd the story might sound to the logical mind, it does provide an insight into the fanaticism of some of the Revolutionary Guards. According to the writer, a captured Iraqi soldier asked to see the 'courageous' commander of the Iranian forces. Taken to see the commander, he objected and insisted on seeing the 'real' commander, 'the one who was leading your (Iranian) forces riding a white horse and using a sword. The one who killed several of us but we could not shoot him' (The bullets would not affect him.) The conclusion of the Revolutionary Guardsman who wrote the letter was that Iran's 'Islamic Army' was led by Imam Mahdi, the Twelveth Imam of Shiites, purportedly absent for some 1100 years to return to earth on Resurrection or Judgment Day.
15. The decision by OAPEC (The Organization of Arab Petroleum Exporting Countries) in October 1973 to reduce its members' production by 5-10 per cent, and also to place selective embargoes against some oil importing countries for supporting Israel, resulted in panic buying which ultimately led to the tripling of oil prices by January 1974. In 1979, the interruption of supplies caused by the revolution in Iran generated another round of oil price escalation in which the price of OPEC Marker Crude increased from $13.34 per barrel in January 1979 to $24 per barrel by the end of the year. The loss of production in Iran and Iraq in 1980 while larger than either of the two previous cases, resulted in no major price increases.
16. In 1979, for example, prices in November were 16 per cent higher than in September.
17. See The *Washington Post*, 27 September 1980. pp. 1, 16.
18. Reference is made, *inter alia*, to 1952, when the loss of Iranian oil was more than compensated by increases in Saudi Arabia, Kuwait, and Iraq. In 1967 and 1973, the decision by Arab producers to curtail their exports resulted in increased production in other countries, notably Iran and Venezuela. Finally, Iran's production cuts in 1978–1979 resulted in increases by other producers, particularly Iraq and Saudi Arabia. All cases are indications of one or a group of producers' misfortunes becoming another group's opportunity to seize, and capture potential markets.
19. According to the provisions of the International Energy Agency, supply shortages of more than 7 per cent in any one member country triggers a system-wide sharing scenario under which all members are expected to share their oil with the affected member or members.
20. See International Monetary Fund, *Direction of Trade Statistics 1981 Yearbook* (Washington DC, International Monetary Fund, 1984) pp. 212–213.

21. It should be noted there that Iran's trade figures for the 1970s were changed in 1981 making any meaningful comparisons between pre- and post-1980 very difficult. Examples: (1) Iran's imports from non-oil LDCs for 1979 had been reported to be $1,713 million. *Direction of trade op. cit.*, *1981 Yearbook*, p. 208. It was changed to $959 million. *Ibid.*, *1982 Yearbook*, p. 207. (2) Iran's imports from the socialist bloc had been reported to be 4.4 per cent of the country's total imports during 1980. *Ibid.*, *1981 Yearbook*, p. 209. It was changed to 8.8 per cent *Ibid.*, *1982 Yearbook*, p. 208.
22. *Direction of Trade, op. cit.*, *1981 Yearbook*, pp. 211–12 and *1982 Yearbook*, p. 211.
23. *Direction of Trade, op. cit.*, *1984 Yearbook*, pp. 214–15.
24. The *Wall Street Journal* 27 November 1981 estimated Iraq's borrowing from Saudi Arabia and Kuwait to be 'between $8 billion and $20 billion' during the first year of the war. The *New York Times* 23 July 1982 estimated that 'Baghdad [has] . . . received more than $16 billion in 'grants' from its Arab neighbors since the war began'. *Newsweek* 26 July 1982 puts the total aid to Iraq from Arab sources at 'more than $22 billion'. *Time* 26 July 1982 estimated the contributions of Persian Gulf states to 'the Iraqi war chest [to be] . . . at least $20 billion.'
25. International Monetary Fund, *International Financial Statistics*, (Washington, DC: International Monetary Fund, October 1984) pp. 246–247.
26. The supposition that the shortage of government income can be equated with foreign exchange deficiencies is true only when there is a high correlation between the two, i.e., in cases where the government receives a very high share of its income from foreign sales of indigenous commodities, usually natural resources. The governments of Iran and Iraq derive more than 90 per cent of their revenues from their foreign oil sales and easily fall within this supposition.
27. Other representatives of the developing countries elected by the Group of 77 were: Algeria, Argentina, Brazil, Cameroon, Egypt, India, Indonesia, Jamaica, Mexico, Nigeria, Pakistan, Peru, Saudi Arabia, Venezuela, Yugoslavia, Zaire, and Zambia.
28. Organizationally, the Conference was divided into four Commissions: Energy, Finance, Development, and Raw Materials. Each Commission was co-chaired by a developing and an industrial country.
29. Other absentees included Argentina, Cameroon, Egypt, Indonesia, Jamaica, Pakistan, Peru, Zaire, and Zambia.
30. Even in the tolerant world of international politics, it is ludicrous to place Ayatollah Khomeini or any of his presidents or prime ministers among the world leaders attending Cancun.
31. OPEC was formed in September 1960 but was anything but a price setter in its first decade, when the oil companies refused to recognize its existence as a 'producers' union' or even to negotiate price changes with it. For a short period in the early 1970s, prices were set by negotiations between OPEC and major oil companies. Only from 1973 has OPEC become the sole determinant of oil prices and hence gained international power.
32. Iran's pre-war production capacity was 6.2 MM b/d and Iraq's was

3.0–3.5 MM b/d. The two countries' respective quotas under OPEC's March 1983 production scheduling scheme were 2.4 and 1.2 MM b/d. Neither country was able to meet its quota. Iran's production in 1983 was 1.9 MM b/d and Iraq's was 1.0 MM b/d. Under the new production scheduling system agreed to by OPEC ministers in October 1984, Iran's quota was set at 2.3 MM b/d and Iraq's kept at 1.2 MM b/d.

33. It is improbable that Saudi Arabia is willing to accede to this demand. In fact, to meet its overall spending goals, including its development plans and defense and foreign aid programs, the country committed itself to exporting in 1982 about 6.5 MM b/d at $34 per barrel. This was a production cut of slightly more than two MM b/d from 1981 and below Saudi Arabia's actual production in 1982. The country's March 1983 quota was set at 5.0 MM b/d and its actual production in that year was 5.1 MM b/d. Saudi Arabia's production in the first half of 1984 was slightly under 5.0 MM b/d and in October 1984 the country agreed to a reduced quota of 4.35 MM b/d. To accommodate any substantial production increases by post-war Iran and Iraq, Saudi Arabia's production has to be further reduced by at least 2.5 MM b/d. This will reduce the country's total production to about 1.8 MM b/d and its exports to 1.1 MM b/d. That being the case, and barring price changes Saudi Arabia's oil income will shrink to $11.6 billion, down from $113.2 billion in 1981.

15 The Afghan State and its Adaptation to the Environment of Central and Southwest Asia
Ashraf Ghani

> Amir Sher Ali . . . left his capital with the intention of bringing in the Russians to get rid of the British. Addressing him we say: how stupid of you. Supposing you were able to force the English out and got your country cleared from aliens, which state will help you to get the Russians out of your house . . . They are not stupid to leave you in control of your country.[1]

So spoke Abdur Rahman (1880–1901) about his uncle whose overthrow by British forces in 1878 eventually resulted in his own ascent to the Afghan throne. His words succinctly enunciated the problem faced by Afghanistan in a geo-political environment overwhelmingly dominated by two imperial powers, Britain and Russia.

EMERGENCE OF A BUFFER STATE

The central problem facing Afghan rulers was that of preserving the state and their own autonomy of decision-making. Translating this policy into practice, they sought to strengthen the institutions of the central government without giving either British or Russian interests a foothold inside the country. A crucial reason for their success was that they were interposed between two European powers, neither of which would allow the other exclusive control over the Afghan state. Afghanistan, therefore, became the classic example of a buffer state.

But for a state to be a viable buffer it must have agreed-upon boundaries. Agreeing to the boundaries of Afghanistan was no easy matter. On 30 March 1885, Russian troops, in full view of members of a British boundary commission, overwhelmed an Afghan garrison stationed on the Panjdeh oasis and occupied the area. For the next several weeks war between Great Britain and Czarist Russia 'seemed inevitable'.² Diplomacy, however, prevailed. In September 1885, the British and Russian authorities signed a protocol defining the frontier between Russian colonies and Afghanistan. After exchange of territory on the two sides of the river Oxus was agreed to in 1893, that river became the boundary between Afghanistan and the Czarist empire and its successor state, the Soviet Union.

Iranian claims on northwestern Afghanistan had been forcefully checked by British forces in 1856, and the boundary between the two countries was fixed through British arbitration in the 1870s. That boundary has subsequently been recognized by both states as an international frontier.

The major remaining difficulty was the demarcation of the southern and eastern frontiers of Afghanistan with 'British India'. This issue was tackled in 1893. On 12 November 1893, an agreement fixing the limit of British and Afghan 'spheres of influence' was signed in Kabul by Abdur Rahman and Sir Henry Mortimer Durand, foreign secretary of the government of India.³ The Durand line, the status of which as an international boundary has been subject to conflicting interpretation by Afghan and Pakistani governments since 1947, has been the most problematic bequest of British imperial policy to twentieth-century Afghanistan.

To understand the reasons for Abdur Rahman's submission to the terms of the agreement, we need to quote article seven of that agreement:

> Being fully satisfied of His Highness's good-will to the British Government, and wishing to see Afghanistan independent and strong, the Government of India will raise no objection to the purchase and import by His Highness of munitions of war, and they will themselves grant him some help in this respect. Further, in order to mark their sense of the friendly spirit in which His Highness the Amir has entered into these negotiations, the Government of India undertakes to increase by the sum of six lakhs [one lakh = 100 000] of rupees a year the subsidy of twelve lakhs now granted to His Highness.⁴

The unequal nature of power between the two contracting parties, the desire not to endanger the internal independence of Afghanistan, the need to insure access to a steady supply of means of destruction, and the wish of the rulers for financial support are underlined by the passage. To understand the nature of the articulation between foreign and domestic policies of the Afghan state through time, the balance between these conflicting tendencies has to be closely examined. To accomplish this task, however, salient features of the structure of the Afghan state in our period of discussion have to be delineated.

CONTINUITY AND CHANGE IN THE STRUCTURE OF THE AFGHAN STATE

Financial basis

In 1908, the income of the Afghan state was estimated at 112–122 lakhs of rupees (£746 704–813 374). The British subsidy of 18 lakhs of rupees (£120 006), therefore, constituted 14-16 per cent of the total domestic income of the state. Between 1880 and 1929, a figure ranging between £500 000 and £1 000 000 may be taken as typical of the domestic revenue of the Afghan state. The bulk of such revenue during this period came from taxes on land, with income from foreign trade constituting the second most important source of revenue.[5]

Figures for 1952 and 1973 reveal a startling reversal in the relative contribution of these two sources of revenue to the income of the state. The total revenue of the government in these two years was $16.59 million and $88.62 million respectively. Taxes from land were respectively $2.08 million and $1.10 million, while those collected from foreign trade were $6.59 million and $38.31 million. In 1973, income from natural gas, which was a state monopoly, amounted to $10.66 million.[6]

The impact of the state on the economy can be grasped from the following comparative figures. In 1953, the ordinary expenditure of the state was Afs. 825 million [$22.23 million] and the expenditure on development Afs. 172 million [$4.63 million]. In 1963, the ordinary expenditure of the state amounted to Afs. 2416 million [$47.09 million] and the development expenditure to Afs. 4663 million [$90.89 million]. The reason for the substantial difference in the scale of the revenue is due to the large influx of foreign aid that began in 1955. In 1963, the foreign debt service already amounted to Afs. 543 million [$10.58 million].[7] The degree of dependence of the state on foreign aid from 1955 to 1978 was substantial. In 1976–77, 67 per cent of the projected Afs. 14 027 million [$309.71 million] that were to be spent on development were to come from foreign sources.[8]

This brief survey of the financial basis of the state enables us to distinguish three periods in the relations between the state and society. These are as follows. First, 1880–1929, where taxes from land constitute the most significant part of the income of the state. Second, 1929–1973, where the relative share of income from taxes on land declined significantly but income from taxes on foreign trade became the predominant source of internal revenue. Third, 1955–1978, where income from foreign aid provided the bulk of the developmental expenditure of the state. Our periodization hints at qualitative changes in time in the relation between the Afghan state and social forces in Afghan society, on the one hand, and the Afghan state and foreign states on the other. The contours of these relations are analyzed below.

State, class and bureaucracy

The formation of the Afghan state in 1747 was a result of transformation of tribal politics. Consequently, during the empire (1747–1818), the power of the monarchs was balanced by that of the *Khans*, a tribal landed elite who commanded their own tribesmen, predominantly organized as a cavalry, in times of conflict. The major internal reason for the demise of the empire was the inability of the monarchs and the *Khans* to reach a political compromise regarding the definition of their respective spheres of interests.

The breakdown of the empire into a number of principalities and the gradual consolidation of these entities into a single state took place between 1818 and 1869. There were two tendencies of this period that were accentuated in Abdur Rahman's reign. The rulers had to derive their revenue from taxes imposed on their subjects rather than external conquest. They also had to expand the size and functions of the standing army, primarily an infantry. Between 1880 and 1896, Abdur Rahman's army was continuously occupied and saw action in four major civil wars and about one hundred rebellions of various scales. Hence his anxiety – as manifested in the Durand agreement – for insuring his access to a regular supply of means of destruction.

The nature of conflict between Abdur Rahman and the social forces in Afghan society was clearly grasped by a perceptive British observer. West Ridegeway, who directed the commission charged with demarcating the boundary between Afghanistan and Russia, wrote to his superiors that '[Abdur Rahman] inflicts savage punishments, but so long as the people are submissive, particularly as regards taxation, he leaves them alone. He wages war on the classes not on the masses'.[9]

Abdur Rahman's war on the classes was primarily directed against the Khans but also involved a head-on collision with the elite of the religious establishment. His policy was not aimed at the elimination of these social forces but their subordination to the institutions of the centralizing state. That he is the only ruler of Afghanistan in the last 100 years to have died of natural causes and to have passed his throne to his chosen successor without a crisis is a commentary on the success of his policies. Bureaucratization of the state-apparatus, both military and civilian, was the major structural change bequeathed by this period.

The internal policies pursued during the reigns of Abdur Rahman's son (1901–1919) and grandson (1919–1929) basically involved attempts at further consolidating the centralizing direction set by him – although within a different symbolic discourse. Yet, for a complex set of reasons that cannot be enumerated here,[10] the political framework allowing for the incorporation of *Khans* and the religious establishment installed by Abdur Rahman was ruptured in 1929. The result was a series of rural revolts that resulted in the overthrow of the dynasty, the brief capture of the throne of Kabul by a rural rebel, and the eventual transfer of state-power to a different family in Abdur Rahman's lineage.

From 1929 to 1973, at which point Prince Daud declared Afghanistan a republic, the rulers of the country were forced to pursue a more cautious policy of centralization. A desire not to confront the landed class as a class became a central assumption of statecraft. The modest sums derived from taxes on land is a vivid commentary on the relative autonomy of the landed class from the state.

In the long run, however, the landed class had to pay the price for its lack of organic ties with the state. Individual landed families played an important role in the micro-politics of their localities and/or regions. But, except for a brief period in the 1960s, there was no national arena for them in which to translate their individual demands into a cohesive positive political program. Furthermore, while the rulers of the state did not choose to confront the landed class on the issue of taxation, they had no hesitation in wielding the power at their disposal to make or break individual landed families.

The mutual suspicion between rulers and landowners, especially between 1929 and 1963, was a pervasive characteristic of the political atmosphere. The nature of the relations between the merchant class and the rulers of the state, however, was different.

Long-distance and inter-regional trade had always been an important source of revenue for the rulers of Afghanistan. In the changed political landscape in 1929, revenue from trade became the dominant source of the income of the state. Vagaries of trade, affecting customs receipts, assumed paramount political significance. Relations between the rulers and the merchants underwent a major change as the merchant class was permitted organizational autonomy and given the power to determine the economic orientation of the country.

The institutionalization of the interests of the merchant class took, in 1932, the form of a joint stock company, later turned into a bank. The scope of the Company's powers can be gathered from the following rights it enjoyed: buying of all the gold and silver currency needed by the government; puchase of all the import items needed by the government; sale of all government mineral and commercial commodities abroad; exclusive right to all internal transactions; and the right of printing money. The government renounced all rights to inspect the checking and savings accounts that were deposited with the Company. And although it bought three thousand shares of the Company, it pledged not to interfere in its administration.[11]

In addition to these vast prerogatives, the Company was given monopolistic control over the import of sugar, gasoline, and other oils for periods of 7 to 8 years. Its major obligations to the government were to guarantee that customs' income from sugar would not fall below the average of the three preceding years and to devote 70–80 per cent of the capital derived from the sale of sugar to the export of Afghan commodities.[12]

Under such favorable conditions, success was not difficult. In the three years between 1934 and 1937, the Company managed to increase its capital from $838 747 to $10 020 555.[13] The Company, subsequently called Bank-i-Mili (the Afghan National Bank), established its control over all aspects of commercial production and circulation, eliminated middlemen by establishing direct ties with producers and international financial networks, and embarked on the first industrial ventures in the country.

The architect of this system was Abdul Majid Zabuli, a Herati merchant who, as the president of the Company and then the Bank, played a major role in shaping the direction of the Afghan economy.

His partnership with the ruling dynasty was given official recognition by his appointment as Minister of National Economy. He maintained that portfolio until 1950.

To understand Zabuli's vision of his task and the categories through which he analysed the world, we need only to quote him. In 1933, he stated that the government had backed the establishment of the Company in order 'to centralize the national capital and bring about a spirit of unity and participation on the part of the capitals of the country'.[14] In 1949, he characterized his intellectual critics as being opposed 'to the principles of capitalism, the merchant class, and its institutions'.[15] Offering a complete plan for the country he argued that,

> neither the merchants, the directors of companies, my person, nor anyone else has the right to stand as an obstacle in the way of the development of the country. Whichever individual or class in whom the government and the nation can place trust should be invited to confront the tasks.[16]

The 1950s, however, were the years in which the merchant class was subordinated to the government. Zabuli was unable to raise the foreign loans to underwrite his ambitious developmental plan. He was dismissed from his post as Minister of National Economy in 1950 and, shortly after, left the country. The government, under the control of the younger members of the royal family, began to play an assertive role in the management of the economy. This trend was especially evident between 1953 and 1963 when Prince Daud, in his capacity as prime minister, exercised dominant power in the country. He was helped in his goals by the climate of cold war, which allowed for an influx of foreign aid to the state without the attachment of any major strings.

The magnitude of this aid, by comparison to the previous revenue of the state, was so staggering that almost overnight the state became the major economic power in the country. The expansion in size and power of the bureaucracy was inevitable. Between 1953 and 1963 the number of bureaucrats rose from about 10 000 to about 60 000 persons.

One of the consequences of the state's access to greater financial resources was the expansion of the educational institutions in the country. The change was dramatic. In 1930, only 1590 students, taught by 53 teachers, were enrolled in 13 institutions. In 1976, by contrast, 928 066 students, taught by 26 687 teachers, were enrolled in 4006 institutions. The peak of expansion occurred after 1955, the year in which large-scale foreign aid started. In 1956, a total of 126 092 individuals were studying in 806 institutions while in 1967 the corresponding figures were 497 911 and 2567 respectively.[17] The upward social mobility achieved through access to governmental bureaucracy played an important role in overcoming the negative attitude towards modern education that was prevalent in many sectors of the Afghan society. But, with the levelling of foreign aid in the 1960s and in the absence of major internal economic changes, the expansion of the bureaucracy came to a halt. Unemployment among high-school and college graduates became a severe problem. In a society where the state was the major, if not the sole employer of the educated, difficulty in finding employment was bound to be a political problem. In the 1960s, ideological groups identifying with different colors of the political spectrum challenged the legitimacy of the regime. The coup of 1973 by Prince Daud, which brought the monarchy to an end, and the coup of 1978 by Khalqi officers, which resulted in the present tragedy of Afghanistan, can both be seen as attempts to find enduring solutions to the crisis. But before examining the complex discourse of the Afghan intellectuals on the legitimacy of the state, we must describe the regional environment in which Afghan politics unfold.

Regions and the Afghan economy

In the 1960s and 1970s, Kabul was not merely the capital of the state; it was the central hub of economic activity and the political nerve center of the country. Things had not always been so. Even in 1945, a knowledgeable foreign observer judged the economic conditions in Kandahar to be better than those in Kabul and the situation in Herat to be quite different from both cities.[18] Analysts of Afghan conditions can only ignore the regional characteristics at their peril.

The already existing classification of Afghanistan into ten or eleven zones which emphasize geographic features must be taken as the initial point of departure.[19] But focus on the changing articulation of economic and political flows among the major regions in Afghanistan and adjacent areas in the surrounding countries through time will throw important light on the nature of the adaptation of the Afghan state to its Central and Southwest Asian environment. Such an extensive analysis is beyond the scope of the present paper but I would like to stress a number of general features.

Transportation by animals, dominant in the nineteenth century and the first quarter of the twentieth century, made the continuation of distinctive regional economies inevitable. Under these conditions the southern and eastern regions were both the key economic and political areas of the country. Northern and northwestern regions, by contrast, had been devastated by warfare and epidemics and were economically and politically marginal.

In 1929, the dominant challenge to the state was from the eastern region; considerable long term economic loss resulted from that political strength. Bank-i-Mili, avoiding this problematic region, concentrated its activities in the northern region and, by the 1970s, that area was, by all criteria, the key economic area of the country, followed by the northwestern region. By 1973, the development of a national market in grain production, though far from complete, had made considerable progress. Furthermore, the 1960s and 70s had witnessed significant changes in the technical organization of agriculture. Response to market conditions in agricultural production was becoming less of an exception and more of a rule. The Afghan economy was by no means static and its uneven regional development was becoming increasingly evident. Given the historical identification between regions and ethnolinguistic groups the issue could not but assume political importance. We can now turn to analyze the social context of Afghan politics.

Ethnolinguistic diversity and legitimacy of the state

Thirty-two languages, belonging to four linguistic families, are spoken in the country. The number of groups claiming distinctive names and identities is even larger. Not surprisingly, ethnic identity has been a salient element in the self-conceptualization of the inhabitants of Afghanistan. The following four major named groups need to be mentioned: Pashtuns who speak Pashtu, and who since 1747, have been the dominant political and, probably, numerical element in the country; Tajiks, who speak Persian; Hazaras, who speak a dialect of Persian, Uzbeks, Turcomans, and others who speak Turkic languages.

Within the present boundaries of Afghanistan, a number of broad correlations between ethnic groups and spatial location is possible.

Central Afghanistan has been predominantly populated by Hazaras, and the majority of the Turkic groups live in the northern region. Until the 1880s, Pashtuns were largely absent from the northern and central regions. Even during the current century, the majority of Pashtuns have lived in the eastern, southern and northwestern areas. Tajiks have formed the major segment of the population in the north-east and north-west as well as in the capital city of Kabul, its surrounding valleys and a number of other urban centers.

Membership of the major ethnic groups is not confined to Afghanistan. Tajiks and all Turkic groups living in the northern region have their co-ethnics living across the border in the Central Asian republics of the Soviet Union. In fact, the republics bear the names of these groups. Small communities of Hazaras live in Iran and Pakistan. Pashtuns, since the drawing of the Durand line, have been divided in almost equal numbers between Afghanistan and 'British India' and then its successor state of Pakistan. The degree to which formal frontiers have been actually open or closed to interaction among people so divided has varied considerably in time and has depended on the political structures of the states involved.

The challenging task of building a legitimate political system out of such diverse socio-cultural material has been the task with which the rulers of Afghanistan have been grappling. Before turning to their strategies, we need to take account of a number of factors that have helped in tempering the existing heterogeneity.

In terms of the number of native speakers, Pashtu and Persian are clearly the two dominant languages, followed by Turkic languages. Under these conditions a large number of people, if not the majority, comprehend one of the dominant languages. Persian, furthermore, for hundreds of years has been the dominant language of bureaucracy, commerce, scholarship, and the media and there has been a clear trend towards its increasing understanding by the majority of the population. Given also the fact that there has been considerable movement of individuals and groups within the country, a simple relation between language and ethnic identity cannot be assumed. And last but by no means least, close to 99.5 per cent of the Afghans are Muslims.

The importance of Islam in Afghanistan has, however, not been confined to the fact that the absolute majority of Afghans have believed in it. In the nineteenth century, Islam provided the model for a centralized state, principles of legitimation of a monarchical regime and, given the threatening presence of imperial powers, the most significant cultural counter-point of reference to the assumed common Christianity of the Europeans.

In the wake of the two British invasions of Afghanistan – 1839–42; 1878–80 – the potency of Islamic symbols assumed overwhelming importance. Abdur Rahman (1880–1901) channeled this orientation into an institutional format that deprived the religious establishment of a large degree of its financial and organizational autonomy and simultaneously made the state more Islamic. *Sharia* (Islamic laws) was bureaucratized and judges became salaried officials of the state but the practice of customary law was forbidden and *Sharia* was declared the sole law of the land. Islam became the major cultural underpinning of the state.[20] Until the end of the monarchy in 1973, the degree of emphasis of the state on Islam changed, but its importance as a principle of the legitimation of the monarchy was never reduced. With the advent of the new dynasty in 1929, Islam became the official religion of the state and no sustained attempt was undertaken to expunge its significance in the juridical sphere.

Assumption of the role of champions of Islam was not the only transformation that the rulers of Afghanistan underwent. The ruling lineage became increasingly Persianized in language and in court culture. Abdur Rahman may have been the last ruler of the country who had equal command of the two dominant and some of the Turkic languages spoken in Afghanistan. Neither King Zahir (1933–73) nor Prince Daud (Prime Minister 1953–63; President 1973–77) ever gave a public speech completely in Pashtu.

Islamization of the state and Persianization of the ruling lineage were, however, only two of the elements in the politics of legitimation. Descent and ethnicity remained equally salient. From 1826 to 1978, state power remained in the hands of members of the Muhammadzai lineage. Solidarity of the lineage as a whole and establishment of a system of internal ranking within it assumed crucial importance for the stability of national politics. The transformation involved a requirement that sub-lineages, which claimed to act as the state in different parts of the country, perceive a centralized state as the organ of their collective interest.

It took two civil wars between Abdur Rahman and two of his cousins, who advocated a different model of politics, for the principle of centralization of power to prevail. The major steps toward the consolidation of the royal lineage were taken in 1892, when the state assigned stipends to all male and female members of the lineage, and in 1896 when the sub-lineages pledged themselves to leave the question of succession to the throne to Abdur Rahman's sons and their descendants.[21]

The dynastic change of 1929 involved the re-ordering of the rank of two sub-lineages within the royal lineage and not a challenge to the principle of the cohesion of the lineage. Between 1929 and 1963, the royal lineage was the government of Afghanistan.

The first element of change came in 1963 when a 'commoner' was appointed prime minister. The change was then formally enshrined in article 24 of the constitution of 1964, preventing the members of the royal family from assuming cabinet-level posts or elective office. As other members of the royal family continued to exercise considerable real power in the country, it seemed that the major intent of the article was that of preventing the return of Prince Daud, first paternal cousin and brother-in-law of the King, to power. Whether the provisions of the constitution of 1964 forced Daud to depart from the monarchical model and declare Afghanistan a republic in 1973 is moot. The formal change of the system did, however, create a very complex situation for the legitimation of the new structure. The principle of succession had, once again, become indeterminate and the Khalqi coup of 1978 made that evident.

The Muhammadzai lineage was a Pashtun lineage and Pashtun clans of the eastern region had played a significant role in the elevation of the new dynasty to the throne in 1929. Therefore, despite its recourse to other principles of legitimation, the royal lineage had to continuously resort to ethnic politics. Its cultural Persianization may, in fact, have been an important asset in enabling its members to revert to different strategies of legitimation in relation to different groups. But Abdur Rahman's legacy was particularly burdensome in this regard. His policies of centralization had brought him to a head-on collision with the tribal organization of the ethnic groups. His ten-year conflict with the Hazaras of the central region was certainly the most brutal of all his campaigns. To subdue their resistance, not only did he rely on levies from other ethnic groups – especially Pashtuns – he also compelled the religious establishment to declare them infidels and fit to be enslaved. Only in the reign of his grandson (1919–29) was slavery legally abolished. Abdur Rahman's crushing of the resistance of other ethnic groups – including the Pashtuns – and the transplanting of these groups was equally severe.

As a result of the 1929 civil war, the Pashtun clans in the eastern region managed to regain a lot of their autonomy, but other groups were incapable of doing so. The changes in the economy of different regions, as already described, showed Pashtun gains to have been largely illusory. Yet, ethnicity and language became important areas of debate and confrontation, especially in the 1960s and 1970s. The historical state was so complex that every ethnic group could declare the other to have benefited and itself to have been victimized by the policies of the state. The cultural ambiguity which had enabled the royal lineage to pursue multiple strategies of legitimation was confronting it with multiple challenges. In 1972, the debate in parliament and the popular press on the status of the 'national language' reached such a point of crisis that the government officially forbade its further discussion. The coup of 1973, resulting at first in the pursuit of an aggressive foreign policy of confrontation with Pakistan, merely managed to drive the discussion underground and render the situation more acute.

An important result of the debates of the 1960s was the reorientation of the Afghan intellectuals from an endeavor to create a national culture towards more narrowly defined postures, be they religious, ethnic or politico-ideological. For the Afghan intelligentsia, despite its small numbers, has played a crucial role in shaping the formal political culture of the country. Its importance has been a result of its small membership and its monopoly of skills of administration, on which the royal lineage was dependent for running the government.

It was the intellectuals who raised the demand for a constitutional monarchy in the first decade of the twentieth century and struggled for its realization until the end of the monarchy. Relations of the intellectuals with the dynasty that came to power in 1929 were particularly complex. Having arisen in the wake of the reformist period of Amanullah (1919–29), the new dynasty was never endowed with legitimacy by the intellectuals. Despite its negative initial reactions and the use of force against the advocates of ideas of reform, the royal lineage usually ended up adopting those ideas as its formal principles, though duly diluting them in practice. Parliamentary democracy within the structure of a constitutional monarchy which was formally functioning between 1963 and 1973, was just one more example of this complex relation: The King agreed to reign but not to rule; yet, his rule eventually prevailed.

The reaction of the intellectuals to this last atrophy of their demands differed significantly from their earlier patterns of reaction. Previously, with a unified voice, they had demanded reform. Now, with multiple voices ranging from extreme left to extreme right, they were demanding the undoing of the entire political structure and the exercise of political power. After seizing power in 1973, Prince Daud attempted different combinations of strategies and domestic and foreign alliances to reign over such diverse movements. His efforts were in vain and initially resulted in the Khalqi coup of 1978, then in the Soviet invasion of 1979. It is time to turn to an examination of the ways in which the Afghan state adapted to its international environment of central and southwest Asia.

RELATIONS WITH GREAT BRITAIN, CZARIST RUSSIA AND THE SOVIET UNION: 1880–1947

The policy of Afghan rulers towards Great Britain and Czarist Russia after 1880 was conditioned by the memories of two Anglo–Afghan wars (1838–42 and 1878–80). In both cases, those Afghan rulers who had counted on vague Russian promises of support which did not materialize in the hours of need, lost their thrones. That the British invasions did not result in the loss of their country was due to the fierce resistance of their countrymen and to a change of British policy in London.

It was such a combination of factors in 1880 that brought about the withdrawal of British forces from Afghanistan. The man the British chose to accept as ruler of Afghanistan in exchange for the control of the foreign relations of his state was Abdur Rahman, who had spent eleven years in exile in the Asian colonies of Russia.

We have already described the process through which the control of foreign relations of Afghanistan allowed the British government to determine the current boundaries of Afghanistan. In the absence of the British power, the probability of Russian forces stopping where they did seems unlikely. But what did the control of the external relations of Afghanistan imply for the determination of relations between the Afghan state and the British power-holders?

An 1891 memorandum drawn by a high-ranking British official provides a useful point of departure. The demands to be put to Abdur Rahman's successor in return for supporting him, in addition to the rectification of some points on the boundary, were to include the following:

(b) obtaining facilities for railway extension when desirable *towards* Kandahar and *to* Jalallabad. (c) The establishment of a

British officer at some convenient point near the Russian border. (d) Construction of telegraph lines. (e) Removal of obstacles to commerce.[22]

Abdur Rahman, whose expected death was to provide the needed opportunity, did not die until October of 1901. Until then, except for the changes resulting in the boundary line arrived at during the Durand agreement of 1893, none of the British demands had been agreed to. In 1899, he was interpreting the agreements to mean 'that the sole obligation which they impose upon the British Government will not interfere with the internal affairs of Afghanistan nor comment upon them'.[24]

By then, Abdur Rahman's policy of internal consolidation was completed and he was clamoring to have direct representation in London. The British government turned down his request. In the meanwhile, making use of the terms of the Durand agreement to buy arms, he had acquired such a stock of arms that the Viceroy was arguing that:

> it appears to us that Afghanistan is rapidly being converted into a vast armed camp, equipped by our aid and largely at our expense, with the latest implements of modern scientific warfare . . . in so unsettled a country as Afghanistan events may occur, either during the lifetime of the Amir or more probably after his death, which may place these arms in the hands of those who may conceivably be arrayed against us.[25]

The dreaded confrontation came in 1919. In that year, Amanullah (1919–29), grandson of Abdur Rahman, went to war against Britain to gain the formal independence of Afghanistan. He eventually succeeded in his goal despite a mixed military performance.

Yet, long before Britain's recognition of Afghanistan's independence, its exclusive control over the external relations of the country had been breached. Czarist Russia, which had agreed during the nineteenth century to consider Afghanistan to be outside its sphere of influence, was no longer satisfied with communicating with its neighbor through the agency of Great Britain. From 1900 on, Russian officials openly argued with their British counterparts that changed circumstances made the existence of direct communications with the Afghan rulers necessary.[26]

At the convention of 1907, which dealt with Persia, Afghanistan and Tibet, Britain agreed that the:

> Russian and Afghan authorities, specially designed for the purpose on the fronier provinces, may establish direct relations with each other for the settlement of local questions of a non-political character.[27]

Amanullah's potential disregard for colonially-imposed boundaries was aptly summarized by the British chief representative to his court who wrote:

> [Amanullah] is greedy for expansion either towards India or towards Central Asia or in both directions; and weakness in either direction will fatally attract him to adventure.[28]

Amanullah was attracted to the Soviet Union partly because of his possible influence over border tribes. The Islamization of the Afghan polity had provided Afghan rulers with the claim of being the only authority that could legitimately declare *Jihad* (holy war). But Amanullah's relations with the Soviets quickly deteriorated especially after the treatment meted by the Republic of Bokhara at the hands of the Red Army. He eventually was persuaded to remain in the Western camp.[29]

Amanullah was overthrown in 1929. It is an article of faith among Afghan intellectuals that the British were instrumental in his overthrow and the ascendency of the new dynasty to power. The record is too complex to be reviewed here but Amanullah's successors did not modify the major contours of Afghan foreign policy. Living up to Abdur Rahman's maxim, they attempted to prevent neighboring powers from gaining a foothold inside the country while trying to take advantage of their resources. And for their technical needs, they relied on the services of nationals from countries believed not to have territorial designs in the area.[30]

The emphasis on foreign trade during this period partly geared Afghan foreign policy. Zabuli forged direct links with the financial networks of London and sought markets for Afghan products there. In 1935, his bank reached an agreement with the Soviet Union allowing it to export 12 000 tons of cotton over three years. The Soviet payment was to be in form of commodities, thus initiating the barter system which was to become ever more important to the Afghan economy.[31]

Zabuli had even more ambitious plans. In 1937, together with the Afghan Minister for Foreign Affairs, he signed an agreement with the American Inland Exploration Company for the exploration of oil in northern Afghanistan. A contract for the exploration of mines in southern Afghanistan was signed with a German firm at about the same time.[32] None of the companies did any exploratory work and the agreements were allowed to lapse. Afghan officials subsequently suspected Great Britain of dissuading the companies from establishing links with Afghanistan.[33]

By then, the clouds of war were looming large on the world. Once again, the survival of the country was at stake. In December, 1939, a British military delegation met with Prime Minister Hashem to discuss the Soviet threat to Afghanistan and India. By March 1940, the British authorities were ready 'to meet Soviet aggression on Afghanistan by declaration of war'[34] and to offer five-year credits for armaments and commercial credit sums not exceeding two and a half million pounds 'unless examination on what Afghan capacity to spend and repay justified.'[35]

The intellectuals, who considered Britain responsible for the rebellion of 1929 and the installation of the new dynasty, looked to Germany with hope. Those who had access to power, as well as the younger generation of the royal lineage, considered the time ripe to act against Britain. The older members of the royal family, who were at the helm, stuck to a pro-British posture and opted for neutrality. A *Loya Jirga* (Grand Assembly) was convened; it ratified the neutrality of the country. By then, the Soviet Union and Great Britain, who had since become allies, had jointly invaded Iran. The danger was felt to be immediate, and all parties in Afghanistan were satisfied with neutrality.[36]

Once the war was over, the Afghan government granted a French company a concession to explore oil in the northern region. The Soviet Union officially objected and despite the Afghan government's protest, work was not undertaken.[37] This rebuff was soon to be followed by an even greater disenchantment. The Afghan leaders were indeed dumbfounded to learn that Britain was withdrawing from India and that the Durand Line was now being claimed as an international boundary by the newly created state of Pakistan.

RELATIONS WITH PAKISTAN, THE SOVIET UNION AND THE UNITED STATES, 1947–1978

The creation of Pakistan made the rulers of Afghanistan acutely conscious of the limitations of their landlocked state. That Pakistan was using the issue of transit as a political weapon in her relations with Afghanistan was asserted as a fact by Zabuli.[38]

His remedy was an ambitious development plan to be financed by the United States. The US Export–Import Bank, to which the loan application was submitted, rejected the major part of Zabuli's request in November 1949 but granted a $21 million loan for a government-sponsored irrigation project in southern Afghanistan, where American firms were involved.[39] This decision had significant repercussions on the internal politics of Afghanistan. The royal lineage realized that it did not need the merchant class as an intermediary with the capitalist world and that it could dispense with their services. Zabuli's political demise was immediate. By the time Prince Daud took effective power as prime minister, the alliance with the merchant class had ended and the state was playing an active role in the economy.

The policy, however, was still based on financing development through the export of agricultural commodities. According to one key participant, the projected annual export of cotton from the northern and south-western regions should have reached, two million tons by the end of the first phase of the new policy.[40]

In 1955, problems between Afghanistan and Pakistan led to the closing of the Pakistani border for five months. During a visit to Kabul in December, 1955 by Khruschev and Bulganin, not only did the Soviet leaders promise a thirty-year credit of $100 million at 2 per cent interest, they also expressed their sympathy 'with Afghanistan's policy on the question of Pashtunistan'.[41] Why should the Soviets be interested in it, and why should the leaders of a lineage-based polity favorably respond to overtures from a regime as radically different from their own as that of the Soviet Union?

The Durand Agreement of 1893 resulted in the division of the Pashtun ethnic group between two states. While the Russian and Soviet governments incorporated the inhabitants of conquered territories into a centralized structure and turned their border with Afghanistan into a 'closed frontier', the British left the tribal areas of the North-West Frontier Province with considerable autonomy and the borders between the two states were completely open. This situation enabled the Afghan decision-makers to maintain active ties with the tribes and hope for their eventual incorporation into Afghanistan.

The establishment of Pakistan and the recognition by the international community of the Durand Line as its international boundary; came as a shock to the Afghan leaders. To make their displeasure public, Afghanistan voted against Pakistan's joining the United Nations. A *Loya Jirga* (Grand Assembly) convened in Kabul in July 1949, repudiated the old frontier agreement with Britain and authorized the government to explore all possible avenues for arming itself.

Both in 1951 and 1954, the Afghan government sought to acquire arms from the United States. Both times, its request was rejected. Meanwhile, Pakistan's close ties with the United States led to its formal membership of what became SEATO in 1954 and the Baghdad Pact in 1955. In the atmosphere of Cold War then prevailing between the United States and the Soviet Union, the political options of the Afghan leaders became very narrow indeed. The options of the Soviets, given the alliances of Turkey, Iran and Pakistan, were equally limited. Afghans and Soviets, in the pursuit of very different goals, had been brought to a marriage of convenience. The consequences of the relations for the two parties, however, were different.

The establishment of links with the Soviet Union transferred the military and ideological training of the Afghan officers and large numbers of bureaucrats to a state whose social system was totally opposed to that of Afghanistan. The impact of this reorientation would be only felt in the long run, as Afghanistan adhered to a foreign policy of neutrality and non-alignment until 1978. A number of important short-term results followed more immediately.

To offset Soviet influence, the United States followed its example and, between 1955 and 1965, gave the Afghan government some $350 million in economic aid. The total amount of US aid until 1979, when it was halted, was $532.87 million, of which $378.17 was in grants or gifts. Soviet economic aid, up to the coup of April 1978, was about $1265 million, almost entirely in loans.[42]

The alliance of the Afghan rulers with the Soviet Union did not deter Pakistani leaders from wielding transit as a weapon. In 1961, they completely closed the border and kept it closed until 1963, when Daud resigned.

The Soviets did not follow up on their initial support for the Afghan position on Pashtunistan and, in the emerging climate of *détente*, they did not even want to be reminded of the issue. But, until 1978, they continued to be the major supplier of military and economic aid, and the dependence of the Afghan government on this aid was ever growing.

Foreign aid enabled the state to emerge as the dominant power in the economic sphere and to expand the size of the educational and bureaucratic establishments. The state, however, failed to pursue a systematic policy of development and the country, as indicated earlier, was undergoing a series of concurrent crises in the 1960s and 1970s. The domestic and foreign policies pursued by Daud, after his re-assumption of power in 1973, brought the situation to breaking point.

Internally, he resumed a more aggressive policy of centralization of power. All banks were nationalized. The implementation of centralization of a land-reform and the collection of substantially higher taxes from rural and urban property-holders was announced. Daud, who had picked a significant number of his lieutenants from among the left-leaning young officers, also unleashed state terror against centrist and radical Muslim groups.

Internationally, he once again put emphasis on the issue of Pashtunistan. The meaning of the demand for Pashtunistan, however, was no clearer this time. He stressed the right of self-determination of the Pashtun and Baluch ethnic groups in Pakistan. The dominant international and domestic interpretation attached to this demand was, however, that of eventual incorporation of these groups in Afghanistan.

Daud, however, had badly misjudged the international and domestic environment in which he was operating. The Soviet Union was in no mood to extend support to his policy and the newly-acquired economic power of Iran and the oil-rich Arab states soon made them central to Daud's plans.

Pakistans' reaction to the Afghan posture was immediate. This time an easy way was found to drive Daud to the negotiating table. When Afghan Muslim radicals moved in large numbers to Pakistan, Mr Bhutto (1971–77), trained them, armed them, and sent them back to Afghanistan. They engaged the forces of the state in a series of operations in rural areas. These operations ceased when Daud agreed to meet with Mr Bhutto. At the time that Bhutto was overthrown by the Pakistani army, the two sides were seriously engaged in a constructive dialogue.

If solutions to the economic and social crises of the country were to be found, the financial basis of the regime had to be significantly changed. In 1955, Daud achieved this goal through the manipulation of the differences between the super-powers. This was not possible in the 1970s. The regional situation, however, contained new possibilities.

Afghanistan's relations with Iran and the oil-rich countries of the Middle East had always been correct, but not particularly close. Anti-Iranian feelings, on the issue of the negotiation of a treaty on the distribution of the waters of the Helmand River had been masterfully exploited by Daud to pave the way for his seizure of power. Yet, once in power, Daud duly announced that the agreement had been properly ratified and there was no outstanding problem between the two countries. Subsequently, the Shah of Iran came with an aid offer of one billion dollars, almost equal to the total amount of Soviet aid since its inception. Possibilities of Arab aid seemed equally plausible.

Awareness of this new regional situation brought a change in Daud's attitude towards his internal allies. Starting in the Spring of 1977, he began an attack on 'imported ideologies'. This was followed by the declaration of a one-party system to which members of the left, with whom he had an implicit alliance at the beginning of his regime, were not admitted, even as individuals. His confrontation with the left was inevitable but his basis of support not strong enough to allow him success. When, in April 1978, he put the leadership of the United Khalq Party in jail, it took the Khalqi officers twenty-four hours to overthrow him. A new chapter in the adaptation of the Afghan state to its central and southwest Asian environment began, in which Abdur Rahman's insight would be radically departed from, with tragic consequences for the Afghan people.

Notes

1. *Nasiehat Namcha* ('Booklet of Advice') (Kabul, 1885), pp. 11–12.
2. Kazemzadeh, F. *Russia and Britain in Persia, 1864–1914.* London, 1968, p. 96.
3. L/P&S/10/125, p. 32.
4. *Ibid.*, pp. 32–3.
5. *Gazetteer of Afghanistan* (Simla, 1908) p. 40.
6. M. Fry, *The Afghan Economy* (Leiden, 1974) pp. 170–1.
7. *Ibid.*, pp. 158–9.
8. *Statistical Information of Afghanistan (1976–77)* (Kabul, 1976) p. 406.
9. Col. Sir West Rideway to Earl of Iddesleigh, 20 December 1886, p. 19.
10. For a descriptive analysis of Amanullah's period see L. Poullada, *Reform and Rebellion in Afghanistan.*

11. *Eqtisad* (Economy) July 1922, pp. 186–8.
12. *Ibid.*, July 1933, pp. 208–10; March 1937, pp. 16–18.
13. *Ibid.*
14. *Ibid.*, September 1933, p. 247.
15. *Ibid.*, September 1949, p. 11.
16. *Ibid.*, October 1949, p. 7.
17. *Education in Afghanistan During the Last Fifty Years* (Kabul, 1968) pp. 12–13; *Education Statistics of Afghanistan 1971* (1972) pp. 4, 12; *Statistical Information of Afghanistan 1976–77* (1977) p. 305.
18. IOR R/12/141 April 26-May 4, 1945.
19. L. Dupree, *Afghanistan* (Princeton, 1980) pp. 3–31.
20. See my 'Islam and State Building in a Tribal Society Afghanistan 1880–1901', *Modern Asian Studies* 12, II, pp. 269–84; and 'Disputes in a Court of Sharia, Kunar Valley, Afghanistan, 1885–1890', *International Journal of Middle East Studies* 15(1983), pp. 353–67.
21. From the file of covenants of the subjects of Afghanistan addressed to His Majesty Amir Abdur Rahman Khan, Archives of the Afghan Foreign Ministry, p. 4, as quoted in H. Kakar, *Afghanistan: A Study in Internal Political Development 1880–1896* (Lahore, 1971) p. 293. For an overall description of Abdur Rahman's period see his *Government and Society in Afghanistan* (Austin, 1979).
22. L/P&S/18/A 81, 'Memorandum by Sir Steuart Bayley on the Question of the Afghan Succession', 1891, p. 1.
23. IOR MSS EUR. F111/287. Lord Curzon to Lord Hamilton, 11 May 1899, p. 4.
24. Abdur Rahman to Curzon quoted in Curzon's proposed letter to Abdur Rahman, *ibid*, p. 4.
25. *Ibid.* Curzon to Hamilton, p. 3.
26. For a review of this issue see L/P&S/A165, 'Question of Direct Relations Between Russia and Afghanistan', 1907.
27. L/P&S/10/125, 'Convention signed on 31 August 1907 between Great Britain and Russia containing Arrangements on the Subjects of Persia, Afghanistan and Thibet', p. 8.
28. L/P&S/18/A194, 'Report on the Kabul Mission by Sir H. R. C. Dobbs', 9 January 1922, p. 8.
29. *Ibid.*
30. For details see Ludwig W. Adamec, *Afghanistan's Foreign Affairs to the Mid-Twentieth Century* (Tuscon, 1974).
31. *Eqtisad*, May 1935, p. 218. For the importance of this trade for Afghan economy see IOR, 'Records of the British Legation, Kabul. Russo–Afghan Trade 7 December 1946–3 January 1948'.
32. *Eqtisad*, March 1937, p. 137.
33. M. H. Maiwandwal [Prime Minister 2 November 1965–12 October 1967], *Maswat*, 16 July 1969, p. 2.
34. IOR R/12/114, p. 38.
35. *Ibid.*, p. 40.
36. M. H. Maiwandwal, *Masawat*, 4 June 1969, p. 2.
37. *Ibid.*, 16 July 1969, p. 2.
38. *Eqtisad*, October 1949, p. 8.

39. P. G. Frank, *Obtaining Aid For a Development Plan* (Washington, DC, 1953) p. 34.
40. A. M. Abdurahimzai, *Afghan Millat*, no. 164, 1970, p. 1.
41. A. Bulganin and N. S. Khruschchev, *Speeches During Sojourn in India, Burma and Afghanistan, November–December 1955* (New Delhi, 1956) p. 175.
42. H. S. Bradsher, *Afghanistan and the Soviet Union* (Durham, NC, 1983) pp. 18, 24.

16 Communism in Afghanistan
Henry S. Bradsher

Two decades ago, two men met in Kabul, in the living room of a minor writer, impecunious translator and political dreamer named Nur Mohammad Taraki. What resulted was celebrated in January 1985, by lengthy statements and anniversary articles in Afghan and Soviet media, as the beginning of a political party which now claims to have 120 000 members and to run Afghanistan. The membership claim is probably a gross exaggeration, and the claim that the party runs Afghanistan is true only in the narrow sense that it is the local link in the transmission of control from elsewhere. The basic significance of that meeting is that it was a step toward the establishment of Russian authority in Kabul and the present Soviet effort to crush Afghan resistance to alien domination. It was a naïve, possibly idealistic, beginning of what has become a savage guerrilla war that is destroying the Afghanistan which those men professed to want to improve.

The meeting on 1 January 1965, is officially regarded as the founding congress of the People's Democratic Party of Afghanistan, (PDPA) 'the party of the working class and all workers of Afghanistan.'[1] In neither its title nor its official publicity does the party call itself Communist, although its public rhetoric is the modern Soviet version of Marxism. In its secret internal documents, however, the party clearly identified itself as part of the world Communist movement led by the Soviet Union and described Taraki at the time of the founding congress as being a 'long-standing Communist'.[2]

USSR ROLE IN FOSTERING A COMMUNIST MOVEMENT

The Soviet Union has been cautious about publicly accepting the PDPA as a Communist party, although there are many reasons to believe that the Soviets played a major – perhaps crucial – role behind the scenes in fostering the development of a Communist movement in Afghanistan. When Soviet leaders describe 'countries of the socialist community', Afghanistan is not listed; it is put in the secondary category of 'countries that have chosen the path of socialist development'.³ This is a more cautious placement that leaves Moscow some room for maneuver on its degree of commitment.⁴ It also helps preserve the fiction that Afghanistan under Soviet domination remains an independent country and a valid member of the non-aligned movement. Nonetheless, the PDPA is proud of its association in the Communist movement, claiming 'relations with more than 52 revolutionary parties, movements, and progressive organizations'.⁵

The Afghan Communist party is one of the newest on the world scene. Its history is remarkable in that the PDPA came to power only 13 years after its official formation.⁶ But within 15 years of that formation, it had collapsed into its present condition of fronting for foreign control. It goes on claiming to be 'a patriotic party' working 'to improve the life of our people and make their progress toward a glorious future and the creation of a just new society irreversible'.⁷ In fact, the party is riven by rivalries, weakened by incompetence, rejected by the majority of Afghanistan's people, and demoralized by a realization that it survives only as the tool of a foreign occupying power.

Communism in Afghanistan, as originally in such other countries as Mongolia and in a sense also China, is an example of the adaptation of Karl Marx's thinking about proletarian power to the conditions of countries too backward to have significant numbers of industrial workers. Not until the 1930s did Afghanistan develop commercial agriculture on a significant enough scale to engage in international trade, and centralized banking began to supplement traditional village moneylending only as an adjunct to that early trade in cotton and a few other products. In the Marxist sense, there was hardly any proletariat, because there was little industry, until the beginning of modernization in the 1950s, and even then it remained small. Communism therefore had to develop out of another class. It lacked even the justification found in some Western countries of bourgeois reformers' arrogating to themselves the task of educating and leading the proletariat, because there was almost nothing to educate or lead.

In the first few years after the Bolshevik Revolution, when enthusiasm was high in Moscow for Communism's sweeping through the world, Afghanistan was not considered fertile ground. It was too feudal, medieval. While beginning there in 1920 their first foreign aid program, the Russians had no interest in creating an Afghan Communist party in the way they were then setting up Communist parties in other countries. The real prize in South Asia was British-ruled India, and Kabul was seen as a base for operations across the Northwest Frontier rather than a target itself, so that it was better not to alarm King Amanullah by political activities in Afghanistan. But Amanullah was ousted in 1929, despite the first Soviet invasion of Afghanistan.[8] His departure ended for 20 years the kind of reforming tendencies that might in modern terms be seen as leftist and therefore claimed as proto-Communist. Afghanistan remained a closed country for most purposes, closed to ideas as well as much travel. Except for the training of Quranic specialists in an Islamic school in India, few Afghans went abroad for education. As a result, there was no opportunity for the Communist International to pursue its usual practice of proselytizing among students from colonial territories attending schools in metropolitan centers like Paris who would go home to such places as Hanoi and eventually become the Communist rulers of newly independent countries.

Other factors militated against the early development of Communism in Afghanistan. The country already had an ideology. It was, and is, Islam. To a degree that most modern Westerners find difficult to comprehend, because they divorce religion from daily life and are only dimly aware of how it has shaped their frame of reference, Islam is an all-encompassing world view. It leaves little room for and is resistant to the materialistic doctrine of Marxism; Islam covers material matters, too, because they are seen as part of a spiritual approach to life. Not until the development of modern, Westernized education in Afghanistan had sapped the Muslim traditions of many people was Marxism able to make significant inroads.

Another factor was the tribal code of the Pushtuns, the people of southern Afghanistan who have been called the true Afghans because their character has been stamped on a land that they dominated politically in recent centuries. Theirs is an inward-looking tradition that has given Afghanistan its unique record of guerrilla warfare against every outsider in the recorded history that begins with Alexander the Great. Their proud reliance on family and clan ties left little room for the Marxist concept of worker solidarity. A parallel factor is the historic hatred held by the Tajik ethnic group that has most strongly influenced Afghan culture and bureaucracy in modern times, and by the less important Uzbeks and Turkmen in Afghanistan. Many of them are descendants of refugees from Bolshevik conquest of what is now Soviet Central Asia, in the early 1920s suppression of the *basmachi* resistance.⁹ Family memories of what Communism did to people just north of the Amu Darya, the border river, insured hostility to Communist ideas to the south.

In a statement for the 20th anniversary of its founding, the PDPA said that 'Some 36 years ago the political, national democratic, patriotic and progressive circles were born among the intellectuals and students in Afghanistan'.¹⁰ This refers to a liberal political movement that developed in 1947 named *Wikh-i-Zalmaiyan* (Awakened Youth).¹¹ Its members were drawn from the small educated elite of very unproletarian government officials, merchants and landowners. They sought an upper-middle-class voice in the government then run by the Pushtun royal family and its feudal retainers in a traditional pre-colonial style more intent upon preventing the wrong things from happening by maintaining rigid controls than accomplishing anything positive by encouraging new initiatives. This was reformism, not revolution. During the 17 months that Taraki was president of Afghanistan, his publicists claimed falsely that his initiative created the late 1940s liberal movement,¹² but in fact he was a minor and junior figure, and the claim has been dropped.¹³

The royal family firmly put down the agitation created by the liberal movement, and a related experiment in allowing the rubber-stamp parliament to question ministers about their corrupt and inefficient ways. About 25 liberal leaders were jailed, plus some other minor figures including a student orator who later became known as Babrak Karmal. But in the slowly expanding school system in Kabul, new ideas had been turned loose. It had become possible to discuss various roads to modernization, including Communism – so long as the discussion was in semi-secrecy.

This discussion was intensified by a fateful decision. Mohammad Daoud, who became prime minister in 1953, wanted to speed up modernization efforts. That required a stronger army for internal security purposes, to prevent the kind of reaction to reforms that had overthrown Amanullah. Daoud also wanted to pursue Afghanistan's irredentist claim against American-armed Pakistan for Pushtun-inhabited areas. With the United States unwilling to fuel both sides of that dispute, and Washington seeing no strategic value in Afghanistan,¹⁴ Daoud turned to Moscow for weapons and military training. The first agreement was concluded in 1956.¹⁵ Daoud's decision to sup with what he considered the devil polarized the emerging intellectual element in Kabul's expanding educational system. By 1958, three views of the country's possible future had developed in identifiable groups in the capital, which was and remained the only center of modern ferment as it drew bright village lads into its government-financed school system. In the late 1950s Afghan politics began to develop into the pattern that it still retains, and Communism in Afghanistan needs to be viewed against this background.

The largest and until 1978 dominant group was the one fostered by Daoud and by his cousin and brother-in-law, King Zahir Shah. The group was composed of technocrats serving the government and businessmen dependent upon it. Its members, educated in an American-guided school system inside Afghanistan and in Western universities, were in general moderate reformers who wanted to bring to their country the benefits of liberal democracy and free enterprise with limited elements of state capitalism. Today this group is the least important of the three. Many of its best people have been killed. The survivors are scattered, a few still serving the government in Kabul, some trying to help the resistance, but most in exile seeking to use their talents in new ways that do not benefit their homeland.

A second group was composed of Afghans with modern, Westernized educations but more traditional Islamic outlooks. While the religious devotion of the technocrats should not be questioned – few Afghans lose their Islamic heritage, even though it might be overlaid with other, seemingly competing or contradictory codes – they did not see in the Quran answers to contemporary problems. The second group, on the other hand, encompassed those whose reaction to Western encroachments was to seek strength in adapting and updating Islamic thought, as had Muslims in Egypt and other Middle Eastern countries in earlier years when faced with similar situations. This fundamentalist group began to coalesce in 1957 as a discussion circle of professors and students led by Ghulam Mohammed Niazi. They included Burhanuddin Rabbani and Abdul Rasool Sayyaf,[16] both of whom are now prominent in resistance politics in Peshawar, Pakistan. Rabbani has said that the first Afghan fundamentalist political organization, the *Jamiat-i-Islam* (Islamic Society), was formed in 1958 in reaction to the move toward Soviet military and economic aid,[17] but reaction to support by traditional Muslim leaders for Daoud's modernization seems also to have been a factor.[18] Within this group there have been varying tendencies, from rejecting most aspects of modernization to willingness to accommodate some Western tendencies so long as leftist and anti-Islamic ideas were prohibited. Today the fundamentalists dominate the resistance organizations based in Peshawar.

The third group is Communist. In the late 1950s there was increasing examination of the Soviet model for economic development among semi-secret groups of Kabul University students and others. How much this was encouraged and financed by the Soviet embassy in Afghanistan remains unclear. Taraki, who might have been subsidized by the Soviets by the late 1950s,[19] later claimed to have met 'clandestinely those whom he trusted in order to equip them with scientific ideology to save the country',[20] and he said in 1978 the PDPA's founding 'was the result of piecemeal activities during the past 25 years'.[21] That there was a fertile field for such preaching need not be doubted. Kabul's schools were full of youths who had been uprooted from their rural and tribal traditions and were looking for new ways to understand the changes all about them. Taraki, a poor boy whose frustration in his ambitions apparently turned him to seek radical ways of retaliating against the royal establishment, was an example of one kind of person to whom Soviet claims of egalitarian progress appealed. By the early 1960s there were some 20 000 students in Kabul University and its feeder high schools in the capital,[22] as well as growing numbers of recent graduates who were dissatisfied with advancement prospects in a stultified, hierarchial bureaucracy.

In March 1963 King Zahir Shah tried to offer broader possibilities to the expanding educated class and thus stabilize a regime that had been narrowly run by Daoud. Daoud resigned, the king named a commoner prime minister, and a decade of constitutional government began. The first meaningful elections for a parliament with some real power were scheduled. This stimulated the Communists formally to establish the PDPA. 'Owing to relatively suitable conditions . . . the endeavors and struggle of the progressive and leftist circles toward unity were realized' the 20th-anniversary statement said.[23] The 1 January 1965, meeting at Taraki's house was held secretly, however, because political parties had not been legally permitted and Communism was in theory forbidden. Parties never became legal, the king shying away from signing legislation to authorize them,[24] thus crippling his cautiously democratic experiment. The Communists had no qualms about operating semi-legally. The fundamentalist Islamic organizations were ostensibly religious in nature, although with political intent, and so could also function. It was only the modern Westernized elements upon whom the king counted for a broad centrist government that were deterred by the inability openly to organize and seek public support for their goals.

The PDPA's founding meeting elected seven full and four alternate (or candidate) members to its central committee,[25] which also filled the role of a political bureau or politburo in larger Communist parties. Taraki and Karmal were full members, and Taraki was elected general secretary. A version of PDPA history issued by Taraki's faction at the time when he was feuding with Karmal does not mention Karmal's having a secretarial position,[26] but for the party's 20th anniversary the claim was made – apparently for the first time publicly – that Karmal had been elected by party founders 'as secretary', or No. 2 to Taraki.[27]

The PDPA constitution proclaimed it to be 'the highest political organ and the vanguard of the working class and all laborers in Afghanistan . . . founded on the voluntary union of the progressive and informed . . . workers, peasants, artisans and intellectuals.'[28] In typical Communist fashion, the party thus claimed to speak for those whom its tiny membership did not themselves include or represent. Most of Afghanistan's estimated 14 million or so people[29] were illiterate villagers with no awareness of politics in the PDPA sense. There was by 1965 still hardly any working class that Marx would have recognized as proletarian. The number of industrial workers was probably only around 20 000, and the bureaucracy numbered some 60 000.[30] By the time the PDPA came to power 13 years later, the number of industrial workers might have expanded to 60 000, and the total working class was claimed by a Soviet writer to number 300 000.[31] But those were not the people targeted for political conversion by PDPA members. It was a party of dissident intellectuals – in the Third World sense of virtually anyone with an education being an intellectual – and later military officers also. These people seem to have made little or no effort to associate themselves with ordinary uneducated workers, farmers or nomads, who were beneath their social class. The PDPA was a party of teahouse political talk.[32] 'A working-class party does not mean that the majority is constituted by workers', a PDPA official explained in 1979, 'but rather that the members are equipped with the ideology of the working class'.[33]

In addition to class distinctions that separated the PDPA from the masses, there were divisions within the new party. While Taraki 'did odd jobs to eke out a living',[34] representing the rise of poor peasants through education, Karmal came from the Afghan aristocracy as the son of a royal general and province governor.[35] They moved in different social circles. This was one factor in the split that developed in the PDPA by 1967. Another was a difference in how to oppose the constitutional government. Karmal, who was proving to be an effective orator in parliament, wanted to work within the royal system to expand Communist influence, while Taraki was the outsider who felt more comfortable seeking supporters from a position of opposition. Yet another factor was the ethnic differences between them and many of their followers. Taraki was Pushtun, while Karmal was Kashmiri but appearing essentially Tajik and claiming Pushtun ancestry; Taraki had grown up speaking Pashto, Karmal speaking Dari (and German, in which he was educated in Kabul). The age-old tribal and ethnic divisions that have always made Afghanistan only a loosely united country (and that in today's war situation are reasserting themselves to put into question any future unity not maintained by force) helped tear the PDPA apart.

It was a messy divorce. Both Taraki's faction, named *Khalq* (People, or Masses) after the short-lived original PDPA newspaper, and *Parcham* (Flag, or Banner) after Karmal's paper that lasted for two years, claimed to be the true party. Four of the seven original PDPA full central committee members joined Karmal's Parchami clique, and a fifth had by 1967 split off to form a Maoist faction, so that Taraki's Khalqis depended upon those added to the party leadership since the founding congress to sustain his claim to majority support.[36]

In its 20th anniversary statement, the PDPA under Karmal's control gave a list of reasons for:

> the appearance of deviationist, tribal, clan, national, sectarian, nationalist and group tendencies, rightist and leftist opportunistic inclinations, adventurism, egoism, deviation from constitutional, organizational and political principles, and other qualities emanating from the backwardness of society and the feudalist and prefeudalist characteristics.[37]

These reasons were listed as:

> the general backwardness of socioeconomic relations in the country; the lack of growth of political and class awareness; the low level of the knowledge of revolutionary theory of the majority of members of the party, along with the shortage of awareness of the experience of the national, progressive, workers and democratic

parties and movements and their creative approach in the specific conditions of our society; weakness in fully and correctly understanding the Afghan society, the characteristics and the level of development of the class composition of the country; and the lack of correct understanding of the tactic and strategy of the working class during the phases of growth and development of the revolution and proletarian internationalism.[38]

The statement added that disunity had weakened party effectiveness and 'temporarily dragged the national democratic movement into perversion and threatened the existence of the party'.[39]

After the split, at a time when the combined strength of the party was later claimed to have been only several thousand,[40] it sought student support and fomented demonstrations. In response, the Islamic fundamentalists were driven to become better organized, creating their own student groups beginning in 1968.[41] There were armed clashes between Communists and fundamentalists not only in Kabul but also in Herat and other towns. The PDPA also sought adherents in the armed forces, working primarily on officers who had been given a large dose of Marxist theory while learning weapons systems in Soviet schools. The Afghan government paid little attention.[42]

In 1973 Daoud led a military coup that overthrew the king and ended the constitutional experiment. He quickly reverted to traditional rule by conservative cronies. Karmal's Parcham, which claimed to have 'played a fundamental role in overthrowing the monarchy',[43] and initially had some of its members in Daoud's presidential government, was soon shunted aside. Meanwhile, Taraki and his deputy Hafizullah Amin were working to build a Khalqi base in the armed forces. With both factions now shut out of any role in government, and with there being no acknowledged successor to the ageing Daoud since he had brought down his own royal family, Khalq and Parcham papered over their differences and united to work against an increasingly right-wing regime. The inspiration seems to have come from the Soviet Union – whose embassy in Kabul had long worked closely with PDPA leaders – and been transmitted at least partly through the Indian Communist Party.[44] Agreement was reached in March 1977 to restore unity, and a unification conference in July 1977 chose a new PDPA leadership shared between the factions.[45] It was insincere unity, the Parchamis in particular later accusing Amin of keeping separate for the Khalqi faction his recruiting efforts in the armed forces.[46]

When a military council overthrew Daoud on 27 April 1978, and three days later turned power over to the PDPA,[47] the party possibly had only about 4000 members, of whom 2500 were Khalqis and 1500 Parchamis,[48] although diplomats' estimates ran as high as 5000 or even 10 000.[49] Its conflicting official claims now, however, are 15 000 or 18 000 members at that time[50] – claims that Soviets in a position to know noticeably avoided repeating for some years.[51] Whatever the number, the party was ill-prepared for power. Its leaders knew little of the public mood, lacked understanding of what was popularly desirable or acceptable, and confused the trappings of authority in Kabul with the ability to exert their will over a traditionally disorganized, unconsolidated governmental structure that was more tolerated than respected among most of the disparate people of Afghanistan.

The PDPA issued on 9 May 1978, the 'Main Directions of the . . . Government's Revolutionary Tasks', a document that the party now claims was 'written and compiled' by Karmal and approved by Taraki.[52] It was the basis for a series of reform decrees covering land, debts, marriage, women's rights, and other subjects, for which Karmal has also claimed at least partial credit.[53] These are surprisingly unwise claims. The Directions and reforms showed how out of touch the party was with the reality of its backward country. Rather than winning the PDPA credit for suddenly transforming life into something better, as the party seemed to expect, they stirred the people into rebellion. The Soviet Communist Party newspaper *Pravda* later conceded that 'Slogans incomprehensible to simple people and far removed from the real situation in the country were advanced. This not only undermined the masses' enthusiasm but also their trust in the leadership'.[54] Another Soviet publication said that 'Ordinary people lost faith in the revolutionary regime'.[55] Karmal himself admitted that there was 'insufficient maturity by the PDPA',[56] which 'lacked the necessary experience in carrying out government affairs'.[57] In short, the PDPA's reforms were economic and social disasters, and the party was exposed as a small group of revolutionary dreamers lacking the toughness or realism to know how to attain those dreams.

FACTIONAL PROBLEMS OF THE PDPA

Karmal was not in Kabul to witness the gradual collapse of the new regime's ability to control the country as both armed and passive resistance to its changes grew. As a result of the 1977 party unity agreement, he emerged as deputy to Taraki after the coup, but within one month signs began to appear of renewed disunity.[58] Within two months, arrangements were made to post Karmal and other key Parchamis abroad as ambassadors,[59] jobs from which they disappeared before being charged by a PDPA central committee meeting on 27 November 1978 with conspiring under Karmal's leadership against the April coup and Khalqi regime.[60] How much truth there was in that charge is unclear and unimportant; the key point is the inability to overcome old differences for the good of the nation – as they interpreted it. Khalqis tortured those Parchamis caught in Kabul.[61]

The party underwent further strains when Taraki, with apparent Soviet connivance, tried to replace Amin and, failing, was himself replaced by Amin and later suffocated.[62] The effect of that September 1979 split among the Khalqis was to put some of them in opposition to Amin and therefore in a position to join with the Parchamis when the Soviet Army installed Karmal in power in December 1979.[63] In the face of overwhelming Soviet arms, these Khalqis joined in the Karmal regime. While some of Amin's closest collaborators were at last report still in Kabul's Pul-i-Charki prison,[64] most Khalqis who had not been directly involved in the Taraki-Amin showdown also rallied to a PDPA that was ostensibly reunited. This unity soon turned out to be no more substantial than the 1977 agreement, however, and the PDPA remains divided to this day.

Khalqi hostility toward Parchami control, always implicit in a situation when the apparent minority faction had been imposed upon the majority by foreign arms, became obvious within 3 ½ months of the invasion. Karmal's regime then disclosed an agreement permitting Soviet troops to remain in Afghanistan.[65] Khalqis reportedly were angered by it both because it guaranteed that Karmal would remain in power so long as the Soviets found him useful and because it violated their nationalistic instincts more keenly than Parchamis'.[66] By the summer of 1980, some Khalqis were reported to be aiding the guerrilla resistance by the *mujahideen* (Islamic 'holy warriors') and even carrying out themselves assassinations of Parchamis that were officially attributed to the resistance.[67] At least four major military coup plots by Khalqi officers were reported by US diplomats between June 1980 and February 1981,[68] all broken up by arrests, and there have been numerous personal and group clashes and shootouts between the two factions.[69] Although the government is basically run by Soviet advisers, this feuding and backstabbing has been frustrating to the USSR. It has complicated and often undercut Soviet efforts to broaden the very narrow base of the regime.

When Karmal returned from his first presidential visit to Moscow, in October 1980, he lectured Afghans in 'high and responsible posts' who had been guilty of 'factionalism, bribery, repression' and other crimes.[70] Since then, he has with regularity harranged the party on its inability to overcome the Khalqi–Parchami split, with the very regularity showing that the problem remains unresolved.[71] At the most recent meeting of the PDPA central committee, on 19 September 1984, Karmal complained that party units were unable to overcome 'the remnants of sectarianism' and 'personal clashes'.[72] The party's 20th anniversary statement warned that the path toward 'organic unity is a very long path . . . a very hard path, and has not yet been reached . . . The anniversary of the party ought to be transformed into a powerful dynamism for the consolidation of party ranks'.[73]

Significantly, Soviet media accounts of Karmal's speeches regularly censor out any mention of PDPA disunity. This probably is partly intended to hide from the Soviet public that it is being forced to support people who cannot even support each other.[74] It might also be an avoidance of something that the Soviets know they have little prospect of solving and therefore prefer not to acknowledge. What Karmal has said are still evident 'signs of clan loyalty, tribal loyalty, loyalty to material gains, to family, group and rank',[75] work against unity. Even if the Soviets were to purge the present PDPA leadership and virtually rebuild the party with new Afghans – which is within their power, so total is it in Kabul – they would not rid Afghan Communism of its ethnic and tribal divisiveness, its traditions of blood feuds and its codes of honor requiring revenge at any cost. New generations of Afghans would pick up the old quarrels. Disunity is natural to the country.

The Soviets also censor repeated complaints by Karmal and others about the PDPA's basic weakness in members' abilities, competence for their jobs, willingness to assume responsibility, and initiative to solve the many daunting problems. On the sixth anniversary of the PDPA's coming to power, Karmal spoke on these problems to the Revolutionary Council, which in theory runs the government but in practice takes party orders – and, ultimately, Soviet directions. Karmal, as council chairman, said that 'so far many successes have not been achieved and fundamental transformations have not taken place' in official work. 'The resistance of the enemies not only prevent this but also the lack of ability of the organizational structure of our party and of ourselves, passivity, taking things easy, slowness in accomplishing the revolutionary duties', and other shortcomings. He denied that 'inadequate experience of party' was an excuse, as had been used in 1980 to justify failures, because 'during the past six years, sufficient experience has been gathered'.[76]

Karmal was even more scathing at the 19 September 1984, PDPA plenum about 'a complacent, arrogant, and bureaucratic approach'. The 31 provincial party committees, 26 city committees, 300 ward committees and more than 200 district and subdistrict committees 'have not yet become the true organizers of the solution of the complex problems of the people', Karmal said. He accused them of 'weak and uninitiated work', paying 'attention to small matters and . . . forgetting important and serious questions', and usually limiting 'their activity in the solution of socio-economic problems to writing letters and demands to Kabul. Thus, they lie in wait and do not display initiative and consistency'. Officials in Kabul, in turn, ignore local committees when making provincial visits, Karmal said.[77] The 20th anniversary statement tried to put a better face on this by claiming that 'The party is being equipped more and more every day and consciously leads social movements.'[78]

This continuing weakness of the PDPA can be explained in several ways. One is that the party did not in its early days attract many of the brightest young Afghans. Its conspiratorial, revolutionary appeal was more to those youths who had little prospect of making it to the top of the country's meritocratic system of the 1960s and early 1970s, and some of its savagery once in power with the technocratic elite apparently is a taking of revenge on those long envied. A second point is that, as PDPA leaders have acknowledged, power was unexpectedly acquired by young people with little experience of managing governmental or business affairs.[79] But the third and most important point is that they have had little opportunity to acquire experience because of Soviet advisers. Even before the Soviet invasion, advisers had assumed a major role in running the civilian administration as well as the armed forces; since then, they have so totally controlled and dominated the regime that PDPA members are effectively discouraged from doing anything. Karmal complained in 1980 that some comrades 'lay all the burden and responsibility for practical work on the shoulders of the advisers'.[80] This seems not to have changed. The natural reluctance to make decisions – when kept in fear of criticism for making mistakes – is one aspect of this.

Another is the vicious circle that few Afghans are willing to take risks in doing the Soviets' work, while the Soviets trust few Afghans.

Efforts to improve PDPA work are being made, although their effectiveness obviously has been low so far. The Social Sciences Institute of the PDPA central committee is claimed by the party politburo to have 'carried out effective activities in training and retraining party and state cadres, military and political personnel, and activists from social organizations' in the five years since its reported founding on 31 December 1979. Karmal has called for its work to be expanded.[81] While the universities at Kabul and Jalalabad have withered, students are being sent to the Soviet Union in an apparent hope of educating a new generation that will accept the necessity of serving as dependable puppets, but the success of this effort is far from assured.[82]

Whatever their quality, the quantity of PDPA members has increased steadily, according to official figures. The membership just before the party's 20th anniversary was claimed to be 120 000 full and candidate members,[83] a claim that has to be taken with some caution. While most party members were reported to have been less than 30 years old in 1980,[84] on 8 July 1984, the PDPA newspaper *Haqiqat-e Enqelabe Sawr* (Truth of the April Revolution) was quoted as saying that half were under 30. It said workers comprised 16.9 per cent of party members and 'peasants and artisans' 33.3 per cent.[85] As already noted, however, PDPA statistics are confusing and often contradictory. Karmal said on 3 July 1983, that the party had 90 000 full and candidate members, of whom 28.4 per cent were workers and peasants – that is, 25 560 of them.[86] The claim of 50.2 per cent workers, peasants and artisans in July 1984, when total party membership was claimed to be past 115 000 and nearing a September claim of 120 000,[87] means that the number of workers and peasants (artisans are few, and probably were lumped in with peasants in 1983) had risen by some 35 000 – while total membership was rising only 30 000! On 16 April 1983, Karmal said more than 50 per cent of a then party membership of 85 000 were in the Afghan armed forces,[88] but on 3 January 1984, the armed forces' chief political commissar said 'one in five servicemen has become a party member'.[89] Reconciling those last two statements would require a military strength of some 200 000, double the claimed 100 000[90] – which claim is itself probably well over double the actual strength.[91] Figures for the PDPA's Komsomol, or youth branch, the Democratic Organization of the Youth of Afghanistan, are similarly uncertain. It was claimed to have 136 000 members by the end of 1983,[92] but in September 1984 Karmal said membership was 'more than 120 000',[93] and in November he complained that it was failing to indoctrinate young people properly, so that they were 'falling prey to the propaganda and deeds of the enemy'.[94]

A strong impression is created that PDPA statistics are fabricated by the same people who kept issuing contradictory statements about how many times some unidentified Afghan authority supposedly invited in the Soviet Army, and when Karmal returned home and was 'elected' to head the PDPA.

The reality behind official statements is that Communism in Afghanistan is limited to a fairly small number of persons who, even if they originally joined the PDPA from some sense of idealism of making their country better, or of adventure, are today almost powerless servants of a colonial power and as a result are detested by most of their fellow countrymen. The party scarcely reaches beyond Kabul – Afghanistan has been dubbed an example of 'socialism in one city' – and in some areas has tried to build nominal local organizations by enlisting traditional leaders who are the antithesis of Communists. The PDPA has not been able to replace the throne as a symbol of national unity for the country's disparate ethnic, tribal and linguistic groups any more than it has been able to overcome its own divisive tendencies because of conflicting ambitions compounded by those ethnic and tribal factors. Any claim that it could have made between April 1978 and December 1979 of representing a new form of national governance, and therefore worthy of public support, has been lost in its post-invasion service to a foreign power. The claim to represent farmers is invalidated by the inability to reach into rural areas, where the *mujahideen* are the only alternative to autarchy or anarchy.

Although a loosely-defined Afghan proletariat might not have grown from the estimated 300 000 in 1978[95] to 550 000,[96] the PDPA's own contradictory figures suggest that only a small proportion of them was willing to join the supposed party of the proletariat. In fact, it has been from its beginnings and remains a middle class party of what are considered intellectuals. The Parchami faction may be a bit more bourgeois, with a larger share of Tajiks from more prosperous Kabul families, and the Khalqis more plebian, with a predominance of members from Pushtun tribal backgrounds, but the party as a whole is not representative of the Afghan population. Probably even less representative are Maoist Communist factions that Soviet sources say maintain clandestine existences in Afghanistan with Chinese help.[97]

Karmal will doubtlessly go on reporting membership increases for the PDPA, because that apparently is considered part of claiming increased popular support for the regime. Although the claim of 120 000 members seems likely to be double or more the true figure, the logic of the situation does suggest that more people will join than desert to the resistance, flee to Pakistan, or be killed either in internecine PDPA strife or *mujahideen* attacks. Partly this is the logic of opportunism, lacking in any appeal of idealism or dedication to helping fellow man that few if any Communists in the Soviet Union or anywhere else believe in any more. So long as Soviet leaders remain determined to hang on to Afghanistan – and, regrettably, there is no visible prospect of a change in that – then opportunity for those who chose to stay in the larger towns and serve the Soviet colonial purpose will lie in joining the PDPA. But there can be few doubts left among PDPA members that their role is a limited one of doing what Moscow says. Another part is the logic of power. The PDPA has used its control to try to coerce people into joining the Party as a price for holding official jobs.[98]

FUTURE OF THE PDPA

The PDPA never did have an opportunity to exist as an independent Communist party, able to deal with Moscow from a position of some internal strength if not as an equal. Aided and encouraged by the Soviets before it unexpectedly and unpreparedly came to power in 1978, the party by its unwise early actions undermined domestic support and immediately fell into a need for Soviet military and economic aid and a stiffening cadre of Soviet advisers in an inept administration. Although Amin defied Soviet advice in further alienating the Afghan people, he never had any alternative to dependence on Moscow because, unlike a Tito or Ceausescu, he could not command either willing or coerced backing of his own people. Any thoughts in the PDPA that independence from Moscow might have been possible were crushed in the 1979 invasion that killed Amin. Since then, with the party indelibly linked in Afghan minds with a Quisling status that betrays millenia of fighting foreign invaders, the PDPA has no chance of breaking away from its Soviet sponsorship. It has no alternative source of support, no ability to exist on its own. It is too tainted to be rebellious as a party. Only as individuals who sabotage Soviet military efforts to tighten the grip on Afghanistan can PDPA members show their contempt for their situation. The material pleasures of being on the side of the occupying power apparently have choked contemptuous feelings in most party members.

The PDPA cannot even hope for the relatively separate position of a Communist country that conducts its own regional policy, like Vietnam, Cuba or North Korea. Geography joins the military, political and economic weakness of total dependence on the Soviet Union to forbid it. Afghanistan can only be an advanced position for Soviet power projection, political if not military, rather than a separate actor on its own.

The future of Communism in Afghanistan, therefore, is to serve as a weak, dependent front for Russian – not Soviet, but Great Russian – control of a mixed collection of people who can agree most readily on despising the PDPA. As more *mujahideen* are killed by the Soviet Army, and as more refugees are driven from a devastated countryside into Pakistan or Iran, more of Afghanistan's dwindling population might appear to rally around the party in battered weariness, more young people decide that there is little alternative to acquiesing in its local fronting for Moscow. But nothing in Afghan history or character suggests that the creation of Taraki, Amin and Karmal will ever become a popular, independent, self-reliant political party, or that Soviet Marxism-Leninism will win widespread acceptance in a land of ruggedly unvanquished people.

Notes

1. People's Democratic Party of Afghanistan central committee document issued for the 20th anniversary of the party's formation, Kabul Radio, 30 (sic – apparently 3) Nov. 1984, in Foreign Broadcast Information Service, Daily Report, South Asia (hereafter FBIS/SA), Washington, DC, 9 Nov. 1984, pp. C1–7. See also Babrak Karmal's speech to anniversary celebrations, Kabul Radio, 10, 11 and 12 Jan. 1985, in FBIS/SA, 14 and 15 Jan. 1985, pp. C1–5 and C1–10.
2. Henry S. Bradsher, *Afghanistan and the Soviet Union*, (Durham, N.C., 1983) p. 43, quoting a 1976 PDPA internal document. For full text of the document, see Anthony Arnold, *Afghanistan's Two-Party Communism: Parcham and Khalq* (Stanford, Calif., 1983) pp. 160–177.
3. E.g., Leonid I. Brezhnev, Report to the 26th Congress of the Soviet Communist Party, Moscow Radio, 23 Feb. 1981, in Foreign Broadcast Information Service, Daily Report, Soviet Union (hereafter FBIS/SU),

Supplement (Washington, DC, 24 Feb. 1981) pp. 6 and 10. See also the listing of *Izvestiya*, (Moscow, 8 Nov. 1984) p. 5, of receptions in various capitals for the 7 Nov. 1984 Bolshevik Revolution celebrations, in (FBIS/SU, 8 Nov. 1984) p. 011.

4. The value of this caution is shown by Brezhnev's 1981 inclusion of Mozambique among countries said to have chosen a socialist path – from which it has since begun to wander.
5. PDPA 20th anniversary document, *op. cit.* Karmal had said on 27 April 1984 that the PDPA maintained 'links with 103 parties and progressive organizations in the world', according to *Izvestiya*, 27 April 1984, p. 4, in FBIS/SU, 1 May 1984, p. D1. The reason for the later claim of only 'more than 52' is not clear but typical of the PDPA regime's conflicting and confusing statistics; see below.
6. The Mongolian Communist party, known as the Mongolian People's Revolutionary Party, ostensibly attained power even quicker, within a year of its formation, but in fact Moscow only used local people as a front for its colonial takeover. See Henry S. Bradsher, 'The Sovietization of Mongolia', *Foreign Affairs*, New York, Vol. 50, No. 3, April 1972, pp. 545–553.
7. PDPA 20th anniversary document.
8. Bradsher, *Afghanistan*, pp. 15–16.
9. See 'The Basmachis: The Central Asian Resistance Movement, 1918–1924', *Central Asian Review*, London, Vol. 7, No. 3, p. 236.
10. PDPA 20th anniversary document.
11. Bradsher, *Afghanistan*, p. 35.
12. A. M. Baryalai, (ed.), *Democratic Republic of Afghanistan Annual, 1979*, (Kabul, 1979) p. 8.
13. See the PDPA 20th anniversary document. Its falsity might not have been the reason it was dropped; its deletion might have been part of an apparent effort to play down Taraki's importance in order to enhance that of Babrak Karmal.
14. Leon B. Poullada, 'Afghanistan and the United States: The Crucial Years', *The Middle East Journal*, Washington, DC, No. 35, 1981, pp. 186–187.
15. Peter G. Franck, *Afghanistan Between East and West* (Washington, DC, 1960) p. 58.
16. Tahir Amin, 'Afghan Resistance: Past, Present, and Future', *Asian Survey*, Berkeley, Calif., Vol. 14, No. 4, April 1984, pp. 376–377.
17. *Le Monde*, Paris, 18 April 1984.
18. Amin, 'Afghan Resistance', p. 377.
19. See Bradsher, *Afghanistan*, pp. 37–39, and Arnold, *Afghanistan's Two-Party Communism*, pp. 18–19.
20. Baryalai, *Democractic Republic of Afghanistan Annual, 1979*, p. 10.
21. Kabul Radio, 2 Aug. 1978, in Foreign Broadcast Information Service, Daily Report, Middle East (hereafter FBIS/ME), Washington, DC, 17 Aug. 1978, pp. S1–4.
22. Louis Dupree, 'Constitutional Development and Cultural Change, Part VIII: The Future of Constitutional Law in Afghanistan and Pakistan',

American University Field Service Reports (hereafter AUFS), South Asia, Vol. 9, No. 10, 1965, p. 6.
23. PDPA 20th anniversary document. After 1978, some PDPA members dated their party memberships to 1963, indicating that some loose organization existed before conditions became suitable for forming a party; see Bradsher, *Afghanistan*, p. 43.
24. *Ibid.*, p. 36.
25. *Ibid.*, p. 43, citing the 1976 internal document. See also the PDPA 20th anniversary document.
26. Bradsher, *Afghanistan*, p. 43.
27. PDPA 20th anniversary document.
28. Constitution text in Airgram No. A-60 from US Embassy, Kabul, 3 July 1978. See also Arnold, *Afghanistan's Two-Party Communism*, pp. 149–159.
29. There has never been a census, and a claim of the Taraki regime to have conducted one in 1978 was later revealed to have been a fraud. See Bradsher, *Afghanistan*, p. 120.
30. *Ibid.*, pp. 44–45.
31. Rostislav A. Ulyanovskiy, 'The Afghan Revolution at the Current Stage', *Voprosy Istorii KPSS*, Moscow, No. 4, April 1982, in FBIS Joint Publications Research Service, USSR Report, Political and Sociological Affairs, Washington, DC, No. 1279, 20 July 1982, p. 6.
32. This is not uncommon for Communist parties, none of which has come to power from such a narrow urban base without external intervention since the Bolshevik Revolution, but some that were driven out of the cities and forces to build rural bases – like the Chinese Communist Party – emerged the stronger.
33. *New York Times*, 9 Sept. 1979, p. A3.
34. Baryalai, *Democratic Republic of Afghanistan Annual, 1979*, p. 10.
35. Bradsher, *Afghanistan*, p. 39.
36. *Ibid.*, p. 50. The only original leader to stick with Taraki was Dr Saleh Mohammed Ziray, a remarkable survivor who is the only person to have sat continuously in the PDPA politburos of Taraki, Amin and Karmal, and is now one of Karmal's most important deputies.
37. PDPA 20th anniversary document.
38. *Ibid.*
39. *Ibid.* Taraki is not accused in the document of factionalism, as Karmal accused him between 1967 and 1977, thus leaving him on a pedestal as party founder from whom Karmal can claim direct and legitimate succession. The party leader in between them, Hafizullah Amin – who was killed in the 1979 Soviet invasion – 'and his group' are accused of a 'treacherous and factionalist role'. Since Amin was the Khalqi leader after Taraki, this blame would seem to contradict Karmal's appeals for overcoming past factionalism.
40. Ulyanovskiy, 'The Afghan Revolution', p. 86. The US embassy in Kabul estimated in 1972 only 300 to 500 total Communists among all factions; see US State Department, *World Strength of Communist Party Organizations*, Washington, DC, 1972, pp. 89–90.

41. Amin, 'Afghan Resistance', p. 377.
42. Airgram No. A-71, US Embassy, Kabul, 26 June 1971.
43. PDPA 20th anniversary document, which does not, however, specify only the Parcham faction.
44. Bradsher, *Afghanistan*, pp. 69–70.
45. Ulyanovskiy, 'The Afghan Revolution', p. 86. The PDPA 20th anniversary document, as transcribed from Kabul Radio by the BBC (for FBIS), dates the unity conference as July 1976, but this apparently is an error.
46. Ulyanovskiy, 'The Afghan Revolution', p. 87. See also Bradsher, *Afghanistan*, pp. 71–72.
47. See *ibid.*, pp. 76–80, for a discussion of whether it was a PDPA-led coup, as the party claims (or, rather, it claims the palace coup was a revolution), or a defensive move by military officers who then turned to the party.
48. Louis Dupree, 'Red Flag Over the Hindu Kush, Part V: Repressions, or Security Through Terror Purges, I–IV', AUFS/Asia, Vol. 28, No. 3, 1980, p. 3.
49. Bradsher, *Afghanistan*, p. 270, footnote 102.
50. The PDPA 20th anniversary statement, *op. cit.*, and numerous official statements say 15 000, but Karmal and others have used the figure 18 000; see Kabul Radio, 25 April 1984, in FBIS/SA, 30 April 1984, p. C2, among many examples.
51. Compare Ulyanovskiy, 'The Afghan Revolution', who avoids the question, with the summary of the PDPA's 20th anniversary document in *Pravda*, 3 Nov. 1984, p. 5, in FBIS/SU, 8 Nov. 1984, p. D4, which quotes the 15 000 figure. On 8 July 1984, *Pravda*, p. 4, had quoted an eve-of-revolution membership of 18 000; see FBIS/SU, 19 July 1984, p. D2.
52. PDPA 20th anniversary document. The claim seems doubtful, probably part of the effort to rewrite history to Karmal's greater glory.
53. Kabul Radio, 7 Jan. 1980, in FBIS/ME, 9 Jan. 1980, p. S2.
54. *Pravda*, 17 Oct. 1980, pp. 2–6, in FBIS/SU, 21 Oct. 1980, pp. D4–11.
55. *Novoye Vremya*, Moscow, 11 April 1980, pp. 5–7, in FBIS/SU, 21 April 1980, pp. D6–9.
56. *Pravda*, 18 Feb. 1980, in FBIS/SU, 21 Feb. 1980, pp. D3–4.
57. Kabul Radio, 28 April 1980, in FBIS/SA, 29 April 1980, pp. C1–3.
58. Arnold, *Afghanistan's Two-Party Communism*, p. 66.
59. Bradsher, *Afghanistan*, p. 87.
60. Kabul Radio, 27 Nov. 1978, in FBIS/ME, 13 Dec. 1978, pp. S1–7. The senior Parchami who was imprisoned in Kabul for the alleged conspiracy, Sultan Ali Keshtmand (who is now prime minister), reportedly confessed (under torture) that 'Karmal argued that the present Khalqi regime was isolated from the people and the latter were dissatisfied' and ripe for an uprising to establish a regime that 'might be able to satisfy the majority'. See Baryalai, *Democratic Republic of Afghanistan Annual, 1979*, pp. 1338 and 1341. If Karmal did actually argue that then, he was right, but he in effect denies it now.
61. Bradsher, *Afghanistan*, p. 230.
62. *Ibid.*, pp. 106–116.
63. For a discussion of the contradictory official accounts of how Karmal

returned from exile and was chosen leader of the PDPA, see *ibid.*, pp. 173–175 and 185–186.
64. The *Times of India*, Bombay, 11 Feb. 1981, p. 1, in FBIS/SA, 23 Feb. 1981, pp. C1–2, which reported 18 Khalqis in prison, including Amin's top deputy, Shah Wali – who has not been seen since then.
65. Kabul Radio, 4 April 1980, in FBIS/SA, 7 April 1980, p. C1.
66. Press Trust of India (news agency) from Kabul, 10 and 14 April 1980, in FBIS/SA, 10 and 14 April 1980, pp. C1 and C9.
67. Foreign and Commonwealth Office (hereafter FCO), London, 'Afghanistan Report', July 1980; FCO, 'Afghanistan: Chronology', undated.
68. Bradsher, *Afghanistan*, p. 231.
69. See the series of US State Department Special Reports issued on Afghanistan every December since the invasion.
70. Kabul Radio, 14 Nov. 1980, in FBIS/SA, 17 Nov. 1980, pp. C1–7.
71. For recent examples, see Kabul Radio, 5 July 1983, in FBIS/SA, 8 July 1983, pp. C1–2; Bakhtar news agency, Kabul, 3 March 1984, in FBIS/SA, 6 March 1984, p. C1; Kabul Radio, 25 April 1984, in FBIS/SA, 30 April 1984, pp. C2–3; and Kabul Radio, 14 May 1984, in FBIS/SA, 16 May 1984, pp. C1–2.
72. Kabul Radio, 21 Sept. 1984, in FBIS/SA, 24 Sept. 1984, pp. C1–5.
73. PDPA 20th anniversary document.
74. For example, compare Kabul Radio, 5 July 1983, in FBIS/SA, 8 July 1983, pp. C1–2, with *Pravda*, 7 July 1983, p. 5, in FBIS/SU, 8 July 1983, p. D1; Kabul Radio, 21 Sept. 1984, in FBIS/SA, 24 Sept. 1984, pp. C1–5, with *Pravda*, 23 Sept. 1984, p. 5, in FBIS/SU, 24 Sept. 1984, pp. D1–3; and PDPA 20th anniversary document, *op. cit.*, with TASS, 31 Oct. 1984, in FBIS/SU, 2 Nov. 1984, pp. D8–9, and with *Pravda*, 3 Nov. 1984, p. 5, in FBIS/SU, 8 Nov. 1984, pp. D3–5. The deceptive dishonesty of censoring out such admissions of PDPA disunity is shown by Soviet media reports claiming the opposite, such as an interview with Karmal's half-brother and alternate politburo member, A. Mahmud Baryalay, who said, 'We can say with pride that our party is now united' – at the same time Karmal was telling a PDPA plenum the opposite; see *Za Rubezhom*, Moscow, 28 Sept. 1984, in FBIS/SU, 11 Oct. 1984, pp. D3–6.
75. Kabul Radio, 5 July 1983, in FBIS/SA, 8 July 1983, p. C2.
76. Kabul Radio, 25 April 1984, in FBIS/SA, 30 April 1984, pp. C2–4.
77. Kabul Radio, 21 Sept. 1984, in FBIS/SA, 24 Sept. 1984, pp. C1–5.
78. PDPA 20th anniversary document.
79. TASS from Kabul, 26 April 1980, in FBIS/SU, 28 April 1980, p. D3.
80. Kabul Radio, 14 Nov. 1980, in FBIS/SA, 17 Nov. 1980, p. C3.
81. Kabul Radio, 28 Sept. 1984, in FBIS/SA, 1 Oct. 1984, p. C2.
82. See Bradsher, *Afghanistan*, pp. 247–248, and Henry S. Bradsher, 'Afghanistan', The *Washington Quarterly*, Washington, DC, Vol. 7, No. 3, Summer 1984, p. 53.
83. PDPA 20th anniversary document, and many speeches and articles.
84. PAP (Polish press agency) from Kabul, 23 Feb. 1981, in FBIS/SA, 25 Feb. 1981, p. C3. Karmal said 65 per cent were under 30 in mid-1983; see Kabul Radio, 5 July 1983, in FBIS/SA, 8 July 1983, p. C2.

85. Quoted by *Pravda*, 8 July 1984, p. 4, in FBIS/SU, 19 July 1984, p. D1. It is more than curious that Karmal used almost the exact figures – 16.9 per cent workers, 33.2 per cent peasants – for the 31 000 new candidate members who he said were accepted by the PDPA in the Islamic year 1982–83; see Kabul Radio, 5 July 1983, in FBIS/SA, 8 July 1983, p. C2. The similarity of figures for supposedly different categories suggests that the worker and peasant proportions are cooked to satisfy some Soviet-set ideological goal, but are then confused in various citations.
86. Kabul Radio, 5 July 1983, in FBIS/SA, 8 July 1983, p. C2. Karmal said the PDPA then had more than 90 000 members, and its membership had increased about 35 per cent in the 'year just ended'. But he also said 31 000 new members 'were accepted last year' – which would be an increase of 53 per cent from the implied previous total.
87. *Izvestiya*, 27 April 1984, p. 4, in FBIS/SU, 1 May 1984, p. D1, said 115 000. One of the earliest claims of 120 000 was on Kabul Radio, 19 Sept. 1984, in FBIS/SA, 20 Sept. 1984, p. C3.
88. Kabul Radio, 16 April 1983, in FBIS/SA, 19 April 1983, p. C2.
89. *Krasnaya Zvezda*, Moscow, 4 Jan. 1984, p. 3, in FBIS/SU, 6 Jan. 1984, p. D1.
90. *L'Unita*, Rome, 6 Jan. 1984, p. 7.
91. 'Afghanistan: Four Years of Occupation', US State Department Special Report No. 112, December 1983, p. 6.
92. TASS from Kabul, 27 Dec. 1983, in FBIS/SU, 28 Dec. 1983, p. D5.
93. Bakhtar news agency, 19 Sept. 1984, in FBIS/SA, 20 Sept. 1984, p. C3. Since the youth organization feeds members into the PDPA, there might not be a contradiction; more youths might have moved up than joined.
94. Kabul Radio, 18 Nov. 1984, in FBIS/SA, 20 Nov. 1984, p. C1.
95. As cited earlier from Ulyanovskiy, 'The Afghan Revolution'.
96. *Pravda*, 27 April 1984, p. 4, in FBIS/SU, 1 May 1984, p. D4, says a 'little more than 550 000 people work in industrial production, construction, transport, and communications in Afghanistan,' and 170 000 belong to trade unions.
97. One Soviet source reported in April 1982 that, 'With the help of Beijing, in January 1979 an attempt was made to unite the scattered groups of Afghan pro-Maoists' at a congress in Herat to plan the overthrow of the pro-Soviet PDPA (Ulyanovskiy, 'The Afghan Revolution', *op. cit.*), and another said in July 1982 that 'Numerous underground pro-Maoist groups planted and directed by Beijing have stepped up their subversive actions', with one of them identified as *Shu'la-yi-Jawed* (Eternal Flame) *Za Rubezhom*, No. 30 for 1982, in FBIS/SU, 29 July 1982, pp. D1–3. The Afghan news agency Bakhtar reported on 15 July 1984, that confessions by two members of a secret Maoist organization, formed in 1979 and named 'Paikar', showed it was engaged in 'broad clandestine activities against the legitimate government'. In FBIS/SA, 17 July 1984, p. C1. Amnesty International heard reports that between July and October 1981, some 500 members of two pro-Chinese groups, *Shu'la-yi-Jawed* and another named as *Sama*, were arrested by Afghan authorities; see *Amnesty International Report 1982*, London, 1982, p. 181.

17 Cultural Determinants of the Afghan Resistance to the Saur Revolution of 1978
Louis Dupree

In general, recent writings on the First Russo-Afghan War (1979–???) fall into the following major categories:
(1) Rationalizations for the invasion of Afghanistan by Soviet writers and Soviet-line sympathizers. The war is currently being more fully covered in Soviet media.[1]
(2) Western specialists on Soviet affairs have written their own interpretations of what happened and why it happened.[2]
(3) A number of 'instant' experts, not only journalists, have arisen to meet the need for news. Accurate reporting has been hampered by the difficulties of access by non-Communists to cover the war from Kabul, for, unlike the Spanish Civil War and the Vietnam War, which were open wars, the conflict in Afghanistan is a closed war. Accurate accounts of what happens inside Afghanistan are difficult to obtain and verify, and even basic mistakes on geographic locations are printed and perpetuated by usually reliable journalists.[3]

Among the better reports in English have come from the typewriter of Edward Giradet of the *Christian Science Monitor*, who has spent several extended periods inside Afghanistan. Another excellent study on the war is John Fullerton (1983).
(4) The works of Western European and American specialists on Afghanistan have been relatively few, the most recent being the best of its kind, M. Nazif Shahrani and Robert L. Canfield (1984). Others of interest are: Anthony Arnold (1981, 1983); Louis Dupree (1979, 1980ab); Willi Steul (1981); Richard Tapper (1983); Vogel[3a] (1980).

In this chapter, however, I propose to examine the post-1978 events in a different perspective: Afghan cultural reaction to the Soviet invasion, but I shall not neglect the preceeding leftist coups that overthrew the Mohammadzai dynasty. In addition, several pertinent historical patterns will be presented in their proper perspectives.

I propose to discuss the patterns in the following contexts:

Period I (April–September 1978): The *Khalqi* Coup, Repression, the abortive reforms, and the lull.

Period II (October 1978–March 1979): The winter civil war, and attempts to exploit ethnic rivalries.

Period III (April–November 1979): The End of the interregnum.

Period IV (December 1979–present): The First Russo–Afghan War, 1979–????[4]

PERIOD I (APRIL–SEPTEMBER 1978)

Seven 'Rs' can be used to characterize the patterns in Afghanistan since the 27–28 April 1978 coup: revolution, repression, rhetoric, reform, revolts, refugees and Russians.

'Revolution' is too strong a term. *Coup d'état* would better describe what happened, but since those who made the coup called it *inqilab* (revolution in Persian) the aliterative use of 'revolution' is possibly justified. No matter, the power elite of the new Democratic Republic of Afghanistan appeared to go out of its way to violate many of the important Afghan cultural patterns, and in so doing made enemies of every element of Afghan society, from the Western-trained (including Soviet-trained) technocrats to peasant farmers and tribesmen.

An initial culturally-oriented mistake of the Democratic Republic of Afghanistan (DRA) was the mass incarceration of the technocrats needed to assist in the building of a new socialist Afghanistan. Almost everyone who had served previous regimes in an official capacity, and did not announce enthusiastic support for the new regime was considered suspect. Few doubt that most technocrats would have worked for the regime, if it had distanced itself from Soviet influence and guaranteed non-alignment in Cold War issues.

The real and pseudo-opposition in jail, the regime once again violated cultural norms. Even in the harshest days of Mohammadzai rule, individuals could personally present petitions for redress or information concerning missing relatives to amirs, kings, and the late Mohammad Daoud, President of the Republic of Afghanistan (1973–1978), overthrown by the 1978 coup. Women who presented petitions in attempts to find the whereabouts of fathers, brothers, husbands or sons were vilely insulted by DRA security officials. Old men, the respected 'white beards' (*rish-i-safid*, Persian; *spingeray*, Pashto) of the society, were similarly treated.[5]

In pre-coup Afghanistan, literate Afghans always practised 'freedom of the mouth'. With a 90 per cent-plus non-literacy the published media had little impact anyway, but most educated Afghans seldom hesitated to express political opinions in tea house debates or in private homes, even those homes of foreigners. Under the Khalqi regimes, freedom of the mouth was blanketed under a curtain of fear.

The reforms (land reforms, women's rights, etc.) announced by the DRA similarly violated Afghan norms, primarily because they were presented in *direct* Persian and Pashto translations from Russian Marxist-Leninist dialectic, which Afghans had heard *ad nauseum* from broadcasting stations out of Soviet Central Asia since at least the mid-1950s. Therefore, most Afghans assumed, right or wrong, that the DRA leaders were pro-Soviet, pro-Communist, and anti-Islamic. It is interesting to note that the reforms of the DRA were remarkably similar to those announced by President Daoud's Republic. But Daoud had presented his reforms in classical Dari – Afghan Persian – and Pashto.[6]

However, in all their public announcements, the two main Khalqis, Nur Mohammad Taraki and Hafizullah Amin, insisted they were not Communists, but of an ideologically distinct Afghan socialist party, *Jamhuriyat-Demokratiki Khalqi Afghanistan* (People's Democratic Party of Afghanistan – PDPA). The ultimate demise of Taraki and Amin as a result of Soviet machinations lends some credence to this claim.

Except for sporadic small-scale attacks from Pakistan, most of the opposition to the PDPA regime was quiet inside Afghanistan until the early fall of 1978. Periodic explosions rocked Kabul, however, and the literate, urban opposition began to clandestinely publish and distribute anti-Government tracts. But winter approached.

PERIOD II (OCTOBER 1978–MARCH 1979)

Several factors account for the relative lack of early reaction against the DRA. For one thing, the coup had come as a surprise; for another, most people were willing to give the regime a chance to succeed under its initially-articulated, socialist-oriented guidelines.

Furthermore, spring and summer months are times of maximum

economic activities (farming, herding, combinations of the two) in the countryside, and it is difficult to farm and fight at the same time. Students of warfare often overlook (or underestimate) the relationships between leisure time and fighting in the annual cycle of pre-industrial peoples.[7]

In late September–early October 1978, regional revolts began right on schedule, at the end of the agricultural cycle and the beginning of the months of winter economic inactivity. Nuristan was the first to launch a traditional attack, quickly followed by other outbreaks.

For its part, the DRA should have also responded in a traditional manner. It should have sent just enough troops into the field to stop the movement of the insurgents, and then call a nation-wide *Loya Jirgah* of regional power elites, religious leaders, high government officials (both civil and military), and prominent intellectuals to talk out the problem.

Instead, the DRA overreacted. The government (and its Soviet military advisers) used its Soviet-trained and equipped military to bomb and napalm villages involved in the fighting. Much blood was shed. Government reprisals continued through the fall and winter of 1978–1979, and the revolts spread to every province in Afghanistan.

During Period II, the DRA leaders tried to take advantage of pre-existing ethnic rivalries to take the heat off their crumbling military. Initially, the gambit appeared to work, but the DRA government found out, just as had the British in the late 19th and early 20th centuries, that groups accept money and then do what they want to. The Wardak Pushtun, accepted arms and ammunition to fight the Hazara, and then kept the weapons to fight the Kabul regime. This breach of promise partly accounted for the well-documented massacre of the civilian population by Afghan government troops and Soviet advisers at Sar-i-Cheshmah.[8]

Another example: the government armed the Gujar in eastern Afghanistan to fight their traditional enemies, the Nuristani. After several reversals, the Gujar joined with the Nuristani to oppose the government.[9] Other examples could be cited, but the above suffice to give the flavor.

PERIOD III (APRIL–NOVEMBER 1979)

Many astute observers predicted that the Afghan peasants and nomads would give up the fight and return to farming and herding as spring of 1979 approached, the familiar pattern to end the annual feud, especially along the Durand Line.[10] But much more blood had been shed, and most ethnic groups had a *badal* (blood feud) with the government in Kabul. So, although some did return to the normal economic cycle, many Afghans remained in the field to fight, another culturally-oriented signal to Kabul. The initial revolts merely expressed an opinion, a traditional way to disagree with a central government's actions. In continuing the fight throughout the spring and summer of 1979, the insurgents indicated that *now* they were fighting to overthrow the regime.

By late summer, early fall 1979, Afghan military units (all draftee) had deserted in large numbers. The war had ceased to be a winter interlude. The military dropped from about 105 000 in April 1978 to between 20–30 000.

As December 1979 unfolded, the Afghan insurgents were everywhere successful in the field. Survival endangered, the DRA leadership requested additional Soviet military advisers and more sophisticated equipment. The Soviets did not want to be accused of deserting a new 'socialist friend' in trouble from 'outside intervention', so most requests were granted. But, the DRA regime, as most observers agreed, could not survive without direct Soviet military intervention.

Some Western observers, more pessimistic, believed that the insurgents could not afford to spend another winter in the field, predicting they would not be able to resist coming to the plains as the snows arrived. But the central mountainous core of Afghanistan is honeycombed with caves, which Afghans use to shelter their livestock in winter. Many caves are named after the number of sheep and/or goats a cave will accommodate, *i.e.*, *Ghar-i-Hazar Gusfand* (Cave of a Thousand Sheep). The farmers and herdsmen involved in the fighting had made the caves comfortable (relatively speaking) for human habitation, and had stored foodstuffs and supplies for the coming winter.

PERIOD 1V (DECEMBER 1979 – PRESENT)

The Socialist interregnum ended with the Soviet invasion, which began on Christmas Eve 1979. By mid-December, the Soviets had two choices: to invade or not to invade. They chose to invade. Many (including me) did not believe they would take such a step, mainly because it would establish a potentially hazardous precedent and damage their image in the non-aligned world. It would be the first direct Soviet aggression since World War II on an independent, non-aligned country.[11]

Evidence indicates that the Soviets planned a Dominican Republic-type[12] operation, a quick slice to eliminate the government in power, replace it with a puppet, smash the resistance, and leave within 90 days, having effectively extended their zone of control to the borders of Pakistan.

When the Soviets invaded Afghanistan, they had either forgotten – or ignored – the historical and cultural patterns of Afghanistan. Twice in the 19th century Afghan tribes and ethnic groups had united to drive British armies from their regions.

Only a small percentage of the Afghan population was actively engaged in the fighting before the Soviet invasion. Why did the bulk of the population rise up against the Soviets and the DRA? And why had the countryside not fought against the reforms of President Daoud (1973–1978)? Both questions can be easily answered within Afghan cultural patterns.

The latter first: Daoud was a member of the royal family (brother-in-law and first cousin of the ex-king), and in the countryside Afghans called him Daoud 'Shah'. But Daoud was a Muslim and he had seized power 'legitimately'. Because in Islamic political theory, an individual rules by 'divine sanction', not 'divine right', as did European monarchs during their heyday. Divine sanction can be withdrawn anytime anyone can overthrow someone in power. Obviously, Allah has withdrawn the mantle from the loser, and given the mantle to the winner.

But, a ruler brought in on bayonets (as was Shah Shuja by the British in 1839) or tanks (as was Shah Shuja II, as Babrak Karmal is called by Afghans) does not have divine sanction and should be resisted.

In addition, the Muslim believes: better a bad king under Allah, than anarchy under the godless. So the Afghans reacted against the Soviets in the 1980s just as they reacted to the British in the 1880s.

Inter-group and extra-group feuds perform valuable positive functions in a number of modern preindustrial societies. Feuds during the off-agricultural, off-herding cycles help channel potential in-group fights over property rights and mate-preference into violence against neighboring groups; *i.e.*, they serve to externalize internal aggressions. The blood feud functions to perpetuate one's own group *not* to destroy other groups. Therefore, blood must be about equally spilled and properties (livestock and other movable objects) equally taken or destroyed. If one side gains materially at another's expense, the seasonal feud might extend into the farming and herding cycle, contrary to the interests of both sides.

If, however, a central government goes beyond the allowable bounds of political and cultural deviance (Period I), Afghan ethnic groups may unite locally to destroy local government offices and kill some bureaucrats (especially tax collectors) and police.

But if a foreign invader enters the equation, the Afghan reactions intensify. Afghan kin units (in all areas, but with varying levels of intensity) are based on vertical, segmentary structures (from nuclear family to extended family to lineage to subtribe to tribe), which are territorially neighbors to other units, with which the annual feud will usually be fought. However, when an outside horizontal force threatens the indigenous vertical structure, regional traditional enemies will unite, and if possible throw out the invaders.

The current situation most resembles the evolution of the Yugoslav partisan movement during World War II.[13] Initially, the seven major Yugoslav ethnolinguistic groups independently resisted the Italians and Germans. As the war prospered, larger units evolved around basic political ideologies: the royalists under Draža Mihajlović, and the leftists under Tito. Although the groups came together in politico-military units, they never lost their ethnolinguistic identities. Out of these patterns emerged Tito's Yugoslav Socialist Federal Republic, comprising seven socialist republics (Slovenia, Croatia, Bosnia and Hercegovina, Montenegro, Macedonia, and Serbia – which also includes two autonomous regions, Vojvodina and Kosovo).

Possibly, the present undivided Afghan resistance elements will ultimately evolve toward the Yugoslav example. Local units may combine into multiethnic regional units, then link up, at a final phase, into a national liberation movement. But this may take a decade or two.

Afghan history is replete with heroic acts by women,[14] and new heroines have arisen during the current war. One, Nahidah, a schoolgirl, was killed leading a demonstration against the regime during the compulsory celebrations for the second anniversary of the coup on 27 April 1980.

During the anti-government demonstrations, girls brought their headscarfs or veils and threw them to the Afghan soldiers blocking their paths. 'Here,' the girls called,' Wear these. Go! Shut yourselves up in your houses. We girls will defend the motherland.'[15]

In colonial situations, women have often used clothing as symbols of protest against the occupying imperialists. Therefore, the European imperialist period in Afro–Asia witnessed two sartorial patterns: the local men who became the bureaucrats, the 'bookkeepers of empire', wore European clothing as they aspired to be like the *sahibs*; their wives continued to wear their native dress, subtly striking back at the imperialist. In contrast, in nations never under the yoke of European imperialism (for long periods of time), the upper-class men and women often adapted European dress styles. Afghanistan is a classic example. Incidentally, Pakistan, in one of its many attempts to assert its identity, now requires all its government civil servants to wear 'national dress' in both official and unofficial capacities.

Islam plays an important role in all Afghan reactions, but it is Islam within an Afghan cultural context. Most Afghans agree that the concept of *shahid* (martyr) is an important feature in Iranian Shia Islam. Afghans will tell you that the concept is also important in their lives, but with a major difference. The Afghan is willing to make you a *shahid*. They prefer to live, and fight another day.

The major religico–political *mujahidin* (freedom fighters) parties with headquarters in Peshawar, Pakistan, are partly based on their own peculiar interpretations of Islam. But ethnic factors and the charisma of the various leaders are also important.

So, Islam is an umbrella under which all *mujahidin* can fight, and also a divisive element, as the antics of the Peshawar merry-go-round illustrate; *i.e.*, several parties unite for brief periods of time, then split up, and re-unite under different alignments.

Mujahidin leaders inside Afghanistan usually put it this way: 'We are all Muslims, and there is no need for us to advertise that fact. We are fighting a godless enemy and that must not be forgotten. At the same time, it is important to realize that we are trying to drive the enemy from our soil, so that we can be free'.

What the Afghans really want is the freedom to make their own decisions (regionally, and rightly or wrongly), with their own culturally-oriented concepts of *group decision-making*, and *not* within the concepts of the inalienable rights of the individual as emphasized in Western political systems.

Afghan cultural attitudes toward the individual play an important role in the current war. The ideal personality type for the Afghan male is the warrior-poet, a man who is brave in battle and can articulate well in the village or tribal council. Afghan history, folklore, folksongs, and literature (mainly poetry) are replete with the idealization of such attitudes. Seldom can a man achieve both statuses, but when he does, he becomes the hero of his age, the prime example being Khushal Khan Khattak (1613–1690 AD).[16]

The First Russo–Afghan War has given the men of Afghanistan a chance to live up to these ideals, and, on the whole, they welcome the opportunity, which partly accounts for the tenacity and longevity of the resistance. With minimal material support from the outside, the *mujahidin* have been fighting the Soviets for longer than the Soviets were in World War II which amounts to a total of four years three months: the Perfidious Polish Campaign (17 September 1939–ca. 1 January 1940): the Great Patriotic War (22 June 1941–7 May 1945); the Japanese Coda (9–21 August 1945). As of 26 December 1984, the Afghan War will have plodded on for five years.

In conclusion, it must be said that even Soviet specialists realize that Afghan cultural patterns are less than favorable for the creation of a modern socialist state. I quote a 'usually reliable source', a diplomat from a non-aligned country. Shortly after the 1978 coup, the diplomat spent an evening over vodka with a Soviet friend, who confided: 'If there is one country in the Third World that is not ready for "scientific socialism," it is Afghanistan.'

Also, much has been published in the Soviet and Western media about 'intervention' (*i.e.*, making weapons available to the *mujahidin*). No one denies that this occurs. But the thrust of this chapter indicates that outside intervention was *not* necessary to precipitate and perpetuate the Afghan reactions to events since April 1978. Afghan society, through its cultural patterns, has spoken loud and clear to the world's conscience. Even so-called objective scholars (and I personally doubt that such a creature exists) cannot deny that with or without 'intervention', the Afghan resistance patterns would have evolved as they have.

The patterns continue, but there is no light at the end of the tunnel, for any of the participants.

Notes

1. Numerous examples can be found in the translations in English language *Foreign Broadcast Information Service* (FBIS). Several English pamphlets also illustrate these themes: *The Truth About Afghanistan: Documents and Eye-witness Reports*, (Moscow: Novosti Press Agency Publishing House, 1980); *Afghanistan, The Target of Imperialism*, (Party Printing Press, (no place of publication is identified), n.d.); *Revolutionary Afghanistan Through Honest Eyes: A Collection of Views Expounded by Foreigners About Revolutionary Transformations in the Democratic Republic of Afghanistan*, Information and Publications Department, Ministry of Foreign Affairs, DRA (Kabul, n.d., ca. 1983).
2. Alvin Z. Rubinstein, *Soviet Policy Toward Turkey, Iran and Afghanistan*, (New York: Praeger, 1982); Henry S. Bradsher, *Afghanistan and the Soviet Union*, (Durham: Duke University Press, 1983); Thomas T. Hammond, *Red Flag Over Afghanistan* (Boulder: Westview Press, 1984).
3. Louis Dupree, 'Tainted news from Afghanistan', *New York Times*, editorial page, 22 June 1984.
4. Hammond op. cit., p. 9–18, refers to three other twentieth-century Soviet 'invasions' (1925, 1929, 1930), but the 1925, 1930 simple border squabbles cannot be compared in magnitude with the Christmas Eve 1979 invasion. And, the Soviet assistance given to Ghulam Nabi Charkhi in his fight against Habibullah II (1929) has been overly exaggerated. Also, the Tsarist period Panjdeh Incident (30 March 1885) could conceiveably be put in the same category as Hammond's mini-incidents. Louis Dupree, *Afghanistan* (Princeton University Press, 1980a), pp. 421–422, 424, 433–434).
5. Many personal communications, plus my own personal experiences while in prison in Kabul (November 1978).
6. Louis Dupree, 'Toward representative government in Afghanistan', Parts I and II, *American Universities Field Staff Reports, Asia*, Nos. 1, 14 (Hanover, NH, 1978).
7. Louis Dupree, 'Militant Islam and Traditional Warfare in Islamic South Asia', *American Universities Field Staff Reports, Asia*, No. 21 (Hanover, NH, 1980); Tribal Warfare in Afghanistan and Pakistan, chapter in *Islam in Tribal Societies*, A. Ahmed and D. Harts (eds) (London: Routledge and Kegan Paul, 1984) pp. 266–288; Afghan and British Military Tactics in the First Anglo-Afghan War (1838–1842), *The Army Quarterly and Defense Journal* 107 (2): 214–221, (Tavistock, Devon, 1977).
8. Personal communication from several independent sources.
9. Richard F. Strand, The Evolution of Anti-Communist Resistance in Eastern Nuristan, chapter in Nazeet Shahrani and Robert L. Canfield (eds), *Revolutions and Rebellions in Afghanistan: An Anthropological View* (Berkeley: University of California Press, 1984), pp. 76–93.
10. See note 7.
11. The Soviet contention that Hafizullah Amin, the less than pro-Soviet Khalqi prime minister, would invite his own executioners into his country strains credulity.

12. Abraham F. Lowenthal, *The Dominican Intervention* (Harvard U. Press,/1972).
13. Personal communications with specialista on Yugoslavia, but mainly with Dennison Rusinow.
14. Nancy Hatch Dupree, Revolutionary Rhetoric and Afghan Women, chapter in Shahrani and Canfield (1984), pp. 306–340.
15. *Ibid.*, p. 33.
16. Dupree, *op. cit.*, pp. 83–89.

18 The Demography of Afghan Refugees in Pakistan
Nancy Hatch Dupree*

No one knows how many Afghan refugees there are in Pakistan.

POPULATION SIZE: THE 'NUMBERS GAME'

Size of population is normally a key to any demographic discussion. Precise figures on the size of the Afghan Refugee population in Pakistan, however, are not available; estimated totals derived from a variety of systems are largely unreliable. Also, the few available 'mathematical observations and measurements' of vital statistics and related subjects may only be used as indicators of evolving physical, cultural and psychological patterns. In short, the statistics included in this discussion should be considered intelligent estimates, or, 'wild guesses based on inadequate data'.[1]

Various factors contribute to this mystery of the 'numbers game' so vigorously played by authorities involved with the care and maintenance of the Afghan Refugees in Pakistan. Some are cultural; some purely administrative. Some rise from pre-exodus traditions; some relate directly to the exigencies of exile.

One attitudinal aspect is of particular importance. Only rudimentary population data collection systems were ever operative in Afghanistan, particularly in the rural areas. None were institutionalized.[2] Nor had an appreciation of the efficacy of reporting deaths and births ever been inculcated successfully. Rather, the general feeling held that it was none of the central government's business who was born, or who died. Further, it was widely held that central

---

* The author wishes to express her gratitude to the Ford Foundation (Grant No. 835–0118), the Universities Field Staff International and the American Institute of Pakistan Studies for their support of the project which made this research possible.

governments sought demographic information for reasons entirely to their own benefit, either to impose local taxes, gain conscripts for the army, or enhance requests for international aid. Because of these attitudes, the bulk of the Afghan population were disdainful of interrogators and typically avoided volunteering information. When confronted, they either withheld or falsified responses so as to minimize expected bureaucratic extractions.

On the government's part, statistics were acknowledged to be a necessary tool for social and economic planning, but the data collection procedures generally did not lead to viable analyses. For instance, as far back as the 1960s a Soviet advisor, V. Chupir, a Russian manpower expert with the Ministry of Planning, was so pressed for a definitive population growth figure that he arbitrarily announced an annual rate of 2.5 per cent.[3] Subsequent governments, regardless of political hue, dutifully increased the Afghan population accordingly. Disregard for preciseness in establishing basic population data, therefore, affected the highest echelons of power, as well as the 90 per cent of the population who were non-literate and rural.

These attitudes seriously affected periodic attempts by pre-DRA (Democratic Republic of Afghanistan; established in April 1978) governments to conduct censuses and demographic surveys, many of which were lavishly funded by UN and inter-government aid.[4] The results were invariably questionable and judged to be of low reliability and validity.[5]

Finding it difficult to work effectively with unreliable figures, some development projects conducted their own sample, project-oriented studies.[6] In many cases these data were remarkably reliable, but their scope was limited.

These few comments serve to point out that there was no traditional respect for demographic accounting systems. Instead, all such efforts were generally perceived as serving vested interests to the detriment of the counted. A change of attitude has occurred among the Afghan Refugee population in Pakistan, however. The same fertile ingenuity once devoted to strategies avoiding enumeration, is now enthusiastically applied to ensuring acknowledgement. The incentive to stand up and be counted arises from the generous disbursements of everything from cash to shoes provided only to those persons listed on registration rolls. On the other hand, the prior reluctance to report deaths has been reinforced by the refugee experience: one less person on the rolls means less food for the family.

Table 18.1 Refugee influx: 1973–1983

After	Population totals
July 1973–April 1978 (following Mohammad Daoud's overthrow of the monarchy and the establishment of the Republic of Afghanistan)	Few hundred
April 1978–September 1979 (following Nur Mohammad Taraki's overthrow of the Republic of Afghanistan and the establishment of the Democratic Republic of Afghanistan)	109 000
September 1979–December 1979 (following Hafizullah Amin's overthrow of Nur Mohammad Taraki)	193 000
December 1979 (following Hafizullah Amin's overthrow by the Soviet army, installation of Babrak Karmal, and Soviet occupation of Afghanistan)	402 100
July 1980	over 1 million
May 1981	over 2 million
January 1982	over 2.5 million
December 1982	over 2.8 million
May 1983	over 2.8 million

Source: CCAR, Islamabad.

Before detailing a few examples of this newfound zest to be enumerated, it is well to consider the enormity of the problem. Official Government of Pakistan (GPO) figures issued by the Chief Commissioner for Afghan Refugees (CCAR) in August 1983[7] summarize refugee population growth (Table 18.1).

Since December 1982, the GOP has held to a consistently rising refugee population of over 2.8 million: claiming 2 846 748 on 30 June 1984. The GOP contends that this figure is inflated by no more than 10–15 per cent. Estimated average monthly arrivals of 2500 to 5000 during much of 1984 rose to 7000[8] in the fall in response to intensified Soviet offensives which began during the spring of 1984.[9] Widespread famine and starvation caused by these offensives it is predicted will force other areas to evacuate to Pakistan.[10] It is imperative, says the GOP, to plan assistance on the basis of the 10–15 per cent inflated figures so as to avoid shortfalls when the anticipated increases materialize.

Monitors of international assistance to the Afghan Refugees, dispute the GOP figures. There is no positive evidence to support the contention of some critics that the GOP profers high population figures in order to defray some of their expenses, but, as the official GOP refugee population figures rose over one million, approached and then passed, two million, evidence of gross malfeasance and overregistration also surfaced. Steps were taken to redress the more blatant malpractices, but the uncertainty of runaway figures made credible assessment of aid requirements next to impossible. It was feared that donor scepticism might possibly degenerate into disinterest and threaten the entire assistance program.

Base planning figures

To establish some measure of credibility, the World Food Programme (WFP) determined (1981) to maintain a mean of 1.7 million in planning food commodity supplies. This figure was arrived at by dividing the amount of wheat actually distributed, by the daily per capita wheat ration of 500 grams. From January 1982 this base figure was raised to 2.1 million, and again to 2.2 million from July 1982. WFP continues to assess needs by this figure as of August 1984. UNHCR (United Nations High Commissioner for Refugees), however, uses a population of 2.3 million to assess other relief needs.

International donors and administrative officials are confident that stocks based on the 2.2–2.3 million figures are very generous and more than adequate as a guarantee against shortfalls and sudden increases in population. Their inflation estimates vary between 25 per cent and 30 per cent.

The evolution of the refugee administration and infrastructure establishment illustrates the confusion which gives rise to these divergent estimates of population inflation. When, in 1979, it became obvious that the influx was growing alarmingly, there were not enough trained personnel in Pakistan to screen and register refugees adequately. Local district administrators did their best, but were soon swamped; recruitment procedures were not only slow, but qualified applicants for government jobs were rare. Abuses were all too soon evident.

Registration: the Malik system

At the same time, it was noted that large groups of Afghan Refugees were normally accompanied by traditional *maliks* (elders; community leaders). This cohesive leadership was immediately called upon by the beleaguered GOP, and gratefully pressed into service to assist in both registration and distribution of relief items.

Initially this system proved reasonably effective. There was a certain amount of altruism; the traditional leaders functioned efficiently and few incidences of gross malpractice surfaced. Unfortunately, those who seek personal gain by manipulating the misfortunes of others soon learn to flourish under emergency situations. Time saw the replacement of many traditional *maliks* by 'ration *maliks*' who, in collusion with some members of the newly established Pakistani refugee establishment perfected 'tricks and deals' encouraging favoritism, discrimination, and inflated population figures.

Examples are legion. Most involve power politics. The more followers a malik has, the more influence he wields, the more influence, the more flexibility he has to bilk the system. Cases are on record of maliks claiming rations for 2000, even 12 000, or 15 000 followers, when in reality there might be no more than a few hundred, or a thousand at the most. Brother maliks conspired to claim additional followers by registering the same names at one or more RTVs (Refugee Tented Village[11]) by using photostats of sanctioned registration lists. There was no way to determine whether the names were entirely fictitious, or double registered. Yet there was danger in cancelling numbers, even on known bogus lists, because legitimate registrants holding these numbers could be penalized unjustly.

Registration: heads-of-families system

As evidence of such innovative subterfuges mounted and became too obviously blatant, a new procedure was devised (1980) which forbade the issuance of rations to tribal heads or any such large groups. As a policy, rations now must be issued only to heads of families.

In order to tighten the rein on inflated registration and, not incidentally, guard against the infiltration of KHAD (the DRA's KGB-styled intelligence system) agents and informers into the legitimate refugee population, GOP policy also requires each head of family to obtain verification of legitimacy from one of the Afghan political parties in Pakistan, either in Peshawar (capital of the North-West Frontier Province [NWFP]) or Quetta (capital of Baluchistan Province). This led to more duplicity. Those wishing to remain independent of party politics will oftentimes seek verification from several parties. Nevertheless, it is on the basis of a party affidavit that the head-of-family obtains a coveted passbook which entitles him to a place on the registered rolls for relief aid.

The family distribution system has corrected many of the more obvious malpractices, but it too is fraught with loop-holes and has not resulted in reliable population figures. Besides, only about 40 per cent of the distribution has yet to be affected by the new system and unscrupulous maliks still manage to intimidate heads of families, demanding they inflate the size of their families in order to provide the maliks with a percentage of all receipts for services rendered or anticipated.

Re-enumeration

A vigorous house by house, tent by tent, re-enumeration was instituted in 1981 (Baluchistan) and early 1982 (NWFP) in an attempt to obtain more reliable population figures. Several factors hinder this process, among which the extraordinary mobility permitted the refugees by the GOP is of particular significance. No barbed wire encloses any of the refugee settlements. No restrictions prevent individuals from moving singly or in family groups anywhere inside Pakistan. The frequent movement of tents naturally creates chaos in the counting system.

In addition, more and more families are returning for short periods to home bases in Afghanistan to attempt some farming to provide food for the *mujahideen* (freedom fighters). Almost all adult males take periodic turns crossing the border to fight in the *jihad* (holy war; resistance) for a month or so, a fact which cannot be admitted because *mujahideen* are expressly forbidden to receive any types of humanitarian aid. Yet in this situation it is impossible to separate a man's role: he is both *muhajar* (refugee) and *mujahid* depending on whether he is in Pakistan taking care of his family, or across the border in Afghanistan fighting for the honor of his country. There are few 'full time' *mujahideen*. So, for these and similar reasons an individual may not be physically present at the time of re-enumeration (to strike such persons off the registration lists would, in my opinion, be unjust).

Multiple-registration ploys

Nevertheless, enumerating a mobile population which disappears and reappears is fraught with many frustrations. Refugees take advantage of their freedom and attempt to register at several sites along their routes of travel. Others have been known to claim newcomer status at the border transit/recording camps every time they return from short sojourns inside Afghanistan.

Other serious obstacles stem from the near impossibility of verifying the number of individuals claimed by family heads. Estimates vary from averages of 6–9 members per family, which tallies with the pre-DRA average household size of 6.2 persons. Each passbook lists the individuals in the family by name, but many listings go far beyond the average and the 'immediate family'. In this the refugees are not without guile, and their imaginative schemes are without bounds. Take, for an example, the experience of one administrator faced with a newly born child who was being passed from family to family for registration. 'All new babies look alike' he moaned.

According to another favorite gambit, a father registers with his women and children, including adult sons with their women and children. Later, each adult son will register as a head of family, and again claims as dependents their immediate women and children and also their father and mother. In this way a single individual may be registered five or six times.

Most importantly, accurate re-enumeration is hindered by the fact that female members may not be paraded before male personnel. At times the number of women per household burgeon beyond belief. Yet the tragedy of the war in Afghanistan has created many widows and custom dictates that they be given haven by male relatives. Without an actual head count, who is to dispute a man's reputed benevolence? Very few female personnel have been employed by the re-enumeration and monitoring authorities, although this problem has been acknowledged since the inception of the assistance program in 1979.

If successful, all these multiple-registration schemes can produce great benefits because disbursements are linked directly to family size. The temptation to engage in these practices, therefore, is often irresistible. Furthermore, some of these ploys appear to be thoroughly justifiable in the minds of those who practice them. Commodities obtained through multiple-registration help sustain the *jihad*, a cause worthy of any finagling. Only through inflating family size is it possible to 'beat the system' beset with overly-long registration procedures. At the very best, it can take 2–3 months before a family qualifies, even though it is the first few months when newcomers are most in need of aid. Some families have been unregistered for over three years. They do not appear in the population count, receive no rations, and must depend on kin for food. In these cases, since the rations are being consumed by legitimate refugees, the logic of complaints and penalties over double registration escapes most of the accused.

Other sizeable (variously estimated from 130 000–150 000) unregistered groups live in urban areas and unauthorized settlements. GOP policy assumes that those who elect not to live in authorized RTVs do so because they have alternate means of livelihood. The regulations specifically state that only those registered in RTVs are eligible for relief assistance. Many of these unregistered refugees, however, are intellectuals and urban entrepreneurs who are unable to adjust to the essentially rural lifestyle provided by the RTVs, even though they find few rewarding opportunities for remunerative employment.

When survival becomes acute, these urban refugees sometimes persuade distant kin or fellow tribesmen living in the RTVs to add their names to passbooks. In addition, some urban refugees are harassed by Pakistani landlords demanding inclusion on refugee rosters in lieu of rent increases. Other Pakistanis are voluntarily added to family lists in order to enhance the local interests and economic advantages of registered refugees.

Improprieties abound. Nevertheless, it is a sad but demonstrable fact that many of the refugees who suffer most are the poor who are unable to manipulate the system. They do not know how to connive, and cannot compete with the crafty who would use them. The more affluent astute, on the other hand, adjust with minor inconvenience, considerable profit, and perverse delight in devising new accommodations to exploit every innovation designed to thwart their devious machinations. When those who succeed flaunt it, eye brows are rightfully raised. Afghans driving new Toyotas stoke local resentment and add credence to the accusation that all Afghan Refugees are capitalists fleeing with their ill-gotten gains, not from fear of political persecution. The legitimate majority are thus unjustly tarred with the brush of opportunism.

Despite all these difficulties, re-enumeration continues and every month the authorities announce that thousands have been 'de-listed'.

Claims of reductions of as much as half a million have been made. There is much see-sawing in this numbers game, however. Reduced totals often rise slowly, sometimes not so slowly, to former levels without visible evidence of comparable arrivals. On the other hand, too much zealous pruning can lead to injustices. In any event, because the unregistered most often take the place of the de-listed, the total registered population has remained fairly stable over the past year or so.

Refugee well-being and program credibility

The monitoring authorities admit to the impossibility of supervising every individual's registration, acknowledge that the unregistered cannot be left to starve, and allow that inflation is in large part balanced by the unregistered. They will even turn a blind eye to stocks crossing into Afghanistan to help avert impending famine and feed the *mujahideen*. Stockpiles must be maintained to meet possible emergencies, and guarantees must be secured to make certain not a single individual dies from starvation.

Multiple-registration and allowable degrees of inflation are tolerated for these reasons. But when bureaucratic duplicity, disingenuous maliks and gross misappropriations create 'phantom' RTVs and stockpiling generates immense individual profits, credibility is severely damaged. Such coupling of maladministration with opportunistic practices produces a quagmire of corruption. Constant efforts to weed out offenders and rectify abuses are made. By November 1984, 17 000 cases had been initiated against employees of CAR/NWFP (Commissioner Afghan Refugees/NWFP) for various charges, including 'inefficiency, indolence, negligence, and gross corruption'.[12]

In Baluchistan, a high official in charge of transport of refugee goods was court-martialed. Others at the highest level of responsibility have resigned rather than be brought up on charges. Despite the fact that these efforts have been widely publicized, outsiders persist in referring to the provincial refugee administrative complexes as 'houses of thieves'.

So, the 'numbers game' must be played on until the day the refugees go home. It is not an esoteric exercise. The numbers cannot be divorced from ration distribution which is the key to refugee survival. While attempting to foil large-scale diversions by unscrupulous refugees and those who are not refugees, the authorities are at the same time determined to allocate sufficient supplies so no vulnerable groups are deprived of their entitlements. It is a matter of considerable satisfaction to all involved that no single individual has died of starvation and that primary malnutrition has never been a major problem. Nevertheless, a fine line divides allocation and disbursements.

For example, if commodities are allocated to the provinces according to the lower base planning figures and then distributed according to inflated figures, individual refugees receive proportionately less. Those who are double-registered make up for the cuts and manage; the honest with no cushion against such manipulations once again suffer. Further, if food cuts based on suspected bogus registration occur, some predict that many refugees will leave established RTVs, and move to swell urban centers and exacerbate the potential for turmoil. It is difficult enough as it is for the refugees to cope since the distribution of commodities such as milk and oil are consistently in arrears. If wheat rations, the diet staple, are cut, it would be impossible for many refugees to survive.

More disturbingly, profiteering from stockpiling made possible by discrepancies between allocations and disbursements, bogus registrations, and overly-inflated population figures is totally unacceptable to the international donor community. To assure strong international support, the 'numbers game' must continue to project program credibility so as to guarantee refugee well-being.

The static base planning population figure has accomplished this. Even though newcomers continue to arrive, there is no evidence of any shortage in wheat disbursements and the inflation cushion functions effectively as a guarantee against starvation.

The exact figure is perhaps not important. What is important is that too many have been forced to leave their homes, and if all the displaced, the registered, the unregistered, urban and rural, and new arrivals are counted, the figure of 'about three million' may not be overly exaggerated. This represents the largest concentration of refugees in a single country anywhere in the world. It is one-third the world's total of over ten million refugees. It also represents one-fifth of Afghanistan's pre-DRA population of about 15 million.[13] And, together with another 1.5 million Afghans living in Iran, plus uncounted hundreds of thousands scattered around the world, about one-third of the Afghan nation waits in exile.

POPULATION DISTRIBUTION: AREA, DENSITY, AGE AND SEX

Area

Refugees arriving during the early part of the exodus, in 1978 and 1979, settled near the Afghan border, in Baluchistan and the NWFP. The disputed Durand Line which separates these Pakistani provinces and Afghanistan divides ethnolinguistically related Pushtun and Baluch tribal groups who account for the majority of the refugees. According to both Islamic injunction and the Pushtun Code of Honor (*Pushtunwali*) it was incumbent on Pakistani tribal leaders to provide succor for their distressed cultural kinsmen. Many instances of spontaneous generosity and genuine gestures of welcome are recorded. These continue.[14] The Government of Pakistan (GOP) also offered lodging in a variety of buildings, including rest houses, schools, hospitals and storage facilities, in addition to some food (wheat, sugar, tea), tents, clothing, bedding and a monthly per capita cash subsistence allowance.

As the flow accelerated, the burden weighed too heavily on both the tribesmen and the GOP. Pakistan appealed to the UNHCR[15] for assistance in April 1979. The refugee population then numbered 85 000. Within the next five months, from May to September, the population rose by 100 000, reflecting an average increase of more than 1000 refugees a day. By September 1979 there were 45 000 (24 per cent) in Baluchistan, 140 000 (76 per cent) in the NWFP, with heavy concentrations in the federally administered tribal agencies (FATAs[16]). Kurram and North Waziristan agencies alone hosted 61 per cent of the refugees in the NWFP (46 per cent of the total refugee population in Pakistan) in September 1979.

From the outset, UNHCR urged the GOP to remove refugee concentrations away from border areas and establish organized settlements so as to discourage DRA incursions and bombings of Pakistan territory,[17] and facilitate orderly aid disbursements. Many large groups had settled as close as 2–4 miles to the border; even closer in the case of some in Kurram and North Waziristan. UNHCR's efforts in this respect were impeded, however, by both the refugees and the GOP.

The refugees were reluctant to move away from tribal affiliates who had been so supportive. To move from the borders was tantamount to admitting that a quick return to Afghanistan was not possible. The GOP cited problems of poorly developed physical and administrative infrastructures, unavailability of government lands, particularly in the NWFP, and scarcity of water and other basic amenities, including grazing areas. By September 1979 there were only 39 organized Refugee Tent Villages (RTVs): 34 in Baluchistan, where more public lands were available, and 5 in the NWFP.[18]

Gradually, however, refugee groups began to move into the interior on their own, making their own arrangements with landlords, or simply setting up encampments near water sources or work opportunities. Fertile Peshawar District (NWFP) became such a magnet that registration was suspended during 1980 in order to encourage refugees to seek accommodation in other districts and agencies.

The situation was chaotic and UNHCR persisted in its efforts to regularize settlement. It was hoped, for instance, that reliable potable water schemes established with the assistance of UNICEF (United Nation's Children's Fund) would lure refugees to RTVs. In addition, an improved administrative infrastructure gradually evolved.

As a result, registration and aid disbursements were limited to a steadily growing number of officially-designated RTVs. By mid–1984 these totalled 349 RTVs in three provinces (Table 18.2); 279 RTVs (with 4 new areas under preparation) in 17 districts/agencies of the NWFP, with 72 per cent of the refugee population (64 per cent in the Settled Districts; 36 per cent in the FATAs); 60 RTVs in the 6 districts of Baluchistan, with 25 per cent of the refugee population; 10 RTVs (10 others under preparation) in Isa Khel sub-district of Mianwali District, Punjab Province, with 3 per cent of the population.

The Punjab Province was requested to accommodate long-term unregistered refugees after registration in the NWFP was officially closed early in 1982 because saturation endangered the total social and economic fabric of that province. The Punjab Government chose a site in Mianwali District not too far from the border with the NWFP, just outside the small town of Kot Chandana on the west bank of the Indus River. For the first time, a permanent water system and other administrative amenities were provided prior to the arrival of the first occupants. This settlement extends for five miles and differs from other RTVs in that the 10 commodity distribution centers, each designated as an RTV with its own Village Administrator catering to about 10 000 persons, cluster around the administrative buildings, instead of being located in separate areas

Table 18.2 Area distribution of Afghan refugees: June 1984

	RTVs	Population
NORTH-WEST FRONTIER PROVINCE		
Settled Districts	*RTVs*	*Population*
Abbottabad	20	135 766
Bannu	7	48 901
Chitral	6	25 448
Dir	14	81 756
D. I. Khan	12	109 215
Kohat	20	221 952
Malakand Agency	3	34 808
Mansehra	9	89 915
Mardan	23	222 009
Peshawar	60	325 501
Swat	3	11 424
	177	1 306 695
FATAs		
Bajaur	30	210 560
Kurram	32	274 802
North Waziristan	31	187 599
Mohmand	1	15 208
Orakzai	2	13 823
South Waziristan	6	38 394
	102	740 386
NWFP TOTAL:	279[1]	2 047 081[2]
BALUCHISTAN		
Districts		
Quetta	4	86 458
Chaman sub-district	5	44 982
Pishin	13	153 664
Gulistan	12	171 142
Zhob	4	35 090
Loralai	7	73 093
Chagai	15	161 744
BALUCHISTAN TOTAL:	60[3]	727 173[4]
PUNJAB		
Mianwali District	10	91 552
PAKISTAN TOTAL:	349	2 864 806

Notes

1. On 25 November 1984 CAR/NWFP announced that the number of RTVs had been reduced to 235 by merging some smaller settlements (The *Muslim*, 25 November 1984, p. 1).

2. Re-enumeration since March 1984 reduced this total to 1 876 000 as of 25 November 1984. Unregistered Afghan refugees in the NWFP numbered 200 000 (*ibid*).
3. In December 1984 the total number of RTVs in Baluchistan was announced to be 61 (personal communication).
4. Officially reduced to 507 000 in November 1984 (personal communication).

Sources: CAR/NWFP fortnightly statement ending 15 June 1984; CAR/Baluchistan fortnightly statement ending 31 May 1984; CCAR/Islamabad 30 June 1984 total was 2 846 748 (Baluchistan 711 367; NWFP 2 043 229).

throughout the settlement. Each family is assigned to one of these distribution points where disbursements are collected, but the family head may construct a dwelling wherever he chooses, usually as close as possible to next of kin who had arrived earlier. A new site at Dara Tang, on the Punjab border 80 km. west of Kot Chandana, is being prepared for future arrivals.

Some unregistered families had been living around the fringes of RTVs in the NWFP without drawing rations for as long as 2–3 years. Still, the move to the Punjab, which began on 15 December 1982[19], was extremely unpopular with the refugees because of ethnolinguistic differences with the Punjabi population, and because the area is renowned primarily for its extreme heat.

Many refugees, therefore, opted to forgo the opportunity to receive rations rather than comply with orders to move. Others registered only to move back to their original sites near kin or established work opportunities, returning periodically to receive rations. As early as January 1983, some administrators estimated that 25–30 per cent of the Punjab registrants would ultimately leave by the back door, and even casual observers have noted that during the summer months the Punjab RTVs are depleted. Even families with established residences typically move to the hills or return to Afghanistan to farm during the summer.

Taking note of the extreme dissatisfaction with the Punjab RTVs, CAR/NWFP has relaxed their rigid requirement that all unregistered groups relocate to the Punjab. Instead, they keep the NWFP population static by alloting de-listed numbers to the nearly 300 000 (1984 estimate) unregistered refugees in their province. Four new RTVs (Nowshera, Akora Khattak, and two near Shabkadar – all in exceptionally lush agricultural areas of Peshawar District) were established in 1984 for this purpose. This is not a new phenomenon. In the spring

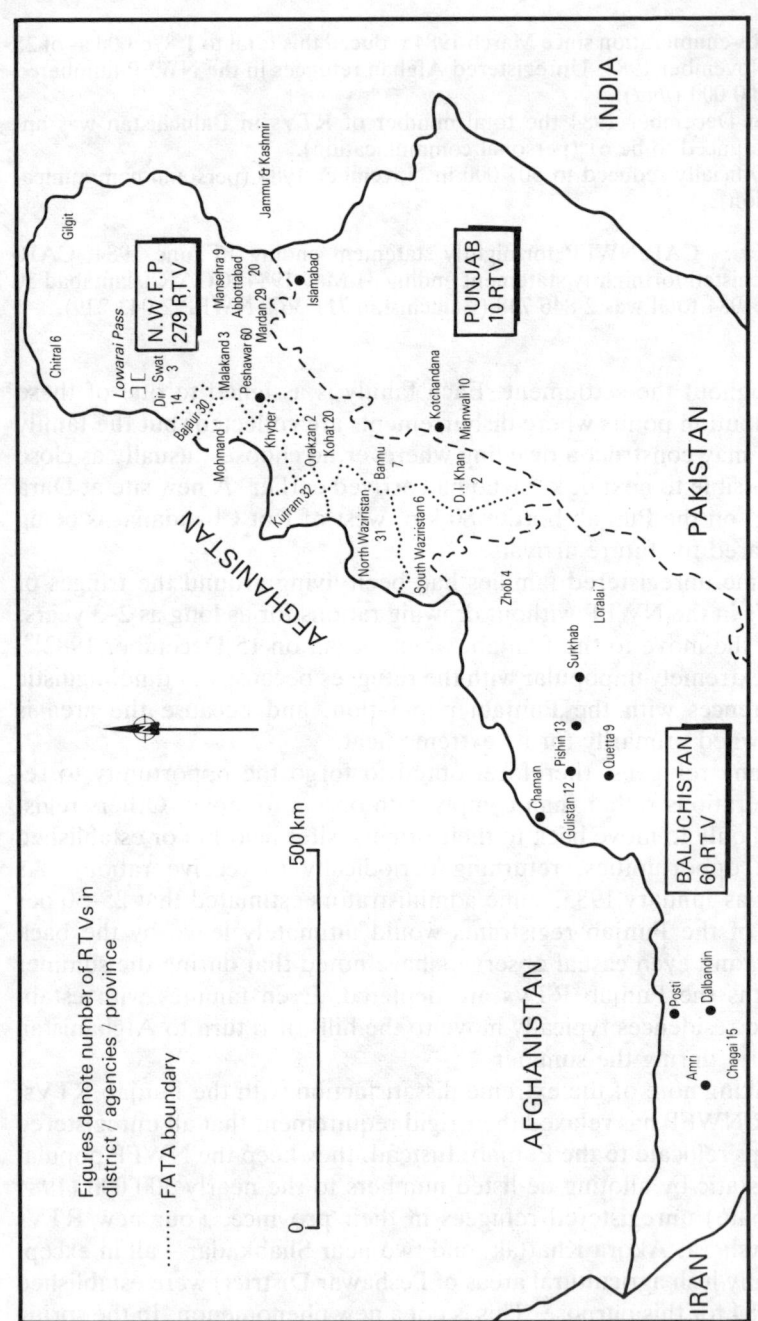

Map 18.2 Afghan refugees in Pakistan, June 1984

of 1982 new RTVs were established in Swat (3) and Malakand Agency (3) to accommodate the unregistered, mainly from Hazara, Mardan, and Peshawar Districts.

All new arrivals, however, will now be directed from border transit camps to the Punjab. Despite the pressures, the concept of *refouler* or rejection of those seeking asylum, is abhorrent to the GOP and most Pakistanis, who will continue to extend a welcome to the Afghans in the traditional manner.

Settlement Patterns
The GOP organization table states that basic RTV units may not exceed a population of 5000 or approximately 1000 families. In reality, most exceed the limit. Single unit populations above 20 000 are recorded in Baluchistan at such sites as Mohammad Khel III (Quetta District) with over 24 000 (total for Mohammad Khel I-IV is 86 458). In addition, contiguous RTVs which began as separate, small encampments of kin-related families have grown and melded to form solid settlements covering vast areas.

Surkhab RTV (Pishin District, Baluchistan), for example, is listed with three units of 9.5, 8.9, and 15.4 thousand individuals respectively. Since there are no visible divisions between these units bordering both sides of a virtually dry river bed for twenty miles, Surkhab RTV give the impression of being one extensive settlement with 4962 households (33 909 total population), complete with neighborhood bazaars. Thus, Surkhab RTV resembles any number of large villages and small towns in rural Afghanistan.

Also, as in Afghanistan, there are many variations in settlement patterns. Some RTVs crowd 15 000 households into a 5-square-mile area (Mardan, NWFP) while others provide 2000 families with spacious homestead-style accommodation over a 25-square-mile area (Kohat, NWFP).

Among the remotest RTVs in Pakistan are those located in Chagai District (Baluchistan) some 220 miles southwest of Quetta, midway between this capital city and the Iranian border.[20] There are 15 RTVs in this bleak area dominated by pebbly deserts and mobile-sand-dunes. One, Posti, is in reality a series of small hamlets, each with only 3–10 close-kin-related households, strung along the length of a narrow 15-mile-long valley hedged in by barren, rocky mountain slopes leading into Afghanistan's Hilmand Valley.

Chitral is another remote area. This northernmost NWFP district sits at the northern end of the 2400 km; 1500 mile arc along which the

RTVs are scattered. Snow blocks the Lowari Pass through which relief supplies from Peshawar must travel, isolating Chitral for as many as five and six months at a time. Rations must be stockpiled well in advance. This creates many logistic and distributional problems.

Elsewhere in the NWFP settlements are equally varied, although there is a higher proportion of smaller concentrations closer to the prescribed 50 000 population maximum. Nevertheless, Pakistan's largest RTV, Barakai (Mardan District), located in the heart of the NWFP, peaked with a registered population of well over 130 000; uncounted unregistered families settled on its outskirts. The social and economic pressure these masses placed on the local population, particularly on the district capital city 35 km. to the east, became so intolerable that a new RTV was established at Haripur (Hazara District) with only the unregistered from Baraki. The Haripur RTVs now threaten to outnumber the parent RTV. In spite of such overcrowding, no major outbreaks of violence with the local population have occurred.

Concentrations of unregistered Afghan Refugees are found in large urban areas such as Peshawar, Karachi and Islamabad. These can be immense. One section of Peshawar, just beside the affluent Cantonment, for instance, is now almost exclusively Afghan and referred to as 'The Afghan Colony'. In Karachi, Afghans rent apartments. Because rents are extremely high, extended families normally crowd into single-family units. Once a family is ensconced, it is not unusual for other kin-related families to rent apartments above and below them, forming what are in effect high-rise RTVs. So many Afghans have gathered to live in Islamabad's G–9/4 sector, that it is now known as the 'little Kabul' of Islamabad. Pakistani's claim Afghans account for 30 per cent of the occupancy of G–9/4.

During the latter part of 1984, concerted efforts were made to force some of these groups to move to RTVs, particularly in Sind, Peshawar and Quetta. Strong emphasis was placed on expunging cities of 'bachelors', who were rounded up from hotels, apartments and private houses and bused to nearby RTVs. Hotels in Peshawar are now forbidden to rent rooms to single Afghan males.[21]

Much of this had to do with a series of bomb blasts[22] set off in Peshawar which were thought to have been the work of KHAD agents and assassination squads sent down by the DRA. In fact, evidence accumulated over a year or more indicates that these agents do rent whole floors in hotels as bases for their nefarious activities.

CAR/Baluchistan began shifting families out of Quetta in October 1984, when about 800 families were moved to Shirin Ab RTV, Chagai District, in the vicinity of Girdi Jangal RTV. It is proposed to move other groups (such as some Ghilzai to Loralai and Muslimbagh RTV and Durrani to Latifabad), but this may take some time as water supplies have not been adequately organized.[23]

Population density ratios

Density ratios vary according to these diverse settlement patterns. In most of the NWFP where the local population density is 164 per square kilometer, the ratio between the local population and the refugees is generally estimated at 6 to 1, but in the FATAs, with a local population density of 77, the ratio rises, occasionally even 1 to 2. Baluchistan's population density is limited to 15 persons per square kilometer because of vast tracks of underdeveloped wasteland. Only 5 million acres out of 50 million arable acres are being farmed because of the absence of adequate irrigation systems.[24] In many areas, therefore, the refugees far exceed the local populations. An extreme example is the town of Chagai with a local population of 3000 surrounded by 18 000 refugees.

Population age and sex distribution

Officially, the age distribution is given as 48 per cent children under 15; 28 per cent adult females and 24 per cent adult males. However, one of several recent surveys found that 57 per cent of the refugee population were children under 15: 22.5 per cent 0–5 years with 98 males to 100 females; 34.5 5–15 years with a male:female ratio of 82:100. Of the adults, 36 per cent of the population was 15–45 years with 88 males:100 females. In the 7 per cent group over 45 years of age, there were 260 males:100 females.

These findings were questioned by some who feared the 260:100 male to female ratio indicated a much greater maternal mortality rate than was suspected. In April 1984, the Centers for Disease Control (Atlanta, Georgia) was contracted by the UNHCR to determine infant and maternal mortality rates. Their findings estimated infant mortality at 156 per 1000 live births. The maternal mortality rate was 1176 per 100 000, which is high but comparable to the Pakistani population.

By comparison, the pre-DRA infant mortality rate was estimated between 182 and 210 per 1000 live births, the highest infant mortality rate in Asia.[25] Also, a 1971 survey[26] found that there was an excess of males over females in all age groups, except from 1–4. The overall sex ratio was 116 males:100 females, but rose as high as 222:100 in the age group 75–79. GOP pronouncements continually stress that the adult male refugee population is primarily 'old men'.

As mentioned above, the reliability of such statistics is questionable, but since it would appear that about 75 per cent of the refugee population is composed of two vulnerable groups, women and children, much attention is now being paid to strengthen programs for them. Health assistance, which has always been of major concern, has effectively staved off major epidemics. Some say it has been overly generous. These critics lament the fact that indiscriminate pill-pushing is creating a deplorable dependency on medical drugs. A number of the voluntary agencies (VOLAGs) are, therefore, focusing on preventive health services, primary health education and maternal-child health (MCH) programs. Training of *dais* (midwives) and lady health visitors (LHV) from the refugee community is also being slowly introduced and expanded.

The birth rate in the RTVs appears to be very high because both men and women express an intense psychological need to replace those who fall on the battlefield. Although acute malnutrition due to insufficient food has never been a problem among the Afghan Refugees in Pakistan, secondary malnutrition noted among children under 5, and pregnant or lactating women is normally due to insufficient intake, traditional weaning habits and eating preferences, or diarrhoea-related illness caused by contaminated food and water, and poor personal hygiene. The health education programs among Afghan women at the MCH are, therefore, of immense importance, particularly in reducing the relatively few cases of severe marasmus noted among infants under one year.

Education has also been receiving intense emphasis recently, particularly among girls and young women. This represents a most encouraging development. In the early days of the exodus even the mere mention of education for girls was anathema and those who advocated it were branded as 'traitors' and 'communists'. These passionate negative attitudes have cooled, but the number of girls attending schools in the RTVs is still minuscule and puberty still signals the end of schooling for most of the students.[27]

The future of teenage girls and young women living with unregistered Afghan refugee families in the urban areas is cruelly bleak. In pre-coup Afghanistan they had taken an education for granted and looked forward to a wide variety of career opportunities. These young women now face the ire of ultra-conservative religious vigilantes who seek to curtail the activities of women outside the home. As a result, urban girls brought up to believe it was their *duty* to contribute to society find that they are now not only denied the facilities to complete their educations, but they are also deprived of opportunities to participate in any activities outside the home. In addition, because of the precarious financial straits in which most of these families find themselves, the urban refugees are hesitant to enter into marriage contracts. Girls of marriageable age are, therefore, often doubly penalized. Most potential female contributors to Afghanistan's future sit at home; an urgent challenge for assistance planners.

Two remarkable institutions seek to ameliorate this situation: the Nazaneen Primary School for Girls assisted by Inter-Aid, a Pakistani-based VOLAG, and, the Nahid Shahid Girls School (8 grades), also assisted by Inter-Aid through the Union of Mujahid Doctors, an Afghan organization. Other VOLAGs, such as the International Rescue Committee (IRC) are currently investigating the feasibility of expanding education programs for boys and girls, men and women. In addition, the UNHCR offers scholarships for men and women to continue college educations, particularly in the fields of medicine, education and engineering.

ETHNIC COMPOSITION AND DISTRIBUTION

Each major component of Afghanistan's kaleidoscope of ethnic groups[28] is represented in the refugee population. They come from every Afghan province. The Pushtun lead with 94 per cent, found in every RTV and representing rural, urban and nomadic backgrounds. Pushtun also dominate urban concentrations.

Semi-nomadic Pushtun groups make up about 29 per cent of the refugee population and are concentrated primarily in NWFP districts such as D I Khan, Kohat and Mansehra, with growing numbers in the Punjab where they occupy the eastern fringe of the settlement at Kot Chandana.

A good number follow patterns established in Afghanistan.[29] They live in houses or canvas tents provided them by the refugee establishment in the RTVs during the winter. In the summer they migrate with their flocks to grazing areas in the hills where they live in their typical black goat-hair tents. The introduction of almost 3 million head of livestock into these mostly barren areas has created a severe strain on an already fragile ecology, necessitating some restrictions by the authorities on the movement of nomadic refugees. Nevertheless, travelling on Pakistan's main highway between Peshawar and Rawalpindi, the famed Grand Trunk Road of Moghul days, is reminiscent of travelling in similar areas of Badakhshan during peak migration periods.

The DRA has always maintained that there are no real refugees in Pakistan and that most of the Afghans outside their borders are nomads who have traditionally crossed back and forth across this border for generations. A recent broadcast in Pashto over Radio Afghanistan accused Pakistan, again, of deceiving world public opinion on 'the question of so-called Afghan refugees, who are fugitives and nomads that Pakistan prevents from returning home by force in order to obtain aid from the western countries'.[30]

The Hazara, from the central mountainous plateaus of the Hazarajat, are found mainly in the city of Quetta (with small pockets in Peshawar) where they are assisted by Pakistani Hazara whose forebears came to Baluchistan as refugees during the reign of Amir Abdur Rahman (1880–1901).[31] They have created a hillside suburban development in Quetta which almost replicates their settlements in Kabul at Deh Mazang and Koh-i-Asmai behind Kabul University.

Almost all Afghan Baluch, primarily from the Hilmand Valley, have settled among their ethnolinquistic cousins in Baluchistan, particularly in Amri and Posti RTVs (Chagai District). These are isolated settlements, far away (104 and 40 miles; $5\frac{1}{2}$ and 2 hours respectively) from the small district town of Dalbandin, 220 miles; 7 hours southwest of Quetta. The Baluch Sardars maintain strong, centralized control.

The Nuristanis were the first major ethnic group to openly revolt in October 1978,[32] and the first rural refugees to settle in Pakistan. Most Nuristanis live in small family groups scattered throughout the many high valleys of Chitral, far away from administrative centers. Others have settled close to the castles of Chitral's former ruling families. Larger RTVs with access to roads and towns exist in Chitral, inhabited by a few Pushtun from the Ningrahar/Laghman, Nijrao/Tago areas as well as Tajik from Parwan, the Panjsher Valley and vicinity of Kabul. Most Tajik, an estimated 3 per cent of the refugee population, are concentrated, however, in Bajaur Tribal Agency.

The Turkoman and Uzbak generally form distinct enclaves with their own bazaars in the larger RTVs in the NWFP. However, the progress of the resistance inside Afghanistan and the 1983–84 Soviet blockage of key passes out of northern Afghanistan has forced refugees from the northern areas into all sectors of Pakistan. A large group of Turkoman in Saranan RTV (Gulistan District, Baluchistan) were unable to use the direct route from Kunduz to the NWFP, for instance. They journeyed the length of Afghanistan, via Bamiyan and the Hazarajat, and crossed over at Chaman (Baluchistan), where they were assigned to Saranan RTV by officials at the border transit camp. Other Uzbak and Turkoman from Aqcha and its environs had lived for twenty years or more among the Pushtun in the Hilmand Valley. They have settled among their Pushtun compatriots in Girdi Jangal RTV (Chagai District, Baluchistan). Still others were relocated in 1982 from Peshawar District to Kot Chandana RTV (Mianwali District, Punjab), where they have established a distinct colony at the western edge of the settlement.

There is another Uzbak colony from the Baghlan area of Afghanistan living among a majority Pushtun population inhabiting an unauthorized settlement in Karachi (Sind Province), at Surkhab Kot which has an interesting history. An Afghan Pushtun family in the business of exporting Afghanistan's famed dried fruits and nuts had developed a long-standing, closely-knit network of connections with the Pakistani business community, and prospered. When a large group of their fellow tribesmen came as refugees to Peshawar and found registration closed, they headed south to claim aid from their affluent cousins. Land was purchased, mosques and schools built, a clinic established, and, most importantly, an imposing *hujra* (guesthouse where leaders entertain, officiate and counsel their constituency) opened. Surkhab Kot thrives in direct defiance of GOP regulations which prohibit refugee settlement outside the designated three provinces of Baluchistan, NWFP and Punjab.

Uzbak who had lived as *hamsaya* (clients) of these Pushtun at Surkhab Kot also migrated south on finding no help forthcoming in Peshawar. Surkhab Kot, continues to grow as refugees attracted by optimum work opportunities at the port and industrial parks of Karachi arrive. The population in 1983 was estimated at 9000. Those newcomers without former ties to the original benefactors, however, are charged a tax for the privilege of residing in Surkhab Kot.

The Kirghiz, another Turkic-speaking people, came down from the high Pamir mountains into Gilgit (Northern Areas) in August 1978. Coming from high-altitude encampments at 12 and 15 000 feet, the

Kirghiz fell victim to newly encountered low-altitude diseases such as malaria, hepatitis and intestinal disorders. Religious conservatism imposed strict seclusion of the Kirghiz women who were used to working freely with their menfolk. Responding to their plight, the Turkish Government offered to resettle the Kirghiz; other Turkic-speaking Afghan Refugees were also given the option of resettlement in Turkey. A 13-flight airlift in August 1982 carried about 4.5 thousand Turkic-speaking Afghan Refugees to Turkey where they are generously accommodated.[33]

OCCUPATIONAL DIVERSITY

About the only restraint the GOP places on the Afghan refugees is to prohibit them from doing what most of them do best – farm. Some do, but only on small plots of government-owned land. The Posti RTV inhabitants have acquired an admirable reputation for their ability to farm vegetables in a relentlessly hostile environment where no one before them had envisaged the feasibility of habitation, much less cultivation.[34] They have accomplished this by applying water-management and engineering techniques perfected over the centuries in Afghanistan. Other groups living in the desert beyond Girdi Jangal RTV (Baluchistan) have performed an equally miraculous agricultural feat. Finding the local melons vastly inferior to the justly famous Afghan melon, they commissioned *mujahideen* to bring back melon seeds from Afghanistan. Crossing these with the hardy, but tasteless, desert melons, they have produced a sensational gastronomical delight. In addition, the ILO (United Nations International Labour Organization) has launched a vegetable seed distribution project so that RTV families may augment the ration diet.

Most Afghans, however, have had to restructure, probably only temporarily, a basic factor in their value system. To till the land and be self-reliant in providing well-being for a family is a matter of pride; a symbol of identity, self-respect, and status to most Afghans. Pushtuns, particularly, look on trade and service to others as somewhat demeaning occupations. Afghanistan was certainly no nation of shop-keepers. To be denied the right to cultivate was a psychological trauma for many. However, Afghans are incapable of sitting around idle while opportunites abound, even if it means twisting a prejudice or two to suit the situation.

Thus, as the Pakistani media regularly complain, the Afghans have maximized opportunities and 'taken over' a number of segments of the economy, especially transport. Also, small sidewalk retail business abound wherever the Afghan Refugees congregate. The plethora of these stands recedes dramatically as snows melt in the passes. Then baubles and satins are exchanged for Kalishnikov assault weapons as the young men again melt into the countryside of Afghanistan to fight the invader.

Rug, antique, and boutique merchants have simply transferred their businesses to Pakistan; large serai have been completely taken over by refugee merchants. Leather workers, potters, weavers, tailors and other artisans have set up going concerns on their own, or with assistance from VOLAGs such as Inter-Aid, Caritas [Pakistan] and the Austrian Relief Committee. The GOP encourages all such self-reliance efforts, except where competition threatens small local industries. Permission to open a soap factory in Mardan, for instance, was denied.

Despite a growing number of these enterprises, the assistance community worries over increasing signs of 'dependency', which threatens to demoralize a people long lauded for their self-reliance who now find themselves forced to depend on hand-outs in order to survive. Such dependency is insidious, and, because it can so easily become an attitudinal habit, it jeopardizes the very essence of Afghan culture.[35]

The emergency phase of the Afghan refugee situation in Pakistan has largely stabilized and emphasis is gradually shifting to focus on income generation, skills training and education. ILO's US$ 2 million program[36] promotes such projects, mainly through established GOP institutions. Most observers agree, however, that those projects which help to prime Afghan initiatives are by far the most successful.

Carpet weaving is a case in point. Turkoman families with capital set up looms in their homes in the RTVs. The whole family works together and the results are admirable. Families in all three provinces who depend on refugee assistance, however, must work with inferior, short-staple wool, harsh dyes and 'new' patterns (including medallions with mosques and other disruptive figures) from the SIDB (Small Industries Development Board). The results are travesties. Even more distressing are the carpet factories set up in some RTVs where Pushtun boys are taught on vertical looms to weave Pakistani adaptations of traditional Turkoman designs. These results are just plain sad.

Afghan skilled labor is much appreciated. It fills the gap of Pakistani laborers who have left to work in the Gulf states. Contractors commend the Afghans for being better workers, more reliable, and less argumentative than local labor. The Afghans are also willing to work for less wages, for which loud abuse is heaped upon them for ruining the labor market for Pakistanis, who must demand an income permitting them to buy the food the Afghans are handed free.

The World Bank's US$ 20 million (funded mainly by the USA and Japan) labour-intensive, income-generating project begun in 1983 seeks to assist both Afghans and Pakistanis by generating employment and compensating Pakistan for refugee-related damage to its ecology. Using a labor force of at least 50 per cent Afghan Refugees, this program includes reforestation in areas of high refugee concentration, the repair of roads damaged by refugee-related transport, and repair and extension of over-used water resources and irrigation systems. In this way it is hoped that the development of Pakistan may be stimulated and the negative aspects of the refugee influx may be offset.

THE FUTURE

These developments in the Afghan Refugee assistance sphere occur at the same time that stewards of global refugee affairs have concluded a new approach must be formulated to deal effectively with the growing tragedy of refugees throughout the world. In essence, the new approach searches for durable solutions accompanied by related development assistance to both host and returnee countries. This is the first time development assistance has been closely related to programs seeking solutions to refugee-related problems.[37]

This is an avenue of bold, innovative thinking because the traditional mandate of UNHCR specifies that the agency is to provide humanitarian relief, with emphasis on relief. Hitherto, the fine line between 'self-reliant schemes', or 'durable solutions' and 'humanitarian relief' has been hard to maintain. Yet in Pakistan, it has been of utmost importance so as to make sure the distinction is discernable at all times. To allow the distinction to be obscured would raise implications fraught with spectres suggesting that Pakistan recognized the legitimacy of the Soviet-puppet DRA regime and sanctioned the occupation of Afghanistan by the Soviets. More explosively, it would suggest that Pakistan has accepted the permanency of the Afghan Refugees in Pakistan. To speak of the 'resettlement' of Afghan refugees in Pakistan is to thoroughly misread present and future objectives.

The Afghan refugees are now welcomed as temporary guests in Pakistan, but it is uncertain what political havoc would be generated if it were determined there was no longer any hope for them to return to their homeland in Afghanistan with honour. For the Afghan refugees in Pakistan, repatriation with honour would seem to be a long way off. But it is well to be prepared. The recent interest in gathering more reliable demographic data on the Afghan Refugee population in Pakistan will greatly assist what must be hoped will be an eventual repatriation and resettlement inside Afghanistan.

Notes

1. Louis Dupree, 'Population Review 1970: Afghanistan', *American Universities Field Staff* (AUFS), South Asia series, vol XV, no. 1, 1970, p.1.
2. For a summary of efforts made by pre-DRA governments to institutionalize data collection, see Graham B. Kerr, *Demographic Research in Afghanistan: A National Survey of the Settled Population*, Afghanistan Council of the The Asia Society (New York), Occasional Paper no. 13, December 1977, Introduction. (May be obtained from Afghanistan Forum, Inc., 201 East 71st Street, 2K, N.Y., N.Y. 10021.)
3. V. Chupir, *Population and Manpower in Afghanistan: 1345–1350 (1966/67–1971/72)*, Royal Afghan Government, Ministry of Planning, (mimeo), Kabul, March 1967. (Discussed in L. Dupree, 'Population Review', *op. cit.* [note 1]).
4. Central Statistics Office, Prime Ministry, Republic of Afghanistan, *A Provisional Gazetteer of Afghanistan: Afghan Demographic Studies*, 3 vols., Kabul, 1975; *National Demographic and Family Guidance Survey of the Settled Population of Afghanistan*, 3 vols., sponsored by the Government of Afghanistan and USAID/Afghanistan. State University of New York at Buffalo (SUNY), 1975; Central Statistics Office, Ministry of Planning, Democratic Republic of Afghanistan, *Statistical Information of Afghanistan (1975–1978)*, Kabul, December, 1978.
5. *Population Policy Compendium: Afghanistan*, Population Division of the United Nations Department of International Economic and Social Affairs and the United Nations Fund for Population Activities, 1984.
6. Rarely published, but see I. Stevens and K. Tarzi, *Economics of Agricultural Production in the Hilmand Valley* (Denver, 1965); Ronald W. O'Comnor (ed.), *Managing Health Systems in Developing Areas: Experiences from Afghanistan* (Lexington, Massachusetts, D. C. Heath and Company, 1980).

7. The Chief Commissionerate for Afghan Refugees, Government of Pakistan, *Humanitarian Assistance Programme for Afghan Refugees*, (Islamabad, August 1983), p. 11.
8. UNHCR Islamabad, interview reported in The *Muslim* (daily newspaper of Islamabad), 3 November 1984, p. 8. On 29 October 1984 the Karachi Domestic Urdu Service reported an influx of 3000 Afghan Refugee families (22 000 individuals) into Northern Waziristan.
9. For monthly eye-witness reports from inside Afghanistan, see *Monthly Bulletin*, Afghan Information Centre, P.O. Box 228, Peshawar, Pakistan, and, *Afghan Realities*, Peshawar Edition, Afghan Information and Documentation Centre (AFC), P.O. Box 324, Peshawar, Pakistan.
10. Frances D'Souza, *The Threat of Famine in Afghanistan*, Afghan Aid, 18 Charing Cross Road, London, WC2N OHR; Edward Giradet's series in the *Christian Science Monitor*, especially 26 September 1984, p. 1; *Time Magazine*, 10 September 1984, p. 26.
11. Although an estimated 60 per cent of the refugee population now reside in *katcha* (pisé or mud brick) housing, the refugee settlements are still referred to as Refugee Tented Villages in order to emphasize their temporary status and promote the principle that the Afghan presence in Pakistan is only a passing phenomenon.
12. Interviews with CAR/NWFP: *Khyber Mail* (daily newspaper of Peshawar), 22 June 1983, p. 1; The *Muslim*, 25 November 1984, p. 1.
13. Variously estimated from 12–19 million; independent observer estimates were much lower. See Kerr, *op. cit.* (note 2), p. 2.
14. A voluntary individual donation of Rs9000 (US$ 540) was made by a local tribal leader in North Waziristan in October 1984 to aid a recently arrived group of 3000 families from the Afghan provinces of Kunduz, Baghlan, Takhar, Logar, Paktyka and Samangan; The *Muslim*, 29 October 1984, p. 1.
15. Headquartered in Geneva. UNHCR is the lead agency responsible for humanitarian aid for the Afghan Refugees.
16. The seven Federally Administered Tribal Agencies (FATA) were mostly created by the British late in the 19th century; only three were created after Pakistan came into being in 1947: Mohmand (1951) and Bajaur and Orakzai (1973). The FATA extend north from Baluchistan Province in the following order: South Waziristan, North Waziristan, Kurram, Orakzai, Khyber, Mohmand, Bajaur. All but Orakzai have a common border with Afghanistan.

    The FATA are administered by the Governor of the NWFP, who acts as the agent of the President of Pakistan, who represents the federal government. Policy concerning the Afghan Refugees is set by the President. For more on the FATA, see Akbar S. Ahmed, *Social and Economic Change in the Tribal Areas*, (Karachi, Oxford University Press, 1977).
17. From 1978 to 11 December 1984 a total of 765 border incursions had been officially noted by the GOP: Afghan aircraft violated Pakistan's airspace 634 times; ground violations (cross-border shellings) totaled 131. The total killed (Afghans and Pakistanis) numbered 158:121 in bombing raids; 37 in shellings. The injured numbered 71: 44 in bombings; 27 in shellings (The *Muslim*, 16 December 1984, p. 1).

18. GOP briefing to UNHCR Mission to Pakistan August–September 1979.
19. For an eye-witness account, see Ekber Menemencioglu, '100 000 Afghans to be moved to the Punjab by the end of 1983', *Refugees Magazine*, August (no. 4), 1983, pp. 7–10.
20. Hanne Christensen, *Sustaining Afghan Refugees in Pakistan*, United Nations Research Institute for Social Development, (UNRISD), Palais des Nations, 1211 Geneva 10, Switzerland, 1983.
21. The *Muslim*, 9 August 1984, p. 1; 6 November, p. 6; 25 November, p. 1. *New York Times*, 25 November, p. 5. According to these accounts, 10 5000 had been shifted by the end of November 1984, and an additional 5000 were expected to be moved by the end of 1984.
22. The *Muslim*, 25 October 1984, p. 1.
23. Personal Communication.
24. F. D. Khan, 'Development of Irrigation and Drinking Water in Baluchistan', The *Muslim Supplement*, 24 October 1984, p. 3. This entire supplement is devoted to Baluchistan and its development.
25. *United Nations Demographic Yearbook for 1982* (34th edition), Department International Economics and Social Affairs, Statistical Office, New York, 1984.
26. Kerr, *op. cit.* (note 2), p. 65.
27. Inger Boesen, *Towards The Self-Reliance of Afghan Refugees?: A study of need and feasibility of establishing income-generating and skill-training programmes for Afghan Refugees in Pakistan, particularly with a view to women*, Danish Refugee Council, P.O. Box 53 DK-1002, Copenhagen K, Denmark; NH Dupree, 'Women Among Afghan Refugees', *Afghanistan Forum*, Vol. XII, no. 2, March, 1984, p. 15.
28. Louis Dupree, 'Anthropology in Afghanistan', *AUFS Reports*, South Asian Series, Vol. XX, no. 3, 1976; also, Louis Dupree, *Afghanistan*, Princeton University, 1980, pp. 68–64.
29. Louis Dupree, *op. cit* (note 28, Princeton), pp. 164ff; Richard Tapper, 'Nomadism in Modern Afghanistan: Asset or Anachronism?', Chapter 8 in L. Dupree, L. Albert eds. *Afghanistan in the 1970s* (New York, Praeger, 1974), pp. 126–143; Bahram Tavakolian, 'Women and Socioeconomic Change among Sheikhanzai Nomads of Western Afghanistan', *The Middle East Journal*, Vol. 38, no. 3, summer 1984, pp. 433–453.
30. 5 November 1984; reported in *FBIS* (Foreign Information Information Service), 8 November 1984. A more extensive diatribe was given by Babrak Karmal to an Indian journalist on 18 September in which he stated specifically, that 'Those who are called by imperialists as "Afghan Refugees" are primarily nomadic people who through centuries move from south and south-west towards north and east and vice-versa with climatic changes. After the April revolution these nomads were the first to fall victim to an international conspiracy . . . traditional routes were closed . . . they were thrown out of their tents and confined within camps installed by the imperialist forces (FBIS, 20 September 1984).
31. Hasan Kawun Kakar, *Government and Society in Afghanistan*, (University of Texas Press, 1979).
32. Richard F. Strand, 'The Evolution of Anti-Communist Resistance in Eastern Nuristan', in M. Nazif Shahrani and R. L. Canfield, eds. *Revolutions and Rebellions in Afghanistan: Anthropological Perspectives*, Institute of

International Studies (Research Series No. 57), University of California, Berkeley, 1984. This work discusses root causes inside Afghanistan which forced the refugee exodus: from Nuristan, Eastern Afghanistan, Qataghan, Badakhshan, Bamiyan, Turkistan, Western, and Southern Afghanistan; with a special chapter on the assault on the honor of women.

33. The *New York Times*, 4 August 1982; Ekber Menemencioglu, 'Afghans Resettled in Turkey', in *Refugees* (newspaper), No. 8, August 1982; N. H. Dupree, 'The Afghan Kirghiz in Turkey', *Afghanistan Forum*, Vol. XII, no. 2, March 1984, p. 21.
34. N. H. Dupree, 'Allah is Pleased' in, 'Baluchistan,' *Afghanistan Forum*, Vol. XIII, no. 1, pp. 23–25.
35. 'Dependency syndromes', *Refugees Magazine*, February (no. 2), 1984, p. 33.
36. UNHCR, International Labour Office, *Tradition and Dynamism among Afghan Refugees*, 1983 Report of an ILO mission to Pakistan in November 1982 on income-generating activities for Afghan Refugees.
37. A major theme at the Conference on Assistance to Refugees in Africa (ICARA II), held in Geneva 9–11 July 1984. For delegate comments, see *Refugees Magazine*, September (no. 9), 1984, pp. 21–32.

19 Superpower Relations with Pakistan, Iran, and Afghanistan
Kail Ellis

This chapter synthesizes the discussions of the panelists' papers on the role of the superpowers and other regional forces in the countries of Pakistan, Iran, and Afghanistan. An attempt has been made to retain the flavor of the discussions by identifying the speakers with their comments, but verbatim quotations have generally been avoided.

Ambassador George McGhee set the tone for the conference by reviewing the current state of diplomacy. McGhee reminisced about his long career in the State Department and his introduction to Pakistan in the 1950s when, as a young diplomat, he was sent to invite Prime Minister Liaquat Ali Khan to visit Washington. In that era, McGhee said, diplomacy justified its existence as a time-honored means of exchanging views and reaching agreements across national borders. The 1980s, he concluded, represents a decline in diplomacy.

Today, McGhee said, the world does not seem to solve its problems by the traditional methods of diplomacy. The United Nations, for example, was created to avert wars, or to stop them, yet many more unnecessary conflicts have occurred. A number of these conflicts are still going on and seemingly cannot be stopped. Diplomacy failed to stop the Iran–Iraq war, the Falklands war, the Grenada invasion, and the current hostilities in Central America. It may startle us to know, he said, that the United States has not concluded a successful negotiation of any importance since 1978, when the Panama Canal Treaty was negotiated. The Camp David Agreement of that same year was a great accomplishment, but turned out to be faulty because there was no real understanding of some of the basic issues. The Reagan Administration has had no successful negotiations in its first five years in office and McGhee feared that this trend will continue.

McGhee speculated that the decline of diplomacy is due to the difficulty with which democracies find the correct way of reaching agreements within their own countries, make correct decisions and give sufficient negotiating authority to heads of state or to secretaries of state to enable them to conduct negotiations. He also said that the news media, although generally very helpful, can also be very harmful, making false accusations and prejudgments that sour issues rather than solve them.

The challenge facing the world, McGhee said, is to change the international environment. The attitude of confrontation, denunciation and unilateralism where nations invade other nations without attempting a negotiation must be avoided. Citing Grenada, McGhee said, 'whether [the US] should have invaded Grenada or not, I don't know, but we certainly made no effort to negotiate with [the Grenadians]'. All attempts should be exhausted to avoid war, McGhee said, and he lamented today's tendency to shoot first and negotiate not at all.

The world must understand that it must have more respect for the rights of other nations and for their interests. The average American, as well as the average foreigner, has to consider that he has to give as well as take, and that the art of compromise is necessary in order to make diplomacy work again. Unfortunately, McGhee observed, politicians in particular don't like to give up anything. Heads of State are embarrassed if they appear to their political mentors to be making compromises. In such situations, war becomes inevitable. McGhee challenged the seminar participants to examine how to revitalize the old processes of diplomacy, which did work at one time. By their example, he said, the participants can show that people who have disagreements can nevertheless respect each other, meet each other half way, and so create an atmosphere in which to solve their problems.

SUPERPOWER RELATIONS WITH PAKISTAN

Mr Agha Shahi, the former Minister of Foreign Affairs for Pakistan, dealt at length with Pakistan's relations with the Superpowers. Shahi stated forcefully Pakistan's opposition to the Soviet military invasion of Afghanistan because it would set a precedent for allowing a larger state to invade and occupy a smaller state. Pakistan, Shahi said, could see no justification for the Soviet Union's military intervention in Afghanistan, including such rationalizations as the failure of the SALT talks, the decline of detente, the US military buildup in the

Persian Gulf, and the Soviet–Afghan treaty which justified military action to quell the Afghan Mujahiddin resistance.

Shahi outlined two issues which have presented difficulties for Pakistan's relations with the United States. The first is Pakistan's nuclear program, the so-called 'Islamic Bomb', and the pressures which the United States has exerted to prevent its attainment. The second is the United States' policy in the Middle East. Shahi explained that Pakistan's concern with the Arab–Israeli conflict is motivated by its fraternal ties to the Muslim states of the region as well as by geopolitical interests. The introduction of Islamic law in Pakistan requires its adherence to the Quranic injunctions governing external relations and resistance to those who drive women and children from their homes. As a consequence, Pakistan regards Israeli expansionism and the US–Israeli strategic alliance as directed against Muslim peoples.

McGhee responded that the United States's policy against nuclear non-proliferation is a cardinal policy of all the nations of the world, with the exception of six or eight, including Pakistan. Pakistan is a long way from the Middle East, he said, and he was not aware that it was so directly involved in the region that when the United States made moves there it was necessary to consult with Pakistan or seek its assistance. Bringing the Middle East into discussions of US–Pakistan relations, McGhee cautioned, would be 'piling unnecessary baggage' on the relationship. It would be better to separate these 'rather extraneous issues' from what may be very real issues between the US and Pakistan. McGhee acknowledged that the US had committed some 'grave sins' in the Middle East. He pointed out, however, that it had sought to resolve the refugee problem and all other outstanding issues such as the question of Israel's borders. McGhee said that the Reagan Plan of 1982 is evidence of the United States's good faith.

Shahi responded that Pakistan, which is faced with unprecedented security problems, is not trying to bring a list of grievances against the United States. It is simply trying to get its viewpoint across. Shahi said he could hardly believe his ears, for example, when one participant said that if Pakistan were to acquire a nuclear capability, it would be 'no less a threat to the Soviet Union than Cuba is to the United States'. Pakistan, Shahi said, is suddenly finding that there is a concerted superpower policy against it. He was shocked to hear American friends say that Pakistan's nuclear capability threatens the Soviet Union when it is obvious to all that the Soviet Union could 'blast Pakistan out of existence'.

The United States must understand that Third World countries must look at problems differently than the Superpowers, Shahi said. Third World countries have no military strength and the only way they can preserve their security is to join together in an act of 'moral solidarity' to deal with the Superpowers.

Shahi protested that Pakistan's criticism of the United States's policies is both responsible and accurate. It is based, he said, on US sources and documentation and is far milder than the criticisms of US policies found in the American press. Besides, since the United States criticizes Pakistan freely, notably with regard to its human rights record and nuclear policy, it should not take umbrage if Pakistan respectfully criticizes US superpower policies.

Pakistan's position regarding the Arab–Israeli conflict in the UN has never been an issue with the United States, Shahi said. Even when Pakistan was the 'most allied ally' or 'client of clients' of the United States, it took a position supporting the Palestinian cause. Now, Shahi said, the United States seems to be making Pakistan's Middle East policy an issue in US-Pakistani relations. But Pakistan's Muslim traditions and the requirements of Islamic law forbid it to change its Middle East policy.

As Pakistan's foreign minister, Shahi tried to develop a 'mature relationship' with the United States. Only a relationship based on mutual respect, not on exaggerated expectations or alliances, he felt, could be durable. The United States and Pakistan cannot have completely identical policies. The United States is far too powerful and its interests as a superpower for too varied, he said, for it and Pakistan to have identical policies.

Pakistan opposed the Soviet military intervention in Afghanistan without prompting, blandishments or threats from the United States, Shahi said. It expected and received no reward from the Carter Administration and even rejected Carter's offer of aid. Shahi was told by one American diplomat, 'Yes we got your message, don't call us, we'll call you'. Shahi said that Pakistan's ambassador in Washington was naturally very anxious that the door be kept open for American aid, but Shahi told him, 'No, don't do anything, just keep quiet'.

Pakistan realized that it was not in a position to exercise influence on the US political system, Shahi said. As a result of having grown a little more 'sophisticated' in understanding US policies, Pakistan has tried to enlist other Third World countries in an attempt to strengthen its international position. Shahi, for example, tried to enlist the moral fervor of the Islamic Revolution of Iran to oppose the Soviet intervention in Afghanistan.

McGhee said that the United States had no desire to keep Pakistan from being non-aligned. The United States does not have a treaty with Pakistan, although relations between the two countries have been very good and the US has given arms on a large scale. If Pakistan wishes to be non-aligned, the United States will respect that choice. The United States has very few treaties in the world and lives with all the non-aligned countries, McGhee added.

McGhee said he thought he understood the origin of some of the 'rather bitter remarks' made by Shahi regarding the United States. Perhaps if the US were in a position similar to Pakistan's, he [McGhee] might have said somewhat the same. McGhee pointed out that the United States has a difficult role to play in the world, and he pleaded for understanding.

James Spain, former US ambassador to Turkey, said that it probably does more harm than good to tie great power ambitions and intentions with the very legitimate and necessary regional concerns for survival of the South Asian countries. Spain doubted that either of the Superpowers would make decisions in South Asia based on the Soviet Union's being dealt in on the Middle East or on a master plan of realignment which would inspire the Soviet Union to withdraw from Afghanistan. Spain thought that when Moscow and Washington get together, Afghanistan is going to be at the bottom of the list. Pakistan, India and the Afghan Mujahiddin will have to work with the situation on the ground, Spain said. They are not going to find any answers from the Superpowers.

Shahi mentioned that the 1959 Executive Agreement between Pakistan and the United States was an irritant in Pakistan–US relations. He was disappointed that the United States was not willing to turn the Agreement into a treaty. When told by a Congressional delegation visiting Pakistan that Congress was ready to pass a concurrent but non-binding resolution, Pakistan was not interested. The 1959 Agreement, Shahi declared, 'is effectively dead'.

Shahi questioned the value of such agreements to Third World countries. He recalled that Henry Kissinger once said to the Israelis, 'Do you think just because there is something on paper that you will hold the United States to its commitment? We will do so only if it suits our interests'. If that was the attitude towards the Israelis, who are 'like lips on the teeth to the Americans', according to Shahi, what hope has Pakistan that any agreement with the United States will have binding force? Even if the 1959 Agreement were to become a treaty with the 'advice and consent' of the Senate, Shahi feared that the stipulation 'the United States will act in any situation to assist Pakistan including the use of military force according to the constitutional processes of the United States', would make the treaty of little value. Pakistan has poor public relations with the Congress, Shahi said. Its relationship with the United States is like 'walking on a tightrope' because the US has reservations about Pakistan's nuclear program and human rights record. The United States, therefore, will intervene on Pakistan's behalf only if it considers that its vital interests are in danger, subject to the interpretation of Congress. The United States may intervene to protect the Gulf States or Saudi Arabia, but not Pakistan. Today, even oil is not vital to the United States. Pakistan, therefore, has no assurance of security from the 1959 Agreement. After withdrawing from the Central Treaty Organization [CENTO], however, Shahi said that Pakistan did not want to say that the 1959 Agreement should be scrapped.

Shahi did not believe there would be a confrontation between the United States or Pakistan with the Soviet Union over the border with Afghanistan. Pakistan has a 1400-mile border with Afghanistan, Shahi said. The Pathan tribesmen have roamed across the mountains from time immemorial and even required tribute from the great Nadir Shah of Iran in the 18th century. Pakistan, would have to engage in a war with the Afghan tribesmen along hundreds of miles and block hundreds of trails, an impossible task. It would be far better for Pakistan, Shahi said, to be threatened by the Soviet Union, suffer the consequences of 'hot pursuit', and 'take it on the chin', than to involve itself in a war with the Pushtun population. The Soviet Union does not offer Pakistan an attractive choice, Shahi said. But given the choice between an internal insurrection and an external threat, Pakistan will opt for the latter. The Soviet Union, Shahi said, must understand Pakistan's great predicament.

Shahi was asked about the seemingly contradictory proposals for solving the Afghan crisis by disassociating it from the East-West conflict on the one hand, and by acquiring 'leverage' for a settlement through an aid package from the United States on the other hand. He was also asked to comment on the effect which a US military aid package would have on Pakistani–Indian relations.

Pakistan, Shahi said, had made it clear that the arms it attained from the United States were not meant to fight India, much less the Soviet Union. They were to be part of the modernization of its armed forces. Unfortunately, they were seen in the context of the Soviet invasion of Afghanistan; and the only objection which India raised against the Soviet invasion was that it enabled Pakistan to obtain arms. Shahi wished that India had been as concerned about the invasion and the disappearance of an independent state.

Whatever one's views on the wastefulness of arms expenditures, Shahi said, it is a practical matter for a political leader to acquire modern arms for his country's armed forces if he wishes to remain in power. That was the situation which faced Pakistan when it was able to get arms only in 1981 through the Reagan offer. Pakistan had been approaching the United States for arms from the time of Yahya Khan in the 1970s. [Prime Minister Z. A.] Bhutto succeeded in getting the arms embargo [imposed after the 1971 war with India] lifted, but he could not persuade the Americans to give him free military aid. Pakistan then went to King Khalid [of Saudi Arabia] and asked for money to buy Mirages. It was unfortunate that Pakistan could get arms from the United States only after the Soviets invaded Afghanistan, Shahi said.

Pakistan's relations with the United States cannot be exclusive, Shahi reiterated. The United States is a global power and it needs to have many 'favorite wives'. Pakistan, therefore, must guard against being tied to the United States to the exclusion of other options. It needs flexibility, for tomorrow the United States may stop delivering the F–16s or cut off its military aid and Pakistan should be prepared.

Pakistan sought arms, Shahi said, not to exercise 'leverage' against the Soviet Union, but because it feared that the Afghan Air Force would attack Pakistan with MIG–21 and MIG–23 aircraft. He did not say so publicly at the time, but Pakistan had no means to counter such attacks. Pakistan also needs Hawkeye surveillance aircraft, Shahi said, but 'God knows what kind of quid pro quo the Americans will demand in return'.

Pakistan's long-standing conflict with India was discussed by Hafeez Malik from Villanova University. Malik proposed some alternate strategies on how 'friendship between Pakistan and India' might be promoted. Developing the concept of war as a continuation of diplomacy, Malik thought that tensions between India and Pakistan can best be eliminated if Pakistan succeeded in developing nuclear weapons. Once India and Pakistan joined the nuclear club, each would have to forego a resort to war and freeze their territorial and other disputes, as for example in Kashmir. The dread of nuclear weapons [Mutual Assured Destruction] would 'induce sanity and reasonableness' if ordinary prudence fails to dampen religious and political fanaticism on both sides. Malik reasoned that a mere 'no war' pact between India and Pakistan would not induce the security which would flow from mutually guaranteed self-destruction.

Shahi addressed India's role in promoting a settlement of the Afghanistan crisis. India was the first country Shahi turned to when Soviet troops intervened in Afghanistan. Shahi said he invited the Indian foreign secretary to Pakistan to exchange views and formulate a common stand on Afghanistan, but he could not come to Pakistan for over a month. Since the issue came before the Security Council, Pakistan was forced to define its position quickly. Shahi said he soon discovered that a big gulf existed between his perception of events in Afghanistan and India's. Pakistan still wants to work with India for a solution to the Afghan problem, but it cannot simply accept Indian good offices or give India a blank check to negotiate with the Soviet Union. India could side with the Soviet Union and tell Pakistan to accept the status quo and if this happened, Shahi said, Pakistan's relations with India would worsen.

Shahi lamented the lack of progress in the Geneva negotiations on Afghanistan. It is unfortunate, he said, that the Soviet Union prefers to deal in terms of 'leverage', as for example, by making the United States concede something in Central America in return for its withdrawal from Afghanistan. He regretted the Soviet Union's rejection of Pakistan's overtures for a settlement on Afghanistan and charged that the Soviets prefer to negotiate with Pakistan as they would with a superpower, that is, by trying to exact advantages. Pakistan's security, and the security of all Third World countries, therefore, lies in its adopting a common position based on international law.

Pakistan's only hope is that the United Nations negotiator, Mr Diego Garcia Cordovez, will make better progress on Afghanistan. Otherwise, Shahi warned, the situation could lead to a confrontation between the United States and the Soviet Union. This would be madness because it could escalate into a nuclear conflict.

Unfortunately, Shahi said, the Soviet Union thinks that Pakistan has come under the control of the United States and so will not negotiate with it. Shahi assured the Soviet Union that if it made a gesture toward the Third World countries by withdrawing from Afghanistan, it would totally outweigh US influence in the region. He jokingly implored his friend, Igor Khalevinski [Political Counselor of the Soviet Mission to the UN], to 'stick his neck out' and advise his country to withdraw from Afghanistan. An agreement on Afghanistan must be independent of East–West tensions. But if the superpowers insist on dealing with Pakistan and other Third world countries as they would with each other, then the matter is out of Pakistan's hands. This places Pakistan in a difficult position. Pakistan, he said, has to be afraid when the superpowers agree as well as when they disagree.

IRAN AND THE SUPERPOWERS

Iran's relations with the superpowers were discussed by Richard Cottam from the University of Pittsburgh, who dealt with US-Iranian relations, and Shireen Hunter, a former Iranian diplomat currently with Georgetown University's Center for Strategic and International Studies, who traced the course of Iran's relations with the Soviet Union. Both presentations generated lively discussions.

Ambassador McGhee commented on the early objectives of US policy in Iran. According to McGhee, the United States recognized the Shah's supremacy in the Middle East, with the exception of Greece, Turkey and Saudi Arabia. The first priority of US policy in 1950–51 was not to lose Iran to the free world. One of the United States' problems, however, was that it was unable to find a way to aid the Shah. When the Shah came to Washington, 'he would ask for the moon', McGhee said. He wanted large armies to protect Iran from Russia. He said that Iran didn't need economic aid, only military aid. Nobody, McGhee said, thought the Shah's requests were realistic. [Secretary of State Dean] Acheson always said that the US's greatest problem was that it couldn't find a way to aid the Shah.

McGhee thought that it was a great mistake for the Eisenhower Administration to have overthrown Mossadegh. Truman's Administration would not have done that, McGhee said. McGhee had good personal relations with Mossadegh and had conducted 80 hours of conversations with him. By McGhee's own account, Mossadegh embarrassed him in London by praising McGhee from the floor of the Majlis. Unfortunately, in McGhee's assessment, Mossadegh was not realistic. Even though the United States could not find a way to work with Mossadegh, McGhee felt that the US should have tried harder rather than overthrown him.

McGhee said he saw the Shah at his lowest, just before he fled the country after the assassination on 7 March 1951 of [General Ali] Razmara, the Shah's prime minister, and at the height of his power, two or three years before his demise. The Shah 'ruled the world' and McGhee said he had never seen a more confident man. But the Shah lost his country himself. Efforts by the US could not have helped him for he had no political base. He was, McGhee said, 'not an Iranian; he was contemptuous of Iranians'.

Hafeez Malik observed that one of the problems faced by a superpower, evident in the US's support of the Shah, is that he was not the only man supported to the hilt by the United States. There are other governments and other leaders in the Middle East who really don't have the support of their own populations, yet the United States deals with them. Perhaps the US has no choice but to support them, but Malik asked, what is the solution to this dilemma?

McGhee responded that we can't support a man against his own country. The US failed in Iran, in McGhee's opinion, by not being able to deal with Mossadegh. This, however, was the fault of the British who were determined to get rid of Mossadegh. McGhee himself was attacked in the House of Commons for trying to deal with Mossadegh, he said. The move to overthrow Mossadegh came from the Anglo–Iranian Oil Company, which convinced Kim Roosevelt to persuade President Eisenhower to mount the campaign to overthrow Mossadegh. These events, McGhee said, were all related in the first edition of Eisenhower's memoirs, but this edition was later recalled. McGhee said this campaign was a very bad mistake; one does not get anywhere by over-throwing governments.

Shahi commented on Cottam's paper, which outlined the three objectives of US policy in the Middle East: (1) containment of the Soviet Union, (2) the safety of the oil lanes and (3) the security of Israel. From Shahi's vantage point, the body politic of the United States makes it practically impossible for the United States to have a coherent Middle East policy which takes into consideration the interests of the region's people. Shahi did not think the political processes in the United States would permit the formulation of a coherent US Middle East policy.

Soviet expansionism, Shahi pointed out, would be effectively contained by neutralizing the region. Iran's foreign policy is 'neither East nor West', and the Revolutionary regime has denounced the Irano–Soviet Treaty of 1921, which gave the Soviet Union the right to interfere in Iran's internal affairs. Just as the United States cannot allow the Soviet Union to dominate Iran, the Soviet Union cannot allow the return of the predominant American influence in Iran. Therefore, Shahi asked, would not the interests of both superpowers be satisfied by a policy of neutrality for the region? Shahi said that the Soviet Union might be induced to consider withdrawing from Afghanistan if it were assured of Iran's neutrality.

Shahi agreed that the safety of the oil lanes is an issue of great interest to the Gulf countries. Shahi proposed, therefore, that a regime be established to guarantee the safety of the Strait of Hormuz.

On Cottam's third point, Shahi asked how Israel's security was to be defined. Quoting Henry Kissinger that 'the United States has undertaken the security of Israel but not its expansion,' Shahi said he was skeptical that the United States could distinguish between Israel's security and its expansion in any concrete situation because of the operations of the American domestic political process. It is a sensitive topic, Shahi acknowledged, but it seemed to him that American goals can be reconciled with the interests of the people of the region and with the legitimate interests of the Soviet Union only when the United States formulates a coherent Middle East policy. Shahi doubted this was possible and, for this reason, he said, the United States has suffered setbacks in the region. As a consequence, the countries of the region feel they must form their own policies and not tie themselves to American policies in the Middle East.

Christopher Van Hollen, former US ambassador to Sri Lanka, attributed significant changes in US foreign policy to Shahi's vision of the region's interests. Thanks to Shahi's negotiation's, Van Hollen said, a new US–Pakistani relationship had developed in the first year of the Reagan Administration. This relationship fully recognized Pakistan's basic non-alignment and role in the Islamic world. Since both Superpowers are somewhat neutralized in Iran, Van Hollen said, he thought that conditions were right for a regime to guarantee the access to the Persian Gulf oil. The one stumbling block, however, is the Soviet Union's role in Afghanistan. It would be difficult for the United States to negotiate a 'zone of peace' in the region with the Soviets still occupying Afghanistan.

Commenting on the remarks by Shahi and Cottam regarding US policy in the Middle East, McGhee said that although it is very easy to criticize US policy in the Middle East, the fact is that it is not possible to develop a policy or strategy to accomplish US objectives. He defied anyone to develop an overall simple strategy that would explain US objectives, and he cited the example of Iran.

Cottam said that he did not 'lament' US policy in the Middle East or the lack of it. The State Department is a hopelessly incrementalist organization, in his view. He did not think the United States could come up with a policy at this time. Cottam told Shahi that if he were to design a US policy for Iran, he would emulate Pakistan's 'hands off' policy. Cottam held little hope that the United States would follow such a policy, however.

Returning to McGhee's comments on US policy objectives for Iran, Cottam said that strategy is the sum of policies carried out over time by different people that adds up to a coherent whole. This happens all the time because systems determine policies. Individuals who are deeply involved in the process of reaching for a goal are sometimes appalled when it is pointed that their little increment was part of this process.

Today, as a result of the falling of a lot of props, the United States simply does not know how to come up with a way of reconciling diverse objectives in the Middle East. If past experience is any indication, Cottam said, a formulated policy will be the result of a lot of increments, not of a single person. Occasionally, at the presidential level or the secretary of state level, we might find an individual who is capable of strategy formation. Strategy, however, never comes from a bureaucracy, although very good increments do. This is not to put down diplomacy, Cottam said, but to distinguish it from strategy.

Jon Anderson, The Catholic University, Washington, DC, suggested that the Islamic revolution in Iran represents not a 'return to religion' but a 'return of religion' in Iran. That is, there is not so much a large turn of the population to religion as a shift of the population that bears the religion.

Cottam agreed with Anderson's observation. Basic social change in Iran is reflected in the people who support the regime. These people are entirely different from those who supported the Shah and identify with a different community, in this case, the religious community. Although their patterns of behavior are bewildering and have to be understood, Cottam thinks the US can deal with them. But trying to understand is important. Cottam cautioned that whenever one hears the term 'irrational' applied to somebody like Khomeini, one should know that person does not understand the worldview of one of the world's most important figures. Khomeini, in Cottam's opinion, is not irrational. He sees the world differently than do we in the West. It is our problem to understand how Khomeini sees the world, not his to see our worldview, Cottam said.

Alvin Rubinstein, a Soviet specialist from the University of Pennsylvania, questioned Cottam's analysis of the factional struggles within the Khomeini regime and the US's ability to affect them. Cottam's analysis, he thought, was based on certain assumptions on the nature of political relationships between governments and the reactions and operations within different regimes. The Khomeini regime might be understood better in terms of family feuds, murders, and intrigues than in terms of a rational view of who, what or how it perceives the world to threaten Iran, he said.

Cottam responded by citing his book *Competitive Interference*, in which he made clear that the person whom you put in power, the client, has an enormous amount of leverage over you. Cottam thinks that the US had almost no control over the Shah. Rather, the Shah controlled the United States, just as do a number of other so-called clients. The Soviet Union also is controlled substantially by its so-called satellites, Cottam said. As to the assumptions of political relationships referred to by Rubinstein, Cottam said was referring to the Shah's personal control system and the very vital role the United States played in it.

Cottam said he did not believe that the United States should involve itself in factional struggles in Iran. The temptation to do so arose when in the process of withdrawing from Iran, the United States hoped that, if Barzagan survived, Iran would move in a 'reformist' direction. Had this happened, the terrible excesses whereby whole sections of the population were purged, involving millions of people, might have been averted. Instead, Cottam said, the State Department had an acute understanding of its limitations, and played a very unobtrusive policy.

One of the areas where the United States is seeing change take place in the Middle East, according to Cottam, is in power or capability change. The capability change taking place in the region amounts to a decline in American influence which we have not recognized. Lebanon was a shock for the US but its lessons have not been learned. The Soviets, according to Cottam, are not any more aware of capability change than is the United States. The nicest thing the Arabs, who counted on Soviet help in 1982, say about the Soviets is 'pathetic'. The Soviet role in the Middle East is more policy-determined than capability-determined. Functionally, Cottam said, the Soviets lack capability because of the strange role they have played in the region's confrontations. They silently allowed their client to be beaten by the US's client, and this did not increase their popularity.

Cottam said that Israel is a declining power in the Middle East. It overextended itself in 1982 and is now being defeated by an indigenous force of Lebanese Shia. No formidable external force, such as Iran, is doing this to Israel. In fact, Iran is actually more under the control of the Lebanese Shia than the other way around. Israel is suffering, in Cottam's view, because it cannot control the whole Middle East with so few people. It is not only Israel, but all the other major determinants, including the Arab secular national states, who are declining. The only force which is not declining in the Middle East, in Cottam's view, is Islam. Islam as a force is inchoate and takes different forms in different areas. However, Iran is the one country that might try to produce unity in Islam since it is the functional Islamic republic in the region. Cottam said that Iran's preoccupations with Iraq has kept it from fulfilling this role.

Igor Khalevinski, Senior Political Counsellor of the Soviet Mission to the UN, conceded that Russian–Iranian relations before the October Revolution were an example of the 'squeezing embrace of the northern Russian Bear' over its southern neighbor. There are, he said, many examples of the 'evil expansionist designs' of the Russian Czars and, as Hunter pointed out in her paper, Iran was an important strategic springboard for spreading Russian influence southward. Such policies, however, are not in the nature of the socialist country that the Soviet Union is today, Khalevinski said. The October Revolution brought about radical change.

Soviet Union's approach to Iran is that of a very close neighbor who respects its southern neighbor's sovereignty. Khalevinski said that the Soviet Union wants only to consolidate the political and economic relationships between the two countries. If one puts aside the past expansionist designs of the Russian Czars, he said, one finds that there are strong cultural links and traditions between the Russian and the Iranian peoples. Russian poets and writers, for example, were known in Iran and the ancient Persian culture is treated with respect in the Soviet Union.

Khalevinski stated that the Soviet Union does not export revolution. The fundamental principle of Soviet foreign policy is that revolution cannot be brought about by outside forces. Revolution is an indigenous phenomena, the result of domestic, social, economic, and political movements and processes. Although some Marxists proclaim that revolutions can be imposed from the outside or exported, that is not true Marxism. It is 'pseudo-Marxism', Khalevinski said. The Communist Parties in individual countries are independent political organizations. What they do or are thinking of doing is their business. To say that they are supervised by the Soviet Union is a distortion of the facts.

Hunter responded that she understood Khalevinski's difficulties in seeing that socialism hasn't been what it was 'cracked up to be'. She protested that she was not judging whether Soviet policy was good or bad, but was trying to explain the Iranian perspective. She had made it quite clear, she said, that initially the Bolshevik Revolution had a very good impact on Iran and had created a lot of sympathy. But the Soviet Union came to behave like a great power, and why shouldn't it? One of the attributes of a great power is opportunism, and great powers cannot commit themselves one way or another, she added.

Khalevinski said he failed to understand the references to the 'opportunistic' attitude of the Soviet Union. The Soviet Union had always maintained a respectful relationship with the Shah, as a head of state, without condoning his ideological bias. It also maintained the same respect for subsequent Iranian leaders, including Barzagan and Khomeini. The Soviet Union regards the nature of the nation's regime as a purely domestic affair, Khalevinski said.

Since the Islamic revolution is not socialist in nature, Khalevinski explained, the Soviet Union has not been very enthusiastic about it. This does not mean, however, that the Soviet Union awaits or promotes revolution in any form in Iran. Iran's form of government is a domestic matter, and Khalevinski reiterated that the Soviet Union wishes only to establish good neighborly relations with Iran.

Khalevinski's remarks prompted Rubinstein to ask if the Soviet Union had accepted the Iranian government's renunciation of Article 6 of the 1921 Treaty, which reserved for the Soviet Union the right to send troops into Iranian territory should the latter become a base for anti-Soviet aggression. If the Soviet Union did not accept the renunciation, Rubinstein asked, what effect would this have on relations between Iran and the Soviet Union?

Hunter responded that the Soviets did not accept the renunciation. She said that it is precisely because Article 6 gives the Soviet Union a free hand to determine the nature of the 'threat' that the Islamic regime is skeptical of Soviet intentions despite the regime's animosity toward the United States.

Khosrow Fatemi, a former senior official in Iran's Ministry of Commerce, was asked to comment on the impact of the Iran–Iraq war on the supply of oil from the Gulf. A study by the Hoover

Institute referred to the loss of 3 million barrels of oil per day because of the war, and of up to 9 million per day if the Strait of Hormuz were to be closed. A related comment by Rodney Jones pointed out that the international energy supply has not been hindered by the Gulf war because price, conservation, and the generation of alternate sources of supply have made up for the shortfall. India, for example, had declined from 75 per cent dependency on oil imports to less than 25 per cent in the last decade.

Fatemi agreed that a closure of the Strait of Hormuz would result in a loss of up to 9 million barrels of oil per day, since this would also involve a cut-off of production from Saudi Arabia, Qatar and the United Arab Emirates. The closure would not be effective for long, Fatemi, said. Although an enormous navy would be necessary to close the Strait, it could easily be reopened by force.

US–Iranian relations and the concept of 'war avoidance' were introduced into the discussion by Jones. He commented on the great risk, especially during the hostage crisis, that the United States might go to war with Iran. He wondered whether we should consider the Carter Doctrine as a substitute for war with Iran. Obviously, it was a statement of American vital interests, and directed implicitly against the Soviet Union. Its latent function, however, was to avoid war with Iran.

Fatemi responded that he did not believe either Carter or Reagan had any clear policy regarding Iran. Their statements, in his opinion, were responses to ad hoc situations which 'hoped for the best'.

The United States's response to terrorism in the Middle East in the context of the Iranian revolution was also raised. Jones discerned a trend toward the 'Sharonization' of US policy, which he defined as the State Department's need to find a more aggressive and more publicly supported response to terrorism in the region. In Jones's opinion this tendency is the result of the clear failure to find ways to deal with the Lebanese situation which, in itself, is symbolic of US policy failures in the Middle East, quite apart from the Iran–Iraq war. In large part, 'Sharonization' is really a response to what Iran is doing in the Middle East, or what elements from Iran appear to be doing in places such as Kuwait and Lebanon. Recent statements from the Secretary of Defense regarding the limits of military power indicate, according to Jones, that a very important debate is going on in the United States. While not agreeing that a tenable response to terrorism is possible, Jones recognized that the compulsion for a response will grow if, in the name of Islam, terrorist activities such as the burning of embassies and the taking of hostages, succeed in re-establishing the order of international relations.

Andrew Kilgore's paper on the Arab-Iranian conflict prompted Hunter to say that very few peoples have interacted so thoroughly as the Persians and the Arabs. Perhaps, she observed, they know each other too well and are too similar to one another. The problem, however, seems to be one of perception. From the Arab side of the Gulf, Iran is seen as a threat. There were, Hunter concedes, elements of truth in that perception, especially after 1974 and the latter years of the Shah. From the Iranian side of the Gulf, however, the perspective is somewhat different. Iran, Hunter said, does not see just the small sheikhdoms of the Gulf, such as Kuwait, Qatar and Abu Dhabi, but the 'Arab West'. Iran perceives itself to be surrounded by the Soviet Union on the north and east and by the Arabs in the west. Arab-Iranian relations, therefore, cannot be explained simply in terms of religion. The conflict is not Sunni–Shia but Arab–Persian.

Kilgore, a former ambassador to Qatar, agreed with Hunter. He said the State Department has always been convinced that the Shia–Sunni division was the cause of all the trouble in the Gulf. While ambassador, he spent three years trying to convince the State Department that it was actually an Arab–Persian conflict.

Iran's relations with the superpowers prompted some observations on how to deal with the Islamic republic. Hunter thought it would be a mistake to think that the Islamic phenomenon will present itself in the same way everywhere. As it affects other forces, she said, it in turn will be affected. Even the most extreme clerical factions have been forced to adapt to the forces of nationalism and international realities, Hunter said, and the Islamic regime is now behaving in some ways like a very traditional and pragmatic government.

Sharaf-ud-Din Ahmed, a Pakistani diplomat, observed that over the last four years a tremendous evolution has taken place in the Iranian leaderships' understanding of the Islamization process in Pakistan. A number of visits to Pakistan by Iranian clerics and mullahs have occurred, including some by such 'notorious' leaders as Ayatollah Khalkhali. Pakistani students are also studying in Iranian theological seminaries. Both countries now realize that they are following different paths for the same objective: Iran, the course of revolution, and Pakistan, the evolutionary path. Pakistan, he thought, is one of the few countries to which Iran does not want to export revolution.

AFGHANISTAN AND THE SUPERPOWERS

The Soviet Union's invasion of Afghanistan and the conditions necessary for its withdrawal dominated the discussions of this panel. Khalevinski stated that the Soviet Union entered Afghanistan at the invitation of the Afghan government. This was prompted by the growing scale of foreign intervention in Afghanistan by Western-supported and trained forces from the refugee camps in Pakistan. It became necessary to introduce Soviet troops, Khalevinski said, to prevent a bloody massacre by these paramilitary forces. It is, therefore, one-sided to approach the Afghan issue only from the presence of Soviet troops and their withdrawal, Khalevinski said. The circumstances which led to their introduction must also be considered.

Khalevinski denied that the Soviet Union is trying to impose Communism in Afghanistan. Communism, he said, is in the very distant future for the Soviet Union, so what kind of 'communism' can exist in Afghanistan? The April Revolution reflected broad social processes which had been taking place in Afghan society for many years. A group of revolutionaries had formed a party and, after taking power, started to restructure Afghan society. The Communist party had never ruled in Afghanistan, so it is natural that many mistakes were made and extreme positions taken. This was also true of the Communist party in the Soviet Union when it attempted to collectivize agriculture. In Afghanistan, Khalevinski said, there were some on the local level who wished to see change occur as soon as possible. They did not take into consideration the real situation. This was true in the agricultural sector during the government of Hafizullah Amin. The present government has a rational approach to reform and is taking care that all the traditional national characteristics of Afghanistan are respected. First in this regard is the respect accorded to Islam. Islam is not in danger in Afghanistan, Khalevinski said. There are no obstacles to its practice and Islamic literature is being published in the country.

Henry Bradsher countered that Islam is respected only in so far as it is prepared to support the state. In the Islamic world, Bradsher said, there is a history of regimes which have wanted the mullahs to support the state. Afghanistan, he said, is a modern case, as indicated by recent reports from Kabul telling of the removal from their mosques of some 22 prominent mullahs because they did not support the state.

Khalevinski acknowledged that there were some problems in Afghanistan. People from across the border, he said, were creating religious problems by terrorizing mullahs, preventing them from delivering their sermons and by destroying mosques. Khalevinski explained that the presence of Soviet advisors in Afghanistan was part of the Soviet Union's policy to assist socialist countries in Asia and Africa in their transformation to socialism. This does not mean that the socialist countries are constructing new societies and a new life for the people themselves, he said, but only assisting. Khalevinski compared this situation to his personal experience in the UN where the Soviet and Afghan delegations maintain a relationship of strict equality. There are differences of opinion between the two, Khalevinski said, but no domination by the Soviet Union. That is also the 'style' of the Soviet advisors in Afghanistan.

Khalevinski was asked if and under what circumstances the Soviet Union would withdraw from Afghanistan. He replied that the withdrawal of Soviet forces is a matter for negotiations. Since the Democratic Republic of Afghanistan is a political reality, he suggested that it would be proper for Pakistan and Iran to talk directly with the Babrak Karmal government. Soviet troops, he said, were invited by Afghanistan in accord with the UN Charter guaranteeing the right of each state to security, and by the relevant article of the Soviet–Afghan treaty. Their presence in Afghanistan is, therefore, legal. According to the report of the Secretary General, the UN negotiations have been making progress. Khalevinski cautioned against undermining these efforts.

The reality of the Afghan situation, in Malik's view, is that the Soviet Union will not withdraw from Afghanistan. The April Revolution was a socialist revolution. The Soviets, therefore, have to be concerned not only for the security of the socialist regime in Afghanistan, but for their own security as well. Withdrawal from Afghanistan would represent a defeat for the Soviet Union on its southern borders. It would also have internal repercussions in Soviet Central Asia. Malik said that we must keep in mind that the insurgents are receiving support from the United States and other countries and that the consequences of a withdrawal for the Soviet Union's prestige would be immense. Malik is convinced that the Soviets will never permit the return of the *status quo ante bellum* in Afghanistan.

Hunter thought that Malik seemed to be advocating a 'Pax Sovietica'. By changing a buffer state into a client state, the Soviet

Union is turning Afghanistan into a Czechoslovakia or, worse, a Bulgaria. Unfortunately, she observed, the Soviets' proclivity is to expand, and the more they expand, the more buffers they need. We have only to think of Aden and Ethiopia, she said. By the time their circular movement is completed, there will not be much left of Saudi Arabia or Pakistan. The Soviets must realize that not every independent Third World country is a threat to them.

Shahi said that he did not know whether the Soviet Union would ever leave Afghanistan, but that Pakistan favors the withdrawal of all Soviet forces from that country. Pakistan, he said, did not take its position out of naïveté. It knew that there could be a Soviet military intervention if Hafizullah Amin and Taraki were at the point of being toppled. Since Pakistan had recognized both Hafizullah Amin and Taraki why, one might ask, did Pakistan not accept Babrak Karmal? Sometimes, Shahi said, 'history turns on what appears to be trivial things'. Shahi related the background to Pakistan's refusal to recognize the Karmal regime.

Shahi said that the Soviet ambassador Azimov brought a note to the foreign ministry and told Shahi that the Soviet Union had intervened in Afghanistan for a limited purpose with a limited contingent for a limited time. The ambassador informed Foreign Minister Shahi that the Soviet forces were invited by the Afghan leadership and as soon as its objectives were achieved, they would be withdrawn. Shahi asked the ambassador, 'Which leadership?' He said, 'Babrak Karmal.' Shahi said, 'But Babrak Karmal was not even in the country.' Shahi said that his meeting with the ambassador had taken place on the 28th of December and the Soviets went into Afghanistan on the 25–26th of December. Shahi told the ambassador, 'Mr Ambassador, you could only have been invited by Hafizullah Amin, but then he has been killed.'

Shahi said that he didn't want to press the issue with the ambassador. However his government debated its course of action for a whole day and concluded that the Soviet Union had not received a legitimate invitation. Pakistan had to consider the consequences of taking a position which would be interpreted as one of direct opposition to the action of a superpower. Pakistan was standing alone, Shahi explained. Internally it had a military regime which was opposed by the political parties. Externally, it was isolated by the pressures brought on by President Carter and the United States over the reprocessing plant and its uranium enrichment program. Nevertheless, he said, Pakistan weighed all the risks, took a conscious decision and called for the Soviet withdrawal from Afghanistan.

Shahi tried to present a note to the Soviet ambassador calling for Soviet withdrawal before the public statement was issued. Ambassador Azimov refused to accept the note and told Shahi, 'I can't believe this is the attitude of your government. This will not be good for you, not good for you personally.' The statement was issued anyway.

Pakistan, Shahi said, was fully conscious that the Soviet Union had never withdrawn from any country to which it had sent its troops. The cases of Austria and Finland, where the Soviets left under certain conditions, were great exceptions. Shahi wanted to develop a common strategy with India but the Indian foreign secretary said he could not come to Pakistan for a month, and events moved on. Some statesmen with long experience in dealing with the Soviet Union have said that under certain circumstances the Soviets might withdraw their troops. Shahi said he was convinced that if the Soviet Union actually withdraws its troops from Afghanistan, it would dramatically increase its prestige in the Third World.

If there is a moral or political basis for the Soviet Union's position in Afghanistan, Shahi asked, then why have all the socialist parties of the world criticized the Soviets' action? He argued that the position of a superpower is so solid that a temporary reversal of its position would not be fatal to its prestige.

Hunter addressed the perception that the Soviet Union intervened in Afghanistan because it feared an 'Islamic threat' emanating from the Iranian revolution to its central Asian Muslim republics. Discounting this theory, she pointed out that the Islamic nature of the Iranian revolution was established sometime after the Soviet invasion, that is, after Bani Sadr left Iran. Certainly during the Barzagan government there was no 'Islamic wave' which could be construed as a threat to the Soviet Muslim republics. Also, as far as the Soviet–Afghan Friendship Treaty is concerned, Hunter recalled that in the past, the Soviet Union has been rather selective in invoking such treaties. A case in point is the Iraqi–Soviet friendship treaty, and the specific clause that whenever there is a threat to one of the signatories the other will help to remove that threat. The Iranians asked the Soviet Ambassador if the clause meant that 'any time Iraq and Iran shout at each other, the Soviets would intervene on behalf of Iraq'. The Soviets, Hunter said, behaved in an utterly opportunistic way during the first two years of the Iran–Iraq war, by trying to court both countries whenever they could. 'Friendship' treaties should not be taken too seriously, she added.

Shahi also commented on the impact of the Islamic revolution on Soviet Central. He pointed out that since the 1917 Revolution, two to four generations have grown up under the Communist regime. He did not believe that Soviet rule and the benefits it has conferred on the peoples of the Soviet Central Asian Republics are so few or superficial that the appeal of the Islamic revolution in Iran could affect the indoctrination of 70 years of Communism. Of the Soviet Union's borders, Shahi doubted that the Afghan border, after the fall of Taraki, would have threatened the Soviet Union. Nor did Shahi believe that an Islamic regime would have been established in Afghanistan had the Soviets not intervened. Even were that to happen, Shahi said, Iran has an Islamic regime and a much longer border with the Soviet Union, so how does that effect the security of the Soviet Union? The Soviet Union, in Shahi's opinion, is hypersensitive about its security.

Nancy Dupree, currently at the US Military Academy at West Point, presented a paper entitled, 'The Demography of the Afghan Refugees', which brought the discussions to the current conditions and future of the refugees in Pakistan. Commenting on N. Dupree's presentation, Malik referred to the Senate Foreign Relations Committee report by John Rich, entitled *The Hidden War: the Struggle for Afghanistan*. Rich's report concluded that any successor to the Zia regime would have to face the practical effect that the refugee population is quite well armed and certainly out to defend its interests if it feels threatened. Malik feared that if Pakistan continues to strengthen the Afghan insurgents and if the US continues to pour in aid, the refugees will become a very serious problem for Pakistan. In Malik's opinion, this problem will be more serious for Pakistan than the Palestinian problem was for Lebanon and other Middle Eastern countries.

Ashraf Ghani, from Johns Hopkins University, disagreed with Malik's assessment. He thought that the Pakistan's policy had been eminently successful in preventing the rise of a 'state within a state' or of any situation which would give the resistance groups autonomy, either to speak in their own name or to pose a major threat to the government of Pakistan. He decried the situation where a regime [General Zia's] that is not elected speaks not only in its own name but in the name of another people as well. This complex issue needs to be addressed, he said, because it is clear that everyone seems to be speaking in the name of Afghanistan.

Shahi replied that Pakistan does not presume to speak for Afghanistan. In fact, he said, Pakistan tried to convince the Mujahiddin leaders to unite and define their policy toward the Soviet Union. The Mujahiddin, however, are divided by political, personal and ideological differences. Some Mujahiddin, Shahi said, want King Zahir Shah, while others are bitterly opposed to him. Some want a fundamentalist Islamic government, while others want a liberal democratic government. This situation obviously presents a problem.

Pakistan would be very happy if the Soviet Union or Babrak Karmal were ready to talk to the Afghan Mujahiddin leaders. But, Shahi said, that is not possible. The Afghan leaders want only to talk to Pakistan and Pakistan wants only to talk to the Soviet Union. The Soviet Union, in turn, tells Pakistan to talk to the Babrak Karmal regime.

Shahi claimed that Pakistan is not interested in the social base of the April Revolution. If the refugees return to their country and if the Afghan regime returns their property and confers on them social benefits, Shahi is convinced that the people themselves would not permit those benefits to be taken away.

Malik's pessimism that the Afghan refugees could ever return led him to propose that they be given the opportunity to become Pakistani citizens. If the refugees should have the opportunity to return to their homes, perhaps no more than 35 to 40 per cent would actually do so. He warned, however, that forcing them to remain in the 'shadow' of Pakistani society would result in dire social consequences, and the government of Pakistan would not have the resources to contain the resulting tensions.

Louis Dupree, also from the US Military Academy at West Point, agreed with Malik. The refugees, he warned, may link up with their fellow Pushtuns and Baluch across the border, or with their fellow Shia groups in Iran, with the result being the Balkanization of the entire area. The borders of Afghanistan and Pakistan are unrealistic, Dupree said. He pointed out that the Durand Line, which became the established border between Pakistan and Afghanistan in 1893, was never considered by the British to be an international boundary. Dupree had checked all the sources in the British India Office files, beginning when the line was drawn in 1893 until partition, and the British annually included in their reports to Whitehall that the

Durand Line was not to be considered an international frontier but rather a line delineating the zones for the maintenance of law and order by the Amir of Afghanistan and the British Indian government. Since the international line was to begin at the end of the settled districts, the Afghans, Dupree said, were right about the issue of Pushtunistan.

The Soviets did not invent the ethnic problems on the international border, L. Dupree said. He cautioned against trying to force the integration of the Afghan refugees into Pakistani society. The refugees he knows all want to go home, even those who have investments in Pakistan. Dupree thinks that these investments will constitute a link with Pakistan.

It is quite possible Pushtunistan may come into being, L. Dupree said. He did not dismiss the potential impact of events in Afghanistan on the Soviet Union, although he did not anticipate massive revolts taking place in Soviet Central Asia. By the year 2000, according to the Soviet Union's own figures, 53 per cent of its population will be non-Russian and of that total, about one-quarter to one-third will be Muslim. 'When you have at least one-third of your population nominally following Muhammad instead of Marx,' Dupree said, 'you might be in a little trouble as far as your economy and political system are concerned, even if you don't have major revolts.'

L. Dupree described the 'bounce-back' effect, which took place regularly between Afghan professors and Soviet Central Asian Institutions from the 1950s to 1978. He said that Afghan professors would return home impressed that intellectuals in Soviet Central Asia had not lost their feelings of cultural identity with the other Muslim peoples of the area. Dupree emphasized the cultural qualifier, 'Central Asian Islam'. The Soviets, he said, realized that a 'religious renaissance' was taking place on its borders with Turkey, Iran and Pakistan, and since Islam is not only a religious force but an overall cultural and political force, the Soviets did not want to see the same phenomenon happen in Afghanistan. Therefore, one reason among many for the Soviet Union's intervention in Afghanistan, Dupree said, was to signal its own Muslim populations that it would not permit this phenomenon to occur in the Soviet Union.

N. Dupree was asked to comment on the increasing tensions between the Pakistani population and the Afghan refugees. There had been complaints, for example, that the refugees had acquired a virtual stranglehold on heavy trucking and that a government crackdown could lead to a strike that would virtually stop half the commerce in Pakistan. It was also mentioned that close to 80 per cent of the Afghan refugee families had people working in the local economy. If the refugees penetrate the local economy, it was pointed out, their chances of returning to Afghanistan would then diminish considerably.

Acknowledging that the refugees are indeed only too willing to maximize any advantage in their competition with the Pakistanis, N. Dupree cited the need to determine the quality of the Afghan refugee population. Once the needs of the Refugee Training Villages and the Afghan community are determined, she said, programs can be developed which would involve the refugees in self-help activities and which would prevent competition with the Pakistani population. The few economic projects which are working well began with Afghan initiative. An International Labor Organization project for $2 million, established through the Small Industries Development Board, and the Austrian Relief Committee which has a pilot project using Afghan university professors and artisans to train young technicians and mechanics were successes.

The Afghan refugees have had a disastrous impact on some economic areas, N. Dupree said. However, there are no reliable cross-section surveys of the economic situation of individual refugee groups which give a comprehensive picture of the situation. Only two or three serious demographic studies have been made. Unfortunately, Dupree said, if the conclusions of such surveys do not tie in with the assumptions which the hierarchy in the establishment likes to hear, someone else is contracted to do the same study and to come up with the desired conclusion.

The discussions on the conditions of the Afghan refugees concluded on a somber note. The panelists were asked to comment on reports which detailed Soviet atrocities in Afghanistan. Citing Mujahiddin literature, General Theodore Mataxis, of the Committee for a Free Afghanistan, described the killing of livestock, crop burnings and the bombings of villages in retaliation for harboring resistance fighters and as a tactic to increase the influx of new waves of refugees into the neighboring countries.

Phyllis Oakley, the US Department of State Desk Officer for Afghanistan, replied that the State Department had looked into these reports. Although the Soviets have increasingly used 'scorched earth' tactics in areas of strategic importance or in areas where the Mujahiddin can count on civilian support, she said it should not be generalized that they are employing such tactics all over the country.

Mataxis agreed that the Soviets have been 'selective' in their targets. Nevertheless, he pointed out, these selective tactics have caused 4 million refugees to leave Afghanistan, and created some 2 million internal refugees, in addition to the killing of large numbers of Afghans.

CONCLUSION

The discussions, although covering familiar themes in the relationship of the Superpowers to Iran, Afghanistan and Pakistan, were enhanced by the recollections, insights and informed comments of the scholars, diplomats and former diplomats who participated. Ambassador McGhee brought to the seminar first-hand knowledge of the United States's involvement in Iran during the Mossadegh era, and of the continuing impact of the decisions made at that time on the United States's relations with Iran.

Mr Shahi's comments provided a unique insight into the thinking of a foreign minister from a Third World country. From Pakistan's perspective, the liabilities of an exclusively bilateral relationship with the United States have come to exceed its benefits. At the same time, according to Shahi, Pakistan must try to distance itself from Superpower rivalry in order to insure its security. Shahi's account of Pakistan's refusal to recognize the Babrak Karmal regime in Afghanistan, his concern over US–Pakistani relations regarding Pakistan's nuclear program, and his attempts to forge a regional coalition of Islamic Third World countries to deal with the Superpowers, provide valuable information to students of the region.

The Soviet military intervention in Afghanistan and its impact on the stability of the region, remains the most challenging problem facing both Superpowers and the countries of the region. The discussion by the participants of these issues, especially those dealing with the impact of the Afghan refugees on the future stability of Iran and Pakistan, add to an understanding of the long-range implications of the continued Soviet intervention in Afghanistan. The danger posed by the continued non-resolution of the Afghan conflict gives new impetus to Ambassador McGhee's exhortation that the old processes of diplomacy, based on compromise, be revitalized.

Appendix: List of Seminar Participants

Mr Agha Shahi (former Minister of Foreign Affairs of Pakistan), Quaid-i-Azam University Islamabad, Pakistan.
H. E. Ejaz Azim, Ambassador of Pakistan to the United States.
Mr George McGhee (former US Ambassador) and Undersecretary of State, Washington, DC.
Dr Igor V. Khalevinski, Political Counselor of the Soviet Mission to the United Nations, New York.
H. E. Dr James Spain, US Ambassador, Rand Corporation, Washington. DC.
Dr Christopher Van Hollen (former US Ambassador), Director, American Institute for Islamic Affairs, The American University, Washington, DC.
Dr Andrew Killgore (former US Ambassador), Washington, DC.
Ms Phyllis Oakley, Desk Officer, Afghanistan, Department of State, Washington, DC.
Mr Craig Karp, Afghan Analyst, INR, State Department, Washington, DC.
Mr Michael Malinowski, Pakistan Analyst, INR, State Department, Washington, DC.
Mr Peter Burleigh, Director of South Asia Division, INR, Department of State, Washington, DC.
Mr Arun B. Patwardhan, Consul General of India, New York.
Dr Craig Baxter (former US Consul General), Juniata College, Huntingdon.
Dr Jon W. Anderson, The Catholic University of America, Washington, DC.
Dr Lawrence Ziring, (Visiting Professor, Oxford University), Western Michigan University, Kalamazoo.
Dr Rodney Jones, Center for Strategic and International Studies, Georgetown University, Washington, DC.
Dr Richard Cottam (former US diplomat), University of Pittsburgh, Pittsburgh, Pa.
Dr Shireen Hunter (former Iranian diplomat), Center for Strategic and International Studies, Georgetown University, Washington, DC.
Dr Khosrow Fatemi (former Senior Official of Iran's Ministry of Commerce), Laredo State University, St. Laredo, Texas.
Dr Ashraf Ghani, The Johns Hopkins University, Baltimore, Maryland.
Mr Henry Bradsher, US Government, Washington, DC.
Dr Louis Dupree, US Military Academy, West Point.
Mrs Nancy H. Dupree, US Military Academy, West Point.
Dr Morris McCain, Research Associate, Russian Research Center at Harvard University and College of William and Mary, Williamsburg.
Dr John Duke Anthony, National Council on US–Arab Relations, Washington, DC.
Major W. Andrew Ritezel, Office of Director for Foreign Intelligence, Pentagon, Washington, DC.

List of Seminar Participants

Major Jerald Thompson, XVIII Airborne Corps, Department of Army, Ft. Bragg, North Carolina.
Major Jerry Mauldin, XVIII Airborne Corps, Department of Army, Ft. Bragg, North Carolina.
Captain Thomas Hedge, XVIII Airborne Corps, Department of Army, Ft. Bragg, North Carolina.
Col Leon T. Hunt, Political Military Officer, Plans & Policy Programs Directorate, Central Command, MacDill AFB, Florida.
Lt Col David Prevost, Rapid Deployment Task Force, MacDill AFB, Florida.
Lt Col Harry F. Johnson, Air War College, Maxwell Air Force Base, Alabama.
Lt Col Lorenzo M. Crowell, Jr., Air War College, Maxwell Air Force Base, Alabama.
Professor J. Bruce Amstutz, Industrial College of the Armed Forces, Ft. Leslie J. McNair, Washington, DC.
Mr Ronald Zwart, Special Assistant for South Asia, Secretary of Defense, Pentagon, Washington, DC.
Mr Yousef Bodonsky, Office of Secretary of Defense, Pentagon, Washington, DC.
Dr Samuel Iftikhar, Reference Librarian, Library of Congress, Washington, DC.
Dr Masood Ghaznavi, Rosemont College, Rosemont, Pennsylvania.
Dr Milan L. Hauner, Foreign Policy Research Institute, Philadelphia, Pa.
Mr H. L. Kephart, Newtown Square, Pennsylvania.
Mrs Dolores Kephart, Newtown Square, Pennsylvania.
Mr John Lee Olsen, Media, Pennsylvania.
Mrs John Lee Olsen, Media, Pennsylvania.
Mr Magdy Barsoum, Newtown Square, Pennsylvania.
Mrs Nadia Barsoum, Newtown Square, Pennsylvania.
Dr Mohammad Yadegari, Albany, New York.
Dr Grant Farr, Portland State University, Portland, Oregon.
Dr Alvin Z. Rubinstein, University of Pennsylvania, Philadelphia, Pa.
Mrs Farzana McCormick, Wilmington, Delaware.
Dr Riaz Ahmad, Secretary, American Institute of Pakistan Studies.
Mr Saeed Shafqat, University of Pennsylvania, Philadelphia, Pa.
Brig Gen (Retd) Theodore C. Mataxis, Southern Pines, North Carolina.

The following participants are from Villanova University:

Dr Hafeez Malik
Dr Kail Ellis
Dr Lynda Malik
Dr Jack Schrems
Dr Fred Khouri
Dr Fritz Nova
Dr Mohammad Zayyan Omar al-Sharqi, Visiting Professor of Middle East Studies, King Abdul Aziz University, Jeddah, Saudi Arabia.

Index

Abu Musa, Island, 16, 17, 98, 287
Acheson, Dean, 218
Afghan Army, 95
Afghan Effective Support Resolution (US Senate) 1984, 139
Afghan Ethnolinguistic diversity, 318–19, 321, 322, 358, 351
Afghan Freedom Fighters, 33, 35–6
Afghan insurgents' inflicted damage in Afghanistan, 139
Afghan joint stock company (1932), 315; see also Bank-i Milli
Afghan national consciousness, 92
Afghan natural gas to USSR (1967), 103
Afghan refugees, 10
Afghan refugees' demography, 25
Afghan regions, 317
Afghan Revolution, 128, 130
Afghans' ideal personality type, 363
Afghanistan in the United Nations, 143–5
Afghanistan, 'Socialism in one city', 347
Afghanistan, Sovietization, 21
Afghanistan's landowning classes, 314; working classes, 339
Afghanistan's Muhammadzai royalty, 321
Afghanistan, relations with superpowers, 412–19
Afshar, Nadir Shah, 245, 269
Agha, Sher (Hazrat of Shor Bazaar), 80
Ahmed, Sharaf-ud-Din, 411
Ali, Akhtar, 211
Ali, Amir Sher, 91, 310
Amanullah, King, 19, 30, 78, 92–3, 137, 322, 325, 335
America replaces Britain in Iran, 218
American aid package (1983) to Pakistan, 133–4

American aid to Afghan insurgents, 35, 139
American covert aid to Afghan insurgents, 34, 47, 139
American Executive Agreement (1959) of Security with Pakistan, 131, 167
American hostages in Iran, 16, 228, 231, 256, 259
American military aid to Pakistan, 63
American–Pakistan relations, 163
American–Pakistan strategic relations, 129–30, 163–71
American policy in the Middle East, 234, 405–6
American policy for Afghanistan and Pakistan, 35–8
Amin, Hafizullah, 20, 24, 33, 107, 108–9, 111–12, 120, 128, 135, 138, 153, 166, 340, 357, 368, 412, 414
Amnesty International, 99
Amouzegar, Jamshid, 101
Anderson, Jon W., 4, 7, 9, 406
Andrapov, Yuri V., 41, 146, 196
Anglo–Afghan Wars, 78, 91, 320
Anglo–Iranian Oil Company, 404
Anglo–Persian Agreement (1919), 217–18
Anglo–Russian Convention (1907), 30
Anglo–Russian Entente (1907), 56
Anglo–Russian Treaty (1887) for Northern Frontier of Afghanistan, 92
Answer to History, Shah's last book, 223
Anti-Americanism in Iran, 217–20
Arafat, Yassir, 239
Arnold, Anthony, 355
Asian Collective Security, 3
Assad, Hafez el-, 234, 238, 277
Ayatollah Khomeini, 6, 7, 14, 15,

16, 17, 28, 35, 46, 49, 51, 102, 113, 115, 116, 219, 222, 225, 227, 228, 231, 234; anti-Khomeini camp, 234, 238, 254, 255, 256, 270, 274, 277, 282, 288, 406, 407
Azerbaijan, Democratic Republic of, 249
Azerbaijan, Iranian province, 32
Azerbaijan, Peoples' Republic of, 8, 16
Azimov, Sarwar, Soviet Ambassador to Pakistan, 414–15
Aziz, Tariq, 258

Baathiste (Iraq), 114, 259
Bachha-i Saqao, Habibullah Khan, 92, 93
Baghdad Pact, 94, 164, 167, 251, 328
Bakthiar, Prime Minister Shahpur, 225, 235
Balance of power, 2, 90
Baluchistan, 5, 32; separatism, 48
Bangladesh, 31, 43, 58, 59, 62, 165, 166, 186
Bani-Sadr, Abolhasan, 117, 227, 231, 232, 256, 257, 259, 260, 415
Bank-i-Mili (Afghan National Bank), 315, 318
Basmachi movement, 93, 136, 336
Baxter, Craig, 6, 7, 54
Bazargan–Brzezinski meeting (in Algiers), 255
Bazargan, Prime Minister Mehdi, 225, 226, 227, 228, 254, 256–7, 407
Beheshti, Ayatollah Mohammad, 223, 232
Bengali nationalism, 151
Bhindranwale, Jarnail Singh, 151
Bhutto, Zulfikar Ali, 98–9, 104, 105, 107, 108, 129, 140, 141, 189; visit to USSR, 190, 207, 211, 213, 329
Bishop, Maurice, 2
Bizanjo, Gaus Baksh, 142

Bolshevik Revolution, 247, 248, 334, 409
Bradsher, Henry, 18, 19, 20, 21, 24, 333, 412
Brezhnev doctrine, 3
Brezhnev, Leonard, 40, 66, 128, 257
British arbitration of Afghan boundary with Iran, 311
Brougham, Lord, 1, 2
Brzezinski, Zbigniew, 131, 155, 223, 224, 225, 227, 231
Buffer State, 9, 90; Afghanistan, Central Asian buffer state, 91–6, 108, 113, 121, 155, 168, 310, 413

Cabinet Mission Plan (1946), 57
Camp David Accords (1928), 173, 273, 395
Canfield, Robert L., 355
Carter, President J., 36, 101, 127, 155, 166, 228, 229
Carter's diplomacy in Iran, 223
Carter Doctrine, 410
Catherine the Great, 245
Center–periphery relations, 75, 76, 79, 80, 83
Central Treaty Organization (CENTO), 33, 60, 95, 96, 168, 178, 188, 254, 400
Centrifuge technology of Pakistan, 203
Chou En-lai, 165
Christopher, Warren, 131, 167
Chupir, V., 367
CIA, 220
CIA sponsored coup in Iran, 218, 219, 271
Cold War, 34, 250, 328
Communist International (Comintern), 335
Communist Party, Afghanistan, 18, 19
Constantinople Accords (1913), 270
Cost of Iran–Iraq War, 284
Cottam, Richard W., 14, 15, 217, 403, 405, 406, 408

Counterpart Advisory System in Afghanistan, 22
Cranston, Senator Alan, 203
Cutler, Ambassador-designate Walter L., 227
Cyrus, the Great, 268

Daoud, Prince Muhammad, 18, 20, 30, 42, 64, 94, 103, 104, 106, 107–8, 133, 314, 317, 320, 321; nationalization and land reforms, 329, 336, 342, 356, 360
Democratic Republic of Afghanistan's culturally-oriented mistakes, 356
Desai, Morarji, 68
detente, 5, 35, 40
Diego, Cordovez, 117, 145, 146, 179, 402
Diego, Garcia Island, 36, 46, 153
Dubs, Adolph (US Ambassador), 111
Dulles, John Foster, 46, 164, 258
Dupree, Louis, 18, 23, 24, 25, 355; Dupree's seven 'Rs', 356, 418, 419
Dupree, Nancy Hutch, 18, 25, 366, 417
Durand Line (1893), 19, 32, 64, 119, 129, 142, 145, 154, 166, 311, 326, 327, 328, 359, 376, 417–18
Durand, Sir Mortiner, 92, 145, 311

East India Company, 30
East Pakistan, secessionist movement, 12
Egyptian–Israeli Peace Treaty (1979), 173
Eisenhower, President Dwight, 218, 222, 403, 404
El Salvadore, 2
Ethnic frontiers, 70, 79, 84
Ethnicity, 70–3, 79, 84

Falklands war, 395
Fatemi, Khosrow, 14, 17, 281, 409

Fatherland Front in Afghanistan, 22
Fedayeen-i-Khalq (Iran), 114
First Russo–Afghan War (1979), 356
Ford, President Gerald, 106
Forward Policy of Britain, 91
'Freedom of the mouth' in Afghanistan, 357
Fullerton, John 355

Gandhi, Indira, 58, 59, 64–5, 67, 68, 121, 150, 151, 183
Gandhi, Mahatma Mohandas, 31
Gandhi, Rajia, 64, 68, 121, 153, 158, 177
Gawader Port, 142
Geneva Negotiations between Pakistan and Afghanistan, 117, 143, 145, 178, 180, 402
Ghani, Ashraf, 18, 19, 79, 311, 416
Gharaieb, Abdel Karim, 231
Giradet, Edward, 355
Graham, Albert, 47
Great Game, 70, 75, 122
Grenada, 2, 395, 396
Gromyko, Andrei, 65, 173, 262
Gulf Cooperation Council, 260

Habibullah Khan, Bachha-i Saqao, 92, 93
Helmand River Valley Project, 95, 320
Helsinki Watch, 34
Hollen, Christopher Van, 405
Horn of Africa, 43
Hunter, Shireen T., 14, 15, 409, 413, 415
Hussein, Saddam, 17, 114, 235, 236, 239, 273–4, 275, 281, 286, 287
Huyser, General Robert, 225

India–Pakistan Joint Commission, 64
India–Pakistan War (1971), 165
Indian Allegations of Interference, 58–9
Indian Foreign Policy, 7

Indian military superiority over Pakistan, 206
Indian National Congress, 31, 43, 61, 94
Indian nuclear capability, 13
Indian Ocean, 28, 43, 45, 50; zone of peace, 52, 91, 98, 127, 153, 183, 252
Indian offer of Treaty of peace, friendship and cooperation with Pakistan, 64
Indira doctrine, 7, 67
Indo–Aryans, 30, 54
Indo–Iranian Joint Commission, 61
Indo–Soviet Treaty of Cooperation (1971), 165, 176, 252
Indus Valley, 121
Indus Waters Treaty, 62
International Economic Cooperation, 300–301; see also North–South Dialogue
International Labour Organization (ILO), 388, 389, 419
Intervention, 1, 2, 3, 4; Soviet intervention in Afghanistan, 5, 12, 16, 18–25, 20, 24; USSR motives, 36, 64, 112, 127; interpretations of, 127–8, 139, 168, 178–81
Iran, relations with superpowers, 403–11
Iran, Soviet–US relations with, 14–18
Iran–Iraq Algiers Agreement (1975), 281, 286, 287
Iran–Iraq foreign exchange shortage, 300
Iran–Iraq foreign trade, 296–7, 298
Iran–Iraq war, 273–6
Iran–US alliance, 250
Iranian army, 96
Iranian National Front, 219
Iranian nationalism, 14, 218
Iranian perceptions of Russian intentions, 244
Iran's oil reserves, 27
Iran's Revolutionary Guards, 288
Iraqi's claim to Kuwait, 271
Islam, a comprehensive world-view, 335

Islamic bomb, 47, 175, 212–3, 397
Islamic feudalism, 44, 48, 51, 101, 109, 128, 136, 277, 279, 338, 341
Islamic fundamentalist theocracy, 42
Islamic League (Jeddah), 109
Islamic legitimacies, 74
Islamic political activism, 237–8
Islamic political theory, 360
Islamic Revolution (Iran), 115, 116
Islamic states, 5
Islamic summit at Lahore, 99
Islamization in Pakistan, 140
Israel, 407, 408
Israeli invasion of Lebanon, 3; Israeli lobby, 17
Israeli invasion of Lebanon, 174

Jamiat-i-Islam (Afghanistan), 337
Jamiat-i-Islami (Afghanistan), 20
Jewish Settlements in West Bank, 173
Jinnah, Mohammed Ali, 31, 172
Jinnah's protest to Truman over Israel's creation, 172
Johnson, President Lyndon, 164
Jones, Rodney, 9, 13, 410

Karakorum Highway, 111, 121
Karmal, Babrak, 20, 107, 108–9, 110, 112, 139, 179, 336, 339; ethnic identity, 340, 342, 344–5, 368, 413, 420
Kashani, Ayatollah Abol Qassem, 220
Kashmir dispute, 7, 43, 61, 62, 97, 121, 142, 150, 163, 164, 177, 208
Kautilya's theory of international relations, 55, 57, 105
Kennedy, President John F., 132, 164, 222
KGB (Soviet Committee for State Security), 112
Khad, Afghan Secret Police, 22, 118, 120, 370, 382
Khaibar, Mir Akbar, 108
Khalevinski, Igor, 408, 409, 412–13
Khalq, 20, 103, 106, 107, 136, 317,

321, 323, 340; Khalqi support to Mujahiddin (1980), 343; Khalqi-Parchami split, 344
Khalq–Parcham disunity, 109
Khan, Abdul Ghaffar, 105
Khan, Abdul Qadir, 203, 205, 211
Khan, Abdul Wali, 105
Khan, Agha Mohammad, 245
Khan, Amir Habibullah, 19
Khan, Liaquat Ali, 163, 187
Khan, President General Mohammed Ayub, 98, 132, 156, 164, 189
Khan, President General Yahya Khan, 132, 189
Khan, Sahabzada Yakub, 196
Khattak, Khushal Khan, 363
Khoram, Ali Ahmed, 106
Khorramshahr, 281
Khrushchev, Nakita, 40, 327
Khudai Khidmatgars, 94, 105
Khuzistan, 16
Khyber Pass, 58
Killgore, Andrew, 14, 17, 411
Kissinger, Henry, 12, 17, 28, 100, 132, 165, 173, 175, 272, 399
Kosygin, Aleksei, 103, 110, 156, 189
Kurdistan, Democratic Republic of, 249
Kurram Agency, 376
Kuzichkin, Uladimir Andreyevich, 261

Lansing, Robert, 217
Lenin, V. I., 40, 185, 248
Liaquat Ali Khan's visit to USSR cancelled, 187

McCain, Morris, 4, 5, 6
McGhee, George, C., 4, 5, 27, 395–6, 397, 399, 403, 405, 420
Mahabad (1943), Peoples' Republic of, 8
Malik, Hafeez, 9, 10, 401, 402, 404, 413, 416
Mangal, Atta Allah, 142
Mataxis, General Theodore, 419, 420
Mogul Empire, 30

Mohammadzai, dynasty, 355, 356
Montagu declaration (1917), 57
Mossadeq, Dr Mohammad, 29, 218, 219, 221, 222, 250, 254, 271, 272, 403, 404
Movement for the Restoration of Democracy in Pakistan (MRD), 141
Mujahiddin (Afghan insurgents), 112, 113, 117, 118, 119, 120, 140, 169, 171, 180, 371, 374, 388, 397, 399, 417, 419
Mujahiddin-Khalq (Iran), 114, 259
Muskie, Edmund, 231
Muslim Brotherhood, 111
Muslim League, 31

Na Sharghi, na gharbi (equi-distance between East and West) in Iran, 254, 404
National Awami Party (NAP), 105, 106
National Democratic Party (NDP) of Pakistan, 141
National Liberation Wars, 40
National Revolutionary Party (NRP) Afghanistan, 106
NATO, 96, 128, 188
Nehru, Jawaharlal, 163, 164
New Jewel Movement, 2
Niazi, Ghulam Mohammed, 337
Nixon Doctrine, 252
Nixon, President Richard, 12, 165, 173, 272
Nizam-i-Mustafa (Rule of the Prophet), 116
Non-Aligned Movement, 61, 62, 66
Non-Aligned Movement, 167, 168, 170, 171, 181, 183, 334
North–South Dialogue, 289, 300–1
North Waziristan Agency, 376
No War Pact between India and Pakistan, 152, 154
Nuclear assistance from China to Pakistan, 205
Nuclear bomb production capacity of Pakistan, 203
Nuclear capability of Pakistan, 130, 199, 203, 213
Nuclear non-proliferation, 166,

175–6, 177, 183; between India and Pakistan, 208–9; 213, 397
Nuclear options for Pakistan, 200–2
Nuclear technologies in Pakistan, 204–5
Nuclear terrorism, 202
Nuclear threat of India to Pakistan, 207
Nuclear-weapon free zone, 175, 183

Oakley, Phyllis, 419
Oil consumption rates, 296
Oil imports (US), 295
Oil price structure, 292; spot prices, 293
Oil production (Iran–Iraq), 289–93; global production, 294–5
Oil stocks, 296
OPEC, 18, 286, 293, 294–5, 301–3, 304

Pahlavi dynasty, 15, 248–9
Pahlavi, Shah Mohammad Reza, 29, 217, 249, 270, 272
Pakistan–Afghan borders closed, 327, 328
Pakistan–China *entente*, 165
Pakistan nuclear threshhold state, 199–200
Pakistan Peoples' Party (PPP), 140
Pakistan proposal for No-War Pact with India, 64
Pakistan State Steel Corporation, 194
Pakistan, superpower relations with, 9, 396, 403
Pakistan's nationalism, 209
Pakistan's nuclear capability, 7, 10, 12, 13
Pakistan's opposition to Israeli expansion, 174
Pakistan's policy towards the Middle East, 171–4
Pakistan's relations with India, 148–50, 176–8
Pakistan's security problems, 131
Pakistan's threat perceptions, 213
Pakistan's western orientation, 43
Palestinian cause, 398

Panjdeh, oasis, 310
Paputin, Victor, 112
Parcham, 20, 102, 103, 106, 107, 108, 340
Parnjsher Valley, 117
Parwareshgah-i-Watan (Fatherhood orphanage), 21
Pasdaran (Irani Revolutionary Guards), 115
Pashtuns, 7, 10; Pashtunistan, 8, 32, 76, 77, 94, 95, 104, 107, 110, 119, 120, 138, 143, 327, 328, 418
Pax Sovietica, 413
PDPA (People Democratic Party of Afghanistan), 20, 21, 22, 103, 333, 334, 336, 338–42, 344; Social Science Institute of, 346; ethnic composition on, 347; future of, 349–50
Peaceful coexistence, 3–40, 180, 182, 186
Persian Cossacks, 246
Persian Gulf, 5, 32, 33, 35, 36, 37, 46–7, 48, 50, 60–1, 91, 96, 114, 127, 128, 142, 166, 169, 177, 181, 183, 230, 236, 241, 247, 252, 260, 262, 282, 287, 292, 297, 298, 397
Persian Mission, 9, 74
Peter the Great, 244, 245
PLO, 235, 237, 239, 252
Primakov, Yevgeni, 260
Proletarian internationalism, 3
Pul-i-Charki prison (Kabul), 343
Pushtunwali (Pushtun Code of Honor), 376

Qaddafi, Muammar, 99
Qajar, Agha Mohammad, 245
Qajar dynasty, 15, 244, 245
Qotbzadeh, Sadeq, 227, 229–30, 231, 258

Rabbani, Burhanuddin, 337
Rafsanjani, Hajatoleslam Hashemi, 116, 259, 261
Rahman, Amir Abdur, 19
Rahman, Amir Abdur, 76, 78, 79,

82, 91, 92, 310, 311, 313, 320, 323, 324
Rajai, Mohammad Ali, 258
Rann of Kutch, 7
Rao, P. V. Narasimha, 65
Rapid Deployment Force (Central Command), 36, 37, 43, 47, 51, 128
Ras al-Khaima, Sheikhdom of, 287
Rastakhiz (National Resurrection Party of Iran), 100
Razmara, General Ali, 403
RCD (Regional Cooperation for Development), 97
Reagan, President Ronald, 2, 10, 36, 127
Refugees (Afghan), 34, 111, 120–1, 135; resettlement in Pakistan, 136–8; repatriation to Afghanistan, 147–8, 168, 170, 179; size, 366–9; enumeration problems, 370–4; programme credibility, 374–5; population distribution, 376–80; settlement patterns, 381–2; population density ratios, 383–4; ethnic composition and distribution, 385–7; occupational diversity, 388–90
Revolution, Islam and War (Afghanistan), 113–22
Reza Shah, 15, 29
Rich, John, 416
Rubinstein, Alvin, 406, 407, 409
Russian–British determination of Afghan boundary, 311
Russo–Iranian Wars (1804–26), 245

Sadat, Anwar el-, 173, 287
Safavid Empire, 244, 245, 269
SALT II Agreement, 128, 396
Sandinistas, 2
Saud, al, King Abdul Aziz, 279
SAVAK (Sazman-i-Amniyat Wa Kishvar), 96, 220
Sayyad, Abdul Rasool, 337
Scorched-earth tactics of USSR, 419

SEATO, 12, 164, 165, 167, 188, 328
Shahi, Agha, 9, 11, 12, 13, 163, 196, 396, 398, 400–1, 402, 404, 405, 417, 420
Shah, King Nadir, 19, 30, 79, 93
Shah of Iran, 98, 99–100, 102, 105, 107, 110, 130, 134, 166, 220, 221, 228, 233, 286
Shah Reza, 248, 249
Shah, Zahir, 18, 20, 30, 93, 94, 102, 103, 166, 320, 337, 338
Shahrani, M. Nazif, 355
Sharia (Islamic laws), 320
Sharja, Sheikhdom of, 287
Sharon-ization of US policy, 410
Shastri, Lal Bahadur, 156
Shatt-al-Arab, 16, 17, 33, 98, 113, 114, 269, 281, 184–5, 286
Sherpao, Hayat Mohammad Khan, 106
Shia population in Gulf states, 270
Shiite Islam, 278
Shor Bazaar, Mulla, 80
Shuster, Morgan, 217
Sikh Nationalism, 11, 151–2
Sikhs, 59, 64
Simla Agreement (1972), 176
Singh, Khushwant, 63
Sino–Soviet conflict, 165
Slavery outlawed in Afghanistan, 321
Smith, Ambassador Gerard, 130
South Asia Regional Cooperation (SARC), 7, 66
Soviet–Afghan Agreement for Stationing of Forces (1980), 121
Soviet–Afghan Friendship Treaty (1978), 110, 128
Soviet–Afghan non-aggression treaty, 94
Soviet–Afghan security treaties (1954, 1956), 94
Soviet-assisted oil exploration in Pakistan, 192–3
Soviet-assisted tractor plant in Pakistan, 194
Soviet economic assistance to Afghanistan, 106

Index

Soviet–Indian cooperation, 43
Soviet–Iran Agreement on Economic and Technical Cooperation, 45
Soviet–Iran rapprochement, 258–9
Soviet–Iran rift, 259–62
Soviet–Iranian detente, 251–2
Soviet–Iraqi Treaty of Friendship, 252
Soviet-made steel mill (Karachi), 191
Soviet military aid to Afghanistan, 94; economic aid, 95
Soviet–Nazi rapprochement, 249
Soviet occupation of Afghanistan, 229
Soviet–Pakistan confrontation, 140
Soviet–Pakistan economic cooperation, 191
Soviet–Pakistan relations, 186–91
Soviet–Pakistan relations decline, 195–6
Soviet–Pakistan trade, 187
Soviet policy for Iran's ethnic minorities, 255
Soviet renunciation of nuclear first strike, 183
Soviet sphere of influence, 45
Spain, James, 399
Stalin, Joseph, 163
State system of Europe, 1
Steul, Willi, 355
Strait of Hormuz, 33, 98, 142, 241, 287, 292, 405, 410
Strategic interest, 4, 5, 27, 30; US interests, 32–3, 37; Soviet interest, 39–42, 49–52
Suez Canal, 46
Sullivan, Ambassador William, 222–3, 224
Symington amendment, 133

Tapper, Richard, 355
Taraki, Nur Muhammad, 20, 24, 108, 109, 110, 135, 136, 166, 333, 336, 338; ethnic identity, 340, 342, 357, 368, 414
Tashkent Agreement (1966), 156, 189

Tehran-Islamabad axis, 95
Teleqani, Ayatollah, 223
Tigris-Euphrates basin, 267, 268
Treaty of Gulistan, 246
Tribes (Afghanistan), 77
Truman doctrine, 60
Truman, President Harry, 218, 222, 403
Tudeh Party, 29, 35, 114, 115, 225, 236, 250, 254, 255, 256, 259, 261
Turkmanchai, Treaty (1829), 15, 246, 247, 248

U-2 reconnaissance flights, 11, 164, 188
United Nations, 395
US Badaber base (Peshawar), 189
US Executive Agreement (1959), with Pakistan, 399, 400
US influence in Iran, 45
US–Israel strategic alliance, 174
US–Pakistan alliance, 164
US–Pakistan Mutual Defense Assistance Agreement (1954), 163
US strategy of graduated compellence in Iran, 230
Ustinov, Demitri, Marshall of USSR, 147

Vajpayee, Atal Behari, 68
Vance, Cyrus, 231, 255
Velayat-e-Faghih, 77

Wakhan Corridor, 92; ceded to USSR (1981), 121
Weber, Max, 70, 84
Wikh-i-Zalmaiyan (Awakened youth), 336
Wilson, President Woodrow, 217

Yazdi, Ibrahim, 227, 255

Zabuli, Abdul Majid, 315, 316, 325–326, 327
Zahedi, General Fazlollah, 219
Zand, Karim Khan, 269

Zia-ul-Haq, President of Pakistan, 62, 64, 65, 107, 111, 116, 131, 132, 133, 139, 140, 150, 152, 178, 195, 416

Zia-ur-Rahman, Bangladesh President, 67

Ziring, Lawrence, 9, 10, 19, 90

Zoroastrianism, 16, 268